# Caring for the Dead

## Your Final Act of Love

## Lisa Carlson

**Upper Access, Inc.**
Hinesburg, VT 05461

Upper Access Books
P.O. Box 457
Hinesburg, VT 05461
800-310-3820

Woodblock illustrations by Mary Azarian
Cover design by Lily Gardner

---

---

Library of Congress Cataloging-in-Publication Data

Carlson, Lisa, 1938–

Caring for the dead : your final act of love / Lisa Carlson.

   p.  cm.

Includes bibliographical references and index.
ISBN 0-942679-21-0 (pbk.)
1. Death--Handbooks, manuals, etc.  2. Funeral rites and ceremonies--
United States.  3. Burial laws--United States--States.
I. Title.
GT3203.C36  1998                    98-27893
393'.0973--dc21                     CIP

# Contents

# Part II
## Caring for the Dead in:

# Part III
## Appendix

To our children—

Stuart, Josh, Joie, Shawn, and Rosalie

—to whom the task of
"final disposition"
may fall

# Acknowledgments

Scores of people provided information and encouragement to make this a more detailed and useful book. State agencies reviewed each state chapter for accuracy—well, most of them did. To them I extend particular appreciation and gratitude.

I owe special thanks, too, to Sally Cavanaugh. Her "How to Bury Your Own Dead in Vermont " (published by the *Vanguard Press,* 1980) was first shared in my writers' group. Because of that article, I had the details I needed just six months later when I had to use them—and to begin the further research that has continued ever since.

People in the funeral profession also provided help. Ellsworth Purdy—now retired from funeral service—sent me a book to add to my death education library years ago: "Stolen from the desk of E.D. Purdy," said the sticker in front. With a renewed friendship, I found Ells on the other end of a warm e-mail correspondence whenever I had questions. Many other industry correspondents added to my education, too, but have requested anonymity in publication.

Lee Norrgard, who for many years monitored the funeral industry for AARP, turned me on to the problems of "constructive delivery"—a way that cemeteries (usually) get to use your money before you can use what they're selling.

Perhaps the person who inspired me most to reach out to all funeral consumers was John Blake in Egg Harbor, Wisconsin. I met him when he was on the board of the national memorial society group and invited me to get involved. He later served as its executive director until his retirement in 1996. Knowing that many elderly were living on limited incomes, John was always seeking ways to make an economical, dignified funeral choice available to more people. He read the industry journals to watch the trends and readily shared his information. At his warm urging, I applied for the position of executive director of FAMSA when he retired. Many of the experiences reported to the FAMSA office over the past two years have clarified for me the huge need for increased funeral consumer protection as suggested in each state chapter.

And some chapters have been contributed by others whose experiences enrich the tale to be told. Their thoughtful sharing adds breadth, diversity, and encouragement. Thank you—Steve, Jan, Chris, and Patsy.

This book never would have seen the light of day without the help of others: Upper Access staffers were avid researchers and careful editors. FAMSA staff and board members were candid critics.[1] Thank you Amy Crawford, Ella Brackett, Jay Kirk, and Kristen Lewis for sharing your sense of humor, too.

The weeping willow woodcut by Mary Azarian has been used again to embellish these pages in charming and appropriate simplicity.

Being married to the publisher, what can I say? Steve's insight, his way with words, made "my" writing so much better. You'll see for yourself that the crafting of this book was an act of love for both of us.

~❖~

"Acknowledgment" has another meaning, too—an "admission," and I'd like to make one. This writing began more than 12 years ago. The recent additions took another five years of writing and then some. It became a pubisher's nightmare to edit because the "voice" with which I wrote changed with each chapter or section that I finished. Sometimes I was "above" it all, a dispassionate reporter and a studious researcher. At other times I was outraged, and it was hard not to let my anger leak through, with flip comments or put-downs or verbal yelling. "Trocar jockeys" seemed the perfect way to characterize the Missouri funeral board whose regs permit a mortician to start embalming after six hours if they can't find a next-of-kin, but I thought better of it later on and took it out. And anyone who knows me knows that I'll find a ready excuse to chuckle whenever I can, even in the face of death and great sadness. Humor and a hearty laugh are therapeutic ways of releasing tension. Or for making difficult subjects just a little easier to broach.

With a publishing deadline to meet, I worried that "it's not done yet," feeling that I should go back and rewrite for better consistency. But I decided not to. Yes, this book may lurch from one "voice" to another, but it is probably nothing more than a microcosm of the range of feelings one is bound to face at a time of death. Maybe that isn't so bad after all.

---

[1] Although I refer to FAMSA throughout, this book is not a publication of FAMSA nor has it specifically been endorsed by FAMSA.

# What you will learn from this book and why I wrote it

After my husband John died, there was a lot of publicity (with my permission) about the fact that I had handled my own "arrangements." Hardly a week went by in the following year without a telephone call or letter from someone else involved in the plans surrounding a death. I also was asked to speak to church groups and classes on "Death and Dying."

People were eager for information. Many expressed a desire to overcome feelings of helplessness or frustration in dealing with death. They expressed a need for more personal identity and control in the choices they made, similar to the decisions regarding "natural" childbirth and hospice.

One of the serious mistakes I made was to remove John's body before others—his mother and his children—had experienced his death first-hand. Over a year later, for example, when my son Shawn was four years old, he asked, "But *where* is my Daddy dead?" The need for involvement of the immediate family was echoed in the various groups with which I spoke. It became clear that all close friends and family should have the opportunity to participate, whenever possible, in ways that lend meaning to each person involved.

I hope this book will encourage people to become more informed about the choices to be made and less afraid to deal with death. By dealing with the physical aspects of death, emotional needs may be handled effectively as well. For me and for many others with whom I have talked, personal involvement at a time of death was significant, meaningful, and even necessary in order to say good-bye to a loved one; examples are shared in the first few chapters.

Almost everything the funeral industry sells interferes with our natural return to the earth, and few know what that involves. By understanding what happens to the body after death and demystifying funeral options, our end-of-life decisions prior to death may be less fearful to face.

The Robert Wood Johnson Foundation spent $27 million to find out that Living Wills were rarely honored. In the situations where such wishes *were* honored, an active family member was usually the critical factor. What information and attitudes did that family member have that made the difference?

My first book on the subject—*Caring For Your Own Dead,* published in 1987—was intended for a relatively narrow audience, primarily those who wished to handle all arrangements themselves, bypassing the funeral industry entirely to the extent possible. The book attracted far more interest and sold far more copies than expected. It did not foment a major "do-it-yourself" movement for funerals at the time, but it did stir pockets of interest around the country. In northern California, Karen Leonard and Jerri Lyons were the moving forces for a group that founded the Natural Death Care Project.

The majority of people in the U.S. and Canada still prefer to hire professional help. In growing numbers, however, people want to understand the process so that they can be educated consumers—making reasoned decisions to pay for only the goods and services they desire—and to personalize the funeral experience in meaningful ways.

The feedback I received prompted me to become a consumer advocate in dealings with the funeral industry, and I now (1998) serve as Executive Director of Funeral and Memorial Societies of America (FAMSA). I've had the privilege of working with families with very diverse needs and values. Many have preferences that are far different from mine. As a result, the scope of this book is greatly expanded. I hope that it will be a useful resource regardless of the rituals that are important to you and your family.

Certainly a religious congregation—the logical support group for a family at a time of death—can provide the resources to return the funeral to the church in a way that emphasizes spiritual rather than material caring. A new chapter has been devoted to this.

For those who—out of necessity or choice—will be using a mortuary, I have included a chapter on the "Tricks of the Funeral Trade." Consumers should be as knowledgeable about funeral industry tactics as they are about the sales techniques of any other business. Yes, there are wonderful, caring funeral directors in this business, and ethical ones welcome—perhaps even prefer—a well-educated consumer, for those will be the easiest to please.

In most areas, however, there are far more mortuaries than can be supported full-time by the death rate. It's a situation that invites abuse. As an editorial in *Mortuary Management* (12/90) put it: "Funeral directors must keep in mind that subtle or direct pressure to encourage client families to consider more elaborate services when a death has occurred has proven to be a primary factor in the success of competitive memorial/disposal organizations."

Perhaps the greatest recent change affecting funeral consumers is the growth of corporate funeral chains as they buy up funeral homes and cemeteries worldwide at break-neck speed. Service Corporation International (SCI), The Loewen Group, Stewart Enterprises, and Equity Corporation International (ECI), are the four largest, with Carriage and Keystone trying to play catch-up. The great majority of complaints that come into the FAMSA office have to do with dealings at chain outfits—from complete lack of sensitivity and questionable tactics to shocking prices,[1] the least-reported of which are happening at cemeteries. FAMSA e-mail from Australia and England contains grim responses to the export of "American" funeral practices via these companies. "We intend to raise the cost of funerals," said one CEO quoted in an industry newsletter.

The FTC chapter points out the role of the Federal Trade Commission in *reducing* consumer choice, and the need for a public outcry. If consumer groups are going to effectively match the high-priced industry lobbyists, they will have to join forces. No one else lobbies for the dead.

No state currently has statutes that are complete or entirely appropriate regarding death. Some states are not clear or specific enough on procedures that are legitimately within the purview of a state's interest. Six states have restrictive statutes which have no place in a society that recognizes the diversity and worth of individuals. Therefore, each state chapter has a list of "consumer concerns," many of which are issues that should be addressed in the statutes. My hope is that private citizens, church groups, and interested others will urge their legislators to consider reform of funeral and cemetery laws. It is unfortunate that attention is usually drawn to these issues only at times of immediate need.

*If there is any overwhelming goal in this edition, however, it is guided by the hope that this book will become a home-study text for parents and other adults of every age. In the last few generations, we have largely failed in teaching an important lesson—the final act of love.*

---

[1] From an on-line mortuary chat: "I was employed by SCI for three years. . . . Once I was at a regional meeting. All were asked if they were funeral directors or sales people. The ones who raised their hands saying they were funeral directors were reprimanded and told they were not funeral directors but sales people. . . . Families do not matter to officials at SCI. Only the almighty dollar, and their prices are high."

I suspect my family is not unlike others in the ways we've responded to the inevitable. . . .

One aunt didn't want to talk about her funeral arrangements at all, even at a time when she was battling cancer; "My sister will know what to do," she said. Did she not think that we cared, too?

My grandmother *did* try to sit me down and talk about such things once. "Oh, Grammy, you're not going to die," I replied, an uncomfortable 20-something-year-old at the time, one who simply wasn't ready to face the idea of losing the special person who took over when my mother died at an early age. How I wish Grammy had insisted! How I wish now that I'd had the benefit of her wisdom—she was "right" about so many other things.

Another relative knows exactly what kind of funeral she thinks the relatives will expect and has a $3,000 insurance policy to pay for it. She's had that policy for years and has no idea that triple that amount would be needed for the kind of funeral she wants.

And then there is my father; he's "taken care of everything" and doesn't mind talking about it at all—well, sort of. He belongs to the Orlando Memorial Society and wants a simple cremation. I admire his no-nonsense approach for a frugal exit, but that's it—it's almost too "frugal" when it comes to the emotional aspects of saying goodbye. I don't object to the idea of a simple cremation—I accept and appreciate that. But there's so much more in the family script for parting that we haven't yet discussed . . . and I don't know if we ever will.

One night a few years ago, I got out of bed and headed for the computer. It suddenly seemed important to "talk" to my own children about this. In the middle of the night, a letter seemed like a good way to begin:

> I'm getting older now. I'm beginning to think about which of my personal things I want each of you to have. Yes, I've written a will, so each of you will share equally in what little is left after I'm gone. There are a few special things, though, I'll want to give you while I'm still alive, because they should not be counted in the sum total of it all. Some of my treasures will mean more to different ones—quite apart from the monetary value—and I hope you'll understand the pattern of my giving, for I *do* have a special place in my heart for each of you.
>
> While I'm dwelling on it, I want to make clear that, when I die, I want the absolutely least expensive funeral you can possibly arrange. I don't want some funeral director telling you that you ought to have "the best" for your mother. If you want to spend

money to show how much you love me—for goodness sake, do it while I'm still alive—you know how much I love flowers! *

But far more than how much you spend on me or anyone else, I hope you know that it's the personal, thoughtful, sometimes little things that count the most. "Considering others" is the major life-lesson I'm sure we all have to learn. Material things don't matter as much as generous caring.

So, contemplating my funeral—because, yes, it will come sooner or later no matter how often I sometimes think I might want to live forever—I got a little silly tonight, given all the possibilities. I certainly had a good laugh . . . and I hope you will, too.

Imagine me, a plain, ordinary, not-very-good-looking, wrinkled, not-in-great-shape-and-therefore-baggy-in-places mom—a mom who got into more mischief than most, with many embarrassments for all of you, I'm sorry to say. (As my favorite pin puts it, "I'm an outrageous older woman." Thank you for enduring through the early years when I was an outrageous younger woman, too.)

I enjoy a good laugh . . . and sometimes I feel entitled to get angry when the world doesn't seem fair. Can you really see me being "comfortable," perfectly-posed in a casket full of satin and crepe? I hear that some of them even have adjustable head-rests! I sit here wondering what it would be like . . . 100 years from now . . . 1,000 years from now . . . to have my body captured inside a metal casket—inside the other box-for-the-box called an "outer burial container"—all of it six feet under, dark as can be. I'm sitting here with my eyes closed, just imagining. Then I peek one eye open, and . . . you know what? I'm still six feet under! I'm howling with laugher now at this even-more-outrageous image . . . what would my pesky spirit do in a situation like that?

I'll tell you what I really want—it's very easy: "Ashes to ashes and dust to dust." I want a plain pine box. No, not plywood with all the glue and formaldehyde. I want a plain wooden box, one that will return naturally to the soil, as I'd like to do.

"Plant" me under an apple tree, or—better yet—a flower garden. (I always did better with the flowers and frivolous things than I did with the vegetable garden and practical matters.) That's

---

* I got a Plant-of-the-Month for my birthday shortly after reading this to one son.

where my spirit would be most happy. It feels strangely warm to "see" myself becoming one with the earth, to picture my elements feeding new life. That's the way I want to go—that's the way I want to come back again—as nourishment for a beckoning flower.

For me, it would be a terrible "sentence" to be stuck with a stopped-in-time expression of religious contemplation forever—that's just not me. I want to laugh, I want to be sometimes naughty and irreverent . . . and, yes, I want to move on when I die—I think there's a much bigger picture out there, bigger than any of us will ever know until we get there. When I'm ready, cremation may be the answer, but I want to be free to go . . . in a plain pine box, one that's not too perfect . . . just like me.

# Part I

# Personal Stories

 # John

1981. It was 2:30 A.M. when I woke up and found the empty space in our bed. John must have gone for a walk, and I wanted to be with him. There were intense, upsetting problems at the small Vermont school where he taught, and John had—for the most part—contained his anger at the situation, always hoping to be the peace-maker. As a result of that effort, he developed a serious stomach pain. He hated what the pain-relieving drugs did to him, and I knew he continued to be depressed. But just that night he'd taken me in his arms—as he so often did—and told me how much he loved me.

I threw on some clothes and tried following his footprints in the shallow March snow, quickly losing them. At the end of the driveway, something made me stop. There was the bright red truck that was his pride and joy. I struggled with the icy door, unprepared for the shock ... his still, cold body was there, his deer rifle beside him! My husband, my love, was dead! His note: "I'm sorry, I can't stand the pain any more."

In hysterical tears I ran to the house, made phone calls to close friends and to the police. The next few hours were a chaotic blur of anguish while I struggled to hold on to some control of what was happening and would happen. I had to answer questions only I could answer and make decisions that I wasn't prepared for but were mine to make. My anger at the school, John's pain, and my loss exploded over and over in sobbing. But there was a fierce need to protect John, to care for him as I never would again.

It was an intimate life John and I had shared, intimate with each other and with the world around us. We were married at home, and John had wanted to be buried at home. But because the ground was still frozen, cremation seemed the only alternative. I would select the simplest procedure.

Opening the Yellow Pages, I reluctantly called a funeral home and inquired about the price of cremation. (There was almost nothing in the bank, and I wasn't even sure if I could cash John's next paycheck. I was panic-stricken about my finances.) The man told me cremation would be $500 including the "required casket." But I didn't have that much money. I called the crematory in St. Johnsbury, 50 miles away. It was very early in the morning, but the telephone was answered by a Mr. Pearl. He did request a box but said it could be of the simplest construction, even something I made myself. And the price of cremation? $85 (1981). I thanked Mr. Pearl and hung up. Did I have the energy in my despair to build John's box? Probably not. My young children would be up soon and they would need me now. So I tried another funeral home.

"Well, the price for cremation, which includes everything, is $700," said the funeral director.

Two more calls gave me costs above my bank balance, but when I pressed for itemized prices, I was given quotes as low as $50 for the box or $50 for transportation. Just in rough averages, I thought my expenses should have been well under $250 for the kind of service I requested, without a viewing, calling hours, or other use of the funeral home. I couldn't understand it.

Because there would be an autopsy, the police called a funeral director to take John's body to Burlington. I plied him, too, with my questions.

"How much is the simplest box for cremation?"

"$60."

"How much is transporting the body to St. Johnsbury?"

"$50."

He saw me reaching a total of $195 on a scrap of paper as I included the $85 for cremation. I was thinking with relief that somehow I'd be able to manage that when he said, "But you'll have to add a $325 service charge to that."

"What is the $325 for?" I asked.

"Oh, there is a lot of paperwork," the funeral director replied.

I pointed out that the death certificate and the permit to cremate would be coming back from the autopsy with the body. That the only other document needed was a burial-transit permit.

"If it will save me $325, I'll go get the permit to transport," I offered, not knowing that this fellow—as a deputy of the town—could sign them himself.

"I'm in business to make money," he said candidly.

Someone offered me money. "Let him do it. Let him do it."

But a quiet realization made me gently but firmly answer, "No," and the undertaker left the house.

Only months before, a friend in my writers' group had brought us her article, "How to Bury Your Own Dead in Vermont." Its historical background had awakened an identity with my own Vermont ancestors. The task of grappling with "arrangements" seemed enormous. I understood just how easy it would be to let a funeral director take over as I drained my body with tears. But I felt a strong need to express my love and caring for John, even in death.

I knew that under Vermont law I could transport the body myself. I would need the permit to do so, and it would mean asking for the help of a friend with a stationwagon or truck. But would I fall apart when I got near John's body? I needed to find out. I grabbed my coat and headed toward the door.

"Where are you going?" someone asked.

"I'll be back in a minute," I answered, not wanting to admit the purpose of my quest.

As I neared the group of officials at the end of the driveway, I could see the green body bag on the gurney, ready to be lifted into the hearse. And then I knew! Not only was I not going to fall apart, I was suddenly overwhelmed with the need to stay close. I knew that for me—and for John—my decision would be the right one.

Would this funeral director be willing to sell just his box? Yes. I asked if there would be a service charge to place the body in his $60 box. There wouldn't. "Then call me when you get back from the autopsy," I said, "and I will pick John up."

That the total cost would now be under $200 had become secondary. I needed to be a part of John's death as I was of his life. If I had had money, I would have lost that—given that away—in a moment of grief and confusion.

When our kids got up, I told them everything, as truthfully as I could. We all cried. The house was full now, and their grandmother took them off to play. (It was months later that their grief and questions finally spilled and continued to flow.) But I went on weeping, for our five-year-old daughter whose father would not be there on her wedding day, and our three-year-old son who would learn to fish without his dad. I moved through that day in a haze, a Tilt-a-Whirl of emotion. And I had calls to make.

I worried about asking my friend Richard to make the drive with me to St. Johnsbury. A sensitive older person who had lost his wife to cancer the year before, would he be uncomfortable on such a trip? It was not the way he had made his arrangements. But perhaps he'd understand. "Of course," he said, "John was my friend."

And so that snowy evening after the children had gone to bed, we drove to the funeral home to pick up John's body. The town clerk met us to sign the transit permit and share a hug. Then Richard and I left on the 50-mile trip, quietly crying, sometimes talking, sometimes silent. It seemed a long trip but one that should not be hurried.

Mr. Pearl had agreed to meet us at the crematory even though it was well after usual business hours. As we unloaded the box, I knew I had to see John one more time, even if his body was now a lifeless one. Richard got a screwdriver from under the front seat of the truck. And as we lifted the cover, I wept for the tender, gentle man I had married, whose life I had shared with so much joy. Then I softly patted his face a final good-bye. The person that I loved was living in my heart. I was ready to let the body go.

~❖~

John had been a rare and special person, not just for me but for the many children he had taught and for those whose lives he had touched. I became aware that others needed to express their love for John, to share his death as well.

In the obituary, I asked the newspaper to announce an "Open House" in his memory two days later. It seemed as if hundreds came. We heard John's favorite music from "Oliver," the show his Children's Theater Group had done so well the year before. And we were surrounded by flowers like the gardens he had loved. Our weeping and our laughing memories blended in a celebration of the gift his life had been to us.

# Raphael

There was no notice in the paper, no formal obituary. But on this early summer evening, the dirt road was lined with cars and trucks. We walked somberly toward the rustic country home. I took a bucket with blooming iris and my shovel. With me were my children—one a next-year's kindergarten classmate of the boy now dead, the other slightly older—and Grandma on a cane.

Familiar people stood in quiet clusters around the yard, for the house was nearly full. I could hear a resonant voice though I did not recognize the reading and, as my children slipped inside, I followed to be near. They found other children sitting on a stairway and moved close beside the dead child's sister, looking down. Their eyes were on the body in the small pine box. Lupines pink and purple in casual arrangements were all around. But my attention sought the sorrow-laden parents—the mother with the youngest daughter in her arms, her husband by her side. I was glad the poem continued on, for I needed the comfort of that metered voice and time to weep my silent tears.

Then the parents shared with us the joy they'd known in this their only son, a child who had cared and understood their march for peace though he had stayed at home that day. Others offered, too, the happiness remembered—the boy who was so proud that his father walked on stilts, the boy who had picked a friend that he would marry when he grew up.

A final reading drew us to the task at hand. An uncle closed the box, secured the lid. In quiet reverence, four assumed the burden of the load and passed on through the door. The children ventured next and led our way, a winding path through fern and woods. A tiny bell his father carried called us, too.

The box was resting by the hole, a careful oblong in the earth beside a birch, and on the boulder at one end a candle burned. His mother read the Song of Mourning in a Hebrew chant that others joined. Then one by one, we laid our flower bouquets upon his box, to share the journey on ahead.

It was his father who made the final move, who tearfully beckoned help to gently guide the box, with ready strings, to rest below. He took a shovel in his hands and stabbed the pile of dirt, then lifted it and cast the dirt into the hole. The shovel soon changed hands, and all of us—the children, too—moved earth to rest upon the flowers and the box. And father hugged a sobbing daughter as we filled the hole, planted iris and a rose.

It was a gentle singing that grew among the many there: songs of God, of Heaven, a lullaby. And though we choked and wept, we sang again—of love and life, in memory of this soul.

~❖~

Raphael, age 5, died sleeping in his mother's arms. He'd had pneumonia, though no one—even doctors—had known. His parents brought his body back from the New York grandparents they had been visiting at the time of the 1982 June peace march. His was a country burial on their own land in Middlesex, Vermont. (First printed in the *Vanguard Press,* September 1982)

# Mary Jane
*by Steve Carlson*

Although my mother was only 63 years old, her death was "expected," at least by the people who worked at the hospital. She had been terminally ill for some time, and her doctors were amazed she held on and remained productive as long as she did.

Yet when the time came for funeral arrangements, we were not well prepared. We had to learn and plan quickly at a time of great stress.

Our failure to plan ahead was not, I suspect, unusual. Before she got sick, Ma was young and healthy, so there seemed to be little reason to discuss death.

Then, when she was stricken by a disease considered 100 percent fatal, she wasn't ready to die. As a teacher and writer, she had projects to complete and people who relied on her to help make meaning of their own lives. So she fought the disease.

Although she was given zero odds by the medical community, Ma was fighting to win. She said more than once she only wanted to be around people "who believe in miracles." Could we doubt her? Did John Henry's family ask him what they should do if the steam drill won?

We weren't just humoring her. Friends and family alike became convinced that if anybody could beat back an incurable disease, Mary Jane could. Funeral planning was a taboo subject which, if it had been brought up, would have hastened her death and ended her hopes of achieving more of her life's goals.

Her foe was the AIDS virus, but the situation would have been the same if she had been stricken by cancer, stroke, heart disease, or any other illness more commonly afflicting people my mother's age.

She did hedge her bets in the final weeks. Weak and bedridden, she asked her four sons to be with her, in shifts, 24 hours a day. In addition to caring for her physical needs, she wanted at least one of us there whenever she was able to summon up the energy to talk. She had things to tell us and, by implication, there was little time left.

It was a difficult time for all of us. My brothers and I had to juggle busy schedules and important commitments, but being with our mother took priority at this time of need.

At her request, on June 16, 1986, Ma was rushed to the hospital in extreme discomfort. She told her doctor she was now able to prepare for death, since she was satisfied that the more important aspects of her life's work would be continued. She said she needed three days of medical care, with her sons at her side, before going home to die. She repeated, for emphasis, her desire to die at home, not at the hospital.

During the three days, she summoned us as often as she was able, straining to speak. She commented on our shortcomings, specific tasks she wanted us to accomplish, political insights, and Biblical interpretations. It was not feasible for us to bring up other issues for discussion. She had only a few words left, which she had to reserve for subjects of her choosing.

She mentioned funeral arrangements only once. She said she wanted a simple burial, not cremation, and specified a location that had spiritual significance for her. The energy she consumed by making the brief request completely exhausted her.

Consistent with the schedule she had set, on June 19th the doctors agreed to send her home. She died a few hours later.

~❖~

Although none of us had experience with funeral arrangements, it didn't occur to us to delegate our final acts of love to outsiders.

In retrospect, that may have been partly because of our experiences when she was bedridden. Ma had preferred that her sheets be changed by family members, for example, even though trained nurses were far more skilled at replacing sheets on an occupied bed. That was because we took the time to rub her feet. She remarked more than once she needed her feet rubbed more than she needed the sheets changed. Yet nurses always seemed too busy to provide that extra attention.

When it came time for burial and tribute, the qualities of thoughtfulness, consideration, and love seemed far more important than professional expertise. Those qualities were abundant among Ma's family and friends.

All official acts had to await completion of a death certificate by my mother's doctor, who was out of state and wouldn't arrive until morning. In the meantime, it was up to us to notify friends and relatives.

Sitting in my mother's apartment, I telephoned as many close friends and relatives as I could. But the telephone calls were emotionally difficult, and I didn't personally know all of the people who should be informed.

My mother did, however, have an address book and a home computer. I was not familiar with her word processing program and am not good at learning new computer languages. But somehow—I think with my mother's help, but I won't try to convince you of that—about 140 letters were written that night.

My wife and I spent the night on the couch in Ma's apartment. Was it just a body in the other room or were we there to be with her? I'm not sure, but we needed to be there.

In the morning, after the death certificate was filled out, I called in an obituary to the local newspaper. The reporter was accustomed to talking with funeral directors who dictate the information in the newspaper's standard format. But she was patient with me as I struggled to recall the maiden name of my mother's mother, the dates of her various leadership positions, and the precise numbers of nieces and nephews.

There was a sense of urgency about burial once the permits were in order. None of us knew how quickly bodies decompose, so we didn't want to leave Ma in her bed any longer than necessary.

The family had been inclined toward cremation, but Ma had specifically requested burial, so two of my brothers built a simple pine casket and brought it to the apartment. Another brother spent an hour with Ma, quietly saying goodbye. Then each of us joined him, lifting a corner of the sheet to place Ma's body in the box.

The burial site my mother had requested was unavailable, so we chose what we guessed would be an equally desirable location for her: a hilltop owned by her brother where she had spent many happy years.

We needed approval from the municipal clerks of the city where Ma died and the town where she was to be buried. Neither clerk was very familiar with the tasks, because the forms are usually filled out by funeral directors, who are deputized for that purpose.

Both clerks, however, were extremely responsive and helpful. After checking with health officers and other officials, they performed their duties with a minimum of delay.

My brothers and I transported the casket in my pickup truck and spent the next eight hours digging the grave by hand. It was hard work, in clay soil with many large rocks. We were eager to meet all legal requirements, so we dug the grave six feet deep. We learned later that the law required only five feet, which would have saved us about an hour of hard labor, but complaints were minimal.

This task culminated weeks of shared work and shared emotions that brought the four of us closer together than anything else we could have possibly done. For many years we had been separated by distance, careers, and individual commitments. By working together at a time of great need we renewed and strengthened our family bonds. For my brothers and me, the private burial was the best way to say good-bye to our mother.

But others also needed a chance to pay their respects. (Although Ma was deeply religious, she was not a church member, so we had no prescribed procedure for honoring her.) We took the easiest route we could think of. We announced a memorial gathering a week after burial, brought a few jugs of cider, accepted offers by others to provide additional refreshments, and played it by ear.

Scores of people showed up, including some who drove great distances. None of us knew everybody else. The only thing we had in common was that Mary Jane had touched each of our lives in profound ways. But that was actually a lot to have in common and, gathering together, at least this one time, was important.

Lacking any formal rituals, we sat around the hillside grave site, saying and doing whatever seemed appropriate. Some spoke words of tribute, some recalled meaningful incidents and experiences, some sang songs, some planted flowers.

As far as I know, nobody felt uncomfortable, out of place, or unfulfilled. There were many comments about what a moving, special experience it was. Some of us remained long after the anticipated two or three hours, conversing and recalling our memories until sunset.

It would be inaccurate to say there were no funeral costs. Wood and nails for the coffin were worth a few dollars, as were the cider and other refreshments. People who drove to the burial site had to fuel up their cars, and I'm sure some of the flowers people brought had been purchased. But overall financial costs were so minimal that nobody kept track of who spent what. We were able to earmark whatever was left of Mary Jane's checking account (after her bills were paid) for publication of a book of her final writings.

We are not a wealthy family, but if any of us had thought that spending two or three thousand dollars for a professional funeral would have made the experience more meaningful for anybody involved, we would have raised the money. We have no regrets over our decision to handle arrangements ourselves.

We also handled probate ourselves, not a difficult task since there were few possessions and no disputes. The court clerk asked if the funeral director had been paid and was astonished to learn we hadn't hired one. No questions were asked about bills due to health care providers, utilities, or other creditors. Those bills got paid, of course, but we found it ironic that funeral expenses were the only obligation not entrusted to the good will and honesty of the family.

This experience with home burial is not offered as a blueprint for others. We were influenced by my mother's wishes, the needs of our family and friends, and the physical possibilities available to us. If Mary Jane's beliefs had been different, or if there hadn't been a rural hilltop that was appropriate for burial, the arrangements would have been far different. Perhaps, in other circumstances, help from a funeral director would have been desirable or necessary.

But since death is a common human experience, there are a couple of general conclusions that may be of use to others. One is the importance of planning ahead if at all possible: in our case, hard decisions were made harder because they were delayed until action became necessary. Another is that personal involvement in death arrangements is a way of fulfilling emotional needs that probably cannot be met in any other way.

# Hospice Didn't Know
*by Jan Buhrman Osnoss*

For the past two years, people have asked me "Why would you want to bury your mother yourself?" We hadn't set out to do it ourselves—it basically evolved as a process of elimination. We're conscious of our environment and try to preserve it any way we can. We do things ourselves whenever we can. When my mother was dying, it was natural that we began preparing for her death by doing some things ourselves.

My mother came to live with us after she was diagnosed with terminal colon cancer. We knew that she would die in our arms in the privacy of our home. My mother's life was a sorrowful one as she had suffered from mental illness for most of her adult life, so it was important that her death be dignified. Arranging for someone else to care for her was not a question—we knew that we would do most of it ourselves.

Choice. We choose how we will give birth, marry, and celebrate life's rituals, so I assumed I would have choices when it was time to bury my mother.

My mother was Catholic. When she was dying we were unable to find a Catholic priest in our area who was available to visit her. A Baptist minister, however, was available to come to visit my mother at our home. Discussion of the funeral arrangements began with him, and he put us in touch with the only funeral home in our area (we live on an island, Martha's Vineyard). We inquired about our options with the funeral home and were presented with a folder of services and prices, but none of the services met our expectations. The least expensive casket was made of particle board and was $700. My husband, Rich, a woodworker and builder by profession, said he would build a nice box himself.

Years earlier, I remember my mother saying that she wanted to be buried in a pine box, and we thought we would try to carry out her wishes. When Rich arrived at a local lumber mill, he found that the owner had just milled some logs of cryptomeria that had been sitting unused for years. Cyrptomeria is a wood which historically had been used in Asia in casket construction. It is cedar-like in its softness, light-weight in color, and exudes a rich aroma. The cost of the wood was under $50. Rich was in the midst of constructing our home at the time, so he built the coffin during the course of his workday.

My sister, whom I see only every few years, arrived from California to be with my mother and help with the arrangements. As Rich was building the coffin, my sister and I began to discuss how the inside should be finished. We decided that it should be lined with blues and reds, as these were my mother's favorite colors. We went to the fabric store and picked out pillow stuffing, satin, a pretty blue and gold fabric, pillows, lace, several small silk roses (her favorite flowers), and red ribbon. We spent the entire afternoon and evening covering pillows and sewing the fabric together. As we sewed and glued, we shared—we talked, laughed and cried. The scent of the box filled the house. It was similar to cedar with an earthy sweet fragrance. It was beautiful. The preparations became the vehicle for us to grieve my mother's impending death.

Then came the actual logistics of pulling off a "do-it-yourself burial." The first person we called was the cemetery caretaker. He thought our plans were feasible and informed us that we needed to purchase a plot, hire a grave-digger, and obtain a burial permit. I called the town clerk who said that I could probably get a burial permit through the Board of Health, but that they weren't meeting for some time. She also said that the funeral home acted as their agent for burial permits and hoped this wouldn't prevent us from doing our "own thing."

The cost of the plot—which has space for three more caskets—was $200. Our next step was to contact the local grave-digger and inform him of our plans. He said that we would have to purchase a concrete box called a grave-liner to be in accordance with the regulations of our town. His fees would be $200 for the digging and $400 for the liner. The price seemed high but not worth haggling about.

Hospice nurses came every day and were wonderfully supportive and encouraging of our plans in theory but voiced concern about the legality of burying my mother ourselves. A day or so after seeing the casket in our dining room, one nurse phoned saying that she had called the State Board of Funeral Directors. She said that what we were planning was completely illegal. She told us that we would have to contact the funeral home. I was reluctant to do this, as I knew the procedure and wanted to avoid the funeral home altogether. We had a casket, a grave digger, a minister, and a plot. I felt confident that we would not be arrested for our actions and could claim our rights through the U.S. Constitution's First and Fourteenth Amendments.

My mother died at 1:15 on Friday, October 15, 1993. My very dear friend Clarissa was with us. As soon as my mother passed away we began to wash her body and get her dressed. We talked about how we could get my mother to look her best, as my brother was due to arrive.

Clarissa remembered visiting her family in Ireland, where they placed pennies on the eyelids to keep them shut. We wrapped mother's head in a scarf to close her mouth. Our attempt at making her beautiful forced laughter through our tears.

The only thing that made the situation uncomfortable was the presence of an uneasy nurse who arrived at our house for the daily hospice visit at about the time my mother died. (This was the same woman who had called the Licensing Board earlier.) Hospice provided wonderful support for the dying but seemed to work against us when it came time to prepare for burial. It didn't make sense to me. I felt this was a very private and meaningful process we had chosen. When my husband carried my mother from the bedroom to the casket, a shoe fell off her foot, and my husband said to the nurse in humor that he was sure this would never happen in a funeral home. If we were breaking a law it wasn't to be malicious, destructive, or harmful. It was because we felt strongly that we could give my mother, even in death, the love that she deserved. At this point, the nurse said she was sorry but that she felt she had to step in. She said that we would have to include the funeral director because we needed a burial permit and the only way we could get one was from him. Relieved that she was gone, I didn't make much of her hurried departure.

We made the burial arrangements for the following morning: We called a bagpipe player, the minister, the gravedigger, and the cemetery caretaker. It was then that I understood the logistics of acquiring a burial permit. A death certificate comes from the doctor, and then a burial permit is issued. I thought I would be able to get the burial permit from the Board of Health after I had the death certificate in my hands. I called the doctor's office to get the death certificate and learned that the nurse who had left our house no more than a half hour earlier was already there at the doctor's office. I asked the receptionist if I could speak to the nurse. I told the nurse that I wanted the death certificate after it was signed. She told me that she had already met the funeral director at the office and had given it to him. She firmly told me that now it was in the hands of the funeral director, and I would have to deal with him! I had a hard time believing that all this signing and handling of papers had happened so quickly.

Feeling we needed to resolve the situation as soon as possible, my husband phoned the funeral director. The director said that we could do most of this ourselves but that we needed a hearse and someone to view the body. The cost would be $1,900. My husband felt at this point we had no choice, and he agreed to the director's proposal. My response, however, was that I was not going to pay someone $1,900 for something I was capable of doing myself. I called the director back and told him $1,900 was too much money and that my mother would never have ridden in a hearse. He said that he "would look the other way" on the hearse but that someone from the funeral home must come to the house, view the body, and witness the burial. He also told me that by law, the body (if it was not going to be embalmed) had to be buried within 24 hours of death. I could compromise but couldn't understand the rationale behind the now-lowered but still very high fee of $1,000.

I was not comfortable with the funeral director's position yet didn't want to make any further decisions that would prevent us from burying my mother the following morning. Questions filled my head. My mother had no money of her own, and I wondered what would happen if I didn't have the money. Would she not be buried? Would she still have a funeral? Who would pay? I decided I would call the chairperson for the State Board of Embalmers and Funeral Directors (the same person the hospice nurse called). He told me that what I was doing was completely illegal and wanted to know where I was calling from so he could turn me in or turn in the funeral director involved. (Turn in to whom, I wondered?) He also said that the absolute lowest possible fee the funeral director could charge was $1,900. I told him the reason I was calling was because I wanted to know what happened if someone was unable to come up with the money. He said he had *never* heard of a family who couldn't come up with $1,900. He told me I could call the state welfare office and that they might provide support. The conversation clearly wasn't moving in my direction, and I didn't want to give him any more information so I hung up.

When I called back to tell the funeral director that we had decided upon a grave-side service at 10 A.M. the following morning, I was told that there would be no one available at that time to come to our home. When I asked about viewing the body and witnessing the burial, the funeral director's response was, "I'm sorry, Ms. Buhrman, no one from our office will be available at that time." I took this to mean that they were stepping out of the way and allowing us to go ahead with our plans without their involvement.

Before we put my mother in the truck on the morning of the burial, our son asked if he could see Grandma. My husband asked him if he wanted to see her head or feet and my son said her feet. Rich lifted up the end of the lid so my son could peek in. His response was, "Oh, wow!" My son was able to satisfy his needs and questions as they presented themselves. I felt truly connected to my mother and knew that our involvement in the entire process was very much a part of life.

The grave-side service was beautiful. The bagpipes played. My son placed five roses on his grandmother's coffin, representing one rose for each of her five grandchildren. There were several children at the service, and my three-year-old son was able to explain to other children his own understanding and meaning of dying and death. He was able to touch her and talk to her both when she was alive in our home and after she had died. The experience and quality of involvement was something very personal. For me and my family, this was the loving and humane way to say good-bye.

A few days after we buried my mother, I received a call from the minister asking me to please call the funeral director, as he could lose his license for allowing us to bury my mother. I agreed to call, and the funeral director asked if I would come to his office and sign a release form and pay $100 for the burial permit. I told him that I thought $100 was a lot of money for typing up a few lines on a state-issued permit. He said that he had allowed us to do our own funeral but certain things, such as the price of the permit and signing of forms, were not negotiable.

I went to the funeral home on October 20, 1993. The director had a form ready for my signature with the date 10/15/93 next to where I was to sign. Then I began to read the agreement:

> I hereby acknowledge that I have the legal right to arrange the final services for the deceased, and I authorize this funeral establishment to perform services, furnish goods, and incur outside charges specified on this Statement. . . .

When I read this, I said to the director, "So here are my legal rights which no one seemed to be able to find when I wanted them, and *now* I am turning them over to you. This is exactly what I wanted from the beginning—my rights."

The director restated what he had said before, that he could lose his license if I didn't sign the form and that it was a set procedure, that this statement came from the State Board of Funeral Embalmers and Directors. He asked if I wanted the funeral home to bill me the $100. I said I would pay him then and there but that this would be the last money he would ever receive from my family for any future death.

I have since begun work with hospice to provide information on how a person can bury a loved one themselves if they so choose. The hospice folks with whom I have talked are now very supportive and eager for the legal details.

Being with my mother when she died and caring for her after her death made me acknowledge the celebration of life. It was a natural process for us. This may not be for everyone, but it should be made available to any family that wishes to be involved. Services, such as those offered by funeral homes, are there for those who need them, but those who wish to take burial arrangements into their own hands should have uncomplicated and dignified options as well.

When I am asked why I chose to bury my mother myself, I wonder why anyone would choose to have someone else care for a loved one's body. We fear death, so therefore we let others handle it—only to rob ourselves of the experience that will help comfort our hearts. I believe, as Jessica Mitford and James Farrell do, that we must experience that which makes us human. I feel more connected to life because of this experience, and it has brought my family together as never before. All families should have this opportunity available to them.[1]

---

[1] In April of 1996, after more than a year of legal research and lobbying efforts by Byron Blanchard of the Boston-based Memorial Society, state health officials announced that indeed local health boards could issue burial permits not only to undertakers but to anyone whose paperwork was in order. Although most have been cooperative, a few have been reluctant. The Memorial Society is prepared to mount a court challenge at any time a family is denied the requested permit.

# A Conflict of Interest?

## 5

The hospice movement has improved the quality of life for the dying. Hospice programs have made it possible for families to care for the dying at home or in a family-oriented respite facility. But there are probably as many different philosophies for operating a hospice as there are hospices. In some, once the moment of death has arrived, the hospice person leaves. In fact, getting "too involved" with families leads to burn-out, the literature says. After-death arrangements are usually left for the family to work out with the funeral director.

It may even turn out to be the funeral director who serves on the hospice board of directors. One has to wonder if having a funeral director on the board might be a conflict of interest. At one hospice facility in Ohio, for example, the local memorial society was not permitted to leave its low-cost-funeral-planning information on a table—the funeral director on the board there objected.

Following is an e-mail that was received in the FAMSA office, edited for anonymity at the request of the writer who feared for his job:

> I don't know. Maybe my perspective is different because I am a social worker, but I would have thought that the hospice movement would have embraced what you are doing. After all, our mutual concern is supposed to be for the patients and their families, right? As a social worker, I have been trained to advocate for the clients and to put their needs above any others.
>
> I'll explain further. I used to work at a hospice on the East coast, and we routinely gave out cost surveys of the various area funeral homes to our patients without any problems from the funeral home industry or from administration. Then my wife and I moved here.
>
> So, not thinking anything was different, I proceeded to call all of our area funeral homes to request the General Price Lists so I would have the information available for our clients. Sounded simple enough. One of the funeral homes, however, refused to send the info. Said if I wanted it, I had to come in to get it. And then he called my executive director to complain. I got called in by my director (not realizing I had done anything contrary to what I was supposed to be doing) and got told

in no uncertain terms that I would refrain from trying to get any more GPLs. I was not to provide the GPLs to anyone. The executive director then tried to take all the GPLs I had collected away from me. (I refused.)

Thanks for letting me vent. I love what I do, but some of these shenanigans bother me.

Perhaps the information in this book will stir more hospice programs that aren't already doing so to make available a wide range of resources on funeral planning. The following chapter demonstrates the value of knowing what the choices are.

# The Most Awful Wonderful Thing

*by Chris Sonnemann, R.N.*
*Pediatric Oncology and Hospice nurse*

## 6

When Yolanda died at age 14 after a 12-year battle with leukemia, her mother described the experience of personally taking her daughter's body to the mortuary—and then a few days later to the cemetery—as "the most awful wonderful thing" she had ever done. It is a sentiment I've heard from many others. It's one I've felt myself.

People who have spent weeks, months, or sometimes years caring for an ill person have done much for their loved one. Caring for them after death is a natural progression in completing the circle of care. In my experience as a pediatric oncology nurse—and most recently as a hospice nurse—I have noticed that families who care for their own dead have an easier time with their grief.

No, taking care of your own dead does not relieve grief altogether. People will continue to feel sad and lonely, and will experience the "fog" and lack of concentration that is part of the grief process. What they will not experience is the regret or "if onlys" that are common when there is no, or only partial, closure. It's important to touch and hold the dead body, and—for some—to wash and dress the body. I remind people that there is no hurry after death to have the body moved. It can remain at home for hours or days, whatever is comfortable. When people are given time, they become accustomed to the idea that the person is really dead, without the anxiety and wondering about whether the person is maybe still alive when the face is covered or the body is put into "the bag." Often, as family and friends gather, the body becomes less and less the focus and people are able to reminisce and remember the loved one's life. Interestingly, there is often a lot of joking and laughter as tension is released and good times are remembered. It is a healing grief.

~❖~

I personally experienced this for the first time 19 years ago when my father-in-law died while planting onions in our garden. Carl, who had been a country doctor for many years, had a history of hypertension and angina. It appeared that when he felt that he was having some sort of fatal episode, he leaned his garden tools against the house and laid down in the soil between the rows of vegetables.

We were told that because Carl had died unexpectedly we would have to wait until the coroner could speak to his doctor and release his body for disposition. We were directed to a local mortuary that could pick up and keep Carl's body until the coroner signed the death certificate.

Once the body had been removed, we had a chance to explore what to do next. Carl's wife Ruth favored burial; my husband Tom and I suggested cremation. We also called his parents' minister for counsel and support. When the minister asked what Carl would have wanted, we realized we really didn't know. We decided to get some sleep and settle things the next day.

Rising in the morning, we found that Ruth had gotten up early. She said she'd felt compelled to find a journal Carl had been keeping when he occasionally couldn't sleep. In this journal she found instructions, written some months earlier, for what he wanted done with his body when he died. He wanted to be cremated and have his ashes scattered among the giant redwoods in a nearby state park or on farm land that they had owned in northern Michigan.

Once Ruth read Carl's journal, our direction was clear as we proceeded to carry out his wishes. We found a crematory and learned what we would need to do to have his body cremated. We were told that we would have to get a death certificate signed by the coroner or his physician. With this in hand, we could then proceed to get a Permit for Disposition which we would need for the crematorium. A container of some sort would be required for the cremation, but it could be as simple as a cardboard box which they could provide for $15.

After much discussion, we decided that—rather than hiring the funeral home—we could do the necessary paperwork and transport the body ourselves. The funeral director was somewhat surprised by our decision but once he understood our determination—that we knew what had to be done, and that we had the right to do this—he became cooperative and helpful. We wrapped Carl's body in a white sheet, lifted his body onto a gurney, and finally loaded it into the back of our van. None of us was sure how we would feel about touching and handling his dead body. Wrestling with that uneasiness and doubt was far more difficult than the actual task proved to be.

As we drove to the coroner's office downtown, Ruth cautioned Tom to drive very carefully. If we got stopped for any infraction we might have an uncomfortable time explaining Carl's dead body. It was amazing how easily we found we could laugh at ourselves and at the situation we found ourselves in. The healing had already begun.

With the proper forms in hand and Carl's body wrapped in the back of the van, we headed for the crematorium. I went in first to pay the fees. The man at the desk told me that his family had owned the crematorium for 45 years and that it was becoming more common for bodies to be brought directly to them without a funeral service first, but this was the first time in his memory that a body had been brought by the family. He helped us remove Carl's body from the van and place it in a box on the gurney. We then each took a few minutes to say our final goodbyes, shed a few tears, and left him there to be cremated the next day.

As we drove home we all expressed a surprised feeling of euphoria. We smiled, laughed, and talked of how pleased Carl would have been knowing that we had done all we could for him by ourselves and that it had cost less than $200. We felt a closeness—defined by having cared for Carl in those last hours. Family members knew of Carl's negative feelings about the funeral industry and his desire to not be taken advantage of, but we knew that few could grasp the meaning of what the three of us experienced and felt.

We learned much from our experience. We learned the importance of writing down wishes—having written instructions was a gift left for us by Carl. We learned the power of knowing what was lawful—what we could and could not do. Being able to be clear and express to others what we did and did not want, we were not influenced—even in a state of shock—by "what is usually done." And most importantly, we learned of the healing that came with doing all that we could for someone we loved.

Since that time, I have helped take my own father to be cremated. After her experience with Carl, Ruth asked that we arrange things in the same fashion for her. I have also assisted numerous times when patients were taken directly to the mortuary or crematory by family members. I let people know that they legally have this choice and encourage them to talk about it ahead of time.

I especially urge parents dealing with the death of a child to take some part in the funeral rituals. The need for constant care and attention when a child is ill is very intense. Death seems inconceivable. The emotional emptiness when the body of a child is abruptly taken away seems to deepen the despair, making it that much more unbearable. But the sense of "having done all I could" has profound healing effects. In my experience, no parent has ever regretted having done at least a portion of the funeral preparations.

~❖~

One of the most profound experiences I have had as a nurse was with Morgan, a young oncology patient, and his family. I developed a special relationship with Morgan. It was not, however, love at first sight. Morgan was not happy about coming to the oncology clinic, and for about nine months he had used a protective cloak of silence to avoid interacting with the clinical staff. I learned long ago not to take such defenses personally, and I don't give up easily. So I kept talking with Morgan—telling him about my own three sons and asking Morgan about his life outside the clinic. One day, Morgan arrived at the clinic carrying a "He-Man" figure. Having had personal experiences with these characters through my own children, I began a discussion that broke the ice between us forever.

When treatment failed and it became clear that Morgan would not survive, I visited his home more and more often according to his needs. That meant there would be no more interruptions of the continuous infusions of morphine that he was receiving to combat the intractable pain due to metastases of his bone, the result of advanced Neuroblastoma.

I sometimes made the trip alone and sometimes with my family, on weekdays or on weekends. My boys played with Morgan and his sisters, and I used those opportunities to talk with Morgan's parents about what to expect as he neared the end of his life and to reassure them that they could help him in dying by just being with him.

As Morgan's disease progressed, he required increased transfusions. I borrowed an IV pole from the clinic, loaded the family ice chest with blood products, and cared for Morgan at home in his own bed.

During this time, Morgan's most comfortable position was propped against the front of his mom or dad. Because his parents alternated this "holding" continuously, it was clearly taking its toll on them. Shortly before he died, I was able to convince Morgan that I could take a shift at holding him so that his parents could take a much needed walk together. In the safety of those moments, Morgan talked with me about his fear of the unknown and sought my assurance that his family would be okay after his death. He wanted to know if dying would hurt and if his family would be sad. He asked if I thought that they would forget him. I told him that I believed that death would relieve him of his pain and that though his family would be very sad, they would never, ever forget him.

The day before Morgan died his parents asked me to talk with his sisters, ages 8 and 14, about his impending death. The parents were concerned that they lacked the strength and energy to make it clear that Morgan would not improve this time as he had always done in the past when he was ill. I took the girls out into the garden to tell them that Morgan was dying and what they could expect when he died. We always try very hard to make the siblings of our patients feel that they are an important part of what is happening. At first they snickered and didn't really believe me. Then, as the reality of what I said sank in, they became angry and ran to their rooms crying. I returned to help care for Morgan so that his parents could comfort his sisters. I still recall this as one of the most difficult things I have been asked to do as a pediatric oncology nurse.

I was called immediately when Morgan died and drove the 40 miles of winding roads to his home that night. After a time of embracing and quiet discussion about the details of what had happened when Morgan died, I asked the family if they had thought about what their next steps would be. The topic of funeral arrangements had been broached before, but the family had never been able to accept making those arrangements.

I was able to share with them their legal choices for handling Morgan's body. I informed them that they could keep his body at home with them until they decided what to do. I reassured them that they needn't call a hearse immediately to come and take his body away but that they could transfer his body themselves when they were ready. Because they had decided that Morgan was to be cremated, I informed them that his body need not be prepared in any special way for disposition. The family seemed very relieved.

They kept Morgan with them at home for two days. During that time, they were able to adjust to his death and say their goodbyes in their own way and their own time. I returned each day to support and encourage what they had chosen to do. I arranged for the death certificate to be signed and the disposition papers to be completed so that Morgan's body could be cremated without complication.

Morgan's dad and uncle built a casket of pine wood. Friends from school, friends from the community, and relatives had time and opportunity to come by and paint a picture or write a message to Morgan on the casket that would be cremated with his body. What a wonderful final gift Morgan's family gave him, and to all those who loved him, by opening their hearts and home to others who needed to say goodbye and grieve. When the time came to take Morgan's body to the crematorium, his parents tenderly wrapped him in a sheet, placed him in his decorated casket, and drove him to the crematory themselves.

Morgan's parents have been a wonderful support for other families who are facing the death of a child. They are able to share how their grief was eased by having done all they could for their son, even in his death. Indeed, those parents who handle all funeral arrangements themselves seem to heal more quickly. The hands-on experience brings an inner peace in spite of their loss.

# General Information

# What is a "Traditional" American Funeral?

## 7

In early America, home funerals were the practice everywhere, and each community had a group of women who came in to help with the "laying out of the dead." In some parts of the country, religious and ethnic groups have maintained the practice of caring for their own dead. (See Chapter 9.)

In the mid-nineteenth century, with the increase of mobility and the onset of the Civil War, preservation of bodies through embalming was sometimes used for the convenience of distant relatives or the shipping of the deceased. Undertaking became at least a part-time job in many towns, often attached to a livery stable or furniture store. President Lincoln's body was embalmed and traveled by train—on display in many states—before burial. This surely contributed to an increased use of embalming in North America, even though this procedure was—and still is—rarely used elsewhere.

Along with the spread of wealth in this country, it became common to include a display of community position and status at the time of a person's funeral. One sociologist, quoted by the editors of *Consumer Reports* in the book *Funerals: Consumers' Last Rights*,[1] states that ". . . because people increasingly lack both the ceremonial and social mechanisms and arrangements that once existed to help them cope with death, monetary expenditures have taken on added importance. . . ." In large cities, this practice prompted sufficient business that undertakers could begin keeping elaborate establish-ments available on a regular basis. Furthermore, crowded urban housing made home funerals more difficult. What once occurred at home was moved to funeral parlors.

By the turn of the century, the term "funeral director" was considered preferable to "undertaker" (at least by those in the business), and the newly formed National Funeral Directors Associa-tion was eagerly pressing its members to consider themselves "professionals," not tradesmen as

---

[1] *Funerals: Consumers' Last Rights.* Copyright ® 1977 by Consumers Union of United States, Inc., Mount Vernon, NY 10553.

the earlier coffin makers had been. Casket manufacturing emerged as a new and separate industry. Preservative or "protective" qualities were being claimed for the new inexpensive-to-produce metal caskets, and—with high mark-up—profits soared. The regular use of embalming was also encouraged, and the new "professionals" used this to suggest that they were keepers of the public health at a time when many diseases were prevalent.[1]

As communities grew more diverse, funeral homes were established to serve specific ethnic or religious groups. There are now two to four times the necessary number of full-time mortuaries in most states. (People seemed willing to pay exorbitant fees for service by "one of their own"—someone from the same social or geographic community.) Just as women at the beginning of this century had turned the management of childbirth over to the medical profession, death was turned over to the undertakers, morticians, and funeral directors.

In the conclusion of his scholarly work, *Inventing the American Way of Death, 1830–1920,* historian James Farrell writes:

> The paraphernalia of the American way of death keep people at one remove from their own feelings. . . . This social convention developed historically, but it continues today, as Americans delegate control of death and the funerals to specialized funeral service personnel. Consequently, funerals are custom-made only in the same sense that automobiles are, and the price we pay for paying our last respects in the American way of death is the price of our personality, which we have purposely withheld from the funeral. By our passive role in directing our funerals, we have transformed an important rite of personal passage into an impersonal rite of impassivity. There have been costs as well as benefits from the American way of death.

No doubt in an effort to make it seem less impersonal in today's world, Michigan funeral director Thomas Lynch offers up vignettes of twentieth-century, small-town lives and deaths in *The Undertaking—Life Stories from the Dismal Trade* (Norton, 1997). His mischievous play with words and his sometimes-earthy romance with life itself generated widespread acceptance for this lyrical penning. Readers—eager perhaps

---

[1] The NFDA web site still claims embalming protects the public health even though no such benefit exists. See "Embalming" chapter.

to be reassured that "the last person to let you down" won't do so—were, with the exception of one *New York Times* review, uncritical.[2]

In fact, if anyone could understand a family's need to care for the dead, I thought that Lynch would:

> . . . Because my father owned a funeral home, it fell to my brother Dan and me to dress Pop Lynch and casket him—the first of my people I ever tended to professionally. I can't remember now if my father simply asked if we would or insisted or offered us the opportunity. But I remember feeling, immediately, relieved that I could do something, anything, to help.

And of his father's death he writes:

> It was something we had always promised him, though I can't now, for the life of me, remember the context in which it was made—the promise that when he died his sons would embalm him, dress him, pick out a casket, lay him out, prepare the obits, contact the priests, manage the flowers, the casseroles, the wake and procession, the Mass and burial. . . .
>
> The bodies of the newly dead are not debris nor remnant, nor are they entirely icon or essence. . . . It is wise to treat such new things tenderly, carefully, with honor.
>
> . . . If the dead are regarded as a nuisance from whom we seek a hurried riddance, then life and the living are in for like treatment. McFunerals, McFamilies, McMarriage, McValues. . . .
>
> Thus tending to his death, his dead body, had for me the same importance as being present for the births of my sons, my daughter.

---

[1] At the start of his book Lynch boasts, "Every year I bury a couple hundred of my townspeople. Another two or three dozen I take to the crematory to be burned." Lynch continues, ". . . you can calculate how big a town this is and why it produces for me a steady if unpredictable labor." And so I did. With a population of 5,511 and a national death rate of 8.4 per thousand, one might expect 46 or so in his town of Milford to die each year—maybe one a week—unless something in the drinking water there is killing folks five times as fast as anywhere else. Assuming that *all* of the 10,000 people in the Highland township area would use Milford's "Lynch & Sons" and *none* of the 12 other funeral homes in a 10- to 20-mile radius of similarly sparse population, business would average 126 funerals a year—about two and a half funerals a week.

Mr. Lynch is a little loose with significant facts in other portions of his book, too. See Chapter 11 on Body Donation.

One has to wonder if Lynch is too close to his topic, however. Has he somehow missed the whole point, or could he simply not resist a parting sales pitch? Regarding his own funeral, he writes:

> On the subject of money: you get what you pay for. Deal with someone whose instincts you trust. If anyone tells you you haven't spent enough, tell them to go piss up a rope. Tell the same thing to anyone who says you spent too much. Tell them to go piss up a rope. It's your money. Do what you want with it.[1] But let me make one thing perfectly clear. You know the type who's always saying "When I'm dead, save your money, spend it on something really useful, do me cheaply"? I'm not one of them. Never was. . . . And if a little upgrade in the pomp and circumstance makes you feel better, consider it money wisely spent. Compared to shrinks and pharmaceuticals, bartenders or homeopaths, geographical or ecclesiastical cures, even the priciest funeral is a bargain.

The Consumer Reports book quotes the late Erich Lindemann, M.D., a Harvard psychiatrist, as saying that the most useful part of the funeral process is "the moment of truth that comes when living persons confront the fact of death by looking at the body." Funeral directors such as Thomas Lynch would choose this as a reason to suggest an open-casket funeral. Caring for your own dead is even more to the point.

With the spread of the hospice movement and the popularity of Elisabeth Kübler-Ross's book *On Death and Dying,* many families are again dealing with death in a more personal way. Some families are now choosing to handle death arrangements privately, without the use of a funeral director. Relatives who have done so share a feeling of spiritual and emotional fulfillment. For many, it has facilitated the grieving process by keeping the family involved. Some have felt they were better able to "let go" when the time came. Fears of not being able to see, touch, and handle a body have proved unfounded: "It was not as difficult

---

[1] As long as it's not cremation, he should have added. Throughout the book is Lynch's subtle and not-so-subtle disdain for those who opt for anything other than the elaborate, body-on-display funeral he unabashedly glorifies. That cremation could be a caring choice is beyond his bias to understand. "We burned the trash and buried the treasure. This is why, faced with life's first lessons in mortality—the dead kitten or bunny rabbit, or dead bird fallen from its nest on high—good parents search out shoe boxes and shovels instead of kindling wood or barbecues." (I wonder what he suggests "good parents" do when they don't have a yard in which to "bury" the kitten?) And while Lynch laments the forgotten boxes of cremated remains never retrieved from the funeral home—as propaganda, no doubt, that those who cremate are indifferent—he fails to mention the graves never visited, equally forgotten.

as I thought it would be,". . ."I had to be close,". . ."I could not give his body to strangers." The Natural Death Care Project in Sebastopol, California helped nearly 60 families its first year, and the program is now spreading to other areas and states.

Undoubtedly one factor that prompts people to care for their own dead is avoiding the "priciest funerals." But of those who have described their experiences, all have felt—after the funeral—that caring for their own was ultimately more important than the dollar saving.

Some, of course, will still choose to work with a mortuary, but they, too, can also take charge—to personalize the funeral observance. A funeral home price list that offers up "Our *traditional* funeral package" is foisting its own ready-made rituals on a family to guarantee a good sale.[1] The Baby-Boomers are unlikely, however, to be so gullible: Just as they took back control of the birthing experience, many will choose to handle death more actively, more distinctively—with or without a funeral director. Sensitive and caring morticians will encourage families to establish and honor their own traditions, regardless of how much or how little is spent. Change is again predictable for "the American way of death."

---

[1] In the truly *traditional* funeral, Grandma was laid out in the front parlor.

# Managing Death: Necessary Information

## 8

## Important!

Persons who choose to handle death privately must take great care to follow all state and local regulations. The requirements are not complex, but failure to meet them can lead to unpleasant situations and create a climate in which professionals become less willing to work with families.

One crematory, for example, was sued for rejecting a body sent by a family. The case was thrown out of court, and rightly so, because the family had merely hired someone to deliver the body without a death certificate, transit permit, or authorization from next-of-kin for cremation. Another crematory will no longer accept bodies directly from families because in one particular case, the family had assumed that medical personnel would fill out the forms properly. While that seems like a reasonable assumption, in this case the cause of death as stated by the medical examiner on the permit to cremate was not written exactly as it had been on the death certificate, and the state later made an issue of it. In short, the procedures are quite simple and straightforward, but it is necessary to pay close attention to the details and to even be vigilant about careless errors that may be made by others.

## Death Certificate

Great care must be taken in completing the death certificate. Whiteout or other corrections are not usually permitted. If an error is made, you may have to start over again with a new certificate.

A death certificate signed by a doctor stating the cause of death must be filed—usually in the county or district where death occurs, or where a body is found, or where a body is removed from a public conveyance or vehicle.

The wording for the cause of death should follow national guidelines as summarized in the Appendix, and any family member acting as a funeral director should check carefully for this. If a doctor felt rushed when signing the form, the wording may not be acceptable or the doctor may have signed the form on the wrong line. These are common complaints of many registrars and funeral directors in almost every state.

Any such errors will necessarily cause a delay in obtaining the final permits for disposition.

If complicated laboratory work is needed to accurately determine the exact cause of death, the physician or medical examiner may write "pending" or a similar phrase for the cause of death and release the body for disposition. In those few cases, a "delayed" or corrected death certificate will be sent to the state registrar by the physician when the cause of death is known.

The death certificate information must be typed or written *legibly* in black ink (in some states, blue-black ink is permissible). In addition to the medical portion, facts such as "mother's maiden name" must be provided by the family. Unless the signature of a licensed funeral director is required by state statute, the family or church member who is handling the arrangements must sign the death certificate in the space marked "funeral director," followed by his or her relationship to the deceased, immediately after the signature.

States vary in the time required for filing the death certificate with the local registrar, but this must usually be accomplished before other permits are granted and before final disposition.

## Fetal Deaths and Miscarriages

A special death certificate, or fetal death report, is required in all but two states for fetal deaths. Eleven states seem to require registration of *all* fetal deaths. In a majority of states, a fetal death must be registered if it occurs after 20 weeks of pregnancy. In Hawaii, the requirement goes into effect after 24 weeks.

Some states gauge pregnancy duration by fetal weight, *e.g.,* 350 grams (12.5 oz.), and since any unattended death—including fetal death—could require a coroner's investigation, a physician should be called.

Even if there is uncertainty as to whether reporting requirements are applicable, reporting a fetal death may be helpful in obtaining insurance benefits in some situations.

## Dealing with a Coroner/Medical Examiner's Office— Autopsy

Autopsies are generally required when cause of death is violent, unexpected, uncertain, or "unusual," including suicide. For this reason, the police should be called when death occurs outside a hospital or nursing home and is "unattended." If an ambulance service has been called first, the medics may notify authorities for you.

Death from a contagious disease may also necessitate involvement with a coroner or local health officer.

When body donation to a medical school has been planned, a family should request that no autopsy be performed. The decision will depend on the circumstances surrounding the death, and the state may prevail in ordering an autopsy in suspicious cases.

The practices in coroners' offices vary widely. In California, it is legal for medical examiners to amputate fingers for identification and remove tissue and organs for study. One woman discovered that her father had been buried without his heart when she arrived at a workers' compensation hearing and saw the heart presented as evidence.

An Alaskan funeral director was concerned that I would suggest family involvement because 20% of the deaths in his state are autopsied. The bodies are not usually closed by the medical examiners there, and he felt this experience would be traumatic for a family.

According to one California mortician, bodies picked up from the Los Angeles county morgue are rarely cleaned up and barely tacked back together, whereas other area coroners (and those in most states or cities) try to restore bodies to intact condition. This mortician cautioned that relatives choosing to handle arrangements when a coroner's office is involved may be treated indifferently and without compassion, as well as kept waiting for what may seem an unreasonable amount of time. There have been instances when such a delay stretched for days, and the body was released only after legal and political maneuvers. In any state, press and public pressure might help to improve state health department regulations and enforcement of them in such situations.

Generally, the funeral director a family has chosen picks up an autopsied body from the coroner's office. Nevertheless, in several states, the state is obligated to cover all costs of returning a body to a family if asked to do so. My request for return was honored here in Vermont. Perhaps if families routinely requested direct return of a body at state expense—even if a funeral director is to be involved later—more care might be taken with the condition in which a body is returned.

The term *medical examiner* is usually reserved for those with medical training, and the person in such a position is often appointed by the department of health. In a few states, the word *coroner* is used interchangeably with *medical examiner.* Generally, however, the term *coroner* implies an elected position. In California, a medical degree is required for a candidate to run for coroner. In other states, however, anyone may run for the office, with or without medical training.

A coroner may have a direct relationship with a funeral home, either as a practicing funeral director or by agreement. To avoid any appearance of impropriety, a coroner or medical examiner will usually rotate pick-up calls among all funeral homes within the jurisdiction, but this is not always the case. For example, one Wyoming funeral director told me that the only time he was called was when there was a disaster and there were more bodies than the other funeral home in town could handle. While law enforcement might, in some cases, choose not to call a particular funeral home if business practices are suspect, no family should feel obliged to continue a relationship with a funeral home just because a body arrived at that destination under state aegis.

Routine handling of dead bodies may harden the sensibilities of some of the people who work in the fields of pathology and forensic medicine. That may explain, but does not excuse, insensitive behavior. I believe that any state government should be obligated to assure that the dead are treated with dignity and that families are treated with courtesy and consideration.

## Home Death, Home Visitation

With hospice support, many persons are able to die at home in familiar surroundings, near familiar faces. In some states, an "expected" death can be certified by an attending nurse.

A home death can allow the family additional time to obtain permits and make necessary arrangements. Turning off the heat in a room or turning on an air-conditioner can make it reasonable to contain a body without further action for 24 to 72 hours or more, depending on the weather. People often ask, "Doesn't the body smell?" No, not usually for the first two or three days, *but* each situation must be considered individually quite apart from the weather and ambient temperature. Often in waning days, a failing person stops eating and drinking, and the body will become somewhat dehydrated even before death. Noxious odors are therefore unlikely during the next few days. The "robust" body of someone who had just finished a meal of corned beef and cabbage prior to death, however, might produce telltale odors.

There appears to be some therapeutic value to keeping the body at home for at least a brief period, allowing the family a chance to congregate and deal with the death, as often occurred in the front parlor two or three generations ago.

## Nursing Home Death

When death is anticipated in a nursing home, it will be important to work out your plans with the nursing home staff ahead of time. If the deceased has had only a semi-private room, for example, the nursing home may have no other location to hold the body while paperwork and other errands are done. Staff members are accustomed to calling a funeral director, regardless of the hour, and expect the removal within a very short time. Out of consideration for other residents, it may not be feasible for the nursing home personnel to allow a long delay while permits, a container, and vehicle are obtained.

## Hospital Death

Disposition of a fetal or infant death can be handled entirely by the hospital as a courtesy if a family so chooses. (Many funeral homes or crematories charge little if anything for an infant death, depending on the arrangements.)

When other deaths occur in a hospital, the relative on hand should ask the nursing staff to remove any life-support articles such as catheters, IV needles, and feeding or breathing tubes. A catheter, for example, is held in place by a "balloon" and is not as simple to remove as an IV needle. Some of the nasal tubes appear especially disfiguring after death and may be of concern to other family members who are expected later to help with the death arrangements. Most hospitals will cooperate with this request, although not all are accustomed to doing so.

Some hospitals may be reluctant to release a body directly to a family without the use of a funeral director. If the death involved is an "expected" death, advising the hospital staff of your intentions ahead of time may be helpful. If hospital personnel are confused or misinformed about their obligations, a telephone call from your lawyer may be in order.

It is important for families to recognize the legitimate needs of hospitals. Some hospitals may have no storage facilities for dead bodies while permits are obtained and may insist on calling a funeral director for immediate removal after death if there is to be any significant delay.

## Body and Organ Donation

Donation of eyes and other organs must be done under sterile conditions and usually within a short time after death. Because organ donor cards may not be immediately available to hospital personnel, next-of-kin should make this decision known to attending staff at the earliest time possible.

Hospital employees are often reluctant to approach a grieving, distressed family. Anyone who can find emotional healing in a gift of life or sight is encouraged to take the initiative in making such an offer even if the time of death is uncertain. The corneas of elderly persons can usually be used, and eyes (and sometimes skin) may be donated even if total body donation to a medical school is subsequently planned.

With the increasing success of organ transplants, persons and families must consider whether organ donation takes priority over body donation. There may develop a competition between those needing body parts and those who need whole bodies. Loss of a major organ involving a thoracic incision usually makes a body unacceptable for a teaching donation because of the difficulty in embalming a system interrupted by recent surgery. My husband and I have written in on the body donation cards we carry that organ donation is to be considered first. If organ donation is not needed, only then should our bodies be considered for body donation. If our bodies are not accepted, a plain pine box exit is what we want.

Body donation to a medical school may be an option even if the deceased has not enrolled in such a program. Check Chapter 11 and the particular requirements for the medical schools in your state. Also check that chapter for cautions about transportation reimbursements if you are not planning to deliver the body.

If a death occurs at home, it is unlikely that organ donation is an option. However, many eye banks have trained staff who can arrive within a relatively short time to remove the corneas.

## Embalming

No state requires routine embalming of all bodies. Special circumstances—such as an extended time between death and disposition—may make it necessary under state law. Interstate transportation by a common carrier may also necessitate embalming, although most airlines will waive that requirement if there are religious objections. Refrigeration or dry ice can take the place of embalming in many instances. Check the Yellow Pages for a source of dry ice. In some states, embalming may be required by law if the person has died of a communicable disease, although this is a seriously flawed requirement. (See Chapter 16.)

## Moving A Body

*Never move a body without a permit (or medical permission)!* Always call ahead before moving a body even if you have a permit. A medical school or crematory staff member who is unprepared, or a town clerk who just isn't sure about family burial plots may need some time and help in doing his or her job. By calling first to make arrangements at the destination, you will be expected and prepared.

The use of a simple covered box allows some dignity for all involved in the handling and moving of a body, regardless of final disposition.

If a family chooses to build the container for delivery of a body for cremation, the size should be considered. A standard cremation chamber opening is 38 inches wide and 30 inches high. A container two feet wide and 14 to 18 inches deep is usually sufficient for most bodies, however. One crematory mentioned that most home-made boxes tend to be too large. Ernest Morgan, in his book *Dealing Creatively with Death,* includes directions and measurements for a plywood container.

Simple cardboard containers (or "caskets") can be purchased from most funeral homes. Or check the internet: www.funerals.org/famsa/caskets.htm for sources. Some boxes are conspicuously more expensive than others because of construction. Some are paraffincoated, others plastic-lined, and some have plywood bottoms.

The length of the box for transporting the body should be considered in choosing the vehicle for transportation.

Most states require a permit for transportation or disposition. The death certificate must usually be completed first, and often a special permit-to-cremate is needed prior to cremation. In most states, funeral directors serve as deputy registrars. If death occurs during an evening, weekend, or holiday—when local municipal offices are closed—a funeral director may be needed to furnish or sign the disposition or transit permit. As a deputy of the state in this function, the funeral director should not charge for this service unless such a charge is already set by the state.

## Body Fluids

After death, the blood in a body settles to the lowest points, leaving the upper portions pale and waxy, with purple mottling below. Some parts of the body may swell a little.

Fluids may be discharged from body orifices. It will be helpful to use absorbent material—such as towels or newspapers—under the deceased. A sheet is convenient for wrapping and moving the dead person. If the person has died from a communicable disease, it will be important to take all health precautions with any discharge and in handling the body. Use a pair of latex rubber gloves. Your state may require the use of a funeral director in such a case. Consult your family doctor for instructions if the information for your state is not specific or if you are concerned.

When an autopsy has been performed or death occurs from trauma, the body may be wrapped in a vinyl body bag—available from a funeral director—to prevent additional leakage or seepage. A plastic, zippered mattress cover might work as well. However, if you plan on cremation, avoid any such materials whenever possible.

## Out-of-state Disposition

All states honor the properly acquired permits of other states when a body is to be moved from one state to another. There may be local regulations with regard to disposition, however. Check by telephone before setting out for the destination.

## Burial

If burial is chosen, the information in Chapters 12 and 13 may be helpful. In some states, when burial will be outside the county or town where death occurred, you will need an additional permit to inter (whether on private land or in a cemetery) from the local registrar in that area.

The statutes and regulations of some states include depth requirements for burial; these are listed in the state-by-state information in Part II. Standard practice in many states places the top of the coffin at least three feet below the natural surface of the earth. A burial location should be 150 feet or more from a water supply and outside the easement for any utility or power lines.

## Cremation

When cremation is chosen, an additional permit is often required from the local coroner or medical examiner. A modest fee is usually charged for this. If the deceased did not sign a cremation authorization (on the right forms) prior to death, authorization from next-of-kin is required by most crematories. Usually this can be obtained by fax, Western Union, or overnight mail if family members live out of state.

Next-of-kin is determined in this order (although it varies slightly from state to state):

(1) surviving spouse
(2) all adult sons and daughters
(3) parents
(4) all adult siblings
(5) guardian or "person in charge."

That is, if there is a surviving spouse, his or her permission is all that is required. If there is no surviving spouse but several children, all adult sons and daughters may be required to grant permission for disposition by cremation. Adult siblings must assume responsibility if no spouse, off-spring, or parents survive.

While some states have laws that specifically grant a person the right to dictate disposition prior to death (and case law often honors such wishes in other states), a crematory will hesitate to accept a body if there is a difference of opinion among survivors. In trying to settle those differences, courts will likely defer to the wishes of the deceased, unless there are unusual circumstances.

A pacemaker must be removed before cremation. The services of an attending physician, the medical examiner, or a funeral director can be requested for this. On the other hand, one funeral director told me, "Anyone can do it." A pacemaker is about the size of a silver dollar, embedded just under the skin, usually near the neck or lower on the rib cage. A shallow incision would make it readily accessible, and the wires to which it is attached should be snipped. If a pacemaker is not removed and explodes during the cremation process, repairing damage to the cremation chamber may be the liability of the person delivering the body. One crematory operator in Washington state claims to cremate pacemakers routinely with no problem. All others I spoke with, however, said failure to remove a pacemaker can cause significant damage.

## Selecting a Crematory

I have chosen to list crematories in the state sections, not because I specifically prefer cremation but because most people don't know where the crematories are. I am told there are about 1,181 crematories in the U.S. at this time and 139 in Canada. But not all are available on any one list. Furthermore, with the increase in the popularity of cremation, there are new ones being built all the time. Check your state funeral board or the Yellow Pages. If there is no separate listing for crematories, there may be mention of such in the mortuary ads in the funeral home section.

## Obituary

When a person dies, it is almost impossible to personally notify everyone who knew or cared about the deceased. Close friends and relatives, of course, should be informed by a phone call or letter before they read about the death in the newspaper. But an obituary will help assure that the news reaches a wider circle of acquaintances in a timely manner. It is the logical place to mention any services planned, even if a memorial gathering is scheduled for a later date.

Although it will be the responsibility of a family managing death privately to arrange for an obituary if one is desired, even those working with a mortician may choose to take on this task as an expression of final tribute.

It is a good idea to telephone the paper, to learn its policies and any costs, before writing the obituary.[1] Your local paper may have a standard format for obituaries or expect certain information to be included. An obituary can generally be phoned in or faxed. If there is no funeral director involved, the person at the paper may ask for a copy of the death certificate just to be sure that the obit is not a practical joke (as has happened from time to time, I'm told).

Some newspapers charge for obituaries, while others print them as a public service. Big-city newspapers generally print obituaries only if the deceased is considered well-known or influential. Most small-to-medium circulation newspapers will accept obituaries if the deceased lived or was known within their circulation area. It should be emphasized that the policies of newspapers vary greatly. Some newspapers, for example, consider obituaries to be "advertising" for funeral homes, and will charge a high price if a funeral home is mentioned. On the other hand, they may run the obituary free of charge if no funeral establishment is named.

It is possible that the newspaper will let you personalize the obituary, to capture the personality and even the sense of humor of the deceased. The son of Frank Simmons did so with obvious affection:

---

[1] In North Carolina, Nancy Spivey ran into a problem with a self-important obit editor named Betty at the *Greensboro News and Record.* With a husband under hospice care and planning for the inevitable, Nancy went to the paper to get the rates and procedures. At first, Betty said they couldn't take an obituary from anyone other than a funeral director. Nancy explained there wouldn't be a funeral director as the family was handling all arrangements. Then Betty said she would want confirmation from the cemetery that Clyde had been buried, which meant that the notice wouldn't run in time to notify folks who might want to attend the graveside service that was planned. Nancy offered to have the hospice nurse call to verify the death when it occurred. Would that satisfy Betty? Nooooo! "Anyone could say they were a hospice nurse." I suggested in a call to Betty that perhaps Nancy should drive up to the newspaper with Clyde's body in the casket so Betty could see for herself. "We're not experts," was her retort. Too bad that Betty didn't have the courtesy to say to Nancy, "Let me see what we can do to help you. This is outside our normal procedures, but I'm sure we can work something out." Nancy has asked the state newspaper association to discuss this issue, to spare the next family from another bureaucratic "Betty."

Frank Cecil Simmons died on Wednesday, March 19, 1997, following a brief illness in the Woodridge Nursing Home in Berlin.

He was born on April 1, 1911 in Larned, Kansas and graduated from Westport High School in Kansas City, Missouri. Frank's varied career included work as a horserace handicapper, professional pool and poker player. During WWII, he worked as a supervisor for Pratt and Whitney Aircraft manufacturing, and after the war, became a jet engine inspector for Westinghouse. He later worked as an inspector for Thikol Chemical Co. on the Minute Man missile. In his 50s and 60s, Frank worked as production manager of Electro Plating Inc., as a bail bondsman, and as an Indian jewelry entrepreneur at the Elephant's Trunk, all in Kansas City. Frank retired and moved to Vermont in 1991, in order to live near his family, and there he began a new career assisting his son, Robert, as senior advisor to the Heaven and Earth Company of Marshfield.

An avid sportsman, he was a champion amateur tennis player and golfer, and he spent many years hunting and fishing throughout the Midwest and Utah. In Vermont, he accompanied family members on trout fishing expeditions, and participated in the raising of both his grandson, Moe, whose acting aspirations he wholeheartedly supported, and the family's golden retriever, Hobbes. Frank was a highly adept dog trainer, and in addition to his work with hunting dogs, he single-handledly trained Hobbes to eat huge quantities of dog biscuits.

After moving into the Woodridge Nursing Home in 1996, Frank took seriously his new avocation of flirting with his nurses and attempting to persuade them to bring him beer and cigars.

Frank was married to Helen Farley from 1940 to 1963. He is survived by his son Robert, daughter-in-law Kathy Helen Warner, and grandson Moebius McCartney Simmons, all of Marshfield. He is also survived by his daughter Patricia Howard and grand-daughter Stacy Howard, both of Las Vegas, Nevada.

May you exist in eternal joy in the clear and living Light that is God.

Frank disliked funerals, so there will be no service. Contributions in his name may be made to the Twinfield Stagelights Fund, Twinfield Union School, Marshfield, VT.

~❖~

## Miscellaneous but Still Important

- It is not uncommon for family members to forget to remove jewelry at the time of death.
- A family using the time of a mortician for advice should find it reasonable to pay a consultant's fee.
- Going back to the crematory to view the body again is expecting an additional service, too, if that is even possible.

- If a person who works in a funeral home or crematory offers to file a death certificate, he or she would be performing a service for which there may be a charge.
- Some crematories expect to be paid at the time a body is delivered, even if the family expects to receive insurance or other death benefits. Some have a 30-day billing period.

~❖~

When private death arrangements are made in an area of the country where the practice is not already established, you can expect some hesitancy on the part of involved persons such as registrars and town clerks. Some hospitals may even be reluctant to release the body to a family. I have tried to include in each state section relevant legal citations enabling family disposition. People in authority, accustomed to delegating their duties to funeral directors, may have to be informed of their responsibilities. That can be frustrating, particularly when you are enduring a time of loss and grief. The majority of these people will probably be concerned with performing their duties appropriately. Few will intentionally want to hinder your choice if you have followed all required procedures and if you seem well-informed.

# A Free Funeral: Starting a Funeral Committee in Your Congregation

## 9

Throughout history, all major religions have established traditions for caring for the dead, and individual congregations have assumed that responsibility for members. When a person died, the local religious community to which he or she belonged provided the needed support to family and friends, making and carrying out appropriate arrangements consistent with their spiritual beliefs.

In twentieth-century America, the professional funeral industry has chipped away at—and in many cases almost obliterated—the traditional role of religious communities. Funeral homes, with their own "chapels," have become surrogate for-profit churches, charging enormous fees for the tasks formerly performed by clergy and fellow congregation members.

As we approach the millennium, many religious groups, representing many different faiths, are giving some thought to reclaiming their traditional roles. In the FAMSA office, I receive frequent calls and letters from people asking for practical information and advice on this issue.

In practice, the funeral industry's takeover of the traditional functions of religious communities has never been quite as pervasive as it might appear. Quietly operating—here and there throughout the U.S. and Canada—are church groups that have continued to provide spiritual and physical support at a time of death. Ernest Morgan writes of his responsibilities serving on the Burial Committee of the Yellow Springs Friends Meeting (Quaker):

> I discovered that what I had anticipated to be a disagreeable chore turned out to be a meaningful privilege—serving one's friends at a time of profound need.[1]

~❖~

---

[1] *Dealing Creatively with Death,* 1996, Zinn Communications, Bayside, NY. Available through FAMSA.

In some situations, however, it hasn't been a simple task. In 1975, a Minneapolis rabbi, Arnold Goodman, became troubled by the Americanizing of Jewish funerals at the expense of traditional Jewish values. In *A Plain Pine Box* he writes:

> The commercialization and professionalization of handling death have removed most of us from really dealing with it. Customs of the past, in which families and friends would assume responsibility for preparing the dead for burial, for making arrangements with—and for—the family, for fabricating coffins and burial garments, have all but disappeared. . . . As people became further and further removed from handling death, a mystique inevitably came to surround it. . . .

Sympathetic to the memorial society emphasis on simplicity and propelled by the rabbinic principle—"In death, we are all equal"—Rabbi Goodman approached his congregation to study the possibility of a Jewish funeral plan. "The response was overwhelming," he wrote, and a committee was formed. In a statement as to why she joined the committee, one person complained that her wish to bury her mother in a simple wood box had brought the reply: "Are you *that* religious?"

Rabbi Goodman goes on:

> A committee member familiar with carpentry commented that a simple coffin consists of six pieces of wood: four sides, a top, a bottom. The cost, he insisted, could not be more than $40 [1975]. Wouldn't it make sense, he wondered, for the congregation to make such a coffin available to every family free of charge? We decided to explore the issue at the following month's meeting.
>
> The committee met [again] in a private home. A simple wood coffin was brought into the living room. Everyone gasped, for this was the first real object of death to be encountered. Tension was high as the box, which was more than a box, was gingerly inspected. Committee members circled it, and the more hardy touched it.
>
> Then it happened: One of the more daring members offered to get in it and try it "for size." Once he lay down in the coffin, it was as if the flood gates had opened. And animated discussion followed.
>
> "Yes, it makes sense to offer a free coffin."
>
> "Why not offer traditional shrouds (tachrichim) as well? There are people who are prepared to sew them."
>
> "Should we not assume responsibility for doing the ritual washing of the body (tahara)?"
>
> "Could we offer a full traditional funeral free to every member?"

The last question reverberated. Suddenly everyone realized that this was the logical conclusion of the committee's deliberations. Could it be done? And at what cost?

The "Jewish" funeral home refused to cooperate, so a Gentile funeral home was used. It split the Jewish community wide open. Some continued to patronize the Jewish funeral home, while others were served by the Chevra (Holy Society). In response to criticism from another rabbi in the area, congregation president Esther Katz wrote, "We have responded to a need within our Congregation. We have fulfilled that need through involvement and with simplicity and dignity."

Although a Chevra still functions at the Adath Jeshurun Congregation in Minneapolis today, it has become increasingly difficult to find volunteers who can drop everything when summoned. The story of how the Chevra began, however—the dedication of one rabbi and a religious group—is well worth reading in its entirety. I found it truly inspiring.[1]

~❖~

Catholic teaching specifically provides for church and family involvement. From the *Order of Christian Funerals:*

> In the celebration of the funeral rites . . . family members should be encouraged to take an active part. . . . Through the celebration of the funeral rites, the Church manifests its care for the dead. . . .
>
> In countries or regions where an undertaker, and not the family or community, carries out the preparation and transfer of the body, the pastor and other ministers are to ensure that the undertakers appreciate the values and beliefs of the Christian community.
>
> The family and friends of the deceased should not be excluded from taking part in the services sometimes provided by undertakers, for example, the preparation and laying out of the body.
>
> . . . The funeral rites should be celebrated in an atmosphere of simple beauty, in a setting that encourages participation.

I discovered one way in which this was being observed when I stopped in to visit Father Walter Miller at St. Jude's in Hinesburg, Vermont. As we chatted in the vestibule between the social hall and the chancery, he mentioned there had been a visitation there the day before, pointing to a large spacious room on the right. "The casket is waiting there now,"

---

[1] *A Plain Pine Box,* copyright 1981 by Rabbi Arnold M. Goodman, KTAV Publishing House, Hoboken, NJ. Available through FAMSA.

he said, "for the funeral tomorrow." Discreetly shielded by partitions, one never would have known. The social hall is available free of charge, he said. When he found that an undertaker had added $100 to the funeral bill for the visitation, he demanded that the charge be removed.

Father Jim Connolly at St. Teresa's in Bellingham Center, Massachusetts allows the funeral directors as far as the front door of the church. The Lazarus Committee and family and friends take over the services from there until it is time to go to the cemetery.

Father Bob Richardson, St. Mary's Church in Cambridge, Vermont tells of a young widow with two children who anxiously approached him before they took her husband's casket to the cemetery:

"Do you think it would be all right if the boys and I helped fill in the grave?" she asked.

"Of course," Father Richardson replied sympathetically.

The funeral director frowned severely and motioned the priest off to one side.

"That's not a good idea," he said. "She might get upset."

"I've got news for you," quipped Richardson. "That's what happens when people die, and it's perfectly okay."

On Prince Edward Island, Father Arsenault—troubled by the high cost of funerals—started a funeral co-op in the early 1980s. By hiring a retired embalmer and using the church facilities, costs were dramatically reduced. Local casket suppliers didn't want to deal directly with the church, however, so another source had to be found.

In the ensuing years, the church purchased a separate building for funeral preparation and visitation. With the mortgage to pay, the cost of funerals began to rise, but it remains less than what it would cost at any of the commercial mortuaries. Industry pressure has made it difficult to find a part-time embalmer, however, for those whose families choose embalming. A new provincial requirement, promoted by the commercial funeral directors, mandates mortuary college and licensing—rather than apprenticeship—for anybody who takes on that task.

Father Arsenault's ideas of almost 20 years earlier are echoed in *The Catholic Cemetery: A Vision for the Millennium* published in 1997 by the National Catholic Cemetery Conference:

To emphasize Church teachings and to promote the universal application of the **Order of Christian Funerals,** the Catholic cemetery may consider operating its own funeral home(s). This would restore its traditional role in funeral ministry .... In addition, this would allow the Catholic cemetery to more fully attend to its mission: ... Fostering an atmosphere more attuned to the spiritual needs of the grieving ... Ensuring a family with limited means that they will be treated with dignity and respect, and accorded a proper funeral and a decent burial.[1]

~❖~

The Muslim tradition involves active participation of those who know the deceased. In Toronto, a Muslim group took over the death and funeral preparations for members there when the local funeral establishments refused to cooperate. In Pittsburgh, another mosque is preparing to serve its members in death. The simplicity and caring of the Muslim rituals and the focus on a natural return to the earth have universal appeal. The following selections are from the "Preparation of the Deceased and Janazah Prayers" from several internet sites:

Washing the deceased's body is obligatory for Muslims. If some members take the responsibility of doing it, the need is fulfilled. But if no one fulfills it, then all Muslims will be accountable.

It brings much thawab [reward of God] to wash the corpse free of charge. ... It is not permissible [to demand payment] if there is no one else

---

[1] The church has had difficulty, however, living up to such high ideals. In 1981, the diocese built a mortuary on church grounds in Denver, CO. After the bishop died in 1985, funeral prices rose drastically, and the mortuary was turned into a "money-maker" for the church under the ensuing leadership.

Catholic funerals saw the most widespread assault in 1997—targeted for take-over by the funeral giants with the apparent collusion of the church. The Los Angeles diocese signed a deal to lease Catholic cemetery space to Stewart Enterprises for the purpose of building funeral homes. According to consumer price surveys, Stewart funeral prices are among the highest. The church, no doubt, will profit greatly from the rent. Other corporations are targeting Catholics, too. SCI has developed a subsidiary—"Christian Funeral Services, Inc."—dedicated to the management of funeral homes, cemeteries and related assets for Catholic dioceses throughout North America. In the fall of that year, it took over management of a major cemetery and new funeral home in Montreal. Earlier in the year, *The Pilot*—a newspaper put out by the Boston archdiocese—ran an ad for Forethought preneed funeral insurance heavily promoted by Loewen-owned funeral homes. Return address for inquiries: The Pilot, Archdiocese of Boston, P.O. Box 282, Batesville, Indiana. *Indiana?*

to wash it free of charge. So is the case with the payments for transporting corpses and digging graves.

Body-washing (Ghusl)
- A man's body should be washed by men and a woman's body by women, but a child's body may be washed by either sex. A husband can wash his wife's body and vice-versa if the need arises.
- One person is needed for washing, with someone to help— preferably those people who know the deceased.
- Remove the deceased's clothes, leaving the private parts covered.
- Only clean water may be used; add some scented oils (nonalcoholic) in the final wash. It is preferable to use warm water.
- Wash three times, but if the body needs more cleaning, continue washing five or seven times, but it must be odd numbers.
- Turn the body on its left side and begin washing the right side. Then turn it on its right side to wash the left side. The first and second washes are done with water and soap, while the last one with water and scent.
- Hair should be un-braided, washed and combed. For women, it may again be braided in three braids.
- Dry the body with a clean cloth or towel.
- Add some perfume on the head, forehead, nose, hands, knees, eyes, armpits, and place perfumed cotton on the front and rear openings.

Wrapping (Kafan)
- The cloth used for wrapping the body must be clean (preferably white) and should cover the whole body.
- Add some perfume.
- Do not use silk cloth for men.
- Use three pieces of cloth for men and five for women (each piece of cloth must cover the entire body).
- Tie the open cloth at the head and feet with a piece of cloth from the same kafan in such a way that one can differentiate the head from the legs.

Prayers are said next. Silence is recommended for the funeral procession. It is forbidden to accompany the body with music or crying. A grave should be deep and the body laid directly on the ground with the head toward Mecca. A casket is not recommended, but the head should be raised up with soil or a stone underneath (not a pillow).

- Fill the pit with soil. It is preferable that each one of those present share in this by pouring three handfuls of soil.

~❖~

When the Buddhist master Rinpoche died in 1987, his body was packed in salt and flown to the Buddhist community, Karme-Choling, in Barnet, Vermont. Seventy days after death, they wrapped the body in silk and placed it in a rosewood coffin. Like the tradition of cremation as practiced in Nepal, an outdoor funeral pyre was built, and the coffin placed on top. The fire burned for three hours, leaving nothing but ashes.

~❖~

From Atlanta, Georgia, Larry Burkett leads an enormous flock via his "Christian Financial Concepts." His weekly and daily programs are aired on more than 600 stations nationwide including the Moody Christian Radio. "Christians should not live in debt," he says, "And that includes funeral debt." A long-time supporter of the memorial society concept of funeral simplicity, Burkett has urged his listeners to plan ahead. "It would be far better if they could do so with the support and involvement of their churches." Burkett is himself a long-time member of the Memorial Society in Atlanta.

~❖~

Not everyone understands another's religious customs. When Doris Fletcher's husband keeled over, she called the rescue squad, even though he had been ill for some time. When it was certain that he was dead and there was no hope for resuscitation, Doris asked for help moving him to a bed. A group from the Fletcher's local ward of the Church of Jesus Christ of Latter-day Saints (Mormon) would be coming to help with the bathing and dressing of the body, she told them. The deputy coroner, however, was sure Mr. Fletcher's body had go to a funeral home. He'd never heard of such a thing. And so, using his police powers, the deputy ordered the body removed. Although the funeral home half-heartedly cooperated with the church group and family members who arrived the next day, Doris is still bitter that the intimacy of home, family, and church was stolen from what should have been a precious final time together.

~❖~

# Problems in the Pulpit

But not all clergy are so willing to get involved in funeral issues. Right after my first book on caring for the dead was published in 1987, I offered a copy to a summer neighbor, a Congregational minister who was on the local Hospice Education Committee. He declined the offer saying, "People aren't going to be interested in that."

Clearly, there are still many clergy who are uncomfortable about dealing with death; who prefer to leave all arrangements to the funeral homes, and have services performed at for-profit chapels rather than the churches to which the deceased belonged. For them, "professional" funerals are now the tradition, relieving them of the pragmatic responsibilities that follow a death.

In fact, in many communities, small-scale but effective financial "arrangements" exist between the local funeral homes and the churches or synagogues. Some of these are ethically suspect:

- One Midwestern funeral director buys a side of beef at the 4-H show each year and puts it in a unit at the local freezer for one of the town's pastors.
- Another funeral director makes his motor home available to a vacationing pastor on a regular basis.
- Several pastors in one town receive beepers to use, paid for by one of the local funeral directors.
- Calendars supplied by one—and only one—funeral home will be passed out at church, even though another funeral home has had calendars to offer.
- At a funeral directors' symposium, the speaker suggested sending apples or other fruit to civic servants—police and fire departments—so they'll remember you, and offer church photos to the clergy, something that could be replicated for a fund-raiser.
- One Chicago-area mortician told a family that $300 cash should be placed in a plain, unmarked envelope for the priest serving at the funeral. When an inquiry was made to the diocese, the woman was told that $175 was "expected."
- The General Price List of a California funeral home states that rabbis in that area expect a $300 honorarium.

Not all situations are so egregious. Many clergy receive no honorarium for a funeral—either because they have refused one, or because it simply slipped the family's mind in the emotions of the moment. And generosity among close and genuine friends, regardless of their respective callings, must be allowed to exist without paranoid scrutiny. But legitimately or not, it is common practice among many funeral homes to provide favors and gifts to help position themselves for profitable business whenever a member of a congregation dies.

Aside from any specific ethical issues, for any congregation that might wish to return the funeral to its spiritual roots in a participatory way, there may be a serious dilemma when there is a mortuary in the same town. What happens to the local funeral director? Chances are that the mortician and his family are all members of your congregation. Chances are, they are well-liked in the community. How can one justify taking over some of the very activities that provide for the livelihood of other members?

I've wrestled with this one, and there is no easy answer; each situation will be fraught with its own peculiarities. The most caring approach I can envision would be for a committee of the congregation to honestly discuss the considered changes with the funeral-home family.

There will always be a need for a mortuary, even if only a very part-time one, so you will want to reaffirm your appreciation for the role your undertaker plays in the community. But in view of the anticipated changes, would the mortician consider selling home-owner's insurance on the side (assuming no one else in the immediate area is already doing that for a vocation)? If so, the entire congregation might be willing to switch to the new "agent" in town. Or does the undertaker have a hobby and interest that could be converted to a money-making proposition? Loves flowers? A green-house-raising with church labor would be a gift of love and support.

Such issues will, of course, be different in every situation. It will be rare for a congregation to take over *all* funeral arrangements for any, let alone all, of its members. And it is rare for a mortician to rely on one congregation for all of his business. But if a local religious community is considering taking over, on a voluntary basis, some of the activities that would otherwise be done for profit by one of its members, discussion of the impact on the funeral-home family is important.

~❖~

## Getting a Funeral Committee Started

**Determine your purpose.** There are probably as many good reasons to start a funeral committee as there are congregations. Your congregation must define why it would be a good idea to have a Funeral Committee. Some suggested purposes:

- By encouraging active involvement of the church members, religious rituals will be preserved and honored.

- By encouraging active involvement of the church, a spiritual focus can be maintained without the distraction or burden of costly material expenditures.

- With the active involvement of those in the larger church family, grieving survivors will find needed support.

- By having something physical to do, the sense of helplessness is diminished.

**Decide on your services.** In any group, there are likely to be limits to the time and effort that volunteers are able or willing to provide. The following are all needed—to one degree or another—at a time of death. You must determine how many of these your funeral committee is able to offer and who will do them:

- **Procure the death certificate and permits.** Requires familiarity with the regulations covering the time and place to file such documents as well as the particulars needed for each document. Are persons available at any hour of the day or night to help with this? Could be done by the transport committee but not necessarily.

- **Transport the body.** Requires a truck, van, or station-wagon, plus two or more people in most cases. Are folks available to be called at any hour including working hours? A list of several should be available from which a parishioner can choose. Are additional people available to handle unique situations such as the death of a 300-lb. person on a second floor with no elevator?

- **Supply a plain pine box or other body container.** Where will you get one? Where will it be kept? Who is responsible for replacing one that is used and who will pay for it? One possibility would be for someone to donate a plain pine box to be stored at the church, to get the project going. When that is used, the family or friends of the family could replace it for the next person to use. You undoubtedly will have local artisans and woodworkers who may be of assistance, especially if a small-sized one were needed for a child, or an extra long or wide one were required. You may wish to check the FAMSA website for casket sources, too:

www.funerals.org/famsa/caskets.htm

- **Bathe the body and dress or shroud.** Where, home or church? Equipment? Who? While this probably would not be necessary in the case of an immediate cremation, it can be a loving ritual in all circumstances.

- **Shelter and care of the body before final disposition.** Is there a place in the church where a body may rest discreetly, without intruding on other church functions if the body will not be kept at home prior to the funeral? Is air conditioning readily available during summer seasons? Would the family appreciate having someone sit in vigil with the body prior to the funeral and final disposition, at home or at the church?

- **Provide for the immediate needs of the family.** This might include house-cleaning, baby-sitting, shopping, scheduling the delivery of meals, or someone to simply sit and listen or answer the phone.

- **Notify and help others close to the family.** Phone calls may need to be made—to employers, to relatives, to friends. Notify others in writing at the request of the family. Pick up out-of-town guests and relatives arriving on public transportation. Provide lodging for out-of-town guests and local transportation while in town. See that pets of the deceased are being cared for, and that mail and utilities are being handled, if the deceased lived alone.

- **Set up a registry of funeral plans.** Members of the congregation, particularly those living alone, should name family members to be called in the event of death. Final disposition preferences should be explained—body donation, body burial, or cremation plus possibilities for disposition of cremated remains. Then register preferences along with additional information, such as the details for any service. A form—"Putting My House in Order"—can be obtained from a memorial society for this purpose.

- **Let others know in advance!** If caring for your own dead is a new concept in your area, and a funeral director will not be participating, it is important to visit—ahead of time—the hospitals, nursing homes, the local town clerks, and anyone else who might be involved. This will avoid delay from those who may not be familiar with the laws that permit people other than a mortician to care for the dead. Many may be skeptical, but it is usually out of their own concern to be responsible in their jobs rather than an effort to thwart your plans.

Establishment of a funeral committee need not be an all-or-nothing decision. In most states, by law, your congregation, working with the family, can provide all of the arrangements when a member dies, and that may be the ideal. But the involvement of the congregation as a support group can be greatly increased, with much benefit to the surviving family and friends, while still leaving some of the responsibilities to a cooperating funeral home. So be realistic in determining the ability to depend on volunteers in your group on an ongoing basis.

Whatever level of involvement you choose, you can expect great appreciation, not only from the family of the deceased but from the participating members. Perhaps the most useful thing to remember in making a commitment to care for the dead is that those of us who have done so—without exception—would never choose to do it any other way. It is, indeed, a meaningful privilege.

# Cremation with Dignity
*by Patsy Santoro with Peter Bilodeau*

## 10

## History of Cremation

The use of fire to prepare the dead for memorialization is not new. Prehistoric people thought of fire as a miracle from their gods. Fire allowed them to cook and keep warm and was possibly used as a method to protect and honor their dead.

The Slavic tribes of the Dniester and Dnieper River valleys of Russia may have been the first to cremate, according to some literature. But the Babylonians ritualized their cremation ceremony. The Babylonians wrapped the bodies of deceased loved ones in a combustible material, then encased them in clay. The clay coffin was then placed on a brick form, and a funeral pyre was built around it and set ablaze.

People of ancient India also used the funeral pyre. They called it the "Sacred Flame" and displayed much of their artistic talents on the urns in which their loved one's cremated remains were memorialized. The word "funeral" comes originally from a Sanskrit word of northern India which means "smoke."

Around the year 1000 B.C., the Greeks began to practice cremation to protect their war dead. Their enemies were known to take buried Greek soldiers' bodies from the ground and desecrate them. The Greeks, after getting wise to their enemies' tactics, cremated the remains of their soldiers and took the cremains back to Greece to be entombed

---

Patsy Santoro is now retired, having served as superintendent of the Evergreen Cemetery and Crematory in New Haven, Connecticut for many years. He has been active in various professional organizations and has spoken on cremation to a number of death education classes.

Peter Bilodeau is an editor for the Jackson Newspapers in New Haven, Connecticut.

Information used in this chapter was also provided by William S. Cook, formerly an operator of a funeral home and crematory in Columbus, Ohio. Resources include an article by Mr. Cook in the now out-of-print trade publication *Casket and Sunnyside;* and "Report on Dental Gold and Cremation," Minnesota Department of Health, 1979.

with great ceremony and honor. Cremation of soldiers soon became a popular tradition of Greek culture, and the tradition spread throughout the country. Later, cremation became the most popular form of preparation of the dead for all Greeks.

The Bible, in I Samuel 31, reports the cremation of Saul:

> (12) All the valiant men arose, and went all night, and took the body of Saul and the bodies of his sons from the wall of Beth'-Shan, and came to Ja'besh, and burnt them there.
> (13) And they took their bones, and buried them under a tree at Ja'besh, and fasted seven days.

Romans, too, practiced cremation from 753 B.C. to 476 A.D. I Ovid (43 B.C.–17 A.D.), the Roman poet, states that the body of Remus, one of the mythological founders of Rome, was cremated, as was that of Julius Caesar (100–49 B.C.). Remains were memorialized in elaborate urns built into the walls around Rome.

The extravagance of cremation during the later years of the Roman Republic made it difficult for the poor to practice it. The affluent of Rome spurned earth burial, preferring lavish funeral pyres and inurnment in beautiful gold and silver urns. Nero used more myrrh, incense, and fragrant oils to cremate his wife than were produced in all of Arabia that year.

The Vikings of the Bronze Age practiced a unique form of cremation. The leaders and dead warriors of the Viking fighting forces were placed into "fire ships," which were ignited and sent out to sea. Also, old German chronicles indicate that Attila, King of the Huns, was cremated fully armed and sitting on his horse.

Cremation, along with Buddhism, came into Japan in 552 A.D. The first recorded cremation in that country was 702 A.D., when a Buddhist priest was cremated. Jitro is considered the first Japanese emperor to be cremated.

Cremation was also the primary means of disposal of deceased persons in England from 787 A.D., when the Danes invaded, until 1066 A.D., when William the Conqueror had defeated Harold the Saxon at the Battle of Hastings. From that time, until 1840 or so, the practice of cremation faded.

The early 1800s brought a revival of cremation in Europe. The English poet Percey Shelley drowned in the Mediterranean, and the Tuscan Quarantine Law stated that cremation was required in such cases to protect the populace from disease. His cremains were buried near Rome, close to the grave of another poet, John Keats.

By 1869, the first modern crematory was constructed by an Italian scientist named Brunetti. After that, the International Medical Congress of Florence urged all nations to promote cremation. The Italian Congress viewed cremation as the most practical method of disposition of the dead. The Congress believed that open land should be for the living.

In England, between 1840 and 1870, people discovered that their country was rapidly becoming urbanized and that cemeteries were deteriorating. In 1874, Sir Henry Thompson formed the Cremation Society of England, with the first modern cremation being performed in that country in 1885. Thirty years hence, cremation became a subject for Parliamentary debate. Finally, the law-making body declared cremation a legal method of disposing of the dead.

Today, in both England and Japan, cremation is the most common form of disposition of the dead. Between half and three-quarters of those who die there are cremated.

A formal American crematory was established in Washington, Pennsylvania, by Dr. Francis Julius Le Moyne in 1876, but the first known cremation of an American colonist was the body of Colonel Henry Laurens in 1792. Laurens presided over the Continental Congress of 1777–78 and was a member of George Washington's military staff.

At least some American Indians preferred cremation to earth burial because they discovered that their deceased often were dug up by animals. In fact, two crude containers with what was believed to be cremated remains of American Indians were discovered in Connecticut in 1974 and are now in the archives of the Connecticut state capital.

Traditional Jewish culture forbids cremation and the terrors of the Holocaust make cremation unacceptable to many Jews. The Catholic Church, however, has removed its ban on cremation.

In 1884 there were 41 cremations in the United States. By the turn of the century the total had risen to 13,281 a year. During the 19th century and into the early 20th century crematories were established throughout the country. From 26 crematories in 1900 the number grew to 585 in 1980, and the number is still growing rapidly, indicating a continuing increase in the choice of cremation for final disposition in America. Today, 22% of deaths end in cremation. By the year 2010, the cremation rate is predicted to be almost 50%.

## Contemporary Cremation Practices

Preparing the body for a wake or visitation hours and arranging church services are to be considered in a cremation, just as they are for earth burial or entombment.

When choosing a casket for cremation, most crematories simply require a rigid combustible container. Rosewood, mahogany, pine or cloth-covered caskets are suitable for cremation. Families who have wake or visitation hours generally are concerned with the appearance of the casket, and most handsome wood caskets are suitable for a cremation.

Few crematories will accept plastic or fiberglass caskets. The intense heat required for cremation will melt the container and interfere with proper cremation. Burning plastic also gives off lethal gases that have made some members of crematory staffs quite ill.

Caskets with polyvinyl chloride filler and lining are not allowed for cremation. The vinyl, when exposed to heat, releases particles of black, sooty, sticky material that pollute the environment. However, once the problem was brought to the attention of casket manufacturers, most of them stopped using the material. Although the increase in the number of cremations has hurt the casket industry, the manufacturers generally have cooperated by not using pollutants in their products. Many manufacturers have marked their caskets "suitable for cremation."

For those concerned with economy or simplicity, there are many types of boxes acceptable for cremation. Some funeral directors build their own cremation containers out of pine, plywood, pressboard, or other combustible material, but these are usually reserved for clients who choose not to have viewing hours. The lowest cost containers are usually labelled as "alternative containers," the expression used in the Federal Trade Commission's Funeral Rule. Many of these containers are made of heavy cardboard, and fulfill the crematory requirements.

If the family were to choose a non-combustible casket for viewing, the crematory would need a simple but sturdy combustible container for the cremation. In such situations, it is often possible to rent an attractive casket for viewing at about half the cost of purchasing the casket.

When a cardboard cremation container is used, a thin piece of pine or plywood should be placed under the deceased to keep the container rigid. The board enables the deceased to be readily moved from a vehicle into a church, for example. Without the board, handling the deceased—particularly a heavy person—is difficult not only for the pallbearers but the staff at the crematory as well.

If handling the deceased becomes difficult for the crematory staff, much of the dignity and respect for the dead will be gone. In one unfortunate experience a very large person was placed in a non-rigid container, and the sides of the container burst just as the deceased was being placed into the cremation chamber. It was unpleasant for the staff; dignity had vanished.

In fact, handling a body in an undignified manner has a psychological effect on the crematory staff. Pouches or body bags, often used to carry disaster victims from the scene of a tragedy, should be discarded and replaced by a rigid container prior to cremation.

Some crematories use a simple, uncovered cremation "tray," with sides about four to six inches high, if the body arrives with no other container. Other crematories require that the body be in a covered receptacle.

It is also important to remove a pacemaker from the deceased prior to cremation. The pacemakers with lithium-type batteries can explode and cause considerable damage to the cremation chamber. The explosion will pollute the environment. Usually a pacemaker is removed at the place of death, or a trained funeral director can be asked to remove one. The person delivering the body for cremation may be liable for any damage to a cremation chamber resulting from a pacemaker explosion.

When making cremation arrangements, you must remember to deal with the valuables that a deceased might have been wearing at the time of death. Too often, and too late, crematory staff members are asked what happened to a ring or other jewelry that was on the deceased at the time of cremation. One young widow managed to retrieve a wedding ring only because the crematory was shut down for the weekend. Cremators generally do not check the deceased for valuables.

With the fluctuating price in precious metals, many families ask what happens to the gold contained in a person's mouth. When the gold alloy is melted during the cremation process it forms small BB-sized pellets. The pellets may possibly fall between the cracks of the fire brick lining in the retort (the cremation chamber). A family can ask that crematory staff check for this metal, but there is no certainty of retrieving it. At some high temperatures gold will vaporize. If saving the gold is important to a family, the metal should be removed from the body before the deceased is taken to the crematory. The services of a dentist might be arranged for this, but the cost would probably be greater than the value of the gold retrieved. Some dentists have refused such requests. While unethical crematories may remove dental gold for personal profit, most claim that no such activity would be worth the unpleasant trouble. Many states, by statute, forbid this.[1]

When the deceased is brought to the crematory, the legal transit documents, burial or cremation papers, and the crematory's authorization for cremation must be presented, along with the cremation fee. The documents are checked very carefully by the crematory staff to be sure the proper authorities have signed them. Signatures of a representative of the state's department of vital statistics or health agency, the medical examiner, the funeral director or whoever is administering the arrangements—usually family, but sometimes a friend—are required. Many crematories require consent from all next of kin. A telegram or fax will often suffice if a family member is not located in the area where the cremation will take place.

A very important element of the documentation is the time of death. Many states require that a person must be deceased for 48 hours prior to cremation. This is a precaution to ensure that any investigation of the cause of death can be completed. Obviously, once cremation occurs, there is no way to determine the cause of death. If a person is buried conventionally, the body can be exhumed if further investigation is required. In some states, if a body is held for cremation beyond 24 hours, refrigeration or embalming may be required by state law.

When the necessary paperwork is completed, the deceased is given an identification number at the crematory. The tag, generally made of stainless steel, is placed in the cremation chamber during the process. Some crematories use a plastic identification tag and place it outside the chamber during the cremation. When the cremation is complete, the tag is placed with the cremains.

Many crematories have chapels. If a family wishes to have a service at the crematory, it is generally done prior to cremation. The casket or container is placed in the chapel as it would be in a funeral home or church. Flowers can be placed around the deceased, with prayers

---

[1] A 1979 study on dental gold done by the University of Minnesota in conjunction with the Minnesota Department of Health determined that there was little value in the dental gold ending up in crematories. That study was cited for "Dear Abby" staff who called the FAMSA office when researching the question in 1996, and her answer reflecting that was printed accordingly in a column. A flood of responses indicated, indeed, that there were crematories retrieving dental gold for significant personal benefit. Undoubtedly, both reports are correct: what's left of dental gold *after* cremation is of little value; dental gold retrieved prior to cremation apparently is quite marketable.

and reading as desired. Some crematory chapels have organs or can pipe in recorded music if the family wishes.

Some families will request to have someone stay in the crematory chapel or waiting room until the cremation is complete. On occasion, a member of the family may ask to see the casket being placed into the cremation chamber. On very few occasions, a family member may ask to view the entire cremation. Because of the way most cremation chambers are designed, it is impossible to view the cremation from the front of the chamber, and there may be other cremations already scheduled or in progress.

Most crematories will allow families to follow their religious beliefs and customs to the extent possible. For example, one family from India, whose loved one died in New Haven, Connecticut, had driven the deceased to the Evergreen Crematory there, stopping about 200 feet away. The family then carried the deceased to the crematory, since it was their custom to carry their loved ones to the funeral pyre. Inside the crematory, they held their religious service, and the cremation followed immediately. In this instance, the family was allowed to view the cremation. Another family from India chose to place branches on and beside the casket of their loved one as it was being placed into the cremation chamber.

Once the casket is placed into the cremation chamber, usually on wooden dowel rollers, the cremation process can begin. Most crematories use natural gas or oil to fuel the cremation. Others use propane gas or electricity as fuel. Many units are designed with flat surfaces, and burners are installed to cremate from two sides and the top. Newer units have burners that also cremate from below the casket.

The cremation chamber is lined with fire brick. These bricks can withstand heat up to 3,500 degrees Fahrenheit, but the units generally cremate at 1,800 degrees. If the chamber has been heated by a previous cremation, the temperature during the subsequent cremation may reach 2,400 degrees.

Cremation time varies with the type of container and the size of the deceased. Generally, a cremation can be completed in one or two hours, but some have taken up to three-and-a-half hours or so. Some of the newer units can cremate in less time because they are built more compactly and take less time to heat up. Many are on timers so they will shut off automatically after a given time. With automatic shut-off and other design features of the newer chambers, the cremains need not be handled extensively during the process.

All of the newer crematory units are constructed with after-burners and scrubbers to prevent air pollution. Crematory operators need to be careful about smoke and usually can control it by opening and closing drafts. In most states, crematories are inspected regularly, either by the Department of Health or an environmental agency.

When the cremation is complete and the burners in the chamber are shut off, the chamber must cool down before the cremains can be removed. In fact, the chamber is so hot that if you were to look at the hearth just after a cremation, the bricks would have a bright pink glow. Once cooled, the cremation chamber can be opened and the cremains—which are three to seven pounds of clean, white bone fragments—can be removed. The staff takes great care to retrieve every particle of the cremains and place them on a metal tray for processing.

Processing cremains begins by taking an electromagnet and withdrawing all the metal from the cremation container—nails, staples, and other small pieces of metal generally mixed with the cremains. Pieces of charcoal from the cremation process are also removed. When all foreign matter is removed, the bone fragments will range in size from minute particles to four-inch-long pieces. They are then placed into a pulverizer, or some type of grinding machine, and converted to very small, unrecognizable fragments. Some machines can convert the cremains to the size of sugar crystals. The cremains then are placed in temporary containers, usually made of tin, plastic, or cardboard, and shipped to their destination.

Most cremains are sent or hand-delivered to local funeral directors who are responsible for getting them to the family. Should the crematory have to hold the cremains for a short time, a fee for storage and insurance is usually charged. When the cremains must be mailed, they are placed in an additional mailing carton. Generally cremains are shipped registered mail to ensure that they arrive at the appropriate destination. UPS—if they know what's in the box—does not, as a matter of policy, accept cremated remains. In some states, Federal Express or Purolator Courier may be used for the delivery of cremains.

During the winter months when the ground is frozen, immediate cremation may be preferable to waiting for a spring earth burial. Furthermore, it is not uncommon for one to die away from a final resting place. Some 8,000 Americans die abroad each year. When the remains must be transported over a great distance, cremation may be a convenient and desirable choice.

---

[1] Sometimes the cremated remains will be more gray than white. The color is determined by the fuel and level of heat used in each retort.

## Memorialization

Cremains can be memorialized in almost every way imaginable, from traditional earth interment to placement in beautiful urns to rest in artistically designed columbaria. You may choose to scatter the cremains or bury them at sea.

Many cemeteries have been able to design lovely sites for cremains in portions of their property not suitable for traditional earth burial, such as shallow earth over ledges. This practice has enabled the cemeteries to utilize valuable land that would otherwise be wasted. Some cemeteries have "scatter gardens" landscaped with paths and planted with roses or other flowers.

Many churches are using their lawns and buildings to memorialize cremains from their congregations. This practice not only brings needed revenue to the churches, it also encourages families to return to church more frequently. A book of remembrance or bronze plaque can be used to record those who are being memorialized there. Some churches have not yet realized the potential of using their facilities for dignified memorials.

In all states but California, cremains may be scattered if they are converted to unrecognizable skeletal remains. Now, many crematories provide the grinding or pulverization process as a standard service, but some may not. You should make sure that process is done before the cremains are scattered. There have been cases in which pieces of recognizable bone that were scattered as cremains have been discovered and reported to law enforcement authorities. The authorities then began investigating the incident, assuming foul play had taken place.

In one unpleasant incident in Connecticut, the family of a deceased person—whose cremains were supposed to have been scattered in Long Island Sound—was notified that a portion of the cremains had floated back to shore and retrieved by local police. The persons charged with burying the cremains at sea had not scattered them nor poked holes in the container so it would sink. The cremains were easily identified because the cremation identification tag was still attached, showing the crematory and a number identifying the deceased. The cremains were eventually disposed of again, properly.

If the deceased has made no plans for memorialization prior to death, cremains may be kept safely until the family completes its plans, unlike regular burials which should be done within a few days after death. Memorial observances can then be planned at the convenience of distant family and friends as well.

~❖~

The rapid rise in the cremation rate nationwide has been of great concern to the funeral industry, as those choosing an immediate cremation followed by a memorial service only (with no casket present) generally spend a great deal less. Be sure to read about the new tactics being used with cremation customers in the "Tricks of the Funeral Trade" chapter.

# Organ and Body Donation
### "Let the dead teach the living"
—Columbia University *et al*

## 11

The above quotation is frequently used by medical schools in their appeals to the public for body donations. The eye banks, kidney foundations, and other organizations that facilitate organ donations might say just as appropriately, "Let the dead heal the living."

All major religions approve of body and organ donations for medical and dental teaching, research, and transplants. According to public opinion polls, most people believe that such donations are desirable. Death provides many of us with a one-time-only chance to make a valuable gift to humanity.

If all of us followed through on our convictions, there would be no medical schools in need of cadavers. Those waiting for the gift of life through organ donation would have their needs met. Tragically, that is not the case.

Unfortunately, morticians tend to resent the loss of a big-ticket funeral, and some have been known to mislead the public about the need for body donation. Michigan funeral director Thomas Lynch was fearless enough to do so in print. In *The Undertaking* he wrote, "The supply of cadavers for medical and dental schools in this land of plenty was shamefully [why shamefully?] but abundantly provided for. . . ." How many has he plied with this lie so the business could enjoy yet another "good year"?[1] Truth of the matter: Of the three medical schools in Michigan, Wayne State and the University of Michigan in Ann Arbor have an "urgent need" of body donors. Michigan State University has a moderate need—"We can always use people."

Lynch is, of course, a brilliant writer whose charming way with words made *The Undertaking* a major best-seller. But a delightful writing style does not add truth to his assertions. The fact is that throughout the U.S. and Canada, body and organ donations are desperately needed.

---

[1] Lynch writes that once he talked his friend Russ out of body donation, Russ next suggested that he'd like to have his ashes flown aloft in a balloon. One has to wonder, then, why or how Russ ended up—shaved and embalmed—in a Batesville casket, as Lynch seemed so pleased to report.

## Organ Donation

Many medical schools request that a Uniform Donor Card be filled out as part of the process of making a bequest. Such cards can also be obtained from many other sources including kidney foundations, eye banks, and funeral planning societies. The card is pictured here:

---

**Uniform Donor Card**

Of_____

In the hope I may be able to help others, I make this anatomical gift, if medically acceptable, to take effect upon my death. The words and marks below indicate my desires.

I give:   (a) ____ any needed organ or parts

          (b) ____ only the following organs or parts

_____

(specify the organs or parts)

for transplantation, therapy, medical research or education;

         (c) ____ my body for anatomical study if needed.

Limitations or special wishes if any _____

_____

---

Signed by the donor and the following two witnesses in the presence of each other:

_____    _____
Signature of Donor               Date of Birth

_____    _____
Date Signed              City and State

_____
Witness

_____
Witness

---

Line (a) identifies "any needed organs or parts." That is, if any organs or other body parts are needed by another living human being, organ donation is to be considered first even if line (c), total body donation, is also checked. It should be remembered that donation of a major organ may preclude body donation to a medical school. Line (b) has a space to identify "only the following organs or parts." This could be "eyes," for example, if donation "for anatomical study"—line (c)—is the primary intent of the donor.

Your signature, on the back, must be witnessed by two other people. The Uniform Donor Card incorporates language that is consistent with the Anatomical Gifts Acts adopted by nearly all states.

If there is only one medical school to which you are willing to entrust your body, you can say that. Medical schools and organizations that facilitate organ transplants are extremely conscious of the need to honor the wishes of the deceased. If there is any doubt, they will err on the side of not accepting the donation.

In most states, there is also a check-off on a driver's license to determine whether or not you are an "organ donor." States expect, however, that an additional card will be carried, establishing the specifics and restrictions regarding that offer.

Most organ donations are now handled with complete privacy, without identifying either the donor or the recipient to the other. Emotional excesses on the part of both donor families and those receiving an organ have made such anonymity necessary. For example, excessive gratitude caused one family to constantly foist itself on the bereaved father of the son whose kidney had been given to their son. The father became sorry that he had made the gesture. Donor families have also intruded into the lives of those now carrying a bit of "my son Johnny," unable to let go. In some unpleasant instances, money has apparently been requested. All hospitals now handle organ transplants discreetly.

At this writing, there is a particular need for corneas and kidneys. The numbers fluctuate, but there are thousands of people waiting for donations of those organs. For any of them, a donation can make the difference between sight and blindness, or life and death.[1] But medical science is advancing. There are laboratory studies being done with the transplanting of the islets of Langerhans, the small cells in the pancreas that produce insulin. If islet transplants become the "cure" for diabetes, another million people would be added to the waiting list for organ donations.

Funeral directors are being trained to enucleate eyes, but the conditions necessary for organ donation—removal of the organ shortly

---

[1] International Cemetery and Funeral Association (ICFA) is working on an "organ donor awareness" program to help with "efforts of preneed marketing." While the goal of improving public awareness is laudable, consumers should not be lulled into purchasing funeral arrangements as a result.

after death in a sterile environment—can be met for the most part only if death occurs in a hospital. Next-of-kin should be aware of the desire for donation or bequest. Family members should be sure the intent is known to medical personnel as well, and that it is included on the patient's hospital chart. Without the advance directive, hospital staff may approach the family with such an inquiry. In his excellent book *Death Notification,* Moroni Leash gives a sample dialog for staff who are placed in the awkward situation of seeking permission from families for organ donation in an unexpected death. A thoughtful family facing a "what if" situation will suggest this first.

When death occurs at home and the family will be handling all funeral arrangements, the area Eye Bank can send a technician to remove the corneas. This is not a disfiguring procedure and will hardly be noticed by those who might wish to see the body afterward.

## Medical and Dental Schools

To satisfy the increased needs for research and education, body donations are in demand in all states. Many people do not realize that even dental schools use entire cadavers in their required anatomy courses.

Some medical schools, either routinely or with permission, will share donations with other schools. Others do not. In many schools—especially the osteopathic and chiropractic schools—over-enrollment of body donors has never occurred.

All schools and state boards of anatomy prefer to receive an enrolled donor—a person who had filed a "bequest" during his or her lifetime. In some states, a bequest can legally take precedence over the wishes of surviving family members, but few medical schools are willing to accept a body if there are objections. For that reason, most bequests must be witnessed, preferably by family members. A bequest may be cancelled at any time.

The body-donor information I surveyed ranged widely in quality of presentation and depth of information. One New England medical school sent a single mimeographed information sheet that covered only the most basic of facts, plus a body-donation form. From a Midwestern medical college I received a many-paged, purple-covered folder in a plastic case. This attractive pamphlet listed, as other schools have, the "Frequently Asked Questions About Body Donation." Almost all medical schools are grateful for such a gift, and assure the donor that the body will be treated with respect.

Most schools issue a donor card that can be carried in a wallet, although a few I saw were too large for a wallet, and several failed to include the necessary telephone numbers or information regarding the procedure to follow at the time of death. It also occurs to me that a conspicuous failing on all such cards is the lack of a place to indicate whether donation may be to the nearest medical school at the time of death or whether a bequest to a specific medical college must be honored (with transportation costs borne by the estate even if a person died in Europe, for example).

In some situations, the next-of-kin may donate a body without prior enrollment, but policies on this vary greatly. Schools that are beginning to receive sufficient donors often restrict donation to those previously enrolled or in "ideal" condition, but a check of other nearby schools— especially the chiropractic and osteopathic—will usually reveal a need.

Almost all medical schools also receive bodies from the state— persons who have died in institutions or alone with no known relatives.

There is no remuneration for body donation. No medical school buys bodies. Some medical schools may pay for all or part of the body transportation at the time of death. Most pay for body preservation, and almost all pay for final disposition. In short, body donation is likely to alleviate, but not completely eliminate, the cost to the family.

Medical schools that pay for transportation may have a contract with a certain transport service or funeral establishment, and many funeral directors will accept less than the usual rate as a commitment to the public good. These practices are not always clear, however. One friend, dealing with the imminent death of her grandfather, contacted a particular medical school about body donation at the suggestion of a neighbor who was also a funeral director. She was told by the school that it would handle all transportation costs. When her grandfather died, she called the same funeral director again. He moved the body from the hospital to his establishment two-and-a-half miles away and filed the death certificate. In the meantime, she notified the medical school. As a result, there were some quick changes in arrangements. The first funeral director was not willing to complete the trip for the rate the medical school normally paid, so another funeral director was sent to pick up the body. My friend later received a bill of $175 from the first funeral director. As can be seen from this example, it is important to ask not only what costs the medical school covers but also how those costs are handled.

A health history is often requested by a medical school, as well as death-certificate information if the medical school is to complete the filing. Families may not request a report of medical findings from the school's examination of the body.

The donor's family is encouraged to consider a memorial service (a service without the physical presence of the body) so that the body can be removed for preservation as soon after death as possible. In some cases, if embalming is done under the direction of the anatomy department, body delivery can be delayed, but this must be arranged in advance with the medical school

Medical schools do not assume the responsibility of filing an obituary.

## Medical Embalming

Medical embalming procedures are considerably different from and far more complex than those used in the funeral industry. Each school of anatomy has developed its own system according to the interests and specialties of the school and staff involved. The thorough embalming needed for long-term preservation requires stronger chemicals and can take as long as three days to complete.

It is important that the methods be as nondisruptive to the body as possible. Blood is not routinely drained from the body since only the arterial system is injected with preserving fluid, allowing the blood to "pool" on the venous side of the system. Any swelling is minimal and not a cosmetic consideration for medical study. Through the arterial system, all capillary beds can still be reached. Organs that would not be affected by the arterial system alone—including the brain—must be separately and carefully perfused with preservatives with a great deal of attention paid to detail. It is necessary to maintain the integrity of the body as a whole, and of entire systems within it. For instance, the circulatory routes can be filled with dyed latex as a marker, but this is not attempted until body preservation is complete. Some medical schools use refrigeration in addition to embalming for preservation.

Most bodies are used within a two-year period. Many medical schools cremate the remains when study is finished and offer a simple memorial service, interring or scattering cremains in a plot reserved for this purpose. *If* the school is notified at the time of body donation or delivery, remains or cremains can be returned to the family, although this option is not available at all schools. A family member expecting remains should notify the school if there is a change of address.

Enrolled body donors should make alternative disposition plans because bodies may be rejected for a variety of reasons. The University of South Alabama, the State Anatomy Board of Maryland, and Southwestern Medical School in Texas will dispose of all enrolled donors regardless of condition, in fulfillment of their contract with a donor. All other schools, however, reserve the right to refuse a donation.

Although some schools share their donors with other schools, usually within the same state, over-enrollment may become a reason for body rejection if donations become more numerous. Skin and eye donations may be considered and are encouraged by most schools, but other organ donations make a body unacceptable for all but a few medical schools. In addition to autopsy, other common reasons for body rejection include:

- missing body parts — extremities, thoracic organs
- age — 76 is too old at one school; below 21, 18, 15, infant or fetal are too young at others
- severe burn victim — preservation is not readily accomplished if there is extreme tissue damage
- decomposition
- emaciation
- trauma or mutilation
- surgery at or near the time of death
- obesity — not only difficult to preserve but difficult to handle and use
- size — over six feet tall (only a few schools) because of limitations in storage facilities
- contagious or diseased — sepsis, TB, hepatitis, AIDS, meningitis, Creutzfeldt-Jacob, Alzheimer's, systemic cancer, and others at the discretion of the institution.

## In Case of Death Abroad

The need in some foreign countries is even greater than in the U.S. In Argentina, for example, 200 medical students must share one cadaver. Because international shipping of scientific cadavers is not allowed (although a private body may be), anatomy classes from an Italian medical school have travelled to Israel for study. If death were to occur abroad, perhaps inquiry about local needs would fulfill the intent of someone who has made an anatomical bequest, either for organs or whole body donation. The tragic death of a child while travelling with his parents in Italy turned into an international diplomacy coup when his parents gave permission for the donation of his life-saving organs.

~❖~

Dr. William Worden, director of a Harvard study of terminal illness and suicide, wrote in *Personal Death Awareness* of the depression of those whose lives will quickly end when no medical intervention is in sight. In one of the examples he cites, a young man—father of two— waiting for a third kidney transplant "began to sit in the hospital hallway and watch the elevator in the hope that an anonymous donor would appear. . . . Finally he realized the donor would never arrive." In making his final preparations for death, the young man's poignant remark was: "I want you to be sure my eyes are donated to people who need them. I lived a little longer because of two kidney transplants, and I want some other people to have the same break I did."

# Tales from a Country Coroner

*by Susan McIver, Ph.D.*

## 12

Coroners' recommendations are often a source of comfort for the grieving family. If something that helps other people arises from the loss of a loved one, then the death is easier to bear. A cherished memory occurred at the conclusion of a two-year-long investigation into the unexpected hospital death of a middle-aged man. The widow and I had gone to dinner to celebrate the resolution of the case. It resulted in procedures for improved patient care at that hospital and, in many ways, marked the end of her acute grieving process. As we parted outside the restaurant she said, "Thanks for giving me my life back." We both had tears in our eyes.

~❖~

My education as a coroner began as an assistant to John, then the coroner, who would be retiring soon. A most pragmatic man, he told me that the first piece of equipment I should acquire was a pair of knee-high rubber boots. "Never know what you'll be walking into," he drawled and proceeded to relate tales of bodies in advanced stages of decomposition.

"And you gotta be careful not to lose the body," John instructed.

"Lose the body?" I queried.

"Yep, a few years ago we were taking this chap off that small island in the big lake. Had him bagged and laid across the gunwales of the police boat." John stopped to fiddle with his pipe. "Trouble started when the cop took off like a bat out of hell. The boat went one way,

---

Susan McIver holds a doctorate in entomology from Washington State University in Pullman. She was a professor in the Faculty of Medicine at the University of Toronto for 17 years. At the University of Guelph, Ontario, McIver was Chair of the Department of Environmental Biology. She now enjoys her back-to-basics country living in British Columbia where she serves as the appointed local coroner. Her dedication for this chapter: "In memory of Elizabeth Siemiller Cooksey, my great grandmother who died in 1890. I wish to hell I could have been the coroner on that case."

the body another." John took a puff. "The divers were forever finding the body."

Not long after, John and I were the guest speakers at a meeting of the local hospice society. A particularly dewy-eyed idealistic young woman asked him, "What's the single most important thing you've learned as a coroner?" From all indications, she was expecting him to reveal some intense spiritual epiphany. Being John, he replied, "If it can be done, people will do it." And he told of the bizarre methods people use to end their own lives.[1] John's stories were a far cry from the rapture of transformation she'd associated with death.

In due course, John retired.

Once I was on the job full-time, I was surprised at the large number of people who commit suicide, even though I guess John had tried to warn me. I always find those deaths to be the most difficult, emotionally and psychologically. Regardless of the horrific sorrow that accompanies the deaths of infants, children, and young adults, or the sickening destruction of the body in certain accidents and homicides, the fact remains that those persons did not choose to die. When someone ends his or her own life, it is because death has become more attractive than life. And that is unutterably sad.

The attractiveness of death can sometimes be for understandable reasons—such as having to face a terminal illness alone and poor, or having suffered years of intense pain with no hope of relief. I've had only two such cases. All the others have been depressed mothers of school-aged children, men tortured by mental illness, teenagers who couldn't see beyond their immediate trials, and people whose lives—for whatever reasons—have collapsed, crushing their desire to live. I always come away from a suicide scene thankful for my mental and physical health, my warm circle of family and friends and comfortable circumstances. As well, I often reflect on how awful it must be to take that final step of pulling the trigger, kicking the stool out from underneath yourself, or drawing the razor blade across your wrist.

A suicide I attended several years ago sticks out among others. It started with a call from the police dispatcher who said, "We have a sudden death in the Twilight Motel." Twilight Motel? How apt, I thought. Arriving at the scene a few minutes later, I was met by a policeman who cautioned me on what I was about to see. I'm glad he did. A middle-aged man of comfortable means who lived in the motel

---

[1] One had used an electric drill.

unit had stripped to his undershorts, neatly folded his clothes, and laid them on the bed. He then went into the living room, sat down in the easy chair, placed a high-powered rifle in his mouth, and pulled the trigger. He had absolutely no idea of the consequences of his action. Yes, of course, he knew he would die and there would be some mess, but he didn't realize that his entire head from the lower jaw up would end up in bits splattered over the ceiling, walls, stove, refrigerator, and kitchen table. How do I know that he didn't realize the extent of the impending mess? Being a tidy and considerate man, he had organized a clean-up kit—a cardboard box containing a bottle of window cleaner, a dish cloth, and a roll of paper towels—and placed it by his feet. The real clean-up was no squirt-and-wipe job; it started with removing the drywall from the entire room.

Dealing with death on an almost daily basis gives one pause for reflection. I have come to appreciate my own mortality even more and try to live accordingly. Only the most shallow could see death after death and not be forced to ponder the meaning of life, if any, and whether or not life continues in some form after death. For the most part, I think encounters with death simply re-enforce our original beliefs.

I do know, however, of at least one conversion, temporary though it may be. A colleague who lives some distance away and is an avowed atheist called.

"Susan, there is a god."

Surprised and curious I replied, "Ohhh?"

"Remember that case I had several months ago where those two scumbags pulled off some dirty tricks that led to that young Smith woman killing herself?" he asked.

"Yes," I said, recalling this particularly tragic case.

"They're dead. Squashed when their car hit a telephone pole. I just came from the scene." I could hear his belief that justice had been done in the tone of his voice as well as in his words. "God got 'em," he said and hung up.

In the public's mind, a cop and coroner go together like a horse and carriage. Although we do work together, police and coroners have distinct roles as reflected in our different powers of investigation. As a coroner in British Columbia, I have legal access without a search warrant to anything or any place that could reasonably be considered to contain information pertaining to a death. In other words, I have much broader powers of investigation than the police. The twist comes in what I can do with the information. The purpose of a coroner's investigation is to elucidate the circumstances associated with a death without assigning guilt. A coroner finds facts. Period. A police officer finds facts also, but those facts may lead to criminal prosecution with loss of freedom.

In my pre-coroner life, my contact with the police was limited to being the recipient of an occasional speeding ticket. I am pleased to say that as a coroner, I have been favorably impressed by the professional conduct of the many Royal Canadian Mounted Police constables with whom I have attended death scenes. They are respectful of the deceased and offer compassionate assistance to family and friends. I am not involved in situations where the tougher side of police officers may be displayed. Whenever I hear a "tough cop story," a touchingly innocent incident comes to mind to contradict it.

A young female constable—whom I will call Linda—and I attended a suicide scene in a fancy motel room. The deceased, a handsome hulk of a guy in his late 20s, had apparently ingested an excess of prescription drugs. He lay on his back in bed covered to mid-chest, so that only his head and bare muscular arms and shoulders were visible. I pulled back the covers to examine his entire body. As I noted that he was clad only in jockey shorts, I heard Linda say with relief, "Thank goodness he has his pants on."

Whether working with the police, medics, or anybody else, coroners must do so in an independent manner. Our job is to speak for those who can no longer speak for themselves; we should speak for no one else. In the last analysis, we are judges employed by the Ministry of the Attorney General. Our usual reports are titled "Judgement of Inquiry," and during inquests we preside over the courtroom.

I'm often asked if I do the autopsies. No, I don't but I authorize them as part of my investigation and always attend. In British Columbia, autopsies are performed only by pathologists—physicians who specialize in the study of the structural and functional changes of the body caused by disease and other misfortunes. I have the good fortune of working with two fine pathologists. They, like myself, are on the shady side of fifty, with bodies that don't lie about our ages. Often at the start of an autopsy, it is apparent that the deceased was not only in much better physical shape than we are but also older. It's always a reminder of how fortunate we are to still be standing.

A few years ago, a lady in her mid-70s broke her hip. After initial examination in a small hospital, she was transferred to a larger one where surgical repair was done. The surgeon placed her on anticoagulants. In a few days, she was taken back to the small hospital where, despite orders from the surgeon, anticoagulation therapy was discontinued. A couple of weeks later, she died from blood clots in the lungs. My recommendations—coupled with the dedication and expertise of medical personnel—led to the development of written protocols for the use of anticoagulants, which—in turn—resulted not only in improved patient care, but also in substantial saving by virtue of reducing the number of days spent in the hospital. And the frosting on the cake? Our local achievements are winning nationwide acceptance.

Knowing that a stretch of highway, a baby's crib, a medical procedure or whatever is safer because of our endeavors is a reward we savor in quiet moments. Coroners' recommendations are not legally binding but do carry considerable moral persuasion.

One such example is told in a clipping I keep in my files. An outdoorswoman had tried to rescue her dog caught in the rapid currents of a river channel, upstream from a vertical drop structure at a dam. Both she and the dog drowned when they were swept over the edge into the whirlpool beneath. Because of my recommendations, fences were installed and danger signs erected. An extensive public education campaign was launched on the dangers of trying to rescue dogs from waterways. A couple of years later, while reading the newspaper of the nearest big city, my eye caught the heading: "Dog Drowns, Boy Lives." The boy said that he had not gone in after his beloved pet because he remembered a warning not to do such a thing.

Then there are the uneventful but necessary encounters. B.C. coroners take a training course in which, among other things, we are given tips on how to conduct interviews. Being able to obtain information from people—sometimes under difficult circumstances—requires tact, persistence, and skill. I prided myself on my interviewing ability until a Sunday afternoon not long ago when I was called to the home of an elderly couple. I was greeted at the door by the husband, an eager and affable gentleman. After examining his wife's body in the bedroom, I sat down with him at the kitchen table to get some pertinent information and to determine the time of death.

"Tell me what happened."

"I went in to change the bed about noon. She'd soiled it. I noticed she was cold and then made myself lunch waiting to see if she'd warm up. At 1:30 P.M. I checked again, and she was still cold, so I called the Fire Department."

"When did you last see your wife alive?" He gave a long-winded answer which made it apparent that he didn't understand my question. "Did she eat breakfast?" I asked.

"She hasn't eaten in three days." I tried not to look surprised.

"Did she speak to you this morning?"

"She's only spoken in guttural sounds for the past three weeks."

With no issue of paramount importance to pursue, I gave up and decided that the lady had died sometime between midnight and 8 A.M.

In spite of the trauma, the violence, and the frustrations I face as a coroner, I treasure some heart-warming moments, too. A woman—in her late 70s—died from an apparent heart attack shortly after admission to the Emergency Room of the local hospital. The attending physician who reported the unexpected death told me that the deceased had a daughter living in Victoria whom he had contacted. A few minutes later, I received a call from the daughter saying that she would be flying in later that day and wanted to see her mother's body. I made arrangements for the body to be moved from the morgue to the adjacent viewing room. At the appointed hour, I met the daughter, a woman in her early 30s who was accompanied by another woman, her friend since childhood.

Once in the viewing room, the daughter sat down at her mother's side and, while stroking her hair, spoke to her mother of their good times together. It was obvious from the reminiscing that the mother had been loving, warm and fun. One particular story involved the mother dancing around the kitchen with a basket of fruit on her head while her husband and daughter cheered. The friend joined into the conversation, too, which for all intents and purposes was three way— except the mother wasn't speaking.

Close to an hour later, the young women left. What a beautiful expression of love, I thought, as I wheeled the mother's body back into the morgue. Whenever I encounter the seamy side of life or the lesser aspect of human nature, I like to think of that woman dancing in her own kitchen with a basket of fruit on her head and the love she passed on to those around her.

---

This chapter illustrates an ideal in forensic medicine. In some U.S. states, coroners are elected—not appointed. There may be no requirement that the coroner have any special training. Funeral directors have often run for such positions, sometimes for self-serving reasons. Perhaps this chapter will motivate states to make appropriate changes where they are needed.

# Burial: Public, Religious, & Family Cemeteries

## 13

Someone once said to me that it's a good thing we have cemeteries—they may be the only open land left in the future. In many countries, including England and Japan, cemetery space is already at a premium.

## Body Burial in Established Cemeteries

Cemeteries are usually administered by a superintendent, the person with whom all cemetery arrangements must be made. The time of interment or burial must meet the cemetery's working schedule. For example, the city cemeteries in Burlington, Vermont allow no burials on Sunday, in order to keep one day totally free for visitations. Other visitation hours are set by these cemeteries as well.

Most established cemeteries require that excavation be handled by cemetery personnel only. This may be true even for the simple excavation needed to bury cremains. On the other hand, it is possible that cemetery workers would agree to oversee a family's personal by-hand excavation in some instances. Filling in a grave by hand is more likely possible—with cemetery supervision. The cemetery folks with whom I have spoken understand a family's need to participate.

Jewish and Muslim cemeteries, honoring the tradition of returning to the earth, rarely require a grave liner or vault. Most other cemeteries, however, require a grave liner (made of concrete slabs, assembled at the site) or a coffin vault (a one-piece unit with a top, also made of concrete, metal, or fiberglass). A grave liner is about half the price of a coffin vault, but many funeral directors claim they "stock" the vaults only. Either item must be lowered into the hole by machine, although the propylene "bell-type" which covers a casket can be handled by two persons without machinery. These outer-burial containers serve the purpose of keeping the earth from settling after burial, thus reducing maintenance.

Funeral directors may suggest that "sealer vaults" provide added protection, but these are the ones that popped out of the ground and floated away during the Midwest flood in '93. Gravediggers would much prefer to work in an older part of the cemetery where digging reveals rich loam: the casket and contents have been absorbed into the soil unhindered by the modern "outer burial containers." Opening a vault is unpleasant business, one told me, if a casket is to be moved. The contents reek of putrefaction when the casket bottom has rusted out.

Veterans, their spouses, and dependent children are entitled to free burial in a national cemetery, including the liner and opening-and-closing. Arlington National Cemetery in Virginia does not require grave liners or vaults. Nearly three-quarters of the other national cemeteries, however, require some sort of grave liner. Some cemeteries require that such an item be purchased from them only. That's not necessarily bad news, as a liner purchased from the cemetery may be less expensive than one purchased through a funeral home.

If the ground is frozen, remains are often placed in a holding tomb until spring. Bodies of those who have died from a contagious disease, however, may be rejected, at least according to the printed policies of some cemeteries.

Specifications for monuments, markers, and planting around graves as well as restrictions on other embellishments such as paths or fencing are described in the policies of most cemeteries. Some cemeteries may tell you that monuments must be purchased only from them. That is an illegal restraint of trade.[1]

*Perpetual care* may be arranged by the payment of a lump sum or may be included in the sale price of the cemetery lot, the most common practice now. In earlier practice, cemeteries billed families annually for the upkeep of grave sites. Most cemeteries have continued care, even when next-of-kin have passed away without making further maintenance provisions, but one cemetery commissioner remarked that "the place ought to look like an asparagus patch if you count everyone who hasn't paid his bill." In many areas, municipal cemeteries have been so poorly managed that cities have considering selling them to private enterprises. While that might be beneficial to the city, it bodes ill for consumers.

Many cemeteries are in churchyards for use by members of the congregation, and larger cemeteries exist for people of specific religious faiths. For many, burial in a religious cemetery is important, and, indeed, a church can provide an extremely important support group for a family dealing with death. At one time, family members not of the same faith were refused burial in such cemeteries, but current policies tend to be more accepting.

---

[1] See the footnote on page 151 regarding anti-tying court decisions.

With the sale of lots as part of a preneed package, many cemeteries are now considered big business and are being purchased by corporations desiring access to the preneed money for investment purposes. The price of a single lot in a small-town cemetery can be as low as $100 including perpetual care. Large commercial cemeteries, however, are likely to charge several thousand dollars for a single lot.

*Many states have provisions that allow a cemetery to declare burial plots "abandoned" if unused after, say, 50 years. If you have moved to another area or if Mom and Dad left you a lot in a town where you are not now known, the cemetery may have no way of locating you before starting the reclaiming procedure. You might want to put the cemetery on your greeting card list, just to be sure the folks there know where to find you.*

## Burial of Cremains

Few states have any restrictions on the final resting place of cremains, which may be buried in any yard or garden or scattered from a mountaintop if a cemetery location has not been chosen. Therefore, when it is consistent with personal and religious beliefs, cremation is a practical choice for many who handle death arrangements themselves, especially in urban or suburban areas.

Sometimes scattering is less satisfying to families than burial of the cremains in a specific location. One mortician told me of a mother who, at the urging of friends, had agreed to ocean scattering because her teenage son had loved surfing. At the time it seemed appropriate. A year or so later, the mother confided to this mortician her feeling of emptiness in not having a "place" by which to remember her son. The funeral director suggested that she purchase a columbarium space and choose some of the son's personal belongings to put into it. The mother gratefully did so, with a certain sense of relief at having a spot that was "his." It is my belief that part of that relief was gained because the mother took a more active role in the "burial" this time.

Some companies offer scattering services, often by air or at sea. On the West Coast, a scandal developed in 1984 involving a California company which merely dumped the cremains in a nearby location instead of providing the service that was contracted. This prompted the passing of a statute to limit scattering on land. In 1996, another scattering business scandal erupted when thousands of boxes of cremains were found in an airplane hangar. The owner ultimately committed suicide. California consumers are now eager to eliminate the law that limits private scattering, which may happen shortly after this goes to print.

Wisconsin requires that the state be notified of final disposition of cremains within 60 days, but there are no limitations as to where that may be. Presumably "at home" is an acceptable alternative to burial or scattering if you have not yet made up your mind or there will be a delay in any disposition.

## Home Burial

Families considering home burial must examine local zoning ordinances. For those with land in rural or semi-rural areas, home burials are usually possible.

Body burial sites must be some distance from any water supply. The slope of the land and the soil conditions must also be taken into account, especially where the earth is shallow, over ledge, or clay. Power lines are to be avoided, because overhead power may be replaced with buried cable at some future time.

There is strong historical precedent in the establishment of a family burial plot, but a family should consider the long-range implications on land value in doing so because a graveyard becomes a permanent easement on the property in many states. In a 1959 Oklahoma case, *Heiligman vs. Chambers,* a grandson sued to keep the new landowner from moving family bodies to a town cemetery. The court decision upheld the right to permanency created by any such family burial ground, at least in that state. Other states have provisions for moving the graves from "abandoned" burial sites.

A family must realize, too, that someone else, in future years, may not maintain a family cemetery after ownership changes. And while visitation rights may be protected by the Oklahoma precedent, how will people feel returning to land no longer in the family?

For many of us, the deterrents are minimal compared to the satisfaction and personal identity that a home burial offers. No one else sets visitation hours, and the plantings or markers can be appropriate to the family or individual.

In my case, I found a rough piece of slate, one too large to be moved easily, but one that I could manage. I used a Boy Scout jackknife and a screwdriver to carve John's name and date on the one flat surface. Acid rain will probably fade the writing in 50 years, but perhaps it won't matter by then. Because John was cremated, I was free to pick the garden site I wanted for his spot, without a permit. But because this is not registered in the town clerk's office as an official home burial site, there will be no guarantee of permanency in preserving recognition there. The slate marker may stay, but then again it may get moved.

I sold the house almost 15 years ago, and it has been sold three times again since then. Perhaps we have been lucky, but a recent visit showed the spot to be well-tended.

## Cemeteries of the Future

An e-mail from South America to the FAMSA office arrived out of the blue one day, seeking partners for a European cemetery project. Several industries, universities, and cemeteries had already agreed to work on the project, it said.

> Recent scientific studies suggest control of the putrefaction process in cemeteries by supplementing nature with non-pathological bacteria and enzymes (bio catalyst) that can decompose bodies more completely and in less time, with no resultant dangerous water contamination. The target is to show the best biological way for proper maintenance of the cemetery and to keep an eye on the main progress of the cemetery's involvement in the equilibrium of the flora and the micro-fauna giving much more value and less risk to the area around it where people live. . . .
>
> It is not easy to challenge all the psychological effects and the old social traditions related to graveyards, but technical and scientific reasons make it a necessity when health and ecological safety of the community are at risk.

FAMSA was in no position to give financial support to this project, but I asked to be kept up-to-date with how it was going.

~❖~

Someone recently asked me what ideas I had for a "green" cemetery, and I'd like to share them. What has been just a private vision perhaps would lend itself as a solution to what you will read about in the next chapter. The idea that a cemetery is run as big business offends me. Cemetery space should be sacred—a spiritual spot that each of us is entitled to, simply for having been alive.

Two hundred acres seems about right—donated by a local citizen or set aside by a municipality, and planted with the most incredible gardens one can imagine—the kind of gardens people would travel to from miles around. And there would be a building—classical and stunning in its design. (I sort of imagine a cross between Pei's chapel at M.I.T. and the "glass house" at Johns Hopkins.) This should be the perfect building for concerts, art exhibits, weddings, and—yes—memorial services.

There would be an attached greenhouse, too, with co-generated heat from the discreetly situated crematory. A fleet of white vans—not black—would be available for body pick-up.

After cremation, a family would be given a personally engraved trowel and would be allowed to bury the cremated remains anywhere on the garden grounds themselves. A "wall of remembrance"—not too prominent, perhaps off to the side by a quiet "prayer garden"—would bear testimony for future genealogists.

Dedicated fund accounts would be set aside to receive "donations in memory of"—for art exhibits, string quartets, tuba concerts, rock concerts, poetry readings, and any of the other arts. (Hasn't someone said that arts are the "balm of the soul"?) The funds would provide a stipend for local artists; an invitation to play or exhibit or present would be an honor, much as it is at the Gardner Museum in Boston.

With land at a growing premium in many parts of the country, this kind of use would allow the dead to honor the living in an environmentally-friendly way. With tax support and private endowment, "burials" would be free to any local resident.

Diane's dad was cremated in New Orleans, but it seemed like a good idea to bury his cremains in the lot where his mother and grandmother were buried in Jacksonville, Florida.

Diane's brother and sister-in-law called the Stewart-owned[1] Arlington Park (Cemetery and Funeral Home) to see about the arrangements. They were visited in their home by one of the cemetery "counsellors," and, by the time he was done, the bill amounted to over $1,800: a "second right of interment" would be $1,025; opening and closing would be $225; vault installation was $40; a memorial marker added $140; and an urn vault was $495—they were told the EPA required the urn vault for sanitary reasons.[2] After Diane's sister-in-law wrote a deposit check for $210, the sales rep said they had three days to cancel the plan if they wished. His company was very easy to work with, he assured them, and they could even take up to 30 days if they wanted.

Diane's brother called her to say everything had been set up, but she nearly choked when she found out how much it would cost. Something didn't seem right. Hopping on the internet to see what she could find out, she quickly located FAMSA's web site and jotted down the phone number, calling me shortly thereafter. She gave me a run-down of what had transpired, and I was aghast. There is, of course, *no* EPA requirement for urn vaults, and saying so would be a clear violation of the FTC Funeral Rule—*if* the Funeral Rule also applied to cemeteries.

"Let me do some checking, and I'll call you back," I said.

I found that the state of Florida gives consumers 30 days to cancel preneed agreements, and a notice to that effect must be printed on the contract.

---

[1] Stewart Enterprises is the third-largest corporate funeral chain.

[2] There is **no** reason to require an urn vault other than to line the pockets of the cemetery folks. It serves no function for maintenance of the cemetery grounds, and it certainly is not required or suggested by any government agency at any level.

Although the family could afford it, Diane felt the money involved was not consistent with her Dad's philosophy of living. We talked about other options—scattering in the ocean where he loved to fish, a veterans' cemetery, her own garden, or quietly scattering his "bone meal" on the sod where her grandmother was buried. We both laughed.

Diane called her brother and clued him in. They had been "had," she said. By this time, her brother had begun to get suspicious, too. On the price list that the counsellor had left behind, it gave a range of prices for urn vaults: "$135 to $495." They had been sold the expensive one without being told they had a choice.

Diane and her brother decided to cancel the arrangements and delay any decisions until later. Checking back with Diane a few months after, I asked what plans had been made. "We still haven't done anything," she said. "My father was restless in life and never quite settled down. I think the same thing is happening in death." But the pressure was now off. Because of Diane's questioning and alertness, she had avoided overpriced arrangements that she would have regretted later.

~❖~

It was announced with some shock in the industry journals. Then it hit the mainstream press: In 1995, Loewen—the second largest funeral conglomerate—made a deal with the National Baptist Convention USA, the largest African-American church group in the country.[1] The church members were to peddle cemetery lots and monuments for a 10% commission. Each sale would generate 11% in additional commissions, divided between the state and local church organization, and the local pastor would get a cut of that as well. Commented the *Funeral Monitor:* "No matter what the short-term financial benefits, such an alliance poses great risk of long-term damage to believers as church leaders implicitly ascribe heavenly virtue to a particular commercial enterprise in which they have a direct financial interest."

Cindy Loose, with her in-depth coverage in the *Washington Post* (August 30, 1997), revealed the script church members were to use.

---

[1] At the time of my final editing, the deal between Loewen and the Baptists has reportedly been called off. But it remains a prime example of the outrageous mischief that can occur if church members and the public are not vigilant.

Charles Johnson is studying the requisite skills of a family life counselor . . . the telephone script prepared for trainees peddling cemetery plots and headstones. It's now Johnson's turn for some role playing.

Johnson tells the potential customer—played by a fellow student—that he would like to come by her house to get her "honest opinion" about a new church-related program.

"What's it about?" asks the customer.

"It's buying power for our community," he says.

The script advises sales agents to avoid mentioning death. If customers insist on knowing what the program is about, the script tells them to answer, "The program is so valuable that it would be unfair to you and the pastor to tell you about it over the phone lines."

. . . A typical contract provides a flat bronze grave marker and a grave vault. It also provides a "double site" at a Loewen cemetery, dug eight feet deep rather than the traditional six in order to conserve space by burying two people atop one another.

With 5 percent down, the program offers an 84-month financing plan at 9.9 percent interest, for a total of $6,417.23.

And the costs wouldn't stop there. For example, at Cedar Hill (owned by Loewen) a family will be hit with an $875 charge for "opening and closing," a fee the cemetery counselor probably forgot to mention. Oh, yes, it goes up to $1,125 if you want a Saturday burial, but it will have to be before 2 P.M. For two, that adds at least $1,750 to the bill—for a new total of $8,167.23. That's if someone in the family were to drop dead today. Six months from now, the price may be even higher, one reason they may not *want* you to prepay for this. Sell you the lot now, and they've got you hooked. If past patterns prevail, they'll raise the other prices later, probably a lot faster than inflation.

A check of several DC, Maryland, and Virginia cemeteries—both religious and municipal—indicated that the same purchases, cash up front, would cost between $3,000 and $4,000 to bury two people. Yes, with the cozy Loewen deal, one of the Baptists' unemployed members would realize a commission of $641.72 and the church people would get to split $705.90. But that's a pretty small return for suckering church members into paying as much as $5,000 more than necessary to bury Mom and Dad.

And once a family has ties to a particular cemetery, is it likely that the family will be steered toward a high-priced funeral home owned by the same corporation (in this case Loewen), which just happens to be conveniently located on the cemetery grounds or nearby? Or can we assume that the "nice" people at the cemetery suggest a more affordable funeral home if cost is a concern?

~❖~

The answer to the above question would appear to be "no," at least in Richmond, Virginia. Although it is against the law in that state for cemeteries to "steer" business to a particular mortuary and accept payment for doing so or to pay money to funeral homes for their cemetery referrals, internal SCI[1] memos sent anonymously to the FAMSA office indicate that is exactly what is happening. On Woody Funeral Home[2] letterhead dated June 29, 1994:

SUBJECT: Synergy Meeting with Forest Lawn 6/30/94

A preliminary meeting was held on Tuesday, June 28, 1994 to plan for the Synergy meeting on Thursday. Those present at this meeting were [names have been deleted]:
General Manager, Richmond Group
Location Manager at Parham Chapel
Location Manager at Laburnum Chapel
Preneed Manager for the Richmond Group
Eastern Region II Sales Director, Sentinel Security Plans

Note: Huguenot Chapel Manager was not present because he is out of town on vacation.

At this meeting, we discussed each point on the directive from the Regional office. The general discussion was as follows and will be included in our meeting Thursday with [name deleted]:

1) "My proactive customer referral program is . . . "
It was the feeling of the assembled group that it would be fairly difficult to convince families using Parham or Huguenot to use Forest Lawn because it [is] so far away from these locations. The best opportunity for referral is obviously at Laburnum Chapel and we are certainly taking advantage of this opportunity whenever it presents itself. . . .

---

[1] SCI—Service Corporation International, the largest worldwide funeral conglomerate.

[2] Owned by SCI, Woody Funeral Home has the highest prices in the Richmond area, according to a Funeral Consumer Information Society survey.

2) "We will track referrals between the cemetery and funeral home by . . ."

It is fairly simple to track referrals from the cemetery funeral home by the number of gift certificates issued by the preneed office to Forest Lawn personnel. On the other hand, our personnel are prohibited by Virginia law from accepting any kind of referral remunerations from the cemetery, so this will be more difficult to measure.

~❖~

Meanwhile, after a lot is purchased, pressure is often placed on consumers to spend even more money. Following is the script approved by a regional SCI manager (name deleted) for milking new money out of existing lot owners at its various cemeteries:

Hello, Mr./Mrs. _____

My name is _____ with _____ Memorial Park, where you own your cemetery property.

Mr./Mrs. _____, the reason why I'm calling is that we are in the process of updating our records prior to placing them in our new computer. We need to set a time when you can come to the office to review your lot owner information with one of our counselors and verify the accuracy of the information we have on file.

Would tomorrow or _____ be convenient for you?

Would afternoon or evening be better? (set specific time)

Great, we will see you _____.

We will be happy to answer any questions you may have at that time, and if you desire, bring you up-to-date on products and services that may not have been available at the time we first talked to you.

Mrs. H. was one of the folks who heard this spiel. She'd seen a similar notice in the newspaper and dutifully made an appointment. Her family had a dozen lots at Forest Lawn, purchased years ago, for $1,100 or so. Now she was being urged to purchase a vault ($700) and pay for the opening and closing charges ($700 on weekdays, but if she wanted to cover all contingencies, she could pay the $990 charge for a weekend death, and the balance would be returned to the family if not needed).

~❖~

"Bolt from on High: L.A. Catholic Archdiocese Enters Funeral Business," reads the headline of the June 16, 1997 issue of *Funeral Monitor.* Stewart Enterprises, it reports, has arranged to lease land on the grounds of cemeteries owned by the diocese in L.A. and Tucson, where it will build mortuaries to serve the Catholic community. Needless to say, independent "Catholic" funeral homes are up in arms. They are not impressed by the Stewart CEO who stated: "Our company has a long-standing reputation of meeting the individual funeral and cemetery needs of families with quality products and services. . . . We consider it a privilege to have been chosen by the Archdiocese of Los Angeles to help them better serve the needs of their congregations." What a slap in the face to the independent funeral homes already serving a Catholic population!

And what a con job on Catholic consumers! Price surveys in the Dallas, Texas area show Stewart-owned funeral homes to be consistently the most costly. Will the L.A. and Tucson Catholics stick with the independent funeral homes? Or will they end up using one of the on-campus, high-priced Stewart ones, simply because "that's where Mom had her lot" and the funeral home has the blessing of the church?

~❖~

By building funeral homes on untaxed, church-owned cemetery grounds, for-profit corporations are taking an unfair advantage over local funeral home owners who do pay property taxes for the land on which their funeral homes sit.

In Pennsylvania, a mortician has built a mausoleum on the grounds of a church cemetery. He pays no property taxes but collects the money from the crypt sales. As he told "Beth Mercer" (I posed as a church person looking for advice), "There's money to be made." Once all spaces are sold, ownership will be transferred to the church. According to an anonymous industry source, substandard materials were used, and by the time the church acquires the mausoleum, it may become a liability. The modest perpetual-care fund may not be enough to even meet the heating bills for the enclosed chapel.

~❖~

Bruce and his daughter were at the VA Hospital for an appoint ment. A stack of colorful red, white, and blue flyers caught Bruce's eye:

Public Notice to All Veterans
FREE BURIAL SPACE

The Military Gardens has been rededicated for veterans, ex-service personnel and their families. Veteran space No Charge. Spouse and family members of veterans 1/2 off burial space. Proof of honorable discharge required.

In the past ten years, thousands of veterans and their families have reserved their property, so a limited number of spaces are still available. Therefore, immediate preregistration is advisable. To receive your eligibility certificate and other valuable veterans information, fill out and mail coupon below or call:

1-800-366-VETS

Bruce and his daughter subsequently visited Sunset Memorial Park in Minneapolis. Although there were no markings to indicate that the section they were shown near the trees was the Military Garden space, it seemed like a good deal from what the counselor said. The veterans cemetery was running out of space, which is why Sunset was making the offer to veterans, he told them. Bruce later learned from the VA that there would be plenty of space in that state's national cemetery—for the next 50 years.

The contract listed a single lot ($1,175), two cremation vaults for Bruce and his wife ($1,010), two urns ($600), two opening and closing charges ($305), and a memorial with vase ($1,084). The total, counting tax, would be $4,244.46 less an $840 "credit." Bruce started making payments on the $3,400 package.

Three months later, a TV show caused him to be suspicious, and he called the FAMSA office. Yes, he'd been sold an over-priced deal at this Loewen-owned facility, I told him. Burial and a marker are free in a veterans cemetery. If he wanted to be buried locally, I thought a municipal or church cemetery would cost considerably less— about a quarter of what he had contracted for—but he could certainly check that out. In a chat later that afternoon, he sheepishly admitted that—after shopping around—he found that lots in a town cemetery were only $200, plus $100 for opening and closing. At that point, he decided it was better to forfeit the $350 he had already paid and walk away from the deal. Given the manipulative sales tactics, he might get it back, I offered.

Why did I suggest that? If Bruce was being offered a free lot by Sunset, there was no need for an additional lot charge for his wife, as there would be plenty of space for the cremated remains of two in a single lot. A call by my office assistant, elicited the information that a Sunset lot for "Aunt Betsy" would cost anywhere from $410 to $820 in the "new" section. In the old section "near the trees," lots were $1,300—but with the current 50% sale, a lot would be only $661.50. Apparently, the veterans' "deal" applied only to the priciest section of the cemetery. That other lots were available for considerably less was never revealed.

This is a good example of why cemeteries should be brought under the FTC Funeral Rule, with a requirement for full price disclosure. Cemeteries should also be required to hand out VA-approved literature delineating veterans' rights and burial benefits. Although many veterans may choose to pay for interment space in a private cemetery because the location is more convenient than the nearest national cemetery, veterans should not be misled into thinking that such sales tactics represent legitimate VA benefits.

It took a letter from the FAMSA office and a letter from a lawyer, but Bruce did get his money back.

~❖~

A dismayed SCI funeral director, who chose to remain anonymous, sent a copy of the script to be used with cremation customers. In an effort to sell niches and cemetery space in the SCI-owned facilities the following illegal ploy was used:

> Memorialization creates an opportunity for family and friends to say good-bye in a dignified manner. It provides a link to the past, future and present by allowing generations of loved ones a permanent place to go to reflect and remember. And most importantly, it provides a time and place for you and your[sic] to go to heal and provide closure. There are specific laws and guidelines that pertain to what can be done with the cremated human body.

This is a blatant lie in every state except California. In California, cremated remains may not be scattered over land. They may be interred anywhere, and the family may even keep them at home. Without cremains police, a family may effectively do anything it wishes—even in California.

And in case the consumer didn't hear the first lie, it was repeated:

> Almost all urns can be buried. Burial can take place in a family plot or urn garden. There are specific laws on where you can bury cremated remains.

~❖~

In Wisconsin (and in a few other states and provinces), it is against the law for a mortuary to own a cemetery or vice versa. SCI and Loewen must have thought their gaggle of high-priced attorneys could out-milk the farmers there and proceeded to purchase both anyway. But they didn't dazzle the Wisconsin judges and, in 1996, SCI was ordered to divest one or the other. Loewen put its funeral homes on the block, it says, and kept the cemeteries. SCI is appealing.

~❖~

As I was researching this book, I received an e-mail from one of my funeral director friends[1] in response to my question about the mad rush by the corporate chains to purchase cemeteries:

> No question about it. Cemeteries are FAR MORE profitable than funeral homes—especially on the preneed front. For a variety of reasons: no sales restrictions as with preneed funerals; up-front money when a sale is made unlike funeral service preneeds; frequent "delivery" of preneed items (warehouses full of bronze markers waiting for the time of installation; also burial vaults warehoused on-site in cemetery sheds and warehouses); income stream from appropriately operated endowment funds, etc.

To give you an idea of what kind of dollars are involved for a "typical" cemetery business, Fort Lincoln Cemetery (owned by Stewart) in Prince George's County, Maryland does an average of 135 interments a month. The least expensive lot costs $1,000. That's down by the stream, Sheryl—the "family service counsellor"—told me. It is a little "moist," she said. Up on the hill, a lot for "traditional ground burial" would be $1,500. The least expensive vaults range from $895 for a cement one to $1,250 for a waterproof variety "guaranteed for 75-100 years." (That's a safe bet. Who's going to be around, curious

---

[1] I am on good terms with a number of funeral directors who resent what the "bad apples" do to the industry. We may not agree on every issue, but the ethical ones are truly embarrassed by the mischief that the others pull.

enough to dig it up then?) The cement one is, of course, porous, Sheryl pointed out, "And most of our families are concerned about that." Opening and closing charges are $895 plus $60 to install the vault. And a minimum marker would be a ten-inch round base with a bronze vase for only $800–$900; installation $60 extra—for a total cost of $3,710 if my "Aunt Bessie" opts for the least expensive view by the old mill stream. (A least-expensive mausoleum or lawn crypt would be $4,000, plus $895 for opening and closing.)

Ten percent of the lot price must be placed in trust for perpetual care, so there goes $100. Although Maryland statutes provide that 55% of the payment for goods and services be placed in trust, "constructive delivery" can evade that requirement. That is, a certificate stating that the vault and marker are yours (and being stored in a warehouse) means that the cemetery has "delivered" and can pocket the rest of the deal. After wholesale costs for the vault (about $350) and a memorial marker (less than $300), the cemetery is clearing almost $3,000 per low-end transaction. "Counsellors'" commissions run about 10%. Perpetual care mows the lawn. Knowing that many will spend more than Aunt Bessie, one can conservatively estimate that sales are generating an income of over $350,000 per month or $4.2 million a year. Oh, yes, property taxes are almost $84,000 a year, but what the heck.

~❖~

Although cemetery operation is restricted to nonprofit entities in many states, the funeral conglomerates have managed their way around that with "two sets of books," as one funeral director described it. A nonprofit sub-corporation set up by the conglomerate is the titular owner of the cemetery to meet statutory restrictions. That corporation then "hires" a management firm to run the cemetery. Guess who gets the contract? The bookkeeping loopholes are big enough for a Goodyear blimp to sail through on a windy day without a pilot. For example, in Oklahoma, statutes declare that 50% of the cemetery income should be used for retiring "debt." Might this be to pay for the expensive-to-be-buried-in mausoleum just erected? And what rate of interest is the debt incurring, payable to whom? Does the sale of vaults and markers come under the "nonprofit" part of the operation, or will those sales list the nearby funeral home at another address? Who does the "opening and closing" of graves—the nonprofit or the for-profit corporation? (The nonprofit price is typically $200 vs. $900 for a for-profit corporation as of this writing.)

~❖~

I have a personal conviction that everyone should be entitled to a simple burial if that's what one wants. That seems like a basic "right" one earns just for existing, even though such an entitlement appears nowhere in any federal or state laws . . . unless one is a veteran or married to one. Fortunately, persons choosing cremation can have their "ashes" placed just about anywhere. But for those who choose body burial, affordable choices are becoming more and more limited.

What would happen if states passed laws that limited cemetery ownership to *real* nonprofit groups such as churches or towns? Well, it would be one heck of a write-off for the corporate chains to donate their cemeteries back to the municipalities and nonprofit groups where some of us think they belong.

Cemeteries in most states are seriously under-regulated. Historically, little regulation was needed because cemeteries were owned by true nonprofit organizations who could be trusted. But with the current rapid trend of takeover by huge corporations, legislative activities need to get under way if cemetery consumers are to get a fair shake:

- When purchased preneed, 100% of the cemetery merchandise and services—*i.e.,* vaults, markers, installation, and opening-and-closing—should be placed in trust. Consumers should be entitled to a full refund of the amount paid—plus interest—if they want to back out of the deal. "Constructive delivery" negates this possibility and should not be permitted.

- Laws should require cemeteries to repurchase an unwanted lot (or crypt or niche) at the original selling price plus 50% of the difference between that and current market price if the value has increased. (Or a lot owner should be free to sell or transfer the lot to another person. Any transfer fee should reflect the real costs to the cemetery, not an inflated "processing fee.") If the value of the lot has decreased below the original selling price, the cemetery should repurchase the lot at 75% of the current worth. One could make a case for subtracting perpetual care or 10%, whichever is less, from the amount to be refunded because the lot has presumably been mowed in the interim. However, at most cemeteries, all lots are mowed regardless of whether they have been sold.

Folks move, remarry, and change their plans with a certain predictability. There is no reason a cemetery should profit excessively from the vagaries of the human condition. The above suggestions are fair to the cemetery operators and consumers alike. The following shows what can happen without such protection.

In 1986, Robert and Melva Shields thought they were doing the responsible thing when they purchased a double-depth lawn crypt at Greenwood Memorial Park (owned by SCI) in San Diego for $1,900. They also paid for endowment care ($75), a granite marker with vase ($455.57), endowment care for the marker ($22), a marker installation fee ($120), an additional flower vase ($35), and sales tax ($26.37)—for a total of $2,637.

In 1997, after their church had established a memorial garden, the Shields decided to opt for cremation. The folks at Greenwood said they couldn't repurchase the lawn crypts, but could issue a credit or refund for the other items, less a $66.22 "revocation fee," for a total credit of $595.80. In the meantime, the sales rep would be happy to sell them two cremation packages for $1,780—which included the "required" $95 copper boxes. Even though the sales rep noted a credit of $595.80 on their paperwork, the full amount of the cremation package—$1,780—was billed to their credit card. When they later asked for a refund check, they were told that there could be no refund or credit for the granite and bronze marker, that it was theirs and they could do whatever they wanted with it. The cemetery was even willing to store it "for a while."

Yes, the Shields had signed an order for engraving the marker when they first purchased the lot, thinking nothing would happen until they died. Three years later, however, the cemetery ordered and installed the memorial, even though neither of them had yet gone to the great beyond.[1] That wasted more than $500 for a marker and installations fees that were no longer wanted.

---

[1] Because the cemetery had "delivered" it, the money could be spent right away. Greed over efficiency. A cemetery worker had actually installed the half-inscribed marker, as a photo showed:

R o b e r t  V.  S h i e l d s
Feb. 9, 1924

M e l v a   J.   S h i e l d s
May 4, 1924

The cemetery would, of course, have had to pull the marker and reinscribe it with the date of death, once either of the Shields had died.

And the value of the double-depth lawn crypts that Greenwood said it could not take back? According to a statement on Greenwood letterhead dated October 17, 1997, the value was now $6,000! Although Greenwood was unwilling to buy back the crypts, the sales rep readily supplied them with the name of a lot broker. He sent a Power of Attorney form authorizing a "Fredric Zarse" to act as their agent in arranging for the sale of the crypts. And how much would the Shields get for this deal? A mere $1,560. . . . There are 4,000 such spaces for sale, they were told, and it might take a while. They decided to donate the crypts to their church instead.

The Shields got their credit card company to reverse the raw deal on the cremation charge, but Greenwood still makes out like a bandit. In the ten years that Greenwood has had the Shields' money, it would have generated $1,874—at 5% compound interest—had all the money been placed in trust. The Shields finally settled their small claims court suit for a refund of $264.88.

If the church donates the lawn crypts to a family in need this year, someone will have to pay $1,151 for a new marker, installation, and tax. The new family will be hit with two opening-and-closing charges of $695 each, if it hasn't gone up. The generous donation by the Shields will still cost the new family a bundle—$2,400 at minimum.

~❖~

With the corporate purchase of cemeteries and the ensuing increase of prices, cemeteries should be required to repurchase unwanted lots, allowing a consumer to take at least a portion of that equity and seek burial space elsewhere. That not only seems fair, it is likely to have a leveling effect on prices by nurturing better competition.

Oh, yes, states may want to check to see if the for-profit cemeteries are paying a fair share of property taxes, if any. In one Mississippi location that I checked, the for-profit cemetery was not.

Abusive and misleading cemetery practices should be stopped, with full price-disclosure required. Only ten states have a cemetery board or cemetery-funeral board combination. The combination board seems most efficient, especially with the growing number of combo operations that the conglomerates are building. A consumer thinks of the funeral experience as encompassing both a funeral home and a cemetery. The regulating agency should likewise have the same continuity of concerns. Changing the existing funeral board to include an equal number of cemeterians who are **not** also affiliated with a mortuary would suggest a balance of interests. Adding an independent crematory operator might also be appropriate for such a board, as well as monument dealer.

For the past few generations, people have depended on funeral homes to care for their dead. In some circumstances, that is still going to be the only practical choice. But how do you care for your own dead when you must use a mortuary? Will you have the opportunity to participate in and personalize this experience? Or will you succumb to a role of dependency and vulnerability that invites the funeral director to take over?

I'm reminded of a Donald Duck cartoon. The first clip shows Daisy alone—zipping down the steep stretch of a roller coaster, purse resting on her lap, and a look of contentment on her face. She gets off and bumps into Donald soon after.

"Wanna go for a ride on the roller coaster?" he asks.

"Sure," says Daisy, and off they go.

The final clip shows Daisy shreaking with fear and holding on to Donald for dear life, as they barrel down the very same hill that Daisy took so calmly before.

Are we expected to play a similar role of helplessness at a time of death while on a roller coaster of emotions? Or is it acceptable to weep and grieve without giving up a sense of control over the final act of love?

Knowing what the "ride" is going to be like may be one way to begin. Of the funeral complaints that are generally filed with state agencies and consumer groups, most fall into the categories of manipulation and excessive price. The following should help you become a less vulnerable funeral consumer.

# Tricks of the Funeral Trade
## A Changing Death-care Industry

## 15

In most businesses, the forces of supply and demand keep goods and services within the affordability range of those who will use them. Not so with funeral and cemetery purchases. According to a 1995 study done by the Wirthlin Group at the behest of the funeral industry, almost 90% do not shop around for a funeral: 45% pick a funeral home that served someone else in the family, 33% call the nearest mortuary (perhaps the only one in town), and 11% pick a funeral home based on the perceived ethnic or religious affiliation.

Years ago, there was a funeral home in every other small town, and death care was acknowledged as a part-time job. When I was growing up, the sign in Craftsbury Common, Vermont read "Upholstery—Hardware—Undertaking." Little by little, morticians found they could raise their prices, and the side-line jobs diminished. If funeral business were indeed a full-time, five-days-a-week job, the following chart shows the number of funeral homes that would be needed for the death-rate in each state, compared to how many there are:[1]

| State | Needed | Existing | State | Needed | Existing | State | Needed | Existing |
|---|---|---|---|---|---|---|---|---|
| Alabama | 173 | 363 | Kentucky | 149 | 495 | North Dakota | 24 | 110 |
| Alaska | 11 | 19 | Louisiana | 162 | 333 | Ohio | 427 | 1,271 |
| Arizona | 146 | 134 | Maine | 47 | 158 | Oklahoma | 133 | 355 |
| Arkansas | 108 | 286 | Maryland | 166 | 263 | Oregon | 115 | 161 |
| California | 904 | 757 | Mass. | 220 | 724 | Pennsylvania | 511 | 1,881 |
| Colorado | 101 | 167 | Michigan | 334 | 805 | Rhode Island | 38 | 127 |
| Connecticut | 117 | 325 | Minnesota | 150 | 498 | SC | 135 | 392 |
| Delaware | 25 | 77 | Mississippi | 109 | 315 | South Dakota | 27 | 135 |
| DC | 27 | 40 | Missouri | 221 | 707 | Tennessee | 207 | 475 |
| Florida | 621 | 794 | Montana | 31 | 87 | Texas | 563 | 1,201 |
| Georgia | 237 | 660 | Nebraska | 62 | 290 | Utah | 44 | 97 |
| Hawaii | 31 | 21 | Nevada | 52 | 31 | Vermont | 20 | 70 |
| Idaho | 34 | 77 | NH | 37 | 103 | Virginia | 211 | 474 |
| Illinois | 430 | 1,388 | New Jersey | 291 | 790 | Washington | 165 | 195 |
| Indiana | 206 | 700 | New Mexico | 52 | 66 | West Virginia | 82 | 289 |
| Iowa | 116 | 582 | New York | 661 | 1,981 | Wisconsin | 180 | 590 |
| Kansas | 96 | 332 | NC | 266 | 686 | Wyoming | 15 | 35 |

---

[1] Compiled from 1995–6 Mortality Statistics, Center for Disease Control, and a report of established funeral homes, 1993 and 1996 figures in the National Directory of Morticians. It is likely that the figures for the number of existing funeral homes are "approximate" only and may be higher, as new funeral homes are being constructed.

There are undoubtedly some funeral homes that can handle more than one funeral a day, which reduces the "needed" number accordingly and probably explains the figures for California, Hawaii, and Nevada. Certainly in rural areas with sparse population, a funeral home does not expect the dying business to be a full-time one, and more establishments will be needed to cover the geographic area than the number generated by a simple death-rate formula. In most states, however, the number of funeral homes far exceeds that which can be reasonably supported—full-time—by the death-rate. In Kansas, Pennsylvania, and Vermont, an average funeral home might get only two funerals a week; in Iowa and Nebraska, there may be only one funeral a week. When that is the situation, the funeral bill is likely to be severely inflated in order to support the under-utilized staff and facilities. Furthermore, there is no need for competition when all can stay in business by charging high fees that people continue to pay. *Ironically, in the areas were there isn't a glut of funeral homes, prices tend to be more moderate, the reverse of what one finds in any other business.* (FTC, please take note!)

## Are You Going to Be a Willing Victim?

From what I hear, most mortuary students go into the business to be of service to the grieving public. It's after they're hit with the hard facts of making a living and the slow rate of business that steering consumers to more expensive options becomes a preoccupation.

There probably are as many exceptional funeral directors as there are exceptional teachers, excellent doctors, and wonderful spouses. Unfortunately, there probably are at least as many bad morticians as there are bad teachers, incompetent doctors, and ill-fated matches. (One retired funeral director told me he thought there were more.) What stacks this law of averages against the funeral consumer is that, although one will move on in school, and one can change doctors or get a divorce, there's only one funeral—there's no second chance.

Therefore, you—the funeral buyer—have a special burden to inform yourself about your choices and educate yourself about the pitfalls. Many of us will never arrange for more than one funeral in a lifetime. In a situation that invites abuse, you won't have much practice. Knowledge is your best self-defense.

## How Much Can You Afford?

When you arrive at a funeral home, the car you drive and how you're dressed will quickly be assessed. (Or the mortician may eagerly offer to come to your home.) If your family is already known in that area, the funeral director probably has a mental calculation of your income and financial worth. But that's part of the funeral director's job—to give you what you want. After all, a car dealer won't try to sell you a Hyundai if it appears you can afford a Cadillac, and a sensitive funeral director isn't going to insult an affluent client by showing bottom-of-the-line merchandise. In fact, no one wants the image of a down-and-outer, so you, too, will probably be on your best behavior in a fancy establishment—one that may be a lot fancier than what we'd find in your home if we walked in on you unannounced just about now.

While the formal aura of a funeral establishment is set to honor the dead, it inherently intimidates the average person. How will you respond?

*"Given your position in the community, I'm sure you'll want to . . ."* Flattery may open your pocketbook, or will it? Unless you flaunt the funeral bill, it's more likely to be the personal and unusual touches that your friends and neighbors remember about a particular funeral.

*"Your mother had excellent taste. When she made arrangements for Aunt Nellie, this is what she chose."* But is that the funeral Dad wanted? Is there a good reason to have the same kind of funeral again this time? Were the prices the same when Aunt Nellie died? Or will the funeral director slip in something "extra" or a little higher-priced if you simply say, "I want one just like Aunt Nellie's. That was nice."?

*"I'm sure you want the best for your mother."* Who doesn't? What is best for your family, however, may not have anything to do with how much you spend.

*"Most of our families pick the **traditional** package."* The emphasis here is on "traditional," as if to imply that anyone who picked anything else would be considered a freak. Morticians have set the "tradition" in direct relation to their profit margin, and a vulnerable public has been unwittingly dragged along.

Most of these sample quotes fall into the category of "controlling with guilt." It may seem easier to go along with the offered suggestions (and high prices) than try to justify that you're not *"cheap"* or unloving.

You're the only one who can determine the most loving and meaningful way to say goodbye. You might want to take a friend with you who would help you resist unwanted sales pressures.

> Suggested response: *"If I spent according to how much I care, I'd be penniless—I'd be paying you for the rest of my life!"*

Funeral directors will usually ask how you plan to pay for the funeral, to see if there is insurance to cover the costs. If a policy is made out to the funeral director, you should find out if any unused portion can be returned to the estate, if money is also needed for other expenses. If a specific funeral home is *not* the beneficiary of an insurance policy, it's probably better not to divulge the amount of any insurance. The cost of an insurance-covered funeral has a strange way of ending up to be just about the same amount as the policy, once that amount is known. One widow told the funeral home her husband wanted "any old wood box." But, knowing that she had walked in with a $12,000 policy in her purse, the funeral director showed her a $6,000 casket and told her it was "the only suitable thing for a man" that they had. The total bill was . . . you guessed it.

If there is no funeral insurance and family funds are limited, there should be no embarrassment in admitting that early in the funeral arrangements—you're not alone. Be careful about obligating yourself for more than you have to spend. You probably don't want the burden of a debt while you're dealing with the grief of a loss. By federal regulations, mortuaries must give prices over the phone. Don't hesitate to shop around—it could save you thousands of dollars. Or, your local funeral planning society may have done some of the price shopping for you.

## Understanding the Paperwork

By federal law, you must be given a General Price List (GPL), a casket price list, and an outer burial container price list when you inquire about arrangements and prices. You may keep the GPL. You must be given an itemized statement of your final choices when contracting for a funeral, as well. Make sure the final statement has only those items you have selected. Take the time to get a total amount in ink, and sign the contract, even if you were not asked to do so. That way, there is no question about which contract is yours and how much you will owe—before the funeral.

## Professional Services Fees

The Federal Trade Commission allows a mortuary establishment to set a *nondeclinable* fee for "Basic services of staff." You must pay this fee in addition to the cost of specific funeral goods and services you select. The consumer gets almost *nothing* for this fee; it is a guaranteed unemployment benefit for the mortician, sort of a "cover charge." As defined by the FTC, this may include the following:

- The funeral director's time in helping you plan the funeral (you're paying to listen to a sales pitch; do you pay your travel agent extra to try to sell you more expensive trips?)
- The time it takes to make arrangements with a cemetery, crematory or other funeral home if the body will be shipped out of the area (but burial, cremation, and shipping are listed elsewhere on the price list)
- The time needed to obtain required permits (most funeral directors sign their own; the car salesman tosses in this kind of service for free)
- The death certificate information (which you must supply)
- Faxing or mailing the obituary (which you probably wrote, and for which you may pay an extra charge to the newspaper for the advertising of the funeral home).

However, in addition to these basic services, the FTC *also* allows this fee to cover "unallocated overhead"—or even "all overhead," according to an FTC staff publication. No other business is so protected; all others must recoup their costs for capital investment, taxes, insurance, answering services, and advertising by the price charged for each item offered. (See the chapter "FTC: Boon and Boondoggle," for a more complete description of this problem. FAMSA has petitioned the FTC to reopen the Funeral Rule, with the intent of getting rid of this fee.)

There is a great deal of inconsistency in how the fee for professional services is established from one funeral home to the next. Some mortuaries may set a high nondeclinable fee and charge very little for use of staff and facilities for a funeral service held at the funeral home, for example. (This may be especially true if there is a retail casket store in the area.) Others may have a lower fee and list other charges and casket prices a lot higher.

To have the greatest control over what you spend for a funeral, determine the type of funeral you want. A memorial service at your church would limit the amount of services required from a funeral home. In that case, finding one with a low charge for the "Basic services fee" may be important to your pocketbook.

## Embalming

Embalming is *not required* for most deaths. In a few states, embalming may be necessitated by law when death occurs from a communicable disease. When burial or cremation will be delayed for several days, refrigeration can substitute for embalming. Not all funeral homes have refrigerated storage, but most hospitals do. Some funeral homes—by policy—will not allow the viewing of a body without embalming,[1] but there is no state law that says the body must be embalmed and restored to a life-like condition for such an observance. In other countries, embalming is seldom done. A more complete description of embalming is given a separate chapter.

The cost of embalming will be listed on the GPL, but there may be additional charges such as "other preparation of the body—dressing and casketing." For some families, dressing Grandma and fixing her hair might be a loving way to say goodbye. You need to remember that all fees are optional once you've paid the nondeclinable fee.

## Shelter of Remains

This may not appear on your price list at all, but, if it does, it should apply only after the four or five days that it might take to complete all funeral arrangements. The FTC does *not* permit a storage fee during usual funeral transactions.

## Forwarding Remains

All general price lists will carry a charge for the handling of a body to be shipped out of the area. The price should include a description of what is covered. This usually includes paperwork, staff time, local transportation of the body, embalming, scheduling shipment, and a shipping container.

Several companies specialize in shipping bodies. Inman Nationwide is one and has contracted with local funeral homes to serve as agents

---

[1] Some of the funeral homes that would require embalming for "public" viewing—"to protect the public health," they often say—are among the culprits requiring family ID viewing without embalming. See "Cremation Mischief" later in this chapter.

in every state. It pays those agents $575 for *forwarding remains* and possibly an additional mileage charge if far from the nearest airport. Airfare is extra, of course.

Why would local funeral directors be willing to accept $575 for a service that might be priced at three times that on its own GPL? Most aren't busy enough, so $575 is better than nothing. They also hope that you will remember the nice folks who came to pick up the body the next time you have a need.

Therefore, if a local funeral home charges much more than $575 for forwarding remains, you would be much better off to call the receiving funeral home and ask if they will be using a shipping company to retrieve the body. (Probably a good idea to let the funeral home know that you know about how much that will cost.)

## Beware of Misleading Package Fees

If you are price-shopping among several funeral homes for a "direct cremation," be sure to ask if the package price includes the cost of a minimum container and the cost for the cremation process and permits. Many funeral homes do not have their own crematories, and this will be an additional expense which may not be apparent on first inquiry. It's hard to imagine how you can have a "direct cremation" without cremation, but this bit of mischief is currently permitted by the FTC—another change that needs to be made.

If you choose "direct burial," one package price may be a lot higher than another because it includes a minimum casket, a grave-liner or vault, and possibly a fee for opening and closing the grave.

However, there may be more insideous tricksterism afoot. In areas where there is a retail casket store, some funeral homes have jacked up their service prices but offer a discounted package if you purchase the casket at the funeral home. This means a "handling charge" has been built into the *a la carte* service fees, a practice outlawed by the FTC. The FTC, however, has been slow to act on complaints of such pricing. If you find deeply discounted packages that require the purchase of a casket, it should alert you to keep shopping for a funeral home with more straightforward and ethical pricing practices. Chances are you'll save money. (Some casket stores are even willing to recommend such a funeral home.)

## Cash Advances

The services of others may be desired when arranging a funeral: an organist, the obituary, special flower arrangements, or cremation.

Some funeral homes add a fee for arranging these, but it must be so stated on the price list, something like, "We charge you for purchasing these goods and services." When a funeral director says, "We'll take care of everything—we'll get the new lettering on the stone," you probably will be paying a lot more. While it may meet your needs to let the funeral home make these arrangements for you, you may wish to consider making the contacts on your own.

### Cremation Mischief

"Yes, [ID viewing] is self-serving," admits the speaker on a tape titled "Keys to Cremation Success." "Often after viewing Mom in a cardboard box, the family will ask if we have something a little nicer." His talk was titled "How to Add $1,400 to Your Cremation Calls," given at a symposium sponsored by the *Funeral Service Insider.* One Florida SCI funeral director pitched a grim mental picture and a guilt trip ahead of time. To a woman phoning for the price of an immediate cremation for her aunt, he said, "You'll probably want to up-grade to a cremation casket [only $350 more, she later learned]. There will be an identification viewing, and most families don't want to see their loved one in a cardboard box."

With the increased cremation rate, mortuaries are scrambling to recover the income they would otherwise be making from what Jessica Mitford called "the full fig funeral." In just a few years, some manipulative tactics have emerged, the most despicable of which is "ID viewing." It is one thing for a family to request a private visitation. It is quite another for the funeral home to *require* such a viewing. But it is couched in such official-sounding terms that few would realize they have a right to refuse.

One Vermont funeral director threatened "to wash my hands of this whole affair" when the family didn't want to view the grandmother's body. Terrified and feeling helpless (this was the only funeral home in town and the body was already there), they agreed. But they were traumatized by what was a most unpleasant experience: Gram's body was on a cold metal table, her blouse undone and hanging open, and splotchy rouge on her cheeks. That was not how they'd wanted to remember her.

Two young California sons who arrived at the SCI crematory before the undertaker did were not prepared for what they found either. Doors were open, with many bodies in clear view. One—dressed in a tuxedo—was "sitting up" in an expensive casket.

The funeral home *knows* whose body it is when picking up the dead person from the hospital, nursing home, or family residence. And the funeral home isn't going to show the family the *wrong body* (unless, of course, its business practices are slip-shod in the first place). Requiring ID viewing is an unnecessary and manipulative tactic, except under the very rare circumstances in which the identity of the deceased may be in doubt.[1]

Some funeral homes have actually charged for ID viewing itself, rather than just using it as a sales tactic for more expensive merchandise. Others charge for "preparation for ID viewing." Any such fee is improper unless the family requested such services.[2]

One SCI-owned funeral home in Wisconsin added five days of high-priced "storage" when a son declined to view his mother's body. The FTC found this "likely deceptive" and therefore in violation of the FTC Funeral Rule.

According to an SCI script to be used with cremation customers (leaked anonymously to the FAMSA office), the family will have to personally select the cremation casket from the container display:

*There are three basic types of cremation containers. There are hardwood caskets, both of a more traditional design as the one depicted here as well as others that are more cremation specific. There are also cremation containers. They are simple in design for those families wanting a dignified unique container to protect their loved one. We also have a minimum cardboard box. This container is quite simply a cardboard box with no pillow and no mattress. Please follow me as we have these containers displayed in a separate room. [Did someone forget that a casket price list must, by law, be offered first?] It is necessary that you accompany me to the room and choose a container as we will not sell anything sight-unseen.*

---

[1] The statutes in several states have specific language to require identification of the deceased by next-of-kin before a cremation can occur. This is not totally unreasonable; a body shouldn't be cremated until any questions are resolved as to whose body it is. But the identification, even in those states, can occur—and usually does—at the hospital, nursing home, private residence, or other place of death. A caretaker is almost always another "qualified person." Every state should require that a body be tagged before removal which would then eliminate the industry's mischief with this ruse and avert mix-up at chain-own businesses that use a central prep facility..

[2] This was confirmed in a staff opinion from the FTC, October 31, 1997. Families who were made to feel this was obligatory and who would not have chosen such a viewing should ask for a refund of any related charges.

Certainly not a cardboard box.

In California, a mid-level manager (different corporation) mentioned to a funeral buddy that when a family comes in and it's clear an immediate cremation is likely to be planned, they have a system for signalling another employee. A bogus call is then placed that rings in the arrangements room. Of course the salesperson—oops, the "counsellor"—interrupts the conversation with the family to answer the phone: "Hello. . . . Yes. . . . I'm sure you do. . . . Well, let me check." The staff person turns to the family and says, "There's someone on the phone checking to see when the visitation will be so they can come pay their respects to your dad." With mischief like this, is it any wonder that consumer activism is exploding?

Oh, yes, consumers are also being told they must purchase a "temporary container" or urn ($45–$85) for the cremains when they do not purchase a more elaborate one. But all crematories supply a modest container for cremated remains. One industry publication suggested stamping either box on all four sides with the marking "Temporary Container" so that families will be more inclined to purchase expensive urns. (By the way, families can save hundreds of dollars by shopping somewhere other than at a funeral home for an urn—Pier I, a pottery shop, the internet. Just make sure it's big enough to hold a five-pound bag of sugar with a little room left over. Weight, for an average adult, is seven pounds.)

## Funeral Conglomerates

Before you finish this book, you will have found many references to the mischief at chain-owned mortuaries—especially SCI, Loewen, and Stewart. (They are the largest, and have been around long enough to have a demonstrated track record.) I know there are sensitive and caring funeral directors in the employ of these businesses,[1] so not all experiences at a corporate-owned funeral home will turn out to be terrible for a family.

One Loewen employee, however, was fired for having a "negative attitude." When a family might be having trouble with what the total funeral would cost, he'd suggest they request a special-order casket because no one would be sure how much to mark it up—and it was almost always less than what was in the showroom.

---

[1] I correspond with some.

In another company, funeral directors were told they were to make sure each funeral averaged at least $10,000. In all such commercial outfits, sales quotas are not uncommon, and the paperwork for reporting or charting of sales increases greatly, according to workers.

Some ex-owners who have stayed on in management positions have become disillusioned with the hard-sell tactics being promoted by the corporations and can hardly wait for their contracts to run out.

*One thing is almost certain: when a corporate chain purchases a funeral home or cemetery, the prices go up even if the name stays the same.* Pierson Ralph of the Memorial Society of North Texas has one of the largest databases of funeral home prices—nearly 300 funeral homes in the southwest. It includes prices at chain-owned mortuaries both prior to and after purchase. The prices charged at these mortuaries are uniformly high—sometimes double the national average. (The major chains now handle 30% of the funeral business nationwide.) Therefore, one should not be surprised by the gross profit margin indicated on the 1997 10-Q reports (available on the internet) or in published reports to stockholders:

Stewart—
    funeral homes—49.8%
    cemeteries—33.3%

Loewen—
    funeral homes—39.7%
    cemeteries—33.6%

SCI—
    funeral homes—22.5%
    cemeteries—37.6%

Loewen—thrilled by its increasing cemetery profits—announced in 1997 that 50% of all new acquisitions would be allocated to amassing more cemeteries.[1] Given Stewart's funeral-home profits, it apparently has decided to build even more funeral homes—particularly on the grounds of the Catholic cemeteries. (Catholic funeral choices are often expensive ones—with several days of wakes or visitation and evening rosaries not uncommon—even though memorial masses are now permitted by the church.)

---

[1] Loewen did suffer losses later in the same year. Some industry analysts attributed this to a tendency of the company to overpay for its acquisitions.

Some of these corporate-owned funeral homes are "Cadillac" operations, an employee noted in a conversation with me. Certainly, there is a place for fancy establishments that offer expensive arrangements for those who can afford them. But that's far from the full picture. The fact is, when a chain buys a funeral home, the prices go up dramatically. The corporate takeovers of the last ten years have caused sticker-shock among consumers.

If a funeral home was "Palmer's Funeral Home" yesterday (owned by John and Mary Palmer, third-generation funeral directors, born and raised in town), it will still be "Palmer's Funeral Home" tomorrow, even if the new owners are stockholders from around the world. The prices and practices of the new owners may not resemble the business considerations of "the Palmers" at all.

In Massachusetts, a new (1998) regulation requires that funeral homes disclose ownership on all signs, price lists, and printed business matter. A similar effort is under way in New Jersey and Florida. In Australia, England, Florida, Maryland, and Virginia, independent funeral directors are banding together with literature proudly proclaiming their establishments as "locally-owned."[1]

This trend should be applauded, as corporate takeovers diminish the choices available to consumers and threaten real price competition when an area is dominated exclusively by conglomerates.

In areas where there are low-priced, independently-owned funeral services actively competing with the conglomerates, the funeral chains have opened up their own low-price operations. Usually, these are run under new names—such as Discount Casket, Cremation and Burial Service (SCI in California) or Funeral Concepts (Loewen in Tennessee)—but work closely with nearby high-price operations, perhaps even using their facilities from time to time. With high-priced funerals subsidizing the discount operations, the corporate funeral home can engage in an unfair price war. "We're just giving consumers choice," is the line usually given to the media, but *none* of the three giant corporations has gone into a new area and opened up such choices for consumers where they didn't exist before. Squashing competition

---

[1] After *60 Minutes* ran a segment in 1998 documenting regular price increases at a Florida funeral home owned by SCI, funeral homes in other parts of the country noticed an immediate interest in ownership from callers and customers. A few began to deny corporate affiliation. One that did so in print may be in deep doo-doo in Oregon. Loewen employees are telling those who ask that the funeral home is employee-owned, because—after all—each one has a few shares of stock.

is the aim. Stewart's April 1997 quarterly report filed with the Securities and Exchange Commission announced it in black-and-white:

> The decline in the average revenue per funeral service performed was attributable principally to selective price reductions in certain of the Company's markets, particularly in the Miami area, in response to competition from low-cost funeral service providers in those markets. This strategy has been successful as the Company has experienced an increase in funeral services performed in the markets affected; furthermore, **price reductions are not expected to continue [emphasis added]**.

No, once competition has been driven out, "price reductions" won't be necessary. In order to keep a range of choices available, some folks will want to make sure they patronize the independent funeral homes—the ones dedicated to serving families, not stockholders. But make sure you check for the ones with the fairest prices. Some of the independent rascals have high prices, too.

## An Educational Obligation

We teach our kids about religion, politics, money, and maybe even sex. But few teach their children about how to shop for a funeral. Said one funeral director, "Picking a funeral home without shopping around is like handing the funeral director a blank check." The most effective way to avoid excessive purchases at a time of emotional vulnerability is to talk about funeral options with your family ahead of time. Local funeral-planning societies have excellent pamphlets on a variety of funeral topics, as well as local price information.

# Embalming
## "A Beautiful Memory Picture"?

## 16

Most people don't know that embalming is almost *never* "required." In some circumstances, state laws may dictate embalming if there will be delayed disposition, but refrigeration can usually suffice and will be a more reliable form of preservation.

Most people don't know that this is the only country where the use of embalming—promoted by the undertakers—has become widespread; it is rarely done in most other countries (although the international U.S. and Canadian funeral conglomerates are now pushing it hard elsewhere, including Japan, England, and Australia).

Most people don't know that the normal funeral-type embalming "holds" a body for only a few days.[1] A stronger solution of chemicals would turn the body to shoe-leather.

Most people probably don't pause to realize that embalming may expose the embalming technician to blood-borne pathogens and highly toxic chemicals.[2] Both go down the drain—in varying quantities—into the common sewer system.[3] In cemeteries where caskets or burial chambers have disintegrated, embalming chemicals have polluted the ground water (especially near old cemeteries containing bodies from an era when arsenic was one of the substances used). Embalming is *not* an environmentally-friendly procedure.

---

[1] S.S.—a 21-year-old only child—died on Friday from an accidental overdose of prescription drugs. He was embalmed on Saturday, and there were visitations for this devastated family all day Sunday, Monday, and half of Tuesday. The stench started on Monday, however, and by Wednesday—while arranging for burial in the next state—it was unbearable.

[2] According to reports from the CDC, embalmers have a higher death rate than the national average.

[3] There has been no environmental damage proven from funeral home effluent, but—given the poisonous chemicals that are bound to leak out in the embalming process, not to mention blood-borne pathogens—there is a growing concern. In all states, hospital waste is treated separately from other municipal waste.

## History of Embalming

The Egyptians began embalming the bodies of wealthy and important people sometime before 4,000 B.C., and the practice spread to other ancient cultures. Generally, the bodies were soaked in a carbonate of soda, and the viscera and brains were removed. Herbs, salts, and aromatic substances were packed into the body cavities. Then the bodies were wrapped in cloth that had been soaked with preservatives. Variations of these procedures were employed as embalming spread to other cultures. For example, Alexander the Great was reportedly embalmed with wax and honey.

Knowledge of embalming moved to parts of Europe about 500 A.D. but was not widespread, although the bodies of several well-known historical figures (including King Canute and William the Conqueror) were preserved.

In the 19th century, Italian and French scientists developed techniques to inject preservatives into veins and arteries. The practice reached the U.S. during the Civil War, when it was used in a few instances to delay decomposition of the bodies of war victims that needed to be transported long distances before burial. When President Lincoln was assassinated, his body was embalmed to allow public viewing in locations throughout the country. It was considered an unusual step to take, in an unusual period of national sorrow.

In his book *Inventing the American Way of Death, 1830–1920,* James Farrell comments: "Before 1880, people viewed embalming only as an historical phenomenon, an exotic custom of the ancient Egyptians." He notes that with organized encouragement from a rapidly emerging funeral industry, ". . . by 1920, almost all dead bodies were embalmed, not just those intended for transport."

As an example of how sophisticated the practice had become in those four decades, Farrell cites a 1920 advertisement by a Boston undertaker:

*For composing the features, $1.*
*For giving the features a look of quiet resignation, $2*
*For giving the features the appearance of Christian hope and contentment, $5.*

The Reverend William L. Coleman, in his book *It's Your Funeral,* notes that "The science of embalming had largely been abandoned for 1,500 years," and its sudden re-emergence in the late 19th and early 20th centuries aroused considerable controversy. "Both Christians and humanitarians often objected strenuously," Coleman writes. "They had visions of bodies being severely mutilated. Ministers denounced it as a desecration of the 'temple of God'." That view continues to be held by some religions, including Orthodox Judaism.

Yet despite such objections, embalming became—and has remained—an expected part of the majority of death arrangement packages offered by U.S. funeral directors. Why? What are the benefits that have come into demand in North America but seem less important to the rest of the world?

## Like Snake Oil?

Embalming was promoted early on as a means of preventing premature burial, a horror that had been verified in several instances in the late 19th and early 20th centuries. Even in 1998, I've heard older folks expressing this concern. Farrell quotes the Portland, Oregon, city attorney in an address to the 1910 convention of the National Funeral Directors Association (NFDA) as saying: "There is consolation in the thought that when a man's undertaker is finished with him, he can be reasonably sure he is not in a trance." That seems a harsher form of "consolation" than the practice of some religious groups which delay body disposition for three days to allow time for the exit of the spirit.

Sanitation was another—and perhaps the most emphatic—argument made by the funeral industry in its early promotion of embalming. The idea put forth was that embalming served to disinfect bodies, preventing the spread of infectious and communicable diseases. The funeral industry, emerging between 1880 and 1920, successfully convinced the public (through the efforts of the newly formed National Funeral Directors Association) that professional services were necessary for proper care of the dead—with compatible laws and regulations quickly following.

Embalming was the centerpiece of that effort. Families could place a body on ice to slow its deterioration, but only an experienced "professional" could embalm. In fact, embalming remains the only specific skill required in the undertaking business. The livery drivers, the carpenters, the furniture sellers (all those who had helped with supplying caskets in the past or delivering the body to the cemetery) quickly found they could—with minimal training in a mysterious "art"— leap to a whole new social status in the community. Most of the time, all it took was the stomach for a little blood-letting.

## Modern Embalming Practices

The major differences between current funeral practices and those used by the Egyptians are the use of modern chemicals and equipment, and an emphasis on temporary cosmetic restoration rather than preservation of mummies. The process consists of both arterial embalming (draining the blood and filling the veins and arteries with pink-colored chemicals) and cavity embalming (emptying fluids from the chest and abdomen, replacing them with sufficient preservatives to afford a temporary delay in decomposition).

The job is performed on an embalming table, which is surrounded by a conduit to catch body fluids and route them to a special container or—more often—the sewer system. First, the body is washed with a disinfectant solution. Then the limbs and joints are massaged to counter the effects of *rigor mortis* so the body can be positioned. The face is "restored," with the use of prickly-topped plastic cups under the eyelids to keep them from sliding open and wire or suture to close the jaws. A little Vaseline or super-glue can keep the lips together, just so.

Then arterial embalming begins. The embalmer chooses one of four (or in some cases all four) locations in which a major artery and vein are in close proximity—the armpits, the neck, and/or the groin—and makes an incision. An injection needle is placed into the artery and drainage forceps into the vein to allow blood to flow into the table trough. An injection machine pumps a chemical solution (dyed for the proper effect on body color) into the artery while body parts are massaged to assist the flow. If the embalming is done too quickly, the features are likely to swell. So far, it's been a relatively "surgical" procedure.

The next step, however, is cavity embalming.[1] A "trocar" (a large-bore hollow needle) is connected to an electric aspirator (a pump that removes fluids from abdominal and chest cavities). The trocar is

---

[1] As justification for elaborate funerals, morticians often cite a quote attributed to Gladstone: "Show me the manner in which a nation or a community cares for its dead and I will measure with mathematical exactness the tender mercies of its people, their respect for the law, and their loyalty to high ideals." One viewing of an actual embalming should be enough to convince anyone that—as practiced today in the western world—it's a totally barbaric procedure bereft of any "tender mercies" whatsoever. The one-hour video, "Embalming Techniques," should be required viewing for every law-maker. To order, call the FAMSA office: 800-765-0107 ($29.96 includes Priority Mail shipping).

inserted near the naval and jabbed around inside the abdomen and chest at random to puncture various organs while the blood and waste are pumped out. The body is then filled with a formalin solution to kill microorganisms and retard decay. "The orifices"—the anus and vagina—are packed with cotton. Or—if the practitioner is up-to-date on the latest devices—the "A/V Closure" (a 4½" white plastic screw) might be used to prevent leakage "while preserving the dignity of the deceased." (What's "dignified" about a butt-plug?) Up to this point, the process has taken about 45 minutes to one hour.

In most cases, the body is then cosmetically restored.[1] The extent of this depends on the condition of the corpse and the wishes of the family. Sometimes a little rouge, face cream, and hair styling will do.

---

[1] The editor of a French magazine had read of an American "funeral cosmetics company" and presumed it to be the only one in the world. (Make-up on a corpse would generally be considered ludicrous in European countries.) An unusual story, he thought, and assigned a Reuter's writer to check it out.

The writer soon found that it didn't stop with cosmetics or one company. There were lots of companies, providing not only cosmetics but burial footwear and burial clothing, too. "But I guess those are just good quality things in the latest styles," she suggested.

"Not exactly . . ." I described the slit in the back so one didn't have to wrestle the whole body into a dress or suit—just drape and tuck. And of course I shared Jessica Mitford's fascination with the "Fit-a-fut" oxfords from "Practical Footware."

By this time we were both giggling. "What else is there?" the writer asked.

"Well, let me check," and I got out my *Blue Book of Funeral Directors*, turning to the "Buyer's Guide" section in the back. "There are 12 companies under 'Cosmetics'," I offered. "Do you have them all?" Then my eye caught a display ad. "Get this. Try Nadene Cover-Up Cosmetics and discover what over 7,000 other funeral directors already know. 100% GUARANTEED. ABSOLUTELY RISK FREE'."

"Absolutely risk free to whom?" she asked in charged disbelief. And the mirth rolled back and forth again on the phone lines. We're only in the "C" section, and already this has been the high point of my week on the laughter scale. When we got to the "H" section, it happened again: there was "Hosiery." With the bottom half of the casket often closed even with an open-casket affair, who's buying enough funeral hosiery to induce eight companies to list their names here? (If there's a choice among "ecru," "taupe," or "support hose," which one do you pick? Knee- highs? Or do they offer panty-hose? Something to go with the "Fit-a-fut" oxfords?)

But the clincher that had us both leaking tears of laughter as we gave in to all-too-vivid imaginations came in the "U" section: "Underwear"—Six funeral clothing companies presumably paid extra for these listings. "Was he a boxer man or did he prefer briefs?" she croaked in funereal concern, gasping between attacks of laughter at the American way of death.

But if the face appears somewhat emaciated, tissue builder is injected with a hypodermic needle, to flesh out the cheeks, for example. If the body is severely mutilated or decayed, the embalmer will do whatever it takes to restore the body to recognizable form, with wax, plaster of Paris, and additional make-up. Dinair Airbrush Systems—a company that touts its equipment for stage and screen—has also been giving demonstrations of cosmetic magic to morticians, even recreating the little crow's feet and wrinkles if need be.

## The Myth of Sanitation

The belief that embalming prevents the spread of disease is still widely held, but public health as a reason for embalming has been refuted by several medical authorities.

The Consumer Reports[1] book on funerals notes that disease does not run rampant in countries where bodies are seldom embalmed. Furthermore, studies show that embalming does not affect certain bacteria or viruses. Tuberculosis, smallpox, anthrax, tetanus, and AIDS have all been found in embalmed bodies shortly after death.

What is even more revealing is the admonition from a Dodge Chemical sales rep (Dodge is one of the major embalming fluid manufacturers): In the case of death from Creutzfeld-Jakobs disease, don't even take the body into the funeral home. One form of embalming fluid keeps the disease alive!

Even back in 1977, a British Columbia deputy health minister was quoted, "It is our view that the process of embalming serves no useful purpose in preventing the transmission of communicable disease. In those few cases where a person dies of a highly infectious disease, a far better procedure would be to wrap and securely seal the body in heavy plastic sheeting before removing it from the room where death occurred." Other Canadian health authorities have gone even further; in several provinces, embalming is *forbidden* for about 12 infectious diseases. Hawaii and Ohio, with similar prohibitions, are the only U.S. states that have recognized the potential health hazard from embalming.

In my 1986 telephone conversations with several people in the Biosafety Department and the AIDS unit at the Centers for Disease Control (CDC) in Atlanta, Georgia, I was unable to find a single official who felt that embalming protects public health. Among the

---

[1] *Funerals: Consumers' Last Rites.* Copyright 1977 by Consumers Union of United States, Inc., Mount Vernon, NY 10553.

notes I took: "I see no reason for embalming for public protection in any circumstances."

Ten years later, I again contacted the CDC. This time I asked for information on the dangers, if any, that a person might risk by contact with an unembalmed body. I was sent a lengthy article from a 1995 British journal, *Communicable Disease Report.* Selected comments include: "Living people with diseases are a far greater hazard to the health than the dead." . . . "Some ethnic groups require that relatives and religious leaders carry out their own hygienic preparation and rituals. . . . It seems unreasonable to restrict such activities unless an obvious hazard exists." The concluding sentence: "There seems little justification for preventing customary cleansings before final disposal, except in rare and obviously dangerous conditions."

The sanitation argument is still widely believed, however, with the help of the NFDA. Its "Consumer Education Series Brochures" (available on its website: www.nfda.org) continue to perpetrate the myth: "The foremost reason for embalming is the protection of public health. . . . Untreated remains pose serious public health concerns."[1]

The most convincing evidence against the sanitation argument for embalming is provided by the current practice of most U.S. medical schools. They all solicit donations of bodies, and many have an urgent need for additional bequeathals. Although all cadavers are embalmed with a far more complete process than that used by funeral directors, bequests are routinely refused if the donor has died of an infectious disease. According to one medical school staffer, the bacteria or viruses become "encapsulated" in the dormant stage and are not destroyed during the embalming process.

In nine states, the statutes still require embalming of people who die of specific diseases, a holdover from the misguided turn-of-the-century efforts of the funeral industry. In other states, embalming may be required at the discretion of the medical examiner or health department. Many funeral directors I interviewed privately questioned these statutes; older embalmers are worried for their sons and daughters who carry on the business. Indeed, the British report notes, "Opening cadavers infected with tuberculosis is dangerous." Because

---

[1] It is ironic that such a blatant lie is posted on a site that has several excellent pages having to do with funeral ethics. Without embalming, there will be no visitation, according to most funeral home policies (no law would prevent the viewing of an unembalmed body—except in Minnesota). Without a viewing, a less-elaborate casket is likely to be chosen. The embalming lie is called "follow the dollar."

*embalming creates a health hazard,* "universal precautions" are now recommended by CDC—gloves, face-mask, and body suit—for *all* instances of embalming. Anthrax has gotten recent media attention as a biological weapon. As more information comes out about how deadly this can be, people may be shocked that anthrax is one of the diseases for which embalming is required in a few states. Those states with embalming requirements for any reason should, I believe, eliminate them.

After reading the chapter on embalming in my earlier book, Mack Smith, executive director of the state funeral board in Kansas, had the good sense to seek amendments to that state's regulations, eliminating the embalming requirement for many diseases including AIDS. (The old embalming requirement had not allowed those who had cared for ailing AIDS friends prior to death to continue their care after death.) Immediate cremation or burial is now an alternative to embalming for the listed virulent diseases such as *Ebola* and rabies.

## Embalming Costs

While embalming fees vary greatly, the national average at this writing is in the neighborhood of $350. The price depends on the amount of restoration that is needed or requested. There might be an additional $150 charge for autopsied bodies, for example. Medical examiners and coroners have a very mixed reputation on the condition in which they release a body, so sometimes an additional charge may be justified. In those cases, more than one injection point will be needed, but that doesn't take a great deal longer. Unfortunately, some mortuaries charge an additional fee after organ donation for the same reasons. Given the generosity of the family, any additional charge after organ donation seems like outrageous opportunism.

A $350 embalming fee strikes me as an extremely modest charge for a service that requires training, significant expertise, overhead expense, is not particularly pleasant, and which puts the funeral folks in jeopardy of blood-borne pathogens as well as exposure to highly toxic chemicals. On the other hand, embalming is usually performed as part of a larger package that includes other items with high-profit opportunity.

## A Perspective on Embalming

In a 1993 issue of *Funeral Monitor,* editor Jean DeSapio noted the modest exit of a famous media executive, but went a step further:

> [There is an] increasing tendency of funeral professionals to go out with the short and quick!
>
> A very upset California funeral director called us . . . : "A long-time funeral director I know just died and had immediate disposition. . . . And the other crazy part of this, his two older brothers had the same deal. These guys were three of the biggest pushers of 'traditional' funeral service you could imagine. So what does this say about us to the community? That we really are the money-grubbing ghouls some of them, including the media, say we are?"
>
> Another funeral director . . . "My own mother, who is a veteran of this business, who loves it, and still lives over our original funeral home, insists that she wants 'nothing. Cremation and that's it.' I can't figure those others out. Is it because they know too much about the behind-the-scenes aspects of funeral service, about what can happen to bodies, so that they reject the funeral process?"

Jean DiSapio herself—a long-time industry observer and promoter— died a short time later and opted for an immediate cremation.

## Why Embalm?

If you donate your body to a medical school, you can expect it to be embalmed, although the procedures are quite different from those used by undertakers. Schools generally keep bodies for six months to two years, and there is no other practical way to keep a body intact for that long.

Laws—until they are changed—may require it. For example, Oregon requires that a body be embalmed or refrigerated if it will not reach its destination within 24 hours of death. One must assume that this was the influencing factor for embalming in the following case, described to me by a funeral director in Bend, Oregon. I was struck, however, by the incongruity of what was surely an unnecessary, unnatural procedure and what followed:

> A young American Indian girl died in the city hospital. When I finished the embalming, the two grandmothers led the procession to the reservation—one riding in my van, the other in a car that followed. I was asked to drive the van around the Long House three times, then left to wait until all was ready. Finally, they carried the body in and circled three times around the inside of the Long House before placing

it on a woven mat in the center of the room. The body was clad only in the undergarments that had been supplied by the family. Women of the tribe then began the Dressing Ceremony, clothing the young woman in gorgeous buckskins. Beside her was a box lined with 15 to 20 blankets that had been woven and dyed by hand. Traditional rituals and ceremonies, including viewing, continued through the night.

Even if there is no statutory requirement in your state, some form of preservation may be desired if there will be a delay of several days in gathering kin and scheduling services. Refrigeration (or air conditioning) creates far less ecological risk. Dry ice can also provide refrigeration in lieu of embalming, and is used, for example, by medical couriers when carrying organs for transplant. Check the Yellow Pages for a source. In the past, people stored bodies on ice for long periods because it sometimes took relatives a week or more to arrive. Because the population has become more mobile, most funerals can be held within two or three days after death.

The most common argument for funeral-type embalming today is that friends and family have an emotional need to see the body one last time before final disposition.[1]

But having spoken with a great many people on the subject, I have heard that viewing a restored corpse did not always fulfill that need. In some cases, the body was made to appear so lifelike that it became even harder to say goodbye. In other cases, it looked like nothing more than a statue or mannequin, a caricature of the departed friend or relative.

My own feeling is that it is far more emotionally fulfilling to participate actively in the funeral arrangements than merely to let a funeral director arrange a viewing. There is much that families can do: filing the death certificate and writing the obituary; helping to build a box and transport it to the grave site or crematory; participating in the digging of the grave or the scattering of "ashes"; helping to comfort survivors and notify other friends and relatives.

Seeing the body one last time may well occur—either by choice or necessity—while performing many of those tasks. Friends have commented that seeing a body that was obviously dead made it easier

---

[1] After sitting in on various on-line funeral director chats, it's clear that some are absolutely and genuinely convinced that viewing a body is necessary for resolving grief. While that is very likely for immediate family members and very close friends dealing with an unanticipated death, those of a more casual acquaintance go only to show the family they care and may stay as far away as they can from an open casket.

to let go: that the spirit may well endure, but not in the physical remains that are devoid of color. Actively participating in the final acts of friendship can be a meaningful way to say goodbye. Holding on to a beautifully restored "memory picture" in eternal sleep may ultimately prove to be a denial rather than an acceptance of death.

## Viewing

After the FTC Rule was passed, funeral homes were required to print the following disclosure on the GPL:

> Except in certain special cases, embalming is not required by law. Embalming may be necessary, however, if you select certain funeral arrangements, such as a funeral with viewing. If you do not want embalming, you usually have the right to choose an arrangement that does not require you to pay for it, such as direct cremation or immediate burial.

While the Rule now keeps funeral homes from requiring or charging for embalming when minimal services are selected, it failed to acknowledge a number of issues including religious or moral objections to embalming for funeral plans that did not call for "immediate" disposition.

FAMSA, in its efforts to seek Rule amendments, will ask that "or other timely arrangements" be added to the above disclosure. Depending on the season, there are significant portions of the country where a body may be kept for two or three days without embalming. Some form of temperature control—air conditioning or refrigeration—is usually quite available. It should be the choice of the family whether or not the body is embalmed prior to viewing, not a funeral industry or state mandate.

## The Difference between Viewing and Visitation

In the case of an *unexpected* death—when a family is grappling with the reality of what has happened—there is a strong need to see the body of the person who died and to hold or touch the person. In most of these situations, the body will have been taken to a hospital for rescue efforts or to determine the cause of death.

Some hospitals will be very cooperative in letting the family spend time with the body over many hours, especially with an infant or child death. Others may have limited space and will expect the body to be moved quickly. When you have out-of-town family that will not arrive for 24 hours or more, another opportunity for "good-bye time" may need to be arranged. If you are not taking the body home and will be using a mortuary, you may want to ask for "private family viewing." Only occasionally is this listed on a General Price List, so there may not be a charge.[1] Sometimes the GPL will limit this to "no more than one hour"—a despicable practice. How dare a funeral director tell you how long or short your grieving time should be! You may certainly demand the time you need but be willing to pay any additional fees for extended use of the facilities.

There is less formality with a private family viewing, and the body is often laid out on a covered table. A casket is distancing, making it more difficult to get close—to cradle one's arms around the dead person.

Whether you choose to have the body embalmed for this private time will be a personal decision. There is no legal reason that would require embalming for such a viewing, and the funeral home may not impose embalming if it is not required by state law for the time period elapsed since death, especially when refrigeration is a better alternative.

In the case of an *expected* death, people have begun to say their "good-byes," and there is less need to see the body to accept the reality of events. When the end comes, it may be seen as a "blessing." Many undertakers insist, however, that a *viewing* is necessary for "closure." That you will probably pick a more expensive casket is surely part of the motivation in promoting a viewing, not just a visitation.

In the past, it was usual to have three days of viewing or visitation. With busy working families, industry reports indicate that only one day of viewing or visitation is now being planned for most funerals. For those who wish to cut expenses even more, a viewing immediately prior to the funeral service can be scheduled—at the church or at the funeral home.

When a public viewing is held, few people admit that they go to peek at the dead body; they are there to support the family and to show they care. Some are uncomfortable with a dead person in the room and will stay as far away from the casket as possible.

On the other hand, a *visitation* also offers informal time for gathering and remembrances, but the casket is either closed or not there at all. A visitation without the casket present can be scheduled anywhere, anytime—without the cost or formality of funeral home involvement. Those who have opted for visitation—not viewing—have found this to be intimate and personal—some would say more comfortable. Whether

---

[1] FAMSA will be asking the FTC to require that this option be offered on each GPL in the future. It is legitimate for the funeral home to make a charge for this service.

in quiet banter, surprised laughter, or tender tears, spontaneous sharing is comforting. There certainly is value for the family to hear friends and colleagues talk freely about the significance of their relationship with the deceased.

# Caskets & Other Boxes
## Memorials & Markers

## 17

In the early years of undertaking, the price on the casket was the total cost of the funeral. The mark-up was often 500–700% to cover the other goods and services such as embalming, viewing, the funeral service itself, and transportation. If funds were limited, for example, you were expected to pick a lesser casket, not skip the embalming or viewing. However, those choosing the least expensive caskets could expect a pretty quick exit.

After the Federal Trade Commission Funeral Rule went into effect in 1984, services had to be listed separately, but many funeral homes never reduced the casket prices to compensate for the other new charges. Consequently, it is not uncommon to see caskets—especially low-end ones—marked up 300–600%, with the cost of a casket accounting for one-third of the total funeral bill.[1]

The funeral industry has studied buying patterns (just like any other business does) and found that people tend to purchase one of the first three caskets they are shown—hurrying, perhaps, through a difficult choice. It isn't hard to figure out that among those first three will be ones with a good profit margin for the mortuary.

When people are shown one casket marked $1,000, one marked $1,800, and one marked $2,500, which would you guess gets picked most often? We are, indeed, a society of middle-of-the-roaders. "I didn't want to pick the *cheapest,*" said one woman about her mother's casket. So if a funeral home wants to make a bigger profit next year, there's a good chance that the first three caskets shown might be listed at $1,800, $2,500, and $3,200—and now the $2,500-casket will become the popular model. Corporate funeral chains seem to be eliminating most if not all low-cost caskets in their inventories. One Florida woman said she was shown only two caskets—a plain pine box and a $4,000 model. At

---

[1] When Fr. Henry Wasieliewski discovered that parishioners were being charged unnecessarily high funeral prices they couldn't afford, he started lobbying for fair funeral pricing. To make his point, Father Henry lists wholesale casket prices on the web: http://www.xroads.com/~funerals.

Chicago and Atlanta Loewen-owned funeral homes the least expensive casket on display is "grasshopper green."

Showing caskets by catalog—with large glossy photos—is becoming more common. It reduces inventory cost and makes another room available for public use. Most funeral directors have such catalogs anyway for use when they visit homes or nursing homes. In states that require a minimum display of, say, "five adult caskets," that may be all you'll find on hand, with others shown by catalog only. Industry reports claim that consumers seem more comfortable with the catalog, and that casket revenues actually *increase!*

The FTC requires that a casket price range be included on the General Price List and that a full casket price list be supplied before showing any caskets. I mentioned this to a *Chicago Sun Times* reporter who was getting ready to take an AARP volunteer "shopping" for a funeral. If the lowest-cost casket is not on display, I suggested, ask to see it anyway. (Many funeral homes hide the low-cost ones.) A couple of weeks later she called back: "You were right. When the nice gentleman I was with asked to see some less expensive caskets, they took us to a hallway on the way to the boiler room." A New Hampshire widow didn't think she could afford a $2,500 casket, the least expensive one on display. Her irate daughter reported that the mother was taken to a dark cold basement full of cobwebs. Half-way down the stairs her mother turned and fled. As a result, her dad's body ended up in the $2,500 casket.

The FTC's "Funeral Rule" makes it illegal for morticians to tout the preservative qualities of a casket, but they've managed to flout the spirit of the law with still-deceptive language that refers to "protective" caskets. It is not uncommon to see the following on GPLs (I've noticed it especially on those from Loewen-owned mortuaries):

> We offer many different styles and prices of caskets and an alternative container from which to select. Since many caskets that appear similar in appearance may differ greatly in quality and construction, we offer the following in order to assist you in making an informed decision.
>
> PROTECTIVE: These caskets are designed by the manufacturer to resist the entrance of air, water and other outside elements. They may be constructed of varying gauges of steel, copper or bronze.
>
> NON-PROTECTIVE: These caskets are not designed by the manufacturer to resist the entrance of air, water or other outside elements. They may be constructed of metal, hardwood, or wood products covered with fabric.

One is tempted to imagine a casket maker sitting down with the designers and saying, "Make sure these won't keep out air, water, or other elements."

The rubber gasket on a so-called protective casket costs the industry about $8, but it may add $800 to the price paid by the consumer. A "sealer"[1]—as many funeral directors call them—will not stop the decomposition of the body; it actually complicates the process. Instead of the natural dehydration that would otherwise occur,[2] the body will putrefy in the anaerobic environment. I can't imagine anyone picking such a casket once they know this. These gaskets are actually supposed to be one-way seals that let out the build-up of gasses inside, I was told by a Batesville representative, but—as described in the company literature—they're subjected to a vacuum test before shipping to make sure no air can get in. I guess you could call them "self-burping" caskets.

If, however, they are closed too tightly, the gasses can't get out and the caskets explode,[3] as one Jacksonville, Florida woman found out three years after her father was entombed in his mausoleum crypt. A new funeral home was then contacted, a new casket was supplied by the manufacturer, and—after a change of clothing and a quick clean-up—a new entombment ceremony was held, sort of, amidst the stench.

---

[1] A Batesville representative said he was uncomfortable with the word *sealer*—"They're water and leak *resistant*," he said.

In *The Funeral Book* (1994), Clarence Miller writes, "Do not for one moment think that just because a casket has a rubber gasket designed to keep out air and water that it will. I have seen caskets disinterred after one month that were full of water though they were sold as 'air and water tight.' . . . In more than 35 years as a mortician, I do not have any faith at all in so-called 'sealer' caskets."

[2] When you put an uncovered plate of food in the refrigerator, the food dries out. When you put something in the refrigerator in a closed mayonnaise jar and forget about it—well, you get the idea.

In Mexico many years ago, it was the practice to charge families rent on the used grave spaces. When a family stopped paying, the body was dug up and the grave re-rented. During a trip to Guadalajara in the '60s, my son discovered some postcards with pictures of "mummies," so we began exploring the cemetery across the street. Descending a spiral stairway to a chamber under the cemetery wall, we saw (through a glass separation) rigid bodies leaning up against a wall—dusty clothes hanging off the skeletal remains, dry wrinkled skin taut against the bones. Yes, life had dissipated for these souls, and—while one might have wished them a horizontal "rest"—it seemed a totally natural condition of demise.

[3] In a state that will remain nameless, disgruntled employees smeared super-glue on the gasket of a casket heading for a mausoleum. Their mean-spirited boss was bound to have a problem on his hands sooner or later.

Knowing that mausoleums are constructed to permit the ventilation of gasses, I was puzzled when another caller to the FAMSA office told me that a Midwest mausoleum wouldn't let him use a traditional Jewish wood casket, only a "sealer." I told him it didn't sound as if folks at the mausoleum knew their business at all. A couple of weeks later when talking to a woman who runs a West Virginia cemetery and mausoleum, I asked if she required sealed caskets. She guffawed. "We don't *allow* sealed caskets. They explode! And if we get one, we send someone back for the crank so we can open the casket a bit."

In addition to the seal, some of the more expensive Batesville steel caskets offer "cathodic protection"—a bar of magnesium serving as a "sacrificial cathode" to deter rusting. Similar mechanisms are used in water heaters, providing protection for three years or so. Batesville, however, is willing to guarantee for up to 50 years its 16-gauge steel caskets.[1]

From an anonymous mortician friend who sends me e-mail "lessons" from time to time, I got this one on casket failure in mausoleums where such problems are more readily noticed than with in-ground burials:

> Mausoleums are marketed as a clean and dry alternative to ground burial. I was able to view first-hand the result of being in a mausoleum. There are no words to describe it. People, dead for only a year or two, covered with mold (I guess it was mold—it was fuzzy), the interior cloth material attached to the lid of the casket usually had fallen down and would lie on their bodies. The contents were always damp. Small insects, usually accompanied by several thousand dead insects, were living in these caskets. The insect's entire life cycle took place in the caskets,

---

[1] The warranty for use with a grave liner is 15 years, with a vault—40 years, with a water-resistant vault or above-ground interment—50 years.

One Indiana company that specializes in cathodic protection for underground storage tanks (made from much heavier gauge steel) gives a "two-year limited warranty," although a ten-year leak detection service is offered. Another company requires inspection every three years. Perhaps these companies should contact Batesville Caskets for advice.

There was interesting technical information on the Allied Corrosion Industries web site: "Another important source of corrosion activity on a structure is differential aeration of the electrolyte (commonly soil). In a situation where part of a structure is in soil having a free supply of oxygen (well aerated) and an adjacent area is in oxygen-starved (poorly aerated) soil, the part of the structure in the well-aerated soil will be the cathode and the part of the structure in the poorly aerated soil will be the anode." I wonder if that means that a casket that keeps air out is *speeding* corrosion by creating an electro-chemical imbalance inside and outside the casket.

so the present living insects were constantly surrounded by their dead ancestors. This gave new meaning, to me at least, that "life goes on."

While working at this mausoleum, I myself witnessed many instances of "casket-failure." This is when the dead people begin to putrefy, and liquid is released from the bodies. The caskets rust out from the inside, and the liquid—on many, many occasions—would run out the front of the chamber.

The company did not count on so many caskets failing. We had to pull them out, put them into an Ensure-a-seal[1] casket enclosure, and reseal the chamber. After that, families were required to purchase these (additional cost to family, about $225.00)—under the lie that it protected the caskets, but—in reality—it kept the goo in the drawer.[2]

~❖~

## The Jig Is Up

There is no amount of embalming or any particular casket that will preserve a body in a life-like condition forever. But perhaps history has to repeat itself several times before the industry will stop perpetrating such myths. One of the cases that Melvin Belli won early in his career resulted in a significant sum for a son whose mother rotted in the bronze sealer casket he'd purchased to protect her.[3] Now a Mississippi funeral home and Batesville Casket Company are facing a multi-million dollar lawsuit charging similar casket fraud.

Barbara Osborne had no reservations about spending $4,000 for Daddy's "protective" copper casket. Two months later—when she went to place flowers for Father's Day—the casket was "stinking to high heaven." Batesville took four months to respond. A video of the rotting flesh confirmed Barbara's worst fears.

"Protective," says the Batesville guarantee that Barbara was given. The Batesville website goes even further: "The urge to keep our loved

---

[1] The company's promotional video shows a giant Tyvek envelope (with a one-way valve to let out gasses) and a tray lined with chemical absorbent material.

[2] Another company, C. A. Joseph, offers Protect-a-Crypt®: "Made of a super absorbent material and shaped like a pillow. Protect-a-Crypt® will absorb and hold up to 10 gallons of liquid. It's an inexpensive yet dignified way to prevent any possibility of leakage damage to your mausoleum . . . and one less worry for you in the future." An illustration shows it just inside the crypt door across the front and up against the casket. Joseph also sells the Crypt Sealer—a polystyrene panel that can be caulked into the crypt opening. "Resists the effects of embalming fluids."

[3] See Chapter 11, "What the Public Wants," in *The American Way of Death Revisited* by Jessica Mitford.

ones protected and safe is fundamental to all of us. No wonder so many families are comforted by the ability to protect their loved ones with the Batesville Monoseal® protective casket." It's going to keep out air, water, and other elements, we're told.

The dictionary definition of protection is "to keep from harm." Yes, the gasketed casket may keep out any bugs that didn't accidently get closed inside in the first place, but Batesville doesn't bother to reveal that—*by keeping air out*—a sealed casket (in anything but the most frigid weather) becomes a slow cooker that will turn the body into a smelly stew.

Some funeral directors are awakening to the problems presented by sealer caskets. One recently wrote to *Mortuary Management* (June '98): "Sealer caskets are in danger of being identified as an alleged consumer fraud that funeral service has been a party to for far too many years. . . . Funeral service should finally divorce itself from this emerging identity."

~❖~

Of course, there are well-made caskets that (should) cost less than $500.[1] But to discourage customers from selecting low-end merchandise, these otherwise perfectly dignified caskets are often ordered in "ugly" colors[2]—dull-gray, cloth-covered being the most common (wholesale cost about $150)—and are sneeringly referred to as the "welfare caskets." When a priest or nun who has taken a vow of poverty dies, this casket might be ordered in burgundy or navy blue. Suddenly, it is no longer the "welfare casket." If the price and basic design of a modest casket seem right for you, ask what other colors can be ordered. Usually a funeral home can get a more attractive replacement within hours. Or you can hop onto the internet and find a casket of your choice available for overnight delivery from a casket retailer or woodworker:

### <www.funerals.org/famsa/caskets.htm>

---

[1] The widow of a well-respected Vermont judge, following his wishes, asked for a plain pine box. She was told that such a casket wasn't available, however. The family was then manipulated into choosing a much more expensive casket—"because of his position in the community."

[2] From an article by David Walkinshaw in the Jan. '98 issue of *Mortuary Management:* "From consumer surveys, it is clear that families select caskets mainly on eye appeal. . . . That is the reason that casket companies produce inexpensive caskets in rather unflattering finishes. If they looked too good, people would buy them."

It is illegal for a funeral home to charge a handling fee (as of July 19, 1994) if you use a family-built casket or purchase one elsewhere. I have seen some GPLs—often SCI ones—that say that any such casket must meet state and cemetery or crematory requirements. Few if any such requirements exist, so you can assume you're dealing with a manipulative company when you see this. Occasionally, a funeral home will state that the casket must be "deemed suitable" by the funeral director. This is manipulative and illegal because the funeral director may not refuse your choice of a casket (unless perhaps the bottom is falling out). Some establishments may make it inconvenient to use another firm's box, insisting that you be present when the casket is delivered, so they won't be "responsible." On the other hand, you just might want to be there—to assure that no one "finds" a torn lining, a dent or scratch, or a smear of dirt and grease on the third-party casket after it is delivered. Retail casket sellers are now routinely taking videos of their caskets before delivery to deter such underhanded and sleazy tactics.

A few states permit only a funeral director to sell caskets, clearly a ploy by the local undertakers to shut out competition and a violation of the intent of the Funeral Rule. C'mon, fellas, what kind of skill does it take to sell a box? As of this writing the states that restrict casket sales—or are actively trying to—are Alabama, Georgia, Idaho, Louisiana, Oklahoma, South Carolina, and Virginia. Until such restrictive laws and regulations are thrown out by the courts or the FTC gets out of a state of limbo, I've suggested that casket artisans and retailers in those states call the boxes they're selling "hope chests"—there is *no* state that forbids a family from burying a body in a hope chest. Of course, consumers in those states may order a casket shipped in from another state, and a mortuary may *not* refuse the family's right to use it.

A "casket" is not required for cremation. All funeral homes must provide a minimum "alternative container." The least expensive would be a cardboard container for perhaps as low as $25 or $50, but some rascals have the nerve to charge $350 for such a box. By law, you have a right to supply your own (check FAMSA's casket page).

Cremation containers are a growing part of the death-care business, and some funeral homes have set up separate displays of cremation caskets. In some cases, they are listed separately on the Casket Price List. While certain containers may be suggested to families who are planning a viewing prior to cremation, any comment that one is "Not suitable for viewing" is strictly manipulative and illegal. *You, the consumer,* get to decide which casket or container you want to use—for viewing, the funeral, and final disposition.[1]

~❖~

## Outer Burial Containers

Outer burial containers (vaults or grave-liners) can be as expensive and fancy as caskets, with some prices going as high as $7,000 or more.[2] Undoubtedly these may offer the caskets some protection from ground water—*if* the cemetery is built near a high-water zone. In that case, it may seem sensible at first blush to choose a "sealer" vault. But unfortunately, a sealer is likely to pop to the surface during a flood and float away. That's what happened during the '93 flood in the Midwest and the '98 flood in the southeast, and cemetery personnel had a terrible time getting everyone buried again where they belonged. Even if high water is not a problem, what is one "protecting" with an expensive vault? Decomposition of the body will occur one way or another.

A grave-liner is usually less expensive than a vault, and a basic concrete model (without the gold-spray paint or the bronze or marble lining) should cost only several hundred dollars. A polypropylene "bell cover" should be another option and is easier to install. The vault or grave-liner keeps the ground from settling after burial so the cemetery people can enjoy easy mowing and maintenance. Because not all cemeteries require liners or vaults, be sure to check the policy for yourself if you'd prefer to avoid this expense. No state has a law requiring an outer burial container and some national cemeteries (including Arlington National Cemetery) do not use them.[3]

---

[1] One SCI salesman suggested a $350 "cremation casket" to the niece. ID viewing would be required, he said, and "most people get upset to see a relative in a cardboard box." *Families may decline such a viewing unless required by law. It is never required if positive identification has been made by next-of-kin or their authorized representatives at the hospital or other place of death.*

[2] In an effort to sell an expensive vault, one Vermont funeral director told the ladies in his arrangements room, "I know a woman who told her husband to buy a cheap casket but an expensive vault because she was afraid of snakes." So were the ladies and the dead grandmother, which made it easier for them to opt for cremation before the transaction was over, much to the funeral director's (financial) dismay.

[3] Perhaps it's what the vault keeps in rather than what it keeps out that makes a case for using vaults. Embalming poisons are less likely to pollute the ground-water from inside a vault.

Many vault companies have refused to sell to consumers or to retailers selling to consumers, or have been boycotted by the local funeral directors if they do. (See the FAMSA website for the story on one that was reported to the FTC.) For Mary Lynn Broe—handling funeral plans for her mother without a funeral director—getting the vault became a huge problem. When she tried to order a vault from a Springfield funeral director, the Illinois funeral home insisted she had to hire their unwanted services as well. Isn't this extortion?

A recent bit of mischief at some cemeteries is the requirement of an "urn vault"—an outer container in which to put the box of cremated remains. This is generally just another ploy to part you from your money. Some cemeterians will say, with a straight face, that it's required in case someone wants to disinter the urn sometime in the future. (Is our society that "mobile"?) The vault will guarantee that the urn or box remains intact or that you won't "put a fork through Mum," as one SCI salesman in Australia put it. An urn vault price of, say, $595 may be mentioned by the sales rep, who is not likely to suggest that less expensive ones are also available. Although you may wish to shop around, any saving could be offset by an "inspection fee," a bogus charge to make up for lost profit, or by an excessive "installation" fee on top of what may already be an outrageous "opening and closing" charge.[1]

Some states restrict who may sell a vault. (Nobody except a funeral director may sell a vault in Tennessee. New Jersey prohibits cemeteries from selling vaults or memorial markers.) Cemeteries that do sell such items may **not** forbid you from purchasing them—or memorials— elsewhere. [2]

---

[1] If you visited the cemetery and just happened to trip while holding an open box of granular remains, are they going to vacuum them up? Gosh, I'd be so embarrassed by such an accident, I'd probably brush them quickly into the grass and sod.

[2] In Moore *vs* Jas. H. Matthews, 550 F.2d 1107 (9th Cir. 1977)—called Moore II, and Nos. 80-3180 & 80-3217 (9th Cir. 1982)—called Moore III, it was determined that cemeteries' exclusive installation rule constituted an illegal tie-in, which violated antitrust laws and was prohibited by the Sherman Anti-Trust Act.

In Rosebrough Monument Co. *vs* Memorial Park Cemetery Association, 666 F. 2d 1130 (8th Cir. 1981), the courts permitted cemeteries to establish "reasonable" rules regarding installation and an inspection fee based on its actual labor costs.

## Memorials & Markers

When a monument dealer lives in an area where there are a great many—too many?—other monument dealers or where there are cemeteries and morticians also selling memorials, there is an inherent business tension among them. Consumer beware!

~❖~

Cemeteries in Massachusetts must be not-for-profit and are not allowed to sell monuments and markers. The folks at Puritan Lawn in Peabody, however, have a "creative" approach for skirting the law, according to a news article by North Shore reporter Heather Anderson. The same family that owns Puritan Lawn also own Endicott Associates, the corporate entity for the monument business. What else does Endicott do? It contracts as a sales agent for Puritan to sell lots as well as markers. And where does Endicott have an office? Why in a building *adjacent* to the cemetery with no road in between. With the same folks making cemetery calls and monument calls,[1] it's not surprising that many of the markers at Puritan have been purchased through Endicott. Except for one factor: Consumers who didn't bother to shop around paid twice as much as they needed to. At Woodlawn Memorials in nearby Everett, a 28" x 16" bronze marker is only $595. At Puritan, it's $1,002.

~❖~

A small-business bronze marker maker had been selling all his plaques to a nearby SCI cemetery. Suddenly, the cemetery stopped purchasing from him, saying that all such memorials now had to be purchased through Matthews Bronze. When he then started selling directly to the public, the cemetery officials became blatant about their intention to put him out of business. They told him that he had no chance of fighting them, reminding him of their big staff of lawyers. He was nearly in tears when he called the FAMSA office—"No one seems to take me seriously." He had been losing business right and left. When customers at the cemetery indicate that they have made arrangements to purchase a memorial through him, the cemetery offers to match his much-lower price and throws in something for free to induce the customers to change their minds.

~❖~

---

[1] One call soliciting a memorial sale was made to an unlisted number that the family had given only to the cemetery personnel.

As a result of a limited survey of a dozen cemeteries in Oklahoma—half of which were owned by SCI and half of which were independent—I found that prices at the SCI cemeteries were conspicuously higher for almost everything. In one case, I was told that the least expensive, simple flat memorial would be $1,000. (I'd already found these on the internet for between $350 and $750, so I had some idea of pricing even though I had never purchased one before.) I asked a second time, just to be sure, if that was the *least expensive*. I was assured it was. When I indicated that I'd probably be purchasing a memorial elsewhere, a lower price was suddenly "remembered," but not very much lower. I wonder how long I could have kept that game going.

(I did learn later that there's a difference between a granite base and a concrete base, but I hadn't known enough to ask which was being quoted or whether that was included. Assuming that SCI's prices were all-inclusive—base and marker—and for "the very best," those prices were still high.)

~❖~

According to an on-line funeral directors chat group, SCI is now managing the Catholic cemeteries in Dallas. Charge for installing a marker purchased from someone else: an outrageous $650!

~❖~

"Perpetual care for memorials" has arrived on the scene as another way to part you from your money. It is totally unnecessary. Unless the spot is in the shade under a tree where moss might grow, Mother Nature does a fine job of washing your marker. In fact, too much scrubbing might mar the finish of the marker if anything abrasive were used.

~❖~

One Pennsylvania funeral director knows that the cemetery nearby is going to charge a "road fee" if an outside monument dealer or funeral director plans to bring in a marker. He feels he has to let families know what all costs will be and tells them about the fee ahead of time. The local monument dealer apparently never mentions the extra $50, however, which means he's sometimes the one who gets the sale. Once the stone has been inscribed and just before heading for the cemetery, the monument dealer calls the family with an "I didn't know" story, asking for the additional $50 so the stone can be delivered. If FAMSA succeeds in bringing cemeteries under the Funeral Rule, we should be able to outlaw any such bogus and discriminatory charges. That should help to level the playing field for consumers.

~❖~

A Boston-area monument dealer faxed me copies of phony invoices that one of his competitors uses to nab business. It seems that the competitor reads the obituaries on a regular basis and notes the cemetery where interment took place. If it's a cemetery with a uniform requirement for markers, the con job is relatively easy because there is little family choice possible. An "invoice" for the standard marker is sent, asking the family to fill in the final data such as birth date, verification of spelling, and the confirming signature. Upon receipt of the total amount "due," it states, the marker will be installed.

## Memorial Alternatives

There are, of course, lots of ways in which to memorialize someone special in your life whether or not you're choosing a cemetery marker—gifts of library books, donations to a particular cause or organization—the possibilities are endless. Here are a few suggestions that might stretch your thinking.

~❖~

In Toledo, you can have a park bench installed for a modest fee. The two slats on the back of the bench provide appropriate space for memorial attribution: In Memory of (Name). I think I'd like to put one outside the Chicago airport where I can never find a place to sit down between flights.

~❖~

Animal lovers might want to consider a granite "dog lick"—sort of a bird-bath on ground level—for a city park. One could have a lot of fun with the inscriptions on the side of this.

~❖~

One Christmas, I joked that I was giving an early gravestone to everyone. I managed to find a bunch of smooth river stones—some big, some small—at a nearby gravel pit, brought them into my kitchen and washed off the snow and mud, then took them to the local monument dealer for engraving. Lots of folks in my family that year got a garden stone that said "Laugh" on it. That's the way I'd like to be remembered.

# The Body Snatchers
## Preneed Greed

## 18

### The Hit

With the glut of funeral homes, mortuaries are fighting over dead bodies—trying to grab market share. If a funeral home has only two or three funerals per week, prospecting for new business makes sense during the slow periods. Selling cemetery lots ahead of time is a long-standing tradition, but the preneed (before you need it) funeral market has exploded in the last 15 years, particularly among the big chains. In the U.S., consumers' concern for Medicaid eligibility (sheltering appropriate assets for funeral expense) has been another driving factor. But most state laws are still woefully lacking in consumer protection.

About half the states allow only funeral directors to sell preneed funeral arrangements. Other states license preneed salespeople who need not be morticians, though in many states they must be affiliated with funeral homes. The larger companies have employees who specialize in selling preneed, with annual commissions often totalling $80,000 or more in states where they can get away with it.[1]

How do they find you? Ann Merchant of Cleveland, Texas was horrified to learn that the Loewen salespeople had laminated her husband's obituary and were delivering it to pallbearers and other friends as a "gift" from her. The sales pitch to her husband's friends at this time of grief was that while the "counselors" were there, it would be a perfect time to make their own arrangements!

From SCI training materials leaked to the FAMSA office:

SUCCESSFUL FAMILY SERVICE COUNSELORS ARE ABLE TO DISPLAY:

... Assertiveness in field follow-up on prearrangement developed from the families they serve.

---

[1] "Sure, the title 'family service counselor' comforts potential preneed buyers. But use it in an an employment ad and your new preneed staff member won't last a year. ... The reason: The word 'counselor' will attract recruits who are too passive to succeed in the fast-paced, high-pressure world of sales. ... Instead, say, 'Looking for an outgoing, assertive, results-oriented salesperson'." —*Funeral Service Insider,* July 20, 1998.

RESPONSIBILITIES AND FUNCTIONS

There are two (2) main functions of a Family Service Counselor. Under each are a series of duties and responsibilities that require a high standard of performance:

1. To counsel, advise and guide at-need families . . .
2. To generate preneed sales through the at-need families using a detailed field follow-up program.

These two main functions incorporate the four "S's".

1. SERVE THE FAMILY
2. SELL THE FAMILY
3. SOLICIT REFERRALS
4. SELL REFERRALS

So prospecting your friends and relatives will be on their minds even during the arrangements for your funeral. From the SCI instructions for handling an initial cremation call:

Tell the family that you will need a list of pallbearers, including phone numbers for us to contact. This will be handled by the primary arranger. If you are given the names over the phone, be careful to ask for correct spelling. This serves to ensure the correct spelling of the names for newspaper notices and pallbearers' letters.

Pallbearers for a cremation? Or just another sales contact?

From the *Funeral Service Insider:* "Require your preneed staff to knock on doors and do in-home follow-up visits after funerals, suggests a Dallas-based manager for Stewart Enterprises. . . . Remember, Stewart's biggest source of preneed business is through at-need leads."

"Aftercare" *can be* a subtle approach. Jim Johnston, a Vermont funeral director, showed a *Boston Globe* reporter how he cranks out "personalized" letters on his computer. He sends one of these along with a booklet on grief supplied by the Dodge Chemical company, maker of embalming fluids. Other funeral homes send annual holiday cards or invite families to attend a holiday memorial at the mortuary— to hang an ornament inscribed with the name of a deceased on the Christmas tree. Some funeral homes sponsor support groups for widows and widowers. Are these genuinely caring and friendly gestures? I certainly wouldn't rule out that possibility. Beyond question, some funeral directors develop real friendships and loyalties toward the families and communities they serve. And if they gain more business in the long run as a result—"doing well by doing good"—I have no complaint. That's one of the basic concepts of capitalism at its best. The follow-through by funeral homes, however, may not always helpful.

At some point, the widow or widower needs to gently put away the past and move on.

Direct mail advertising for preneed funeral and cemetery purchases jams mail boxes in many areas, especially where there is a high population of retirees. From the *Funeral Service Insider:* "The [preneed] team manages a marketing database that downloads 1,500 names [per] month from an automated lead-management system. They send mailings to all names on the list, then follow up with a phone call a week later. The funeral home also promotes preneed at regular seminars at local nursing homes and social-group meetings." With so much direct mail these days, list managers can tailor mailings to targeted households—those with residents older than 45, for example, who live in certain neighborhoods. The mailing may offer a free planning guide, but you're likely to get someone offering to help you fill it out in person.

To their credit, Ontario and Virginia forbid in-person solicitation—including phone calls—for preneed funeral prospecting. Ontario has a similar ban for cemeteries. Although Virginia legislation is underway to expand that ban to cover cemeteries, too, the corporate lobbyists are trying to derail the bill. It would cramp the style of their preneed sales people who now can pitch cemetery offers over the telephone, and—once they are face-to-face with the consumer—they can make the pitch for funeral services.

## Preneed Insurance Policies

There is no such ban on insurance sales reps, but perhaps there should be. The following e-mail from a fellow who works for Loewen in Ontario describes what happened there:

> Have had a really shitty 48 hours. Now they want us to rescind our funeral directors' licenses and get insurance licenses instead so we can be more aggressive. Apparently, if we dump our licenses, the corp. will send us to insurance school, one whole month!!! Sorry, but I think I'm going to be out of here or this business. THIS SHOULD BE EXPOSED! Get a new license after four-plus years of school so you can hit up little old ladies??? THE WORLD REALLY SUCKS!!! And you can print that, I'm sooooo f__king mad!!! I wasn't the only one. All the funeral directors got up and left, but they were devastated. Now the big boys will get vacuum salesmen off the street to sell their Purple Shield or whatever the hell it is!!! Selling funerals like vacuums, and it's going to be a free-for-all. I thought I was going to help someone through the most difficult time in their life . . . . WRONG . . . MONEY, MONEY, MONEY!

And what about funeral insurance? Heck, an envelope for "Physicians' Insurance" ($5,000, no physical) falls out of my Sunday newspaper three or four times a year, and Montgomery Ward just began aiming for the Boomers with a funeral insurance plan. Four states forbid insurance-funded funeral arrangements—Connecticut, Georgia, Maryland, and Wisconsin, whereas New Mexico permits *only* insurance-funded preneed. While insurance may have more portability than many other plans, it is a high-commission industry that offers only a modest increase in value from year to year—3% or so which may match general inflation but is less than funeral inflation. If cashed in before using it, there will be far less returned than paid. There are many different kinds of insurance, and, as the *Funeral Monitor* noted, "The devil is in the details." An insurance purchase may have high premiums and all sorts of limitations, such as no coverage for the first two years. A bank takes no commissions, and you can get your money back any time.

The bottom line? If someone contacts you by phone or mail for cemetery or funeral arrangements, they want your body—and your money. You, the consumer, should initiate the contact—but only after learning what it's all about *and* after shopping around.

### "Guaranteed" Mischief

Funeral inflation is running about 5–7% a year for a full, one-of-everything funeral. It's much higher at the chains. Protection from inflation is, of course, the major selling pitch for "guaranteed-price" funerals. But your potential saving will disappear fast if your survivors are manipulated into paying additional charges, *as they usually are.* Funeral sales people are not working for charities; they aren't about to lock in prices unless they think they can get that inflation difference later. Caskets, for example, come out in new models every year like cars. If your arrangement states that you've selected the "Windsor 123" casket, the chances are that that specific model won't be available when you die. Your survivors will be asked to pick out another—and, oh, by the way, there's an additional charge.[1] While funeral directors in some states are supposed to substitute a casket of *equal quality* if the one selected is not available, only two (Virginia and Idaho) stipulate that

---

[1] Be sure to read Peggy Porter's appalling story in the chapter on prepaid funerals in Jessica Mitford's *American Way of Death Revisited.* A class action suit has been filed against Loewen in Louisiana as a result.

the survivor or a representative has the right to approve a substitution. A casket of *equal value* (price) may leave you with a high-priced plywood box if there's been a jump in prices for the oak and velvet Dad picked out long ago.

How else do they hit up survivors? In Massachusetts, an additional $100 was added for a "carrying assistant." A more common racket is the markup on third-party "cash-advance" items such as flowers, the fee for the organist, or the charge for arranging the obituary. It's not surprising that these prices are not locked in by the contract, as they are goods and services provided by others. But the contract probably also places no cap on how much extra the funeral director can charge for making arrangements for those goods and services. The result can be a huge increase in the amount of money your survivors will be asked to contribute to your funeral. Of course, your survivors could arrange for all of the "cash-advance" items themselves. But in practice, many grief-stricken survivors welcome a funeral director's offer to "take care of everything." And for a few phone calls they may pay dearly.

With the emergence of casket retailers and low-cost, no-frills operations, more options are becoming available in some areas, options that would be far less costly than what you might arrange for today. The ultimate goal of the FTC Funeral Rule is to lower costs through competition. It would be too bad to be locked into a high-priced funeral today when it *might* cost you less in the future.

## Better Not Move, Travel, or Change Your Mind!

Only a few states and provinces guarantee you a full refund or right to transfer arrangements with the interest included. In almost half the states, the funeral director or cemeterian can take a commission right away.

Even in the states that require the funeral director to put 100% of your money in trust, there's a magical way around that: it's called "**Constructive Delivery.**" This is perhaps the most insidious problem for prepaid funeral and cemetery consumers who later need or want to change their plans. If you have been given a certificate or statement of ownership, the item is *supposed* to be placed in storage with your name on it. In the legal sense, it has been "delivered" even though no names are engraved on the marker and you've not yet occupied the vault or casket. Cemeteries and funeral homes like this because it gives them immediate access to your funds, including the large markup over wholesale cost. States rarely—if ever—check to see if the committed items are in the warehouse. Even if they are, the greater problem is that once the items are "delivered," you're not entitled to a refund if you move or change your mind.

One Florida woman paid for her funeral there but died during a trip to New Jersey. The service funds were transferred, but the New Jersey funeral director was told that the casket was in a warehouse in Florida and he would have to make arrangements to pick it up. In order to be sure they had a casket in time for the viewing, the family ended up buying a new one in New Jersey. There was no refund on the casket they didn't use. Had the woman died in Florida, there probably would have been no mention of the warehouse; a different ploy is usually used instead. Survivors would be told that such-and-such a casket model was no longer available, and a "comparable" but ugly one would be offered. Many families will then pick out a new casket—for more money, of course.

And if the woman had purchased her funeral in Mississippi? Only 50% of what she had paid would have been sent to the New Jersey funeral home—the selling funeral director having legally pocketed a whopping commission first.[1]

When funds ran out to ship her aunt's body from Florida to Iowa, Claire and the other relatives decided to opt for an immediate cremation. The SCI-owned funeral home refused to change the $3,000-plus ship-out arrangements to their pricey $2,100 cremation "because it's irrevocable." (Funny thing—funeral homes are always eager to *upgrade* "irrevocable" arrangements, but never willing to *downgrade* to anything less expensive.) Claire then found an independent cremation service for less than $500. She'll apply for the refund permitted under state law. After all, a funeral home certainly shouldn't be allowed to just pocket the money if survivors learned about a prepaid arrangement after the fact and never used it. Will Claire get back everything her aunt paid? Well, if the funeral home claims that the (now musty) casket is in the warehouse and the state inspectors can't back it up, a class-action suit may be in order.

Gary was contacted by a Mt. Auburn Memorial Park representative while he was still living in Illinois. A prudent, plan-ahead kind of guy, he liked the idea of getting his final affairs in order. The price wasn't too bad: $470 for a marker and $575 for a lawn crypt. But he hesitated to make any purchase, telling the sales rep that he probably would be moving to another state when he retired. No problem, the sales rep told him. If he moved outside a 75-mile radius, his plan could be

---

[1] Each state chapter will tell what protection you may, or may not, have.

transferred to another cemetery. The sales rep even marked his contract clearly: "Do not inscribe marker until contacted by the buyer."

By the time Gary retired and had moved to West Virginia, he changed his mind about body burial and decided cremation was the way to go. He approached a local cemetery about niche space with the intent of moving his cemetery arrangements there. Just one problem: Mt. Auburn said his memorial marker was in the warehouse with his name on it. The folks there would be happy to ship it at his expense if that was what he wanted. That it wouldn't fit the niche Gary had selected was *his* problem, not theirs, they said. And how much money are they going to send to the cemetery in West Virginia? Only 50% of Gary's original lot price was put in trust, with the annual interest (or 3%, whichever is less) available to the cemetery.

As smart as Gary was, the final irony didn't hit him until much later. His $1,040 agreement was paid for in installments—at an interest rate of 10%! He'd paid $329 in finance charges for something he'd never used, and the cemetery had been claiming another 3% each year from the interest on what he'd paid.[1]

Some situations are worse. In 1997, the following was faxed to Maridel Freshwater in the regional office of the FTC by Pierson Ralph, executive director, Memorial Society of North Texas.

> Simplicity Plan of Texas, a subsidiary of Stewart Enterprises, Inc., sells preneed cemetery space and funeral plans for Stewart funeral homes, including Restland, Laurel Land, Anderson Clayton, and Bluebonnet Hills, among others. Simplicity seeks to sell cemetery space/markers and a funeral plan concurrently, and offers time payment terms to cover the purchases.
>
> Simplicity encourages purchasers who buy both items to combine payments on one account. There are, however, potentially adverse consequences to such combination if the purchaser defaults or chooses to cancel a contract. Simplicity **does not** warn purchasers of such adverse consequences. . . .
>
> In April 1995, a woman of modest financial means and relatively unsophisticated about time purchases—and with essentially no knowledge at all about funeral purchases—became concerned about funeral arrangements for her father. She contacted Restland Funeral Home in Dallas and purchased two contracts, one for a cemetery space at $1,850, the other for a funeral at $4,040. She paid $100 down and

---

[1] These states permit interest to be charged on preneed funeral or cemetery purchases: Florida, Illinois, Indiana, Michigan, Nebraska, North Carolina, and Texas. Virginia specifically forbids such charges.

financed the balance at 7% interest—on first appearance, a relatively low finance rate. As it turned out, this supposedly favorable rate was an illusion, as is shown later.

Although she had two contracts, Restland graciously offered to combine these under a single payment plan under terms of the cemetery space purchase contract: "For your convenience, the payments on the (cemetery purchase) Contract may be combined with payments for any additional purchase(s), including any pre-paid funeral arrangements, on one account."

Restland normally sets up payments for a funeral purchase for a maximum of seven years. Under this arrangement, however, the funeral purchase was tacked onto the end of the cemetery purchase. The payment schedule called for 119 payments of $68, extending the payout period to one month shy of **ten years!!!**

The total time payment price, thus, was $8,192: the $100 down payment and 119 time payments of $68. The total finance charges included in this price, if paid according to the schedule, come to $2,302. This increased the total cost by 39%, ignoring for this calculation the subtleties of the "time value of money."

In late 1996, the woman began to have financial problems. The sight drafts for the monthly payments, among other things, caused several overdrafts at her bank account. She closed the account, and, by 1997, no regular payments were being made. In September, she turned to Senior Citizens of Greater Dallas for help, and they referred her to the Memorial Society.

By this time, the father was failing and could die any time. The woman had equity of only $835 (according to Restland) toward the contract of $5,890. All the rest of her payments had gone to carrying charges and penalties. Upon maturity (the death of her father), she would have to come up with over $5,000 to complete the purchase. This seemed virtually impossible considering the trouble she was having just making the $68 monthly payments.

The best the Memorial Society could suggest was that she cancel, essentially forfeiting everything she had paid, including the $835 equity in the cemetery space, and choose a less expensive package of goods and services from a less costly provider. . . .

There is a possibility that the packaging of the single payment for the two contracts constitutes a deceptive trade practice. As noted above, there were two separate contracts, one for purchase of cemetery space, the other for purchase of the funeral. There are substantial differences in protection to the consumer under these contracts. The cemetery property sale is a retail installment contract, governed by Texas law pertaining to such contracts. One provision of the contract is that "If a payment to be made by Purchaser on this Contract is not paid within 60 days of the date the payment is due, Seller may, as a matter of its sole discretion, (i) declare that all payments made by Purchaser on this Contract are forfeited to and shall remain the property of Seller as and for liquidated damages." This indicates that the cemetery property would revert entirely to the seller in the case of default or cancellation. The funeral contract is governed by a special law which restricts what the seller can retain in case of cancellation.

The provision for combination of the payments is in the contract for purchase of the cemetery space. It goes on to state, "All payments will be applied first, to accrued finance charges and insurance premiums, if applicable, secondly, to purchases of cemetery property and any memorial until fully paid, and lastly to other purchases." In the case cited, the other purchase was for the funeral.

If, instead of these provisions, the payments had been allocated proportionally to the amount financed, the equity would have been only $262 in the cemetery property and $573 in the funeral purchase. The seller could retain only half this amount or $286.50. The other $286.50 would be returned to the purchaser. A small amount, but significant to a financially-strapped buyer.

It would take a person with thorough knowledge of the difference in the cancellation provisions between the two contracts to catch the significance of allocating principal payments first to the cemetery property debt and only after this is paid in full, to the funeral contract. The effect is to minimize what the purchaser can recover upon cancellation, and, conversely to maximize what the seller can keep. It seems very unlikely that the attorneys and other professionals at Restland were not aware of this distinction and structured the provisions to benefit their own interests at the expense of the purchaser.

## Trusting and Reporting: Who's in Default?

If you have already prepaid for a funeral and are *not* getting an annual report of where your money is and how much is actually there, you might want to check right away. Ethical funeral homes will have this documentation readily available; *I hope you won't be disappointed.* You will probably have a much harder time finding out whether your cemetery funds are in safe-keeping.

Here's one example of the problem and the temptation that can lead to disaster for consumers even in a state where 100% of prepaid funeral money is supposed to go into a trust: A small-town Vermont funeral director whined to me that he hadn't had a funeral in 13 weeks; he was sweating his mortgage payments, he said. He probably is well-intentioned, but the next person through the door with a check for a prepaid funeral could certainly rescue his cash-flow problem. Instead of putting 100% in trust as required by Vermont law, it's easy enough to imagine him saying, "I'm a good-guy. I'll take care of Annie when she dies, but I'm going to pay my mortgage now."[1]

In Colorado, a couple—working as preneed sales people registered with the Department of Insurance—sold $150,000 worth of funeral plans one year. The proper amount (85%) was even in the bank when the state audited their preneed account. Within weeks of the audit, however, the bank account was closed. Destination of the couple: unknown. In Pennsylvania, millions disappeared in the Meacham case—where some of the preneed funds were "invested" in rare coins at far above their "rare" value.

In state after state, there has been an increasing number of defaults by funeral directors who can't meet the obligations they hold for servicing prepaid funeral contracts. A few states have set up some form of "guarantee fund": Florida, Indiana, Iowa, Missouri, North Carolina, Oregon, Vermont, and West Virginia. (A bond, as required in Virginia, is a start but not ideal.) When the default fund was used in West Virginia a few years ago, the system worked very well.

## Planning Ahead, Not Paying Ahead

Given the lack of completely consumer-oriented preneed laws in most states, it is probably a mistake to ever pay a funeral home or cemetery ahead of time. The safest place for your money is a pay-on-death account (Totten trust) at a bank, with next-of-kin—*not the funeral home*—as the beneficiary. (Be sure to go to the "trust" department of your bank, not just one of the tellers at a counter.) Many states will accept this if it is in an irrevocable trust, when setting aside assets in

---

[1] When Annie died, the granddaughter was told, "It will cost more than $895, you know." That was the amount Annie had been quoted for a funeral 20 years ago by the funeral director's dad who'd run the Woodstock business way back then. She'd told her kids it was "all taken care of," and—being the pragmatic, no-nonsense Yankee that she was—no one doubted her word for it. It must surely never have occurred to Annie, either, that by sending cash there would be a problem (whether or not she ever got receipts); it was simply the way honorable, small-town Vermonters did their transactions in those days—when everyone knew everything about everyone else. The new generation of owners did seem to acknowledge that Annie had paid the full amount, hinting that the family would have to pay even more. But did the $895 (and interest) show up as a credit on the funeral bill? Nope. Because of other mischief, too, that funeral director was obliged to take a course on ethics, mandated by an agreement with the Attorney General's office, the state Funeral Board, and his lawyer. The family paid nothing more.

order to be eligible for various social benefits such as Medicaid. That way, you won't have to worry about the funeral home going out of business, and you can readily transfer the funds if you move, perhaps to be with an adult child in another state. Or, if ownership of the local funeral home changes and it's no longer the one you would choose a year from now, you won't be locked in.

Preneed contracts are now being promoted by the funeral industry with more and more hucksterism. "Hurry, hurry, hurry! Look how much you'll be saving if you buy your funeral now! After Ground-Hog Day, these prices will be going up!" Funeral directors wouldn't be trying so hard to sell these contracts if they didn't bring about an increase in revenues by capturing more of the market share (plus the expectation that survivors can be squeezed for more at the time of death). The fact is, we're all going to need funeral arrangements of one type or another, sooner or later. It always pays to plan ahead, but it rarely pays to pay ahead.

There's a psychological reason for not rushing out to buy a funeral, too. Yes, I've heard people say with satisfaction (just as Annie did), "It's all taken care of." And I've heard adult children say, "My Mom took care of everything—it was wonderful, just one phone call." But "taking care of everything" *may* deprive your survivors of a therapeutic involvement. Find out what funeral rituals will be important to others and let them know what seems important to you. If cost is a concern, be sure to teach the others how to shop for a funeral. In the process, you'll be giving them a lesson they can pass along—the final act of love.

## Of Death & Taxes

For years, the IRS has held that—because it is supposed to be used for your benefit—you must declare on your Income Tax Return the interest income from any prepaid funeral trust. In 1997, a new provision went into effect that allows the funeral home or trustee to declare the interest and pay any tax due from the proceeds of the trust. Because in states such as Texas you are unlikely to get your interest if you were to cancel a preneed contract or die somewhere else, you may wish to return the 1099 tax form that the funeral home sends you and politely tell the funeral home that you wish to take advantage of the new provision and let the mortuary report the interest. Although the funeral home may not be forced to do so under current rules, it would be a terrible public relations mistake if it refused.

## Ideal, Consumer-friendly Preneed Laws

- Not counting the cost of the lot, crypt, or niche, 100% of all monies paid for *cemetery* and *funeral* merchandise and services should be placed in trust, with interest to accrue. "Delivery" of merchandise should not be permitted prior to the time of need, and finance charges should not be allowed.

- A consumer should have the right to cancel any cemetery or funeral purchase, on 15-days notice, with a full right of refund including all interest. If a contract is made irrevocable to shelter assets, those funds should be transferable to another cemetery or mortuary without penalty or administrative fees.

- A cemetery should be required to buy back any unwanted lot at 50% of the difference between the original purchase price and the current market value, if the owner has not found another buyer.

- A detailed description of all merchandise should be included in a preneed contract. If the selected merchandise is not available at the time of death, survivors should approve any substitution from others of like quality and construction.

- The consumer should receive an annual report from the institution holding trust funds. Any administrative fee should be *minimal:* actual expenses or 0.5%—whichever is less.

- A state-sponsored, industry-funded guarantee program would protect consumers against provider default.

## When Might It Make Sense to Pay Ahead?

- When your funeral plans will cost more than $2,500 or so (states differ) and you need to legitimately shelter assets to pay for your funeral before applying for Medicaid, *and* . . .

- When you're *sure* you're not likely to move or travel, perhaps because you're going into a nursing home, *and* . . .

- When you're *sure* of the funeral options you and your family want or there's no penalty for changing your mind, *and* . . .

- When it is unlikely that the ownership of the funeral home and staff will change.

# Federal Trade Commission: Boon and Boondoggle

## 19

Government regulation of business activity in the U.S. is always controversial and often clumsy. This is a capitalistic country, and the prevailing view is that market forces, at least in the long run, serve the interests of consumers better than does government regulation.

However, throughout American history, we have found that some industries have immunized themselves from marketplace competition, resulting in exorbitant prices for essential services and lack of choices for consumers. Therefore, some form of government intervention is needed, not to micro-manage the industry but to allow competition on a fair playing field, and to ensure that consumers have a choice in the goods and services they wish to purchase.

Federal attention to the funeral industry occurred because consumers demanded it. Members of the general public were sick and tired of the abusive practices, and they called their congressional representatives. Members of the funeral and memorial societies throughout the U.S. led the charge.

It took ten years of public pressure to convince the Federal Trade Commission (FTC) to pass consumer protection for funeral purchases.[1] The National Funeral Directors Association (NFDA) fought tooth-and-nail, every step of the way.[2]

The major goal of consumer advocates was itemization—a menu of funeral goods and services from which one could choose only the items that were wanted, including low-cost ones. No one should be locked into a funeral package based on the selection of a particular casket as had been the practice in the past. Someone who didn't want embalming or a viewing should not have to pay for it. If someone

---

[1] The original Funeral Rule was passed in 1982 and went into effect in 1984.

[2] This was not with the full support of their membership. The California funeral directors dropped out of the organization, embarrassed by the rigid intransigence of the national office. Ironically, the worm has turned. In 1998, NFDA voiced public approval for bringing all funeral-related vendors—including cemeteries—under the Rule, one of FAMSA's major goals. Other issues will be more divisive, however.

wanted a different casket or other services than those listed with the casket, one should be free to choose.

Once it became apparent that itemization would prevail, the industry insisted that the list include a nondeclinable charge for planning the funeral. Planning was, after all, providing a service, the industry said, and everyone should have to pay for that. (In contrast, car salesmen and travel agents don't charge for their sales pitches, or even the paperwork involved in the transactions. These costs are rolled into the price for goods and services you purchase.)

When it became obvious that the Funeral Rule would be weakened, several of the more consumer-oriented and passionate FTC staff members gave up and left. One has to assume that the rest of the FTC lawyers had become weary by this time.[1]

The new nondeclinable charge on the General Price List (GPL) was called "Basic Services of *Staff*." (That word *staff* is important in understanding what happened next.) This was defined as the time it took to plan the funeral, to get the permits, and to collect the obituary and death-certificate information—those things common to most or all funeral arrangements. But it was also the *only* place on the GPL where the word "staff" was used. "Facilities for viewing" and "Facilities for a funeral" had to be listed, but "staff" was not mentioned in connection with those items.

Undoubtedly the FTC thought "staff" was implied for the various services from which to choose. But an industry that *loves* the concept of a nondeclinable fee—a fee that you *must* pay regardless of the choices you make—quickly embellished what this "basic" fee was to cover. For the next ten years, many price lists read: "This fee also includes staff prior to, during and after the funeral." This was in complete violation of the intent of the Rule. Someone opting for a simple graveside service was being charged at the same rate as someone choosing a funeral with viewing and a church ceremony. That was not supposed to happen.

On average, this nondeclinable fee increased by 73% in the next six years, according to the FTC studies. And yet, the commentary in the 1988 FTC reports wondered why the cost of funerals was rising faster than inflation. When a single item (the one item for which there was no accountability at all) had risen from 11% to almost 20% of the

---

[1] Jessica Mitford has a most interesting chapter on the FTC Rule in *The American Way of Death, Revisited.*

total funeral cost, one has a hard time imagining how the FTC staff missed it!

In 1988, a review of the Funeral Rule began. I testified at one of the hearings in Washington, DC, pointing out the documented abuse of this fee. (There was also a huge amount of additional anecdotal evidence.) After six years of oral and written testimony, the FTC *finally* issued an amended Rule that went into effect July 19, 1994.

Lo and behold, the required items on the GPL had new references to "staff": *"Staff* and facilities for viewing," *"Staff* and facilities for a funeral," and *"Staff* and Equipment for a Graveside Service."

Consumers who had hoped that costs would shift accordingly were soundly disappointed, however. The NFDA—long enamored of the nondeclinable fee concept—wanted "unallocated overhead" included in this fee. "Where else do we put [the cost of] the parking lot?" asked one. In spite of written testimony from objecting consumers, the undefined "unallocated overhead" was allowed.

Not only was "unallocated" not defined in the Rule, FTC staff appear to have effectively gutted the anti-packaging portions of the Rule with the following expansion of what this might cover:[1]

> The basic services fee also may include overhead from various aspects of your business operation, such as the parking lot, reception and arrangements rooms, and other common areas. It also may include insurance, staff salaries, taxes, and fees that you must pay. Alternatively, instead of including all overhead in your basic services fee, you can spread the overhead charges across the various individual goods and services you offer. . . .

How did "unallocated overhead" suddenly become "all overhead"? If a funeral home is allowed to put *all overhead* in the nondeclinable fee, someone picking minimal services is paying for staff and facilities that were not used, negating the principle that was supposed to be guiding the Rule:[2]

> Itemization permits consumers to decline the use of various provider facilities.

---

[1] From "Complying with the Funeral Rule, A Business Guide Produced by the Federal Trade Commission," June 1994, page 15.

[2] *Federal Register,* p. 42261, v. 47, no. 186, 9-24-82, and p. 1608, 1-11-94.

Someone arranging a direct cremation over the telephone or planning all services at a church is not filling the parking lot or using the reception rooms and should not be forced to pay for such. The consumer gets no tangible benefit for this fee. *What other industry is given government permission to charge a nondeclinable fee that is unrelated to the goods and services selected?* (Few people shop around for medical services either, but each item on a hospital bill must represent a specific service or item that was actually supplied.)

The nondeclinable "basic" fee could also be called a waiting-around-until-you-die charge or an unemployment benefit for the morticians. If people were to die Monday through Friday with only one funeral a day and two weeks off for the mortician's vacation, the number of funeral homes needed to handle 2,322,000 deaths (in '96) would have been 9,288. Yet we have 22,000+ funeral homes in this country. What other business is so completely insulated from the modest forces of supply and demand that might otherwise prevail?

How has the industry responded? The FTC pegged this fee at $459 in 1987. In 1996, the industry reported that the "average" charge for this "Basic" fee was $1,025. But what happened at individual funeral homes is more telling, especially the corporate-owned ones. In 1993, Laurel Land in Fort Worth, Texas charged $1,198. By 1996, this now Stewart-owned mortuary had upped it to $1,995. At Sparkman-Hillcrest in Dallas, Texas, this fee was $1,495 in '94 but jumped to $1,990 by '96; it's owned by SCI. At a Loewen-owned funeral home in Springfield, Massachusetts, this fee was $2,465 on a 1997 GPL. In fact, once a mortuary has been purchased by a corporate funeral chain, this fee tends to rise every six months.

In areas where there are retail casket sellers, funeral homes follow the advice of trade journals and lower their casket prices to compete, then raise their service prices. In other words, competition and market forces lower the price of the casket itself, but this does no good to the consumer who must make up the difference in the nondeclinable fee to the funeral home.

The nondeclinable fee has, in practice, voided all expectations of the original Rule (*Federal Register,* p. 42298, v. 47, no. 186, 9-24-82):

> . . . to the extent that itemization allows consumers to choose less than traditional funerals, the increased demand for less than full funerals may stimulate innovative new services and allow the market to respond. As a result, the long run effect of *itemization is expected to drive all prices down to the competitive level* [emphasis added].

Of course, funeral prices won't go down if a hefty nondeclinable fee is permitted to replace the bloated casket prices of yore.

How do Americans fare compared to other countries? According to a '96 issue of *Funeral Monitor*, the "average" funeral at the high-priced SCI-owned mortuaries in Britain is $1,650; in France, $2,200; and in Australia, $2,100. The U.S. average cited by the Federated Funeral Directors of America is $4,700 for the same year. (These figures do not include cemetery costs.) One has to assume that Brits care as much about their dead as Americans do. Why are we paying so much more?

Funeral and Memorial Societies of America (FAMSA), along with a coalition of other consumer groups, has asked the FTC to hold hearings during its next review of the Rule scheduled for '99 if the FTC is unwilling to begin earlier. The goal will be new amendments to the Rule:

- Abolish any nondeclinable fee. (Replace current charges with an *optional* per-hour fee, for assisting consumers with insurance and benefit applications if they desire these services.)
- Add an option for private viewing without embalming, with a per-hour charge permitted.
- List the cost for body donation to a medical school.
- List the cost of the cremation process. (The current listing implies that one may pick an immediate cremation only.)
- Include the cost of cremation in package pricing for all cremation options. (How can one have a direct cremation without cremation, as is now permitted by the FTC in the price listings? Later, a $100-$300 crematory charge is added as a cash-advance item, but consumers shopping for prices would have no way of anticipating this.)
- Standardize the description of the immediate burial option, so that consumers can compare prices charged by different funeral establishments.
- Require disclosure of any service charge for obtaining or mark-up on cash-advance items purchased by the funeral director. This would apply to things like placement of the obituary, ordering of a floral tribute, or any other third-party item that the consumer could purchase independently. For clarification, there should be no need to reveal the funeral home's profit margin on things like acknowledgement cards or rosaries that are stocked for resale. But when a funeral director offers to take care of ordering goods and

services, the customer should know how much is being charged for that service.
- Expand the Rule to also cover cemeteries, casket vendors, and monument dealers. They, too, should be required to disclose the prices they are charging consumers, and should be forbidden from committing deceptive practices or restraint of trade.
- Require disclosure of all conditions and cancellation risks on preneed contracts: trusting, "constructive delivery," interest income, fees and commissions, penalties, and substitution of merchandise.

On the whole, casket sellers and monument dealers are eager to see the Rule expanded and have expressed their support for FAMSA's position. The National Funeral Directors Association and many independent funeral homes may not be too happy with some of these changes but they do want to see cemeteries brought under the Rule, especially with the growth in corporate ownership and increasingly restrictive practices.

However, the International Cemetery and Funeral Association (ICFA)—a remake of the old American Cemetery Association with funeral homes added—has sent a letter to the FTC expressing objection to FAMSA's claims, stating that there is no evidence of consumer abuse. Hardly a credible source, when one considers that almost all the officers of this organization come from corporate-owned funeral and cemetery chains. Will deep pockets be the determining factor for how this FTC battle plays out? Not if enough voices demand a change. But it will be an up-hill battle. In the first five months of 1998, ICFA raised close to $1 million for its war chest—for "some of the brightest and best legal minds in the industry." Their lawyers are wooing AARP in "frank discussions." The industry managed to get Capitol Hill to limit the FTC in 1980 and may try that again.

How can you help in working for needed change? A little outrage is a good beginning. But please don't stop there. The best way to enact change is to become a member of your local memorial society and to devote time and effort to the cause or make a donation. There are millions of people who are angry about the abuses of the funeral industry, but only a handful actively doing anything about it. Join the handful. You can make a difference. Your membership and donations will help to build FAMSA's Legal Fund, too.

# A Consumer's Right to Choose: Funeral Planning Societies

## 20

The practice of group planning for funeral arrangements started early in the century, in the Farm Grange organization in the Northwestern United States; members formed burial co-ops. From there the idea spread to the cities, mainly under church leadership. The People's Memorial Association of Seattle, organized in 1939, was the first such urban group. Organizations spread gradually up and down the West Coast, then eastward across the United States and northward into Canada.

By 1963, the societies had become a strong continent-wide movement, and the Cooperative League of the U.S.A. called a meeting in Chicago, where Canadian and U.S. societies together formed the Continental Association of Funeral and Memorial Societies [CAFMS]. Canadian societies later dropped out, and the membership voted to change the name to Funeral and Memorial Societies of America [FAMSA] in 1996.[1]

Although the original reason why many joined funeral planning societies was to cut costs through cooperative buying power, a sense of social activism emerged when societies began to compare their experiences. Low-cost options were sometimes not offered by the local mortuaries, for example. The national organization (then CAFMS) led the effort to require that simple arrangements be made available and to improve consumer protection, and—after other consumer groups added their support to the cause—the FTC Funeral Rule finally went into effect in 1984. Once the Rule was in place, many thought their needs had been met, and energy to keep the societies alive faltered in areas where the societies were still small. Even AARP cut back its staff studying funeral matters after review of the Rule in 1988, reassured—perhaps—that federal protection would stay in place.

Those who kept watch, however, found consumers facing new problems that limited choice and kept costs high. By 1997, the need for new regulation was obvious. A petition to re-open the Funeral Rule

---

[1] From *Dealing Creatively with Death* by Ernest Morgan.

for amendment was submitted on behalf of FAMSA in October of that year.

Today, perhaps the most compelling reason to join a funeral information or memorial society (or *Friends of FAMSA* if there is no society in your area) is to lend strength and political clout to the fight for more funeral consumer choice—both on the national level and on the state level. People join, contribute to, or volunteer for the Environmental Defense Fund or Greenpeace or the Sierra Club because of a concern for an environment threatened by the big-money interests of giant corporations. So must there be a lobby speaking for the interest of individuals caring for the dead. At a time when the consumer may be feeling the most vulnerable, funeral-related businesses—which inherently seek monetary gain—should be held accountable for ethical standards and fair play that will enhance consumer choice.

There are more than 100 nonprofit societies in the U.S. and 25 in Canada, representing half a million people. Membership offers personal benefits, as well as support for a cause. Volunteers in many societies do regular price surveys of area funeral homes and cemeteries. The society may have negotiated a discount for members with cooperating, ethical mortuaries. Planning forms, such as a Living Will and "Putting My House in Order," are also available as a benefit of membership. And if you are reading this book in the library and want one of your own, you'll be able to get it at a discount through your local society or *Friends of FAMSA*.[1]

You will be able to keep on top of what is happening through regular newsletters, information that will be helpful to share with your family, your local AARP, Gray Panthers, civic and church groups. Be prepared to let your legislators know your concerns—especially if the well-oiled lobby of the funeral industry starts raising a ruckus in DC. By joining a society, you will swell the count of people to be heard: Every consumer should have a right to choose a meaningful, dignified, and affordable funeral.

---

[1] Contact information for societies is listed at the end of each state chapter. Or call the FAMSA office: 800-765-0107.

# Part II

# Caring for the Dead

# State by State

I am indebted to the many public agencies that took the time to review their own state chapters. They were under no obligation to do so for a private citizen—especially an out-of-state one—and one who may not have been too complimentary in the text. ("Does your author always write in that tone of voice?" asked one irked lawyer.) Each of those who helped was offered a finished copy of the book; many said they were looking forward to seeing how their state stacked up against others.

If your state did not respond to my request to review for accuracy, please keep in mind that there may be regulations that exist of which I was not aware prior to publication. However, my writing was taken directly from the existing statutes and should be reasonably accurate. If these states have no interest in what is going to be published about them, one has to wonder how responsive they are to the needs of consumers.

~❖~

If you want to check your state's statutes for the latest version, most can be found on-line. For Vermont's home page, it would be:

<http://www.state.vt.us>

Change the two-letter abbreviation for other states, then look for the "legislative" section.

# In Alabama

*Please refer to Chapter 8 as you use this section.*

Persons in Alabama may care for their own dead. The legal authority to do so is found in:

*Title 22-9-70: . . . The funeral director or other person in charge of interment shall be responsible for obtaining and filing the certificate of death . . .*

There are no other statutes that might require you to use a funeral director when no embalming is desired. A 1986 letter from John Wible, General Counsel, Alabama Department of Health verifies this interpretation.

## ❖ Death Certificate

The family doctor or a local medical examiner will supply and sign the death certificate within three days, stating the cause of death. The remaining information must be supplied, typewritten or in permanent ink. The death certificate must be filed with the local registrar within five days and prior to cremation or removal.

## ❖ Fetal Death

A fetal death report is required if death occurs after 20 weeks of gestation. All other procedures apply.

## ❖ Transporting and Disposition Permit

A receipt for burial, removal, or other disposition must be obtained from the county health department. (Someone should be available—on call—even on weekends and holidays.) This receipt must be obtained prior to the release of a body from a hospital or nursing home and one copy must be left with that institution. Another copy must be delivered to or mailed to the local registrar within 72 hours. The remaining copy must stay with the body to its final destination. If disposition is planned in another state, make sure to ask for the out-of-state form, which is slightly different from the one used for local disposition.

## ❖ Burial

Check with the county or town registrar for local zoning laws regarding home burial. There are no state burial statutes or regulations with regard to depth. A sensible guideline is 150 feet from a water supply and three feet of earth on top.

## ❖ Cremation

A permit for cremation must be signed by a local medical examiner. If no medical examiner is available, the county sheriff will secure a licensed physician for this purpose. Most crematories insist that a pacemaker be removed, and authorization by next-of-kin is usually required. The crematory will return the burial-transit permit to the registrar. All crematories are affiliated with mortuaries. Some may resent your desire to bypass their other funeral operations. You may wish to get the assistance of your family physician in negotiating arrangements ahead of time if the crematory fails to acknowledge your rights.

## ❖ Other Requirements

Alabama has no requirements controlling the time schedule for the disposition of unembalmed bodies. Weather and reasonable planning should be considered.

If the person died of a contagious or communicable disease, the doctor in attendance should be consulted.

Embalming or cremation is required before removing a body from the state.

## ❖ Medical Schools for Body Donation

Alabama Anatomical Board*
Department of Anatomy
College of Medicine
University of So. Alabama
Mobile, AL 36688
334-460-6490, 8-5 M-F only
(Check hospital hold facility or use a
local funeral director on weekends
and holidays.)
Low need

Cost to family: transportation unless from USA Medical Center; embalming if weekend or holiday death
Prior enrollment: not required
Over-enrollment: shared
Disposition: cremation; cremains returned by request
Body rejection: none for prior enrollees

* Also serves University of Alabama in Birmingham

## ❖ Crematories

Atalla

Morgan Funeral Chapel
625 Gilbert Ferry Rd., 35954
205-538-7834

Birmingham

Johns-Ridout's Funeral Parlors
2116 University Blvd., 35202
205-251-5254

Dothan

Byrd Funeral Home
3409 W. Main St., 36301
334-793-3003

Huntsville

Laughlin Service Funeral Home
2320 Bob Wallace Ave SW, 35805
205-534-2471

Jacksonville

K.L. Brown Funeral Home
322 Nisbet St. NW, 36265
205-435-7042

Mobile

Pine Crest Cemetery
1939 Dauphin Island Pkwy.
P.O. Box 5347, 36605
334-478-5227

Additional crematories may have been established in this state after the date of publication.

## ❖ State Governance

The Alabama Funeral Board has seven members; no more than four may be of the same race. There are **no** consumer representatives.

No license is required to open a crematory at this time. Crematories are not inspected by the state.

## ❖ Prepaid Cemetery and Funeral Funds

Preneed *funeral* purchases and *cemetery* purchases are **not** protected in Alabama as of this writing. It is the only state where consumers have no protection at all.

Cemeteries are required to post a complete list of prices for all burial services and merchandise offered.

## ❖ Restrictive Casket Sales—Not exactly . . . yet

This heading shows up in only seven state chapters: Alabama, Georgia, Idaho, Louisiana, Oklahoma, South Carolina, and Virginia. (An Oklahoma state court determined in 1997 that restrictions on casket sales were illegal, a decision now under appeal by the funeral board.)

For years, caskets have been the major profit-maker for an undertaker, and mark-up on caskets was often 500–700% or more. As word leaked out about actual casket costs, some entrepreneurs saw an opportunity to cut the price and still make a "fair" profit, knowing that consumers were growing resentful. In the mid '90s, the retail casket business was born. Although I certainly support a free-market concept, I—for one—didn't think the public would shop anywhere but at a funeral home for a casket. Boy, was I wrong! The retail casket market is exploding, and consumers are now saving thousands of dollars on overnight delivery of attractive, well-made, quality caskets when casket prices at the funeral homes are too high.

The Federal Trade Commission encourages this, permitting consumers to purchase from a funeral home *only* those goods and services wanted. As of 1994, it forbids a funeral home from charging a handling fee if a consumer purchases an item or service elsewhere.[1]
The FTC does not address who may sell a casket, but it has very specific language that does oblige a funeral home to accept a casket provided by the consumer.

So what's the scoop in Alabama? At one time, anyone selling caskets but who would not be handling the disposition of the body had to include a copy of the state laws with the casket. That statute was repealed in 1992. (I guess legislators didn't want consumers to become too well educated.) And now—if you ask—the executive director for the funeral board will say that only a funeral director may sell a casket. He refers to the following statute: *Title 34-13-1 Definitions: Funeral Directing. The practice of . . . the selling of or offering for sale funeral merchandise or funeral supplies or the making of financial arrangements for the rendering of said services or the sale of such merchandise or supplies . . . .*

Of course funeral directors sell funeral merchandise, but it doesn't say they are the only ones who can. (All Catholics are Christians, but not all Christians are Catholics.) In fact, the cemetery business is exempted

---

[1] Funeral homes with nearby casket stores have been dropping their casket prices and upping their service charges to off-set the loss. Others offer a discounted package if you purchase the casket from the funeral home. The National Casket Retailers Association has filed a complaint with the FTC charging that falsely inflated service charges—that are conditionally discounted later—are hiding the illegal handling fee.

from the funeral directing law. And wholesalers and distributors of caskets aren't required to be funeral directors. So, someone in Alabama must be aware that it doesn't take any special training, knowledge, or skill to sell a box and that the state would look foolish if it tried to take a narrow interpretation of the law based on what the funeral board thinks.

One person who didn't ask and doesn't care what the funeral board thinks is Tommy Long. As an insurance rep, Long was familiar with what families—including his own—had been paying for caskets. After careful research, he decided that Alabama consumers needed more reasonable choices and started selling caskets out of his home. With four years of steady but limited business, better exposure made sense, and in 1998 Long opened a store-front outlet in Mobile: Premier Casket Company. Surrounded by chain-owned funeral homes with high prices, business has been brisk. It's not surprising that "What do we do about that kid in Mobile?" was the major topic of conversation at the last state funeral directors' meeting.

There are rumors afoot that the state may try to put Long out of business. Consumers may want to monitor legislative activities carefully from now on. In the meantime, anyone looking for attractive caskets for less than $1,000 can check out Premier Casket Company, 334-345-1771. Another shop is scheduled for Fairhope. Long will deliver anywhere in the surrounding areas. (And if the state succeeds in temporarily closing Premier Caskets? Too bad to send your money out of state, but you can call the FAMSA office for the nearest casket retailer shipping over-night.)

## ❖ Consumer Concerns

- The death rate in Alabama can support approximately 157 full-time mortuaries; there are, however, 394. Funeral prices tend to be higher in areas where there are "too many" funeral homes.
- There is no state board governing cemeteries.
- If no other buyer is found, laws should require cemeteries to repurchase an unwanted lot at the original selling price plus 50% of the difference between that and current market price.
- The make-up of the funeral board should be amended to include consumer representation, preferably a majority.
- There is no provision for an adequate description of funeral goods selected preneed nor for a substitution of equal quality—for

approval by survivors—if the selected item is no longer available at the time of death.

- There are no laws providing for transfer or cancellation of prepaid funeral accounts.

- Separate accounting should be required for all prepaid funeral funds, with annual reporting to the consumer. The seller should not be entitled to any funds until the time that services are rendered.

- There is no state protection in the case of default on prepaid funeral monies.

- Until the Alabama laws are changed, it is probably a *terrible* idea to prepay for a funeral or any cemetery merchandise and services, given the lack of adequate protection for consumers. Your own pay-on-death account in the bank will be safer.

- The standards for ethical, professional conduct should be strengthened. That would make it easier for a consumer to prevail when filing a complaint. (See Appendix.)

- Complaint procedures are unclear and inadequate.

- The executive director of the funeral board told me he had no intention of enforcing the FTC Funeral Rule. If the feds are going to pass laws, let them enforce them, he said.

- Identification and tagging of the body at the place of death before removal should be required.

- As of this writing, current Alabama regulations require "a card or brochure in each casket stating the price of the funeral service using said casket and listing the services and other merchandise included in the price." It does permit the funeral home to attach separate prices to each item on the list in the casket, but the total-funeral-per-casket package pricing is not in compliance with the FTC Rule; only the basic service charge may be included in the casket price in some instances. Alabama consumers, then, are probably not receiving a separate itemized list of funeral options from which to choose. If you decided not to have embalming, for example, how much would that save? If you chose to use your own vehicles instead of a limo to the church, how much would that save? The FTC permits a family to choose funeral goods and services separately, selecting only those options they want. That may not be happening, however, in Alabama.

- The regulations require that at least eight adult caskets be on display, but there is no requirement that low-cost caskets be included in that display.

- The law requiring embalming or cremation when crossing state lines should be repealed. This is not only an offense to some religious groups, it is entirely unnecessary when only a short distance is being travelled.
- There is no provision either forbidding a mark-up on cash advance items or requiring the disclosure of how much the mark-up would be if permitted.
- There is no law that allows you to state your funeral preferences or for naming a designated agent to make your final arrangements. In situations where you are estranged from next-of-kin, this could be important.
- Coroners are elected. Some are medical people but, according the executive director of the funeral board, nearly 75% are funeral directors or have an affiliation with a funeral home. When that is the case, there is a serious conflict-of-interest. Consumers should feel free to have a body moved to the funeral home of their choice if a coroner has sent the body to a funeral home that otherwise would not have been selected.
- There is legislative interest in Alabama for requiring that a crematory be operated by an undertaker. Such a law, were it to pass, is clearly a self-serving effort to control the industry. There are only five other states where crematories must be run by a funeral director. In Michigan, a funeral director may not even own a crematory. There is nothing on the national funeral directors exam about running a crematory. There is nothing in the curriculum of mortuary schools on running a crematory. To make sure that some price competition remains in the deathcare industry, crematories should be independently licensed.

❖ **Miscellaneous Information**

- Educational requirements for becoming a funeral director: 18 years of age, two years of apprenticeship, and passing an exam. For an embalmer: mortuary college (2 yrs.), two years of apprenticeship, and a passing exam grade of 70%.
- Casket manufacturers and casket dealers must pay a license tax.
- Funeral directors may not hold a body for payment.
- It is unprofessional conduct to use "profane, indecent, or obscene language" in the presence of the family or a dead human body "not yet interred." After that, watch out?

## ❖ Nonprofit Funeral Consumer Information Societies

Although there are no memorial societies in Alabama as of this writing, you may check the internet directory—

**www.funerals.org/famsa**

—or call the national office to see if any have since been started: 1-800-765-0107. Or let the FAMSA office know if you are willing to help start one. The FAMSA office may have a limited list of ethically-priced mortuaries in Alabama to which referrals can be made while monitoring consumer satisfaction.

~❖~

*This chapter was sent for review to the Alabama Department of Health and the state Board of Funeral Service. I received no response.*

# In Alaska

*Please refer to Chapter 8 as you use this section.*

No Alaska statute requires the use of a funeral director for body disposition. Indeed, AS-08.42.020(c) states that unlicensed persons may be granted a permit to dispose of the dead if no embalming is required.

## ❖ Death Certificate

The family doctor or a local medical examiner will supply and sign the death certificate within 24 hours, stating the cause of death. The remaining information must be supplied, typewritten or in black ink. The death certificate must be filed with the local registrar or subregistrar within three days and prior to disposition. The registrar may grant a time extension in situations of hardship but this provision should not be abused.

## ❖ Fetal Death

A fetal death certificate is required if death occurs after 20 weeks of gestation and must be filed with the registrar within three days and before final disposition. A physician must sign the fetal death certificate except in special problem cases handled by the Department of Health and Social Services.

## ❖ Transporting and Disposition Permit

The local registrar or subregistrar will issue a burial-transit permit. The death certificate must be obtained first. The person in charge must keep a copy of all records.

## ❖ Burial

Check with the county or town registrar for local zoning laws regarding home burial. There are no state burial statutes or regulations with regard to depth. A sensible guideline is 150 feet from a water supply and at least two feet of earth on top.

If the death occurred outside the district where burial will take place, the burial-transit permit must be filed with a magistrate of the court in that district.

Property used exclusively for cemetery purposes is not taxed.

## ❖ Cremation

Approval for cremation must be granted by a local medical examiner or magistrate. Most crematories insist that a pacemaker be removed, and authorization by next-of-kin usually is required.

## ❖ Other Requirements

When the body will not reach its destination within 24 hours after death, embalming is required.

Human remains shipped into or out of Alaska must first be embalmed. If body donation to a medical school is considered, have a funeral director check with the medical school first regarding acceptable procedures.

When death occurs from smallpox, plague, anthrax, diphtheria, meningococcal meningitis, cholera, epidemic typhus, or any unusual and highly communicable disease, the body shall be embalmed. A physician shall advise appropriate precautionary measures in other deaths from a communicable disease.

The rate of autopsied deaths runs close to 45% in Alaska. According to the Health Department regulations now being considered, a medical examiner is not required "to make the head, face, and hands of the deceased presentable..." after autopsy. Indeed, according to a funeral director, the body may not even be closed after autopsy. Any family choosing to handle a death personally under such circumstances may wish to ask for the assistance of a funeral director to at least place the body in a covered container.

## ❖ Medical Schools for Body Donation

There are no medical schools in Alaska. Check the nearest states and consider the time required for transportation. A body shipped out of state must be embalmed which may make the body unacceptable to a medical school if the school's procedures are not followed. Preliminary embalming may be at the expense of the family.

## ❖ Crematories (all crematories in Alaska are owned by mortuaries)

Anchorage

Evergreen FH & Crematory
P.O. Box 100537, 99510
907-279-5477

Kehl's Forestlawn Mem. Crem.
Box 111127, 99511
907-344-1497

Witzleben Family Funeral Home
P.O. Box 140975, 99514
907-274-7576

Fairbanks
Northern Lights Mortuary
2318 Yankovich Rd., 99701
907-479-2545

Juneau

Alaskan Memorial Park
P.O. Box 33103, 99803
907-789-0611

Wasilla

Valley FH & Crematory
151 E. Herning Ave., 99654
907-373-3344

Additional crematories may have been established in this state after the date of publication.

## ❖ State Governance

Alaska has no state funeral board. The Department of Commerce and Economic Development, Division of Occupational Licensing issues the license to a funeral director.

Crematories must be run under licensed funeral establishments

There is no state board governing cemeteries.

## ❖ Prepaid Cemetery and Funeral Funds

Prepaid *cemetery* money and perpetual care funds are entrusted to the care and integrity of the cemetery association without any state trusting requirements. Nonprofit cemeteries are tax-exempt.

Prepaid *funeral* money must be placed in a **trust** in an insured financial institution within five days. The trust must be in the name of the person on whose behalf the purchase is made, with **interest** and any excess accruing to the estate of that person if not used for funeral purposes. There appear to be no **reporting** requirements.

When **cancelling** a revocable funeral account, the seller may retain 15%.

## ❖ Consumer Concerns

- The death-rate in Alaska can support approximately 9 full-time mortuaries; there are, however, 21 commercial establishments—a modest number of facilities considering the vast geography of this state. Funeral prices do tend to be higher in areas where there are "too many" funeral homes or funeral homes that are under-utilized.
- If no other buyer is found, laws should require cemeteries to repurchase an unwanted lot at the original selling price plus 50% of the difference between that and current market price, if the value has increased. If the value of the lot has decreased below the original selling price, the cemetery should repurchase the lot at 75% of the current worth.
- Any preneed funeral purchase that indicates a particular casket should include a picture of the selected casket or a detailed description. There should be a provision for substitution, approved by the survivors, of like quality and construction if the casket selected is not available. It is not uncommon for families to be told, "We don't have anything like that any more—" with subsequent pressure to purchase something more expensive.
- There are no laws providing for transfer of irrevocable prepaid funeral accounts. The 15% permitted to the seller when cancelling should be eliminated.
- An annual report of prepaid funds should be sent to the consumer, paperwork that may be useful to survivors. Such reporting would also help to enforce the trusting requirement and deter any temptation for embezzlement.
- There is no state protection for consumers in case of default on prepaid funeral funds.
- Until the Alaska laws are changed, it is probably a *terrible* idea to prepay for a funeral or any cemetery merchandise and services, given the lack of adequate protection for consumers. Your own trust account in the bank will be safer.
- There is no law that allows you to state your funeral preferences or for naming a designated agent to make your final arrangements. In situations where you are estranged or distant from next-of-kin, this could be important.
- A proposed regulation (1986)—that all human remains be treated in a respectful manner—was never adopted.
- Identification and tagging of the body at the place of death before removal should be required.

- The regulation requiring embalming when death involves communicable diseases should be repealed. Not only will the funeral staff and possibly the public health be at risk, such a regulation does not acknowledge religious or personal objections to embalming.
- The regulations requiring embalming within 24 hours or if being shipped out of state should also be repealed. This is not only an offense to some religious groups, it is entirely unnecessary for at least several days given the Alaska climate or when the destination will be reached quickly by plane.
- There is no requirement that low-cost caskets be included in any display.
- There is no provision either forbidding a mark-up on cash advance items or requiring the disclosure of how much the mark-up would be.
- Although there are other mentions of FTC regulations in the statutes, there is no specific reference to the Funeral Rule. Adoption of this would make it more enforceable in Alaska.
- Because crematories must be run only through licensed funeral establishments, this option is likely to be more expensive than it needs to be. There is nothing on the national funeral directors' exam with regard to crematory operation nor does the subject appear in mortuary curricula.

### ❖ Miscellaneous Information

- Educational requirements for becoming a funeral director: one year of college (30 hrs.) and one year of apprenticeship. For an embalmer: mortuary college (2yrs.) and one year of apprenticeship.
- Alaska has a comprehensive Trade and Commerce statute to protect consumers which clearly identifies "Unlawful acts and practices." Some provisions are specific to funeral dealings, but facets of all others may apply as well.
- Medical examiners are appointed and must be licensed physicians.
- Fraternal benefit societies may not own funeral homes.
- Five or more persons of the same district may form a cemetery association. Land, not exceeding 80 acres, may be set aside for cemetery purposes and will not be subject to taxation.
- Coal mining is not permitted within 100 feet of a cemetery.

## ❖ Nonprofit Funeral Consumer Information Societies

These consumer groups are run mostly by volunteers. Consequently, contact information may change. If you have difficulty reaching a society or you are interested in starting a society in your area, call the FAMSA office: 800-765-0107. Or you may check the internet directory—

**www.funerals.org/famsa**

Anchorage
  Cook Inlet Memorial Society
  P.O. Box 102414, 99510
  907-248-3737

~❖~

*This chapter was reviewed by the Alaska Division of Occupational Licensing (Mortuary Science Section) and the Department of Health and Social Services.*

# In Arizona

*Please refer to Chapter 8 as you use this section.*

Persons in Arizona may care for their own dead. The legal authority to do so is found in:

> *Title 36-831-A.: The duty of burying the body of a dead person devolves in the following order:*
>> *1. If the dead person was married, upon the surviving spouse . . . [goes on to other next-of-kin]*

> *Rule 9-19-102(9): "Person acting as a funeral director" means a person other than a licensed funeral director who has assumed the responsibility for the disposition of a dead human body.*

There are no other statutes that require you to use a funeral director.

## ❖ Death Certificate

The family doctor or a local medical examiner will supply and sign the death certificate within 72 hours, stating the cause of death. The remaining information must be supplied, typewritten or in black ink. The death certificate must be filed with the local registrar within three days and prior to cremation or removal.

If death has occurred without medical attendance on an Indian reservation and if no medical examiner is available, tribal law enforcement authority may certify the cause of death.

Arizona is researching electronic death registration. When that is adopted the procedure will change somewhat. Check with the local registrar or health department.

## ❖ Fetal Death

A fetal death certificate is required if death occurs after 20 weeks of gestation or when the weight is 350 grams or more. If there is no family physician involved, the local medical examiner must sign the fetal death certificate.

### ❖ Transporting and Disposition Permit

The local registrar will issue a burial-transit permit. If the death has occurred after usual business hours, a funeral director may be asked to supply the permit. The death certificate must be obtained first.

The "state copy" must be mailed immediately to the state registrar as a notification of death. After disposition, the original page of the burial-transit permit must be signed and returned to the clerk of the county where it was issued or to the state registrar within ten days of disposition.

### ❖ Burial

Check with the county registrar for local zoning laws regarding home burial. Title 36-333 reads, "Any person who inters dead human remains in a burial ground where there is no person in charge shall endorse, sign and file the permit and write across the face of the permit the words 'No person in charge'." There are no state burial statutes or regulations with regard to depth. A sensible guideline is 150 feet from a water supply and at least two feet of earth on top.

Only cemetery personnel may open and close a grave in an established cemetery.

### ❖ Cremation

When cremation is chosen, the permit for cremation must be obtained from a local medical examiner before the burial-transit permit can be issued. If no medical examiner is available, the county sheriff shall secure a licensed physician for this purpose. A fee may be charged. Most crematories insist that a pacemaker be removed, and authorization by next-of-kin usually is required.

### ❖ Other Requirements

If disposition does not occur within 24 hours, the body must be embalmed or refrigerated.

The body of a person who died from smallpox, Asiatic cholera, plague, typhus, yellow fever, glanders, anthrax, meningitis, or Hansen's disease must be embalmed. If the person died of any other contagious or communicable disease, the doctor in attendance should be consulted.

## ❖ Institutions for Body Donation

University of Arizona
College of Medicine
Department of Anatomy
1501 N. Campbell Ave.
Tucson, AZ 85724
520-626-6084
    626-6443, after 5 & page
Moderate need

Cost to family: transportation outside
    35-mile radius
Prior enrollment: preferred
Over-enrollment: shared
Disposition: cremation; return of cre-
    mains by request
Body rejection: standard,* under 18,
    previous embalming, obesity, sys-
    temic cancer

* autopsy, decomposition, mutilation, severe burn victim, meningitis, hepatitis, AIDS, and other contagious or communicable diseases

## ❖ Crematories

Bullhead City

Dimond & Sons Funeral Homes
Mohave Cremation Service
2620 Silver Creek Rd.
520-763-5440

Chandler

Valley of the Sun Mem. Crem.
19040 E. Chandler Hgts. Rd., 85248
520-249-1100

Flagstaff

Flagstaff Mortuary
302 W. Oak Ave., 86001
520-774-1467

Glendale

Resthaven Park Cemetery
6290 W. Northern Ave., 85302
520-939-8394

Kingman

Beller-Sutton Crematory
2215 Northern Ave. 86401
602-757-4022

Mesa

East Valley Crematory
Bunker Mortuary/Crematory
33 N. Centennial, 85201
520-964-8686

Meldrum Mortuary & Chapel
52 N. MacDonald St.
520-834-9255

Payson

Mount. Meadows Mem. Park
Payson Funeral Home
Upper Round Valley Rd., 85547
520-474-2800

Peoria

Heritage Funeral Chapel
6830 W. Thunderbird Rd., 85381
602-974-3671

Phoenix

Brown's Colonial Mortuary
4141 N. 19th Ave. 85201
602-263-7944

Greenwood Memorial Park
2300 W. VanBuren St. 85009
602-254-8491

Greer-Wilson Funeral Home
5921 W. Thomas Rd. 85033
800-322-1936

Valley of the Sun Crematory
348 W. Chandler Hgts. Rd., 85061
602-249-1100

Prescott

Mountain View Cemetery
1501 Willow Creek Rd.
602-445-4990

Scottsdale

Green Acres Crematory
401 N. Hayden Rd. 85257
602-945-2654

Paradise Memorial Gardens
9300 E. Shea Blvd.
602-860-2300

Sedona

Sedona Funeral Home
701 W. Highway 39A, 86340
602-282-3253

Sierra Vista

Hatfield Funeral Home
830 Highway 92 So., 85635
520-458-5120

Sun City

Menke Funeral Home
12320 N. 103rd Ave., 85351
602-979-6451

Sunland Mem. Park/Mortuary
15826 Del Webb Blvd., 85351
602-933-0161

Camino Del Sol Funeral Home
13738 Camino Del Sol Dr., 85375
602-584-6299

Tucson

Adair Funeral Homes
El Encanto Crematory
1050 N. Dodge Blvd., 85716
520-326-4343

Bring's Crematory/Mortuaries
236 S. Scott, 85701
520-623-4718

Daltons Palms Crem/Mortuary
5225 E. Speedway Blvd., 85712
520-327-4565

Evergreen Mortuary/Cemetery
3015 N. Oracle Rd., 85705
520-888-7470

East Lawn Palms Mort./Cemetery
5801 E. Grant Rd., 85712
520-885-6741

South Lawn Cemetery
5401 S. Park Ave., 85734
520-294-2603

Yuma

Johnson Mortuary
Desert Lawn Memorial Park
1415 S. First Ave., 85364
520-782-1633

Additional crematories may have been established in this state after the date of publication.

## ❖ State Governance

The Arizona State Board of Funeral Directors and Embalmers has seven members. Three are consumer representatives.

Cemeteries are supposed to be regulated by the Real Estate Commission.

Crematory authority is issued by the Real Estate Commission, but a crematory must also be licensed by the Funeral Board. One does not need to be a funeral director to run a crematory.

## ❖ Prepaid Cemetery and Funeral Funds

The Real Estate Recovery Fund covers claims stemming from the sale of cemetery lots. Cemeteries are required to prove financial responsibility for continued maintenance. However, there are **no trusting** requirements for prepaid *cemetery* goods and services and apparently no procedures for dealing with cemetery complaints.

Responsibility for monitoring prepaid *funeral* funds is shared between the funeral board and the State Banking Department. Safe investment in a federally insured trust, inspections, and clear disclosures on the funeral agreement are well-defined. The agreement names the institution *and* account number into which monies will be deposited. (How do they know ahead of time? Is that often left blank?) The Department of Insurance is responsible for regulation of funeral insurance.

A funeral establishment *may* pocket 15% as an initial service fee, although that would be refunded if the consumer cancelled the arrangement within three days. The balance must go into **trust**. If you are making **installment** payments, the seller may keep up to half of each payment until the 15% commission has been claimed. The mortuary may also withdraw up to 10% of the **interest** each year for administering the funds. Consumers may ask to withdraw funds to reimburse themselves for taxes on the interest, once the taxes have been paid. Someone **cancelling** a prepaid account will lose the 15% service fee and at least some, if not all, of the interest.

If a prepaid plan is a "fixed price" plan, all interest goes to the seller, with the agreement stipulating that the purchaser has agreed to this. If it is not a fixed-price plan, the excess is distributed to the estate. Let's hope survivors know enough to check the account balance listed on the prepay agreement before making the actual arrangements.

The seller of prepaid funeral plans must **report** on such funds annually to the state.

The seller must provide for a **substitution** of "substantially equivalent" funeral merchandise if the item selected—such as a casket—is no longer available. A description of the construction material and lining must be included in the preneed contract.

The difference between cemetery sales and funeral sales is easily demonstrated by the practices at Sunland Memorial Park and Mortuary. One Arizona man and his wife arranged for immediate cremations preneed. Each received a "Preneed Funeral Arrangement Agreement" indicating a total cost of $806—$1,612 for the two of them; that covered the funeral director, refrigeration, body pick-up, body container, and miscellaneous items such as memorial cards and a guest book. 85% of that money was, presumably, placed in trust. On another sheet marked "Cemetery Arrangement Agreement," the total was $1,280.28; this covered the cost of two urns ($846), two cremation chamber fees ($300), with the balance for engraving and tax. *None of this money was required to be placed in trust.* Four years later—after receiving a hand-made wooden urn from a friend—the husband asked to cancel the urn purchase and get his money back. The Sunland manager—with calculating indifference but "most sincerely"—replied that the purchase of the urn was a *cemetery* contract and was binding. No refund, not even 85%, even though the items were sold by a salesman making the *funeral* arrangements. In fact, this slick cemetery-mortuary combo operation had pocketed more than half of what the couple paid by writing up a portion of the purchase as a cemetery agreement.

A two-inch thick report that documents the failure of the Real Estate Commission to deal with cemetery regulation was issued July 1, 1998 by the Executive Director of the Funeral Board. A public outcry would help to instigate legislation for better protection of cemetery consumers.

## ❖ Consumer Concerns

- The death rate in Arizona can support approximately 124 full-time mortuaries; there are, in fact, 133. This is one of the very few states where there is not a significant glut of funeral homes. Prices should be somewhat competitive.
- If no other buyer is found, laws should require cemeteries to repurchase an unwanted lot at the original selling price plus 50% of the difference between that and current market price.
- All preneed payments for cemetery goods and services should be placed into trust.

- There is desperate need for cemetery regulation and a procedure for dealing with cemetery complaints.
- There are statutory provisions for vacating a cemetery. While they are thoughtful provisions, it seems a little disconcerting that a cemetery isn't necessarily a permanent easement on the land.
- Although preneed funeral trust accounts are to be considered the property of the beneficiary and revocable arrangements may be cancelled, there should be a statutory provision for transfer of irrevocable funeral arrangements.
- There is no annual reporting requirement to the purchaser of prepaid funeral goods and services, paperwork that might be useful to the family of a deceased to indicate prepayment and that would help to "enforce" trusting requirements.
- While there is a cemetery recovery fund for lot purchases, there is no state protection in case of defaulting funeral providers.
- Until the Arizona laws are changed to require 100% trusting of all money and interest for prepaid funeral and cemetery goods and services and better provisions for transfer, it is probably a *terrible* idea to prepay for these arrangements. Your own trust account in a bank will be safer.
- The standards for professional conduct could be strengthened. That would make it easier for a consumer to prevail when filing a complaint. (See Ethical Standards in Appendix.)
- The statute requiring embalming when death involves certain communicable diseases should be repealed. With low incidence of these diseases, it is out of date, but in the rare occurrence of such, not only will the funeral staff and possibly the public health be at risk, this statute does not acknowledge religious or personal objections to embalming.
- Identification and tagging of the body at the place of death before removal should be required.
- The State Board of Funeral Directors and Embalmers is due to be eliminated as of July 1, 2004. Unless it is replaced by an administrative law office, new enabling legislation will be needed for it to continue.
- There is no requirement that low-cost caskets be included in any display.
- Although a mortuary must mail a price list on request (a postage and handling fee not to exceed two dollars may be charged), it is not required to supply a price list when making arrangements with

someone who is out-of-state. In an age of fax machines, this exemption should be eliminated.

- Although there is a statutory obligation to comply with the written wishes of the decedent, it also would be helpful to have provisions for a designated deathcare agent. In situations where you are estranged or distant from next-of-kin, unanticipated situations might be easier to resolve.

## ❖ Miscellaneous Information

- Educational requirements for becoming a funeral director/embalmer: mortuary college (2 yrs.), pass national exam, and one year of apprenticeship.
- Cash advance items may not be marked up with a commission for the mortuary. They must be billed to the consumer in the same amount the funeral home is billed.
- A statement that a casket is not required must appear on the funeral purchase agreement.
- Reference is made to the FTC Funeral Rule which allows those provisions to be enforced by the state.
- Prices must be disclosed in a standardized format that makes it easy for consumers to shop and compare.
- Medical examiners are appointed and must be licensed physicians.
- In compliance with the statutes, Arizona funeral directors must give out a pamphlet describing a funeral consumer's rights, and it is quite good. It may also be obtained by writing or calling:

  Arizona State Board of Funeral Directors and Embalmers
  1400 Washington, Room 230
  Phoenix, AZ 85007
  602-542-3095

## ❖ Nonprofit Funeral Consumer Information Societies

These consumer groups are run mostly by volunteers. Consequently, contact information may change. If you have difficulty reaching a society or you are interested in starting a society in your area, call the FAMSA office: 800-765-0107. Or you may check the internet directory—

**www.funerals.org/famsa**

Phoenix area

Valley Memorial Society
Box 0423
Chandler, AZ 85244-0423
602-929-9659

Prescott

Memorial Society of Prescott
P.O. Box 1090, 86302-1090
520-778-3000

Tucson

Memorial Society of SW AZ
P.O. Box 12661, 85732-2661
602-721-0230

~❖~

*This chapter was sent for review to the Arizona Board of Funeral Directors and Embalmers, the Department of Health Services, and the Department of Real Estate.*

The executive director of the funeral board, George Beard, was most interested in this chapter and took the time to share a draft of new statutes under consideration at the time of my correspondence. He shared his concerns about the lack of cemetery oversight to enforce existing statutes, and was eager to see FAMSA succeed in bringing cemeteries under the FTC Funeral Rule. It was nice to meet such a consumer-oriented funeral board director!

Don Schmid, administrative counsel for the Health Department, however, simply suggested that I hire a lawyer to read this chapter (that figures, one lawyer recommending another). Because the laws from which I drew the material are written in plain English, I didn't bother.

Apparently, the Department of Real Estate—which controls cemeteries and crematories—has no interest in what Arizona consumers will be reading on these topics—no response was received. Consumers may find that department equally unresponsive when seeking redress for cemetery complaints. Perhaps it's time for legislative change—to put cemeteries and funeral homes under a combined board. Suggested representation: three funeral directors, three cemeterians who have NO funeral home affiliation, one crematory operator, one independent monument dealer, and three consumer representatives.

# In Arkansas

*Please refer to Chapter 8 as you use this section.*

Persons in Arkansas may care for their own dead. Wording for such is found in the following statute:

> *Title 20-18-601(b): The funeral director or person acting as such who first assumes custody of the dead body shall file the death certificate.*

However, Rule II promulgated by the Board of Embalmers and Funeral Directors states:

> *1. Every funeral conducted within the State of Arkansas must be under the personal supervision and direction and in charge of a Funeral Director who holds a valid license from this Board. To conduct a funeral shall require the direct personal supervision of a Licensed Funeral Director until final disposition is completed.*

Statutory mandate gives the board authority only over those in funeral-related businesses. This rule—which would limit the actions of church groups and private citizens if applied to them—is outside the authority of the board. Therefore, persons in Arkansas may care for their own dead, provided that all permits and other health regulations are in compliance.

## ❖ Death Certificate

The family doctor, a local medical examiner or coroner, or a hospice nurse will sign the death certificate within 24 hours stating the cause of death. The remaining information must be supplied, typewritten or in black, unfading ink. The death certificate must be filed with the local registrar within ten days and before final disposition.

Arkansas is researching electronic death registration. When that is adopted the procedure will change somewhat. Check with the local registrar or health department.

## ❖ Fetal Death

A fetal death report is required when death occurs after 20 weeks of gestation or when the weight is 350 grams or more. The certificate may be prepared by the physician or other person in attendance or the father or mother. However, when gestation has reached a period of 28 completed weeks, the cause of death must be certified by a physician. The fetal death certificate must be filed within five days.

## ❖ Transporting and Disposition Permit

A body may be moved with the consent of a physician, medical examiner or county coroner. A burial-transit permit, obtained from the local registrar, is required when a body is transported into or out of the state or for cremation. No burial-transit permit is required for burial within the state.

## ❖ Burial

Family graveyards are exempt from taxation and must be registered with the county clerk before burial. There are no state burial statutes or regulations with regard to depth. A sensible guideline is 150 feet from a water supply and three feet of earth on top.

## ❖ Cremation

If the death was investigated by a coroner or medical examiner, a Cremation Authorization must be obtained from that agent. Otherwise, a Cremation Authorization must be submitted by the person who has the right to control disposition, usually next-of-kin.

Most crematories insist that a pacemaker be removed.

No member of the public may witness the cremation, unlike Delaware law, which specifically permits family members to attend the cremation. This seems unfortunate, especially for those of any religious persuasion in which the family members, by tradition, are actively involved.

If cremated remains are scattered on private land, the written permission of the landowner is required. There are no other limitations on the disposition of cremated remains.

## ❖ Other Requirements

When disposition has not occurred within 24 hours, the body must be embalmed or refrigerated. Embalming or refrigeration is not required for 48 hours if cremation is the method of disposition.

A body to be shipped by common carrier must be embalmed.

If the person died of a contagious or communicable disease, the doctor in attendance should be consulted.

## ❖ Medical Schools for Body Donation

University of Arkansas
Department of Anatomy
School of Medicine
Little Rock, AR 72205-7199
501-905-5180 or 905-5000
Moderate need

Cost to family: transportation outside the state
Prior enrollment: preferred
Over-enrollment: sharing can be arranged
Disposition: cremation; return of cremains by request
Body rejection: autopsy, burn victim, decomposition, missing body parts, obesity, destruction of internal organs

## ❖ Crematories

Bella Vista

Bella Vista Funeral Home
2258 Forest Hills Blvd. 72714
501-855-1611

Conway

Crestlawn Crematory
8th & Vine, 72032
501-327-7727

Fayetteville

Nelson's Memorial Crematory
3939 N. College Ave. 72703
501-521-5000

Harrison

Coffman Crematory
501 Old Bellefonte Rd., 72601
501-743-2021

Hot Springs

Caruth Funeral Home
Sunset Crematory
655 Park Ave. 71901
501-623-2533

Gross Funeral Home
120 Wright's Lane, 71913
501-624-1244

Huntsville

Brashears Funeral Home
509 N. Gaskill St.
501-738-2123

Little Rock

Arkansas Central Crematory
1514 Maryland Ave. 72202
501-374-5019

Forest Hills Memorial Park
Rest Hills Memorial Park
5800 W. 12th St., 72204
501-661-9111

Tri-State Mortuary Service
1219 Bowman Rd., 72201
501-375-8100 Mountain Home

Baxter Mem. Gdns./Crematory
Highway 5N, 72653
501-425-2161

Kirby's Memorial Crematory
Tucker Cemetery Rd. 72653
501-425-6978

Rogers

Benton Co. Memorial Park
3800 W. Walnut St., 72756
501-636-2412

Van Buren

Southern Crem./Mort. Svcs.
P.O. Box 1396, 72956
501-474-6364

Additional crematories may have been established in this state after the date of publication.

## ❖ State Governance

The Arkansas State Board of Embalmers and Funeral Directors has seven members. There are two consumer representatives, including one senior citizen.

The Arkansas Cemetery Board has seven members: the Securities Commissioner or designee; four cemeterians; and two public members, at least one of whom must be over the age of 60.

The Department of Insurance regulates all preneed transactions.

The Board of Embalmers and Funeral Directors licenses and inspects crematories. One does not have to be a funeral director, however, to run a crematory.

## ❖ Prepaid Cemetery and Funeral Funds

Before a cemetery may be established, the Department of Health must determine if there is a potential threat of groundwater pollution. What a sane provision!

Cemeteries must make an annual report of the perpetual care funds to the Cemetery Board. Ten percent of each lot, niche, or mausoleum sale must be set aside in the permanent maintenance fund.

A lot owner wishing to sell cemetery space must first offer it to the cemetery at the going rate for similar space (20-17-1019).

The Arkansas Insurance Commissioner oversees prepaid *funeral* contracts. The contracts must specify the specific goods and services being purchased at a contract or **guaranteed price**. With funeral inflation exceeding general inflation, this may be asking for mischief. Although the funeral home must provide goods and services of "a like kind and quality" to those chosen—regardless of the price at a later date, it would not be difficult for a mortician to coerce family members into picking something else, probably at an additional cost—"I simply don't have anything *like* it anymore"—because of all the new casket styles appearing each year. A clear description of the quality and construction for any merchandise selected should be included in all prepaid plans, and the survivors should approve any **substitution**.

The seller must establish "a **trust** account" into which all prepaid funds are deposited; it does not specify a separate trust in the name of each buyer. Statutes provide that "net **investment income** or surplus" may be withdrawn by the seller at any time. However, the Insurance Department regulations provide that excess funds will be returned to the buyer or buyer's estate.

**Annual reporting** to the Insurance Department is required giving the total invested and the people it covers. People may contact that department to inquire about the value of their contract. If you have not checked on this, the mortician may be the only one who knows exactly how much your account is "worth," and your survivors could be in the dark about what "excess funds" will be due for refund.

Contracts made after July 1995 may be **cancelled** or **transferred** at any time. However, the following note will appear on your contract: "If this contract is irrevocable and you choose to transfer this contract to a substitute provider, the entire amount of the contract will not be transferred and you may have to pay more to obtain 100% of the services provided for in the contract." That actually applies to a revocable one, as well, because all you will get back is the principal amount paid, **not the interest.** If an irrevocable account is transferred, 100% of what you paid—less the interest—will be transferred.

## ❖ Consumer Concerns

- The death rate in Arkansas can support approximately 100 full-time mortuaries; there are, however, 278. Funeral prices tend to be higher in areas where there are "too many" funeral homes.
- It appears that "constructive delivery" (warehousing) is permitted for prepaid cemetery merchandise such as vaults and markers. This should be eliminated, with 100% of all such prepaid monies put into trust against the possibility of cancellation.
- Although Arkansas law is unique in requiring a lot owner to offer to return the lot to the cemetery at the going rate, if that offer is not accepted and no other buyer is found, cemeteries should be *required* to repurchase an unwanted lot at the original selling price plus 50% of the difference between that and current market price, if the value has increased. If the value of the lot has decreased below the original selling price, the cemetery should repurchase the lot at 75% of the current worth.
- There is no annual reporting requirement to the purchaser of prepaid funeral goods and services, paperwork that might be helpful to the family of a deceased to indicate prepayment and would help to "enforce" trusting requirements.
- There is no state protection in the case of default on prepaid funeral funds.
- Until the Arkansas laws are changed to require survivor approval for substitution of funeral merchandise and full trusting of cemetery purchases, it is probably a *terrible* idea to prepay for these goods and services, given the lack of adequate protection for consumers. Your own trust account in a bank will be safer.
- The standards for ethical, professional conduct should be strengthened. That would make it easier for a consumer to prevail when filing a complaint. (See Ethical Standards in Appendix.)
- Complaint procedures are unclear and inadequate.
- Identification and tagging of the body at the place of death before removal should be required.
- The regulations require that at least five caskets be on display, but there is no requirement that low-cost caskets be included.
- As of this writing, current Arkansas regulations permit several methods of funeral pricing that seem in conflict with the FTC Funeral Rule. The Rule requires itemization for all but a specified few options—direct cremation and immediate burial. In Arkansas, however, the following are permitted: Single Unit (all costs of the

206 ~ *Caring for the Dead in Arkansas*

funeral are quoted in a single price including the casket), Bi-Unit (1. professional service fees and use of facilities, and 2. casket), and Tri-Unit (1. professional services, 2. facilities, and 3. merchandise). Regulations require "a card or brochure in each casket therein stating forth the price of the service using said casket and listing the services and other merchandise included in the price." Regulations do permit the funeral home to attach separate prices to each item on the list in the casket, but the total-funeral-per-casket package pricing is not in compliance with the FTC Rule; only the "basic" service charge may be included in the casket price for that method of pricing. Although the regulations include a reference to the FTC Rule, Arkansas consumers may not be receiving a separate itemized list of funeral options from which to choose. If you decided not to have embalming, for example, how much would that save from the price in the casket if it didn't mention embalming specifically? If you chose to use your own vehicles instead of a limo to the church, how much would that save? If you purchase a casket elsewhere, what would the funeral charges be? The FTC permits a family to choose funeral goods and services separately, selecting only those options they want. That may not be happening, however, in Arkansas.

- The requirement for embalming or refrigeration within 24 hours is unnecessarily restrictive and should be increased to 48 hours or eliminated to permit families to more readily care for their own dead.

- The wishes of the decedent will govern if arrangements have been made prior to death, unless—in the case of cremation—there is a conflict with the next-of-kin, who have a right to choose an alternative method of disposition. If you are estranged or distant from your next-of-kin, a designated deathcare agent might be preferable, but there is no such statutory provision at this time.

- As stated earlier, no member of the public may witness a cremation. Such a restriction is not sensitive to those for whom active involvement is a religious tradition.

- The State Funeral Board licenses body transport services. However, a transport service firm may act only at the request of a mortician, effectively limiting use by consumers.

- There is no provision either forbidding a mark-up on cash advance items or requiring the disclosure of how much the mark-up would be.

## ❖ Miscellaneous Information

- Educational requirements for a funeral director are a high school degree and two years of apprenticeship. One year of mortuary school may replace one year of apprenticeship. For an embalmer, high school and mortuary college (2 yrs.) plus one year of apprenticeship are required.
- Coroners are elected. There is nothing in the statutes to require that the coroner be a physician.

## ❖ Nonprofit Funeral Consumer Information Societies

These consumer groups are run mostly by volunteers. Consequently, contact information may change. If you have difficulty reaching a society or you are interested in starting a society in your area, call the FAMSA office: 800-765-0107. Or you may check the internet directory—

**www.funerals.org/famsa**

Fayetteville

NW Arkansas Memorial Society
P.O. Box 3055, 72702-3055
501-443-1404

~❖~

*This chapter was reviewed by the Cemetery Board and the Insurance Department. It was also sent to the Arkansas Funeral Board and the Department of Health, but I received no response.*

# In California

*Please refer to Chapter 8 as you use this section.*

Persons in California may care for their own dead. The legal authority to do so is in the California statutes, Chapter 3, section 7100-1003:

> The right to control the disposition of the remains of a deceased person, unless other directions have been given by the decedent, vest in . . . (a) the surviving spouse, (b) the surviving adult child or adult children of the decedent, (c) the surviving parent or parents of the decedent, (d) the person or persons respectively in the next degree of kindred . . .

There are no other statutes that require you to use a funeral director.

## ❖ Death Certificate

The family doctor will sign the death certificate within 15 hours, stating the cause of death. A coroner will supply a death certificate within three days.

In practice, those caring for their own dead must pick up a death certificate look-alike at the local health department, fill that out and then apply for the real thing to fill out all over again and take to the doctor for a signature. It is hard to understand why the Health Department insists on such annoying busy-work for grieving next-of-kin unless, perhaps, the funeral industry is pulling bureaucratic strings to make life more difficult for the do-it-yourselfers. C'mon, the kind of information a family fills in is "mother's maiden name" or the name and address of the deceased. How much practice does it take to get that right? Doctors have a poorer track record when filling out a death certificate than families do. The information must be typewritten or in black ink, without white-out or corrections. It makes more sense for the Department of Health to make unlimited copies of the real thing available to whomever asks. A blank death certificate is of no use until it is filled out and signed by a doctor. Perhaps doctors will accommodate consumers by keeping a ready supply. If funeral directors are allowed to have them in advance, surely doctors should have them, too. The death certificate must be filed with the local registrar within eight days and before final disposition.

California is researching electronic death registration. When that is adopted the procedure will change somewhat. Check with the local health department.

## ❖ Fetal Death

A fetal death certificate is required when death occurs after 20 weeks of gestation. If there is no family physician involved, the local medical examiner must sign the fetal death certificate.

## ❖ Transporting and Disposition Permit

Upon presentation of a completed death certificate, the local registrar in the county health department will issue the permit for disposition. This must specify the cemetery, at sea, or crematory with final resting place for cremains. (It's fine to say you'll be taking them home.) One copy must be filed with the registrar of the county where disposition takes place and one must be returned to the issuing registrar within ten days. The charge for this permit is $7. After-hours service may not be available in all counties. Therefore, a family trying to make arrangements when death occurs during a weekend may find the process difficult. (Funeral directors seem to be given some latitude in dealing with such requirements in that situation.)

## ❖ Burial

Body burial must have 18 inches of earth on top; with a double-depth burial (one vault on top of another), at least 12 inches of cover is required. Burial must be in an established cemetery, so you will need to check with the county registrar for local zoning laws to see about establishing a cemetery for home burial. According to a 1939 statute, six or more bodies buried in one place—not the cremated remains of six—constitutes a "cemetery." One must wonder if they all have to die at once to start a new cemetery. Local municipalities are given jurisdiction over cemetery matters, and it will be up to local officials to okay home burial in rural areas.

## ❖ Cremation

No additional state-mandated permit for cremation is required. Most crematories insist that a pacemaker be removed.

Although crematories in all states require authorization by next-of-kin if a person has not authorized his/her own cremation prior to death, new mischief from the chain-owned funeral homes in California seems designed to delay an otherwise routine process. The problem? If you were to write out instructions authorizing the cremation of your body after death—knowing the statutes have given you that right— chain-owned funeral homes are likely to refuse your direction merely because it was not on *their* particular form. Anyone making the arrangements will then have to hope that *all* of your next-of-kin with the right to control disposition are easily reachable and that all will agree to sign and fax back the new paperwork promptly. If your brother is on a one-month polar trek, I'm not sure what the funeral home would do.

Let's say you know about the funeral home policy ahead of time and ask for one of their forms so everything will be in order. Forget it—unless you want to pay ahead of time, too. No pay, no form. I think this is called extortion or blackmail—take your pick. If such a form were leaked to consumer groups, no doubt the wording would be quickly changed.

What possible purpose is there for this paperwork hanky-panky? Additional charges for body storage can be slapped on survivors while they scramble to get the paperwork done. More angering, however, these tactics are eradicating the right to arrange for one's own disposition prior-to-death in a tidy way, as granted by law.

The California legislature needs to act quickly to institute a generic cremation authorization form that all funeral homes *must accept.* Let the big boys offer what they want to see on the form, then pass the bill so quickly their lobbyists will wonder how to collect the next pay check. (Forgive my wishful thinking.)

Cremains, having been removed from any container, may be scattered at sea. A verified statement must be filed with the local registrar nearest the point where scattering occurred. Otherwise, cremated remains may be interred—but not scattered—on land; or they may be kept in the dwelling of the person having the right to control disposition. There are, however, no "cremains police" visiting to see if they are still on the mantle, so you may effectively do as you wish (no fines have ever been levied on those who did . . . whatever they wished). The scattering restriction was passed after a scandal was exposed in the late '80s: a scattering-at-sea service had been blithely dumping them on the back forty instead of in the ocean. California consumer societies are actively seeking legislative change to permit private scattering, which is permissible in *all* other states. With the help of consumers who are speaking up, the scattering restriction will probably be lifted by the time this book gets into print (Fall 1998), but the industry boys—with niches to sell—are working against this, too. If the legislation fails to pass, you can pretty much assume that legislators were bought by the industry.

May I suggest a bit of revenge that might put the whole thing in perspective? Plan a "scattering" party. Get a little bonemeal at the local garden store. Could be the remains of a horse named "George." Call the cops and tell them you're going to defy California law about scattering remains and you just want to 'fess up front; you have this *irresistible* urge to scatter "George's" leftover bones at such-and-such public park and you want to warn them. One package is probably enough to share with twenty others if you can find a few free spirits who'd like to "warn" the cops, too, about this "illegal" plan. What are the cops going to do, arrest all of you for fertilizing the park gardens with bonemeal?[1]

## ❖ Other Requirements

California has no other requirements controlling the time schedule for the disposition of unembalmed bodies. Weather and reasonable planning should be considered.

Before a mortician may embalm a body, the person arranging for the body disposition must sign an authorization that discloses that embalming provides no permanent preservation.

If the person died of a contagious or communicable disease, the doctor in attendance should be consulted.

---

[1] Molly Ivins says the airport DEA dogs never did figure it out. It started with an innocent "little white lie" about the tin box wrapped in brown paper that she was hesitant to open during the security check. "Mr. McDuff," it was marked. But one little white lie led to another. With crocodile tears running down her face and a plane to catch, Molly finally convinced the armed officers to let her take the unopened box—the cremated remains of her mother's dog—onto the plane. But you really had to have heard Molly's version of this story to see what mischief a little bonemeal can cause.

If the body is to be shipped by common carrier, it must be embalmed or shipped in an airtight container.

## ❖ Natural Death Care Project

In 1995, Jerri Lyons invited a group of people in Sebastopol to set up an alternative death care resource for their community. She was inspired after helping with the death arrangements for a friend the year before. With Karen Leonard of the Redwood Funeral Society acting as an advisor, Lyons offered to assist families in caring for their own dead. Whether it was teaching the family about bathing the body, instructions for paperwork, the loan of a van, or locating a casket, the Natural Death Care Project was quickly successful. More than 300 families in three years have been helped. Others who might wish to set up such a project in another area can reach Jerri at the Natural Death Care Project, 707-824-0268.

## ❖ Medical Schools for Body Donation

University of California
School of Medicine
Department of Cell Biology/Anatomy
Davis, CA 95616
916-752-2100
Moderate need

Cost to family: transportation outside 30-mile radius
Prior enrollment: required
Over-enrollment: never occurred
Disposition: cremation; no return of cremains
Body rejection: standard,* previous embalming, Kuru, Alzheimer's, MLS, Creutzfeldt-Jakob, ALS

University of California
Department of Anatomy/Neurobiol.
364 Medical Surge II
Irvine, CA 92717-1275
714-824-6061
714-379-8538 (24 hr.)
High need

Cost to family: transportation outside 100-mile radius
Prior enrollment: required
Over-enrollment: never occurred
Disposition: cremation, scattering off coast; return of cremains by request
Body rejection: standard,* previous embalming, Hepatitis B, Kuru, Alzheimer's, MLS, Creutzfeldt-Jakob, ALS

University of California,
   San Diego
School of Medicine
La Jolla, CA 92093
619-534-4536
Low need

Cost to family: transportation outside
   San Diego county
Prior enrollment: required
Over-enrollment: shared
Disposition: cremation; return of cre-
   mains on request at expense of
   family
Body rejection: autopsy, previous em-
   balming

Loma Linda University
School of Medicine
Loma Linda, CA 92354

Repeated requests for information
from this school have gone unanswered.

University of California
Department of Anatomy
Los Angeles, CA 90024
310-825-9563
Moderate need

Cost to family: transportation outside
   50-mile radius
Prior enrollment: required
Over-enrollment: shared
Disposition: cremation; no return of
   cremains
Body rejection: standard,* previous em-
   balming

University of So. California
School of Medicine
1333 San Pablo St.
Los Angeles, CA 90033
213-222-0231
Current donations meet need.

Cost to family: transportation outside
   50-mile radius
Prior enrollment: required
Over-enrollment: shared
Disposition: cremation; return of cre-
   mains by request and at expense of
   family
Body rejection: standard*

California State Polytechnic Univ.
Pomona, CA 91768

Repeated requests for information
from this school have gone unanswered.

Western University of Health Sciences
309 E Second St.
Pomona, CA 91766
909-469-5431
213-690-0739 (eves/weekends)
Urgent need.

Cost to family: none within so. Calif.
Prior enrollment: not required
Over-enrollment: shared
Disposition: cremation; return of cre-
   mains by request
Body rejection: standard* (will accept
   some autopsied bodies

University of California-SF
School of Medicine, AC-14
San Francisco, CA 94143-0902
415-476-1981
Urgent need

Cost to family: transportation to university
Prior enrollment: not required
Over-enrollment: not happened
Disposition: cremation, scattering; no return of cremains
Body rejection: under 18, standard,* Creutzfeldt-Jacob, infectious disease, trauma

Stanford University
School of Medicine
Division of Human Anatomy
Stanford, CA 94305
650-723-2404
Urgent need

Cost to family: transportation outside 70-mile radius
Prior enrollment: required
Over-enrollment: never occurred
Disposition: cremation; return of cremains by request
Body rejection: standard*

Los Angeles College of
Chiropractic
16200 E. Amber Valley Dr.
P.O. Box 1166
Whittier, CA 90609
562-947-8755 ext. 252, 221
Moderate need

Obtains donations from other medical colleges as it does not have body preparation facilities.
Disposition: cremation; return of cremains by request

* autopsy, decomposition, mutilation, severe burn victim, meningitis, hepatitis, AIDS, infectious diseases

## ❖ Crematories

Many of these are owned by corporate chains. Although most had said they would work with a family in 1986, some are now refusing to do so.

Alameda

Alameda Cremations
1516 Oak Street, #208, 94501
510-965-3435

Altadena

Mountain View Cemetery
2400 N. Fair Oaks Ave., 91001
818-794-7133

Anaheim

The Atlantis Society
1440 S. State College Blvd. #2E, 92806
714-758-3848

Cremar Crematory
2303 S. Manchester, 92802
714-634-3836

Antioch

Oak View Mem. Pk. Cemetery
2500 E. 18th, 94509
510-757-4500

Arcata

Pierce Mortuary Chapels Inc.
1070 -H- Street, 95521
707-822-2445

Arroyo Grande

Arrroyo Valley Crematory
134 Nelson Street, 93420
805-489-4717

Bakersfield

Mish Funeral Home/Crem.
120 Minner Ave., 93308
805-399-9391

Beaumont

Weaver Mortuary & Crem.
690 Euclid Ave., 92223-2293
909-845-1141

Berkeley

Sunset View Cemetery Assn.
101 Colusa Ave.
El Cerrito, 94530
415-525-5111

Brawley

Frye Crematory Mortuary
799 S. Hwy. 86, 92227
619-344-1414

Brea

Memory Garden Mem. Park
455 W. Central Ave., 92621
714-529-3961
714-990-9543

Burbank

The Valley Funeral Home
2121 W. Burbank Blvd. 91506
818-845-3766

Neptune Society
930 West Alameda Ave., 91506
818-845-2415

Calimesa

Desert Lawn Park
11251 Desert Lawn Dr.
P.O. Box 485, 92320
714-795-2451

Camarillo

Conejo Mt. Memorial Park
2052 Howard Rd., 93012
805-482-1959

Castro Valley

Jess C. Spencer Mortuaries
21228 Redwood Rd., 94546
510-581-9133

Ceres

Ceres Cemetery Assn.
1801 E. Whitmore St., 95307
209-537-9013

Chatsworth

Oakwood Memorial Park
22601 Lassen, 91311
818-341-0344

Chico

Chico Cemetery Assn.
881 Mangrove Ave., 95296
916-345-7243

Newton-Bracewell Fun'l Home
680 Camellia Way, 95926
916-342-9003

Colma

Cypress Lawn Cemetery
El Camino Real, 94014-0397
415-755-0580

Olivet Memorial Park
1601 Hillside Blvd.
P.O. Box 457, 94014
415-755-0322

Woodlawn Memorial Park
1000 El Camino Real
Colma, 94014
415-755-1727

Compton

Angeles Abbey Memorial Park
1515 E. Compton Blvd., 90221
310-631-1141

Concord

Memory Gardens Inc.
2011 Arnold Industrial Way
P.O. Box 5756, 94524
510-685-3464 or 510-685-3466

Costa Mesa

Harbor Lawn-Mount Olive
   Memorial Park
1625 Gisler Ave., 92626
714-540-5554

Crescent City

Wier's Mortuary Chapel &
   Crematorium
408 -G- Street, 95531
707-464-2011

El Cerrito

Sunset View Cemetery Assn.
101 Colusa Ave., 94530
P.O. Box 7007, 94707
510-525-5111

Eureka

Ocean View Cemetery
Sunset Memorial Park
Broadway at S. City Limits, 95501
707-445-3188

Fairfield

Fairmont Memorial Park, Inc.
Bryan-Baker Funeral Home
1900 Union Ave., 94533
707-425-4697

Fremont

Cemetery of the Pioneers
Irvington Memorial, Inc.
41001 Chapel Way, 94538
510-656-5800

Cedar Lawn Cemetery
48800 Warm Springs Blvd., 94539
510-656-5565

Lima Family Cedar Lawn
48800 Warm Springs Rd., 94539
510-656-5565

Fresno

Belmont Memorial Park
201 N. Teilman Ave., 93706
209-237-6185

Chapel of the Light
1620 W. Belmont Ave., 93728
209-233-6254

Central Valley Crematory
475 North Broadway, 93701
209-233-2101

Fullerton

Loma Vista Memorial Park
701 East Bastanchury Rd., 92635
714-525-1575

Garden Grove

Dimond Service Corp.
10630 Chapman Ave., 92640
714-537-1038

Gardena

Roosevelt Memorial Park
18255 S. Vermont Ave., 90247
213-321-0482

Gilroy

Gavilan Hills Crematory
Habing Family Funeral Home
129 Fourth St., 95020
408-847-4040

Glendale

Forest Lawn Memorial Park
1712 Glendale Ave., 91209
213-254-3131

Grand View Memorial Pk.
1341 Glenwood Rd., 91201
818-242-2697

Glendora

Oakdale Memorial Park
1401 S. Grand Ave., 91740
818-335-0281

Hayward

Chapel of the Chimes
Memorial Park & Mortuary
32992 Mission Blvd., 94544
510-471-3363

Bay Area Crematory
1051 Harder Road, 94542
510-537-6939

Hemet

Miller-Jones Mortuary
1501 W. Florida St., 92343
909-658-3161

Hollywood

Hollywood Cemetery Assn.
6000 Santa Monica Blvd., 90038
213-469-1181

Hughson

Lakewood Mem. Park & FH
900 Santa Fe Ave., 95326
209-883-4465

Inglewood

Inglewood Park Cemetery
720 E. Florence Ave., 90301
310-412-6500

Lafayette

Oakmont Mem. Park & Mortuary
2099 Reliez Valley Rd., 94549
510-935-3311

Laguna Beach

McCormick Crematory
1795 Laguna Canyon Rd., 92651
714-494-9415

Laguna Hills

O'Connor Laguna Hills Mortuary
25301 Alicia Parkway, 92653
714-581-4300

Lake Elsinore

Pacific Crematorium Inc.
571-J Crane Street, 92530
909-674-1962

Lakeport

Jones Mortuary
115 S. Main St., 95453
707-263-5389

Lancaster

Antelope Valley Crematory
44802 Date Ave., 93534
805-942-1139

Oakmont Memorial Park
2099 Reliez Valley Rd.
P.O. Box 417, 94549
650-935-3311

Livermore

Roselawn Cemetery/Crem.
1240 N. Livermore Ave, 94544
510-443-3200  or 581-1206

Livermore Crematory
Callaghan Mortuary
3833 East Avenue, 94550
510-447-2942

Lodi

Cherokee Memorial Park
Hwy. 99 at Hamey Ln., 95240
209-334-9613

Loma Linda

Loma Linda Cremations Inc.
Hughes Loma Linda Mortuary
24684 Barton Rd., 92354
909-796-0125

Lompoc (& Santa Barbara, Santa Maria)

Starbuck-Lind Mortuary
123 N. -A- St., 93436
805-735-3773

Long Beach

Dilday-Mottell Crematory
1250 Pacific, 90813
213-436-9024

Long Beach Crematory
Stricklin-Snively Mortuary
1952 Long Beach Blvd., 90806
310-426-3365

Los Angeles

Evergreen Cemetery & Crem.
Los Angeles, 90033
213-268-6714

Heritage Alternative Inc.
3223 East Pico Blvd., 90033
213-222-8100

L.A. Odd Fellows Cemetery
3640 Whittier Blvd., 90023
213-261-6156

Pierce Brothers Mortuaries
1605 S. Catalina St., 90006
213-731-5179

Roosevelt Memorial Park
18255 S. Vermont Ave., 90247
213-329-1113

Rosedale Mortuary/Cemetery
1831 W. Washington Blvd., 90007
213-734-3155

Manteca

P.L. Fry & Son
290 N. Union Rd., 95336
209-239-1242

Marysville

Sierra View Memorial Park
4900 Olive Ave., 95901
916-742-6957

Merced

Evergreen Memorial Park
1480 -B- St., 95341
209-383-7488

Mill Valley

Daphne Fernwood Cemetery &
Mortuary
301 Tennessee Valley Rd., 94941
415-383-7100

Modesto

Lakewood Mem. Park & FH
900 Santa Fe Ave.
Hughson, 95326
209-883-4465

Monrovia

Like Oak Memorial Park
200 East Duarte Rd., 91016
818-359-5311

Morro Bay

Benedict-Rettey Crematory
1401 Quintana Rd., 93442
805-772-7382

Newport Beach

Pacific View Memorial Park
3500 Pacific View Dr., 92663
714-644-2700

Zornex International Inc.
4000 MacArthur Blvd. #3000, 92660
714-955-1490

Novato

Valley Memorial Park
650 Bugeia, 94947
415-897-9609

Oakland

Chapel of the Chimes, Inc.
4499 Piedmont Ave., 94611
510-654-0123

Evergreen Cemetery-Crem.
6450 Camden St., 94605
415-632-1602

Mountain View Cemetery
5000 Piedmont Ave., 94611
510-658-258

Oceanside

Eternal Hills Mem. Pk./Mort.
1999 El Camino Real, 92054
619-757-2020

Oceanside Mortuary
602 South Hill St., 92054
P.O. Box 542, 92049
619-722-4264

Oildale

Mish Funeral Home
120 Minner Ave., 93308
805-399-9391

Pacific Grove

The Little Chapel-by-the-Sea
65 Asilomar Blvd.
408-375-4191

Palm Springs

Wiefels & Son Mortuary
666 Vella Rd., 92264
619-327-1257

Palmdale

Antelope Valley Crematory
3359 E. Palmdale Blvd., 93550
805-947-4155

Palo Alto

Alta Mesa Memorial Park
695 Arastradero Rd., 94306
415-493-1041

Paradise

Paradise Chapel of the Pines
5691 Almond St., 95969
916-877-4991

Rose Chapel Mortuary & Crematory
6382 Clark Rd., 95969
916-877-4923

Petaluma

Cypress Hill Memorial Park
430 Magnolia Ave., 94952
707-762-6683

Placerville

Chapel of the Pines FH
2855 Cold Springs Rd., 95667
916-622-3813

Pomona

Pomona Valley Mem. Park
502 East Franklin Ave., 91766
909-622-2029

Porterville

Myers Funeral Servc. & Crem.
248 N. -E- St., 93257
209-784-5454

Rancho Palos Verdes

Green Hills Memorial Park
27501 S. Western Ave., 90275
310-831-0311

Red Bluff

Hoyt-Cole Chapel of Flowers
North Valley Crematory
816 Walnut St., 96080
916-527-1174

Redding

Redding Memorial Park
1201 Continental St., 96001
916-241-2256

Redondo Beach

Pacific Crest Cemetery Co.
2701 - 182nd St., 90278
310-370-5891

Richmond

Rolling Hills Memorial Park
4100 Hilltop Dr., 94803
510-223-6161

Riverside

Pierce Brothers Crestlawn
Memorial Park & Mortuary
11500 Arlington Ave., 92505
909-689-1441

Evergreen Cemetery
4414 - 14th St., 92501
909-683-1840

Sacramento

Argus Crematory
3030 Fruitridge Rd., 95820
916-421-5864

Camellia Memorial Lawn
10221 Jackson Road
PO Box 277008, 95827
916-363-9431

East Lawn Memorial Park
Folsom Blvd. at 43rd St., 95819
916-732-2000

Lombard Company
2930 Auburn Blvd., 95821
916-483-3297

Mt. Vernon Memorial Park
8201 Greenback, 95628
916-969-1251

N. Sacramento Mem. Crem.
725 E. Camino Ave., 95815
916-922-9668

Sacramento Mem. Lawn
6100 Stockton Blvd., 95824
916-421-1171

Salinas

Garden of Memories Mem. Pk
768 Abbott St., 93901
408-422-6417

San Bernardino

Mt. View Mortuary & Cem.
570 E. Highland Ave., 92404
909-882-2943

San Diego

Caring Cremation Services
5252 Balboa Ave. #708, 92111
619-282-0505

Cypress View/Bonham Bros.
3953 Imperial Ave., 92113
619-264-3168

Greenwood Memorial Park
Market & 43rd St., 92112
619-264-3131

Holy Cross Cem. & Mausoleum
4470 Hilltop Dr., 92102
PO Box 620367, 92162
619-264-3127

San Francisco

Neptune Society of N. CA
Telophase Society
2740 Hyde St., Ste. 110, 94109
415-771-1805

Pacific Interment
2100 Folsom St., 94110
415-431-9940

Neptune Society of N. CA
1275 Columbus Ave., 94133
415-771-1805

San Jose

Los Gatos Memorial Park
2255 Los Gatos-Almaden Rd., 95124
408-356-4151

Oak Hill Memorial Park
300 Curtner, 95125
408-297-2447

San Luis Obispo

Los Osos Valley Mem. Park
2260 Los Osos Valley Rd., 93402
805-528-1500

San Mateo

Skylawn Memorial Park
Route 35 at Highway 92
10600 Skyline Blvd., 94402
415-349-5047

San Pedro

Green Hills Memorial Park
27501 South Western Ave., 90275
310-831-0311

Santa Ana

Fairhaven Mem. Pk. & Mort.
1702 E. Fairhaven Ave., 92705
714-633-1442

North American Crematory
1020 North Fuller St., 92705
714-835-9313

Santa Barbara

Welch-Ryce-Haider Funeral Chapels
15 East Sola St., 93101
805-965-5145

Santa Cruz

Santa Cruz Mem. Park & FH
1927 Ocean St., 95060
408-426-1601

Santa Maria

Dudley-Hoffman Mortuary/Crem.
1003 E. Stowell Rd., 93454
805-922-8463

Santa Rosa

Chapel of the Chimes Crem.
2601 Santa Rosa Ave., 95401
707-545-0196

Santa Rosa Memorial Park
Franklin Ave. & Poppy Dr., 95404
707-542-1580

Sebastopol

Pleasant Hill, Inc.
1700 Pleasant Hill Rd., 95472
707-823-5042

Soquel

Soquel Crematory
P.O. Box 655, 95073
408-476-2888

Stockton

Park View Mem. Mausoleum
3661 E. French Camp Rd., 95201
209-982-1611

Turlock

Allen Mortuary & Crematory
247 N. Broadway, 95380
209-634-5829

Turlock Memorial Park
P.O. Box 1666
575 N. Sodorquist, 95380
209-632-1018

Ukiah

Evergreen Memorial Garden
141 Low Gap Rd., 95482
707-462-2206

Vallejo

Skyview Memorial Lawn
200 Rollingwood Dr., 94590
707-644-7474

Ventura

Mayr Funeral Home & Crem.
3150 Loma Vista Rd., 93003
805-643-9977

Ivy Lawn Cemetery Assn.
5400 Valentine Rd., 93003
805-642-1055

Victorville

Victor Valley Memorial Park
17150 -C- St., 92392
619-245-4291

Visalia

Miller Memorial Chapel
1120 W. Goshen Ave., 93291
209-732-8371

Walnut Creek

Hull's Walnut Creek Chapel
1139 Saranap Ave., 94595
510-934-5400

Watsonville

Pajaro Valley Memorial Park
127 Hecker Pass Rd., 95076
408-724-7524

Westlake Village

Pierce Brothers Valley Oaks
Memorial Park & Mortuary
5600 Lindero Canyon Rd., 91362
818-889-0902 or 805-495-0837

Westminster

Peek Colonial Funeral Home
7801 Bolsa Ave., 92683
714-893-3525

Westminster Memorial Park
14801 Beach Blvd., 92683
714-893-2421

Whittier

Rose Hills Memorial Park
3900 S. Workman Mill Rd., 90601
310-699-0921

White-Emerson Crematory
13304 Philadelphia St., 90601
310-698-0304

Yuba City

Ullrey Memorial Chapel
817 Almond St., 95991
916-673-9542

Additional crematories may have been established in this state
after the date of publication.

### ❖ State Governance

The California legislature voted in 1995 not to fund the State Funeral and Cemetery Boards in an effort to boot the incumbent administration. Depending on who's doing the talking, the office was incompetent *or* it was the consumer's best chance to see some changes. At least there were public meetings at which consumers could freely air their concerns.

As of this writing, the Consumer Affairs Division of the Attorney General's Office is handling funeral and cemetery issues. It is overworked and understaffed, and one has to wonder whether the public is well-served by this change.

Crematories were regulated by the now-defunct cemetery board; the Department of Consumer Affairs presumably is overseeing crematory operation, too. Does the DCA understand this responsibility? Stacks of rotting bodies were found at a southern California crematory in early 1998. It was allowed to continue operation until a public outcry demanded that the place be shut down.

### ❖ Prepaid Cemetery and Funeral Funds

100% of *cemetery* goods and services must be placed in **trust.** **"Constructive delivery"** can bypass the trusting requirement. "Delivery" usually is accomplished by issuing a certificate of ownership and warehousing the vault and/or marker, although the state is not checking to see if the goods are actually there. Once "delivered," it is almost impossible to get a refund even if the items and services have never been used.

If the price for cemetery goods or services sold preneed is not guaranteed, a **disclosure** must appear on the contract indicating that additional charges may be due at the time of death.

A city or county cemetery may not sell markers or monuments.

Cemeteries must make an annual **report** to the state accounting for all preneed and endowment funds. California has had some serious problems with cemeteries going out of business, due to lack of adequate maintenance or endowment funds. One has to wonder what the state has been doing with the reports or whether the reporting is even enforced.

California requires that 100% of all prepaid *funeral* funds be deposited in **trust** in a federally insured institution. A 10% revocation fee may be charged by the seller if the plan is cancelled or transferred. 4% of the original amount may be withdrawn from the earnings each year by the seller, which leaves little to accumulate for covering inflation.

Commingled preneed trust funds "shall be subject to an annual, independent certified financial audit" which is then to be filed with the state. There is no way for the state to know, however, if some funds were never put in trust.

### ❖ Consumer Concerns

- The death rate in California can support approximately 904 full-time mortuaries; there are, in fact, 757. This is one of the very few states where there is not a significant glut of funeral homes, and prices are competitive in some areas. Consumers will have to shop around, however, as there is a huge difference from one funeral home to the next.
- There are statutory provisions for vacating a cemetery. While they are thoughtful provisions, it seems a little disconcerting that a cemetery in California isn't necessarily a permanent easement on the land.
- Laws should require cemeteries to repurchase an unwanted lot at the original selling price plus 50% of the difference between that and current market price, if the value has increased. If the value of the lot has decreased below the original selling price, the cemetery should repurchase the lot at 75% of the current worth.
- 100% of prepaid cemetery goods and services should be placed in trust, with full right of cancellation or transfer. "Constructive delivery" should not be permitted.
- There is no requirement for annual reporting to the purchaser of prepaid funeral and cemetery goods and services, paperwork that might be helpful to the family of a deceased to indicate prepayment. Such reporting would help to "enforce" the required trusting, as well.
- The laws should provide for full transfer or cancellation of prepaid funeral accounts without penalty or loss of interest.
- There should be a requirement that any preneed funeral purchase which indicates a particular casket should include a picture of the selected casket or a detailed description, along with brand and model number. There should also be a provision for substitution of like

quality and construction, approved by survivors, if the agreed-upon merchandise is not available.

- There is no guarantee fund to protect prepaid funeral money in case of default.
- Until the preneed loopholes are changed, it is probably a *terrible* idea to prepay for a funeral in California.
- Identification and tagging of the body at the place of death before removal should be required.
- There is no requirement that low-cost caskets be included in any display.
- Prices must be disclosed in a standardized format that makes it easy for consumers to shop and compare, but apparently the state is not checking on this, as surveys of area funeral homes show many differences.
- Information on funeral industry violators is no longer available to the public since the Department of Consumer Affairs took over. This takes away the consumer's right-to-know, the normal self-defense against unscrupulous businesses.
- High ethical standards in competence, honesty, and business practice are mandated by statute but they should be more clearly defined so that it would be easier for a consumer to prevail when filing a legitimate complaint. (See Appendix.)
- Provisions for a designated deathcare agent should be added to the personal preference laws. In situations where you are estranged or distant from next-of-kin, a designated agent would be able to handle unanticipated circumstances.

## ❖ Miscellaneous Information

- Educational requirements for becoming an embalmer (funeral director): Mortuary college, two years of apprenticeship, and an exam.
- Cash advance items may not be marked up with a commission for the mortuary. They must be billed to the consumer in the same amount the funeral home is billed.
- A statement that a casket is not required must appear on the funeral purchase agreement. There is also a regulation that requires the following statement to appear on each casket that has a sealing device:

  *There is no scientific or other evidence that any casket with a sealing device will preserve human remains.*

- There is a statutory duty to comply with the written wishes of the decedent. Although the laws are not specific about the ability to delegate the decision-making to other than a next-of-kin, you may want to go ahead and name a designated deathcare agent.
- In compliance with the statutes, California funeral directors must give out a pamphlet describing a funeral consumer's rights. It may also be obtained by writing or calling:

> California Department of Consumer Affairs
> Cemetery & Funeral Programs         800-952-5210
> 400 -R- St., Sacramento, CA 95814

- The Federal Trade Commission Funeral Rule has been incorporated by statute.
- Anyone responsible for the disposition of a body who fails to do so "within a reasonable time" is liable for three times the cost of another person's actually doing so in his or her stead.
- Undertakers are subject to disciplinary action for "using profane, indecent or obscene language in the course of the preparation for burial, removal or other disposition of or during the funeral service for a dead human body or within the immediate hearing of the family or relatives of a deceased, whose body has not yet been interred or otherwise disposed of." After burial, watch out?
- Coroners are elected. A medical examiner—a physician—may be appointed.
- A body may not be held for debt.

## ❖ Nonprofit Funeral Consumer Information Societies

These consumer groups are run mostly by volunteers. Consequently, contact information may change. If you have difficulty reaching a society or you are interested in starting a society in your area, call the FAMSA office: 800-765-0107. Or you may check the internet directory—**www.funerals.org/famsa**

Arcata

> Humboldt Funeral Society
> P.O. Box 856, 95518
> 707-822-8599

Berkeley

> Bay Area Funeral Society
> P.O. Box 264, 94701-0264
> 510-841-6653

Bakersfield

> Kern Memorial Society
> P.O. Box 1202, 93302-1202
> 805-854-5689 or 366-7266

Fresno

> Valley Memorial Society
> P.O. Box 101, 93707-0101
> 209-268-2181

Los Angeles

Los Angeles Funeral Society
P.O. Box 92313, 91109-2313
626-683-3545 or 683-3752

Modesto

Stanislaus Memorial Society
P.O. Box 4252, 95352-4252
209-521-7690

This society is in desperate need of new volunteers. It may no longer be in operation when you read this.

Palo Alto

Funeral & Memorial Planning Soc.
P.O. Box 60448, 94306-0448
650-321-2109 or 888-775-5553

Riverside

The society in Riverside dropped out of the national organization a number of years ago. At the time of this writing, it was not monitoring consumer satisfaction with the SCI-owned mortuary it recommends to members. The FAMSA office has located independent, affordable services for that area, however. Call the FAMSA office for more info.

Sacramento

Sacramento Valley Memorial Society
P.O. Box 161688, 95816-1688
916-451-4641

San Diego

San Diego Memorial Society
P.O. Box 16336, 92176
619-293-0926

San Luis Obispo

Central Coast Memorial Society
P.O. Box 679, 93406-0679
805-543-6133

Santa Barbara area

Channel Cities Memorial Society
P.O. Box 1778, Ojai, 93024-1778
805-640-0109 or 800-520-PLAN

Santa Cruz

Funeral & Mem. Soc./Monterey Bay
Box 2900, 95063-2900
408-426-3308

Sebastopol

Redwood Funeral Society
7735 Bodega Ave. #4, 95473
707-824-8360

Stockton

San Joaquin Memorial Society
Box 4832, 95204-4832
209-465-2741

~❖~

*This chapter was sent for review to the California Department of Consumer Affairs and the Department of Public Health. No response has been received.*

# In Colorado

*Please refer to Chapter 8 as you use this section.*

Persons in Colorado may care for their own dead. The legal authority to do so is found in:

*Title 25-2-110 (3) The funeral director or person acting as such who first assumes custody of a dead body or dead fetus shall be responsible for the filing of the death certificate.*

*Title 12-54-119 [re statutes regulating the funeral profession] (2) This part shall not apply to, nor in any way interfere with, any custom or rite of any religious sect in the burial of its dead, and the members and followers of such religious sect may continue to care for, prepare, and bury the bodies of deceased members. . .*

Note: The Funeral Board for the State of Colorado no longer exists, and no other state agency has been assigned the task of licensing morticians. Therefore, anyone may make funeral arrangements in Colorado provided the death certificate is in order.

## ❖ Death Certificate

The family doctor or a local medical examiner will supply and sign the death certificate within 48 hours, stating the cause of death. The remaining information must be supplied, typewritten or in black ink. The death certificate must be filed with the local registrar within five days and prior to disposition.

## ❖ Fetal Death

Each fetal death in Colorado must be reported. A "Report of Spontaneous or Induced Abortion" is used when gestation is less than 20 weeks. A "Certificate of Fetal Death" is used when gestation has been more than 20 weeks. A physician's signature is required.

## ❖ Transporting and Disposition Permit

The county registrar or coroner will issue a disposition permit. The death certificate must be obtained first. The permit must be endorsed by the sexton or crematory and returned within five days to the person authorizing disposition.

## ❖ Burial

Check with the county registrar for local zoning laws regarding home burial. There are no state burial statutes or regulations with regard to depth. A sensible guideline is 150 feet from a water supply and at least two feet of earth on top.

## ❖ Cremation

The disposition permit serves as the permit to cremate. No additional permit is required. Most crematories insist that a pacemaker be removed, and authorization by next-of-kin usually is required.

## ❖ Other Requirements

If disposition does not occur within 24 hours, the body must be embalmed or refrigerated.

If the person died of a contagious or communicable disease, the person acting as the funeral director must consult with the local or state health officer concerning disposition.

A body to be transported by common carrier must be prepared by a mortuary science practitioner.

## ❖ Medical Schools for Body Donation

State Anatomical Board
University of Colorado
4200 E. 9th St.
Denver, CO 80262
303-315-8554
399-1211, after hours
Moderate need

Cost to family: transportation outside 100-mile radius; return of cremains—$110
Prior enrollment: required
Over-enrollment: not yet
Disposition: cremation; return of cremains by request
Body rejection: standard,* emaciation, obesity, other dangerous diseases

* autopsy, decomposition, mutilation, severe burn victim, meningitis, hepatitis, AIDS

## ❖ Crematories

Canyon City

Holt-Dixon Funeral Home
806 Macon Ave., 81212
303-275-4113

Colorado Springs

Colorado Springs Crematory
225 N. Weber St., 80903
303-632-7600

Evergreen Shrine of Rest
1730 E. Fountain, 80910
303-634-1597

Denver

All Mortuary & Crematory
3200 Wadsworth, 80033
303-766-7007

Colorado Crematory Services
8600 E. Hampton, 80231
303-771-4636

Crown Hill Cemetery/Mortuary
7777 W. 29th Ave., 80215
303-233-4611

Denver Crematory
6425 W. Alameda Ave., 80226
303-232-1239

Fairmont Cemetery Assn.
E. Alameda & Quebec, 80231
303-399-0692

Hamden Memorial Park
Clarkson & 17th, 80218
303-832-7832

Horan & McConaty
3020 Federal Blvd., 80211
303-477-1625

Mile High Cremation Service
2406 Federal Blvd., 80211
303-458-8331

Monarch Society
1534 Pearl St., 80203
303-837-8712

Tower of Memories
8500 W. 29th Ave., 80215
303-455-3663

Englewood

Englewood Crematory
1375 E. Hampden Ave., 80110
303-789-2535

Fort Collins

Reager Funeral Home/Crematory
1530 Riverside Dr., 80524
303-482-2425

Fort Collins Crematory
121 W. Olive St., 80524
303-482-4244

Glenwood Springs

Western Slope Crematory
P.O. Box 45, 81601
303-945-6468

Grand Junction

Martin's Crematory
550 North Ave., 81501
303-243-1538

Greeley

Northern Colorado Crematory
700 8th St., 80631
303-351-0130

Lakewood

Aspen Crematory
1350 Simms St., 80401
303-232-0985

Montrose

Montrose Valley Crematory
505 S. Second
303-249-3814

Pueblo

Almont Crematory
401 Broadway, 81004
719-542-4434

Davis Memorial Crematory
128 Broadway, 81004
719-542-1984

Southern Colorado Crematorium
1317 N. Main St., 81003
P.O. Box 1572, 81002
719-542-1552

Sterling

Tennant Funeral Home
330 S. 2nd St., 80751
303-522-3544

Wheat Ridge

All States Cremation
3200 Wadsworth, 80033
303-234-0202

Additional crematories may have been established in this state after the date of publication.

## ❖ State Governance

The Colorado funeral board was eliminated by sunset laws in 1983. The Colorado Funeral Directors and Embalmers Association, a trade organization, has established the Mortuary Science Commission. The commission "certifies" those applying for recognition who have successfully completed training and apprenticeship. The commission has five members. Three are funeral directors, one represents the clergy, and one is a consumer representative.

The Insurance Division regulates preneed sales. Crematories are regulated by the environmental agency.

## ❖ Prepaid Cemetery and Funeral Funds

Fifteen percent of the sales price of any grave and at least ten percent of the sales price of any crypt or niche must be put into an endowment fund in a state-authorized institution.

85% of *cemetery* goods and services must be placed in **trust**. "**Constructive delivery**" can bypass the trusting requirement. "Delivery" usually is accomplished by issuing a certificate of ownership and warehousing the vault and/or marker, although the state is not checking to see if the goods are actually there. Once "delivered," it is almost impossible to get a refund even if the items and services have never been used.

Preneed *funeral* sales and sellers are regulated by the Colorado Division of Insurance. A consumer may **cancel** a preneed contract and get a full refund within seven days. After that, however, only 75% of prepaid funeral money is required to be put in **trust**, which—in effect—permits the seller of preneed funeral goods and services to pocket an up-front "commission" of 25%. With that kind of immediate financial gain, Colorado must be a "hot" place for preneed funeral merchants. Once the amount of the trust exceeds the total that the buyer has paid, **interest** income is considered "excess funds" and may be withdrawn by the seller. If the full amount is deposited, the seller starts earning the interest right away.

The law is a little vague about what happens if you change your mind. You may **cancel** (or, presumably, **transfer**) a preneed policy after seven days, "for **return** of consideration." How much "consideration" you'll get seems iffy but surely will be missing the interest. If you default on payments, the funeral home is permitted to keep 15% of the contract price (not 15% of what you actually paid) as **liquidated damages**. The math doesn't work very well here, as the seller may have already pocketed 25%. I guess that means forking over the other 10% whether it's in the trust or not.

Not all those selling preneed funeral arrangements are morticians. Agents are required to make an **annual report** to the trustee holding prepaid funeral monies (such as a bank) so that the trustee or state can compare all accounts outstanding against funds being held. However, there seems to be no way for the state to check if all preneed sales are actually deposited and included in the report. In the case of one pair of agents, at least some money had been deposited, and—once the state had audited the account—they emptied the account, with over $100,000 in prepaid funeral money now missing. The funeral homes named as the suppliers for these arrangements have been gracious enough to honor them. Not a nice situation, however, for anyone.

### ❖ Consumer Concerns

- The death rate in Colorado can support approximately 90 full-time mortuaries; there are, however, 155. Funeral prices tend to be higher in areas where there are "too many" funeral homes.
- Laws should require cemeteries to repurchase an unwanted lot at the original selling price plus 50% of the difference between that and current market price.

- 100% of prepaid cemetery goods and services should be placed in trust, with full right of cancellation or transfer. Constructive delivery should not be permitted.
- Preneed contracts must be printed in at least eight-point type. Elderly who prepay may have failing eyesight; this should be increased to ten or eleven.
- The amount of funeral funds going into trust should be increased to 100%, with interest to accrue, to permit consumers to transfer the account to another mortuary without penalty—as would be needed if one moved to another geographic location.
- Although a preneed contract is to "specify the services or merchandise, or both, to be provided," and substitution of equivalent quality must be provided, casket models vary from year to year. Survivors have already heard, "We don't have anything like that any more. You'll have to pick a new casket. . . " for which the family was charged an additional fee. A photograph and adequate description of construction should be attached to any agreement specifying merchandise selected, with family approval required for any substitution if the item selected is no longer available.
- Preneed funeral consumers should get an annual report indicating the institution of deposit and value (purchase price plus interest) of all prepaid funeral monies. Such documents could be important to survivors who might not know about prepaid accounts otherwise and would help to "enforce" trusting requirements.
- There is no statutory provision to protect consumers against default of prepaid agreements if funds were never put in trust.
- Until the laws are amended, it is probably a *terrible* idea to prepay for a funeral in Colorado.
- Identification and tagging of the body at the place of death before removal should be required.
- The requirement for embalming or refrigeration within 24 hours is unnecessarily restrictive and should be increased to 72 hours or eliminated to permit families to more readily care for their own dead and to honor individual preferences and religious tenets.
- Although there is a statute that requires "a broad selection of caskets reflecting a price range sufficient to meet the various financial means of the clientele served or expected to be served," this seems easily manipulated without further definition or state inspection.
- Without a licensing board, Colorado has no way to put unethical mortuaries out of business. The laws provide for a $5,000 fine and/or two years in jail for a limited list of "unlawful acts," but it would appear that no one is inspecting funeral homes or dealing with

funeral consumer complaints on a general basis. (See Appendix for Ethical Standards.)

- The FTC Funeral Rule should be adopted by reference to make it more enforceable in this state.
- There is no law that allows you to state your funeral preferences or for naming a designated agent to make your final arrangements. In situations where you are estranged or distant from next-of-kin, this could be important.

## ❖ Miscellaneous Information

- Cash advance items may not be marked up with a commission for the mortuary. They must be billed to the consumer in the same amount the funeral home is billed. Anecdotally, however, there is evidence that this statute is being ignored.
- Coroners who have an interest in a funeral home may not, as a rule, direct business to their own establishments in the course of performing as a coroner unless there is an emergency.
- Embalmers and funeral directors are not currently licensed in Colorado. A trade organization offers such recognition, but it is strictly voluntary. Anyone may set up a business in funeral directing in this state.

## ❖ Nonprofit Funeral Consumer Information Societies

These consumer groups are run mostly by volunteers. Consequently, contact information may change. If you have difficulty reaching a society or are interested in starting a society in your area, call the FAMSA office: 800-765-0107. Or check the internet directory—
**www.funerals.org/famsa**

Denver

Funeral Consumer Society
4101 E. Hampden Ave., 80222
303-759-2800

~❖~

*This chapter was sent for review to the State Registrar and the Division of Insurance. No response was received.*

# In Connecticut

*Please refer to Chapter 8 as you use this section.*

Church groups and individuals in Connecticut will have difficulty in caring for their own dead. The statutes not only conflict with each other— inviting a court challenge—they fail to protect the interest of its citizens with responsible state mandates while limiting individual choices in ways that benefit the special interests of the funeral industry:

*Title 45a-318 Custody of remains of deceased persons. (a) The custody and control of the remains of deceased residents of this state shall belong to the surviving spouse of the deceased. If the surviving spouse had abandoned, and at the time of death was living apart from, the deceased, or if there is no spouse surviving, then such custody and control shall belong to the next of kin, unless the decedent, in a duly acknowledged writing, designated another person to have custody and control of his remains.*

*Title 7-62b. Death certificates. (b) The licensed funeral director or licensed embalmer in charge of the burial of the deceased person shall complete the death certificate. . . and file it . . . . Only a licensed embalmer may assume charge of the burial of a deceased person who died from a communicable disease, as designated in the public health code.*

*Title 7-64. Disposal of bodies. The body of each person who dies in this state shall be buried, removed or cremated within a reasonable time after death. The person to whom the custody and control of the remains of any deceased person are granted by law shall see that the certificate of death required by law has been completed and filed. . .*

*Title 7-69. Removal of a body from one town to another. . . . [N]o person except a licensed embalmer or funeral director licensed by the Connecticut board of examiners of embalmers shall remove the body of a deceased person from one town to another. . .*

*Title 19a-295. Ownership and management of burial grounds. Towns and ecclesiastical societies may procure and hold lands for burial grounds and provide a hearse and pall for the burial of the dead.*

Compared to all other states, the statutes in Connecticut are a conspicuous exercise in prolixity, scattering statutory responsibility far and wide among various titles that other states have gathered under a few limited sections. When they do show up, statutory directives seem incomplete, vague, and even misguided.

Title 7-62b—re Death certificates—refers to the "licensed funeral director or licensed embalmer in charge of the burial." What if the family doesn't want a funeral director in charge? Title 45a-318 specifically gives custody of the deceased to the family. Other states use the statutory wording "funeral director or person acting as such." This would be more to the point for the purpose of ensuring accurate vital statistics in the least restrictive manner possible. None of the information on the death certificate comes from the funeral director. The physician fills out the medical portion and the family has to supply the "mother's maiden name"-type details. Indeed, the language in 7-64 indicates that only the family or "person granted by law" shall be the one to file the death certificate.

Title 7-69—requiring a funeral director to move a body—is in conflict with 45a-318 that specifically gives custody to family. Furthermore, all one needs to drive a motor vehicle is the appropriate driver's license. I know of no special skills required for riding in the front seat when there is a body in the back. If a hearse or van is supplied by a church group (per 19a-295), presumably one still must have a funeral director doing the driving. Title 7-69 is unnecessarily restrictive and of benefit to a special interest group only (*i.e.,* funeral directors).

Until these laws are changed, church groups and others wishing to care for their own dead in Connecticut will have to pay a mortician to drive the body if going from one town to another. Once that is done, however, the services of the funeral director could be terminated, as Title 45-253 gives control to next-of-kin and Title 7-64 gives that person the responsibility to oversee disposition and file the death certificate.

## ❖ Death Certificate

The death certificate must be signed by a physician within 24 hours and filed, prior to disposition, in the town where death occurred.

## ❖ Fetal Death

A fetal death report, signed by a medical examiner or physician, is required when death occurs after 20 weeks of gestation.

## ❖ Transporting and Disposition Permit

The local registrar will issue a burial permit or a removal permit—to a funeral director only—when disposition is planned outside the town or state. If cremation is planned, obtain the cremation *certificate* from the medical examiner before applying to the registrar for a cremation *permit*. A funeral director may serve as a sub-registrar for use on holidays and weekends but may not issue a cremation permit.

## ❖ Burial

A burial permit must be obtained from the registrar of the town in which burial will occur. Burial must be 350 feet from a dwelling place, one-half mile from a reservoir, 600 feet from an ice pond, and the top of the casket must be 2½ feet from the surface of the earth. The sexton will return the burial permit to the registrar in a monthly report.

## ❖ Cremation

There is no fee for a cremation *certificate* if the death is under the jurisdiction of a medical examiner. In all other cases, a cremation certificate from the medical examiner must be obtained. The fee for this is $75. Once the cremation certificate has been obtained, a registrar will issue a cremation *permit*. The charge for this is $3. Sub-registrars may not issue cremation permits.

There is a 48-hour wait before cremation unless death was from a communicable disease. A crematory may charge for storage or refrigeration if the body is delivered much before that time. Most crematories insist that pacemakers be removed, and authorization by next-of-kin usually is required.

## ❖ Other Requirements

Disposition must occur within a "reasonable time."

If the person died of a communicable disease, disposition must be handled by a licensed embalmer.

## ❖ Medical Schools for Body Donation

University of Connecticut
School of Medicine
Farmington, CT 06030-3405
860-679-2117
860-223-4340
Urgent need

Cost to family: transportation outside of state
Prior enrollment: not required
Over-enrollment: not yet occurred
Disposition: cremation; return of cremains by request
Body rejection: standard,* emaciation, obesity, under 18, widespread cancer

Yale University
Anatomy Dept./School of Med.
310 Cedar St.
P.O. Box 208023
New Haven, CT 06520-8023
203-785-2813
Low to Moderate Need

Cost to family: transportation outside of state
Prior enrollment: not required
Over-enrollment: not yet occurred
Disposition: cremation; return of cremains by request
Body rejection: standard,* emaciation, obesity, under 18, widespread cancer

* autopsy, decomposition, mutilation, severe burn victim, meningitis, hepatitis, AIDS, and other communicable or infectious diseases

## ❖ Crematories

Bridgeport

Mt. Grove Cemetery
2675 North Ave., 06604
203-336-3579

Park Cemetery Crematorium
620 Lindley St., 06606
203-334-8165

Danbury

Danbury Area Cremation Co.
2 Homestead Ave., 06810
203-743-2624

Deep River

Fountain Hill Cemetery/Crematory
6 River St., 06417
203-526-2498

Hartford

Cedar Hill Cemetery
453 Fairfield Ave., 06114
860-522-3311

New Haven

Evergreen Cemetery
92 Winthrop Ave., 06511
203-624-5505

Hawley Lincoln Mortuaries
493 Whitney Ave., 06511
203-787-4101

Norwich

Maplewood Cemetery
184 Salem Pike, 06360
860-887-2623

Stamford

Connecticut Crematory
104 Myrtle Ave., 06902
203-324-9711

Stamford Crematory
2900 Summer St., 06905
203-327-1313

Waterbury

Pine Grove Cemetery
850 Meriden Rd., 06705
203-753-0776

West Haven

Oak Grove Crematory
760 First Ave., 06516
203-934-6050

West Haven Funeral Home
662 Savin Ave., 06516
203-934-7921

Windsor

Carmon Community Funeral Home
807 Bloomfield Ave., 06095
860-688-2200

Mt. Laurel Crematory
807 Bloomfield Ave., 06095
860-688-2200

Additional crematories may have been established in this state after the date of publication.

## ❖ State Governance

The Department of Public Health and Addiction Services is the agency that is given the responsibility to license and inspect funeral homes—*not* the Board of Examiners of Embalmers and Funeral Directors. And what importance *does* the state of Connecticut see in having a Board of Examiners of Embalmers and Funeral Directors? From a statutory point of view, attendance at board meetings is of concern:

*Title 20-208. Examining board. (b) Said board shall meet at least once during each calendar quarter . . . Any member who fails to attend three consecutive meetings or who fails to attend fifty per cent of all meetings held during any calendar year shall be deemed to have resigned from office.*

Is there any mandate to set ethical standards and protect funeral consumers? Not that I could find. The board *is* empowered to adjudicate complaints and impose sanctions, but that would be *after-the-fact*.

The Examining Board has five members. Three are embalmers and two are public members. When I tried to get the names of the consumer representatives, I was sent the names of all five members, with no indication of which were which. Furthermore, although I had asked for the addresses of the consumer reps, I was told to direct all communication to that office. One has to wonder how responsive to the public these members are if consumers can't readily reach them. I have received no response to my mailing to these members in care of the department.

Crematories may be established on cemetery grounds or on other lots with the approval of selectmen.

### ❖ Prepaid Cemetery and Funeral Funds

There is no state cemetery board. Perpetual care funds for cemeteries are usually entrusted to the town or state, as most cemeteries are municipal ones. Religious cemeteries are expected to put perpetual care funds into trust also.

Prepaid *funeral* funds must be placed into federally insured accounts and both the consumer and seller must receive an **annual report**. Comingling of accounts is permitted.

The seller of a funeral contract is allowed to collect a 5% **administrative fee** if the purchaser defaults or moves the contract to another firm.

The funeral establishment is obligated to **subsitute** merchandise "similar in style and at least equal in quality" for any items selected preneed, but there is no indication that an adequate description of merchandise will be included in any such contract.

### ❖ Consumer Concerns

- The death rate in Connecticut can support approximately 113 full-time mortuaries; there are, however, 326. Funeral prices tend to be higher in areas where there are "too many" funeral homes.
- The laws in Connecticut should be amended to protect the rights of individuals who might wish to care for their own dead.
- Laws should require cemeteries to repurchase an unwanted lot at the original selling price plus 50% of the difference between that and current market price, if the value has increased.

- Laws should provide for full transfer or refund of prepaid funeral accounts without penalty or "administrative" withdrawal.

- There is no default fund to protect prepaid funeral accounts. With annual reporting, it is likely that few defaults will occur—but only if consumers know that they must get the annual report.

- A detailed description of merchandise selected preneed should be required to guarantee adequate substitution. Survivors should approve any substitution.

- Although the preneed laws in Connecticut are better than in some states, it probably is very *unwise* to prepay for a funeral until the penalty for transferring an account is eliminated and the subsitution of merchandise is approved by survivors.

- There is no statute or regulation that requires a display of low-cost caskets.

- The law should distinguish between those dying of a "contagious" disease and a "communicable" disease. Immediate disposition without embalming would be a responsible requirement for contagious or infectious diseases. That provision, however, would be unnecessary for a communicable disease such as AIDS, and the family should be permitted to make all arrangements.

- The 48-hour wait before cremation serves no useful purpose for consumers. *If* all next-of-kin are in agreement, *or* the deceased signed a cremation authorization prior to death, *and* there are no suspicions surrounding the circumstances of death, then the 48-hour wait is simply a ploy of the industry to announce, "It is the policy of this funeral home that a body must be embalmed or refrigerated if it is held beyond 8 hours," as I found on some SCI general price lists. Consumers will be stuck with an unnecessary charge for a procedure many consider an indignity.

- The medical examiner's permit for cremation in the case of an *anticipated* death from natural causes is totally unnecessary and creates an additional burden and charge for families.

- Identification and tagging of the body at the place of death before removal should be required.

- The FTC Funeral Rule should be adopted by reference to make it more enforceable in this state.

- The standards for ethical conduct should be well-defined and strengthened. That would make it easier for a consumer to prevail when filing a complaint. (See Ethical Standards in Appendix.)

- There is inadequate public information on how to file a funeral complaint.

- Consumers should have ready access to the consumer representatives on the state Board of Examiners.
- There is no law that allows you to state your funeral preferences or for naming a designated agent to make your final arrangements. In situations where you are estranged or distant from next-of-kin, this could be important.

## ❖ Miscellaneous Information

- The educational requirement for becoming a funeral director/ embalmer is an associate degree (usually two years) and one year of apprenticeship. Applicant must also pass the national board exam.
- Cash advance items may not be marked up with a commission for the mortuary. They must be billed to the consumer in the same amount the funeral home is billed. (This restriction is not always honored by corporate chains, or a "processing fee" may be assessed.)
- Funeral homes may not operate on cemetery grounds.
- Medical examiners are appointed; they must be physicians.

## ❖ Nonprofit Funeral Consumer Information Societies

These consumer groups are run mostly by volunteers. Consequently, contact information may change. If you have difficulty reaching a society or are interested in starting a society in your area, call the FAMSA office: 800-765-0107. Or check the internet directory—

**www.funerals.org/famsa**

Funeral Consumer Information Society of CT
P.O. Box 34
Bridgewater, CT 06752
860-350-4921
800-607-2801 (CT only)

~❖~

*This chapter was sent for review to the Connecticut Board of Examiners of Embalmers and Funeral Directors, the Department of Public Health and Addiction Services, and the Attorney General's Office.*

Assistant Attorney General Felicia Suggs wrote back, "Please be advised that the Board is considering whether it wishes to review the draft you provided. . . . Thus, until such time as a final decision is made by the Board, it would be inappropriate for you to represent that said chapter was reviewed by the Board, the Department of Public Health, or my office."

Attorney Suggs included with that correspondence a copy of a letter she had written to the chair of the embalmers board in which she writes, "After reading the draft, it is clear that Ms. Carlson's overall perception of Connecticut laws governing the disposition of deceased persons is negative and that is how she intends to characterize our statutes. For example, she begins the Connecticut chapter by incorrectly stating that Connecticut statutes concerning the disposition of deceased individuals are in conflict with each other."

I quickly responded to Attorney Suggs: "If I am wrong about this and if, indeed, families in Connecticut may care for their own dead, I would be **delighted** to change my text. In fact, I was hoping that a review of the draft might prompt some changes so that it could be a less negative chapter." I received no reply.

# In Delaware

*Please refer to Chapter 8 as you use this section.*

Church groups and residents in Delaware who might wish to care for their own dead may be faced with growing difficulty if they are not vigilant. After a family chose to handle a death privately, Delaware statutes were amended in 1993 to delete "the person in charge" and the phrase "funeral director or persons acting as such" from the Registration of Death statutes.[1] That section now reads:

> *Title 16§ 3123 Registration of Deaths. . . (a) A certificate of death for each death which occurs in this State shall be filed with the Office of Vital Statistics . . . (b) The funeral director who assumes custody of the dead body shall file the certificate of death.*

Although this would imply that a paid "funeral director" must be involved, there are no statutes actually forbidding families or church groups from caring for their own dead. Indeed, it is usually the clergy who help the family in directing the funeral and whose congregations would lose out if a narrow interpretation of the law were to prevail. According to one Dover official, the Amish take over once the totally unnecessary embalming[2] has been done.

Although morticians were the instigating force to alter the statutes (with the intent to limit caring for one's own dead, no doubt), Delaware's Professional and Occupational statutes begin the section on funeral directing with distinctively laudable aims:

---

[1] One can assume that any legislator who voted for the change was as uninformed as most citizens are, letting their fears and lack of knowledge succumb to the ploys of a greedy industry. Any legislator who knew otherwise should be totally ashamed and embarrassed.

[2] There is *no* public health purpose served by embalming, and—in some circumstances—it may *create* a health problem. See Chapter 16.

*Recognizing that the practice of funeral services is a privilege and not a natural right of individuals, it is hereby deemed necessary . . . to provide rules and regulations . . . that the public shall be properly protected against price fixing and unprofessional, improper . . . unethical conduct . . . . Accomplishment of that purpose shall be the primary objective of the Board of Funeral Services.*

This would seem to document a consumer's right to choose. Church groups and families, however, may wish to seek new statutes to guarantee such a right. There are no other statutes that would require you to use a funeral director.

### ❖ Death Certificate

The family doctor or medical examiner will supply and sign the death certificate within 72 hours, stating the cause of death. The remaining information must be supplied, typewritten or with ball point pen in black ink. (There are four carbons which must be clear.) The death certificate—copies one and two—must be filed in any one of the three Vital Statistics offices (Dover, Georgetown, or Wilmington) within three days and before final disposition. Copy four may be retained by the hospital or physician. Although an attending nurse may "declare" a death, the cause of death must be certified by a physician.

### ❖ Fetal Death

A fetal death report is required when death occurs and the weight is 350 grams or more. If there is no family physician involved, the local medical examiner must sign the fetal death certificate.

### ❖ Transporting and Disposition Permit

A body may be moved with medical permission. Copy three of the death certificate must be retained as a burial-transit permit.

### ❖ Burial

Home burial is permissible outside town limits in Kent and Sussex counties. Check with the local registrar or health officer. The top of the casket must be 18 inches below the natural surface of the earth. Although not mentioned in the laws, a burial site should be 150 feet or so from a water supply.

## ❖ Cremation

A permit for cremation may be obtained from the Office of Vital Statistics or from a funeral director. This permit must then be signed by the medical examiner (or deputy medical examiner). There is no fee for this authorization. These signatures could be difficult to obtain over a weekend. However, both parties involved—as officers of the state—can be expected to serve at any time. The telephone numbers to contact may be obtainable through a funeral director or a local law enforcement person. The authorization must also be signed by the next-of-kin or legal representative of the deceased. Most crematories insist that a pacemaker be removed.

Delaware statutes permit a family to view cremation.

## ❖ Other Requirements

Body disposition must be accomplished within five days. If disposition does not occur within 24 hours, the body must be embalmed or refrigerated.

Embalming is required if a person has died of smallpox, plague, anthrax or "other disease which the State Board of Health may specify." Check with the physician involved.

## ❖ Medical Schools for Body Donation

There is no medical school in Delaware. Those considering body donation should check the nearest neighboring state.

## ❖ Crematories

Dover

Capitol Crematory
61 S. Bradford St., 19904
302-734-3341

Hockessin

Hockessin Crematory
Lancaster Pike
P.O. Box 480, 19707
302-478-7100

Lewes

Parsell, Atkins & Lodge
119 W. 4th St., 19958
302-645-9520

Wilmington

Chandler FH and Crematory
2506 Concord Pike, 19803
302-478-7100

Doherty Funeral Homes
1900 Delaware Ave., 19806
302-652-6811

Silverbrook Cemetery
3300 Lancaster Ave., 19805
302-658-0953

Additional crematories may have been established in this state after the date of publication.

## ❖ State Governance

The Delaware Board of Funeral Service Practitioners has seven members, three of whom are public members, not connected with funeral service. "Such public members shall be accessible to complaints, inquiries and comments from the general public."

Prepaid funeral transactions are regulated by the State Bank Commissioner. Preneed sellers are licensed by the Banking Commissioner and are not necessarily morticians. Funeral and burial insurance is regulated by the Insurance Department.

There is no state board overseeing cemetery operation. The Attorney General may inspect cemetery records. Cemeteries may be run by nonprofit organizations only.

Crematories are regulated by the Delaware Department of Health.

## ❖ Prepaid Cemetery and Funeral Funds

10% of the cemetery lot price must be placed in the perpetual care fund.

100% of prepaid *funeral* funds are to be placed in **trust**—in "an insured depository institution, or insured credit union, authorized to do business in Delaware"—along with accumulated **interest**. The seller must maintain records of all such agreements and make the records available for inspection.

If the preneed funds are placed in a revocable account, the purchaser has the full right of **refund**, with interest, upon giving 15 days notice. Irrevocable accounts may not exceed $10,000.

❖ **Consumer Concerns**

- The death rate in Delaware can support approximately 24 full-time mortuaries; there are, however, 77. Funeral prices tend to be higher in areas where there are "too many" funeral homes.
- Laws should require cemeteries to repurchase an unwanted lot at the original selling price plus 50% of the difference between that and current market price.
- Although Delaware requires 100% of prepaid funeral money to be put in trust, preneed funeral consumers should get an annual report indicating the institution of deposit and value (purchase price plus interest) of all these funds. Such documents could be important to survivors who might not know about prepaid accounts otherwise. Embezzlement of funds that never made it into trust accounts has already happened in Vermont, Colorado, Massachusetts, and Pennsylvania. This reporting would be an additional discouragement.
- There is insufficient statutory provision to protect consumers against default of prepaid funeral agreements if funds were never put in trust. A guarantee fund should be established.
- There is no statutory provision to allow the transfer of an irrevocable account should a person move or want to change which funeral home to use.
- When a prepaid funeral policy specifies particular merchandise, there is no protection for consumers if that item is no longer available. An adequate description (or photo) should be required, and consumers should be guaranteed a substitution of equal quality, with the approval of survivors.
- Until the preneed loopholes are closed, it is probably an *unwise* idea to prepay for a funeral in this state.
- There is no requirement that low-cost caskets be included in a casket display.
- The law requiring embalming in case of disease should be repealed. This is not only an offense to some religious groups, it puts the funeral professionals at risk and possibly the environment.
- The embalming or refrigeration requirement should be changed to 72 hours or eliminated—to permit a family more choice. At 24 hours, funeral homes are likely to make an additional and unnecessary charge, even for the most minimal of arrangements. There has been no public health problem in the states without an embalming requirement.
- There is no law that allows you to state your funeral preferences or for naming a designated agent to make your final arrangements.

In situations where you are estranged or distant from next-of-kin, this could be important.

- Ethical standards should be clearly defined in order for valid consumer complaints to prevail. See Appendix.

- The FTC Funeral Rule should be adopted by reference in the statutes or regulations to make it enforceable in this state.

- Delaware requires identification by next-of-kin, a person authorized to make funeral arrangements, or a medical examiner prior to cremation. "ID viewing" has been used by the industry to tack on additional charges or for manipulative sales tactics to sell more expensive cremation containers. Until this law is modified, persons with relatives choosing cremation should insist on identifying the body *before* it goes to a Delaware funeral home. A more appropriate statutory provision would be to require—as does the state of Washington—that all bodies be identified at the place of death and tagged before removal. This would be a responsible procedure if, for example, Mom died in a nursing home while her children were all out-of-state and where it would be reasonable for a caretaker to identify the body. Cremation could then be readily arranged without delay, prior to any memorial plans. Body tagging is probably a more reliable method to keep from mistaking identities, which has happened *after* ID viewing in at least a few instances.

## ❖ Miscellaneous Information

- Educational requirements for becoming a funeral director in Delaware are: two years of college plus one year of mortuary college, pass a state exam with a score of 70%, and one year of apprenticeship after college.

- Cash advance items may not be marked up with a commission for the mortuary. They must be billed to the consumer in the same amount the funeral home is billed.

- No mortuary may be operated on cemetery grounds or connected with a cemetery.

- Funeral complaint procedures are spelled out in the statutes, with a time schedule for response. The Funeral Board will accept both written and oral complaints, including anonymous ones.

- "Any licensed funeral director may obtain a duplicate funeral director's certificate upon proof of satisfactory evidence to the Board that the original has been lost or destroyed . . ." Let's see, how does one "prove" that something has been lost?

## ❖ Nonprofit Funeral Consumer Information Societies

These consumer groups are run mostly by volunteers. Consequently, contact information may change. If you have difficulty reaching a society or are interested in starting a society in your area, call the FAMSA office: 800-765-0107. Or check the internet directory—
**www.funerals.org/famsa**

The Maryland Memorial Society serves Delaware as of this writing:

Bethesda

    Memorial Society of Maryland
    9601 Cedar Ln., 20814
    800-564-0017

~❖~

*This chapter was reviewed by the Delaware Department of Public Health—Vital Statistics and the Department of Banking. It was also sent to the state Funeral Board, but I received no response.*

# In District of Columbia

*Please refer to Chapter 8 as you use this section.*

Persons in DC may care for their own dead. The legal authority to do so is found in:

> *Title 6-211: The funeral director or person acting as such who first takes custody of the dead body shall file a certificate of death.*

There are no other statutes that might require you to use a funeral director when no embalming is desired.

## ❖ Death Certificate

The family doctor or a local medical examiner will supply and sign the death certificate within 48 hours stating the cause of death. The remaining information must be supplied, typewritten or in black ink. The death certificate must be filed with the local registrar within five days and before final disposition.

## ❖ Fetal Death

A fetal death report is required if death occurs after 20 weeks of gestation or when the weight is 500 grams or more. If there is no family physician involved, the local medical examiner must sign the fetal death certificate.

## ❖ Transporting and Disposition Permit

A body may be moved with the consent of the physician or medical examiner certifying death. The next-of-kin must authorize final disposition.

## ❖ Burial

Because of the metropolitan nature of the District of Columbia, home burial generally is not feasible. When cemetery burial is arranged, the family member acting as the funeral director must sign the authorization for disposition and file it with the mayor by the end of the month.

## ❖ Cremation

A permit for cremation must be obtained from the medical examiner. There may be a fee for this. Most crematories insist that a pacemaker be removed, and authorization by next-of-kin usually is required.

## ❖ Other Requirements

Disposition of a body must occur within one week. Weather and reasonable planning should be considered.

If the person died of a contagious or infectious disease, disposition must be handled by a licensed funeral director.

## ❖ Medical Schools for Body Donation

George Washington University
Department of Anatomy
2300 -I- St. NW
Washington, DC 20037
202-994-3511
High need

Cost to family: transportation beyond a 50-mile radius
Prior enrollment: not required
Over enrollment: has not occurred
Disposition: cremation, return of cremains on request
Body rejection: under 18, autopsy, missing thoracic organs, burn victim, decomposition, AIDS, infectious disease

Georgetown University
School of Medicine
Department of Anatomy
3900 Reservoir Rd. NW
Washington, DC 20007
202-687-1219 8:50-5 M-F
202-625-0100 (other times)
Urgent need

Cost to family: transportation beyond 25-mile radius
Prior enrollment: not required
Over-enrollment: has not occurred
Disposition: cremation, no return
Body rejection standard*, under 20, previously embalmed, widespread cancer

Howard University
College of Medicine
Department of Anatomy
Washington, DC 20059
202-806-6555
202-726-1089
Moderate need

Cost to family: transportation beyond 50 miles
Prior enrollment: preferred
Over-enrollment: shared
Disposition: cremation
Body rejection: standard*

*autopsy, decomposition, mutilation, severe burn victim, meningitis, hepatitis, AIDS, infectious diseases

## ❖ Crematories

Cedar Hill Cemetery
4000 Suitland Road S.E.
Washington, DC 20023
202-568-5400

Additional crematories may have been established in this state after the date of publication.

## ❖ District Governance

The District of Columbia Funeral Board has five members. Three are funeral directors, one is the director of the Department of Human Services, and one is a consumer representative.

Cemeteries must register with the Department of Human Services. Cemetery land is tax-exempt.

Crematories must be built on cemetery grounds unless permission is granted in writing from more than half the property owners within a radius of 200 feet of the property line.

## ❖ Prepaid Cemetery and Funeral Funds

There is no protection for prepaid cemetery or funeral transactions in the District.

## ❖ Consumer Concerns

- The death rate in DC can support approximately 27 full-time mortuaries; there are 40.
- Laws should require cemeteries to repurchase an unwanted lot at the original selling price plus 50% of the difference between that and current market price, if the value has increased. If the value of the lot has decreased below the original selling price, the cemetery should repurchase the lot at 75% of the current worth.
- 100% of prepaid funeral money and prepaid cemetery goods and services should be placed in trust, with interest to accrue.
- There is no requirement for reporting to the consumer annually where the money is and how much is there, paperwork that would be useful to survivors and which would help to enforce any trusting requirements once they are established.

- There is no provision for an adequate description of funeral goods selected preneed nor for a substitution of equal quality and construction if the selected item is no longer available at the time of death. Any substitution should be approved by the survivors.
- There is no provision for cancellation of prepaid funeral contracts with a full refund of principal and interest, nor for transfer to another funeral home if the agreement is irrevocable.
- Until there is a District effort to regulate preneed sales of cemetery and funeral purchases, it is a *terrible* idea to prepay for either in the District.
- The coroner or medical examiner's permit for cremation in the case of an *anticipated* death from natural causes is totally unnecessary and creates an additional burden and charge for families.
- Identification and tagging of the body at the place of death before removal should be required, given the regular mix-ups that have been happening at chain-owned establishments with central prep facilities.
- There is no requirement that low-cost caskets be included in a casket display.
- The standards for ethical conduct should be strengthened. That would make it easier for a consumer to prevail when filing a complaint.
- Detailed and explicit procedures should be available to anyone wishing to file a complaint.
- The FTC Funeral Rule should be adopted by reference in the regulations to make it more enforceable by the District.

## ❖ Miscellaneous Information

- Educational requirements for becoming a funeral director: mortuary college (at least one year), two years of apprenticeship, and an exam. If the applicant has a two-year degree, only one year of apprenticeship is required.
- The District maintains a crematory at the Washington Asylum and Jail for disposition at public expense.
- The mayor may pay a maximum of $450 for funeral services and a plot for indigents.
- Cash advance items must be billed in the amount paid. Interest may be charged for a balance unpaid beyond 30 days.
- No person may engage in the practice of funeral directing while employed either part-time or full-time by a nursing home, hospital, morgue, or ambulance service.

- Preference is given to the written wishes of the deceased. A person may also designate an agent to make after-death arrangements.
- Medical examiners are appointed physicians.

## ❖ Nonprofit Funeral Consumer Information Societies

These consumer groups are run mostly by volunteers. Consequently, contact information may change. If you have difficulty reaching this society, call the FAMSA office: 800-765-0107. Or check the internet directory—

**www.funerals.org/famsa**

Memorial Society of Metropolitan Washington
1500 Harvard St. NW
Washington, DC 20009
202-234-7777

~❖~

*This chapter was sent for review to the District Funeral Board. I received no response prior to publication.*

# In Florida

*Please refer to Chapter 8 as you use this section.*

In 1987, immediately after publication of my first book, the Florida statutes were amended to delete "or other person acting as such" from the statute I cited and from related statutes.

> *Old statute: FS 382.061 Burial-transit permit— (1) The funeral director or person acting as such who first assumes custody of a dead body or fetus shall obtain a burial-transit permit prior to final disposition . . .*

> *New statute: FS 382.006 Burial-transit permit— (1) The funeral director who first assumes custody of a dead body or fetus must obtain a burial-transit permit . . . . The application for a burial-transit permit must be signed by the funeral director and include the funeral director's license number.*

This does not have to be construed restrictively, however. In checking this chapter prior to publication, the Vital Statistics Administrator, Kenneth Jones, pointed out that the definition of "funeral director" now reads:

> *Chapter 382.002(7) "Funeral Director" means a licensed funeral director or direct disposer licensed pursuant to Chapter 470 or **other person who first assumes custody** [emphasis added] of or effects the final disposition of a dead body or a fetus as described in subsection (5).*

Therefore, next-of-kin and designated death care agents claiming custody of the body may care for their own dead in Florida.

## ❖ Death Certificate

It is the responsibility of the person acting as a funeral director to prepare a typewritten death certificate with all required information and take to the physician or medical examiner for completion of the medical certification of death. The attending physician or district medical examiner will sign the death certificate within 72 hours after presentation. The death certificate must be filed in the county of death within five days of death and before final disposition.

Florida is researching electronic death registration. When that is adopted the procedure will change somewhat. Check with the local health department.

## ❖ Fetal Death

A fetal death certificate is required when death occurs after 20 weeks of gestation. If there is no family physician involved, the district medical examiner must sign the fetal death certificate.

## ❖ Transporting and Disposition Permit

The local registrar or deputy registrar in the county health department will issue the burial-transit permit after you file the death certificate. There is no fee for this permit. The permit must be obtained within five days after death and prior to final disposition of the body. It must be filed in the county where disposition takes place, within ten days.

## ❖ Burial

Check with the county zoning commission regarding home burial. Cemeteries of less than five acres do not need to be registered with the state Board of Funeral and Cemetery Services. There are no state burial statutes or regulations with regard to depth. A sensible guideline is 150 feet from a water supply and three feet of earth on top.

When burial is arranged, the family member acting as the funeral director must sign the burial-transit permit and deliver it to the local registrar within 10 days. If there is no person in charge, the words "no person in charge" must be written across the face of the permit.

## ❖ Cremation

A medical examiner's authorization on the burial-transit permit is required for cremation. The usual charge for this varies from one county to the next. There is a 48-hour wait before cremation. After the first 24 hours, refrigeration is required. Most large hospitals have refrigeration facilities, but if the storage becomes crowded, removal may be requested. All but a few crematories have refrigerated storage for which a fee is charged.

Most crematories insist that a pacemaker be removed, and authorization by next-of-kin usually is required. The crematory will sign the disposition permit which must be filed with the local registrar within 10 days.

## ❖ Other Requirements

Refrigeration or embalming is required after 24 hours.

If the person died of a contagious or communicable disease, the doctor in attendance should be consulted.

## ❖ Medical Schools for Body Donation

There is one agency for body donation in Florida:

Fla. State Anatomical Board
P.O. Box 100235
Health Science Center
Univ. of Florida
College of Medicine
Gainesville, FL 32610-0235
352-392-3588 (Gainesville)
305-547-6691 (Miami)
800-628-2594
High need

Cost to family: transportation to Gainesville or Miami and embalming
Prior enrollment: not required
Over-enrollment: has not occurred
Disposition: cremation; return of cremains by request
Body rejection: autopsy, crushing injury, decomposition, contagious disease

## ❖ Crematories

Avon Park

> Highlands Crematory
> 111 E. Circle, 33825
> 813-453-3101

> Lake Forest Crematory
> 507 U.S. 27 North, 33852
> 813-453-3134

Beverly Hills

> Memorial Gardens
> 5891 N. Lecanto Hwy.,32665
> 904-746-4646

Big Pine Key

> Memorial Gardens
> Mile Marker 31, 33043
> 305-743-5177

Boynton Beach

> Palm Beach Memorial Park
> 3691 Seacrest Blvd., 33435
> 305-585-6444

Bradenton

> Griffith Cline FH
> 720 Manatee Ave., 34205
> 813-748-1011

Brandon

> TampaBay Crem/Stowers FH
> 401 W. Brandon Blvd., 33511
> 813-689-9156 or 1121

Brooksville

> Brewer Memorial FH
> 1190 S. Broad St., 34601
> 904-796-4991

Cape Coral

Griffith Kilne
P.O. Box 9420, 34206
813-748-1011

Clearwater

Bay Area Crematory
5862 Ulmerton Rd., 34620
813-531-8200

National Cremation Society
4945 E Bay Dr., 34624
813-536-0494

No. Amer. Cremation Soc.
P.O. Box 895, 34617
813-733-0073

Rhodes Funeral Directors
800 E. Druid Rd., 34617
813-446-3055

Sylvan Abbey Mem. Park
2860 SR 588, 33510
813-796-1992

Coral Gables

Caballero Woodlawn FH
1661 Douglas Rd., 33145
305-444-6511

Cocoa

Cocoa Cremation Service
6 Poinsettia Dr., 32922
407-636-2441

Crestview

Mclaughlin-Aultman FH
429 E. Pine Ave., 32539
904-682-2252

Daytona

Tri-City Diversified Svcs.
3713 Old Deland Rd., 32114
904-255-7623

Volusia Co. Cremation Soc.
1425 Bellevue Ave., 32014
904-252-3100

Delray Beach

Delray Crematory
320 N. 5th, 334444
305-276-7474

Deltona

Stephen R. Baldauff FH
1233 Saxon Rd.
P.O. Box 128, 32727-0128
904-775-2101

Dunnellon

Fero FH/Crematory
US 41 N., 34465
904-746-4551

Roberts Funeral Home
19939E. Penn Ave., 32630
904-489-2429

Ft. Lauderdale

All State Cremation Service
6061 NE 14th Ave., 33334
305-523-6700

Broward Crematory
4343 N. Federal Hwy, 33308
305-492-4000

Cremation Systems
225 SW 21st Terr., 33312
305-581-6666

Fairchild FH & Crematory
3501 W.Broward Blvd, 33312
305-581-6100

Gold Coast Crematory
796 NW 57th St., 33309
305-491-0490

Kalis Funeral Home
2505 N. Dixie Hwy., 33305
305-566-7621

Ft. Meyers

Ft. Meyers Crematory
2200 Crystal, Dr., 33907
813-936-1053

Harvey Crematory
1600 Colonial Blvd., 33907
813-936-2177

Ft. Pierce

Ft. Pierce Crematory
1101 U.S. #1, 33450
305-461-7000

Haisley-Hobbs Crematory
3015 Okeechobee Rd. 33450
305-461-5211

Gainesville

Colonial Crematory
404 N. Main St., 32601
904-376-7557

Johnson-Hayes FH
311 S. Main St., 32601
904-376-5361

Golden Gate

Casto Funeral Home, Inc.
2772 Santa Barbara, 33999
813-455-2221

Hollywood

Boyd's Family Funeral Home
6400 Hollywood Blvd., 33024
305-983-6400

Cremations Inc.
6107-A Miramar Pkwy 33023
305-989-1550

Fred Hunter FH/Crematory
6301 Taft St., 33024
305-989-1550
800-835-7070

Homosassa

Fountains Mem. Park
5635 W. Green Acres, 32646
904-628-2555

Inverness

Davis FH/Crematory
3075 S. Florida Ave., 34450
904-726-8323

Hooper FH/Crematory
501 W. Main St., 32650
904-726-2271

Jacksonville

Evergreen Cemetery
4535 Main St., 32206
904-353-3649

Key Largo

H.W. Beyer Funeral Home
P.O. Drawer 3000, 33037
305-451-1444

Key West

Dean-Lopez Funeral Home
418 Simenton St., 33040
305-573-4310

Lady Lake

All Faiths Cremation Soc.
18 LaGrande Blvd., 32159
904-753-2612

Lake Worth

All County Mortuary
1107 Lake Ave., 33460
407-627-9482

Callaway Vault/Crematory
1933 8th Ave. N., 33460
407-582-1964

Earl Smith East Chapel
1032 N. Dixie Hwy., 33460
407-582-3341

Earl Smith West Chapel
3772 S. Military Trail, 33463
407-964-3772

Necron Cremation Srvcs.
429 S. Dixie Hwy., 33460
407-582-2273

Lakeland

Central Fla. Crematory
717 Griffin Rd., 33805

Lakeland Crematory
1833 S. Florida Ave., 33806
941-682-3155

Polk Co. Crematory
328 S. Ingraham Ave., 33801
941-682-0111

Leesburg

Beyers Funeral Inc.
1123 W. Main St., 32748
904-787-4343

Lehigh

Lee Memorial Park
Highway 82, 33970
813-334-4880

Miami

Caballero Funeral Homes
2546 SW 8th St., 33135
305-642-6716

J.B. Cofer Funeral Home
10931 NE 6th Ave., 33161
305-754-7544

Lithgow Funeral Centers
485 NE 54th St., 33137
305-757-5544

S. Florida Crematory, Inc.
1495 NW 17th Ave., 33125
305-325-1171 / 800-252-7385

VanOrsdel Funeral Chapels
3333 2nd Ave. NE, 33137
305-573-4310

Woodlawn Park Cemetery
3260 SW 8th St., 33135
305-445-5425

Miramar

Cremations, Inc.
6107 Miramar Blvd., 33023
305-925-7577

Mt. Dora

AAA Cremation Services
550 S. Highland St., 32757
904-735-1288

Naples

Beachwood Society
2900 14th St. N. #21, 33940
800-368-0960

E.G. Hodges Funeral Chapel
3520 Tamiami Tr. N., 33940
813-261-1237

D. K. Johnson Crematorium
4424 E. Tamiami Trail 33962
813-774-3444

New Smyrna Beach

Baldwin-Hughey FH/Crem.
Halifax Cremation Society
1 N. Causway, 32169
904-428-2424

Ocoee

Quality Vaults
751 S. Bluford Ave., 34761
407-656-8781

Orange Park

Rivermead FH & Crematory
950 Park Ave., 32073
904-264-2481

Orlando

Atlas Crematory-Vaults
6452 E. Colonial Dr., 32853
407-277-0841

Baldwin-Fairchild
301 N. Ivanhoe Blvd., 32804
407-898-8111

Orange Co. Crematory
600 Wilkinson, 32803
305-898-7882

Palm Beach

Royal Palm Mem. Gardens
5601 Greenwood Ave., 33407
407-848-8659

Palm Bay

Fountain Head Mem. Park
2929 S. Babcock St., 32906
305-724-2861 or 727-3993

Palm Harbor

Curlew Hills Mem. Gardens
1750 Curlew Rd., 33563
813-785-4428

Pinellas Park

Internat'l Mortuary Services
4617 73rd Ave. N., 34665
800-228-8844

Pompano Beach

R. Jay Kraeer Crematory
200 N. Federal Hwy., 33062
305-941-4111

Port Charlotte

Robertson Crematory
2151 Tamiami Tr., 33949
813-629-3141

Punta Gorda

Charlotte Memorial Gardens
5200 Indian Spgs Rd., 33950
813-639-1171

Royal Palm Mem. Gardens
27200 Jones Loop Rd., 33950
813-639-2381

Quincy

Adams-Sasser FH/Crematory
22 S. Madison St., 32351
904-627-7535

San Mateo

Southern Crematory
US Hwy. 17 S., 32088
904-328-1919

Sarasota

Jackson-Lew Funeral Home
5750 Swift Rd., 33581
813-922-3551

Manasota Mem. Park
P.O. Box 3109, 33578
813-755-2688

Sara-Mana Crematory
135 N. Lime Ave., 33597
813-365-1767

Universal Cremation Society
2944 Constitution Blvd., 34231
813-795-7000

Sebring

Warren-Morris FH
307 S. Commerce Ave., 33870
813-385-0101

Seminole

Pinellas Crematory
6767 Seminole Blvd., 34642
813-391-9954

Spring Hill

Turner Crematory
14360 Spring Hill Dr., 34609
904-796-3588

St. Petersburg

Anderson-McQueen FH
2201 9th St. N., 33704
813-822-2059

Directors Services
3121 44th Ave. N., 33714
813-527-5667

Woodlawn Mem. Gardens
101 58th St. S., 33707
813-345-9393

St. Petersburg Beach

Beach Memorial Chapel
301 Corey Ave., 33736
813-360-5577

Stuart

Tri-County Crematory
505 S. Federal, 30497
305-287-1717

Sunrise

Leo Arsenault
2001 NW 98th Ave., 33322
305-742-6068

Tampa

F.T. Blount
5101 Nebraska Ave., 33603
813-237-3336

Florida Mortuary
4601 N. Nebraska Ave., 33603
813-237-2900

Garden of Memories
4207 E. Lake Ave., 33610
813-626-3161

Hillsboro Memorial FH
2323 W. Brandon Blvd., 33511
813-689-8121

Venice

Crematory of Venice
265 S. Nokomis Ave., 33595
813-488-2291

Vero Beach

Cox-Gifford Funeral Home
1950 20th St., 32960
407-562-2365

West Palm Beach

Northwood Funeral Home
5608 Broadway, 33407
407-844-4311

Royal Palm Mem. Gardens
5601 Greenwood Ave., 33407
407-848-8695

Winter Garden

Woodlawn Mem. Park
400 Woodlawn Rd., 34787
407-293-1361

Winter Park

Baldwin-Fairchild FH
1201 W. Orchard Ave., 32789
407-740-7000

There may be additional crematories established after the date of publication.

## ❖ State Governance

There are two "funeral boards" in Florida—one that covers general funeral business (what could be described as at-need services), and one for cemetery and preneed transactions. Because preneed contracts are ultimately used at a time of need, one has to wonder how efficient this dual regulation is.

The Board of Funeral Directors and Embalmers is under the Department of Business and Professional Regulation. Of the seven members, five must be funeral directors, with no more than two of those having an interest in a cemetery. Two are public members, at least one of which is 60 years of age or older. This board regulates funeral homes, funeral directors, direct disposers, refrigeration facilities, body transport services, embalming facilities, and crematories. One does not need to be a funeral director to run a crematory.

The Banking and Finance Department covers preneed and for-profit cemetery transactions. Its Board of Funeral and Cemetery Services has seven members. Two must be funeral directors with no relationship to a cemetery; two must be cemeterians, but there is no equivalent restriction for a relationship with a mortuary; three are consumer representatives, one of whom must be over the age of 60.

## ❖ Prepaid Cemetery and Funeral Funds

All cemetery goods and services available must be disclosed on a printed or typewritten price list. 10% of the grave, columbaria, or mausoleum price must be set aside for perpetual care.

100% of all money for cash advance *cemetery* items must be placed in **trust**. Only 70% of prepaid *funeral* and *cemetery* services and 110% of the wholesale cost of *cemetery merchandise* must be placed in **trust**. The seller may withdraw the **interest**. "**Constructive delivery**" can bypass this requirement for monuments, markers, outer burial containers, "and similar merchandise . . . commonly sold or used in cemeteries." This is accomplished by issuing a certificate of ownership and warehousing the merchandise. (Although a person at the state board says it is checking to see if the goods are in the warehouse, it's a rare board that is actually doing so.) Once "delivered," it is almost impossible to get a **refund** even if the items have never been used. Trusting requirements can be avoided if a bond or evidence of financial responsibility has been filed with the state.

The only **reporting** requirement seems to be from the trustee holding prepaid funds to the seller. Cemeteries are to be inspected once a year, however, including a review of preneed contracts.

**Substitution** of merchandise of equal or greater quality is required if the specified items are not available.

A consumer may get a full **refund** within 30 days of signing any cemetery or *funeral* contract. At any time after that, a consumer may get a full refund of services, facilities and cash advance items—*not merchandise*—by providing a written request. However, FS 497.421 provides that "In the event that the funeral merchandise or service or burial merchandise or service contracted for is not provided or is not desired by the heirs or personal representative of the contract beneficiary, the trustee shall return, within 30 days after its receipt of a written request therefore, funds paid on the contract to the certificate holder" (seller). No mention of returning **interest.** Refund on merchandise is clearly a problem; one family, whose mother died in New Jersey, was told to come and get the casket in Florida. Another woman moved to California. Service fees were transferred, but the Florida funeral home has kept $900 for her casket—a casket she no longer wants, now that she has decided on cremation.

Florida has a Preneed Funeral Contract Consumer **Protection Trust Fund** to provide restitution in the case of a delinquent provider.

## ❖ Consumer Concerns

- The death rate in Florida can support approximately 621 full-time mortuaries; there are, however, 794. Funeral prices tend to be higher in areas where there are "too many" funeral homes.
- In some areas of Florida, all—or almost all—funeral homes are owned by one of several corporations, leaving limited choices for price-sensitive consumers.
- A law to permit church groups and families to care for their dead should be enacted so their rights are protected and clear.
- Laws should require cemeteries to repurchase an unwanted lot at the original selling price plus 50% of the difference between that and current market price.
- Finance charges are permitted for installment purchases of prepaid cemetery arrangements. This is outrageous and should be repealed immediately! When you finance a car, house, or other retail

purchase, you get to use the item. But a finance charge on a lay-away plan before they lay you away?

- All money (100%) for prepaid funeral goods and services should be placed in trust, with better provisions for transfer or refund of monies paid plus interest. "Constructive Delivery" should not be permitted.
- There is no annual reporting requirement to the purchaser of prepaid funeral and cemetery goods and services, paperwork that might be helpful to the family of a deceased to indicate prepayment. Such reporting would help to "enforce" the required trusting, as well.
- Until the Florida laws are changed, it is probably a *terrible* idea to prepay for a funeral or any cemetery merchandise and services, given the lack of adequate protection for consumers. Your own trust account in a bank will be safer.
- While Florida requires that the least expensive casket be displayed in the same manner as the more expensive caskets, there is no requirement that low-cost caskets be carried by a funeral home. (One woman said she was shown only two caskets—a plain pine box and a $4,000 casket.)
- A system of body identification is required for various funeral or disposition services, but a more responsible requirement would be identification and tagging at the place of death prior to removal.
- Cash advance items must be listed in the amount charged to the funeral home, *but* an escape clause in the regulations says that disclosure of "a discount or rebate" is not necessary. Consumers may wish to ask for the invoice for each cash advance item.
- To its credit, Florida indicates that advertising would be misleading if it "makes only a partial disclosure of relevant facts." Taken at face value, that would seem to mean that any funeral home citing a price for "Direct Cremation" that does not include the cost of the cremation process would be in violation of the state regulations. Apparently, however, the state is not cracking down on this, given the many General Price Lists I've seen that fail to include this cost.
- Although Florida has some excellent points in its ethical standards, additional requirements could be added that would make it easier for a consumer to prevail when filing a complaint. (See Appendix.)
- Telephone complaints to the Board of Funeral and Cemetery Services have resulted in "See if you can work it out" advice, not especially reassuring to consumers who would not have called if they thought that was possible in the first place.

- While many of the Florida requirements parallel those of the FTC, there is no adoption of FTC requirements by reference. A few have been omitted (*e.g.,* the timing of when price information must be given), and—without specific reference—any future amendments of the Funeral Rule will have to be acted on separately in Florida, not an efficient use of legislative time.
- You may state your funeral preferences prior to death, but there is no law permitting you to name a designated agent to make your final arrangements. In situations where you are estranged or distant from next-of-kin, this could be important.

## ❖ Miscellaneous Information

- Educational requirements for becoming an embalmer: mortuary college and a passing grade on the national exam; one year of internship after school is also required. An associate's degree (two years) is required for a funeral director's license, plus exam and internship.
- Direct disposers and body transport services are licensed by the Department of Business and Professional Regulation. One does not need to be a funeral director, but an exam is required covering state laws and determination of death.
- The Funeral and Cemetery Board's toll-free number for help or complaints is 800-323-2627, but take note of the concern above.
- Medical examiners are physicians who are appointed to the position.

## ❖ Nonprofit Funeral Consumer Information Societies

These consumer groups are run mostly by volunteers. Consequently, contact information may change. If you have difficulty reaching a society or are interested in starting a society in your area, call the FAMSA office: 800-765-0107. Or check the internet directory—
**www.funerals.org/famsa**

Cocoa

   Funeral Mem. Soc. Brevard Co.
   P.O. Box 276, 32923
   407-453-4109 or 636-3363

DeBary

   Funeral So. of Mid-Florida
   P.O. Box 392, 32713-0392
   904-789-1682 or 407-668-6822

Ft. Myers

   Funeral Mem. Soc. SW Florida
   P.O. Box 7756, 33911-7756
   941-743-0109

Gainesville

   Mem. Soc. of Alachua Co.
   Box 14662, 32604-4662
   352-378-3432

Orlando

Memorial Soc. Grtr. Orlando
P.O. Box 953
Goldenrod, 32733-0953
407-677-5009

Palm Beach Gardens

Palm Beach Funeral Society
P.O. Box 31982, 33420
561-659-4881

Pensacola & Ft. Walton Beach

Funeral Mem. Soc. W. Florida
7804 Northpointe Blvd., 32514
904-477-8431

Sarasota

Memorial Society of Sarasota
P.O. Box 15833, 34277-5833
941-953-3740

St. Petersburg

Suncoast-Tampa Bay Soc.
719 Arlington Ave. N., 33701
727-898-3294

Tallahassee

Funeral Mem. Soc. Leon Co.
1006 Buena Vista Dr., 32304
850-224-2082

~❖~

*This chapter was sent for review to*
*the Florida Board of Funeral Directors and Embalmers,*
*the Department of Health, and the Department of Banking and*
*Finance—Board of Funeral and Cemetery Services.*

Kenneth Jones in the Department of Health, Vital Statistics was extremely helpful in tidying up facts in this chapter, as was staff for the Board of Funeral Directors and Embalmers. Apparently, people at the Board of Funeral and Cemetery Services found this chapter of no interest whatsoever. I've not yet heard from them. One has to wonder if they are watching out for the interest of consumers.

# In Georgia

*Please refer to Chapter 8 as you use this section.*

Persons in Georgia may care for their own dead. The legal authority to do so is found in:

> *Title 31-10-15 (b) The funeral director or person acting as such who first assumes custody of the dead body shall file the certificate of death . . .*

There are no other statutes that might require you to use a funeral director.

## ❖ Death Certificate

The family doctor or a local medical examiner will supply and sign the death certificate within 48 hours, stating the cause of death. The remaining information must be supplied, typewritten or in black ink. The death certificate must be filed with the local registrar within 72 hours and before final disposition.

## ❖ Fetal Death

A fetal death report is required for each fetal death. If there is no family physician involved, the local medical investigator must sign the fetal death certificate.

## ❖ Transporting and Disposition Permit

A body may be moved with the consent of a physician or county coroner. After receiving the death certificate, the local registrar will issue a final disposition permit if cremation or out-of-state disposition is planned. No burial-transit permit is required by statute for in-state burial, although a local ordinance may require one.

## ❖ Burial

Check with the county or town registrar for local zoning laws regarding home burial. If a local ordinance requires a disposition permit for burial, the family member acting as the funeral director must sign the authorization for disposition and retain it on file. There are no state burial statutes or regulations with regard to depth. A sensible guideline is 150 feet from a water supply and three feet of earth on top.

## ❖ Cremation

The registrar's permit for disposition is required before cremation. There is no fee for this. Most crematories insist that a pacemaker be removed, and authorization by next-of-kin is usually required. The crematory will return the burial-transit permit to the registrar.

Within 50 days, cremated remains may be buried at sea. They must be removed from their container and scattered, at least three miles from shore. There are no statutes dictating the method when disposition occurs on land.

## ❖ Other Requirements

Georgia has no other requirements controlling the time schedule for the disposition of unembalmed bodies. Weather and reasonable planning should be considered.

If the person died of a contagious or communicable disease, the doctor in attendance or the local health officer should be consulted.

## ❖ Medical Schools for Body Donation

Emory University
Department of Anatomy
School of Medicine
Atlanta, GA 30322-3030
404-727-6242
Moderate need

Cost to family: transportation
Prior enrollment: required, 90-day wait
Over-enrollment: not occurred
Disposition: cremation; cremains returned by request
Body rejection: standard*, under 18, embalming

Morehouse School of Medicine
720 Westview Dr. SW
Atlanta, GA 30310
404-752-1560, 9-5 M-F
404-752-1500, other times

Cost to family: transportation beyond 50 miles
Prior enrollment: not required
Over-enrollment: not occurred
Disposition: cremation; cremains returned by request
Body rejection: standard*, under 10

Medical College of Georgia
Augusta, GA 30912

Repeated requests from this school have been unanswered.

Mercer University
School of Medicine
1550 College St.
Macon, GA 31207
912-752-4050

Cost to family: transportation to funeral home where embalming will occur (check w school)
Prior enrollment: not required
Over-enrollment: shared
Disposition: cremation; cremains returned by request
Body rejection: standard*, demyelinating diseases.

Life College School of Chiropractic
Anatomical Donor Program
Dept. of Anatomy
1269 Barclay Cir.
Marietta, GA 30060
770-426-2718
770-805-9777
High need

Cost to family: transportation to funeral home/initial embalming
Prior enrollment: required
Over-enrollment: shared
Disposition: cremation; cremains returned by request
Body rejection: standard*, 250 lbs.

* autopsy, decomposition, mutilation, severe burn victim, meningitis, hepatitis, AIDS, and other communicable and contagious diseases.

❖ **Crematories** (all crematories must be run by a funeral director)

Albany

Kimbrell-Stern, Inc.
1503 Dawson Rd.
P.O. Box 92, 31702
912-883-4152

Athens

Master Cremation Service
234 Fairfield Cir.
P.O. Box 201, 30603
404-353-1115

Atlanta

Atlanta Crematory
100 Main St.
P.O. Box 605, 30086
404-469-5577

G A Cremation Service
195 Mendell Dr. SW, 30336
404-691-9414

Austell

Cremation Soc. of the South
5754 Harrison Ave., 30001
770-941-5352

Blairsville

Cochran Funeral Home
32 Hospital St., 30512
706-492-3321

Brunswick

Miller & Sons Funeral Home
P.O. Box 1555, 31520
912-265-3636

Mableton

Mount Harmony Crematory
581 Bankhead Hwy.
P.O. Box 352, 30059
404-739-1751

Macon

Harts Crematory
765 Cherry St., 31201
912-746-4321

Marietta

Medford-Peden Crematory
1408 Canton Hgwy. NE, 30066
770-427-8447

Martinez

Elliott Sons Crematory
4255 Columbia Rd., 30907
706-868-9637

Rossville

Lane Funeral Home
833 Chickamauga Ave., 30741
706-866-5151

Savannah

Fox & Weeks Crematory
7200 Hodgson Mem'l Dr., 31406
912-352-7200

Tucker

Bill Head Funeral Homes
6101 Lawrenceville Hwy 30084
770-564-2726

Additional crematories may have been established in this state after the date of publication.

## ❖ State Governance

The Georgia Board of Funeral Service has seven members—six funeral directors and embalmers and one consumer representative.

Cemeteries are regulated by the Secretary of State.

Crematories are licensed and inspected by the Funeral Board. A crematory must be under the supervision of a licensed funeral director.

## ❖ Prepaid Cemetery and Funeral Funds

100% of *cemetery services* and 35% of *cemetery goods* must be placed in **trust**. "**Constructive delivery**" can bypass the trusting requirement. "Delivery" usually is accomplished by issuing a certificate of ownership and warehousing the vault and/or marker, although the state is not checking to see if the goods are actually there. Once "delivered," it is almost impossible to get a refund even if the items were never used.

Only a funeral establishment may sell prepaid *funeral* arrangements. 100% must be deposited in **trust** and allowed to accrue **interest**. The funeral agent must **report** on these funds annually to the state.

Although Georgia law requires that "excess funds" be returned to the estate if more is in the account at the time of death than needed to pay for the goods and services selected, it is unlikely that any is ever refunded if the family is simply told, "It's all taken care of."

Consumers have full right of **refund** for money paid plus interest when cancelling an agreement.

At the time of death, the merchandise supplied may not be of "lesser quality" than that selected, but there are no rules indicating how survivors would know the difference. It would not be difficult for a mortician to coerce family members into picking something else, at an additional cost—"I simply don't have anything *like* it any-more"—because of all the new casket styles and construction materials appearing each year. An adequate description should be included in the preneed contract, and survivors should approve any **substitution**.

### ❖ Restrictive Casket Sales? . . . Depends who's talking.

This heading (or one similar) shows up in only seven state chapters: Alabama, Georgia, Idaho, Louisiana, Oklahoma, South Carolina, and Virginia. (An Oklahoma state court determined in 1997 that restrictions on casket sales were illegal; the ruling is now under appeal by the funeral board.)

For years, caskets have been the major profit-maker for an undertaker, and mark-up on caskets was often 500–700% or more. As word leaked out about actual casket costs, some entrepreneurs saw an opportunity to cut the price and still make a "fair" profit, knowing that consumers were growing resentful. In the mid '90s, the retail casket business was born. Although I certainly support a free-market concept, I—for one— didn't think the public would shop anywhere but at a funeral home for a casket. Boy, was I wrong! The retail casket market is exploding, and consumers are now saving thousands of dollars on overnight delivery of attractive, well-made, quality caskets that are available from sources all around the country.

The Federal Trade Commission encourages this, permitting consumers to purchase from a funeral home *only* those goods and services wanted. Since 1994, it has forbidden a funeral home from charging a handling fee if a consumer purchases an item or service elsewhere. The FTC does not address who may sell a casket, but it has very specific language that does oblige a funeral home to accept a casket provided by the consumer.

What's the problem in Georgia? The funeral board refers to the following statute to claim that one has to be a funeral director to sell a casket. But the wording is so faulty that—if the intent was to restrict the trade of funeral merchandise—an English teacher could render it unenforceable without bothering to hire a lawyer or face a judge: *Title 43-18-1 Definitions*: *(13) "Funeral merchandise" means the goods that may **only be sold or offered for sale** by a funeral director working in a funeral establishment and includes, but is not limited to, a casket or alternative container, but does not include an outer burial container or cemetery marker.*

Funeral merchandise is merchandise *that may **only** be sold or offered for sale* in a funeral establishment. If it's *rented,* it's apparently not funeral merchandise. If the word *only* were moved and the definition read *merchandise that may be sold **only** by a funeral director working in a funeral establishment* or *merchandise that may be sold by a funeral director working in a funeral establishment **only**,* we have two other meanings. Yet none of these would address someone who is not a funeral director working elsewhere.

About the only other place where the word *casket* appears is in a preneed statute, and the context is far more logical: *Title 43-18-92. Definitions (1) "Burial supplies and equipment" means those articles used for burial, normally provided by funeral directors, including but not limited to articles of clothing used for burial, caskets, and subterranean crypts or vaults not affixed to real property at the time of sale.* Of course funeral directors normally sell funeral merchandise.

But funeral merchandise and burial supplies aren't sold *only* by funeral directors. Casket sales reps, wholesalers, or manufacturers sell caskets and aren't usually funeral directors. Florists sell funeral flowers, and stationery stores sell guest books and prayer cards used at funerals—funeral merchandise, if you will.

As *definitions,* the current Georgia statutes simply don't address what a non-funeral director may or may not sell, especially working somewhere other than a funeral home. If a new law were introduced that said "Only a funeral director may sell a casket to the public," the attempt at restraint of trade would be despicably obvious. Generally, burdensome laws will be sustained by the courts only if there are reasons of public health, vital statistics, or legal/criminal concerns. The funeral board would have a hard time justifying who may or may not sell a box—which is all a casket is. (What if we called it a "hope chest" instead? Who may sell it then? No law against burying someone in a hope chest.)

As of this writing, I've heard from three Georgia folks planning to sell caskets directly to consumers at great prices. It would be too bad if the powers-that-be decide to fight them, for that would surely force Georgia money out of state. On the other hand, the free publicity might be worth the tussle for the new enterprises. They'll surely prevail in the long run.

If there is no casket retailer near you, you can order your casket via the internet or get directions for building your own:

### www.funerals.org/famsa/caskets.htm

Or call Catskill Casket Co. in East Meredith, New York: 888-531-5151. Joe White, a minister, and his wife Gail, a teacher, ship affordable caskets for overnight delivery anywhere in the country. They'll be glad to send you a brochure of their casket selection or refer you to another retailer if they don't carry what you want. By federal law, the funeral home must accept a casket of your choice, regardless of where it's purchased.

### ❖ Consumer Concerns

- The death rate in Georgia can support approximately 237 full-time mortuaries; there are, however, 603. Funeral prices tend to be higher in areas where there are "too many" funeral homes.
- There is little or no oversight of cemetery sales practices. Reconstructing the make-up of the Funeral Board would be one way to begin. Suggested possibility: two funeral directors, two cemeterians who are not funeral directors or affiliated by business interests to a mortuary, two consumer representatives, and an independent monument dealer.
- Laws should require cemeteries to repurchase an unwanted lot at the original selling price plus 50% of the difference between that and current market price.
- 100% of prepaid cemetery goods and services should be placed in trust, with full right of cancellation or transfer. "Constructive delivery" should not be permitted. Until the laws are changed to require this, it is probably a *terrible* idea to prepay for cemetery goods and services.

- Survivors should approve any substitution of merchandise if selected items are not available at the time of death.
- Preneed funeral consumers should get an annual report indicating the institution of deposit and current total of all prepaid funeral monies. Such documentation could be important to survivors who might not otherwise know about prepaid accounts and might help to "enforce" the trusting requirements.
- There is no statutory provision to protect consumers against default of prepaid agreements if funds were never put in trust.
- Until there is better reporting and survivor-approved substitution of merchandise, consumers in Georgia may not want to prepay for their funerals.
- The statute that requires a crematory to be under the supervision of a licensed funeral director is clearly aimed at limiting competition and low-cost funeral alternatives. Cremation costs to consumers are generally higher in the few states where independent crematories are not allowed. The knowledge and skills for running a crematory do not require 3,120 hours as an apprentice funeral director, a college degree, nor training in embalming. Mortuary curricula do not generally cover the running of a crematory, nor is the operation of a crematory covered on the national funeral directors' exam, which further indicates the absurdity of this restriction. Therefore, Title 43-18-71 and related statutes should be amended. Training by the manufacturer and apprenticeship at, say, ten cremations—in-state or out—would be consistent with the task involved.
- Although identification tagging of the body prior to disposition is required, this should occur at the place of death and before removal.

- The regulations require that at least eight adult caskets be on display, but there is no requirement that low-cost caskets be included in that display.
- There is no provision either forbidding a mark-up on cash advance items or requiring the disclosure of how much the mark-up would be. Consumers may wish to ask for an invoice for such charges.
- There is no law that allows you to state your funeral preferences or for naming a designated agent to make your final arrangements. In situations where you are estranged or distant from next-of-kin, this could be important.
- The standards for unprofessional conduct should be strengthened. That would make it easier for a consumer to prevail when filing a valid complaint. (See Ethical Standards in the Appendix.)

## ❖ Miscellaneous Information

- Educational requirements for funeral directors and embalmers: one year of mortuary school, passing grade on the national exam, and an exam on state laws for funeral directors. Apprenticeship of eighteen months is also required—3,120 hours (recently reduced from two years). This still seems excessive compared to other states but is undoubtedly a source of cheap labor for the industry.
- The FTC Funeral Rule has been endorsed by statutory reference.
- Medical examiners are appointed; coroners are elected.
- It is an unlawful act to hold a body for debt.
- The Secretary of State's office has a brochure on how to file a complaint.

## ❖ Nonprofit Funeral Consumer Information Societies

These consumer groups are run mostly by volunteers. Consequently, contact information may change. If you have difficulty reaching a society or are interested in starting a society in your area, call the FAMSA office: 800-765-0107. Or check the internet directory—

**www.funerals.org/famsa**

Atlanta

Memorial Society of Georgia
1911 Cliff Valley Way NE, 30329
404-634-2896
800-840-4339

Macon

Middle Georgia Chapter
4825 Brittany Dr., 31210
912-477-1691

~❖~

*This chapter was sent for review to the Secretary of State's Office, Department of Health—Vital Statistics, and the Board of Funeral Service. Only the latter responded with a minor correction and without further comment.*

# In Hawaii

*Please refer to Chapter 8 as you use this section.*

Persons in Hawaii may care for their own dead. The legal authority to do so is found in:

> *Chapter 338-1 "Person in charge of disposition of the body" means any person who . . . disposes thereof.*

> *Chapter 338-9 (a) The person in charge of the disposition of the body shall file with the department of health in Honolulu or with the local agent . . . a certificate of death.*

There are no other statutes which might require you to use a funeral director.

### ❖ Death Certificate

The family doctor or a medical examiner will supply and sign the death certificate within 24 hours, stating the cause of death. The remaining information must be supplied, typewritten or in black ink. The death certificate must be filed with the local registrar or health agent within three days and before final disposition.

### ❖ Fetal Death

A fetal death report is required if death occurs after 24 weeks of gestation. If there is no family physician involved, the local health officer must be notified. All other procedures apply if disposition is handled by the family.

### ❖ Transporting and Disposition Permit

A burial-transit permit must be obtained within 72 hours of death from the local registrar or deputy and prior to final disposition of the body. There is a modest charge—$5 as of this writing.

The family member acting as the funeral director must sign the permit and within 10 days file it with the registrar of the district where disposition took place.

## ❖ Burial

Check with the local registrar for zoning laws regarding home burial. Burial must be on land approved as a cemetery by the county council. A written certificate of dedication exclusively to cemetery purposes must be filed with the registrar along with a map. Burial depth must be sufficient to avoid a public health nuisance and to make it impossible for animals to disturb the grave. A useful guideline is 150 feet from a water supply and at least two feet of earth on top.

## ❖ Cremation

The burial-transit permit is sufficient for cremation and no additional permit is needed. Most crematories insist that a pacemaker be removed, and authorization by next-of-kin usually is required.

## ❖ Other Requirements

A body shall be embalmed, cremated, or buried within 30 hours after death or release by the medical examiner or placed in a refrigerated storage in a state-approved hospital.

Bodies dead from the following diseases may not be embalmed: plague, Asiatic cholera, smallpox, epidemic typhus fever, yellow fever, or louse-borne relapsing fever. Check with the director of health for other possible restrictions. *This is the only U.S. state that has recognized the potential hazard from embalming.*

## ❖ Medical Schools for Body Donation

University of Hawaii
Department of Anatomy
1960 East-West Rd., T311
Honolulu, HI 96822
808-948-7132 or 941-4734 (mortuary)

Cost to family: transportation outside Oahu
Prior enrollment: not required
Over-enrollment: not shared
Disposition: cremation; return of cremains by request
Body rejection: standard*, over-enrollment, cancer, possibly if outside Oahu

* autopsy, decomposition, mutilation, severe burn victim, meningitis, hepatitis, AIDS

## ❖ Crematories

Kauai

Kauai Mortuary
3168 Poipu Rd.
Koloa, HI 96756
808-332-7321

Maui

Borthwick-Bulgo Mortuary
524 Waiale Dr.
Wailuku, HI 96793
808-242-6841

Borthwick-Norman's Mortuary
105 Waiale Dr.
Wailuku, HI 96793
808-244-4065

Oahu

Mililani Memorial Park
94-560 Kamehameha Hwy.
Mililani Town, HI 96789
808-677-5631

Hawaii

Borthwick Mortuary
1330 Maunakea St.
Honolulu, HI 96817
808-531-3566

Diamond Head Mortuary
529 18th St.
Honolulu, HI 96816
808-735-2872

Dodo Mortuary
199 Wainaku Ave.
Hilo, HI 96720
808-935-5751

Homelani Memorial Park
388 Ponahawai St.
Hilo, HI 96720
808-961-6051

Memorial Mortuary
297 Waianuenue Ave.
Hilo, HI 96720
808-935-1257

Kona Community Crematory
Kuakini Highway 11
Kealakekua, HI 96750
808-322-3524

Additional crematories may have been established in this state after the date of publication.

## ❖ State Governance

There is no Hawaii State Funeral Board. Funeral directors are no longer licensed by the Professional & Vocational Licensing Division of the Department of Commerce and Consumer Affairs (DCCA). The DCCA's Cemetery and Pre-Need Funeral Authority Program regulates and monitors prepaid cemetery and funeral trusts only. The DCCA does not approve contract format.

Crematories are regulated by the Department of Health.

### ❖ Prepaid Cemetery and Funeral Funds

For perpetual care, $1 per square foot of interment space, $50 for each mausoleum crypt, and $15 for each niche must be placed in trust.

*Cemetery* and *funeral* preneed sellers may retain the lesser of "acquisition costs" or 30% of the contract, placing in **trust** at least 70%. **Interest** may be withdrawn by the seller as long as the Authority deems that sufficient funds are there.

Preneed sellers must make an annual "audited financial statement" to the director of DCCA. The DCCA *may* require **reports** to clients.

A general price list must be provided for all cemetery and funeral transactions, signed by the purchaser. Prices must be the same for at-need and preneed purchases. A "clear and concise statement" of all purchases must be included in the preneed contract, but this falls short. There is no provision for a satisfactory **substitution** of unavailable merchandise (i.e., caskets) without an extra charge.

There is no provision for **transfer** of irrevocable contracts in the preneed statutes, although the implications are that a consumer may cancel at will. While terms for a **refund** must be disclosed in the preneed contract, the state apparently does not require a full refund over and above the 70% in trust when the contract is cancelled. What happens to the interest is unclear.

Preneed sellers must carry a $50,000 **bond** proof of surety. This is a relatively paltry sum, given the aggressive preneed marketing these days. Default on just ten $5,000 funerals would wipe that out, leaving untold numbers uncovered.

### ❖ Consumer Concerns

- The death rate in Hawaii can support approximately 31 full-time mortuaries; there are, in fact, only 21. This is one of the very few states where there is not a significant glut of funeral homes, and prices are competitive in some areas. Consumers will have to shop around, however, as there is a huge difference from one funeral home to the next.
- Laws should require cemeteries to repurchase an unwanted lot at the original selling price plus 50% of the difference between that and current market price.

- Substitution of merchandise purchased preneed should be permitted only with the approval of survivors.
- Constructive delivery (warehousing) should not be permitted to bypass the trusting requirement for preneed purchases.
- There is insufficient statutory provision to protect consumers against default of prepaid funeral agreements if funds were never put in trust.
- Until the Hawaii laws are changed to require 100% trusting of all money and interest for prepaid funeral and cemetery goods and services and adequate provision for transfer, it is probably a *terrible* idea to prepay for these arrangements. Your own trust account in a bank will be safer.
- There is no requirement that low-cost caskets be included in any display.
- There is no provision either forbidding a mark-up on cash advance items or requiring the disclosure of how much the mark-up would be. Consumers may wish to ask for a copy of the invoice for each cash advance item.
- There is no law that allows you to state your funeral preferences or for naming a designated agent to make your final arrangements. In situations where you are estranged or distant from next-of-kin, this could be important.
- Ethical standards and unethical conduct should be clearly defined in order for valid consumer complaints to prevail.
- More detailed and explicit procedures should be available for those wishing to file a complaint.
- The FTC Funeral Rule should be adopted by reference to make it more enforceable in this state.
- Identification and tagging of the body at the place of death before removal should be required.

## ❖ Miscellaneous Information

- There are several possibilities for qualifying as a funeral director in Hawaii: five years of apprenticeship, *or* a high school diploma and two years of apprenticeship, *or* mortuary school and one year of apprenticeship. A written exam is also required.
- The chief of police and deputies serve as coroners. The medical examiner serves in that capacity for the city of Honolulu.

- Complaints regarding cemetery and funeral trusts may be filed with the Regulated Industries Complaints Office (RICO), DCCA, Suite 600A, 828 Fort Street Mall, Honolulu, HI 96813; 808-587-3222.

## ❖ Nonprofit Funeral Consumer Information Societies

These consumer groups are run mostly by volunteers. Consequently, contact information may change. If you have difficulty reaching a society or are interested in starting a society in your area, call the FAMSA office: 800-765-0107. Or check the internet directory—

**www.funerals.org/famsa**

Honolulu

> Memorial Society of Hawaii
> 2510 Bingham St., Room A
> Honolulu, HI 96826
> 808-946-6822

~❖~

*This chapter was reviewed by the Hawaii Health Department. No response was received from the Department of Commerce and Consumer Affairs.*

# In Idaho

*Please refer to Chapter 8 as you use this section.*

Persons and religious groups in Idaho may care for their own dead. The legal authority to do so is found in:

> *Title 39-260: (re death registration) . . . the person in charge of interment or of removal of the body from the district shall be responsible for obtaining and filing the certificate.*

> *Title 54-1104: Exemptions from provisions of act (re licensing of morticians) . . . Any duly authorized representative of any church, fraternal order or other association or organization honoring the dead who performs a funeral or other religious service . . .*

There are no other statutes that might require you to use a funeral director.

### ❖ Death Certificate

The family doctor or local medical examiner will supply and sign the death certificate within 72 hours, stating the cause of death. The remaining information must be supplied, typewritten or in black ink. There are two carbons, so do not use a felt-tip pen. The death certificate must be filed with the local registrar within 5 days.

### ❖ Fetal Death

A certificate of stillbirth is required when death occurs after 20 weeks of gestation or when a weight of 350 grams is attained, and must be filed as above.

### ❖ Transporting and Disposition Permit

A body may be moved with medical permission. The death must be recorded with the local registrar within 24 hours, in person or by mail. Use the third (pink) page of the three-copy death certificate for this purpose. Even if some items on the death certificate are not yet complete, be sure that the name of the deceased, the date of death, the name of the doctor and the person acting as the funeral director have been filled in. The second (blue) page serves as the burial-transit permit. It is necessary to have a physician's or coroner's authorization before removing a body from the state.

## ❖ Burial

Home burial is permissible in Idaho. Check with the county or town clerk for local zoning laws. There are no state burial statutes or regulations with regard to depth. A sensible guideline is 150 feet from a water supply and three feet of earth on top.

Three or more residents may organize a nonprofit rural cemetery association.

## ❖ Cremation

A cremation permit from the coroner is required. There is no fee for this. Authorization by next-of-kin is usually required, and a pacemaker must be removed. A person may authorize his/her own cremation as part of a preneed plan.

## ❖ Other Requirements

Embalming is no longer required. Weather and reasonable planning should be considered.

If the person died of a contagious or communicable disease, the doctor in attendance should be consulted.

Bodies transported by commercial carrier must be embalmed.

## ❖ Medical Schools for Body Donation

There are no medical schools in Idaho. However, Washington, Wyoming, Alaska, Montana and Idaho participate in the WWAMI Medical Education Program which accepts bodies for anatomical study in a variety of programs:

University of Idaho
WWAMI Medical Program
Moscow, ID 83844-4207
208-885-6696
509-878-1221 (fun'l home in no. ID)
208-983-0740 (fun'l home in so. ID)
Moderate need.

Cost to family: WWAMI pays for transportation and must make the arrangements, within 150 mi.
Prior enrollment: not required
Over-enrollment: shared
Disposition: cremation; return of cremains by request
Body rejection: standard*, budgetary restriction

Idaho State University
Anatomical Donation Program
Life Science Bldg., Room 421
Pocatello, ID 83209
208-236-3993 or 236-3765
After death:
208-233-0686 (funeral home) or
236-3165 (Biol. Sci.) 233-4451 (home)
Moderate need.

Cost to family: program pays transportation within 200 mi.
Prior enrollment: not required
Over-enrollment: shared
Disposition: cremation; return of cremains by request
Body rejection: standard*, embalming, death beyond 200 miles from Pocatello (except Boise)

* autopsy, decomposition, mutilation, severe burn victim, meningitis, hepatitis, AIDS, and other contagious or communicable diseases

## ❖ Crematories (All crematories are run by funeral homes in Idaho.)

### Blackfoot

Grove City Crematory
288 N. Shilling, 83221-2399
208-785-0230
800-343-0434

Hill Hawker Sandberg Funeral Home
SE Idaho Crematory
214 S. University Ave., 83221
208-785-1320

### Boise

Alden-Waggoner Funeral Chapel
5400 Fairview Ave., 83706
208-376-5400

Cloverdale FH & Memorial Park
1200 N. Cloverdale Rd., 83704
208-375-2212

Cremation Society of Idaho
5541 Overland Rd., 83705
208-322-3590 or 800-550-3590

Mt. View Crematory
8209 Fairview, 83704
208-322-3999

### Caldwell

Flahiff Funeral Chapels
415 S. 6th, 83605
208-459-0833

### Coeur d'Alene

Coeur d'Alene Memorial Chapel
7315 N. Government Way, 83814
208-772-4015

English Funeral Chapel
North Idaho Crematory
1133 N. 4th, 83814
208-664-3143

Yates Funeral Home/Crematory
744 N. 4th St., 83814
208-664-3151

### Kellogg

Shoshone Funeral Services
106 S. Main St., 83837
208-786-5121

### Lewiston

Lewis Clark Memorial Gardens
7th & Cedar, 83501
208-743-9464

Valley Crematory
920 21st Ave., 83501
208-743-6541

### Meridian

Cloverdale Crematory
4225 E. Fairview, 83642

Sandpoint

Coffelt Funeral Service
109 N. Division, 83864
208-263-3133

White Mortuary
136 4th Ave. E., 83301
208-733-6600

Twin Falls

Parke's Magic Valley Crematory
2551 Kimberly Rd., 83303
208-735-0011

Additional crematories may have been established in this state after the date of publication.

## ❖ State Governance

The Idaho Board of Morticians has three members. There are no consumer representatives.

Public cemeteries are generally regulated by county commissioners. Private cemeteries are supposed to be regulated by the Idaho Board of Cemeterians, but the board has never been established.

As of 1996, crematories became regulated by the Board of Morticians. Prior to that, the Department of Health licensed crematories.

## ❖ Prepaid Cemetery and Funeral Funds

Only 50% of the funds for prepaid *cemetery* merchandise must be placed in **trust**. **"Constructive delivery"** can avoid any trusting requirements at all.

Only 85% of all other preneed *funeral* and cemetery services and merchandise must be placed in **trust**. The trustee holding the funds may withdraw from the **interest** "reasonable" expenses for administering the funds.

A purchaser may **cancel** a revocable preneed plan and collect "all payments made, plus accrued interest thereon, less *reasonable* administrative expenses and taxes incurred." Obviously, the purchaser is going to be missing the interest on the 15% that was never deposited. There is *no* provision for **transferring** an irrevocable contract.

The preneed seller must make an annual **report** to the state.

Preneed solicitations at hospitals, rest homes, or similar institutions are forbidden unless specifically invited. Such in-person solicitation is *sort of* forbidden elsewhere if it "comprises an uninvited invasion of personal privacy at the personal residence." Why didn't the law just come right out and say no in-person or telephone solicitation?

If selected merchandise is not available at the time of death, the seller must supply a **substitute** equal in quality of material and workmanship satisfactory to the person making the arrangements. If the seller is unable to provide an acceptable substitute, the person handling the arrangements may transfer to another provider all funds in the trust (85% of what was paid, plus interest, less expenses).

## ❖ Restrictive Casket Sales

This heading shows up in only seven state chapters: Alabama, Georgia, Idaho, Louisiana, Oklahoma, South Carolina, and Virginia. (An Oklahoma state court determined in 1997 that restrictions on casket sales were illegal, now under appeal by the funeral board.)

For years, caskets were the major profit-maker for an undertaker, and mark-up on caskets was often 500-700% or more. As word leaked out about actual casket costs, some entrepreneurs saw an opportunity to cut the price and still make a "fair" profit, knowing that consumers were growing resentful. In the mid '90s, the retail casket business was born. Although I certainly support a free-market concept, I—for one— didn't think the public would shop anywhere but at a funeral home for a casket. Boy, was I wrong! The retail casket market is exploding, and consumers are now saving thousands of dollars on over-night delivery of attractive, well-made, quality caskets that are available from sources all around the country, when casket prices in their areas are too high.[1]

---

[1] Funeral homes with nearby casket stores have been dropping their casket prices and upping their service charges to off-set the loss. Others offer a discounted package if you purchase the casket from the funeral home. The National Casket Retailers Association has filed a complaint with the FTC charging that falsely inflated service charges which are conditionally discounted later are hiding the illegal handling fee.

The Federal Trade Commission encourages this, permitting consumers to purchase from a funeral home *only* those goods and services wanted. As of 1994, it forbids a funeral home from charging a handling fee if a consumer purchases an item or service elsewhere. The FTC does not address who may sell a casket, but it does have specific language that requires a funeral home to accept a casket provided by the consumer.

What is the problem in Idaho? The following appears in *Title 54-1102 Definitions. A. "Mortician" means any person engaged in or conducting, or holding himself [sic] out as engaged in or conducting, any of the following activities: . . . (5) Selling funeral supplies to the public."*

If one is going to enforce this restrictive *funeral supplies* law, it wouldn't be fair to apply it selectively, would it? Wouldn't that also mean the corner stationery store may no longer sell guest books or thank-you cards? What about burial clothing? And funeral flowers? Generally, burdensome laws will be sustained by the courts only if there are reasons of public health, vital statistics, or legal/criminal concerns. Just how does the state of Idaho justify controlling who may sell a box—which is all a casket is? What if we call it a "hope chest" instead? Who may sell it then? No law against burying someone in a hope chest.

Clearly, any restriction on who may sell caskets or other funeral supplies in Idaho is a restraint of trade which subverts the FTC's provision specifically permitting consumers to purchase *only* the goods and services desired from the funeral provider. Until legislators get down to business and change the laws or the Mortuary Board changes its interpretation, there is nothing to stop you from ordering your casket from another state via the internet or getting directions for building your own:

**www.funerals.org/famsa/caskets.htm**

Not on the internet? Call Catskill Casket Co. in East Meredith, New York. Joe White, a minister, and his wife Gail, a teacher, ship affordable caskets for overnight delivery anywhere in the country. They'll be glad to send you a brochure of their casket selection or refer you to another retailer if they don't carry what you want: 888-531-5151.

## ❖ Consumer Concerns

- The death rate in Idaho can support approximately 34 full-time mortuaries; there are, however, 76 such establishments. Given the low density of population over a vast geographic area, mortuary careers are not likely to be full-time work. Unfortunately, because of the low volume of business per mortuary, funeral prices will tend to be higher than elsewhere.

- Laws should require cemeteries to repurchase an unwanted lot at the original selling price plus 50% of the difference between that and current market price.

- Annual reporting to the consumer should be required for all prepaid funeral trust accounts, paperwork that might be helpful to the family of a deceased to indicate prepayment and which would help to "enforce" trusting requirements.

- Irrevocable preneed contracts should be fully transferable.

- There is no state protection in the case of default of prepaid funeral monies. (There have been defaults even in states requiring 100% trusting.)

- Until the Idaho laws are changed to require 100% trusting of both cemetery and funeral purchases, it is probably a *terrible* idea to prepay for any merchandise and services, given the lack of adequate protection for consumers. Your own trust account in a bank will be safer.

- Only a funeral establishment may now run a crematory in Idaho. This is clearly a restraint of trade effort by undertakers to limit competition and low-cost choices. Cremation cost for a consumer is generally higher in the few states where independent crematories are not allowed. The knowledge and skills for running a crematory do not require apprenticeship as a funeral director, a college degree, nor training in embalming. Mortuary curricula do not generally cover the running of a crematory, nor is the operation of a crematory covered by the national funeral directors' exam. Therefore, Title 27-305 and related statutes should be amended. Training by the manufacturer and apprenticeship at, say, ten cremations—in-state or out—would be consistent with the task involved.

- The coroner's permit for cremation in the case of an *anticipated* death from natural causes is totally unnecessary and creates an additional paperwork burden.

- Identification and tagging of the body at the place of death before removal should be required.

- Any laws requiring embalming should be repealed. This is an offense to some religious groups, and refrigeration is a safer method of body preservation. Depending on the season, even that may not be needed for the first 72 hours.
- There is no requirement that low-cost caskets be included in any display.
- There is no provision either forbidding a mark-up on cash advance items or requiring the disclosure of how much the mark-up would be. Consumers may wish to request a copy of each invoice for such.
- The standards for ethical, professional conduct should be strengthened. That would make it easier for a consumer to prevail when filing a complaint. (See Ethical Standards in the Appendix.)
- Complaint procedures are unclear and inadequate.
- The FTC Funeral Rule should be adopted by reference to make it more enforceable in this state.

## ❖ Miscellaneous Information

- Educational requirements for becoming a mortician: two years of college, an embalming course, one year of apprenticeship, and a passing grade on an exam.
- Coroners are elected. They need not be physicians.
- Unprofessional conduct includes: "using profane, indecent or obscene language in the presence of a dead human body, or within the immediate hearing of the family or relatives of a deceased, whose body has not yet been interred or otherwise disposed of." Then watch out?
- A person may establish funeral preferences in a preneed plan. A person may also delegate disposition authority to a survivor.

## ❖ Nonprofit Funeral Consumer Information Societies

These consumer groups are run mostly by volunteers. Consequently, contact information may change. If you have difficulty reaching a society or are interested in starting a society in your area, call the FAMSA office: 800-765-0107. Or check the internet directory—

**www.funerals.org/famsa**

Boise

Idaho Memorial Association
P.O. Box 1919, 83701-1919
208-343-4581

~❖~

*This chapter was sent for review to the Department of Health—Vital Statistics and the Board of Mortuary Science. The Department of Health was kind enough to make some corrections, but no response was received from the Board of Mortuary Science.*

# In Illinois

*Please refer to Chapter 8 as you use this section.*

Church groups and families in Illinois may care for their own dead. The legal authority to do so is found in:

> *55 ILCS 5/3-3021. [Coroner] Public policy—Release of body to next of kin. As a guide to the interpretation and application of this Division it is declared that the public policy of the State is as follows:*
> *That as so as may be consistent with the performance of his duties under this Division the coroner shall release the body of the decedent to the decedent's next of kin, personal representative, friends, or to the person designated in writing by the decedent or to the funeral director selected by such persons, as the case may be, for burial, and none of the duties or powers of coroners enumerated in this Division shall be construed to interfere with or control the right of such persons to the custody and burial of the decedent upon completion of the coroner's investigation. (1990)*
>
> *410 ILCS 535/21(1). The funeral director or person acting as such who first assumes custody of a dead body or fetus shall make a written report to the registrar of the district in which death occurred . . . .*

There are no other statutes which would require you to use an undertaker.

## ❖ Death Certificate

The attending physician, medical examiner, or coroner will supply and sign the death certificate within 24 hours, stating the cause of death. The remaining information must be supplied, typewritten or in black ink. The death certificate must be filed with the registrar within five days and prior to burial, cremation or removal from the state.

Illinois is researching electronic death registration. When that is adopted the procedure will change somewhat. Check with the local registrar or health department.

### ❖ Fetal Death

A fetal death report is required when death occurs after 20 weeks of gestation. If there is no family physician involved, the local medical examiner or coroner must sign the fetal death certificate.

### ❖ Transporting and Disposition Permit

The local registrar will issue a permit for disposition once the death certificate has been filed.

### ❖ Burial

Home burial may be permissible in Illinois and an additional permit may be required. Check with the county registrar for zoning laws and burial procedures. The top of the coffin must be covered by 18 inches of earth. A sensible guideline is 150 feet from a water supply.

### ❖ Cremation

A permit for cremation must be obtained from the county coroner, and there is likely to be a fee, although it varies from one county to the next. This must be obtained before the permit for disposition. Most crematories insist that a pacemaker be removed, and authorization by next-of-kin or other authorizing agent is required.

### ❖ Other Requirements

Illinois has no other requirements controlling the time schedule for the disposition of unembalmed bodies. Weather and reasonable planning should be considered.

When death occurs due to a contagious or communicable disease, embalming is required. In deaths due to smallpox, cholera, or plague, the local health officer must sign the "Permit for Disposition."

### ❖ Medical Schools for Body Donation

All body donations in Illinois are handled through one agency.

Anatomical Gift Association
2240 W. Fillmore St.
Chicago, IL 60612
312-733-5283
800-734-5283
Urgent need

Cost to family: transportation
Prior enrollment: not required
Over-enrollment: shared
Disposition: cremation
Body rejection: under 18, embalming, autopsy, decomposition, infectious and communicable diseases

## ❖ Crematories

Alton

Elias-Smith Funeral Home
2521 Edwards St., 62002
618-465-3571

Arlington Heights

Memory Gardens Cemetery
2501 E. Euclid Ave., 60004
708-255-1010

Batavia

River Hills Mem. Park
E. River Rd., 60510
312-879-7400

Belleville

Valhalla Gardens of Memory
3200 Old St. Louis Rd., 62223
618-233-3110

Lake View Mem. Gardens
5000 N. Illinois St., 62221
618-233-7200

Belvidere

No. Ill. Wilbert Vault
845 E. Jackson, 61008
815-625-0077

Bloomington

Bloomington-Normal Crem.
1001 E. Front St., 61701
309-827-2325

Chebanse

Countyline Crematory
320 Oak St., 60922
815-697-2321

Chicago

A & Z Cremation Service
2500 N. Cicero Ave., 60639
312-278-8485

Acacia Park Cemetery
7800 W. Irving Pk., 60634
312-625-7800

American Cremation Soc.
2616 W. 38th St., 60632
312-273-6283

Cremation Society of Ill.
1374 E. 53rd St., 60615
312-752-6400

Cremation Society of Ill.
736 W. Addison, 60613
312-281-5058

Evergreen Cemetery
W. 87th & Kedzie 60642
312-776-8434

Graceland Cemetery
4001 N. Clark, 60613
312-525-1105

Matz Funeral Home
3440 N. Central Ave., 60634
312-545-5420

Oakwoods Cemetery
1035 E. 67th St., 60637
312-288-3800

Rago Brothers
5120 W. Fullerton, 60639
312-276-7800

Parkside Chapels
5948 Archer Ave., 60638
312-767-9788

Rosehill Cemetery
5800 N. Ravenswood, 60660
312-561-5940

Zefran Funeral Home
1941 W. Cermak Rd., 60608
312-847-6688

Danville

Sunset FH & Mem. Park
3940 N. Vermillion, 61832
217-442-2874

Decatur

Graceland-Fairlawn Cem.
2101 N. Oakland Ave., 62525
217-429-5439

Dixon

Chapel Hill Mem. Park
1121 N. Galena Ave., 61021
815-284-3322

Dolton

Oakland Mem. Lanes
15200 Lincoln Ave., 60419
708-841-5800

Downers Grove

G & S Cremation Co.
4800 Pershing Rd., 60515
708-969-0305

Toon Funeral Home
4920 Main St., 60515
708-968-0408

East St. Louis

Nash Funeral Home
P.O. Box 6407, 62202
618-874-9225

Elgin

Twin Pines Crematory
1240 Kingman Ct., 60123
708-695-8849

Elmhurst

Elm Lawn Mem. Park
401 E. Lake St., 60126
708-833-9696

York Crematory
435 N. York, 60126
312-834-1133

Forest Park

Woodlawn Cemetery
7600 W. Cermak, 60130
708-442-8500

Hazel Crest

S. Suburban Cremation Svc.
17065 S. Dixie Hwy. #47, 60429
708-335-4884

Highland Park

Kelley & Spaulding
1787 Deerfield Rd., 60035
708-831-4260

Hillside

Hursen Funeral Home
4001 W. Roosevelt, 60162
708-547-8200

Hinsdale

Samaritan W. Suburban Crem.
7508 County Line Rd., 60521
708-654-0306

Joliet

Rivers Edge Crematory
459 N. Ottawa, 60432
708-722-0524

Woodlawn Mem. Cemetery
23060 W. Jefferson, 60435
815-725-1152

Kankakee

Countyline Crematory
1151 E. Court St., 60901
815-932-1214

Lake Bluff

Lakewood Crematory
28835-217 N. Herky Dr., 60044
708-362-3303

Lombard

Phoenix Crematory
229 S. Main St., 60148
708-951-2690

McHenry

Omega Limited/Justen FH
3519 W. Elm St., 60050
815-385-2400

Mt. Prospect

Cremation Soc. of Illinois
770 E. Northwest Hwy., 60056
708-577-6505

Oak Brook

Geneses Cremation Service
122 W. 22nd St. #333, 60521
312-571-7390

Park Forest

Lain-Sullivan Funeral Home
50 Westwood Dr., 60466
708-747-3700

Pekin

Abel Vault & Monument
1917 N. 8th St., 61554
309-346-4186

Peoria

Davison-Fulton Crematory
2021 N. University, 61604
309-688-5700

Mid-state Funeral Service
1800 N. Knoxville Ave., 61603
309-682-3923

Quincy

Quincy Wilbert Vault Co.
4128 Wismann Ln., 62301
217-224-8557

Rock Island

Chippiannock Cemetery
2901 12th St., 61201
309-788-6622

Rockford

Greenwood Cemetery
1010 Brown, 61103
815-962-7522

Rosemont

Cremation Services Inc.
9669 Allen St., 60018
708-671-7868

Salem

Merz Vault Co.
Rte. 37 South, 62881
618-548-2859

Schaumburg

Ahlgrim & Sons
330 W. Golf Rd., 60195
708-882-5580

Skokie

Memorial Park Cem.
9900 Gross Point Rd., 60076
708-864-5061

Springfield

Charles T. Bisch & Son
505 E. Allen, 62703
217-544-5424

Springfield Crematory
437 N. 6th St., 62702
217-544-5755

Streator

    Schultz Wilbert Vault Co.
    115-127 S. Shabbona St., 61364
    815-672-2049

Sycamore

    Butala Funeral Home
    145 Dekalb Ave., 60178
    815-895-2833

Urbana

    Kelley Vault Co.
    406½ N. Lincoln Ave., 61801
    217-367-1844

Zion

    Mt. Olive Mem. Park
    1436 Kenosha Rd., 60099
    708-562-5476

There may be additional crematories that have been established after the time of publication.

## ❖ State Governance

The Illinois State Funeral Board has five members. There are no consumer representatives.

The Office of the Comptroller regulates cemeteries, crematories, and both cemetery and funeral preneed sales.

## ❖ Prepaid Cemetery and Funeral Funds

Only 50% of preneed *cemetery* purchases must be placed into **trust**. "**Constructive delivery**" can bypass the trusting requirement. The seller may withdraw "a reasonable fee" from the trust fund annually for administrative purposes, not to exceed the lesser of 3% or the **interest** earned.

"Delivery" is usually accomplished by issuing a certificate of ownership and warehousing the casket, vault or marker, but few states are checking to see if the goods are actually there. Once "delivered," it is almost impossible to get a **refund** even if the items have never been used. If a person opted for cremation at a later date, a burial vault would not be needed, for example. (See Gary's story on page 160.)

All preneed cemetery contracts must guarantee the price.

If installment payments are made to cover both interment rights and cemetery merchandise or services, the payments may be allocated to the lot purchase first. Those funds will not be placed in trust and are not required to be refunded if you change your mind. If you are paying

$2,000 for a lot, $1,000 for a vault, $1,000 open-and-closing, and $1,000 for a marker—$5,000 total—the first $2,000 goes directly to the cemetery. After that, only $1,500 of the remaining $3,000 will go into trust . . . maybe.

A consumer wishing to **cancel** the contract is entitled to receive the amount in the trust, but only after the last payment is made. At best, this is likely to be $1,500 in the case above or 50% of what was initially paid for merchandise and services, the interest having been withdrawn each year. If the vault and marker have been "delivered," then say goodbye to that money, too. If a consumer defaults on payments for cemetery goods and services, the cemetery *may* retain all that was paid as **"liquidated damages."**

There are additional statutes addressing the advance sale of undeveloped interment space. If construction has not begun, the purchaser may, within 12 months of purchase, cancel the agreement and get a full refund.

**Finance charges** are permitted on preneed cemetery and funeral purchases. This hits the poor the hardest. Besides, why should anyone pay interest on something they aren't yet using? Consumers should refuse to pay any preneed finance fees until this practice is outlawed.

The state requires that a booklet describing related Illinois law be given to each consumer prior to purchasing a preneed *funeral* contract. (It does not cover and is not required to be given prior to making preneed *cemetery* purchases.) Fine as far as it goes, but it does not fully describe the pitfalls of constructive delivery.

For preneed *funeral* goods and services, a commission of 5% is permitted, with 95% going into **trust**. A 15% commission is permitted on outer burial containers, 85% going into trust when sold through a funeral home. **"Constructive delivery"** can bypass the trusting requirement. (Your casket may end up in a warehouse, with no refund possible if you change your mind or move.)

The initial payments of installment purchases may be allocated entirely to the commission and finance charges, rather than making such allocations proportionately. This limits the amount earning interest at the beginning. A consumer may **cancel** a preneed funeral arrangement after it is fully paid for. In that case, the seller may retain 10% or $300, whichever is less. However, the seller may retain 25% of the payments or $300, whichever is less, as **"liquidation damages"** if a purchaser defaults in completing the purchase. If you have paid $1,000 toward a $5,000 funeral, you'll get back only $750, assuming that none of the $1,000 was allocated to finance charges.

If merchandise is not available at the time of death, **substitution** of one similar in style and equal in quality of material and workmanship is required.

Funeral insurance or annuities are transferable.

Sellers of preneed arrangements must **report** annually to the state Comptroller. The seller of preneed arrangements may manage up to $500,000 of the money. Thereafter, a new trustee must be selected.

Five dollars of each preneed cemetery sale goes into the **Cemetery Consumer Protection Fund** for reimbursement against loss. In 1997, the manager of Valley View Cemetery in Edwardsville was found to have diverted cemetery money into his own account. Similar problems have been found at Mt. Hope Cemetery in Belleville and Warren County Memorial Park Cemetery in Monmouth. If restitution is not made, consumers will be protected by this fund.

## ❖ Consumer Concerns

- The death rate in Illinois can support approximately 430 full-time mortuaries; there are, however, 1,385. Funeral prices tend to be higher in areas where there are "too many" funeral homes.
- Finance charges should not be permitted for installment purchases of prepaid funeral arrangements. When you finance a car, house, or other retail purchase, you get to use the item. But under current practice, you'll be paying a finance charge on a lay-away plan before they lay you away.
- Laws should require cemeteries to repurchase an unwanted lot at the original selling price plus 50% of the difference between that and current market price.
- Constructive delivery (warehousing) should not be permitted. The trusting requirement for preneed purchases should be increased to 100% for all goods and services—both cemetery and funeral expenses. Funeral agreements should be fully transferable, and—in the case of revocable contracts—fully refundable.

- There is no annual reporting requirement to the purchaser of prepaid funeral goods and services, paperwork that might be helpful to the family of a deceased to indicate prepayment.
- In spite of the Cemetery Consumer Protection Fund and until the Illinois laws are changed, it is probably a *terrible* idea to prepay for a funeral or any cemetery merchandise and services, given the raw deal a consumer would get in trying to transfer or back out of such a purchase. Your own trust account in a bank will be safer.
- There is no requirement that low-cost caskets be included in any display.
- There is no provision either forbidding a mark-up on cash advance items or requiring the disclosure of how much the mark-up would be if there is one. Consumers may want to ask for a copy of the invoice for each cash advance item.
- There is no clear "personal preference" law to assure that the wishes of the deceased will prevail. While the cremation statutes provide for a person to authorize his or her own cremation and make reference to a "designated survivor" as having some authority to handle such arrangements, next-of-kin in order of usual priority are likely to prevail if there are objections. A succinct law for naming a designated agent would clarify such rights for all funeral transactions.
- The standards for ethical, professional conduct should be strengthened. That would make it easier for a consumer to prevail when filing a complaint. (See Ethical Standard in the Appendix.)
- The FTC Funeral Rule should be adopted by reference to make it more enforceable in this state.
- Identification and tagging of the body at the place of death before removal should be required.
- The coroner's or medical examiner's permit for cremation in the case of an *anticipated* death from natural causes is totally unnecessary and creates an additional burden and charge for families.

### ❖ Miscellaneous Information

- The educational requirements for becoming a funeral director/ embalmer in Illinois are one year of college and one year of mortuary school (or two years of mortuary school) plus one year of apprenticeship. All must pass a state-approved exam.
- Coroners are elected. They must pass a law enforcement training program and are not necessarily physicians.

- Complaints are handled by a Complaint Intake Unit covering all regulated businesses and professions. (It is difficult to get through on the phone.)

## ❖ Nonprofit Funeral Consumer Information Societies

These consumer groups are run mostly by volunteers. Consequently, contact information may change. If you have difficulty reaching a society or are interested in starting a society in your area, call the FAMSA office: 800-765-0107. Or check the internet directory—

**www.funerals.org/famsa**

Chicago

   Chicago Memorial Association
   P.O. Box 2923, 60690

Urbana

   Champaign County Memorial Society
   309 W. Green St., 61801

~❖~

*This chapter was reviewed by the Illinois Department of Health—Vital Records. It was also sent to the Office of the Comptroller and the State Funeral Board. The Comptroller's office sent another set of laws, the preneed booklet, and a couple of other publications—without comment.*

# In Indiana

*Please refer to Chapter 8 as you use this section.*

Church groups and individuals in Indiana may have difficulty in caring for their own dead. While the majority of the statutes in the Indiana Code clearly recognize the rights of families to control the disposition of a body—including those laws dealing with public health, one statute stands out in conflict, inviting a court challenge. This one was surely passed to benefit the special interests of the mortuary industry and is buried in the Embalmers and Funeral Directors section of the Code:

> *IC 25-15-8-25. A local health officer may issue a [disposition] permit under IC 16-37-3-10 only to a funeral director . . . .*

The Public Health Code, however, has no such restrictions and deals only with the necessary concerns of the state:

> *IC 16-37-3-2. As used in this chapter, "person in charge of interment" means a person who places or causes to be placed a stillborn child or dead body or the ashes, after cremation, in a grave, vault, urn, or other receptacle, or otherwise disposes of the body or ashes.*

> *IC 16-37-3-3. The person in charge of interment shall file a certificate of death or of still birth with the local health officer. . . .*

> *IC 16-37-3-10. Upon receipt of a properly executed certificate of death or stillbirth or, when authorized by rule of the state department, a provisional certificate of death, a local health officer in the county in which the death occurred shall issue a permit for the disposal of the body.*

Even under the funeral directors' statutes a family's rights are acknowledged:

> *IC 25-15-9-18. The following persons, in the order of priority indicated, have the authority to designate the manner, type, and selection of the final disposition and interment of human remains:*

*(1) The decedent's surviving spouse.*
*(2) The decedent's surviving adult child or children. However if the children cannot agree on the manner of final disposition, the personal representative of the decedent's estate.*
*(3) The decedent's surviving parents.*
*(4) The personal representative of the decedent's estate.*

*IC 25-15-8-1 Grounds for Discipline . . . A licensee that . . . takes possession of human remains without authorization from the person legally entitled to custody of remains . . . may be disciplined. . . .*

Certainly, ethical legislators will want to repeal 25-15-8-25, the offending statute, and I suspect funeral directors might decide that's in their best interests, too. I have yet to see an Indiana funeral home price list with a charge *only* for obtaining the disposition permit. Perhaps it's a public service funeral directors are willing to do for free.

On the other hand, a family wishing to care for its own dead may be able to convince a local health officer to issue a permit directly—as permitted by 16-37-3-10—assuming that the death certificate is in order and given the other substantiating statutes that empower a family to retain control of the body.

## ❖ Death Certificate

The family doctor or a local health officer will sign the death certificate, stating the cause of death. The remaining information must be supplied, typewritten or in black ink. The death certificate must be filed with the local health officer prior to final disposition.

Indiana is testing electronic death registration. When that is adopted the procedure will change somewhat. Check with the local health department.

## ❖ Fetal Death

A death certificate is required in a case of stillbirth after 20 weeks of gestation.

## ❖ Transporting and Disposition Permit

The local health officer will issue the authorization for disposition upon receipt of a properly executed death certificate. A burial transit permit (two copies) is required if the body is to be transported by common carrier. An out-of-state transit permit, for bodies brought into Indiana, must be filed with the local health officer.

## ❖ Burial

Burial in Indiana must occur in an "established cemetery," and have a cover of not less than two feet of earth.

Cemetery personnel may not sell markers or monuments for a profit if any public funds are accepted by that cemetery.

## ❖ Cremation

There is a 48-hour wait prior to cremation unless waived by the local health officer. (One might wish to seek this waiver if the crematory intends to charge a holding fee.) A pacemaker must be removed, and authorization by next-of-kin or other authorizing agent is required.

An authorizing agent must sign a statement saying that arrangements have been made for viewing the body (or for holding it until other services with the body present have been arranged first). Some funeral homes will interpret this to mean that they can require ID viewing and charge for it. Identification and tagging of the body at the place of death prior to removal would be a more responsible requirement.

Cremated remains may legally be disposed of in a crypt or cemetery, on the property of a consenting owner, on uninhabited public land or a waterway. A form recording the disposition must be filed with the county recorder within ten days of the final disposition.

## ❖ Other Requirements

Disposition must occur within "a reasonable time" after death. When death has occurred from a communicable disease, consult the doctor in attendance.

## ❖ Medical Schools for Body Donation

All body donations in Indiana are handled through one agency.

Anatomical Education Program
635 Barnhill Dr.
Medical Science 259
Indianapolis, IN 46202-5120
317-274-7450 or 852-4965
Urgent need.

Cost to family: embalming and transportation minus $200 paid to funeral director
Prior enrollment: not required
Over-enrollment: not yet
Disposition: cremation; return of cremains by request
Body rejection: standard,* under 16, over 200 lbs., over six feet tall, amyotrophic lateral sclerosis, other infectious diseases

* autopsy, decomposition, mutilation, severe burn victim, meningitis, hepatitis, AIDS

## ❖ Crematories

Crown Point

Northwest Indiana Cremation
10101 Broadway, 46307
219-662-0661

Evansville

Alexander Mem. Park
2200 Mesker Pk. Dr., 47720
812-422-1674

Fort Wayne

Klaehn-Fahl & Mellon
420 W. Wayne St., 46802
219-424-1525

Lindenwood Cemetery
2324 W. Main, 46808
219-432-4542

Greenwood

Gr'tr South Side Crematory
481 W. Main St., 46142
317-632-9431

Indianapolis

Amer. Midwest Crematory
740 E. 86th, 46240
317-844-3966

Crown Hill Cemetery
700 W. 38th, 46208
317-925-8231

Flanner & Buchanan
2950 N High School Rd., 46224
317-925-9871

Muncie

Meeks & Sons
415 E. Washington, 47305
317-288-6669

Portage

Calvary Cemetery
2701 Willowdale Rd., 46368
219-762-5885

South Bend

Michiana Crematory
52803 US 33N, 46616
219-232-4857

Riverview Cemetery
2300 Portage, 46616
219-233-2420

Terre Haute

Terre Haute Crematory
3000 Lafayette, 47805
812-466-5204

There may be additional crematories that have been established since publication of this book.

## ❖ State Governance

There are eleven members on the Funeral and Cemetery Board—four funeral directors, four cemeterians, two consumer members, and one member from the public health department. (No more than five may be of the same political party.) However, cemeterians may not vote on funeral issues and funeral directors may not vote on cemetery issues. This seems to negate the positive aspect of having a combined board.

Crematories are licensed by the Funeral and Cemetery Board and may be operated by anyone so licensed—not necessarily a mortician.

## ❖ Prepaid Cemetery and Funeral Funds

A portion of ground interment rights or crypt sales must be placed in perpetual care: 8% for crypts, 15% for lots.

100% of all money paid preneed for *funeral* or *cemetery* goods and services must be placed in **trust** and the **interest** allowed to accumulate. "**Constructive delivery**" can bypass the trusting requirement. "Delivery" usually is accomplished by issuing a certificate of ownership and warehousing the casket, vault and/or marker, although few states are checking to see if the goods are actually there. Once "delivered," it is almost impossible to get a refund even if the items have never been used. If a person opted for cremation at a later date, a burial vault would not be needed, for example.

All preneed funeral policies are irrevocable after 30 days, although a consumer may **transfer** a prepaid funeral contract to another funeral home. (The seller is entitled to keep 5% as a transfer fee.) The irrevocable requirement seems a strange limit on consumer choice.

All prepaid funeral contracts must guarantee to supply goods and services of **equal value** at the price paid, without additional charge. Current industry literature warns against guaranteeing prices because funeral inflation is so rampant—6% a year—which exceeds the interest usually received on such contracts. Therefore, one must wonder if folks in Indiana have a great deal going or whether funeral homes are finding mischievous ways around the law to collect the difference. The word "value" is an obvious problem. A $795 casket ten years ago would have been far fancier than a $795 casket today.

Excess monies left over after the contract services have been provided "may"—but not necessarily will be—returned to the family, an unlikely event, given funeral inflation.

Sellers of preneed funeral plans must make an annual **report** to the state board of prepaid funds collected.

Indiana has a preneed **consumer protection fund** that may accumulate up to $1 million. It is financed by a fee for each preneed contract written—$2.50 for those under $1,000 in value and $5 for those $1,000 and over. This fund will be used in the case of default by a funeral provider.

## ❖ Consumer Concerns

- The death rate in Indiana can support approximately 206 full-time mortuaries; there are, however, 700. Funeral prices tend to be higher in areas where there are "too many" funeral homes.
- Laws should require cemeteries to repurchase an unwanted lot at the original selling price plus 50% of the difference between that and current market price, if the value has increased. If the value of the lot has decreased below the original selling price, the cemetery should repurchase the lot at 75% of the current worth.
- Finance charges are permitted for installment purchases of prepaid funeral services and merchandise. This is outrageous and should be repealed immediately! When you finance a car or house, you get to use either. But a finance charge on a lay-away plan before they lay you away?
- Although a funeral home must supply "services and merchandise similar in style and quality of material at least equal in value" to those chosen preneed, there is no guarantee that an adequate description will be listed on the preneed contract. Survivors should be allowed to approve any substitution.

- Constructive delivery (warehousing) should not be permitted to bypass the 100% trusting requirement for preneed purchases.
- There is no annual reporting requirement to the purchaser of prepaid funeral goods and services, paperwork that might be useful to the family of a deceased and which would help to "enforce" the trusting requirement.
- Given the loopholes, it is probably a *terrible* idea to prepay for cemetery and funeral expenses in Indiana. Money in your own bank account will be safer, is more transferable, and allows for a change in plans.
- Identification and tagging of the body at the place of death before removal should be required.
- There is no requirement that low-cost caskets be included in any display.
- The statute on mark-up of cash advance items is vague and does not appear to forbid a mark-up or require disclosure of the exact amount of any mark-up if there is one.
- The FTC Funeral Rule should be adopted by reference to make it more enforceable in this state.
- There is no law that allows you to state your funeral preferences or for naming a designated agent to make your final arrangements. In situations where you are estranged or distant from next-of-kin, this could be important.
- Ethical standards should be clearly defined in order for valid consumer complaints to prevail. (See Appendix.)
- More detailed and explicit procedures should be available to anyone who wants to file a complaint.

## ❖ Miscellaneous Information

- The educational requirements for becoming a funeral director in Indiana are one year of college and one year of mortuary school (or two years of mortuary school) plus one year of apprenticeship. All must pass a state-approved exam.
- A crematory may not sell inorganic matter (*e.g.*, gold) retrieved from a body.
- A county coroner is elected and may appoint deputies.

## ❖ Nonprofit Funeral Consumer Information Societies

These consumer groups are run mostly by volunteers. Consequently, contact information may change. If you have difficulty reaching a society or are interested in starting a society in your area, call the FAMSA office: 800-765-0107. Or check the internet directory—

**www.funerals.org/famsa**

Bloomington

> Bloomington Memorial Society
> 2120 N. Fee Ln., 47408
> 812-332-3695

Indianapolis

> Indianapolis Memorial Society
> 5805 E. 56th St., 46226

Valparaiso

> Memorial Society of NW Indiana
> P.O. Box 329, 46384-0329
> 219-464-3024

~❖~

*This chapter was sent for review to the Funeral and Cemetery Board, the Department of Health, and the Attorney General's office. No response was received by the time of publication.*

# In Iowa

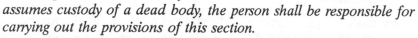

*Please refer to Chapter 8 as you use this section.*

Families and church groups in Iowa may care for their own dead when no communicable disease is involved. The legal authority to do so is found in:

> *Title 144.27 (re filing a death certificate) — When a person other than a funeral director assumes custody of a dead body, the person shall be responsible for carrying out the provisions of this section.*

> *Title 156.2 Persons excluded (from the Practice of Funeral Directing and Mortuary Science regulations) (5) Persons burying their own dead under burial permit from the registrar of vital statistics.*

## ❖ Death Certificate

The family doctor or a local medical examiner will supply and sign the death certificate within 24 hours stating the cause of death. The remaining information must be supplied, typewritten or in black ink. The death certificate must be filed with the local registrar within three days and before final disposition.

Iowa is researching electronic death registration. When that is adopted the procedure will change somewhat. Check with the local registrar or health department.

## ❖ Fetal Death

A fetal death report is required when death occurs after 20 weeks of gestation. If there is no family physician involved, the local medical examiner must sign the fetal death certificate. All other procedures apply if disposition is handled by the family.

## ❖ Transporting and Disposition Permit

The local registrar, medical examiner, or a funeral director will issue the burial-transit permit. This authorization must be obtained before moving the body from the place of death.

## ❖ Burial

Check with the county registrar for local zoning laws regarding home burial. The top of the casket must be three feet below the natural surface of the earth. Although not mentioned in the law, a burial site should probably be 150 feet from a water supply.

When burial is arranged, the family member acting as the funeral director must sign the burial-transit permit and return it within 10 days to the issuing registrar.

## ❖ Cremation

A cremation permit must be obtained from the medical examiner. The cost will not exceed $35. Most crematories insist that a pacemaker be removed, and authorization by next-of-kin is usually required. The crematory will return the disposition authorization to the issuing registrar.

## ❖ Other Requirements

Embalming is required if disposition will not occur within 48 hours.

Embalming is required if death was from a communicable disease. Only a funeral director may handle such deaths. Embalming or a sealed casket is required when shipping a body by common carrier.

## ❖ Medical Schools for Body Donation

Palmer College of Chiropractic
Dept. of Anatomy
1000 Brady St.
Davenport, IA 52803
319-323-9712 (8-4:30 M-F)
319-355-4433 (all other times)
Moderate need

Cost to family: transportation beyond 250 miles
Prior enrollment: not required
Over enrollment: not occurred
Disposition: cremation; return of cremains by request
Body rejection: standard*, under 18, bypass surgery, missing parts

University of Osteopathic Medicine & Health Sciences
3200 Grand Ave.
Des Moines, IA 50312
515-271-1481 (8-4:30)
515-271-1400 (all other times)

Cost to family: transportation over $150 inside Polk Co.; over $250 outside Polk Co.
Prior enrollment: required
Over enrollment: not shared
Disposition: Cremation; return of cremains by request
Body rejection: standard*, under 18, missing limbs

University of Iowa
Dept. of Anatomy, BSB
Iowa City, IA 52242
319-335-7762
319-356-1616 (after hours)
Moderate need

Cost to family: transportation; embalming if not delivered within 10 hours
Prior enrollment: required
Over enrollment: shared by request
Disposition: cremation; return of cremains by request
Body rejection: standard

\* autopsy, decomposition, mutilation, severe burn victim, meningitis, hepatitis, AIDS

## ❖ Crematories

Ankeney

Cremation Society of Iowa
128 SE Shurfine Dr., 50021
800-830-3464

Cedar Rapids

Cedar Memorial Park
4200 1st NE, 52406
319-393-8000

Creston

Larkin Funeral Home
604 W. Adams St., 50801
515-782-8428

Davenport

Fairmont Cemetery
3902 Rockingham Rd., 52802
319-322-8663

Quad Cities Crematory
838 E. Kimberly Rd., 52807
319-391-6202

Des Moines

Dunn's Funeral Home
2121 Grand, 50312
515-244-2121

La Porte

Heisman Funeral Home
606 Main St., 50651
319-342-3131

Marion

Roland Crematory
1210 Blairs Ferry Rd., 52302
319-377-4834

Sioux City

Siouxland Crematory
805 10th St., 51105
712-258-4576

There may be additional crematories that were established after the date of publication.

## ❖ State Governance

The Iowa Board of Mortuary Science Examiners has seven members. Two are consumer representatives.

Cemetery funds are monitored by the Insurance Department.

Crematories are inspected by the Department of Health.

### ❖ Prepaid Cemetery and Funeral Funds

Iowa has both perpetual care cemeteries and non-perpetual care cemeteries, although all cemeteries established after 1995 must provide for perpetual care. A contract with a non-perpetual care cemetery must be clearly marked as such.

Twenty percent of the lot purchase must be put into a **guarantee fund** when sold by a perpetual care cemetery. A cemetery may not require that you purchase cemetery merchandise only from that cemetery, something to keep in mind as the for-profit companies move in.

Corporate chains are purchasing and building cemeteries in Iowa. Cemeteries are tax-exempt, which gives the corporations a huge incentive to invest in such. The cost of cemetery space and services—when owned by a for-profit corporation—tend to be extremely high.

Eighty percent of all money prepaid for *funeral* and *cemetery* service and merchandise must be placed in **trust** in a federally insured institution. An annual **report** of each trust fund must be made to the state Insurance Department every year. Each preneed contract must carry a disclosure indicating that the consumer may contact the Insurance Department to verify the whereabouts and amount of the fund being held.

The seller may withdraw up to 50% of the **interest,** not to exceed the amount needed to keep up with inflation as measured by the consumer price index and as set by the commissioner. Unfortunately, the insurance commissioner is probably not aware that funeral inflation is at least twice the rate of general inflation. If the funeral home does not perform the services, the purchaser may reclaim any interest withdrawn. No clear rights on **transfer** or **cancellation** exist.

The trusting requirement does not apply to merchandise (other than caskets and vaults) that has been **"delivered"** to the consumer—even if stored by the seller—provided it is clearly identified. The most common example of this kind of merchandise would be a marker or headstone.

Although a prepaid funeral plan must disclose the terms under which **substitutions** "may" be made, there is *no requirement* for a full description of the merchandise and *no requirement* for the undertaker to supply merchandise of equal quality and construction when it is a guaranteed-price arrangement.

Iowa has authorized the establishment of an Insurance Division **Regulatory Fund**—capped at $200,000—to protect consumers against the default of prepaid funerals among other things. This is apparently a serious concern in Iowa, as there are 12 pages of statutes covering "liquidation" of a funeral firm, far more than in any other funeral-related section. It is not at all clear that the Regulatory Fund will be available to everyone left holding the bag if a mortuary goes out of business, however. To wit, the liquidator may "prefer the claims of certain at-need and preneed funeral customers . . . considering the relative circumstances" when assigning assets of the funeral home. (Oh, yes, witnesses and lawyers get paid before funeral consumers.) Is the short-fall guaranteed to be made up by the Regulatory Fund so that no funeral customer experiences a loss and everyone is "made whole"? What if $200,000 isn't enough? At an average of say $5,000 each, $200,000 would cover just 40 funerals. A funeral home doing 50 calls a year probably has 15 of those prepaid if it is within the industry norm. If people prepay within five years of death or so, then the funeral home could be sitting on 75 or more prepaids, not 40!

### ❖ Consumer Concerns

- The death rate in Iowa can support approximately 116 full-time mortuaries; there are, however, 582. Funeral prices tend to be higher in areas where there are "too many" funeral homes, and there is likely to be a greater default on prepaid funeral monies.
- There is little or no oversight of cemetery sales practices. Reconstructing the make-up of the Funeral Board would be one way to begin. Suggested possibility: two funeral directors, two cemeterians who are not funeral directors or affiliated by business interests to a mortuary, an independent monument dealer, and two consumer representatives.
- Laws should require cemeteries to repurchase an unwanted lot at the original selling price plus 50% of the difference between that and current market price.
- The trusting of prepaid funeral money and cemetery merchandise should be increased to 100%, with no withdrawal of interest.

- Rights of transfer and cancellation should be established.
- A full description of funeral and cemetery merchandise should be spelled out in prepaid contracts, with an obligation to supply merchandise of equal quality and construction if not available at need. Survivors should approve any substitutions.
- Although funeral homes must report on prepaid accounts to the state each year, it would be more helpful if the report were also sent to consumers. This would provide a record that may be useful to survivors and would help to enforce the trusting requirements.
- Until the laws have been improved for prepaid funeral and cemetery purchases, it is probably a *terrible* idea to prepay for a funeral or for cemetery services and merchandise in Iowa.
- Identification and tagging of the body at the place of death before removal should be required.
- The regulation requiring embalming when death involves communicable diseases should be repealed. Not only will the funeral staff and possibly the public health be at risk, such a regulation does not acknowledge religious or personal objections to embalming.
- The state should distinguish between "communicable" and "contagious" diseases. Those who have cared for someone dying of AIDS, for example, should not be forbidden from personally handling the funeral arrangements.
- There is no requirement for a display of low-cost caskets.
- There is no required disclosure of how much mark-up will be charged on cash advances nor is a mark-up forbidden.
- The ethical standards for funeral directors should be more detailed and explicit, with clear procedures available to anyone wishing to file a complaint.
- If you have signed a permit for cremation, the "authorizing person" has the authority to cancel that after your death. The authorizing person would be a next-of-kin if you have not given the power-of-attorney-for-healthcare to someone else. According to the Board of Mortuary Science rules, the person whom you have named as attorney-in-fact for a durable power of attorney for health care has first priority in making funeral decisions. The usual order in next-of-kin follows after that. This would be more enforceable if it were in statute, not merely regulations that govern mortuary practitioners.

## ❖ Miscellaneous Information

- Two years of college plus a course in mortuary study are required to become a funeral director. One year of internship after school is required.
- A county medical examiner must be an MD and is appointed by the medical examining board. A medical examiner may not influence the choice of a mortuary.
- The FTC Funeral Rule has been adopted by reference in the Mortuary Science Board Rules.
- A public official who is otherwise forbidden from accepting gifts of value may, however, accept funeral flowers and memorial gifts designated for a nonprofit organization.
- Cemetery commissioners may subscribe to cemetery publications paid for by the cemetery fund.
- Coal mining is not suitable if it is within 100 feet of a cemetery.

## ❖ Nonprofit Funeral Consumer Information Societies

There is one nonprofit society in Iowa:

Memorial Society of Iowa River Valley
120 N. Dubuque St.
Iowa City, IA 52245
319-338-2637

Iowans outside this area may wish to join *Friends of FAMSA*, 800-765-0107. FAMSA has negotiated an arrangement with a commercial provider to serve the rest of the state. If you are interested in starting a society in your area, call the FAMSA office: 800-765-0107.

~❖~

*This chapter was reviewed by the Iowa Board of Mortuary Science Examiners. It was also sent to the Department of Insurance and the Consumer Affairs Department of the Attorney General's office, but no response was received from those agencies.*

# In Kansas

*Please refer to Chapter 8 as you use this section.*

Persons in Kansas may care for their own dead. The legal authority to do so is found in:

*Title 65-1713b. Every funeral service or interment, or part thereof, hereafter conducted in this state must be in the actual charge and under the supervision of a Kansas licensed funeral director or of the duly licensed assistant funeral director. Provided, however, that this shall not prevent a family from burying its own dead where death did not result from a contagious, infectious or communicable disease, nor shall it prevent a religious group or sect whose religious beliefs require the burial of its own dead from conducting such services where death did not result from a contagious, infectious or communicable disease.*

There are no other statutes that might require you to use a funeral director.

## ❖ Death Certificate

The family doctor (or a coroner) will supply and sign the death certificate within 24 hours, stating the cause of death. The remaining information must be supplied, typewritten or in black ink. The death certificate must be filed with the state registrar within three days and before final disposition.

## ❖ Fetal Death

A fetal death report is required when the weight of the fetus is 351 grams or more and death did not result from an induced termination of pregnancy. If there is no family physician involved, the local coroner must sign the fetal death certificate.

## ❖ Transporting and Disposition Permit

A body may be moved with medical permission. If out-of-state disposition is planned, the state registrar will issue a transit permit.

## ❖ Burial

Home burial is permissible in Kansas. Check with the county or town for local zoning laws regarding home burial. There are no state burial statutes or regulations with regard to depth. A sensible guideline is 150 feet from a water supply and at least two feet of earth on top.

## ❖ Cremation

A cremation permit from the local coroner is required. There is no fee for this. Authorization by next-of-kin is usually required, and a pacemaker must be removed.

## ❖ Other Requirements

If disposition will not take place within 24 hours, embalming or refrigeration is required. A reasonable extension of this may be permitted if no health hazard or nuisance will result.

When death has occurred from meningococcal infection, Ebola virus infection, Lassa fever, anthrax, rabies, brucellosis, or any other infectious or contagious disease, the body must be handled by an embalmer. (The list of specified diseases was reduced in 1997.) In the case of immediate burial, the body must be in a sealed metal casket.

A body to be shipped by common carrier or for burial in a mausoleum must be embalmed.

## ❖ Medical Schools for Body Donation

University of Kansas
Department of Anatomy
Medical Center
39th & Rainbow
Kansas City, KS 66103
913-588-7000 8-5 M-F or
913-588-5000
Low need

Cost to family: transportation beyond Kansas City area
Prior enrollment: not required
Over-enrollment: shared
Disposition: cremation; return of cremains by request
Body rejection: standard,* missing body parts

* autopsy, decomposition, mutilation, severe burn victim, meningitis, hepatitis, AIDS, and other contagious or communicable diseases

## ❖ Crematories

Dodge City

Burkhart Funeral Chapel/Crematory
1901 N. 14th Ave., 67801
800-279-8791

Great Bend

Great Bend Family Mortuary/Crem.
5220 10th St., 67530
316-793-8690

Olathe

Frye & Son Mortuary/Crematory
105 E. Loula, 66051
913-782-0582

Salina

Ryan Mortuary
137 N. 8th St., 67401
785-825-4242

Shawnee Mission

Shawnee Mission Crematory
Amos Family, Inc.
10901 Johnson Dr., 66203
913-631-5566

Topeka

Mount Hope Cemetery
4700 W. 17th, 66604
785-272-1122

Shawnee Co. Crematory
1321 W. 10th, 66601
913-354-8558

Wichita

Cochran Mortuary & Crematory
1411 N. Broadway, 67214
316-262-4422

Downing & Lahey Crematory
6555 E. Central, 67206
316-682-4553

Lakeview Funeral Home/Crematory
12100 E. 13th, 67206
316-684-8200

Quiring Old Mission Mortuary
3424 E. 21st., 67208
316-666-7311

Additional crematories may have been established in this state after the date of publication.

## ❖ State Governance

The Kansas State Board of Mortuary Arts has five members. Two are consumer representatives.

The Secretary of State regulates cemetery preneed transactions.

There is no state agency regulating crematories.

## ❖ Prepaid Cemetery and Funeral Funds

Kansas statutes do not address how prepaid *cemetery service* money should be handled, but there are some pretty wild provisions for what a cemetery can do with the money you prepaid for *cemetery merchandise*—presumably vaults and markers. "**Constructive delivery**" can bypass any **trusting** requirements altogether, so the cemetery is likely to give you a certificate of ownership and call it "delivered" (in the warehouse, though few states are checking to see if your vault and marker really are). Otherwise, 110% of the wholesale cost must go into trust. But it doesn't go into trust right away: the cemetery can pocket 35% of your purchase price before allocating any payments to your lay-away trust account. If any of your prepaid money actually ends up in the bank, "reasonable" amounts may be withdrawn from the income to administer the account. How much does it cost to watch the **interest** grow?

I have a sneaking suspicion after wading through the legalese of the Kansas statutes that the state also permits preneed funeral and cemetery installment sales to come under the "actuarial method." That would mean that **finance charges** are permitted, and your payments will be applied to the carrying charges before they will be applied to the merchandise and services you're purchasing.

There are no provisions for simply **cancelling** a purchase of cemetery goods and services and getting a refund unless you move 150 miles away. If you can't afford to keep up the payments, you can probably kiss whatever money you've already paid goodbye.

But listen to the statutory plan if you do move more than 150 miles away and the vault and marker have not yet been installed or "delivered": In that case, you may ask the cemetery to send the merchandise to a new cemetery but you'll have to pay the transportation costs! Hey, the lid on an average vault is 900 pounds, and that's just the lid! What's it going to cost to ship the whole thing to, say, Vermont?

If you do want to **cancel**—but, remember, you have to be 150 miles away first—you are entitled to—*ta-da!*—85% of what's in trust (if there's anything really there). In case you're feeling muddled (I was for a while), the most that the cemetery ever had to leave in the trust was 110% of the wholesale cost for your vault and marker! If you paid $1,000 for the vault but it cost the cemetery only $350, then $385 might have been put into trust. Not counting interest—which can be withdrawn for "reasonable" expenses—you get 85% of that or $327.25! What a deal the Secretary of State has arranged for you!

All payments for preneed *funeral* goods and services (including vaults but not markers) must be placed in **trust,** with **interest** to accumulate.

Payment checks must be made out to the depository bank or institution unless the mortuary carries an insurance policy of at least $100,000 against employee dishonesty. The state may audit accounts on a random basis.

A **report** of preneed arrangements must be made by the funeral home to the Mortuary board every two years.

A prearranged contract may be **cancelled** by the buyer at any time. An irrevocable policy (of no more than $3,500) may be **transferred** to another provider at any time.

## ❖ Consumer Concerns

- The death rate in Kansas can support approximately 96 full-time mortuaries; there are, however, 332. Funeral prices tend to be higher in areas where there are "too many" funeral homes.
- There is no state board governing cemeteries.
- "Constructive delivery" of cemetery merchandise should not be permitted. Trusting requirements should be increased to 100% of cemetery goods and services, with a full right of cancellation and refund including interest.
- Laws should require cemeteries to repurchase an unwanted lot at the original selling price plus 50% of the difference between that and current market price.
- If finance charges are permitted for installment purchases of prepaid funeral services and merchandise, this is outrageous. When you finance a car or house, you get to use what you are buying. But a finance charge on a lay-away plan before they lay you away?
- There is no annual reporting requirement to the purchaser of prepaid funeral goods and services, paperwork that might be helpful to the family of a deceased to indicate prepayment and would help to "enforce" trusting requirements.
- There is no guarantee fund to protect prepaid funeral money in case of default. The $100,000 insurance policy against employee dishonesty is not mandatory nor likely adequate.
- There is no requirement that when merchandise is selected for a guaranteed-price preneed agreement that a clear description be given and that merchandise of equal quality and construction must be substituted if the original item selected is not available. Survivors should approve any substitution.

- Until the laws governing preneed cemetery and funeral purchases have been changed, it is probably a *terrible* idea to pay for either ahead of time in Kansas.
- The coroner or medical examiner's permit for cremation in the case of an *anticipated* death from natural causes is totally unnecessary and creates an additional burden for families.
- Identification and tagging of the body at the place of death before removal should be required.
- All laws requiring embalming should be repealed. When death occurs from a communicable disease, funeral professionals and possibly the environment are at risk. Refrigeration is a more reliable method of body preservation and should not be needed for 72 hours under normal circumstances. This would allow for most funeral rituals to occur according to religious preference.
- There is no provision either forbidding a mark-up on cash advance items or requiring the disclosure of the mark-up. Consumers may want to ask for a copy of the invoices for such charges.
- There is no requirement that low-cost caskets be included in any display.
- The FTC Funeral Rule should be adopted by reference to make it more enforceable in this state. Furthermore, the statutes that describe funeral pricing bundled with the casket price should be eliminated, as the FTC Rule requires itemization of funeral services.
- There is no "personal preference" law to assure that the wishes of the deceased will prevail.

## ❖ Miscellaneous Information

- Educational requirements for becoming an embalmer: mortuary college (2 years), national exam, and one year of apprenticeship. For a funeral director: two years of college, state exam, and one year of apprenticeship prior to exam.
- Ethical standards for morticians are fairly comprehensive, but additional ones will be found in the Appendix.
- Complaint information is spelled out in a pamphlet put out by the Mortuary Board.
- District coroners are licensed physicians who are appointed.

## ❖ Nonprofit Funeral Consumer Information Societies

Although there are no memorial societies in Kansas as of this writing, you may check the internet directory—**www.funerals.org/famsa**—or call the national office to see if any have since been started: 1-800-765-0107. Or let the FAMSA office know if you are willing to help start one. The FAMSA office may have a limited list of ethically-priced mortuaries in Kansas to which referrals can be made while monitoring consumer satisfaction.

There is a society in Kansas City, Missouri:

Funeral and Memorial Society of Greater KC
4500 Warnick Blvd., Kansas City, MO 64111
816-561-6322

~❖~

*This chapter was reviewed by the Kansas Department of Health and Environment—Vital Statistics, the Secretary of State, and the Kansas State Board of Mortuary Arts.*

# In Kentucky

*Please refer to Chapter 18 as you use this section.*

Persons in Kentucky may care for their own dead. The legal authority to do so is found in:

> *Title 213.080 Certificate of Death . . . The statement of facts relating to the disposition of the body shall be signed by the undertaker or person acting as such.*

There are no other statutes which might require you to use a funeral director.

## ❖ Death Certificate

If the deceased was not attended by a physician, the death must be reported to the coroner, regardless of the cause of death. The death certificate, obtainable from the health department or a funeral director, must be presented to the physician, dentist, or chiropractor in charge of the patient's care within five days. The nonmedical information must be supplied, typewritten. The physician will return the completed death certificate within five working days to the funeral director or person acting as such. The death certificate must then be filed with the Office of Vital Statistics.

A provisional death certificate will serve as the burial-transit permit. This may be procured from the county coroner or facility releasing the body.

## ❖ Fetal Death

A fetal death must be reported when death occurs after 20 weeks of gestation or when the weight is 350 grams. If no physician is in attendance, the coroner must be notified.

## ❖ Transporting and Disposition Permit

The local registrar (within the county health department) or a deputy will issue the Provisional Report of Death. The top copy serves as the burial transit permit. This must be obtained prior to final disposition of the body. After disposition, it must be filed with the local registrar within five days.

## ❖ Burial

Check with the county zoning commission for laws regarding home burial. There must be three feet of earth over a box unless the casket is impervious, in which case the container must be covered by two feet of earth. Although not mentioned in the law, a burial site should be at least 150 feet from a water supply.

When burial is arranged by the family, the family member acting as the funeral director must sign the authorization for disposition and return it to the registrar of that locale within 10 days.

## ❖ Cremation

A coroner's signature on the Provisional Report of Death is required for cremation. As of 1996, physicians accounted for only a dozen or so of those serving as coroners. The majority of the rest were associated in some way with funeral homes. This may put a family wishing to care for its own dead in an awkward and difficult position if the mortician doesn't understand a family's rights.

State law requires that a pacemaker be removed. Persons may authorize their own cremation or designate an authorizing agent; otherwise authorization from all next-of-kin of the same order is required. The crematory may offer to file the paperwork.

## ❖ Other Requirements

Kentucky has no other requirements controlling the time schedule for the disposition of unembalmed bodies. Weather and reasonable planning should be considered.

If the person died of a contagious or communicable disease, the physician or local health officer should be consulted.

## ❖ Medical Schools for Body Donation

University of Kentucky
College of Medicine
Body Bequeathal Program
MN 224 Medical Center
Lexington, KY 40536-0084
606-323-5160
Urgent need

Cost to family: none from central and
eastern KY
Prior enrollment: not required
Over-enrollment: shared in KY
Disposition: cremation, burial on
grounds; return of cremains by
request
Body rejection: infectious/contagious
disease, recent surgery, autopsy,
obesity, trauma, organ donors
(except eyes), death outside KY,
objection by family

University of Louisville
Health Science Center Rm. 916
Department of Anatomy
Louisville, KY 40292
502-852-5165
after hours: 368-3396
Moderate need

Cost to family: transportation outside
Jefferson, Clark, Floyd counties;
over $1.25 per mile outside 50-mile
radius
Prior enrollment: preferred
Over-enrollment: used, not shared
Disposition: cremation and burial in
University plot; return of cremains
by request
Body rejection: autopsy,
decomposition, burn victim,
mutilation, organ donor,
contagious disease, obesity

## ❖ Crematories

Bowling Green

Vogt Vault Company
Molamish Park, 42701
502-491-0946 (Louisville)

Elizabethtown

Vogt Vault Company
4650 Louisville Rd., 42101
502-491-0946 (Louisville)

Lexington

The Lexington Crematory
833 W. Main St., 40508
606-255-5522

Louisville

Funeral Directors Vault
817 E. Jefferson St., 40201
502-585-4401

Resthaven Memorial Park
4400 Bardstown, 40218 ◂
502-491-5950

Vogt Vault Company
6010 Action Ave., 40218
502-491-0946

Owensboro

Owensboro Memorial Gardens
Hardinsburg Rd., 42303
502-926-1881

West Paducah

> 4-K Corporation
> 1170 Fisher Rd., 42086
> 502-554-4436

Additional crematories may have been established in this state after the date of publication.

## ❖ State Governance

The Kentucky Board of Embalmers and Funeral Directors has five members. One is a consumer representative.

The Attorney General's office oversees cemetery companies, preneed sellers, and crematories.

Crematories are licensed by the Attorney General's Office. Sound crematory practices are well-defined in the statutes passed in 1994.

## ❖ Prepaid Cemetery and Funeral Funds

A cemetery must deposit 20% of each lot sale, 5% of each crypt sale, and 10% of each niche sale in its perpetual care fund.

100% of preneed *cemetery services* must be placed in **trust**. 40% of the payments for *cemetery merchandise* must be placed in **trust** unless the merchandise has been "delivered" (stored in a warehouse) with a certificate of ownership supplied to the purchaser. This is called "**constructive delivery**." Once the merchandise has been so "delivered," it may not be possible to get a refund. **Bonding** may be used in lieu of the trust fund.

All (100%) prepaid *funeral* money must be placed in **trust** in a federally controlled financial institution. Funds may be co-mingled, but separate accounting must be maintained.

A preneed contract may be **cancelled** with 15 days notice and all principal and **interest** returned to the purchaser.

Preneed licensees and cemetery companies must file annual **reports** of all sales with the state.

A fee of $5 for cemetery sales of $500 or less and $10 for sales over $500 in value must be paid to the Attorney General's office for the "consumer security account" to provide restitution to consumers who have been defrauded by cemetery companies and preneed sellers.

## ❖ Consumer Concerns

- The death rate in Kentucky can support approximately 149 full-time mortuaries; there are, however, 507. Funeral prices tend to be higher in areas where there are "too many" funeral homes.

- Laws should require cemeteries to repurchase an unwanted lot at the original selling price plus 50% of the difference between that and current market price.

- 100% of all prepaid cemetery merchandise should be placed into trust with the right to cancel and receive a refund. Constructive delivery should not be permitted.

- There is little or no oversight of cemetery sales practices. Reconstructing the make-up of the Funeral Board would be one way to begin. Suggested possibility: two funeral directors, two cemeterians who are not funeral directors or affiliated with a mortuary, one crematory operator who is not a funeral director or affiliated, and two consumer representatives.

- Although prepaid funeral purchases must be placed into a trust account with an annual report to the state, there is no way to be sure that all funds are included. Such paperwork could be useful to survivors and would help to enforce the trusting requirements.

- There is no requirement that when merchandise is selected on a guaranteed-price, preneed agreement that a clear description be given and that merchandise of equal quality and construction must be substituted, with approval of survivors, if the original item selected is not available at the time of need.

- Until there is better protection for preneed funeral and cemetery funds, it is probably a *terrible* idea to prepay for these in Kentucky.

- Identification and tagging of the body at the place of death before removal should be required.

- There is no requirement that low-cost caskets be displayed along with others.

- There is no provision to either disclose the mark-up on cash advance items or to forbid such a practice.

- The Funeral Board does not have a clear mandate to set and enforce ethical standards. Clear statutes would make it easier for a consumer to prevail when filing a valid complaint. The $500 limit on fines should be raised a significant amount in order to act as a deterrent.

- The FTC Funeral Rule should be adopted by reference to make it more enforceable in this state.

- There is no requirement that coroners must be medical personnel, and yet a coroner is required for at least preliminary judgment regarding medical investigation. The fact that this is an elected position is demeaning of the role. A medical investigator should not have to run in a popularity contest; the position should be filled via appointment based on medical training and competence. A mortician holding this position is facing a clear conflict of interest. If families and church groups plan to bypass the local funeral establishment, one can only hope that it will not be difficult to obtain cremation permits from the local coroner/funeral director.

- Next-of-kin may challenge in court the wishes of the deceased to be cremated even if there is a preneed authorization, but deference must be given to the deceased "unless extraordinary circumstances exist." Laws to allow for a designated deathcare agent would be helpful, when estranged or distanced from next-of-kin or when dealing with unexpected circumstances.

## ❖ Miscellaneous Information

- The educational requirements for becoming an embalmer are an associate's degree from a mortuary college plus one year of apprenticeship. For funeral directors, the only requirement is a high school diploma or equivalent plus three years of apprenticeship. One or two years of mortuary college may be substituted for up to two years of apprenticeship.

- This is the only state where a dentist is authorized to sign a death certificate.

- Funeral consumer complaints should be filed with:

  Consumer Protection Division
  Office of the Attorney General
  1024 Capital Center Drive
  Frankfort, KY 40601
  502-696-5395

## ❖ Nonprofit Funeral Consumer Information Societies

These consumer groups are run mostly by volunteers. Consequently, contact information may change. If you have difficulty reaching a society or are interested in starting a society in your area, call the FAMSA office: 800-765-0107. Or check the internet directory—

**www.funerals.org/famsa**

Memorial Society of Greater Louisville
P.O. Box 5326
Louisville, 40255-5326

~❖~

*This section was reviewed by the Board of Embalmers and the Attorney General's Office.*

# In Louisiana

*Please refer to Chapter 8 as you use this section.*

Persons in Louisiana will have difficulty in caring for their own dead. The laws are contradictory and invite a court challenge.

> *R.S. 8 Chapter 10 Human Remains § 655. Right of disposing of remains—A. The right to control interment . . . of the remains of a deceased person, unless other specific directions have been given by the decedent in the form of a written and notarized declaration, vests in and devolves upon the following in the order named: (1) The surviving spouse, if not judicially separated from the decedent. (2) A majority of the surviving adult children of the decedent . . .*

and so on.

Existing public health statutes—as they do in most states—refer to "the funeral director or person acting as such." In 1986, however, the funeral industry influenced self-serving legislation to take away the rights granted above—and then some. Most of the changes appear in the Professions and Occupations statutes:

> *R.S. 40 Public Health and Safety § 32 Definitions—(17) "Funeral director or person acting as such" is a licensed funeral director or embalmer . . .*

> *R.S. 37 Chapter 10 Embalming and Funeral Directors § 831. Definitions—(23) "Funeral directing" means the operation of a funeral home, or, by way of illustration and not limitation, any service whatsoever connected with the management of funerals, or the supervision of hearses or funeral cars, the purchase of caskets or other funeral merchandise, and retail sale and display thereof, the cleaning or dressing of dead human bodies for burial, and the performance or supervision of any service or act connected with the management of funerals from time of death until the body or bodies are delivered to the cemetery, crematorium, or other agent for the purpose of disposition.*

*R.S. 37 Chapter 10 Embalming and Funeral Directors § 848 Unlawful practice—C. It shall be unlawful for anyone to engage in the business of funeral directing or embalming . . . unless such business is conducted by a duly licensed funeral establishment. D. (5) Every dead human body shall be disposed of and prepared through a funeral establishment and under the supervision of a licensed funeral home or embalmer.*

Indeed, one has to wonder how legislators can face their own clergy, as any who preside at funerals are clearly in violation of 37 §848 if one uses the definition in § 831. What about religious groups that routinely bathe and shroud the dead? Not in Louisiana? Certainly a family caring for its own dead is not "in the business"—probably less so than clergy—and it seems a valid argument that the Professions and Occupations statutes should not apply to individuals and situations when there is no monetary transaction involved.

## ❖ Death Certificate

The family doctor will sign the death certificate within 24 hours, stating the cause of death. If the death is a coroner's case, the coroner may take 48 hours. The remaining information must be supplied, typewritten or in black ink. The death certificate must be filed with the parish registrar within five days and before final disposition.

## ❖ Fetal Death

A fetal death report is required if death occurs after 20 weeks of gestation or when the weight is 350 grams or more. If there is no family physician involved, the local coroner must sign the fetal death certificate.

## ❖ Transporting and Disposition Permit

Once the death certificate has been filed, the local registrar will issue a burial-transit permit which is a separate document, not attached to the death certificate, and for which there is a modest fee. This permit must be obtained prior to final disposition of the body.

## ❖ Burial

Burial must occur in a duly authorized cemetery. Home burial would probably be permissible if the property were dedicated as such with local authorities and registered with the Louisiana Cemetery Board. Check with the parish registrar for local zoning laws. The casket must have a covering of two feet of soil unless a burial vault or lawn crypt is used. Although not mentioned in the law, burial should be at least 150 feet from a water supply.

When burial occurs, the burial-transit permit must be filed within ten days with the registrar of the parish where disposition takes place.

## ❖ Cremation

A permit to cremate must be obtained from the coroner in the parish where death occurred. The charge for this varies and may be nothing in one parish, $5 in the next, $25 in another. Most crematories insist that a pacemaker be removed, and authorization by next-of-kin is usually required. The crematory will sign the burial-transit permit. This permit must be filed with the parish registrar within ten days.

## ❖ Other Requirements

If disposition is not arranged within 30 hours of death, the body must be embalmed or refrigerated below 45º.

If the person died of a contagious or communicable disease, the doctor in attendance should be consulted.

## ❖ Medical Schools for Body Donation

Dept. of Health & Human Resources
Anatomical Services
1901 Perdido St.
New Orleans, LA 70112-1393
504-568-4012 days
504-861-0383 or 522-1441
(J.T. Willie Funeral Home)
Moderate need

Shreveport area:
    Anatomy Dept, LSU
    318-226-3312 days
    318-226-3369
    (LSU Security office)

Cost to family: none if previously registered and death is in state or within 100-mile radius
Prior enrollment: not required, but priority given to registered donors
Over-enrollment: shared within state
Disposition: cremation; cremains returned by request
Body rejection: autopsy, burn victim, embalming if trocar is used, decomposition

## ❖ Crematories

Bossier City

Memorial Crematory
2156 Airline Dr., 7111
318-742-5361

Denham Springs

Evergreen Crematory
1710 S. Range Ave., 70726
504-665-9020

Lafayette

Lafayette Crematory
2920 N. University Ave., 70507
318-896-8966

New Orleans

Metairie Cemetery
5100 Pontchartrain
P.O. Drawer 19925, 70179
504-486-6331

St. John Cemetery
4841 Canal St., 70119
504-486-6651

Tharp-Southeimer
4117 S. Claibourne Ave.
P.O. Box 750140, 70175
504-821-8411

Additional crematories may have been established in this state after the date of publication.

## ❖ State Governance

The Louisiana Board of Embalmers and Funeral Directors has seven members. Three are licensed embalmers, three are licensed funeral directors, and one—over the age of 60—represents the elderly.

The Louisiana Cemetery Board oversees all cemeteries in Louisiana. There are seven members, two of whom shall not have any direct or indirect interest in a cemetery or funeral business. There is a separate board—the Louisiana Unmarked Burial Sites Board—to preserve historical grave sites.

Crematories are regulated by the Environmental Quality department.

## ❖ Prepaid Cemetery and Funeral Funds

10% of the purchase price of a cemetery lot must go into a perpetual care trust fund. Only 50% of the money for prepaid *cemetery* merchandise, such as a vault or memorial, must be placed in **trust.** "**Constructive Delivery**" can bypass the trusting requirement. Therefore, it is highly unlikely that you would get any money back if you were to change your mind.

All prepaid *funeral* monies (100%) must be deposited in a separate savings or **trust** account for each purchaser with **interest** to accrue and a **report** filed annually with the state. Unless the account is made irrevocable, the purchaser may **cancel** the agreement and withdraw the funds at any time.

There is no provision for the substitution of merchandise if the selected item is not available at the time of death. There is now a class action suit against the Loewen Group in Louisiana because of the problems this has created for consumers.[1] Burial policies sold back in the '40s, '50s, and '60s had a low face value—$350 to $500 or so. But in those days, $500 purchased a pretty darned good funeral. With interest accumulating, those accounts today should be worth $6,000 or more, sufficient to cover the services and merchandise listed in the policies. When consumers tried to use these policies to pay for a funeral, however, they were shown poor-quality caskets—"It looked like a flimsy stage prop," said one. "The lid fell off," said another. When the families opted to pay for another casket, they were told that any substitution voided the policy. The families then faced funeral bills of over $7,000.

## ❖ Restrictive Casket Sales

This heading shows up in only seven state chapters: Alabama, Georgia, Idaho, Louisiana, Oklahoma, South Carolina, and Virginia. (An Oklahoma state court determined in 1997 that restrictions on casket sales were illegal, now under appeal by the funeral board.)

For years, caskets have been the major profit-maker for an undertaker, and mark-up on caskets was often 500-700% or more. As word leaked out about actual casket costs, some entrepreneurs saw an opportunity to cut the price and still make a "fair" profit, knowing that consumers were growing resentful. In the mid '90s, the retail casket business was born. Although I certainly support a free-market concept, I—for one— didn't think the public would shop anywhere but at a funeral home for a casket. Boy, was I wrong! The retail casket market is exploding, and consumers are now saving thousands of dollars on over-night delivery of attractive, well-made, quality caskets that are available from sources all around the country.

---

[1] The text of this suit is posted in the "Consumer Alert" section of the FAMSA web site: <**www.funerals.org/famsa**>. The class-action portion of the first suit was thrown out, with the deft shenanigans of Loewen lawyers, one of whom just happened to be a relative of the local DA. Individual suits are proceeding, however, and a new class-action has been filed in another parish.

The Federal Trade Commission encourages this, permitting consumers to purchase from a funeral home *only* those goods and services wanted. As of 1994, it forbids a funeral home from charging a handling fee if a consumer purchases an item or service elsewhere.[1] The FTC does not address who may sell a casket, but it has very specific language that does oblige a funeral home to accept a casket provided by the consumer.

What is the problem in Louisiana? Well, the statutory definitions of "funeral directing" and "funeral merchandise" are so globally loose that one has to guess at the intent of the legislature. *"Funeral merchandise" means those consumer goods used in connection with the casket, vault, or box, clothing, and any other merchandise used for the funeral of a dead human body, including but not limited to, the receptacle in which the body is directly placed. . . .*

Should the corner stationery store still be allowed to sell guest books and thank-you cards? What about stores selling clothing that will be used for burial even though a dress doesn't have that slit up the back? And funeral flowers or casket sprays? Or the flag-case to hold a veteran's flag?

Yes, all funeral directors may do the things listed in the definition of funeral directing, but not all people doing those things need to be funeral directors. (All Catholics are Christians, but not all Christians are Catholics.)

No such logic prevails in the Louisiana state offices. Bluster from the Board of Embalmers and Funeral Directors has shut down two casket retailers so far. But mild-mannered, no-nonsense, ex-banker Ashton Long has no intention of closing shop. In 1997, he opened his retail outlet in Shreveport—Caskets Direct. The board quickly filed a "cease and desist" order that Mr. Long has appealed. As of this writing, the case is still rattling around in the court system. In the meantime, Caskets Direct is still in business, and anyone in Louisiana looking for a fair

---

[1] Funeral homes with nearby casket stores have been dropping their casket prices and upping their service charges to off-set the loss. Others offer a discounted package if you purchase the casket from the funeral home. The National Casket Retailers Association has filed a complaint with the FTC charging that falsely inflated service charges which are conditionally discounted later are hiding the illegal handling fee.

price on a casket might want to check it out: 318-671-9100. Or check the FAMSA casket page

**http://www.funerals.org/famsa/caskets.htm**

for his web link. Long will deliver caskets anywhere in the state.

Generally, burdensome funeral laws will be sustained by the courts only if there are reasons of public health, vital statistics, or legal/criminal concerns. Just how would the state of Louisiana justify limiting who may sell a box—which is all a casket is?

## ❖ Consumer Concerns

- The death rate in Louisiana can support approximately 151 full-time mortuaries; there are, however, 333. Funeral prices tend to be higher in areas where there are "too many" funeral homes.
- Church groups and individuals should get the right to care for their own dead clearly established in the statutes.
- The amount going into trust for cemetery merchandise should be increased to 100% to permit consumers to withdraw the account—as would be needed if one moved to another geographic location and sold or did not use the lot.
- Laws should require cemeteries to repurchase an unwanted lot at the original selling price plus 50% of the difference between that and current market price.
- Preneed funeral consumers should get an annual report indicating the institution of deposit and value (purchase price plus interest) of all prepaid funeral monies. Such documents could be important to survivors who might not know about prepaid accounts otherwise and would help to enforce the trusting law.
- There should be a requirement that any preneed funeral purchase that indicates a particular casket should include a picture of the selected casket, along with brand, model number, and full description of construction materials. There should also be a provision for substitution of like quality and construction, on approval of survivors, if the selected item is not available at the time of death. It is not uncommon for survivors to be told, "We don't have anything like that any more—" with subsequent pressure to purchase something a lot more expensive. Corrective consumer legislation is being pursued by one irate citizen who got stung by a funeral home that didn't honor the preneed contract. If you'd like to lend your support, you can reach Teresa Fox of Kenner at 504-443-2363.

- There is no statutory provision to allow the transfer of an irrevocable account should a person move or want to change which funeral home to use.
- There is no statutory provision to protect consumers against default of prepaid funeral agreements if funds were never put in trust. Consumers in other states have experienced a loss of funds in spite of trusting requirements.
- Because of all the loopholes and the difficulty Louisiana families have had with substitution of merchandise, it is probably a *terrible* idea to prepay for a funeral in this state.
- The restrictive interpretation on who may sell caskets is a restraint of trade which subverts the FTC's provision specifically permitting consumers to purchase *only* the goods and services desired from the funeral provider.
- Identification and tagging of the body at the place of death before removal should be required.
- The regulations require that at least six adult caskets be on display, but there is no requirement that low-cost caskets be included in that display.
- The standards for ethical, professional conduct should be strengthened. That would make it easier for a consumer to prevail when filing a valid complaint.
- The FTC Funeral Rule should be adopted by reference to make it easier to enforce in this state.

## ❖ Miscellaneous Information

- Educational requirements for becoming a funeral director: one year of college (30 hrs.) and one year of apprenticeship. For an embalmer: mortuary science program (15 mos.) and one year of apprenticeship.
- When a funeral home changes ownership or more than 50% of the stock is sold, the state Funeral Board must be notified and a new license acquired.
- Wishes of the decedent will prevail, if written and notarized.
- Cash advance items may not be marked up with a commission for the mortuary. They must be billed to the consumer in the same amount the funeral home is billed.
- The Board of Embalmers and Funeral Directors employs an investigator to handle complaints and violations.

## ❖ Nonprofit Funeral Consumer Information Societies

These consumer groups are run mostly by volunteers. Consequently, contact information may change. If you have difficulty reaching a society or are interested in starting a society in your area, call the FAMSA office: 800-765-0107. Or check the internet directory—

**www.funerals.org/famsa**

Memorial Society of Greater Baton Rouge
8470 Goodwood Ave.
Baton Rouge, LA 70806
504-926-2291

~❖~

*This chapter was sent for review to the Louisiana Board of Embalmers and Funeral Directors, the Cemetery Board, and the Department of Vital Statistics. No response was received.*

# In Maine

*Please refer to Chapter 8 as you use this section.*

Persons in Maine may care for their own dead. The legal authority to do so is found in Chapter 707 of Title 22. The following section is pertinent:

> §2846—Authorized person. For the purposes of this chapter, the "authorized person" responsible for obtaining or filing a permit or certificate shall mean a member of the immediate family of the deceased, a person authorized in writing by a member of the immediate family of the deceased if no member of the immediate family of the deceased wishes to assume the responsibility, or in the absence of immediate family, a person authorized in writing by the deceased.

There are no other statutes that might require you to use a funeral director.

## ❖ Death Certificate

The family doctor or a local medical examiner will supply and sign the death certificate within 24 hours, stating the cause of death. The remaining information must be supplied, typewritten or in black ink. The death certificate must be filed with the local town or city clerk within three days.

## ❖ Fetal Death

A fetal death report is required when death occurs after 20 weeks of gestation. If there is no family physician involved, the local medical examiner must sign the fetal death certificate.

## ❖ Transporting and Disposition Permit

The municipal clerk will issue a Permit for Disposition of Human Remains. The fee for this permit is $4. The death certificate must be obtained first, as well as a medical examiner's release if cremation, burial-at-sea, or out-of-state disposition is planned. If a permit is needed when the municipal clerk is not available, one of the clerk's sub-registrars (some of whom are funeral directors) may be asked to issue the permit. For issuance of this permit to an authorized person, the death certificate must indicate that the doctor personally examined the deceased after death.

The Disposition Permit must be filed, within seven days, with the clerk of the municipality where burial or cremation takes place. If this is in another district, an additional fee may be charged to file the permit.

### ❖ Burial

Check with the city or town for local zoning laws regarding home burial. Family burial grounds of not more than a quarter of an acre are protected as a "burial place forever." This plot must be recorded in the registry of deeds in the county where burial takes place and enclosed by a fence to be "exempt from attachment and execution." There are no state burial statutes or regulations with regard to depth. A sensible guideline is 150 feet from a water supply and three feet of earth on top.

### ❖ Cremation (or Burial at Sea)

A permit (usually called a "release") for cremation or burial at sea must be signed by a local medical examiner. The usual fee for this is $15. There is a 48-hour waiting period prior to cremation. A rigid combustible container must be used, without a canvas or plastic bag. Authorization by next-of-kin is usually required. A pacemaker and other non-combustible items must be removed prior to cremation.

### ❖ Other Requirements

There are no other requirements affecting the time schedule of disposition of an unembalmed body. Weather and reasonable planning should be considered.

Death from a "disease" may require the involvement of a medical examiner. Check with the attending physician to be sure.

## ❖ Medical Schools for Body Donation

University of New England
College of Osteopathic Medicine
11 Hills Beach Rd.
Biddeford, ME 04005
207-283-0170 ext. 2206 or 2202
Moderate need.

Cost to family: none; transportation for several hundred miles
Prior enrollment: preferred
Over-enrollment: not shared
Disposition: cremation; return of cremated remains by request
Body rejection: standard,* previous embalming, over-enrollment

* autopsy, decomposition, mutilation, severe burn victim, meningitis, hepatitis, AIDS, and other contagious or communicable diseases

## ❖ Crematories

Auburn

> Gracelawn Memorial Park
> 980 Turner, 04210
> 207-782-3741

Bangor

> Mt. Hope Cemetery Group
> 1038 State, 04401
> 207-945-6589

Portland

> Brooklawn Memorial Park
> P.O. Box 1176, 04104
> 207-773-7679

Saco

> Laurel Hill Cemetery
> 293 Beach, 04072
> 207-282-9351

Additional crematories may have been established in this state after the date of publication.

## ❖ State Governance

The Maine Board of Funeral Service has eight members. There are two consumer representatives.

Cemeteries are usually owned and operated by municipalities, churches, or voluntary nonprofit associations, although a few are for-profit businesses. There is no state cemetery board.

Crematories must be registered with the Department of Human Services. One does not have to be a licensed funeral director to run a crematory.

## ❖ Prepaid Cemetery and Funeral Funds

Preneed sellers may not solicit sales (the consumer must initiate the contact), although advertising is permitted.

All money for prepaid *cemetery* products and services (*i.e.,* cremation or opening-and-closing charges but not the lot) must be placed in **trust**. If the purchaser cancels the arrangement, the cemetery may keep the **interest**, but the principal will be **refunded**.

All money for a prepaid *funeral* contract must be deposited in a separate account, with **interest** to accrue. The financial institution must send a **confirmation of the deposit** to the purchaser within 30 days. If funds are transferred to another institution, the purchaser must be notified.

The preneed agreement may be **cancelled** for a **refund**—*if* permitted by the contract.

## ❖ Consumer Concerns

- The death rate in Maine can support approximately 47 full-time mortuaries; there are 106 such establishments. However, given the low density of population over a large geographic area, mortuary careers are not likely to be full-time work. Unfortunately, because of the low volume of business per mortuary, funeral prices will tend to be higher than in busier mortuaries.
- Laws should require cemeteries to repurchase an unwanted lot at the original selling price plus 50% of the difference between that and current market price.
- Although there is an initial notification, there is no requirement for an annual report to the purchaser of prepaid funeral goods and services, paperwork that might be useful to the family of a deceased to indicate prepayment and which would help to "enforce" trusting requirements.
- There is no state-administered fund to reimburse consumers in case of default on prepaid funeral funds that were never put into trust.
- There is no provision for an adequate description of funeral goods selected preneed nor for a substitution of equal quality and construction if the selected item is no longer available at the time of death. Any substitution should be approved by survivors.
- While individual contracts may cover the issue of cancellation or transfer, there are no statutory provisions reserving a consumer's right to cancel or transfer prepaid funeral arrangements with full benefit of the amount paid plus interest. In other states, it's not uncommon to lose a portion of what you paid if there is a need to change your plans.

- Until there is better reporting, a provision for the substitution of merchandise when not available, and better cancellation/refund guarantees, it is probably an *unwise* idea to prepay for a funeral in Maine.
- The 48-hour wait before cremation is totally unnecessary when survivors are in agreement and may be causing additional charges to families for "storage."
- The coroner or medical examiner's release for cremation in the case of an *anticipated* death from natural causes is totally unnecessary and creates an additional burden and charge for families.
- Identification and tagging of the body at the place of death before removal should be required.
- There is no provision either forbidding a mark-up on cash advance items or requiring the disclosure of how much the mark-up would be. Consumers may wish to ask for a copy of such invoices.
- There is no requirement that low-cost caskets be included in any display.
- The ethical standards for funeral directors should be more detailed and explicit.
- Complaint procedures are unclear and inadequate.

## ❖ Miscellaneous Information

- Educational requirements for becoming a funeral director: one year of college and one year of mortuary college (or two years of mortuary college) plus 2,000 hours of apprenticeship. Applicants must pass a written exam and a practical exam.
- The 1984 FTC Funeral Rule, as amended, has been adopted by reference.
- Prior to death, and in the absence of immediate family, individuals may designate a person to serve as a legally authorized agent for funeral arrangements and indicate directions for such.
- Medical examiners are physicians appointed to the position.
- A cemetery may not employ a funeral director to arrange funerals. A cemetery may, however, employ a funeral director to be its landscaping foreman or accountant, provided the funeral director is not paid more than $500 per year.

## ❖ Nonprofit Funeral Consumer Information Societies

These consumer groups are run mostly by volunteers. Consequently, contact information may change. If you have difficulty reaching a society

or are interested in starting a society in your area, call the FAMSA office: 800-765-0107. Or check the internet directory—
**www.funerals.org/famsa**

Memorial Society of Maine
Box 3122
Auburn, ME 04212-3122
207-786-4323

~❖~

*This chapter was sent for review to the Department of Health—Vital Statistics and the Board of Funeral Service, but I got no response.*

My sincere thanks, however, to Ernest Marriner of the Memorial Society of Maine for doing meticulous fact-checking with various local agencies to correct some initial errors.

# In Maryland

*Please refer to Chapter 8 as you use this section.*

Persons and church groups in Maryland may care for their own dead. In 1987, Charles R. Buck, Jr., Secretary of Health and Mental Hygiene at the time, wrote to me:

> *Under English Common Law, which is carried over in our State law, the immediate families may dispose of their dead either by burial or cremation. They must, however, conform to the laws. . . .*

Indeed, the following remains in the statutes in almost poetic diction:

> *Chapter 3 § 62. There is no universal rule regarding the right of persons to bury the dead, but each case must be considered in equity on its own merits; and, no matter in whom the right of burial rests, it is in the nature of a sacred trust for the benefit of all who may, from family ties or friendship, have an interest in the remains.*

> *Generally, the right to bury a body and the right to preserve the remains is a legal right which the courts will protect, and the next of kin or surviving spouse has the legal right to designate the place of burial.*

## ❖ Death Certificate

When death occurs in a hospital or nursing home, the death certificate will be supplied by the institution. In the case of a home death, contact the office of Vital Records, Division of Field Services, to obtain a blank death certificate: 410-764-3173. On weekends a field rep can be paged at 410-909-4810. Enter the phone number at which you may be called.

The attending or certifying physician—or a local medical examiner—will sign the death certificate within 24 hours, stating the cause of death. The remaining information must be supplied, typewritten or with black ball-point pen. There is one carbon. The first page of the death certificate must be filed with the Department of Health and Mental Hygiene, Division of Vital Statistics, within 72 hours.

Maryland is researching electronic death registration. When that is adopted, the procedure will change somewhat. Check with the local registrar or health department.

### ❖ Fetal Death

A fetal death report is required if death occurs after 20 weeks of gestation or when a weight of 500 grams or more. It is also required at any age if the fetus is transported from the place of delivery for cremation or private burial. If there is no family physician involved, the local medical examiner must sign the fetal death certificate.

### ❖ Transporting and Disposition Permit

Page two of the death certificate serves as the burial transit permit. The physician's or medical examiner's signature is required.

### ❖ Burial

Contact the county Health Department and Zoning Board for local ordinances or regulations that may apply to home burial. There are no state burial statutes or regulations with regard to depth. A sensible guideline is 150 feet from a water supply and at least two feet of earth on top.

When burial is arranged, the family member acting as the funeral director must sign the burial-transit permit and return it to the Department of Health and Mental Hygiene, Division of Vital Records, within 10 days.

### ❖ Cremation

The burial-transit permit serves as the permit for cremation. There is a 12-hour waiting period prior to cremation. The body must be identified[1] and cremation approved by the next-of-kin or other person who is authorized to arrange for final disposition. Most crematories insist that a pacemaker be removed. The crematory may offer to file the burial-transit permit.

---

[1] "ID viewing" is being used as a sales ploy to sell more expensive cremation caskets—"Most families don't want to see their loved-one in a cardboard box." A more appropriate requirement would be identification and tagging at the place of death before removal. That way, there should be fewer mix-ups at the mass-production embalming centers used by the conglomerates.

## ❖ Other Requirements

Maryland has no other requirements controlling the time schedule for the disposition of unembalmed bodies. Weather and reasonable planning should be considered.

If the person died of a contagious or communicable disease, the doctor in attendance should be consulted.

## ❖ Medical Schools for Body Donation

The State Anatomy Board
Dept. of Health & Mental Hygiene
655 W. Baltimore St.
Bressler Research Bldg., Rm. B-026
Baltimore, MD 21201
410-547-1222
Moderate need.

Cost to family: none if death occurs within the state; transportation paid
Prior enrollment: preferred
Over-enrollment: shared within state
Disposition: cremation; return of cremains by request
Body rejection: none if pre-enrolled; otherwise, autopsy or diseased

## ❖ Crematories

Baltimore

    Green Mount Cemetery
    Greenmount & Oliver, 21202
    410-539-0641

    Metro Crematory
    P.O. Box 2966, 21229
    410-455-0100

Bethesda

    Montgomery Crematory
    7557 Wisconsin Ave., 20814
    301-652-2200

Brentwood

    Fort Lincoln Cemetery
    3401 Bladensburg, 20722
    301-864-5090

Cambridge

    Cambridge Crematory
    2272 Hudson Rd., 21613
    410-228-2645

Catonsville

    MacNabb Funeral Home
    301 Frederick Rd., 21228
    410-747-4770

Clinton

    Lee Crematory
    6633 Old Alexander Ferry Rd., 20735
    301-868-0900

Cumberland

    Cumberland Crematory
    404 Decatur St., 21502
    301-722-5700

Frederick

    Resthaven Memorial Gardens
    9501 Rte. 15N, 21701
    301-898-7177

Hagerstown

    Hagerstown Crematory
    415 E. Wilson Blvd., 21740
    301-739-6800

Hampstead

Carroll Cremation Service
934 S. Main St., 21074
301-239-8163

Laurel

Baltimore-Washington Crematory
7601 Sandy Spring Rd., 20707
301-776-1243

Riverdale

Chambers Crematory
5801 Cleveland Ave., 30737
301-699-5500

Salisbury

Salisbury Crematory
501 Snow Hill Rd., 21801
410-742-4440

Silver Spring

Chambers Funeral Home/Crematory
8653 Georgia Ave., 20910
301-565-3200

Suburban Crematory/Rapp
933 Gist Ave., 20910
301-565-4100

Smithsburg

Smithsburg Crematorium
Pennsylvania Ave. 21783
301-791-1230

Suitland

Cedar Hill Cemetery
4111 Pennsylvania Ave., 20746
301-568-5400

Additional crematories may have been established in this state after the date of publication.

## ❖ State Governance

The Maryland Board of Morticians has twelve members. Four are consumer representatives.

The Office of Cemetery Oversight regulates cemeteries and burial goods businesses including preneed sales. The Office's Advisory Council has eleven members, five of which are consumer members.

Crematories are not regulated in Maryland except by the air quality control agency.

## ❖ Prepaid Cemetery and Funeral Funds

One has to wonder what was in the statehouse drinking water when the preneed statutes were passed. Half of the funds for preneed *cemetery merchandise and services* must be placed in **trust**—but only the "second 50%"—if you are paying by installments! The cemetery may pocket your first payments right away. The statutes go on to say that within 30 days of your last payment, a tad bit more should be deposited to bring the account up to 55% of the contract. Why didn't they just say 55% in the first place? By a process of deduction it would seem that this 55% refers to the cost of a marker, a grave liner or coffin vault, and the opening-and-closing charges because the next statutory paragraph says the trusting requirement for a "casket or casket vault" sold by a cemetery is 80% (even though funeral directors must put 100% of their casket sales in trust).[1] However, the trusting requirements apply only if the cemetery hasn't taken advantage of the **constructive "delivery"** loophole, handing you a certificate that says the merchandise is yours and is in storage—a common ploy to get their hands on all your money now.

That's bad enough, but get this: If the cemetery is dutifully putting your installment payments into trust, it may not charge you interest on the purchase. *However,* if the cemetery plans to put your vault or marker (or even a casket) into its warehouse—to "purchase" it now for you—then the cemetery may levy a **finance charge!** You could also end up with a finance charge if the cemetery sells the contract to a lending institution. If you are offered a contract with a "Notice to Consumers" clause, watch out! You have a right to refuse to sign any such contract or scratch out the parts that are unacceptable.

If you default on your installment payments before getting to the half-way mark, kiss your money goodbye—the first 45% never had to go into trust anyway, remember? After that, the cemetery may withhold "reasonable expenses" before returning what might be in the trust.

And what does happens if you change your mind about needing a vault—if you've decided to be cremated instead? Forget it. In the existing statutes, there is no provision for any such change of heart and a **refund**. If you move more than 75 miles away, you might possibly get 55% of what you paid plus interest that's in the trust—*if* the vault isn't already in the warehouse with your name on it or waiting in the ground; in which case, you won't even get the installation service charges refunded.

A bill that passed in the 1998 legislature requires a 100% refund for the sale of a casket or "casket vault" (80% in trust, plus interest, plus an additional contribution from the seller to bring your refund check

---

[1] A "casket vault" is a one-piece unit that combines the features of both a casket and a vault. In limited usage where cemeteries may sell vaults but not caskets.

up to the amount of your initial payment only—not initial payment plus interest).

Each cemetery must make an annual **report** of its sales, including preneed sales, to the Board of Cemetery Oversight.

Your protection for prepaid *funeral* contracts is somewhat better: 100% must be placed in **trust**. The funeral home must also send you an annual **report** of the **interest** income for tax purposes. But have you been getting one? Many consumers have been angered by this, figuring it's the funeral home's money—why should they have to declare it—especially if the money is in an irrevocable arrangement.[1] Given the public resentment over declaring interest on money that's already signed away, one has to wonder if all funeral homes have been complying with the statutes. Or have they quietly been declaring the interest themselves as a favor to their patrons? A 1997 IRS ruling does permit the seller to declare the interest income. If the Maryland statutes are changed to reflect that new ruling, the only reporting-to-the-consumer requirement will be eliminated unless another report is instituted in its place.

Maryland has an excellent provision that I've seen in only a few other states: When a funeral home is going to be sold, you must be notified and given a choice of either continuing with the new owner or asking for a refund or transfer. Before assuming that you will want to continue with the new owner, you may wish to see what kind of reputation the new one has for honoring preneed arrangements. If you weren't paying attention when you first got a notice—or suddenly discover that you were never notified—you might want to check that out now. Unless it is an irrevocable agreement, you may cancel a contract and request a **refund** of all funds paid, plus interest, at any time. Irrevocable funeral trusts may be **transferred** to a new provider.

### ❖ Consumer Concerns

- The death rate in Maryland can support approximately 166 full-time funeral homes; there are, however, 260. Funeral prices tend to be higher in areas where there are "too many" funeral homes.

---

[1] Sorry, folks, Uncle Sam, too, says it's your money, for your benefit.

- Laws should require cemeteries to repurchase an unwanted lot at the original selling price plus 50% of the difference between that and current market price.
- "Constructive delivery" should not be permitted, and 100% of all prepaid cemetery merchandise and services should be placed into trust. Until the cemetery laws are changed, it is probably a mistake to prepay for such goods and services in Maryland.
- A funeral home must substitute "comparable merchandise" if the item selected preneed is no longer available at the time of death, but there is no provision for an adequate description to make sure that the substitution is, indeed, "comparable" and for the survivors to approve such a replacement. Savvy consumers should add these provisions to any prepaid contract.
- Although there is supposed to be annual reporting of interest income, not all consumers may be getting this. In any event, a 1099 tax form does not give the family a report on the total asset in the prepaid account. This would be useful information for survivors at a time of death and would help to enforce the trusting requirement.
- There is no state protection for consumers in case of default on prepaid funeral funds that were never put into trust. With that in mind, you may prefer to keep your preneed money in your own bank account.
- Identification and tagging of the body at the place of death before removal should be required.
- There is no provision either forbidding a mark-up on cash advance items or requiring the disclosure of how much the mark-up would be. Consumers may wish to request a copy of the invoices for such items.
- There is no requirement that low-cost caskets be displayed along with others.
- $3,500 from a limited estate is given reserve priority for funeral expenses over other debts. The morticians are trying to increase this to $4,500, which would leave even less for rent, utilities, medical bills or other such final expenses.
- Although provisions for honoring advance directives are well-established, there is no reference to specifying after-death disposition or delegating authority for such. A designated agent for deathcare may be important when one is at a distance or estranged from next-of-kin.
- There are no ethical standards for funeral directors. These should be detailed and explicit. (See Ethical Standards in the Appendix.)

- The FTC Funeral Rule should be adopted by reference to make it more enforceable in this state. (Licensees are given a copy of "Complying with the Funeral Rule," however.)

## ❖ Miscellaneous Information

- Educational requirements for becoming a mortician: associate's degree (2 yrs.) and 1,000 hours of apprenticeship. A state and national exam are also required.
- Complaints against funeral practitioners are handled by the Board of Morticians.
- Medical examiners are physicians who are appointed to the job.

## ❖ Nonprofit Funeral Consumer Information Societies

These consumer groups are run mostly by volunteers. Consequently, contact information may change. If you have difficulty reaching a society or are interested in starting a society in your area, call the FAMSA office: 800-765-0107. Or check the internet directory—

**www.funerals.org/famsa**

Memorial Society of Maryland
9601 Cedar Lane
Bethesda, MD 20814
800-564-0017

~❖~

*This chapter was reviewed by the Department of Health and Mental Hygiene—Vital Statistics, the Office of Cemetery Oversight, and the Board of Morticians.*

# In Massachusetts

*Please refer to Chapter 8 as you use this section.*

Persons and church groups in Massachusetts may care for their own dead. The legal authority to do so is found in:

> *Title 46 § 9. Death certificates. A physician . . . shall immediately furnish for registration a standard certificate of death . . . to an undertaker or other authorized person or a member of the family of the deceased. . . .*

There are no other statutes that might require you to use a funeral director.

## ❖ History

The Board of Registration in Embalming issued a regulation in 1905 stating:

> *No permits for . . . burial . . . shall be issued . . . to any person . . . not registered . . . [by] the state board of registration in embalming.*

That regulation was found invalid by the Supreme Judicial Court of Massachusetts in 1909, *Wyeth v. Thomas, 200 Mass. 474, 86 NE 925.* The court wrote:

> *There is no doubt that the . . . refusal to permit one to bury the dead body of his relative or friend, except under an unreasonable limitation, is also an interference with a private right that is not allowable under the Constitution of the Commonwealth or the Constitution of the United States.*

The regulation remained on the books until 1998, even though it was invalid and unenforceable. The Board of Registration insisted until 1996 that the regulation was valid and even convinced the Vital Statistics department of the Massachusetts Department of Public Health (MDPH) in 1989 to change the wording on one box on the death certificate form to "funeral service licensee" and to tell local boards of health that burial permits could be issued only to undertakers.

The Memorial Society in Boston was also fooled into believing that people were forbidden to care for their own dead in Massachusetts. Jan Burhman Osnoss, whose experience is recounted in Chapter 4, asked the Memorial Society to try to get the law changed. After a bit of simple research, it became apparent that the law had *never required* the use of an undertaker.

The MDPH, on reviewing the court opinion, agreed privately that persons could care for their own dead but was unwilling to say so publicly. The Board of Health of the Town of Lexington, after considering the matter for 13 months, voted in April 1996 to issue burial permits to non-undertakers.[1] The Board of Registration went to the MDPH seeking its support in opposing the Lexington decision, but the MDPH said that Lexington was correct. Two days later the Board of Registration agreed to drop their opposition to issuance of burial permits to non-undertakers.

The MDPH in August 1996 sent a memo to all 351 towns telling them it *is* legal to issue burial permits to non-undertakers. With the memo was a set of guidelines from the MDPH to be given to persons caring for their own dead, explaining the law and suggesting appropriate precautions. In 1998, the Board of Registration modified its regulation.

## ❖ Death Certificate

The family doctor or a medical examiner will "immediately" supply and sign the death certificate, stating the cause of death. The remaining information must be supplied, typewritten or in black ink. The death certificate must be filed, within five days, with the Board of Health in the town where death occurred in order to obtain the "burial" permit.

## ❖ Fetal Death

A fetal death report is required when death occurs after 20 weeks of gestation or when the weight is 350 grams or more. If there is no family physician involved, the local medical examiner must sign the fetal death certificate.

---

[1] Byron Blanchard, treasurer of The Memorial Society in Boston, handled the negotiation with the MDPH and Lexington.

## ❖ Transporting and Disposition Permit

The local board of health (or town clerk if there is no board of health) will issue the burial permit. (This is actually a transportation and disposition permit.) This authorization must be obtained prior to moving a body or final disposition. After normal business hours, check with the local police to determine who the after-hours agent is.

Although most boards of health are now willing to work with those caring for their own dead, there are a few recalcitrant ones. If you run into difficulty, suggest that the clerk contact the Department of Health at 617-753-8603. As a member of the public, you may call 753-8604. If that doesn't help, call Howard Wensley at 617-983-6761. The Memorial Society in Boston may be able to assist in seeking an emergency court hearing if necessary.

## ❖ Burial

The Board of Health in each town regulates burial grounds, whether on private land or established cemeteries. There are no state burial statutes or regulations with regard to depth. A sensible guideline is 150 feet from a water supply and at least two feet of earth on top.

When burial is arranged, the sexton or family member acting as the funeral director must sign the coupon on the burial-transit permit and return it to the issuing registrar.

## ❖ Cremation

A cremation permit from the medical examiner is required. The fee for this is $50. There is a 48-hour waiting period prior to cremation unless the death was due to a contagious or infectious disease. Authorization by next-of-kin or designated agent is required, and a pacemaker must be removed.

Where there is no spouse or next-of-kin and the decedent did not appoint an agent to authorize cremation, the crematory may demand that a court-appointed guardian sign the authorization to cremate. Where there is an estranged or separated spouse or there are next-of-kin opposed to cremation, it is essential for the decedent to have appointed an agent in writing. The form to appoint an agent is called a Declaration of Intent for Cremation and is available from the crematory; it should be witnessed and notarized.

New regulations (1998) permit a funeral home to require that the next-of-kin view a body *at the funeral home* prior to cremation. This is a blatant ploy to sell cremation caskets. As one funeral director told a niece, "You'll probably want to upgrade to a cremation casket. Most families don't want to see their loved one in a cardboard box." A more responsible requirement would be identification and tagging at the place of death prior to removal, especially with all the body mix-ups that are becoming endemic at chain-owned mortuaries. For them, it is standard practice to send bodies to a central location for embalming and preparation, and the incidence of negligent body-swapping has spawned a rash of expensive lawsuits that continue afresh as of this writing.

## ❖ Other Requirements

Massachusetts has no other requirements controlling the time schedule for the disposition of unembalmed bodies. Weather and reasonable planning should be considered.

If the person died of a contagious or communicable disease, the doctor in attendance should be consulted.

Regulations—which apply only to the bodies handled by undertakers—require that, if there will be no embalming, all orifices must be stuffed with treated cotton, the body washed, then wrapped in a sheet. Off the record, funeral directors tell me this is rarely done unless there is to be a private family viewing. But by having such a requirement in the regulations, mortuaries may charge for this service, and none is the wiser if it's never done prior to an immediate burial or cremation. (Anyone who considers the cotton-stuffing an indignity may wish to skip the use of a funeral home altogether.)

## ❖ Medical Schools for Body Donation

There was at one time a coordinated donor program for all schools, but it is without a director at this time.

Boston University School of Medicine
80 E. Concord St.
Boston, MA 02118
617-638-4245
After hours: 638-4144
Low/moderate need

Harvard Medical School
25 Shattuck St.
Boston MA 02115
617-432-1735
After hours: 432-1379
Low/moderate need

Tufts University School of Medicine
136 Harrison Ave.
Boston, MA 02111
617-636-6685
After hours: 636-6610

University of Mass. Medical School
55 Lake Ave. N.
Worcester, MA 01605-2397
508-856-2460 24 hrs.
Low/moderate need

Cost to family: a modest sum for transportation within the Commonwealth is supplied by the school
Prior enrollment: required
Over-enrollment: shared
Disposition: cremation for donors at
University of Mass.; return of cremains by request; for other three,
burial or return of remains by request and expense of family
Body rejection: standard,* previous embalming, missing body parts

* autopsy, decomposition, mutilation, severe burn victim, meningitis, hepatitis, AIDS, and other contagious or communicable diseases

## ❖ Crematories

Cambridge

Mt. Auburn Cemetery
580 Mt. Auburn, 02138
617-547-7105

Duxbury

Duxbury Crematory
774 Tremont St., Rte. 3A, 02331
781-934-5261

Everett

Woodlawn Cemetery
302 Elm, 02149
617-387-0800

Haverhill

Linwood Crematory
41 John Ward Ave., 01830
978-374-4191

Jamaica Plain

Forest Hills Cemetery
95 Forest Hills, 02130
617-524-0239

Newton Center

Newton Cemetery
791 Walnut, 02159
617-332-0047

Pittsfield

Pittsfield Cemetery
203 Wahconah, 01201
413-447-7953

Salem

Harmony Grove Cemetery
30 Grove, 01970
978-744-0554

Springfield

Springfield Crematory
171 Maple, 01105
413-732-0712

Worcester

New Swedish Crematory
7 Island Rd., 01603
508-753-8842

Rural Cemetery
180 Grove, 01605
508-754-1313

Additional crematories may have been established in this state after the date of publication.

## ❖ State Governance

The Massachusetts Board of Registration in Embalming and Funeral Directing has five members. One is a consumer representative.

Most cemeteries are town or city cemeteries and are regulated by their municipalities. The Board of Health must approve new cemeteries and crematories.

Crematories are generally considered part of a cemetery's operation, and those on cemetery grounds are not licensed separately. The statutes permit, however, that an independent, nonprofit crematory could be established elsewhere with the permission of the local health department. One does not need to be a funeral director to run a crematory.

## ❖ Prepaid Cemetery and Funeral Funds

Cemeteries (and crematories) in Massachusetts established after 1936 must be run by not-for-profit corporations. They may not sell monuments. Several have set up separate companies to vend markers but have been caught making sales on cemetery grounds. Funeral directors may not be employed by a cemetery or crematory.[1] There are no statutes regulating prepaid *cemetery* purchases.

This is one of the few states, however, where there are *no* straight-forward *statutory* protections for preneed *funeral* consumers either. The Board of Registration has enacted some *regulations,* but they are full of such gigantic loopholes and convoluted escape clauses that an industry lawyer no doubt gets the credit for wangling this "creative" writing into the record. Consequently, The Memorial Society of Boston has increased its vigilance in monitoring the Board of Registration. If you'd like to help, be sure to offer your time and assistance. (Meetings can be quite interesting. Initially, board members had not been used to having vocal consumers watch what they do or challenge closed-

---

[1] That may or may not be a good restriction. It's one way to avoid a monopoly in the industry. On the other hand, if funeral directing is a part-time job, what more logical place to work. Better to get an outside job to supplement an undertaker's income than to raise funeral prices to consumers and just sit around.

meeting sessions.) This will be an important consumer project until the legislature comes to its senses and puts funeral consumer legislation on the front burner.

Preneed sellers may not solicit sales in a nursing home, hospital, or other care facility unless invited in writing by the prospective customer. Telephone solicitation is just fine, however. Arrrgh!

Only funeral directors may sell preneed funeral arrangements. A buyer may **cancel** a preneed contract within ten days for a full **refund**. After that time, only 90% must be placed in **trust**. The name of the trustee where the money will be deposited must be disclosed to the buyer. . . .

*Unless!* Unless the agreement is paid in full and the buyer "has received satisfactory evidence that those goods or services will be furnished at the time of death. . . ." Lo and behold: Then there is **no trusting requirement**. One has to wonder what constitutes "satisfactory evidence" or whether an unsophisticated buyer would even know what was "satisfactory." Would you get a **refund** should you change your mind? I doubt it.

Preneed sellers must make an annual **report** of all preneed accounts to the state Board of Registration. (Does this include the "satisfactory evidence" ones?) The beneficiary of any funeral *trust* must also receive an annual **report** unless waived in writing. If you prepaid for your funeral and are not getting an annual report, find out why. Did the undertaker think you'd gotten "satisfactory evidence" promising delivery? Or did you sign away your rights in some tiny print you didn't notice? If so, simply send a letter to the funeral home stating that you want the annual report to which you are entitled. (There are no annual reports required for funeral insurance.)

Any preneed contract must disclose what penalties might apply if transferred, cancelled, or not fully paid-for at the time of death. They aren't limited in imposing penalties, they just have to tell you what they are. So be sure to read the fine-print on that, too. Preneed agreements must also disclose whether or not the funeral provider is obligated to **substitute** merchandise of equal or greater "value." That word "value" is a real problem. Substitution should be of equal quality and construction, not price, and any new merchandise that is substituted should be contingent on the approval of survivors. After all, a $750 casket ten years ago was pretty snazzy. Today, for $750 an undertaker would show you the "welfare casket."

Preneed funeral arrangements—whether revocable or irrevocable—may not be altered after death, even at the request of the family. The regs do not anticipate what should happen if insufficient funds are available to complete the arrangements (or there's no one around to come to the wake).

If the preneed contract is a guaranteed-price agreement, the seller may retain all **interest** income or earnings. On a non-guaranteed agreement, the estate gets a refund if funds exceed the actual cost (highly unlikely with the rate of funeral inflation). If the cost exceeds what's in the trust, the estate (or survivors) are liable for the additional costs. If a family may not alter the arrangements as mentioned above, the funeral director may try to stick the family with a funeral bill that wasn't expected.

A funeral establishment must notify preneed customers no later than ten days after a change in ownership.

A preneed seller may amend the funeral contract "at any time"—just let the buyer know ten days prior to the effective date and get the buyer to agree. Do not assume that any such amendment is in your best interest. If, for example, trust funds are being converted to insurance, be to you decline such a change. Insurance has diddley-squat cash value if you want to change your mind and turn it in.

If funeral directors want to sell funeral insurance, they must be licensed by the Division of Insurance. Funeral directors must supply "A Buyer's Guide to Pre-Need Funeral Contracts" before you sign any contract. (Don't assume it's going to tell you the real skinny, though.)

### ❖ Consumer Concerns

- The death rate in Massachusetts can support approximately 220 full-time funeral homes; there are, however, 725. Funeral prices tend to be higher in areas where there are "too many."
- Cemeteries should be regulated.
- Laws should require cemeteries to repurchase an unwanted lot at the original selling price plus 50% of the difference between that and current market price.

- There is no requirement that when merchandise is selected on a guaranteed-price, preneed agreement that a clear description is given and that merchandise of equal quality and construction must be substituted—to the satisfaction of survivors—if the original item selected is not available.
- There is no state protection to reimburse consumers in case of default on prepaid funeral funds that were never put into trust. One Massachusetts funeral director managed to spend $200,000 of his preneed funds before he landed in jail.
- Until there are statutory protections for preneed funeral consumers that eliminate the mischief cited, it is a *terrible* mistake to prepay for a funeral in Massachusetts unless you absolutely must prior to entering a nursing home. At that point, make sure it's a guaranteed-price funeral, that you get a full description of what you are paying for and what you will get, and that you know exactly where your money is with an annual report to verify it.
- The 48-hour wait before cremation is totally unnecessary when survivors are in agreement. Not to mention the additional charges to families for "storage."
- The coroner or medical examiner's permit for cremation in the case of an *anticipated* death from natural causes is totally unnecessary and creates an additional burden and charge for families.
- Identification and tagging of the body at the place of death before removal should be required.
- There is no requirement that low-cost caskets be included in any display.
- The standards for ethical, professional conduct should be strengthened. That would make it easier for a consumer to prevail when filing a complaint. (See Ethical Standards in the Appendix.) Furthermore, the board has no ability to levy a fine for most offenses; the only punishment available is yanking a license—something that is rarely done. The one fine permitted: $1,000 for failing to give an itemized price statement when arranging a funeral. The FTC considers this a $10,000 violation.
- The FTC Funeral Rule should be adopted by reference in the statutes or regulations to make it more enforceable in this state.
- Complaint procedures are unclear and inadequate.
- While case law will give preference to the written wishes of the deceased, there is no law that allows you designate an agent for death care. In situations where you are estranged or distant from next-of-kin, this could be important.

### ❖ Miscellaneous Information

- Educational requirements for becoming a registered funeral director or embalmer: mortuary college (9 months), an exam, and two years of apprenticeship. This apprenticeship period seems excessive compared to other states and more likely imposed as a source of cheap labor for the industry. The board of health for each town where a funeral director has an establishment must issue the actual funeral director's license. An interesting concept . . . Overkill or appropriate local control?
- Medical examiners are physicians who are appointed.
- Cash advance items must be billed in the same amount as is billed to the funeral director.
- Unprofessional conduct includes: "the use of profane, indecent or obscene language in the presence of a dead human body, or within the immediate hearing of the family or relatives of a deceased, whose body has not yet been interred or otherwise disposed of." Then watch out?
- Each funeral home must have a "chapel"—a for-profit church blessed by the Board of Registration?
- Ownership of a funeral home must be disclosed on all stationery and advertising materials.
- A funeral business may not represent itself as a society, fund, trust or other not-for-profit unless it is, in fact, not-for-profit.
- Undertakers registered with the board "shall be fair with present or prospective customers with respect to quality of merchandise, freedom of choice, quality of service, and reasonableness of price, and shall not misrepresent any material fact with respect to such matters." Wow! Perhaps consumers should start filing complaints against funeral homes that do not have "reasonable" prices!
- One may not picket within 500 feet of a funeral home when a funeral is in progress.
- Rendering funeral services may not be made contingent on payment or expectation of payment.
- The Commonwealth will pay $1,100 toward the burial of indigents, provided the total cost is not more than $1,500.

### ❖ Nonprofit Funeral Consumer Information Societies

These consumer groups are run mostly by volunteers. Consequently, contact information may change. If you have difficulty reaching a society

or are interested in starting a society in your area, call the FAMSA office: 800-765-0107. Or check the internet directory—

**www.funerals.org/FAMSA**

Boston

  The Memorial Society
  66 Marlborough St., 02116
  781-859-7990 or 888-666-7990

New Bedford

  Memorial Society of SE Mass.
  71 8th St., 02740

East Orleans

  Memorial Society of Cape Cod
  P.O. Box 1375, 02643-1375
  508-862-2522 or 800-976-9552

Springfield

  Memorial Society of Western Mass.
  P.O. Box 2821, 01101-2821
  413-783-7987

~❖~

*This chapter was sent for review to the Massachusetts Department of Public Health, the Attorney General's Office for Consumer Affairs, and the Board of Registration in Embalming and Funeral Directing. No response was received.*

# In Michigan

*Please refer to Chapter 8 as you use this section.*

Persons in Michigan may care for their own dead. The legal authority to do so is found in:

> *MCL 52.205(5) . . . The county medical examiner shall, after any required examination or autopsy, promptly deliver or return the body to relatives or representatives of the deceased . . . .*

> *MCL 333.2848(1) . . . a funeral director or person acting as a funeral director, who first assumes custody of a dead body, . . . shall obtain authorization for the final disposition.*

> *MCL 339.1810 Prohibited conduct. (n) . . . sending or causing to be sent to a person or establishment licensed under this article the remains of a deceased person without having first made inquiry as to the desires of the next of kin and of the person who may be chargeable with the funeral expenses of the decedent. If kin is found, the person's authority and directions shall govern the disposal of the remains of the decedent.*

Although section 333.2843 states, *A funeral director or his or her authorized agent who first assumes custody of a dead body shall report the death,* it does not say that *only* a funeral director must report the death. Indeed, per 333.2848, a *person acting as such* may obtain the authorization for final disposition. A 1995 federal court decision, Whaley v. County of Tuscola,[1] reaffirmed the right of next-of-kin to possess a body "for the purpose of preparation, mourning and burial." With

---

[1] 58 F.3d 1111 (C.A. 6 1995) (applying Michigan law), *certiorari* denied, 116 S.Ct. 475, 133 L.Ed.2d 404, *on remand* 941 F. Supp.1483. The three-judge panel discussed the quasi-property nature of a dead body. One certainly cannot sell a body, but, said the judges, "If a woman's husband dies in a neighbor's yard, the neighbor cannot simply keep the body. . . . Just because the woman cannot technically 'replevin' her husband's body does not mean she has no legitimate claim of entitlement to it."

undertakers fighting over dead bodies in Michigan, however, consumers should be concerned that there will be a legislative effort to take away any such rights as soon as this information becomes widely known. There are no other statutes that might require you to use a funeral director.

### ❖ Death Certificate

The attending physician, registered nurse, or county medical examiner must sign the death certificate within 48 hours, stating the cause of death. The remaining information must be supplied, typewritten or in black ink. The death certificate must be filed with the local registrar within 72 hours.

### ❖ Fetal Death

A fetal death report is required for all such deaths and must be filed with the state registrar within five days. A physician or medical examiner must fill out the cause of death.

### ❖ Transporting and Disposition Permit

A body may be moved with the consent of the physician or medical examiner who certifies the cause of death. The local registrar will issue the authorization for disposition in the form of a burial-transit permit. This authorization must be obtained within 72 hours of death and prior to final disposition. Funeral directors can also issue permits after hours.

### ❖ Burial

Family graveyards under one acre outside city or village limits are permissible. Such land is exempt from taxation and must be recorded with the county clerk. Permission from the local health department is required to establish a private cemetery. There are no state burial statutes or regulations with regard to depth. A sensible guideline is 150 feet from a water supply and at least two feet of earth on top.

### ❖ Cremation

A signature of the medical examiner in the county where death occurred is required on the burial-transit permit for cremation. Authorization by next-of-kin is usually required, and a pacemaker must be removed.

## ❖ Other Requirements

A body which will not reach its destination within 48 hours must be embalmed.

A body of one who has died of diphtheria, meningococcic infections, plague, poliomyelitis, scarlet fever, or small pox must be embalmed. The attending physician may determine the appropriate precautions to be taken in the case of AIDS.

## ❖ Medical Schools for Body Donation

University of Michigan
Medical School
Dept. of Anat. & Cell Biology
Medical Science II Bldg.
Ann Arbor, MI 48109
313-764-4359 8-5 M-F
313-936-6267 page person carrying
beeper for the donation program.
Urgent need

Cost to family: transportation to
   medical school
Prior enrollment: not required
Over-enrollment: shared
Disposition: cremation; return of
   cremains by request ($25)
Body rejection: standard,* obesity

Wayne State University
Medical School
Department of Anatomy
540 E. Canfield
Detroit, MI 48201
313-577-1188
nights: 577-1198
Urgent need

Cost to family: transportation outside
   SE lower Michigan
Prior enrollment: not required
Over-enrollment: shared
Disposition: cremation; return of
   cremains by request
Body rejection: standard,* recent major
   surgery, metastatic cancer,
   previous embalming

Michigan State University
Willed Body Program
Dept. of Anatomy
East Lansing, MI 48824-1316
517-353-5398
Moderate need

Cost to family: transportation to
   medical school
Prior enrollment: not required
Over-enrollment: shared
Disposition: cremation; return of
   cremains by request
Body rejection: standard,* obesity,
   severe emaciation, recent major
   surgery

* autopsy, decomposition, mutilation, severe burn victim, meningitis, hepatitis, AIDS, and other contagious or communicable diseases

## ❖ Crematories

Ann Arbor

Southern Michigan Crematory
4495 Jackson Rd., 48103
313-665-3650

Bay City

Northern Michigan Crematory
1500 N. Henry St., 48706
517-686-7400
800-258-2339

Bay City

Sunset Valley Crematory
210 Au Sable State Rd., 48706
517-684-0262

Berkley

Roseland Park Crematory
3401 Woodward Ave., 48072
810-541-1154

Clarkson

Ottawa Park Cemetery
6180 Dixie Hwy., 48346
810-623-9112

Detroit

Evergreen Cemetery
19807 Woodward, 48203
313-368-1330

Forest Lawn Cemetery
11851 Van Dyke, 48234
313-921-6960

Meadowcrest Memorial
5800 E. Davidson, 48212
313-891-2429

Woodlawn Cemetery Assn.
19975 Woodward, 48203
313-368-0010

Woodmere Memorial Park
9400 W. Fort, 48209
313-841-0188

Flat Rock

Michigan Memorial Park
P.O. Box 610, 48134
313-782-2473

Grand Rapids

Graceland Memorial Park Cemetery
4341 Cascade SE, 49546
616-949-0660

Rosedale Memorial Park
0-50 Lake Michigan Dr. NE, 49504
616-453-2411

Hagar Shore

North Shore Memorial Gardens
P.O. Box 294A, 49039
616-849-1100

Kalamazoo

Mount Ever Rest Memorial Park
3941 S. Westnedge Ave., 49008
616-343-6820

Manislee

Oak Grove Cemetery
330 Fifth St., 49660
616-723-2727

Mount Morris

Flint Memorial Park
P.O. Box 157, 48458
810-666-3660

Muskegon

Sunrise Memorial Gardens
2188 Rememberance Dr., 49442
616-777-2422

West Michigan Cremation Service
1600 Creston St., 49442
616-773-6631

Negaunee

Northland Chapel Gardens
239 Midway Dr., 49866
906-225-0716

Okemos

East Lawn Memory Gardens
2400 Bennett, 48864
517-349-9180

Royal Oak

Oakview Cemetery
1032 N. Main, 48067
810-541-0139

Traverse City

Northern Cremation Services
3575 Veterans Dr., 49684
616-946-8613

Troy

White Chapel Memorial Cemetery
621 W. Long Lake Rd., 48098
810-362-7670

Additional crematories may have been established in this state after the date of publication.

## ❖ State Governance

The Michigan Board of Mortuary Science has nine members. There are three consumer representatives.

The Cemetery Commission in the Department of Licensing governs for-profit cemeteries and crematories.

## ❖ Prepaid Cemetery and Funeral Funds

For *cemetery* merchandise—vaults and markers—130% of the wholesale cost must be placed in **trust**. If "**delivered**" to storage, the actual cost may be withdrawn, with the remaining 30% left in trust until the death of the purchaser.[1] There are no trusting requirements for cemetery services.

**Finance charges** are permitted for installment sales—for both cemetery and funeral purchases. This is absurd! Consumers would be wise to

---

[1] Is a casket "cemetery merchandise" when sold by a cemetery? The Fenton Corporation in the Flint area owns five cemeteries. It started selling caskets and giving warehouse receipts to consumers to avoid trusting requirements. The Michigan Funeral Directors Association brought suit, contending that Fenton was violating trust requirements for "funeral merchandise." And where was the State of Michigan all this time? As it turns out, only about 200 of the 500 caskets sold were in the warehouse.

demand an adjustment to any contract, deleting finance charges before signing an agreement. Tell the sales person it would be silly to pay interest on something you don't have yet.

Unlike cemetery sales, all prepaid *funeral* funds must be placed in **trust.** (For those wishing to make an irrevocable plan—to be eligible for social services, the amount may not exceed $2,000.) A preneed seller may charge an *additional* 10% in commission. Yes, ladies and gentlemen, step right up. Pay now, and it will cost you only 10% more than if you wait and pay later. I wonder if only 90% goes into trust, with the 10% taken from the contract price and the paperwork adjusted to keep everyone happy. Two checks would do the trick: one for 90% of the charges of which all (100%) goes into trust, and another for 10%—the commission.

To its credit, Michigan has required since 1986 that an annual **report** of preneed funds be sent to the purchaser *unless waived in writing.* One can only hope that slick sales people haven't convinced unwitting purchasers to sign away their rights with a simple, "Just sign here, and here, and here."

Although Michigan has no **guarantee fund** to protect against default by a preneed seller, the annual reporting requirement to the purchaser should be a compelling factor for keeping funds properly invested and for reducing the chance of consumer loss. Any consumer *not getting an annual report,* however, should immediately demand one, even if—or perhaps especially if—the agreement was made prior to 1986.

Every three years preneed sellers must make audited reports to the state. Records must be open for inspection any time.

Fees not to exceed 1% of the trust may be withdrawn (or accumulated to the credit of the fund trustee) for "reasonable fees and expenses."

If excess funds remain after services have been provided, there is a complicated formula for how much gets refunded to the heirs or estate, ranging from 0% to 100%—varying with how big the initial commission was and whether or not it was a guaranteed-price funeral. In practice— with funeral inflation generally exceeding bank interest, one shouldn't fret about how big a refund you might get on grandma's funeral. There isn't likely to be one.

If you want to **cancel** a preneed contract (30 days notice), you should pay attention to the issue of "commission." If no commission was acknowledged on the preneed agreement, the seller may retain 10% before issuing a **refund**. There is no statutory provision guaranteeing that you may **transfer** an irrevocable contract. If permitted, it will be out of the goodness of the mortician involved.

If you've been making only intermittent payments, a seller may cancel an installment contract that is more than 90 days in default and retain 10% of the amount in escrow.

The department of licensing may promulgate rules to "protect against solicitations which are intimidating, vexatious, fraudulent, or misleading, or which take unfair advantage of a person's ignorance or emotional vulnerability." Sounds wonderful, but I didn't find any such rules. I understand that the Michigan Funeral Directors Association is conscientious about policing its own, but the state should not leave that to a trade organization that has no authority to fine an entity or suspend a license.

## ❖ Consumer Concerns

- The death rate in Michigan can support approximately 334 full-time mortuaries; there are, however, 805. Funeral prices tend to be higher in areas where there are "too many" funeral homes.
- 100% of all cemetery merchandise and services should be placed in trust; a purchaser should have a full right of refund at any time, along with the interest. "Constructive delivery" should not be permitted.
- Laws should require cemeteries to repurchase an unwanted lot at the original selling price plus 50% of the difference between that and current market price.
- Finance charges are permitted for installment sales of prepaid funeral and cemetery arrangements. This is outrageous and should be repealed immediately! When you finance a car or house, you get to use either. But a finance charge on a lay-away plan before they lay you away?
- There is no statutory requirement that when merchandise is selected on a guaranteed-price preneed contract that a clear description is given and that merchandise of "equal quality and construction" must be offered if the merchandise selected is not available (although

this provision *may* appear on individual contracts). Survivors should be allowed to approve any substitutions.

- Annual reporting to a preneed funeral customer should be required, not sign-away-able.
- Until the Michigan laws are changed to require 100% trusting of all money and interest for prepaid goods and services and adequate substitution of funeral merchandise that meets the approval of survivors, it is probably a *very unwise* idea to prepay for these arrangements. Your own trust account in a bank will be safer and will be transferable.
- The coroner or medical examiner's permit for cremation in the case of an *anticipated* death from natural causes is totally unnecessary and creates an additional burden and charge for families.
- Identification and tagging of the body at the place of death before removal should be required.
- The law requiring embalming after 48 hours or when death occurs from a communicable disease should be repealed. This is not only an offense to some religious groups, it puts the funeral professionals and possibly the environment at risk. Refrigeration is a more reliable means of body preservation.
- There is no provision either forbidding a mark-up on cash advance items or requiring the disclosure of how much the mark-up would be. Consumers may wish to ask for a copy of those invoices.
- There is no requirement that low-cost caskets be included in any display.
- Rental or reuse of any part of a casket is not permitted. This creates an absurd financial burden for a family when cremation is the final method of disposition. With removable liners, there is no public health concern if a casket shell is reused.[1]
- Casket-funeral-package pricing is still permitted by administrative rules, in violation of the FTC's itemization requirements.
- Although there is reference to using FTC pricing methods when selling preneed arrangements, the full FTC Funeral Rule should be adopted by reference to make it enforceable in this state.

---

[1] The executive director for MFDA assured me that such wrap-around shells were not considered part of a "casket" and that some funeral directors were, indeed, offering these. The law should be clarified, however, to make sure this option is being made available to all.

374 ~ *Caring for the Dead in Michigan*

- The standards for ethical, professional conduct should be strengthened. That would make it easier for a consumer to prevail when filing a valid complaint. (See Ethical Standards in the Appendix.)

## ❖ Miscellaneous Information

- Educational requirements for a license in mortuary science: mortuary college (3 years), one year of apprenticeship, and an exam.
- Funeral directors may not own or have an interest in a cemetery[1] or a crematory (which is considered part of a cemetery function). Crematories on cemetery grounds do not need to be licensed separately. Someone who is not a mortician may, however, be licensed by the Cemetery Commission to run an independent crematory if zoning and environmental concerns are met.
- One may name a personal representative in a will to carry out written instructions for funeral arrangements and body disposition.
- From the mortician statutes, prohibited conduct includes: "using profane, indecent or obscene language in the presence of a dead human body, or within the immediate hearing of the family or relatives of a deceased, whose body has not yet been interred or otherwise disposed of." Then watch out?
- From the "Rural Cemetery" statutes: ". . . no saloon or place of entertainment shall thereafter be set up or established for the sale of intoxicating drinks, and no sporting festival shall be held within ¼ of a mile of the entrance to the grounds . . . . No person shall enter into such inclosed cemetery by climbing or leaping over or through any fence or wall . . . ."
- One office handles complaints for 27 different occupations. The complaint form is relatively easy to fill out.
- Coroners are no longer elected. County medical examiners must be licensed physicians and are appointed.

## ❖ Nonprofit Funeral Consumer Information Societies

These consumer groups are run mostly by volunteers. Consequently, contact information may change. If you have difficulty reaching a society

---

[1] Loewen and SCI have purchased or are trying to purchase cemeteries in violation of the statutes. The Michigan Funeral Directors Association has filed a suit to halt such acquisition. The State of Michigan, however, may be the only entity with a legal right to intercede. Stay tuned.

or are interested in starting a society in your area, call the FAMSA office: 800-765-0107. Or check the internet directory—
**www.funerals.org/famsa**

Ann Arbor

  Memorial Advisory & Planning Society
  2030 Chaucer Dr., 48103
  313-665-9516

Flint

  Memorial Society of Flint
  P.O. Box 4315, 48504-4315
  810-239-2596

Detroit

  Greater Detroit Memorial Society
  P.O. Box 14054, 48224-04954
  313-886-0998

~❖~

*This chapter was sent for review to the Department of Public Health,
the Cemetery Commission, the Board of Examiners in Mortuary
Science, and the Michigan Funeral Directors Association.
No response was received.*

# In Minnesota

*Please refer to Chapter 8 as you use this section.*

Families and church groups in Minnesota may care for their own dead. The legal authority to do so is found in:

> *Chapter 149A [re disposition of bodies and funeral directing] Subd. 3(b) This chapter does not apply to or interfere with the customs or rites of any culture or recognized religion in the final disposition of their dead, to the extent that the provisions of this chapter are inconsistent with the customs or rites.*
>
> *(c) Noncompensated persons related by blood, adoption, or marriage to a decedent who chose to remove a body of a decedent from the place of death, transport the body, prepare the body for disposition, except embalming, or arrange for final disposition of the body are not required to be licensed, provided that all actions are in compliance with this chapter.*

There are no other statutes that might require you to use a funeral director.

## ❖ Death Certificate

The family doctor or a local medical examiner will supply and sign the death certificate, stating the cause of death. The remaining information must be supplied, typewritten or in black ink. The death certificate must be filed with the local registrar within five days and before final disposition.

Minnesota is beginning to implement electronic death registration. When that is adopted the procedure will change somewhat. Check with the local health department.

## ❖ Fetal Death

A fetal death report is required when death occurs after 20 weeks of gestation or more and must be filed as above.

## ❖ Transporting and Disposition Permit

The local registrar, health officer, clerk of district court, or city administrator will issue the burial-removal-transit permit. Morticians serve as sub-registrars after hours. This authorization must be obtained within five days and prior to final disposition of the body. The vehicle used to move the body must be enclosed.

## ❖ Burial

Any private person and any religious corporation may establish a cemetery on their own land. The land must be surveyed and a plat recorded with the county recorder. Family graveyards so dedicated are exempt from taxation. Check with the county or town registrar for local zoning laws regarding home burial. There are no state burial statutes or regulations with regard to depth. A sensible guideline is 150 feet from a water supply and at least two feet of earth on top.

The original copy of the burial-transit permit is to be filed with the place of disposition. In the case of home burial, the original should be retained with your deed unless the clerk of the court requires it to be recorded with official land records. The second copy of the burial-transit permit must be filed with the Department of Health.

## ❖ Cremation

A permit for cremation must be obtained from the coroner or medical examiner. There is no fee for this. Authorization by next-of-kin is usually required, and a pacemaker must be removed.

## ❖ Other Requirements

Disposition must be within a "reasonable time." New statutes are more specific, intrusive, and unreasonable with regard to embalming:[1] The body must be embalmed if disposition will not be accomplished within 72 hours. There is no allowance for refrigeration, a far superior method of body preservation. Embalming is also required in the case of infectious diseases, the worst possible circumstances under which to require embalming. A body must be embalmed prior to shipping via public transportation, even though most airlines are willing to make exceptions for religious reasons if the casket is tightly closed. But the most offensive requirement is embalming for public viewing. Such a

---

[1] 149A.91 Subd. 3.

stricture has no allowance for religious conviction that embalming is an indignity upon the "temple of the soul," as some believe.

## ❖ Medical Schools for Body Donation

Northwestern College of Chiropractic
2501 W. 84th St.
Bloomington, MN 55431

Does not accept cadaver donation.

University of Minnesota
Bequest Program
4-135 Jackson Hall
321 Church St.
Minneapolis, MN 55455
612-625-1111
Donations meet need.

Cost to family: transportation outside metropolitan area
Prior enrollment: required
Over-enrollment: not shared
Disposition: cremation; return of cremains by request and expense of family
Body rejection: standard,* obesity, over-enrollment

Mayo Clinic Foundation
Rochester, MN 55901
507-284-2511

Cost to family: transportation beyond 200 miles or $.75/mi.
Prior enrollment: not required
Over-enrollment: not shared
Disposition: cremation; return of cremains by request and expense of family
Body rejection: standard,* over-enrollment

* autopsy, decomposition, mutilation, severe burn victim, meningitis, hepatitis, AIDS, and other contagious or communicable diseases

## ❖ Crematories

Brainerd

Lake Area Cremation Services
2120 Excelsior Rd., 56401
507-828-5051

Coleraine

Peterson Funeral Chapel
422 Roosevelt Ave., 55722
218-245-1441

Coon Rapids

Anoka County Cremation Soc.
1827 Coon Rapids Blvd. NW, 55433
612-767-1000

Duluth

Park Hill Cemetery Assn.
2500 Vermillion Rd., 55803
218-724-7149

Eagan

Eagan Cremation Service
1580 Century Pt., 55121
612-454-9488

Faribault

Southern Heights Crematory
300 Prairie Ave., 55021
507-334-4481 or 800-657-7095

Fergus Falls

Olson Funeral Home/Crematorium
711 Pebble Lane Rd., 56537
800-530-8937

Hopkins

Washburn-McReavy Funeral Chapels
1400 Main St., 55343
612-938-9020

Long Prairie

Stephan-Stein Funeral Home
333 1st Ave. N., 56347
612-732-2629

Madison

Zahrbock Funeral Home
108 2nd Ave., 56256
612-598-3339

Mankato

Glenwood Crematory
1001 N. Riverfront Dr., 56001
507-388-2202

Woodland Hills
1605 Woodland Ave., 56001
507-387-5504

Minneapolis

Cremation Society of MN
4343 Nicollet Ave., 55409
612-825-4567

Crystal Lake Crematory
Penn & Dowling N., 55412
612-521-7619

Hillside Memorium
2600 19th Ave. NE, 55418
612-781-3391

Lakewood Cemetery Assn.
3600 Hennepin Ave., 55408
612-822-2172

Sunset Memorial Park
St. Anthony Blvd. & 22nd, 55418
612-789-3596

Washburn-McReavy-Welander-Quist
2301 Dupont Ave. S., 55405
612-377-2203

Mound

Fairview Crematory
RFD #1., Box 157, 55364
612-472-3925

Richfield

Morris Nilsen Funeral Chapel
6527 Portland Ave., 55423
612-869-3226

Rochester

Anderson's Rochester Crematory
2843 S. Broadway Hwy. 63S., 55904
507-282-9101

Southern MN Crematory
1705 Elton Hills Dr. NW, 55901
507-289-3600

St. Cloud

Central MN Cremation Service
1111 25th Ave. S., 56301
320-252-3132

St. Paul

Forest Lawn Memorial Park
1800 Edgerton St., 55117
612-776-6420

Virginia

Greenwood Cemetery/Crematory
1126 9th St. N., 55792
218-741-9413

Northern MN Crematory
516 1st St. S., 55792
218-741-9593

Additional crematories may have been established in this state after the date of publication.

## ❖ State Governance

The Minnesota Advisory Council in Mortuary Science has five members. There is one consumer representative.

There is no state board governing cemeteries.

Crematories are licensed and regulated by the Department of Health.

## ❖ Prepaid Cemetery and Funeral Funds

Cemeteries larger than ten acres must send a report of perpetual care funds annually to the county auditor.

There are **no statutes** governing or protecting other portions of a *cemetery* purchase such as opening-and-closing charges, vaults, and markers—no trusting requirements whatsoever. That means the cemetery can spend your money the minute you pay it, and you'll have to hope they're still in business when you need what you've paid for. There is no provision for changing your mind and getting a refund, either. With the for-profit cemeteries moving into Minnesota, this should be of considerable concern.

All of the money paid preneed for a *funeral* purchase must be placed into **trust.** The purchaser must be given the name of the financial institution and the account number where the money will be deposited.

A purchaser may get a full **refund,** including interest, of a revocable plan. Although the statutes are a little vague, it would appear that one has a full right to **transfer** an irrevocable agreement, as well.

Under the disbursement of funds portion of the statute is an interesting provision: "The funds shall be distributed for the payment of the actual *at-need value* [emphasis added] of the funeral goods and/or services selected with any excess funds distributed to the estate of the decedent." This would imply that funeral homes may not sell a guaranteed-price funeral. The general sales lure to buyers, however, is to select a casket and all other details of the funeral service now, to lock in prices. I fear that the "at-need value" clause leaves a funeral home free to imply that a family must honor a particular casket choice, for example, even if there is not sufficient money to pay for it at today's prices. With the rate of funeral inflation, "excess funds" are unlikely, and survivors would—presumably—be billed for an additional amount if they felt such arrangements were binding. A more responsible provision would be for the **substitution** of equal quality merchandise at no extra cost (and with the approval of the survivors).

When a funeral home has been sold to a new owner—especially a funeral chain, the at-need prices are likely to increase dramatically. Because the state guarantees a full right of refund, you may want to move any prepaid account to another funeral home if what is in the account will not cover the new prices—even if the body is already at the funeral home.

The funeral home must make an annual **report** to the commissioner of all prepaid accounts.

## ❖ Consumer Concerns

- The death rate in Minnesota can support approximately 150 full-time mortuaries; there are, however, 520. Funeral prices tend to be higher in areas where there are "too many" funeral homes.
- There is no state board governing cemeteries.
- There is no provision for placing preneed cemetery services and merchandise in trust.
- Laws should require cemeteries to repurchase an unwanted lot at the original selling price plus 50% of the difference between that and current market price.
- There is no annual reporting requirement to the purchaser of prepaid funeral goods and services, paperwork that might be useful to the family of a deceased to indicate prepayment and which would help to "enforce" trusting requirements.
- There is no state protection for consumers in case of default on prepaid funeral funds that were never put into trust.
- With no adequate provision for cemetery trusting or for substitution of funeral merchandise selected preneed, it is probably a *terrible* idea to prepay for cemetery and funeral arrangements in Minnesota until the laws are changed.
- The coroner or medical examiner's permit for cremation in the case of an *anticipated* death from natural causes is totally unnecessary and creates an additional burden for families.

- Identification and tagging of the body at the place of death before removal should be required.
- The laws requiring embalming for any purpose should be repealed. This is not only an offense to some religious groups, it puts the funeral professionals and possibly the environment at risk when death occurs from a contagious disease.
- There is no provision either forbidding a mark-up on cash advance items or requiring disclosure of how much the mark-up would be.
- There is no requirement that low-cost caskets be included in any display.
- While the standards for ethical, professional conduct aren't too bad, they could be strengthened. That would make it easier for a consumer to prevail when filing a valid complaint. (See Ethical Standards in the Appendix.)
- Complaint procedures are not clear.
- Although there is a statutory duty to comply with the written wishes of the decedent, if your wishes are challenged in court, the next-of-kin may be given priority over a designated agent.

### ❖ Miscellaneous Information

- Educational requirements for becoming a funeral director or embalmer (effective January 1999): bachelor's degree (4 years) in mortuary science, the national and state exams, and one year of internship.
- The language of the FTC Funeral Rule has been adopted in statute.
- Rental caskets are specifically permitted by law.
- Medical examiners are appointed physicians. Coroners are elected and may be funeral directors, but there has been, in practice, a shift of coroner's duties to medical examiners.
- It is a misdemeanor to hold a body for debt.

### ❖ Nonprofit Funeral Consumer Information Societies

These consumer groups are run mostly by volunteers. Consequently, contact information may change. If you have difficulty reaching a society or are interested in starting a society in your area, call the FAMSA office: 800-765-0107. Or check the internet directory—

**www.funerals.org/famsa**

Minnesota Funeral and Memorial Society
717 Riverside Dr. SE
St. Cloud, MN 56304
320-252-7540

~❖~

*This chapter was sent for review to the Minnesota Department of Health Mortuary Science Section and the Attorney General's Consumer Division.*

The Mortuary Standards Supervisor declined to review this chapter, "because of the limited time and resources available." He sent a duplicate of some of the Minnesota laws I already had. Some state bureaucrats are timorous about being quoted or named in publication, so one must hope that the supervisor does find the time to reflect on several of the serious funeral consumer issues raised in this chapter. Otherwise, one has to wonder, exactly what are the priorities of the supervisor? No response was received from the Consumer Division.

# In Mississippi

*Please refer to Chapter 8 as you use this section.*

Persons and church groups in Mississippi may care for their own dead. The legal authority to do so is found in:

> *Health Department Rule 41: Filing of death certificate (a) The funeral director, or person acting as such, who first assumes custody of a dead body, shall review and correct any items completed by an institution or the medical examiner, complete the death certificate and file it with the Office of Vital Records . . . .*

> *MS Code 73-11-55 (1) . . . In case of funeral services held in any private residence, church, cemetery, cemetery chapel, cemetery facility, or lodge hall, no license [as a funeral establishment] shall be required.*

There are no other statutes which might require you to use a funeral director.

### ❖ Death Certificate

The attending physician or local medical examiner will sign the death certificate within 72 hours, stating the cause of death. The remaining information must be supplied, and the use of a typewriter is preferred. There are three carbons. The original (white copy) must be filed with the Office of Vital Records within five days and before final disposition. The third page may be retained by a hospital or nursing home and the fourth page by the physician.

The medical examiner will certify the cause of death in violent or unexpected circumstances and when a physician was not in attendance within 36 hours, except in cases where terminal illness has been diagnosed.

## ❖ Fetal Death

A fetal death report is required when death occurs after 20 weeks of gestation or when weight is 350 grams or more. If there is no family physician involved and the death is not subject to the jurisdiction of the coroner or medical examiner, the person attending or the parents may file the fetal death report with the State Registrar within five days. A fetal death report may be obtained from a physician, hospital, or the county health department.

## ❖ Transporting and Disposition Permit

A body may be moved with the consent of a physician, coroner, or medical examiner. If the body is moved out of state, it must be accompanied by a burial-transit permit signed by the doctor or medical examiner certifying the death. This is the yellow page of the four-copy death certificate.

## ❖ Burial

Check with the county Board of Supervisors for local zoning laws if home burial is planned. The top of the coffin must be 24 inches below the natural surface of the earth.

When burial is arranged, the family member acting as the funeral director must sign the death certificate and file it with the Office of Vital Records within five days.

## ❖ Cremation

The death certificate must be filed with the Office of Vital Records before cremation. Most crematories insist that a pacemaker be removed, and authorization by next-of-kin usually is required.

## ❖ Other Requirements

When the destination cannot be reached within 24 hours or disposition does not take place within 48 hours, a body must be embalmed or refrigerated.

When death is from a contagious disease that may constitute a public hazard, the matter must be referred to a medical examiner.

## ❖ Medical Schools for Body Donation

University of Mississippi
Medical Center
Jackson, MS 39216
601-984-1000
Moderate need

Cost to family: transportation beyond 300 miles
Prior enrollment: not required
Over-enrollment: shared
Disposition: cremation/burial at University; return of cremains by request
Body rejection: autopsy, communicable and infectious diseases, decomposition, burn victim, severe trauma, embalming unless under the direction of the University

## ❖ Crematories

Bay St. Louis

South Mississippi Crematory
229 Hwy. 90 E., 39520
601-467-4242

Biloxi

Mississippi Gulf Coast Crematory
314 E. Howard Ave, 39530
601-374-5650

Brookhaven

Cremation Services, Inc.
505 Storm Ave., 39601
601-833-6680

Jackson

Southern Mortuary Services
245 W. Lorenz Blvd., 39216
601-366-5239

Verona

Lee Memorial Crematory
Old Hwy 45 S., 38879
601-566-8769

There may be additional crematories that were established in this after publication.

## ❖ State Governance

The Mississippi State Board of Funeral Service has seven members. One is a consumer representative.

No state agency governs cemeteries or crematories.

## ❖ Prepaid Cemetery and Funeral Funds

There is no requirement that all *cemeteries* have a perpetual care fund; it is strictly optional. If a cemetery has opted to be a "perpetual care cemetery," then 15% of all lot sales, and 5% of crypt and niche sales must be placed in trust.

Prepaid funds for vaults, urns, memorials, scrolls, vases, foundations, and bases are exempt from any trusting requirements if the seller has delivered "a valid warehouse receipt." This **"constructive delivery"** makes a refund nearly impossible if you were to move or change your mind.

All cemetery land is exempt from taxation per MS Code 27-31-1. I found at least one for-profit cemetery that was not paying property taxes in 1997.

Only 50% of prepaid *funeral funds* must be placed in **trust,** and—from the income—the trustee may withdraw funds to cover "reasonable expenses." The trustee must report annually to the seller, but there is no **reporting** requirement to the purchaser or to the state.

Mississippi Code still contains statutes (dated mostly in the '30s) for "burial associations" that are governed by the state insurance commissioner. As of 1996, no new burial associations may be established. On certain policies, there is a restriction as to which funeral home may be used or a limit on benefits, the maximum being $500. As the elderly owning these contracts die, there will be a rude shock: there was no provision for the interest on the amount paid to cover inflation. On the other hand, if the policy was supposed to cover a casket and all services and if survivors select a more expensive casket than the el-cheapo flimsy one that is usually shown (a blatant "bait and switch" tactic), any substitution may void the policy altogether or yield only the face value, not the full funeral cost as intended. If a person stops making payments on one of these burial policies, there will be no refund. Either way, the seller benefits while the consumer is cheated!

Unless you have only six months or so to live and don't mind being buried in something not much better than a giant shoe-box, it's probably a good idea to stop making any more payments to a burial association. Put your money in the bank with a next-of-kin on your account. There it will be readily available at a time of death along with all the interest.

Mississippi is one of the states where funeral consumers are at serious risk and poorly protected, far more so than in many other states. It should come as no surprise, then, that the funeral conglomerates are buying up funeral homes at a great rate. The cost of funerals in Mississippi can be expected to soar until consumers seek and support alternatives such as church-run funerals or ethically-priced independent mortuaries.

### ❖ Consumer Concerns

- The death rate in Mississippi can support approximately 109 full-time mortuaries; there are, however, 306. Funeral prices tend to be higher in areas where there are "too many" funeral homes.
- At least some cemeteries run by for-profit corporations were not paying property taxes as of 1997. This places an unfair burden on the local taxpayers.
- Laws should require cemeteries to repurchase an unwanted lot at the original selling price plus 50% of the difference between that and current market price.
- The law should be changed to require 100% trusting of all prepaid funeral *and* cemetery funds—to allow for adequate interest to build against inflation and for a full refund if the consumer were to move to another location or simply change funeral plans.
- A law providing for substitution of funeral merchandise of equal value is needed, with an adequate description—to allow for the satisfaction of the family. A common ploy of morticians—especially on a "guaranteed" funeral package—is to announce that the selected casket is no longer available or to display a particularly shoddy model as the one that comes with the package. Family members invariably pay additional funds for a better casket.
- Preneed funeral consumers should get an annual report indicating the institution of deposit and value (purchase price plus interest) of all prepaid funeral monies. Such documents could be important to survivors and would help to enforce the trusting requirements.
- A guarantee fund should be established to serve consumers in case of funeral home default on prepaid arrangements.
- Until the preneed laws are strengthened in Mississippi, it is probably a *terrible* idea to prepay for any funeral or cemetery arrangements (except perhaps a plot). A personal bank account is much safer.
- Identification and tagging of the body at the place of death before removal should be required.
- There is no requirement that low-cost caskets be included in any display.

- There is no restriction on taking a mark-up on cash advance nor a requirement to disclose how much it is if a mark-up is taken.
- There is no statutory provision for giving priority to the wishes of the deceased if expressed in writing before to death.
- The ethical standards for funeral directors need to be defined and expanded. That would make it easier for a consumer to prevail when filing a valid complaint. (See Ethical Standards in the Appendix.)
- Complaint procedures are unclear and inadequate.
- The FTC Funeral Rule should be adopted by reference so it could be more enforceable in this state.
- Coroners are elected, and—while they must attend State Medical Examiner Death Investigation Training School—a potential conflict of interest is raised when the person holding a coroner's job is also a funeral director rather than a physician.

## ❖ Miscellaneous Information

- The educational requirements for becoming a funeral director in Mississippi are: a high school diploma, two years of apprenticeship, and passing a state-approved written or oral exam. For being licensed in funeral service (as an embalmer) the requirements are: high school, one year of mortuary school, one year of apprenticeship, and passing a state-approved written or oral exam.
- The body of a person with an infectious or communicable disease must be tagged. These diseases include infectious hepatitis, tuberculosis, AIDS, and any venereal disease.

## ❖ Nonprofit Funeral Consumer Information Societies

Although there are no FAMSA-affiliated funeral-planning societies in Mississippi as of this writing, you may check the internet directory—**www.funerals.org/famsa**—or call the national office to see if any have since been started: 1-800-765-0107. The FAMSA office may have a limited list of ethically-priced mortuaries in Mississippi. And let the office know if you are interested in starting a consumer organization in your area.

~❖~

*This chapter was sent for review to the Mississippi Department of Insurance, the Attorney General's Office, the Department of Public Health, and the State Board of Funeral Service.*

Wrote Shepard Montgomery of the Department of Insurance: "I was very impressed with the materials you forwarded. . . . We are very aware of the critical nature of the solvency problem surrounding burial associations, yet our success in taking proactive legislative steps to address the situation has been frustrated by a limited number of very influential funeral home owners who seek to preserve the burial association system." Perhaps it's time for consumers to speak up.

# In Missouri

*Please refer to Chapter 8 as you use this section.*

Persons in Missouri may care for their own dead. The legal authority to do so is found in:

> *Title 193.145 . . . 4. The funeral director or person acting as such shall file the certificate of death.*

There are no other statutes that might require you to use a funeral director.

## ❖ Death Certificate

The family doctor or a local medical examiner will supply and sign the death certificate within 72 hours, stating the cause of death. The remaining information must be supplied, typewritten or in black ink. The death certificate must be filed with the local registrar within five days. A "notification of death" must be filed with or mailed to the local registrar prior to disposition if the death certificate has not been completed. This form can be obtained from the registrar or a funeral director.

## ❖ Fetal Death

A fetal death report is required when death occurs after 20 weeks of gestation or when the weight is 350 grams or more. If there is no family physician involved, the local medical examiner must sign the fetal death certificate. The fetal death certificate must be filed within seven days.

## ❖ Transporting and Disposition Permit

A body may be moved with the consent of a physician, medical examiner, or coroner. An out-of-state disposition permit can be obtained from a funeral director or the Bureau of Vital Records if the body will be removed from the state.

## ❖ Burial

Home burial is permissible in Missouri. Land, not to exceed one acre, must be deeded in trust and the deed filed with the county court within 60 days. Check with the county or town registrar for local zoning laws regarding home burial. There are no state burial statutes or regulations with regard to depth. A sensible guideline is 150 feet from a water supply and at least two feet of earth on top. There is no permit required for burial if the notification of death or death certificate has been filed.

## ❖ Cremation

The death certificate must be completed and filed with the registrar prior to cremation. The physician completing the death certificate will authorize cremation. Authorization by next-of-kin is also required, and a pacemaker must be removed.

One may authorize one's own cremation prior to death.

## ❖ Other Requirements

For families handling a "normal" death on their own, there are no statutory embalming requirements.

Regulations promulgated by the Board of Embalmers and Funeral Directors, however, require embalming or refrigeration after 24 hours. If next-of-kin have not yet been located or if waiting any longer would make the embalming job more difficult, the mortuary may go ahead and embalm the body after six hours. This seems outrageously presumptive, with such disparate religious or personal views on embalming and when refrigeration is a more reliable method of body preservation.

If a person dies of a communicable disease, the body must be tagged and labeled with the disease. This seems at odds with the advice from the Centers for Disease Control which says *all bodies* should be handled with universal precautions. And given the constant mix-ups at mortuaries with mass-preparation facilities, all bodies should be tagged at the place of death anyway, prior to removal.

When death is due to an infectious disease, burial or cremation must occur within 24 hours unless the body is embalmed.

If shipping by common carrier, a body which will not reach its destination within 24 hours must be embalmed or encased in a sealed casket. If death is due to Asiatic cholera, typhus, typhoid or ship fever, yellow fever, bubonic plague, diphtheria, scarlet fever, glanders, anthrax, leprosy, small pox, TB, puerperal fever, erysipelas, measles or "other dangerous or communicable diseases," embalming is required prior to shipping. Alternatively, the body may be wrapped in a disinfectant-saturated sheet before being placed in a sealed casket.

## ❖ Medical Schools for Body Donation

Logan College of Chiropractic
1851 Schoettler Rd.
P.O. Box 100
Chesterfield, MO 63017
314-227-2100 ext. 135
314-962-0271
Moderate need

Cost to family: transportation over $75
Prior enrollment: not required
Over-enrollment: not shared
Disposition: cremation; no return of cremains
Body rejection: AIDS, autopsy (rare exceptions)

University of Missouri—Columbia
Dept. of Pathology & Anat. Sciences
School of Medicine
Columbia, MO 65212
314-882-2288
Moderate need

Cost to family: transportation
Prior enrollment: preferred
Over-enrollment: shared
Disposition: cremation; no return of cremains
Body rejection: standard,* under 18, obesity

Cleveland Chiropractic College
6401 Rockhill Rd.
Kansas City, MO 64131

Obtains bodies through other schools.

Kirksville College of Osteopathic Med.
800 W. Jefferson
Kirksville, MO 63501
660-626-2468
Moderate need

Cost to family: transportation and embalming
Prior enrollment: required
Over-enrollment: shared
Disposition: cremation; return of cremains by request
Body rejection: standard,* under 12

St. Louis University
School of Medicine
Dept. of Anatomy
1402 S. Grand Blvd.
St. Louis, MO 63104
314-577-8271
Moderate need

Cost to family: transportation
Prior enrollment: required
Over-enrollment: shared
Disposition: cremation; no return of cremains
Body rejection: standard,* previous embalming—unless school permission is granted

Washington University
Dept. of Anatomy
4566 Scott Ave.
St. Louis, MO 63110
314-362-3597
Moderate need

Cost to family: transportation
Prior enrollment: required
Over-enrollment: shared
Disposition: cremation; no return of
    cremains
Body rejection: standard,* previous em-
    balming

* autopsy, decomposition, mutilation, severe burn victim, meningitis, hepatitis, AIDS, and
other contagious or communicable diseases

## ❖ Crematories

Anderson

Ozark Funeral Home
(crematory in Arkansas)
Main & Spring St., 64831
417-845-3393

Arnold

Schaefer Mortuary Services
2061 Hwy. 21, 63126
314-487-2366

Bismark

Sunset Memorial Crematory
371 Wallen Rd., 63080
314-468-4171

Camdenton

Hedges Funeral Home
148 N. Hwy. 5, 65020
314-346-2090

Columbia

Memorial Funeral Home
1217 Business Loop 70W, 65202
314-443-3173

Parker Funeral Service/Crematory
10th & Walnut, 65201
573-449-4153

Independence

Carson Crematorium
Winner Rd. & Fuller St., 64052
816-252-7900

Jackson

Cape Crematory Service
3520 Matthew St., 63755
314-335-8681

Joplin

Ozark Memorial Park
415 N. St. Louis, 64802
417-624-0184

Kansas City

Carson Crematorium
Winner Rd. at Fuller, 64052
816-252-7900

Central States Mortuary/Crematory
4437 R NW Gateway, 64150
816-746-1321

D.W. Newcomer's Sons
1331 Brush Creek Blvd., 64110
816-561-0024

Mt. Moriah Crematory
10507 Holmes, 64131
816-942-2004

Parklawn Funeral Home
8251 Hillcrest Rd., 64138
816-523-1233

St. Joseph

Heaton-Bowman-Smith-Sidenfaden
3609 Frederick Blvd., 64506
816-232-3355

St. Louis

Hillcrest Abbey Crematory
3211 Sublette Ave., 63139
314-645-4305

Cremation Society of St. Louis
740 N. Mason Rd., 63141
314-434-3933

Hoffmeister Broadway Fitzgerald
7814 S. Broadway, 63111
314-638-0107

Memorial Park Cemetery
5200 Lucas Hunt Rd., 63121
314-389-3500

Mt. Hope Cemetery
1215 Lemay Ferry Rd., 63121
314-544-2000

Oak Grove Chapel & Crematory
7800 St. Charles Rock Rd., 63114
314-721-7260

St. Louis Cremation Service
2909 Chouteau, 63103
314-721-7260

Schaefer Mortuary Service
2061 Hwy. 21, 63010
800-296-9360

Valhalla Chapel
7600 St. Charles Rock Rd., 63133
314-721-4900

Springfield

Gorman-Scharpf Funeral Home
Spring-Green Crematory
1947 E. Seminole, 65802
417-886-9994

Greenlawn Funeral Home
3506 N. National Blvd., 65803
417-833-1111

Ozark Wilbert Vaults
2850 Barton, 65804
417-883-2355

Sullivan

Eaton Funeral Home
Meramec Regional Crematory
347 N. Clark St., 63080
314-860-3473

Warrensburg

Warrensburg Memorial Gardens
617 N. Maguire, 64093
816-747-9114

Additional crematories may have been established in this state after the date of publication.

## ❖ State Governance

The Missouri Board of Embalmers and Funeral Directors has six members. There is one consumer representative.

The Division of Professional Registration is responsible for regulating cemeteries.

Crematories are licensed, regulated, and inspected by the Board of Funeral Directors and Embalmers. One does not need to be a funeral director to run a crematory. A limited license is given.

## ❖ Prepaid Cemetery and Funeral Funds

Only 110% of the wholesale cost for prepaid *cemetery merchandise* must be placed in trust. "**Constructive delivery**" can bypass the trusting requirement, but the chances are that the state isn't checking to see what's in the warehouse. There is **no trusting** requirement for prepaid cemetery *services* such as the opening-and-closing fee. If there is anything in trust, the **interest** may be withdrawn by the cemetery. This is piddley protection for consumers who are unlikely to get any refund if they were to change their minds. For example, if you decide on cremation later, a coffin vault would not be needed, but you'd get no refund.

The cemetery must make an **annual report** to the Division of Registration.

Only 80% of prepaid *funeral funds* must be placed into **trust**. If you are purchasing an installment plan, the seller gets to keep the first 20% right off. The seller is entitled to all income from preneed trusts and may withdraw the **interest** annually.

A purchaser may cancel a preneed contract, but if done so after 30 days, the **refund** will be only 80% of the total contract, without any interest. Likewise, for anyone wishing to **transfer** an irrevocable contract, all that gets moved is 80%.

On the other hand, a seller may suggest, in lieu of a trust, a **joint deposit account**—in the names of both the seller and the purchaser. In this case, 100% must be placed in the account. The "deposited funds" in such an account are fully **refundable** if it has not been made irrevocable. (Whether that includes interest "deposited" is questionable. Read the fine-print in your contract.) Why a preneed seller would suggest this plan over the 80% plan, one can only speculate. Is the joint account an asset against which the seller may borrow?

A seller must **report** preneed sales to the state funeral board annually.

### ❖ Consumer Concerns

- The death rate in Missouri can support approximately 221 full-time mortuaries; there are, however, 707. Funeral prices tend to be higher in areas where there are "too many" funeral homes.
- Laws should require cemeteries to repurchase an unwanted lot at the original selling price plus 50% of the difference between that and current market price.
- All (100%) money prepaid for cemetery goods and services should be placed into trust, with full right of refund.
- There is no provision for an adequate description of funeral goods selected preneed nor for a substitution of equal quality and construction if the selected item is no longer available at the time of death. Substitution should require the approval of survivors.
- There is no annual reporting requirement to the purchaser of prepaid funeral goods and services, paperwork that might be useful to the family of a deceased to indicate prepayment and which would help to "enforce" trusting requirements.
- There is no state protection for consumers in case of default on prepaid funeral funds that were never put into trust.
- Until the laws are changed to require 100% trusting for preneed cemetery and funeral purchases and other loopholes are closed, it is probably a *terrible* idea to prepay for any such arrangements other than perhaps a plot. A personal bank account is much safer and can easily be transferred.
- Body tagging of all bodies should occur at the place of death before removal, given the regular mix-ups that have been happening at chain-owned establishments with central prep facilities.
- All laws and regulations requiring embalming should be repealed, especially those for when the death has occurred from a communicable or contagious disease. This is not only an offense to some religious groups, it puts the funeral professionals and possibly the environment at risk.
- There is no requirement that low-cost caskets be included in any display.
- Although one may authorize cremation prior to death, there is no law that allows you to state other funeral preferences or for naming a designated agent to make your final arrangements. In situations where you are estranged or distant from next-of-kin, this could be important.

- The standards for ethical, professional conduct should be strengthened. That would make it easier for a consumer to prevail when filing a valid complaint. (See Ethical Standards in the Appendix.)
- The FTC Funeral Rule should be adopted by reference to make it more enforceable in this state.
- Complaint procedures are unclear and inadequate. Complaints against funeral establishments are kept secret.

## ❖ Miscellaneous Information

- Educational requirements for becoming a funeral director: high school, one year of apprenticeship, and a state and practical exam. For an embalmer: mortuary college (2 years), one year of apprenticeship, the state and national exams.
- Cash-advance items must be billed to the customer in the same amount as they were billed to the funeral home.
- Coroners are elected. They need not be medical personnel.

## ❖ Nonprofit Funeral Consumer Information Societies

These consumer groups are run mostly by volunteers. Consequently, contact information may change. If you have difficulty reaching a society or are interested in starting a society in your area, call the FAMSA office: 800-765-0107. Or check the internet directory—

**www.funerals.org/famsa**

Funeral & Memorial Society
  of Greater Kansas City
4500 Warwick Blvd.
Kansas City, KS 64111
816-561-6322

Funeral Consumer Information Society
216 E. Argonne Ave.
St. Louis, MO 63122-4310
314-997-9819

~❖~

*This chapter was sent for review to the Department of Public Health and the Division of Professional Registration, but no response was received. Staff at the Board of Embalmers and Funeral Directors were kind enough to make some small corrections.*

# In Montana

*Please refer to Chapter 8 as you use this section.*

Persons in Montana may care for their own dead. The statute granting the right to control disposition of remains was repealed in 1993, and no other statute or regulation has been enacted. By common law, next-of-kin would prevail, unless other provisions have been made by the decedant prior to death. There are no statutes that would require you to use a funeral director.

### ❖ Death Certificate

The clerk and recorder's office or the local registrar can supply a death certificate. (Ask for the the removal authorization form at the same time.) The doctor last in attendance, the county coroner, or the state medical examiner will sign the death certificate, stating the cause of death. The remaining information must be supplied, typewritten or in black ink. The death certificate must be filed with the local registrar within 10 days or within two days of when the cause of death has been determined, if after 10 days.

### ❖ Fetal Death

A fetal death report is required when death occurs after 20 weeks of gestation (or when a weight of 350 grams) and must be filed as above. A midwife or other person "in attendance" may fill out this report.

### ❖ Transporting and Disposition Permit

A body may be moved with medical permission, but a "Dead Body Removal Authorization" must be signed by the physician or coroner (or a mortician) within 24 hours. One copy must be filed with the registrar of the district where the death occurred.

### ❖ Burial

Check with the county or town registrar for local zoning laws regarding home burial. There are no state burial statutes or regulations with regard to depth. A sensible guideline is 150 feet from a water supply and at least two or three feet of earth on top. Six bodies constitute a "cemetery."

When burial is arranged, the family member acting as the funeral director must sign the authorization and file it with the local registrar.

## ❖ Cremation

The Dead Body Removal Authorization is sufficient for cremation, but there is a 24-hour waiting period after death. Authorization by next-of-kin (or the deceased before death) is required, and a pacemaker must be removed. Cremation must be in a licensed crematory.

"Unauthorized persons" may not witness the cremation. The next-of-kin or other authorizing agent must specify "the ultimate disposition of the cremated remains, if known." Apparently—if you have not made up your mind yet—that will not be a problem.

## ❖ Other Requirements

A "proper covering" is required when a body is transported by a private carrier.

A body that will not reach its destination within 48 hours must be embalmed or refrigerated.

The local health officer must be notified, and embalming is required, if death is due to small pox, cholera, pneumonic plague, lassa fever, ebola fever, Marburg virus disease, TB, AIDS, hepatitis, and any undiagnosable febrile disease occurring shortly after returning from international travel.

## ❖ Medical Schools for Body Donation

There are no medical schools in Montana. However, Washington, Wyoming, Alaska, Montana, and Idaho participate in the WWAMI Medical Education Program:

WWAMI Medical Education Program
Montana State University
Leon Johnson Hall
Bozeman, MT 59715
406-994-4411 or 994-3230
Needs adequately met at the time of
this writing

Cost to family: transportation outside
200-mile radius (some, but not all,
funeral homes will make additional
service charges)
Prior enrollment: preferred, not required
Over-enrollment: not shared
Disposition: burial in county lot
Body rejection: standard,* under 18,
cavity embalming, unhealed
wounds, over-enrollment

* autopsy, decomposition, mutilation, severe burn victim, meningitis, hepatitis, AIDS, and other
contagious or communicable diseases

## ❖ Crematories

Billings

Billings Crematory
48 Riverside, 59102
406-248-8527 (not always there;
sells vaults, too)

Cremation & Caskets
Gallery of Choices
114 Florine Ln., 59101
406-254-2474
888-254-2414

Michelotti-Sawyers Mortuary
1001 Alderson Ave., 59102
406-252-3417

Terrace Gardens
304 34th St. W., 59102
406-245-6427

Bozeman

Dahl Funeral Home
P.O. Box 1063, 59715
406-586-5298

Butte

Butte Crematories
2415 S. Montana St., 59701
P.O. Box 4266, 59702
406-782-1503

Great Falls

Hillcrest Lawn Memorial Assn.
1410 13th St. S., 59403
406-453-3847

O'Connor Crematory
2425 8th Ave., N.
P.O. Box 2374, 59403
406-453-7257

Hamilton

Daly Leach Memorial Chapel
1010 W. Main, 59840
406-363-2010

Dowling Funeral Home
415 S. 2nd St.
P.O. Box 666, 59840
406-363-1111

Helena

Sunset Memorial Gardens
7100 N. Montana, 59601
406-458-5732

Kalispell

Hillside Crematory
525 Main St., 59901
406-752-6666

Buffalo Hill Funeral Home/Crematory
1890 Highway 93 N, 59901
406-752-0336

Miles City

Bullis-Graves
1806 Main St., 593401
406-232-4840

Eastern Montana Cremation Service
Waterplant and Logan Dr.
406-665-1207

Missoula

Garden City Funeral Home
1705 W. Broadway
406-543-4190

Sunset Memorial Cemetery
7405 Mullan Rd., 59802
406-549- 2857

Additional crematories may have been established in this state after the date of publication.

## ❖ State Governance

The Montana Board of Funeral Service has five members. One is a consumer representative, one a crematory operator, and three are morticians.

The Department of Commerce receives annual reports of prepaid cemetery and funeral plans.

Crematories are licensed, regulated, and inspected by the Board of Funeral Service, but one does not need to be a funeral director to run one.

## ❖ Prepaid Cemetery and Funeral Funds

Most of the cemetery laws in Montana deal with municipal or county *cemeteries* and are relatively mundane. Another set of laws deals with private cemetery associations, with the implication that these are not-for-profit without bothering to say so, other than that they are exempt from property taxes. A few new laws (1997) address for-profit cemeteries, a growing concern if conglomerate funeral chains buy up any of the private "associations" or start new cemeteries.

A lot owner wishing to sell a lot must offer it to the cemetery first, at the going rate.

All (100%) of prepaid *funeral and cemetery* purchases (excluding the price of a lot) must be placed in individual **trust** accounts. The institution holding these funds must **report** annually to the Department of Commerce the income and amount in each account, along with the name of the beneficiary.

There are no statutory provisions for **cancellation** or **transfer** of prepaid funeral arrangements.

### ❖ Consumer Concerns

- The death rate in Montana can support approximately 28 full-time mortuaries; there are 87 such establishments. With the low density of population over a large area, mortuary careers are not likely to be full-time work. Unfortunately, because of the low volume of business per mortuary, funeral prices may tend to be high.
- There is no state board governing cemeteries.
- There is no provision for an adequate description of funeral goods selected preneed nor for a substitution of equal quality and construction if the selected item is no longer available at the time of death. Survivors should approve any substitutions.
- There are no statutory provisions for a refund or transfer of preneed accounts. With some contracts being made irrevocable to shelter assets when applying for SSI or Medicaid, transferability is a concern if death occurs outside the area. If the ownership of the funeral home has changed, you may wish to change providers. Current statutes do not guarantee you that right.
- There is no law specifically forbidding "constructive delivery," which has been used in other states to avoid trusting requirements.
- There is no annual reporting requirement to the purchaser of prepaid funeral goods and services, paperwork that might be useful to the family of a deceased to indicate prepayment and which would help to "enforce" trusting requirements.
- There is no state protection for consumers in case of default on prepaid funeral funds that were never put into trust.
- Until there are more preneed protections, it is probably a *terrible* idea to prepay for a funeral in Montana.
- As of this writing, current Montana regulations permit three methods of funeral pricing, all of which seem clearly in violation of the FTC Funeral Rule: 1) "a single price which includes professional services, the use of facilities, and the casket;" 2) "a two-part price made up of (i) the price of professional services and the use of facilities" and "(ii) the price of the casket selected;" and 3) "itemized—the prices for the various facets of the funeral according to their general

functions or use . . . (i) professional services, (ii) facilities, (iii) equipment, (iv) casket." The next Rule, however, states that, "An itemized listing of the service charges must be disclosed and made available to the consuming public." (The FTC requires that prices be made available to anyone who asks, not just the "consuming public." One inquirer was told by an undertaker, "I don't have to give prices unless you go into the showroom." When the person said he was quite willing to go into the showroom, the response was, "I choose not to let you go in. Now get out.") The regulation also provides that "if the quoted price includes a basic component of a funeral or a part thereof which is not desired, then a credit therefore shall be granted."

One walk-in inquirer—whose father was ailing at a local hospital—asked for prices and was given one price list. When he said he had been thinking about cremation, he was given another funeral price list. When he asked about the use of alternative containers, he was given yet another funeral price list.

After learning of these difficulties, I called a Montana mortuary and began asking for their prices in the order and terminology used by the FTC. But after just a few items, the undertaker quickly said, "Well, a full traditional funeral would cost . . ." I never did get the exact price or a clear difference between the facilities and staff for a "memorial service" and a "funeral service."

It would appear that Montana consumers probably are not receiving itemized lists of funeral options in the FTC-approved format nor in a timely way per FTC requirements. If one chose not to have a viewing (which involves both facilities and staff), would it be easy to quickly see how much could be deducted from the other prices given?

- The FTC Funeral Rule should be adopted by reference in the statutes or regulations to make it more enforceable in this state.
- The laws on embalming should be repealed, especially when death occurs from a communicable disease. This is not only an offense to some religious groups, it puts the funeral professionals and possibly the environment at risk.
- Identification and tagging of the body at the place of death before removal should be required.
- There is no provision either forbidding a mark-up on cash advance items or requiring the disclosure of how much it would be.
- Ethical standards should be expanded and clearly defined in order for valid consumer complaints to prevail. The only penalties now

amount to a slap on the wrist unless a license is revoked. The board should have the ability to levy a fine large enough to deter unethical practices.

## ❖ Miscellaneous Information

- Educational requirements for a funeral director: two years of college plus mortuary school, one year of apprenticeship, and an exam.
- Pets and other animals may not be cremated in a crematory used for humans.
- Regulations require that the least expensive casket be shown on display or by photograph.
- Preference regarding disposition is given to the expressed wishes of the deceased. It may be helpful, however, to also name a deathcare agent, if you are distant or estranged from next-of-kin.
- Coroners are elected and need not be physicians, although some training is required.
- A body may not be held for debt.

## ❖ Nonprofit Funeral Consumer Information Societies

These consumer groups are run mostly by volunteers. Consequently, contact information may change. If you have difficulty reaching a society or are interested in starting a society in your area, call the FAMSA office: 800-765-0107. Or check the internet directory—

**www.funerals.org/famsa**

Billings

Memorial Society of Montana
1024 Princeton Ave., 59102
406-252-5065

Missoula

Five Valleys Burial Memorial Assn.
405 University Ave., 59801
406-543-6952

~❖~

*This chapter was reviewed by the Montana Department of Public Health. No response was received from the Board of Funeral Service or the Department of Commerce.*

# In Nebraska

*Please refer to Chapter 8 as you use this section.*

The laws in Nebraska might make you a little angry. Not only will families have a difficult time caring for their own dead, they may be stuck with a funeral bill for an estranged relative, and—whether they like it or not—it'll have to be the kind of funeral that the person asked for prior to death, as the written or oral wishes of the deceased regarding disposition must be honored.

> *Chapter 71-1339—The right to control the disposition of the remains of a deceased person, unless other directions have been given by the decedent, vests in the following persons in the order named: (1) The surviving spouse; (2) if the surviving spouse is incompetent or not available, or if there be no surviving spouse, adult child of the decedent; (3) a surviving parent of the decedent; (4) an adult brother or sister of the decedent; or (5) an adult person in the next degrees of kindred in the order named by the laws of Nebraska as entitled to succeed to the estate of the decedent. The liability for the reasonable cost of interment devolves jointly and severally upon all kin of the decedent in the same degree of kindred and upon the estate of the decedent.*

> *Chapter 71-605(1)—The funeral director and embalmer in charge of the funeral of any person dying in the State of Nebraska shall cause a certificate of death to be filled out . . . (7) No dead human body shall be removed from the state for final disposition without a transit permit issued by the funeral director and embalmer having charge of the body . . . (8) The interment . . . shall be performed under the direct supervision of a licensed funeral director and embalmer . . . (9) All transit permits . . . shall be signed by the funeral director and embalmer in charge . . .*

The primary concern of 71-1339 seems to be an effort to nail down who will pay for the "reasonable cost of interment." What if the cost isn't "reasonable" (and by whose standards is "reasonable" measured)?

What remedy do families have then? Certainly not caring for their own dead, if these conflicting laws are allowed to stand.

The restriction in 71-605 was undoubtedly passed at the behest of a self-serving funeral industry. Without a court challenge, people in Nebraska will have far fewer burial rights than in almost any other state. Yet a court challenge would certainly be decided in favor of a family's right to custody of the body, according to legal precedents.[1]

In the meantime, it will be a most unusual undertaker who might cooperate with a family or church group wishing to handle their own funeral arrangements. Legally, you could get the death certificate signed by the funeral director; you could then transport the body home or to a church for final "good-byes" and a service. But then, you'll have to call the funeral director again to meet you at the cemetery or crematory for final "interment," or out on the back forty if home burial is planned. It may be easier to change the laws.

One other curious law—71-609—appears in the statutes. Casket retailers must include a copy of the laws and a blank death certificate. Doesn't that give the impression that families have the right to care for their own dead?

### ❖ Death Certificate

The family doctor or a local medical examiner will sign the death certificate within 24 hours, stating the cause of death. The remaining information must be supplied by the family, typewritten or in permanent ink. The death certificate must be filed with the Bureau of Vital Statistics within five business days—by a funeral director.

### ❖ Fetal Death

A fetal death report is required if death occurs after 20 weeks of gestation. If there is no family physician involved, the county attorney must be notified.

---

[1] Court cases from the early 1900s are clear about this, but it seems that consumers must be forced to fight for this right over and over. As recently as 1995, a Michigan court again confirmed a family's right to possession of the body "for preparation, mourning and burial." The legal premise on which this is based is fundamental and constitutional, not one that can be taken away by the states.

## ❖ Transporting and Disposition Permit

A transit permit is required only for a body shipped out of state. A funeral director will issue this permit. You may have difficulty getting the funeral director to grant the permit if you are driving the body to another state, but you do have a legal right to do so; there are no statutes in Nebraska restricting who may transport a body. You would not need a mortician at the receiving end if delivering a body to a medical school.

## ❖ Burial

Check with the county registrar for local zoning laws regarding home burial. Family graveyards are exempt from taxation and must be registered with the county clerk. When burial is arranged—even on private land—it must be under the direct supervision of a licensed funeral director.

There are no state burial statutes or regulations with regard to depth. A sensible guideline is 150 feet from a water supply and two or three feet of earth on top.

## ❖ Cremation

A permit for cremation must be obtained from the county attorney. There is no fee for this. Most crematories insist that a pacemaker be removed, and authorization by next-of-kin is usually required unless authorized by the decedent prior to death.

Cremation is considered final disposition, "the same as interment."

## ❖ Other Requirements

Nebraska has no other requirements controlling the time schedule for the disposition of unembalmed bodies. Weather and reasonable planning should be considered.

If the person died of a contagious or communicable disease, the doctor in attendance should be consulted.

A body shipped by common carrier must be embalmed.

## ❖ Medical Schools for Body Donation

Anatomical Board
State of Nebraska
600 S. 42nd St.
Omaha, NE 68198
402-280-2914 (Creighton)
402-559-4030 (U. of NE)
    or 559-6249
    or 331-2839
Moderate need

Cost to family: Anatomical Board pays $1 per mile up to 250 miles. The mortuary may levy additional charges.
Prior enrollment: required
Over-enrollment: shared within Neb.
Disposition: cremation, burial of cremains in university plot; return of cremains by request and at expense of family
Body rejection: autopsy, decomposition, TB, obesity, emaciation, mutilation

## ❖ Crematories

Gibbon

Miller & Godberson
P.O. Box 10, 68840
308-468-5621

Kearney

Central NE Cremation Service
2155 2nd Ave., 68847
308-234-3500

Lincoln

Lincoln Memorial Park
6800 S. 14th St., 68512
402-423-1515

Roper & Sons
4300 -O- St., 68510
402-476-7037

Omaha

Catholic Cemeteries
7710 W. Center Rd., 68124
402-391-3606

Elmore Crematory
c/o Omaha Wilbert Vaults
2660 Gomez Ave., 68107
402-731-1452

Forest Lawn Mem. Park
7909 Mormon Bridge Rd., 68152
402-451-1000

West Lawn Hillcrest Mem. Pk.
5701 Center St., 68106
402-556-2500

Paxton

CNCS West
101 N. Elm St., 69155
308-2239-4343

Additional crematories may have been established after publication.

## ❖ State Governance

The Nebraska State Board of Embalmers and Funeral Directors has four members. There is one consumer representative.

The Department of Insurance regulates preneed funeral and cemetery purchases.

Cemeteries have the right to erect crematories, but crematories are otherwise unregulated in this state.

### ❖ Prepaid Cemetery and Funeral Funds

Nebraska statutes provide that cemeteries must be operated "in nowise with a view to profit." Only municipalities, churches, and nonprofit cemetery associations may operate cemeteries. "The establishment of a cemetery by any agency other than those enumerated herein shall constitute a nuisance, and its operation may be enjoined at the suit of any taxpayer in the state." With corporate funeral chains finding greater profits in cemetery operations than in mortuaries, Nebraskans need to be alert. An operation that is technically "nonprofit" on the surface can easily siphon off exorbitant sums—to a holding company for rent of the land, perhaps—or in management fees. A definite "nuisance," indeed.

Preneed marketing "agents" are not necessarily morticians but must be working for a preneed "seller," the one who will be providing funeral or cemetery services.

A seller may charge and pocket interest on installment purchases. This is absurd—**finance fees** for a lay-away plan before they lay you away.

Only 85% of prepaid money for *funerals and cemetery* merchandise (*i.e.,* markers and vaults) must be placed in **trust**, reducing the amount that otherwise might generate interest against inflation. "**Constructive delivery**" can bypass trusting requirements. This is usually accomplished with a title showing ownership or a document stating that the marker or vault is in the cemetery warehouse with your name on it. Few states verify such documents.[1]

---

[1] In Washington state, less than half of what was supposed to be there was in the warehouse of one cemetery. (A preneed examiner for the Nebraska Insurance Department pointed out that this footnote has no relevance with regard to her state. She didn't say whether Nebraska was actually checking the warehouses, however.)

The seller may withdraw annually any **income** in excess of the National Consumer Price Index. That is, if the national inflation rate is 2%, then 2% of the income must be left in the account. If the account generated 5% interest, the preneed seller may withdraw the remaining 3%. As you can see, interest growth will be minimal unless general inflation runs wild. Obviously, Nebraska legislators arc out of touch with what's really happening in the industry: funeral inflation is running between 5% and 7% a year; more for low-cost funeral selections, and more still if "your" funeral home has been purchased by a chain.

The financial trustee may also withdraw "reasonable costs incurred in the administration of the trusts." This little statement is a sneaky one, as many state trade organizations have set up "master" trusts through which to invest preneed funeral funds. The state funeral directors association usually gets a monthly commission as does the funeral director who sold the preneed arrangement. In most states, growth for the consumer's interest in these accounts is usually between 3.6% and 4.9%, still less than funeral inflation and a CD at the bank. The state is not aware of any such master trust at this time, but the idea may catch on later.

Anyone seeking to **cancel** or **transfer** a preneed agreement can throw 15% of the initial payment to the prairie winds. What you get will also be depleted by the price of whatever has already been "delivered" and the annual "cxccss" income or administrative fees withdrawn. Oh, yes, don't expect a refund or transfer for 90 days—less a permitted service charge from the bank. (Any financial institution taking that long to process a transaction shouldn't be allowed to charge for it.)

An irrevocable funeral trust is limited to $3,000.

There is no provision for an adequate description of merchandise selected preneed. While the seller "*may*" **substitute** merchandise of like or better quality if the item selected is not available, this is not a *requirement.*

The preneed seller must make an annual **report** to the director of the Insurance Department.

## ❖ Consumer Concerns

- The death rate in Nebraska can support approximately 62 full-time mortuaries; there are, however, 290. Funeral prices tend to be higher in areas where there are "too many" funeral homes.

- Laws should require cemeteries to repurchase an unwanted lot at the original selling price plus 50% of the difference between that and current market price.

- There is no provision for an adequate description of funeral goods selected preneed nor a *requirement* for the substitution—approved by survivors—of equal quality and construction if the selected item is no longer available at the time of death.

- Constructive delivery should be eliminated. Trusting requirements should be increased to 100%, with all interest to accrue. The consumer should get full benefit of all interest and amounts paid when cancelling or transferring an arrangement.

- Preneed funeral consumers should get an annual report indicating the institution of deposit and value (purchase price plus interest) of all prepaid funeral monies. Such documents could be important to survivors who might not otherwise know about prepaid accounts and could serve to enforce the trusting requirements.

- There is no state protection for consumers in case of default on prepaid funeral funds that were never put into trust.

- Until the preneed loopholes and omissions have been fixed, it is probably a *terrible* idea to prepay for a funeral or cemetery goods and services in this state. Money in the bank will be safer.

- There is no requirement to have low-cost caskets on display.

- There is no requirement to disclose how much a cash advance item may be marked up or forbidding such a mark-up.

- Identification and tagging of the body at the place of death before removal should be required.

- The cremation permit from the county attorney is an unnecessary burden on families in the case of an anticipated death.

- The definition of "funeral directing" in the statutes sounds as if morticians were clergy: "counseling families or next of kin in regard to the conduct of a funeral service for a dead human body. . . ." Not everyone wants the funeral director to call the shots.

- Ethical standards should be expanded and clearly defined in order for valid consumer complaints to prevail.

- The FTC Funeral Rule should be adopted by reference in the statutes or regulations to make it more enforceable in this state.

## ❖ Miscellaneous Information

- The educational requirements for becoming an embalmer/funeral director are 60 semester hours of college (two years), plus mortuary "college" (could be one year), and one year of apprenticeship.
- Under standards for funeral directors and embalmers, no "indecent, profane, or obscene language" may be used in the presence of the body or family and friends "prior to the burial." After that, watch out?
- Written or oral wishes of the deceased regarding disposition must be honored. Better hope he or she left the funds to pay for it.
- There are no restrictions on who may sell caskets at retail. The casket retailer, however, must keep a record of each sale including the name, place, and date of death. In each casket, the retailer must supply a notice of the law and a blank death certificate.
- Coroners are elected.

## ❖ Nonprofit Funeral Consumer Information Societies

There are no funeral consumer information societies in Nebraska at the time of this writing, although perhaps the revelations in this chapter will stimulate more consumer activity there. If you are eager to help, call the FAMSA office (800-765-0107) or check the FAMSA website—

**www.funerals.org/famsa**

—to see if one has since been started. In the meantime, the FAMSA office will be looking for low-cost Nebraska mortuaries to which it can refer consumers.

~❖~

*This chapter was sent for review to the Nebraska Department of Health and Human Services and the Nebraska Board of Examiners in Funeral Directing and Embalming, but no response was received. The Department of Insurance was also sent a copy.*

Wrote Timothy Hall, director of insurance, "While the Department of Insurance has reviewed the information pertaining to our agency, we do not endorse the statements made in your publication."

# In Nevada

*Please refer to Chapter 8 as you use this section.*

Persons in Nevada may care for their own dead.[1] The relevant statutes are found in:

*NRS 440.370: Signature of statements as to disposition of the body. The statement of facts relating to the disposition of the body must be signed by the funeral director or person acting as undertaker. . . .*

*NRS 642.550: Applicability of chapter (re funeral directors and embalmers). Nothing in this chapter shall be construed to apply: 1. To persons engaged as layers-out or to those who shroud the dead.*

## ❖ Death Certificate

The family doctor, local health officer, or coroner will sign the death certificate, stating the cause of death. The remaining information must be supplied, typewritten or in black ink. The death certificate must be filed with the local registrar within 72 hours and before final disposition.

## ❖ Fetal Death

A fetal death report is required for each fetal death. If there is no family physician involved, the local health officer or coroner must sign the fetal death certificate.

## ❖ Transporting and Disposition Permit

A body may be moved with the permission of the person certifying death. The local health officer will issue the final burial or removal permit. This must be obtained within 72 hours of death.

---

[1] The Office of Vital Statistics (Department of Human Resources, Health Division) accepts a liberal interpretation of the statutes. According to 1986 correspondence, "The funeral industry has hotly contested this viewpoint. . . ."

## ❖ Burial

Check with the county registrar for local zoning laws regarding home burial. There are no state burial statutes or regulations with regard to depth. A sensible guideline is 150 feet from a water supply and three feet of earth on top.

When burial is arranged, the family member acting as the funeral director must sign the burial permit and file it with the local health officer within 10 days.

## ❖ Cremation

No additional permit is required for cremation. Authorization by next-of-kin or designated agent is required unless a cremation order is signed prior to death by the deceased. A pacemaker must be removed. Cremation must be in a licensed crematory.

## ❖ Other Requirements

Embalming may not be required for the first 72 hours unless ordered by the board of health. If the person died of a contagious or communicable disease, the doctor in attendance should be consulted for state health guidelines. In this case, embalming may be required.

## ❖ Medical Schools for Body Donation

University of Nevada
Department of Anatomy
School of Medicine
Reno, NV 89557
702-784-6113 or 784-6169
Moderate need

Cost to family: transportation costs above $75
Prior enrollment: required
Over-enrollment: few shared
Disposition: cremation
Body rejection: autopsy, decomposition, mutilation, missing body parts, suicide, AIDS, infectious diseases

## ❖ Crematories

Carson City

  FitzHenry's Funeral Home
833 N. Edmonds Dr., 89702
702-882-2644

Las Vegas

  Memory Gardens
7251 Lone Mountain Rd., 89108
702-645-1174

Neptune Society of NV
1111 Las Vegas Blvd. N., 89101
702-474-6699

Nevada Funeral Service
726 S. Casino Center Blvd., #208, 89101
702-382-7378

Palm Mausoleum/Memorial Park
1325 N. Main St., 89101
702-382-1340

Paradise Valley Chapel
6200 S. Eastern Ave., 89119
702-736-6200

Reno

Mountain View Cemetery
435 Stoker, 89504
702-329-9231

Sierra Crematory
227 Vine St., 89503
702-323-1836

Additional crematories may have been established after publication.

## ❖ State Governance

The Nevada Board of Funeral Directors, Embalmers and Operators of Cemeteries and Crematories has five members: one funeral director, one cemeterian, one crematory operator, and two consumer representatives. What a comprehensive, well-balanced board.

Crematories are licensed and regulated by the funeral board. One does not need to be a funeral director to run a crematory.

The commissioner of insurance regulates preneed cemetery and funeral purchases, as well as crematories and pet cemeteries.

## ❖ Prepaid Cemetery and Funeral Funds

There are statutory provisions for moving a cemetery—with the consent of "known heirs." Kind of too bad a cemetery isn't a permanent place.

Cemeteries, including pet cemeteries, must be eleemosynary, not-for-profit organizations. Funeral conglomerates are finding ways around this, and SCI owns at least one cemetery as of this writing.

Preneed agents must be registered with the Department of Insurance. Boy, is Nevada generous to its preneed sellers. Preneed must be a booming business in this state. Only 60% of preneed *cemetery* goods and services must be placed in **trust**. 60% of the **income** may be withdrawn annually by the seller after administrative fees are paid.

If you paid $1,000 for a vault, $1,000 for opening-and-closing, and $1,000 for a marker, then only $1,800 will go into the trust. If you change your mind and decide on cremation and won't need the expensive vault or hefty opening-and-closing, there's no telling what provision for **cancellation** there might be. On the other hand, if you move, the statutes do allow the cemetery to **transfer** the $1,800 or so that's left in the trust from your original $3,000.

But wait. Somebody really has it in for the struggling buyer. If you are paying on an installment plan, statutes provide that the 40% commission *may* be retained before any is put in trust. I am told by one of the Insurance Department staffers that the commissioner is now preparing a regulation that would require a proportionate share of each payment to be placed into trust.

If you default on *"any"* payment, the cemetery may terminate the contract and keep "as damages not more than 40% of the total purchase price." Not 40% of what is paid, but 40% of what you *would* have paid. In plain talk, if you have paid $1,000 of the $3,000 and hit a month of hard times missing a payment, you'll get back nothing, not one red cent. If you've paid $2,000, you'll get back $800. What a deal!

Only 75% of preneed *funeral* expenses must be placed in **trust**. If you are paying on an installment plan, the 25% commission may be retained before any is put in trust. That is, if you have negotiated for a $5,000 funeral, the seller may keep the first $1,250 you pay before the remaining $3,750 is put aside for your funeral (unless the commissioner's new regulation requires proportionate deposits here, too). But the seller's preneed income doesn't stop there. Let's say your trust earns 5% interest each year. After the trust institution has deducted any administration fees, the seller may withdraw 75% of the **income** from the trust annually. Suppose the trustee takes 1% for administration; that leaves 4% of which the seller may claim the 3% share, and your account keeps 1%. With funeral inflation running about 5-7% a year, 1% is hardly adequate to keep up. Once the account has built up to 125% of the initial amount, the trust will be capped—at the grand sum of $4,687.50 in this case—and the seller may withdraw all income after that.

Although the preneed contract must carry a "clear and unambiguous statement of the services and property to be supplied," there is no provision for **substitution** of merchandise equal in quality and construction if the item selected is not available. This has been a source of some mischief around the country. Typical ploy: "I'm sorry, we no longer have that model. You'll have to pick another casket. And, oh, yes, there'll be an additional charge."

Apparently, the only way you can **cancel** a preneed arrangement is to move "to another geographic area." At that point, you'll get "all the money in the trust fund"—75% of what you initially paid plus whatever piddley interest has been left in the account. There is a strange provision that if you die and your account is all paid up, your survivors could transfer the contract to another provider and expect "all money paid"— $5,000 in the case above. That won't include the **interest**, but it's more than you'd get if you moved and cancelled the agreement yourself.

Trustees for preneed funeral and cemetery accounts must make quarterly **reports** to the insurance commissioner.

Preneed cemetery and funeral sellers must carry a **bond** of $50,000. That is hardly adequate protection as it would barely cover ten people with funeral plans of $5,000 each. It would cover a few more contracts for cemetery services and merchandise if those averaged only $3,000 a piece.

I found one interesting provision in the Nevada statutes that doesn't seem to appear anywhere else in the country: The funeral director or cemetery authority must give a copy of any preneed agreement to the person making final arrangements. Failure to do so may result in a fine three times the amount of the preneed sales agreement. This seems like a great idea if there weren't already so many loopholes.

### ❖ Consumer Concerns

- The death rate in Nevada can support approximately 52 full-time mortuaries; there are 34 such establishments. This is one of the few states where there is not a significant glut of funeral homes, and prices are competitive in some areas. Consumers will have to shop around, however, as there are huge differences from one funeral home to the next.
- Laws should require cemeteries to repurchase an unwanted lot at the original selling price plus 50% of the difference between that and current market price.
- There is no provision for an adequate description of funeral goods selected preneed nor for a substitution of equal quality and construction if the selected item is no longer available at the time of death. Survivors should approve any substitution.
- Preneed funeral consumers should get an annual report indicating the institution of deposit and value (purchase price plus interest)

of all prepaid funeral monies. Such documents could be important to survivors who might not otherwise know about prepaid accounts. This report would also help to enforce the trusting requirements.

- Until trusting requirements are increased to 100% with interest income kept intact and adequate provisions for cancellation or transfer, it is probably a *terrible* idea to prepay for a funeral or any cemetery services and merchandise in Nevada.
- Identification and tagging of the body at the place of death before removal should be required, given the regular mix-ups that have happened at chain-owned places with central prep facilities.
- There is no provision either forbidding a mark-up on cash advance items or requiring the disclosure of how much any mark-up is.
- There is no requirement to have low-cost caskets on display.
- Ethical standards should be expanded and clearly defined in order for valid consumer complaints to prevail.
- A person may authorize his/her cremation prior to death, but there is no provision for naming a designated death care agent, something that might be important if you are at a distance or estranged from next-of-kin.

❖ **Miscellaneous Information**

- Educational requirements for becoming a funeral director or embalmer: two years of college, one year of mortuary college, one year of apprenticeship, and an exam.
- Unless it is run by a society for the purpose of preventing cruelty to animals, only a cemetery authority may operate a pet crematory.
- The FTC Funeral Rule has been adopted by reference.
- Livestock may not be pastured in a cemetery.
- It is unprofessional conduct to use "profane, indecent or obscene language in the presence of a dead human body, or within the immediate hearing of the family or relatives of a deceased whose body has not yet been interred or otherwise disposed of." After that, watch out?
- It is a misdemeanor to hold a body for debt.

## ❖ Nonprofit Funeral Consumer Information Societies

These consumer groups are run mostly by volunteers. Consequently, contact information may change. If you have difficulty reaching a society or are interested in starting a society in your area, call the FAMSA office: 800-765-0107. Or check the internet directory—

**www.funerals.org/famsa**

Reno (also serves Las Vegas)

Funeral Consumer Information Society of Nevada*
Box 8413, Univ. Station, 89507-8413
702-329-7705

**\*PLEASE NOTE:** This all-volunteer, nonprofit society recently changed its name from Memorial Society of Western Nevada to the one listed above. There is a for-profit rascal using the name "Northern Nevada Memorial Cremation and Burial Society," not to mention the "Neptune Society." These commercial outfits have no endorsement or affiliation with the nonprofit consumer group. Unfortunately, there is no legal recourse in most states to keep businesses from becoming a bogus "society" or poaching the name used by nonprofit groups.

~❖~

*This chapter was reviewed by the Department of Insurance. It was also sent to the Department of Health and to the Board of Funeral Directors, Embalmers and Cemetery and Crematory Operators. No response was received from the Health Department.*

The review copy of this chapter elicited an angry call from the chair of the funeral board, however. She was particularly incensed that I would refer to any funeral business as a "rascal." I pointed out that using a variation on the name of a nonprofit consumer group was cause to question motives, and it did seemed rather rascally to try hitching a ride on the reputation of a bunch of do-gooding volunteers. Senior Deputy Attorney General Robert Auer—an attorney for the funeral board—followed up in writing: "Where we live such a term [rascal] has a negative connotation which I believe is inappropriate." Regarding the chapter as a whole, he went on to say, "I found statements of opinion which should not have been made. . . ." Has the constitutional right to free speech been suspended in Nevada? Attorney Auer did make one factual correction—which I appreciated—but he didn't want any credit for it: "I strongly suggest that you delete any reference to the alleged and false statement that the Nevada State Funeral Board has reviewed the proposed chapter. . . ." I did, but it's obvious the chapter was read and got poor "reviews."

# In New Hampshire

*Please refer to Chapter 8 as you use this section.*

Families in New Hampshire may have difficulty in caring for their own dead—at least for a while. A 1996 addition to the New Hampshire statutes clearly recognizes the rights of families and designated agents to control the disposition of a body. This is consistent with English ecclesiastic and common law and case law in every U.S. state. Other New Hampshire laws remain in conflict, however, inviting a court challenge.

> *Title 290:16 II. "Custody and control" means the right to make all decisions, consistent with applicable laws, regarding the handling of a dead body, including but not limited to possession, at-need funeral arrangements, final disposition, and disinterment. (1996)*
>
> *Title 290:17 Custody and Control Generally. The custody and control of the remains of deceased residents of this state are governed by the following provisions:*
> *I. If the subject has designated a person to have custody and control in a written and signed document, custody and control belong to that person.*
> *II. If the subject has not left a written signed document designating a person to have custody and control, or if the person designated by the subject refuses custody and control, custody and control belong to the next of kin. . . . (1996)*
>
> *Title 290:11 Release; Transfer of Body.*
> *I. No dead body of a human being may be released or transferred from any residence, hospital, or other facility to any person other than a funeral director or his designee.*
> *II. The body of any deceased person may be transferred to another town for preparation or for burial or cremation only under the direction of a funeral director . . . . (et al, 1935)*

The rest of the legislative effort in 1996 to eliminate any barriers to families caring for their own dead was thwarted in committee hearings by negative testimony from the New Hampshire Hospital Association, concerned about hospital "liability" when releasing a body. Somehow, it never occurred to those folks that releasing a body to the one who has a right to *custody and control* is hardly a legal soft-spot, that *not* releasing a body would be more so. Furthermore, family management of funeral arrangements has a better track record than the industry does, judging by the current rate of lawsuits against mortuaries around the country. The hearing on this bill was poorly publicized, so few supporters showed up.[1]

Courts usually sustain restrictive statutes only when there is a prevailing concern for the public good—in the case of death: health, vital records, and questions of criminality or other issues needing legal resolution (*e.g.,* worker comp claims). As they are now written, the restrictive statutes in New Hampshire fail all these tests while benefiting a specific industry. That all the surrounding states and provinces have responsible yet sensitive legislation to allow families to care for their own dead (with families who have done so in increasing numbers without legal or health problems) makes New Hampshire stick out as a lone exception. One can "live free" but one can't "die free" in New Hampshire.

The next session of the New Hampshire legislature is bound to see new efforts to give funeral control back to families after this has gone to print. I will write the rest of this chapter with the assumption that that, too, shall come to pass. Call the FAMSA office if you need to make sure: 800-765-0107. We'll be following this issue closely.

## ❖ Death Certificate

The family doctor or a local medical examiner will supply and sign the death certificate, stating the cause of death. The remaining information must be supplied by the family, and all information "immediately" filed with the Bureau of Vital Records and Health Statistics electronically via computer. Town clerks have the appropriate computer program as do many funeral directors. The state's computer will generate a burial-transit permit and return it to the sending computer.

---

[1] Representative Amanda Merrill's enabling bill in 1992 was scuttled in House hearings by the chief medical examiner—"Death is messy," he said. The embalmer-legislator on the House committee was hotly against the bill, too. The standing-room-only crowd of consumers who were there to testify in favor of Mandy's bill was unable to sway the day.

### ❖ Fetal Death

A fetal death report is required for all stillbirths and must be filed in the same manner as a death certificate if death is outside a hospital.

### ❖ Transporting and Disposition Permit

The burial-transit permit that was furnished by the state must be returned to the town clerk or board of health where death occurred within six days after burial.

Ironically, the funeral board regulations permit nonlicensed personnel to transport a body at the behest of a funeral director. This would further verify that restrictive statutes are self-serving to a specific industry and without merit for the public health and safety.

### ❖ Burial

Check with the town clerk for zoning laws regarding home burial. A few cities, including Keene, do not allow home burial. The location of private burial sites must be recorded with the deed. No cemetery can be laid out within 100 feet of any dwelling or school, store or other place of business without the consent of the owner, and may not be laid out within 50 feet of the right-of-way of highways. There are no burial statutes with regard to depth. A sensible guideline is 150 feet from a water supply and three feet of earth on top.

### ❖ Cremation

A cremation permit from the medical examiner is required. The fee for this is $35. There is a 48-hour waiting period prior to cremation unless the person died of a communicable disease. Authorization by next-of-kin is usually required, and a pacemaker must be removed.

### ❖ Other Requirements

New Hampshire has no other requirements controlling the schedule for disposition of unembalmed bodies. Weather and reasonable planning should be considered.

If the person died of a contagious or communicable disease, the doctor in attendance should be consulted.

## ❖ Medical Schools for Body Donation

Dartmouth Medical School
Department of Anatomy
Hanover, NH 03756
603-646-1636
646-5000 after hours (ask for donor
program representative)
Moderate need

Cost to family: none
Prior enrollment: required
Over-enrollment: not shared
Disposition: cremation; return of cremains by request
Body rejection: under 21, previous embalming, over-enrollment, autopsy, decomposition, mutilation, severe burn victim, contagious or communicable diseases

## ❖ Crematories

Concord

Granite State Crematory
RFD 10, Industrial Park Dr., 03301
603-225-6291

Derry

Southern New Hampshire Crematory
15 Birch St.
P.O. Box 1264, 03038
603-432-6090

Epping

Brewitt Funeral Service
18 Pleasant St., 03042
603-679-5391

Hampton

Phoenix Crematory
811 Lafayette Rd., 03842
603-926-6500

Heights Station

Concord Crematory
Broken Bridge Rd.
P.O. Box 7114, 03301
603-224-5041

Lebanon

Connecticut River Valley Crematory
P.O. Box 549, 30766
603-448-1568

Manchester

Phaneuf Funeral Home & Crematory
243 Hanover St., 03104
603-625-5777
800-742-6383

Merrimack

Geo. R. Rivet Funeral Home
425 Daniel Webster Hwy., 03054
603-424-5530

Additional crematories may have been established in this state after the date of publication.

## ❖ State Governance

The New Hampshire Board of Funeral Directors and Embalmers has five members. One is a consumer representative.

Public cemeteries are governed by the trustees of the municipality in which they are located. Private cemeteries are not regulated.

## ❖ Prepaid Cemetery and Funeral Funds

All money paid for a preneed *funeral* arrangement must be placed in **trust,** with **interest** to accrue. (There are no **reporting** requirements, however.)

A purchaser may cancel a preneed contract for a full **refund**.

Although these two provisions are excellent as far as they go, New Hampshire residents may be missing adequate consumer protection given the consumer concerns which follow.

## ❖ Consumer Concerns

- The death rate in New Hampshire can support approximately 37 full-time mortuaries; there are, however, 103. Funeral prices tend to be higher in areas where there are "too many" funeral homes.
- There is no state board governing private cemeteries. With municipal management of most cemeteries, this is not likely to be an immediate concern. However, with funeral conglomerates moving into the state, residents can anticipate that for-profit cemeteries will be on the horizon before long.
- Laws should require cemeteries to repurchase an unwanted lot at the original selling price plus 50% of the difference between that and current market price.
- There is no annual reporting requirement to account for prepaid funeral investments. Such paperwork might be helpful to the family of a deceased, to indicate prepayment, and might help to "enforce" the trusting requirements.
- There is no state protection in the case of default of prepaid funeral monies. Although the New Hampshire Funeral Directors Association has publicly promised this assistance, such social "obligations" of a trade organization cannot be enforced.[1] Would NHFDA provide the same resources if the defaulter were not an NHFDA member or if the funeral consumer wished to spend the reimbursement with other than an NHFDA member?

---

[1] The Vermont Funeral Directors Association made a similar promise when the Calderwood Funeral Home in St. Johnsbury was closed by the state in 1995. The two nearby morticians who came to the aid of shafted consumers—at their own expense—saw not a penny from VFDA. But then, they were not VFDA members.

- There is no requirement that when merchandise is selected on a guaranteed-price, preneed agreement that a clear description is given and that merchandise of equal quality and construction must be substituted if the original item selected is not available. Survivors should have a right to approve any substitution.
- There are no laws allowing for a transfer of an irrevocable preneed arrangement to another provider.
- Until there is better protection for preneed arrangements, it is probably a *terrible* idea to prepay for a funeral in New Hampshire. (Your own trust account in a bank will be safer and may be made irrevocable if you need to shelter assets.)
- The 48-hour wait before cremation is totally unnecessary when survivors are in agreement and is causing additional charges to families for "storage."
- The coroner or medical examiner's permit for cremation in the case of an *anticipated* death from natural causes is totally unnecessary and creates an additional burden and charge for families.
- Identification and tagging of the body at the place of death before removal should be required.
- There is no provision either forbidding a mark-up on cash advance items or requiring the disclosure of how much the mark-up would be. Consumers may wish to request a copy of the invoices for these charges.
- There is no requirement that low-cost caskets be included in a casket display.
- The standards for ethical, professional conduct should be strengthened. That would make it easier for a consumer to prevail when filing a complaint. (See the Appendix.)
- Complaint procedures are unclear and inadequate.
- The FTC Funeral Rule should be adopted by reference to make it more enforceable in this state.

## ❖ Miscellaneous Information

- Educational requirements for becoming a funeral director or embalmer: one year of college, one year of mortuary college, and one year of apprenticeship.
- Crematories are regulated by the Department of Health. They may be erected on the grounds of a cemetery or other location approved by the selectmen. In practice, there are no cemeteries currently

operating crematories. One does not need to be a funeral director to run a crematory. The funeral board inspects crematories.

- The owner of any stock found trespassing on public or private graveyards is guilty of "a violation." Ironically, in Vermont, sheep were tried for reducing the cemetery's mowing costs.
- Preference is given to the expressed wishes of the deceased if sufficient funds are made available to carry out those wishes.
- Medical examiners are physicians who are appointed.
- Anyone wishing to make grave rubbings must get the permission of the selectmen or mayor first.

## ❖ Nonprofit Funeral Consumer Information Societies

These consumer groups are run mostly by volunteers. Consequently, contact information may change. If you have difficulty reaching a society or are interested in starting a society in your area, call the FAMSA office: 800-765-0107. Or check the internet directory—

**www.funerals.org/famsa**

Vermont Memorial Society
(covers western and northern NH)
1630 Clark Rd.
East Montpelier, VT 05651-4529
800-805-0007

New Hampshire Memorial Society
P.O. Box 941
Epping, NH 03042-0941
603-679-5721

~❖~

*This chapter was sent for review to the State Board of Funeral Directors and Embalmers, the Department of Health and Human Services, and the New Hampshire Hospital Association.*

No response was received from the first two agencies. I changed a couple of words that were bothering the Hospital Association (although I may not have changed them enough). In addition, the letter from NHHA said, "We do not have the resources to verify the information in your chapter." That's okay, it was a courtesy copy. I hope they will some day.

# In New Jersey

*Please refer to Chapter 8 as you use this section.*

Families in New Jersey may care for their own dead. The legal authority to do so is found in the Cemetery Act:

> *8A:5-18 Disposition of remains of deceased persons; right to control; priorities. The right to control the disposition of the remains of a deceased person, unless other directions have been given by the decedent or by a court of competent jurisdiction, shall be in the following order:*
> > *a. The surviving spouse.*
> > *b. A majority of the surviving children . . .*
> > *c. The surviving parent or parents of the decedent.*
> > *d. A majority of the brothers and sisters . . .*
> *A prepaid funeral agreement or a preneed funeral arrangement . . . shall not constitute "other directions" for the purposes of this section, nor shall it bind those with the right to control the disposition of the remains.*

The Vital Statistics statutes for the registration of death and obtaining permits refer to the duties of a "funeral director" in this regard and might be misleading. (Most states use the statutory language "funeral director or person acting as such.") However, there are *no New Jersey statutes* which say that *only* a licensed funeral director may perform these functions when one is not in the business or trade of caring for the dead.

It should be noted that *regulations*—not statutes—promulgated by the Board of Mortuary Science require a mortuary science practitioner in attendance at every "interment, cremation or other disposition of a dead human body." However, the Mortuary Science Board was given statutory authority only over those "in the practice of" or in the "occupation" of embalming and funeral directing. Requiring the involvement of a funeral director at a cremation—when the crematories are regulated by the Health Department—would appear to be outside its authority.

*Such boards have no statutory authority over private individuals, either.*[1] For example, you don't have to be a licensed physician to treat your child's cold or other physical ailments, and you can represent yourself in court without being a lawyer. The authority of the state comes into play only if one is in business.

## ❖ Death Certificate

Within 24 hours, the doctor in attendance, a registered hospice or nursing home nurse, or the county medical examiner must sign the death certificate, stating the cause of death. The remaining information must be supplied, legibly written in blue or black ink. The death certificate must be filed with the local registrar where death occurred or where disposition will take place.

New Jersey is researching electronic death registration. When that is adopted the procedure will change somewhat. Check with the local health department.

## ❖ Fetal Death

A fetal death certificate is required if death occurs after 20 weeks of gestation. If there is no physician involved, the medical examiner must sign the certificate.

## ❖ Transporting and Disposition Permit

Upon receipt of a properly filled-out death certificate, the local registrar will issue a burial or removal permit. The cost is $1. If no registrar is available, a judge or magistrate may issue an emergency permit.

## ❖ Burial

Check with the county or town registrar for local zoning laws regarding home burial in rural areas. Family burial grounds should not have to comply with the same conditions that govern public cemeteries. The top of an adult casket must be covered by four feet of earth; a child's casket by three and a half feet of earth. When a vault is used, the depth requirement is reduced to six inches. A sensible guideline for a gravesite is 150 feet from a water supply.

---

[1] The New Jersey statutes do grant some rather broad powers to the board that may not have been intended: " . . . and improvement of the public health, morals, safety and welfare." Morals police?

When burial is arranged, the burial permit must be filed with the local registrar within 10 days. When there is no person in charge of the burial ground, "No Person in Charge" must be written across the face of the permit.

## ❖ Cremation

The burial permit is sufficient for cremation. (The New Jersey legislature had the good sense in 1983 to eliminate the requirement for a medical examiner's permit.) There is a 24-hour waiting period prior to cremation. Authorization by next-of-kin is usually required, and a pacemaker must be removed.

## ❖ Other Requirements

Within 48 hours of death a body must be embalmed or refrigerated to 45° or less, if disposition has not yet occurred.

If death is due to cholera, plague, smallpox, typhus fever, or yellow fever the body must be handled by a funeral director. If disposition of a diseased body is not made within 24 hours, the body must be embalmed. If a person died from any of these diseases—or from diphtheria, meningococcal meningitis, poliomyelitis, streptococcic sore throat including scarlet fever—the Department of Health must be consulted before a funeral is scheduled. In those cases, a sealed casket must be used.

A body to be shipped by common carrier must be embalmed unless the destination will be reached within 24 hours.

## ❖ Medical Schools for Body Donation

UMDNJ
Robert Wood Johnson Medical School
Anatomical Association
675 Hoes Ln. Rm. 114-1
Piscataway, NJ 08854-5635
800-GIFT-211 (24 hrs.)
Moderate need

Cost to family: transportation
Prior enrollment: preferred
Over-enrollment: shared or referred
Disposition: cremation/burial in college plot; return of cremains by request ($25)
Body rejection: standard,* under 18, previous embalming, extreme obesity or emaciation, fresh major surgery, missing organs

* autopsy, decomposition, mutilation, severe burn victim, meningitis, hepatitis, AIDS

## ❖ Crematories

Basking Ridge

Somerset Hills Memorial Park
Mount Airy Rd., 07920
908-766-0522

Bordentown

Cremation Burial Associates
517 Farnsworth Ave., 08505
609-298-0330

Camden

Harleigh Cemetery
1640 Haddon Ave., 08103
609-963-0122

Cape May

Cape May Crematory
3214 Bayshore Rd., 08204
609-886-7112

Elizabeth

Rosemount Memorial Park
1109 Neck Ln., 07201-1705
201-824-6871

Harrison

Cremation Funerals of NJ
336 Cleveland Ave., 07029
201-678-3336

Hillside

The Evergreen Cemetery
1137 North Broad St., 07205
908-352-7940

Linden

Rosedale & Rosehill Cemetery
355 E. Linden Ave., 07036
908-862-4990

Neptune

Monmouth Memorial Park
4201 State Hwy. 33, 07753
908-922-1515

Newark

Fairmount Cemetery
620 Central Ave., 07107
201-623-0695

North Bergen

Garden State Crematory
4101 Kennedy Blvd., 07047
201-867-0219

North Brunswick

Franklin Memorial Park
Rt. 27 & Cozzens Ln., 08902
908-545-4184

Orange

Rosedale Cemetery/Crematory
367 Washington St., 07051
201-673-0127

Paterson

Cedar Lawn Cemetery/Crematory
McLean Blvd. & Crooks Ave., 07513
201-279-1161

Ridgewood

Valleau Cemetery
660 E. Glen Ave., 07450
201-444-3230

Toms River

Ocean County Memorial Park
1722 Silverton Rd., 08753
908-255-1870

Trenton

Greenwood Cemetery
1800 Hamilton Ave., 08619
609-587-4993

Additional crematories may have been established in this state after the date of publication.

## ❖ State Governance

There are seven members of the state Board of Mortuary Science; two of those are public members. (At the time I inquired, at least one of the public seats was vacant.) I was not permitted to contact the public member directly, only through correspondence to the board address. One has to wonder how these persons can truly serve the public if contact information is not readily available. Paul Brush, Executive Director for the Board of Mortuary Science responded:

> I feel it is an unfair characterization that Board member contact information is not available. Every licensee's name and address is a matter of public record, and I would certainly provide this information. The misunderstanding may have arisen if I advised a caller to correspond on Board business through the Board office rather than directly to the Board member. In this way, the matter is placed on the agenda and read and deliberated by all members.

The New Jersey Cemetery Board oversees the cemetery business—well, it's supposed to.

## ❖ Prepaid Cemetery and Funeral Funds

As of 1971, all newly established New Jersey cemeteries must be run by nonprofit organizations. "Plenty" of private, for-profit cemeteries had been established prior to that, I was told. Cemeteries may not be affiliated with a funeral home, nor may cemeteries sell vaults and markers. In spite of that, Loewen has managed to purchase at least two. What is the Cemetery Board doing? Nothing as far as I could tell.

In-person **soliciting** for the purpose of selling funeral services is not permitted. Prices charged for preneed purchases may not exceed those on the current price list.

Unless one is purchasing funeral insurance, all prepaid *funeral* money must be placed in **trust** with the **interest** to accumulate. If the money is to be deposited in a pooled trust account, the trustee (financial manager) may withdraw a 1% **commission** annually. In the case of these "master trusts"—which are heavily promoted by morticians—the commission is often shared with morticians or with their state associations. The purchaser has a right to an annual **report** reflecting the amount and interest accrued. This does not seem to be mandatory, and there appear to be no reporting requirements for individually trusted accounts.

If a provider converts a trust account to funeral insurance, the commission and any other differences must be disclosed to the purchaser.

A person may **transfer** or **cancel** a prepaid arrangement at any time, for a full **refund** including interest (less the 1% annual commission that probably has been withdrawn). "**Constructive delivery**" is not permitted.

If merchandise selected preneed is no longer available at the time of death, the provider *may* **substitute** "goods of equal quality, value and workmanship." The word "value" may be a problem, however. A casket that cost $750 ten years ago was quite a fancy casket and probably costs $1,000 more today. For $750 today, many funeral homes would offer up a gray cloth-covered "minimum" casket with the goal of getting the survivors to ante up some extra dollars for something "nicer."

## ❖ Consumer Concerns

- The death rate in New Jersey can support approximately 291 full-time mortuaries; there are, however, 790. Funeral prices tend to be higher in areas where there are "too many" funeral homes.
- Laws should require cemeteries to repurchase an unwanted lot at the original selling price plus 50% of the difference between that and current market price.
- Preneed arrangements should carefully describe the merchandise selected and permit survivors to choose an alternative of equal quality and construction if not available at the time of death.
- Annual reports to a consumer should be required for all trust funds.
- There is no guarantee fund or other protection against default of prepaid funeral funds.
- While the preneed regulation in New Jersey is not too bad, it is probably an *unwise* idea to prepay for a funeral until adequate provision for substitution and reporting.
- All embalming laws should be repealed, especially the law requiring embalming when death occurs from a communicable disease. This is not only an offense to some religious groups, it puts the funeral professionals and possibly the environment at risk. Refrigeration is a better form of preservation. A sealed casket can be used for

long-distance transportation; for short inter-state travel, such measures are totally unnecessary.

- There is no requirement that low-cost caskets be included in any display.
- Identification and tagging of the body at the place of death before removal should be required.
- The standards for ethical, professional conduct should be strengthened. That would make it easier for a consumer to prevail when filing a valid complaint. (See Ethical Standards in the Appendix.)
- Complaint procedures are unclear and inadequate.
- The language of the 1984 Funeral Rule was incorporated into the regulations. That has not been updated to reflect the changes of 1994. Adopting the Rule by reference would save the state from having to update its own laws every time there's a change.

## ❖ Miscellaneous Information

- Educational requirements for becoming a mortuary science practitioner: two years of college, one year of mortuary school, and two years of apprenticeship. Three years of college reduces the apprenticeship requirement to one year. A state exam and practical exam are also required.
- Crematories are licensed, regulated, and inspected by the Department of Health.
- Cash advance items must be billed at the actual cost to the funeral director.
- Preference is given to the expressed wishes of the deceased.

## ❖ Nonprofit Funeral Consumer Information Societies

These consumer groups are run mostly by volunteers. Consequently, contact information may change. If you have difficulty reaching a society or are interested in starting a society in your area, call the FAMSA office: 800-765-0107. Or check the internet directory—

**www.funerals.org/famsa**

Cherry Hill

Memorial Society of S. Jersey
401 Kings Hwy. N., 08034

East Brunswick

Raritan Valley Memorial Soc.
176 Tices Ln., 08816
732-572-1470

Lincroft

Memorial Assn. Monmouth Co.
1475 W. Front St., 07738
732-842-2251

Madison

Morris Memorial Society
Box 509, 07940-0409
973-540-9140

Montclair

Memorial Society of Essex
P.O. Box 1327, 07042-1327
973-783-1145

Paramus

Central Memorial Society
156 Forest, 07652
201-664-3072

Princeton

Princeton Memorial Assn.
48 Roper Rd., 08540
609-924-5525 or 1604

~❖~

*This chapter was reviewed by the Executive Director of the Board of Mortuary Science. It was also sent to the state Cemetery Board and the Department of Public Health. No answer was received.*

# In New Mexico

*Please refer to Chapter 8 as you use this section.*

Persons in New Mexico may care for their own dead. The legal authority to do so is found in:

> *Title 24-14-20: Death Registration. The funeral science practitioner or person acting as a funeral science practitioner who first assumes custody of the dead body shall file the death certificate.*

> *Title 24-14-23: Permits; authorization for final disposition . . . A burial-transit permit shall be issued by the state registrar or a local registrar for those bodies which are to be transported out of the state for final disposition or when final disposition is being made by a person other than a funeral service practitioner or direct disposer.*

There are no other statutes which might require you to use a funeral director.

## ❖ Death Certificate

The family doctor or a medical investigator will sign the death certificate within 48 hours, stating the cause of death. The remaining information must be supplied, typewritten or in black ink. Do not use a felt-tip pen; there are five copies. The death certificate must be filed with any registrar within five days and before final disposition.

## ❖ Fetal Death

A fetal death report is required when death occurs and the weight is 500 grams or more. If there is no family physician involved, the state medical investigator must sign the fetal death certificate. The fetal death certificate must be filed with the state registrar within ten days.

## ❖ Transporting and Disposition Permit

A body may be moved with medical permission. No burial-transit permit is required if disposition is under the direction of a funeral service practitioner or direct disposer and if disposition occurs within the state. In other cases, the local registrar must sign the burial-transit permit (page four of the death certificate) before final disposition.

## ❖ Burial

Check with the county registrar for local zoning laws regarding home burial in rural areas. Prior arrangements must be made with the county clerk's office to record a map designating the burial site. Burial must be 50 yards from a stream or other body of water and five feet from the property line; minimum depth is six feet. Unless the registrar in the district of disposition requests the burial-transit permit, persons acting as the sexton should retain it for their records.

## ❖ Cremation

A permit for cremation must be obtained from the state medical investigator. There is no charge for this when a family is handling arrangements. Most crematories insist that a pacemaker be removed, and authorization by next-of-kin usually is required.

## ❖ Other Requirements

As of 1993, bodies must be embalmed or refrigerated to a temperature below 40° if disposition has not occurred within 24 hours.

If the person died of a contagious or communicable disease, the Office of the Medical Investigator should be consulted. Embalming or a sealed casket may be required.

## ❖ Medical Schools for Body Donation

University of New Mexico
Department of Anatomy
Albuquerque, NM 87131
505-277-1111 or
medical investigator—
505-272-3053
Moderate need

Cost to family: none in state
Prior enrollment: required
Over-enrollment: not shared
Disposition: burial or cremation by request of family
Body rejection: autopsy, missing extremities, infectious diseases, embalming if not under direction of school

## ❖ Crematories

Albuquerque

Fairview Memorial Park
700 Yale Blvd., 87106
505-262-1454

Sunrise at Vista Verde
Sara Rd./Meadowlark, 87124
505-892-9920

Sunset Memorial Park
924 Menaul NE, 87125
505-843-6333

Artesia

Twin Oaks Memorial Park
412 W. Chisum, 88210
505-746-9231

Carlsbad

Sunset Gardens
505-885-3325

Deming

Mimbres Crematorium
820 S. Gold St., 88031
505-546-9671

Dona Ana

Memory Gardens of the Valley
4900 McNutt Rd., 88032
504-589-2371

Las Cruces

Mesilla Valley Crematory
555 W. Amadore, 88205
505-526-6891

Santa Fe

Berardinelli Family Funeral Svc.
1399 Luisa St., 87505
505-984-8600

McGee Memorial Chapel
1320 Luisa St., 87501
505-983-9151

Santa Teresa

Memory Gardens of Valley
P.O. Box 1287, 88008
505-546-9671

Additional crematories may have been established in this state after publication.

## ❖ State Governance

The New Mexico Board of Thanatopractice has six members. Three are funeral directors, two are consumer representatives, and one is a direct disposer.

There is almost no regulation of cemeteries in New Mexico and no cemetery board. Cemeteries must register with and report on their endowment funds to the Director of Financial Institutions.

The Superintendent of Insurance regulates preneed sales.

## ❖ Prepaid Cemetery and Funeral Funds

25% of cemetery lot sales and 10% of crypt, vault, or niche sales shall be set aside in trust (presumably for endowed care, but the law doesn't say).

Only the "special care" fund for *cemetery* markers must be placed in trust, which essentially means that a cemetery can spend all other income from marker sales and—presumably—declare a memorial "delivered" with a certificate of ownership. Just 10% of vault sales must be placed in trust, which makes the possibility of **cancellation** and a **refund** bleak. There is no statutory mention to protect other prepaid cemetery service charges, such as the opening-and-closing fee, often a significant expense.

Prearranged *funerals* must be financed only through **insurance** and only by those licensed by the Superintendent of Insurance. Funeral directors may not sell funeral prearrangements unless also licensed as insurance agents. Anything labelled "insurance" usually means that someone is getting a **commission**. Consequently, there is likely to be fine-print denoting limitations on the policy, such as reduced benefits if death occurred within two years.

Insurance is usually easily **transferred**, assuming that it is not a policy that is restricted to "approved providers."

Strangely, the statutes indicate that money paid ahead for a funeral must go into a **trust,** with **interest** to accrue. No one in the state insurance offices has been able to explain why this statute exists if only preneed insurance is permitted, nor why only insurance is allowed as a funding vehicle for a funeral.

An annual **report** to the superintendent may be required of all prearranged funeral sellers.

## ❖ Consumer Concerns

- The death rate in New Mexico can support approximately 52 full-time mortuaries; there are, however, 66. Funeral prices tend to be higher in areas where there are "too many" funeral homes, although this is a modest number to cover such a large geographic area.

- Laws should require cemeteries to repurchase an unwanted lot at the original selling price plus 50% of the difference between that and current market price.
- There is no requirement that—when merchandise is selected as a part of a guaranteed-price, preneed agreement—a clear description be given and that merchandise of equal quality and construction be substituted if the original item selected is not available. Substitutions should be approved by survivors.
- Unless there is a clear provision for substitution on each individual preneed agreement and unless there will be no limitations on the benefits you expect—regardless of when death occurs, it may be *unwise* to prepay for a funeral in New Mexico. With no state protection for prepaid cemetery expenses, it is definitely a *terrible* idea to prepay for these.
- Identification and tagging of the body at the place of death before removal should be required.
- The requirement for embalming or refrigeration within 24 hours is unnecessarily restrictive and should be eliminated. Air-conditioned facilities make it possible to keep a body for two or three days without embalming.
- There is no provision either forbidding a mark-up on cash advance items or requiring the disclosure of how much the mark-up is.
- A casket display of at least 12 caskets "in a range of models and prices" is required. "Range" is not defined to include low-cost caskets, however.
- There is no mandate for the Board of Thanatopractice to set ethical standards. Such practices need to be set and clearly defined in order for valid consumer complaints to prevail. (See Appendix.)
- The Board of Thanatopractice receives complaints and can issue letters of reprimand. Formal disciplinary actions may be taken under the Uniform Licensing Act: the board can order restitution to a consumer, revoke a license, levy a fine of $1,000, or impose various other remedies. The amount of the fine should be increased to make it a more effective deterrent to unethical conduct once such conduct has been adequately defined.
- The FTC Funeral Rule should be adopted by reference to make it more enforceable in this state.
- A funeral home may hold a body if the bill has not yet been paid. This could incur unnecessary "storage" charges over a weekend, for example, before insurance or social benefits are received. Such tactics should not be permitted.

## ❖ Miscellaneous Information

- Educational requirements for funeral director: two years of college (60 semester hours) plus mortuary college, national exam, exam of state laws, a practical exam, and one year of apprenticeship.
- Direct disposers are licensed by the Board of Thanatopractice and do not have to be funeral directors or embalmers. They may not conduct funerals. New Mexico has excellent statutory provisions for this low-cost option for body disposition. However, there have been an increasing number of complaints filed against the existing direct disposers (not by consumers, mind you, but by competitors)— complaints that appear to be frivolous. Consumer vigilance will be necessary to keep this affordable option available in the future.
- Crematories are licensed by the Board of Thanatopractice. They do not need to be operated by a funeral director.
- Medical investigators must be licensed physicians and are appointed.
- There is a statutory duty to comply with the written wishes of the decedent. Any adult may authorize his own cremation and disposition of cremated remains. In situations where you are estranged or distant from next-of-kin, you may wish to also indicate a designated deathcare agent.

## ❖ Nonprofit Funeral Consumer Information Societies

These consumer groups are run mostly by volunteers. Consequently, contact information may change. If you have difficulty reaching a society or are interested in starting a society in your area, call the FAMSA office: 800-765-0107. Or check the internet directory—

**www.funerals.org/famsa**

Albuquerque

Funeral Consumer Info. Soc./No. NM
9701 Admiral Dewey NE
Albuquerque, NM 87111

Las Cruces

Memorial and Funeral Soc./So. NM
P.O. Box 6531
Las Cruces, NM 88006-6531

~❖~

*This chapter was sent for review to the Board of Thanatopractice, Office of the Medical Investigator, Superintendent of Insurance, and the Registrar of Vital Records. Only the Medical Investigator's Office responded.*

# In New York

*Please refer to Chapter 8 as you use this section.*

Until there is a court challenge or other change in the laws, families and church groups in New York will be limited in caring for their own dead. Some statutes seem contradictory or defy logic; others are restrictive and intrusive.

> *Article 41 Vital Statistics Sec. 4140. Deaths; registration 2. . . . the registrar of the district in which the death occurred shall then issue a burial or removal permit to the funeral director or undertaker.*

In addition, the Sanitary Code—"Practice of Funeral Directing" states:

> *77.7 (b)(1) In no case shall a dead human body be released from any hospital, institution or other place where the death occurred or from the place where the body is held by legal authority to any person not a duly licensed and registered funeral director or undertaker.*

Later in the same code, however, is found:

> *77.7(f) Nothing contained in this section shall be deemed to require that a mere transporter, to whom or to which a dead human body has been duly released for the sole purpose of transportation or transfer, shall be a duly licensed and registered funeral director or undertaker.*

So the State of New York has determined that there is no health problem with someone other than a funeral director transporting bodies. What, then, is the rationale that would require a licensee to pick up the accompanying paperwork and add his/her signature? The doctor fills out the medical portion; the family supplies the personal data. But the undertaker's signature will cost the family a nondeclinable fee of $1,025—if New York prices match the national average at this writing. Just for a signature! Was the industry more than a little involved in the construction of these statutes?

But back to the statutes in 77.7 to see how the industry has literally promoted itself:

> *(a)(2) A licensed funeral director or undertaker shall be present and personally supervise the conduct of each funeral service.*
>
> *(a)(3) Nothing herein shall be construed as prohibiting religious supervision of the funeral service by a member or members of the clergy designated by the family of the deceased person.*

Apparently, New York funeral directors—with a mere two years of mortuary school (that most likely did not include any training on religious funeral rituals and services whatsoever)—have now become pseudo-clergy, usurping a role that traditionally was religious in nature.[1] That legitimate clergy would not be *prohibited* from supervising funerals smacks of poorly worded after-thought that—if penned by industry hands as I suspect—borders on arrogance. There will, of course, be an attending charge, regardless of whether the presence of a funeral director is wanted or needed.[2]

And an undertaker can keep the meter running with another bit of statutory help:

> *77.7(a)(4) A licensed funeral director or undertaker shall be present and personally supervise the interment or cremation . . . .*

The undertaker isn't needed to transport the body, but the undertaker must be at a crematory when that method of disposition has been chosen? Rather strange. Crematory operation is *not* included in mortuary curricula; crematory operation is *not* mentioned on the national exam for funeral directors. What kind of supervision is the undertaker qualified to do at the crematory?

---

[1] E-mail received in the FAMSA office: "I am a Catholic priest. About three years ago, while still a seminarian, I was doing a feature story on the most prominent mortician in the diocese, a Catholic active in just about everything. In the interview, I asked him if the curriculum at mortuary school included courses about religious practices. I was floored when he said 'No'."

[2] A Bruderhof Christian community in New York handles all aspects of the funeral for a member—the preparation and bathing of the body, as well as conducting the service and burial. "Oh, yes, the funeral director comes out and spends the day with us, has lunch with us, and sort of hangs around," one member told me.

Oh, yes, if you are planning home burial as permitted in New York, you'll have to pay a funeral director to hang around under the apple tree.

A movement is afoot to get the limiting statutes changed—through legislation or court action. It shouldn't be hard. In a 1909 federal case, *Wyeth v. Cambridge Board of Health,* the court ruled:

> . . . *the refusal to permit one to bury the dead body of his relative or friend, except under an unreasonable limitation, is also an interference with a private right that is not allowable under the Constitution of the Commonwealth or the Constitution of the United States.*

The same ruling referred to an earlier case, *Lochner v. New York, 198 U.S. 45, 57,* in which the opinion said:

> . . . *the mere assertion that the subject relates though but in a remote degree to the public health does not render the enactment valid. The act must have a more direct relation, as a means to an end, and the need itself must be appropriate and legitimate, before an act can be held to be valid which interferes with the general right of an individual to be free in his person. . . .*

## ❖ Death Certificate

The doctor last in attendance, county coroner, or medical examiner will supply and sign the death certificate, stating the cause of death. The remaining information must be supplied, typewritten or in black ink. The death certificate must be filed with the local registrar within 72 hours and before final disposition.

## ❖ Fetal Death

A fetal death report is required for each fetal death and must be filed as above. If there is no family physician involved, the local medical examiner must sign the fetal death certificate.

## ❖ Transporting and Disposition Permit

The local registrar will issue the burial and removal permit to a licensed funeral director only (until the statute has been challenged). This authorization must be obtained within 72 hours of death and prior to final disposition. Once this permit has been obtained, a family may handle the moving of a body, although you will need a mortician at the other end to oversee disposition if burial or cremation will occur in New York. Make sure that the undertaker you initially use will be willing to relinquish custody, however; more than one family has had difficulty when the undertaker did not understand the law. During transportation, the body must be obscured from public view.

## ❖ Burial

Any person may dedicate land to be used as a family cemetery provided that it is less than three acres and not closer than 100 rods (1,650 feet) to a dwelling. Such land must be registered with the county clerk. Check with the county or town for local zoning laws regarding home burial. There are no state burial statutes or regulations with regard to depth. A sensible guideline is 150 feet from a water supply and at least two feet of earth on top.

When a person is buried in a cemetery or other burial place where no person is in charge, the undertaker will sign the permit and write across the face of the permit, "No person in charge." The permit must be filed within three days with the registrar of the district in which burial took place.

Because towns are obliged by law to "provide for the removal of grass and weeds at least twice in each year" from cemeteries that are not being maintained, the town may want you to provide for some sort of perpetual care fund when seeking permission to establish a new cemetery, even if it's a family one. Dedicating the entire site as a "wildflower garden" might possibly avert the need for such a fund.

## ❖ Cremation

No additional permit is needed for cremation. Authorization by next-of-kin is usually required, and a pacemaker must be removed. The crematory will file the disposition permit with the local registrar. If there is no licensed funeral director on the crematory staff, the family must arrange for a funeral director to be present at the time of delivery, a totally unnecessary and burdensome requirement.

## ❖ Other Requirements

A body must be buried or cremated within a "reasonable time after death." Weather and reasonable planning should be considered.

If the person died of a contagious or communicable disease, the doctor in attendance should be consulted.

## ❖ Medical Schools for Body Donation

Union University
Albany Medical College
Albany, NY 12208
518-262-5379
Moderate to high need

Cost to family: transportation beyond 120 miles or $150
Prior enrollment: not required
Over-enrollment: shared
Disposition: cremation; return of cremains by request
Body rejection: decomposition, contagious and communicable diseases

Yeshiva University
Albert Einstein College of Medicine
Bronx, NY 10461

Repeated requests for information have not been returned from this school.

S.U.N.Y
Health Sciences Center/Brooklyn
450 Clarkson Ave.
Brooklyn, NY 11203
718-270-1014 or 2379
    227-1402 or 235-0505

Cost to family: transportation beyond 100 miles
Prior enrollment: not required
Over-enrollment: shared
Disposition: cremation; return of cremains by request and at the expense of the family
Body rejection: standard,* under 10, previous embalming

S.U.N.Y
University at Buffalo
Dept. of Anatomy & Cell Biol.
Buffalo, NY 14214
716-829-2912
    834-8128 other times
Moderate need

Cost to family: transportation beyond 100 miles
Prior enrollment: preferred
Over-enrollment: shared
Disposition: cremation; return of cremains by request
Body rejection: standard,* under 18, previous embalming

NY Chiropractic College
Glen Head, NY 11545

Repeated requests for information have not been returned from this school.

City University of NY, Mt. Sinai
New York, NY 10029

Repeated requests for information have not been returned from this school.

Columbia University
College of Physicians and Surgeons
630 West 168th St.
New York, NY 10032
212-305-3451

Cost to family: transportation beyond
  100 miles
Prior enrollment: not required
Over-enrollment: shared
Disposition: cremation; return of cre-
    mains by request and at the ex-
    pense of the family
Body rejection: standard,* under 21,
    previous embalming

Cornell University Medical College
Dept. of Cell Biol. & Anatomy
1300 York Ave.
New York, NY 10021
212-746-6140
212-674-3630 (funeral home)
Moderate to high need

Cost to family: transportation beyond
  60 miles
Prior enrollment: not required
Over-enrollment: not occurred
Disposition: city cremation or burial;
    no return
Body rejection: standard,* under 18

New York University
School of Medicine
New York, NY 10016
212-263-5378
Always needed

Cost to family: transportation outside
    Manhattan, case by case
Prior enrollment: not required
Over-enrollment: not occurred
Disposition: burial or cremation; return
    by request
Body rejection: standard,* previous em-
    balming

New York Institute of Technology
Old Westbury, NY 11568

Repeated requests for information have
not been returned from this school.

University of Rochester
School of Medicine
Rochester, NY 14642

Repeated requests for information have
not been returned from this school.

S.U.N.Y
School of Medicine
Stonybrook, NY 11794
516-444-3111 or
    599-0041
Moderate need

Cost to family: transportation outside
    Suffolk & Nassau counties
Prior enrollment: not required
Over-enrollment: shared
Disposition: cremation; return of cre-
    mains by request
Body rejection: standard,* under 16,
    previous embalming

S.U.N.Y
Health Sciences Center/Syracuse
Dept. of Anatomy & Cell Biology
750 E. Adams St.
Syracuse, NY 13210
315-464-5120 or 4349
Moderate need

Cost to family: transportation over $100
    + $.23 /mi.
Prior enrollment: not required
Over-enrollment: shared
Disposition: cremation; return of cre-
    mains by request
Body rejection: standard,* under 13

New York Medical College
Dept. of Cell Biology & Anatomy
Valhalla, NY 10595
914-993-4025 or
  735-4849 nights/weekends
Urgent need

Cost to family: transportation beyond
  50 miles
Prior enrollment: not required
Over-enrollment: not occurred
Disposition: cremation; return of cre-
  mains by request
Body rejection: standard,* previous em-
  balming

* autopsy, decomposition, mutilation, severe burn victim, meningitis, hepatitis, AIDS, and other contagious or communicable diseases

## ❖ Crematories

Albany

  Albany Rural Chapel & Crematory
  Cemetery Ave., 12204
  518-463-7017

Bronx

  The Woodlawn Cemetery
  20 W. 233rd & Webster, 10470
  718-920-0500

Brooklyn

  The Green-Wood Cemetery
  5th Ave. & 25th St.
  718-783-8776

Buffalo

  Buffalo Cremation Co.
  901 W. Delavan Ave., 14209
  716-885-3079

  Cutler Cremation Co.
  1386 Love Joy Ave., 14212

  Forest Lawn Cemetery
  1411 Delaware Ave., 14209
  716-885-1600

  Sheridan Park Crematory
  2600 Sheridan Dr., 14150
  716-836-6500

Central Square

  Traub Crematory
  684 N. Main St., 13036
  315-668-2688

Cheektowaga

  Mt. Calvary Cemetery
  800 Pine Ridge Rd., 14225
  716-892-6660

Cherry Valley

  The Leatherstocking Crematory
  22 Church St., 13320
  607-264-8141

Chester

  Oxford Hills Crematory
  Black Meadow Rd., 10918
  914-783-1811

Coram

  Washington Memorial Park
  Canal Rd., 11727
  516-473-0437

Dryden

  Cayuga Crematorium
  55 W. Main St., 13053
  607-844-8161

Earlville

Chenango Valley Crematorium
Preston St., Box 92, 13132

Ellenburg Depot

Whispering Maples Mem. Gardens
13 Cemetery Ln., 12935
518-594-7500

Elmira (Pine City)

South Port Crematorium
1050 Pennsylvania Ave., 14904
607-734-7373

Endicott

Twin Tiers Crematory
P.O. Box 244, 13760
607-754-0144

Falconer

Southern Tier Memorial Crematory
46 E. Falconer St.
716-665-4455

Glens Falls

Pine Crematorium
Quaker Rd., 12801
516-796-4726

Hartsdale

Ferncliff Cemetery Assn.
Secor Rd., 10530
914-693-4700

Kenmore

Elmlawn Cemetery & Crematory
3939 Delaware Ave., 14217
716-876-8131

Kingston

Wiltwyck Rural Cemetery Assn.
321 Fair St., 12401

Lewiston

Niagara Falls Memorial Park
5871 Military Rd., 14092
716-297-0811

Livonia

Fingerlakes Crematory
P.O. Box 59, 14487
716-346-5401

Monroe

Hickory Cremation Service
139 Stage Rd., 10950
914-783-1811

Newark

Pleasant Valley Crematorium
Box 131, 14513

Newburgh

Cedar Hill Cemetery Assn.
706-720 Rt. 9W North, 12550
914-562-0505

Niagara Falls

Niagara Falls Memorial Park
5871 Military Rd.
716-297-0811

Oakwood Cemetery Assn.
763 Portage Rd., 14301
716-284-5131

Pittsford

White Haven Memorial Park
210 Marsh Rd., 14534
716-586-5250

Poughkeepsie

Poughkeepsie Rural Cemetery
342 South Rd., 12602
914-454-6020

Rochester

Mt. Hope Cemetery & Crematory
1133 Mt. Hope Ave., 14620
716-473-2755

Schenectady

Mohawk Cemetery Assn.
1867 State St., 12304

Parkview Crematory
Fehr Ave., 12309
518-346-3217

Syracuse

Oakwood-Morningside Cemetery
1001 Comstock Ave., 13205
315-475-2194

Theresa

Frederick Bros. Crematory
38422 NYS Rt. 37, 13691
315-628-4451

Tonawanda

Tonken Crematory
417 Kenmore Ave., 14233
716-835-4522

Troy

Gardner-Earle Memorial Chapel
Head of 101 St., 12180
518-272-7520

Vestal

Vestal Hills Memorial Park
3997 Vestal Rd., 13850
607-797-8407

Watertown

Brookside Cemetery
19000 County Rte. 165, 13601
315-788-5668

Waterville

Waterville Cemetery Assn.
4883 Waterville Rd., 13480
315-841-4883

West Babylon

Long Island Cremation Co.
91 Eads St., 11704
516-293-6664

Additional crematories may have been established in this state after the date of publication.

## ❖ State Governance

The Funeral Directing Advisory Board, under the Department of Health, has ten members. There are three consumer representatives, one cemetery operator, and six undertakers.

Cemeteries are governed by the Cemetery Board and the Division of Cemeteries. The board is made up of the Secretary of State, the Attorney General, and the Commissioner of Health.

Crematories are regulated by the Cemetery Board. One does not need to be a funeral director to run a crematory, but a funeral director must be present for cremation. Why?

A few funeral homes were permitted by the Cemetery Board to construct what are supposed to be not-for-profit crematories. That practice will no longer be allowed once the governor signs the bill on his desk.

### ❖ Prepaid Cemetery and Funeral Funds

Cemeteries must be run not-for-profit. Both Loewen and SCI have tried to get into the cemetery business in New York by purchasing cemetery mortgage certificates for which they have paid wildly-inflated sums compared to the face value. Loewen paid between $45 and $50 million for certificates worth a mere $2 million. SCI paid $2 million for a face value of $30,000. (Ownership of such certificates yields a voice in cemetery operations.)

The Cemetery Board found that financial practices at these cemeteries have not always stayed within the law. Thanks to tight regulations and vigilant oversight, those practices were quickly corrected.

The state board has won the first round of litigation with Loewen over its attempt at cemetery control, but—given the huge investment at risk—there's bound to be a continuing saga. Stay tuned. And if you want to know whether "your" cemetery is at risk, call the Division of Cemeteries at 212-417-5713.

If a lot-owner wishes to sell a lot, it must first be offered back to the cemetery at the original sale price plus 4% per year.

Cemeteries may not sell monuments or vaults; they may sell grave-liners. If there is a religious objection to the use of a liner or vault, the cemetery may not require one but it may impose a "reasonable" maintenance fee for refilling a settling grave, such fee having been approved by the Cemetery Board. Cemeteries must be available for interments six days a week.

100% of all prepaid *funeral and cemetery* purchases must be placed in **trust**, with the **interest** to accrue. The purchaser must be notified within 30 days of the institution where the funds have been deposited.

The seller must **report** annually to the purchaser where the funds are held, along with the current total. Administrative fees may not exceed .75 of 1%. Although there is no guarantee fund to protect funeral consumers against default, the annual reporting should go far in enforcing the trusting requirement.

Prepaid funds are considered the property of the purchaser and may be withdrawn at any time for a full **refund** if it is a revocable contract. An irrevocable agreement may be **transferred**.

If a funeral home changes ownership, the owner of a preneed agreement must be notified. With the mad scramble of chains to purchase funeral homes, it would be interesting to see if they are obliging. The Bureau of Funeral Directing should be able to tell you who owns the one where you prepaid for your funeral: 518-402-0785. Be sure to file a complaint if you were not notified.

A preneed contract must specify whether or not it is a guaranteed-price agreement. It must "fully describe" the service and merchandise selected, but there is no clear provision for how detailed that should be. There might be a $1,000 difference between the least expensive "20-gauge steel" and the highest. I am told that the agreement is supposed to stipulate **substitution** obligations, but there is no statutory directive for this. Excess funds must be returned to the estate or the purchaser, if it is not a guaranteed-price arrangement.

A funeral home may not sell or be the beneficiary of funeral insurance. However, funeral homes are likely to ask you to sign over such a policy to cover the deceased's funeral expenses at a time of need. It's better not to let the funeral home even know how much the policy is for. Otherwise, if there is a surplus of funds, you may not get a refund. The cost of the funeral has a strange way of rising to the amount of insurance available. Get the bill from the funeral home and then have the insurance company mail any check to you so you can pay the funeral bill from that.

### ❖ Consumer Concerns

- The death rate in New York can support approximately 661 full-time mortuaries; there are, however, 1,949. Funeral prices tend to be higher in areas where there are "too many" funeral homes.
- The laws should be changed to permit families and church groups to care for their own dead.
- There is no provision for an adequate description of funeral goods selected on a guaranteed-price agreement nor for a substitution of

equal quality if the selected item is no longer available at the time of death. Substitutions should meet the approval of survivors.

- There is no requirement that low-cost caskets be included in any display.
- The format for pricing is in conflict with FTC requirements. New York requires a separate charge for *supervision* and another for *facilities* for viewing, for example. The FTC requires a single fee— *facilities and staff for viewing*. Consequently, many funeral homes list prices both ways in order to be in compliance with both state and federal requirements. This is cluttering the General Price List (GPL) and definitely confusing to consumers. New York may *certainly* require that additional options be offered on the price list— as does Vermont—but the standard pricing format of the FTC should be adopted.
- The New York GPLs are now required to include a statement, "The direct cremation prices do not include the crematory charge," probably because most crematories are on the grounds of cemeteries and are not owned by funeral homes. This should be changed to require the inclusion of the crematory fee. How can you have a "direct cremation" without cremation? Who would think to ask if it were extra? For someone shopping over the phone, the disclosure will never be seen. If a funeral home uses more than one area crematory, and prices differ from one to the next, an appropriate disclosure would be, "There will be an additional $50 charge if the crematory at Mt. Such-and-Such is used."
- Identification and tagging of the body at the place of death before removal should be required, given the regular mix-ups that have been happening at chain-owned establishments with central prep facilities.
- There is no law that allows you to state your funeral preferences or for naming a designated agent to make your final arrangements. In situations where you are estranged or distant from next-of-kin, this could be important.
- Complaint procedures are unclear and inadequate.
- The FTC Funeral Rule should be adopted by reference to make it fully enforceable in this state. Fortunately, most provisions are identical to the wording of New York's funeral statutes.

## ❖ Miscellaneous Information

- Educational requirements for becoming a funeral director or embalmer: mortuary college (60 semester credits) and one year of apprenticeship.
- The law states, "Upon receipt of satisfactory evidence that a license or certificate has been lost, mutilated or destroyed, the department may issue a duplicate license. . . ." How does one prove something is lost?
- Cash advance items must be billed at the actual cost to the funeral director.
- Misconduct in funeral directing is defined in a fairly comprehensive listing, although additional factors will be found in the Appendix of this book.
- The state office has funeral consumer information pamphlets available:

  Bureau of Funeral Directing
  NY State Dept. of Health
  Hedley Park Plaza
  433 River St., 6th Floor
  Troy, NY 12180

- It is a misdemeanor to hold a body for debt.
- Medical examiners are physicians who are appointed. Coroners are elected.

## ❖ Nonprofit Funeral Consumer Information Societies

These consumer groups are run mostly by volunteers. Consequently, contact information may change. If you have difficulty reaching a society or are interested in starting a society in your area, call the FAMSA office: 800-765-0107. Or check the internet directory—
**www.funerals.org/famsa**

Albany

  Mem. Soc. of Hudson-Mohawk Region
  405 Washington Ave., 12206-2604
  518-465-9664

Buffalo

  Greater Buffalo Memorial Society
  695 Elmwood Ave., 14222-1601
  716-837-8636

Binghamton

  Southern Tier Memorial Society
  183 Riverside Dr., 13905

Corning

  Memorial Soc. of Grtr. Corning Area
  P.O. Box 23, Painted Post, 14870-0023
  607-962-7132 or 936-6563

Farmingdale

Memorial Society of Long Island
P.O. Box 3495, 11735
516-541-6587

Ithaca

Ithaca Memorial Society
Box 134, 14851
607-273-8316

New Hartford

Mohawk Valley Memorial Society
P.O. Box 322, 13413
315-797-2396 or 735-6268

New York

Community Church Funeral Society
40 E. 35th St., 10016
212-683-4988 (membership open to all)

Poughkeepsie

Mid-Hudson Memorial Society
249 Hooker Ave., 12603
914-229-0241

Rochester

Rochester Memorial Society
220 Winton Rd. S., 14610
716-461-1620

Syracuse

Syracuse Memorial Society
P.O. Box 67, DeWitt, 13214
315-446-0557

White Plains

Westchester Funeral Planning Assn.
Rosedale Ave. & Sycamore Ln., 10605
(This one is desperate for volunteers.)

~❖~

*This chapter was reviewed by the New York Division of Cemeteries
and the Bureau of Funeral Directing.*

# In North Carolina

*Please refer to Chapter 8 as you use this section.*

Persons in North Carolina may care for their own dead. The legal authority to do so is found in:

> *Title 130A-420. Authority to dispose of body or body parts. (b) If a decedent has left no written authorization for the disposal of the decedent's body as permitted under subsection (a) of this section, the following competent persons in the order listed may authorize the type, method, place, and disposition of the decedent's body:*
>
> *(1) The surviving spouse.*
> *(2) A majority of surviving children.*
> *(3) The surviving parents . . . .*

There are no other statutes that might require you to use a funeral director.

## ❖ Death Certificate

A Notification of Death can be obtained from the local registrar. This must be completed within 24 hours. The registrar will keep one copy; the other is for your records.

Within three days, the family doctor or a local medical examiner will supply and sign the death certificate, stating the cause of death. The remaining information must be supplied, typewritten or in black ink. The death certificate must be filed with the local registrar within five days and before final disposition.

## ❖ Fetal Death

A fetal death report is required when death occurs after 20 weeks of gestation and must be filed as above. If there is no family physician involved, the local medical examiner must sign the fetal death certificate.

## ❖ Transporting and Disposition Permit

The physician or local medical examiner will authorize disposition. A burial-transit permit is required only if the death is under the jurisdiction of the medical examiner or if the body is to be removed from the state. It is the third copy of the medical examiner's death certificate. In other cases, the burial-transit permit may be obtained from the local registrar at no cost.

## ❖ Burial

Check with the county or town registrar for local zoning laws regarding home burial. The top of the casket must be 18 inches below the surface of the earth. Another sensible guideline is 150 feet from a water supply.

## ❖ Cremation

A permit from the medical examiner is required before cremation or burial at sea. This fee may not exceed $50. There is a 24-hour waiting period prior to cremation that may be waived in case of death from an infectious disease. Unless you have authorized your own cremation prior to death, authorization by next-of-kin will usually be required. A pacemaker must be removed.

Families and authorized agents may witness a cremation.

## ❖ Other Requirements

There are no other requirements controlling the time schedule for the disposition of unembalmed bodies. Weather and reasonable planning should be considered.

If the person died of a contagious or communicable disease, the doctor or medical examiner should be consulted. The body must be encased.

## ❖ Medical Schools for Body Donation

University of North Carolina
314 Berry Hill Hall 219-H
Chapel Hill, NC 27599-7520
919-966-1134 8:30-4:30 or
   966-4131
Moderate need

Cost to family: transportation
Prior enrollment: not required
Over-enrollment: shared
Disposition: cremation; return of cremains by request
Body rejection: standard,* obesity

Duke University Med. Center
Dept. of Biol. Anth. & Anat.
Durham, NC 27710
919-684-4124
    684-8111 after hours
High need

Cost to family: transportation
Prior enrollment: not required
Over-enrollment: shared with permission
Disposition: cremation; return of cremains by request
Body rejection: standard*

E. Carolina University
School of Medicine
Anatomy & Cell Biol. Dept.
Greenville, NC 27834
919-816-2849 8-5, M-F
    816-2246 after hours
Low need

Cost to family: transportation outside eastern NC
Prior enrollment: preferred
Over-enrollment: shared
Disposition: cremation; return of cremains by request
Body rejection: infectious disease, autopsy, amputation or constriction of limbs, over 170 lbs.

* autopsy, decomposition, mutilation, severe burn victim, AIDS, meningitis, hepatitis, other infectious diseases

## ❖ Crematories

Asheboro

    Central Carolina Crematory
    437 Sunset Ave., 27203
    800-793-0438

Asheville

    Asheville Mortuary Services
    89-A Thompson St., 28803
    828-254-0566

    Maple Springs Crematory
    304 Merrimon Ave., 28804
    704-254-6197

Candler

    Cremation Services
    2239 Smoky Park Hwy, 28715
    704-665-0520

Charlotte

    Sharon Memorial Park
    P.O. Box 220346, 28222
    704-537-5011

    Yates Cremation Service
    2828 Rosemont, 28208
    704-399-8453

Clemmons

    Vogler Crematory
    Middlebrook Dr., 27012
    910-766-4714

Coats

    Coats Crematory
    P.O. Box 656, 27521
    910-897-6303

Concord

    Carolina Memorial Park
    P.O. Box 3257, 28025
    704-786-2161

Durham

    Cremation Soc. of Carolinas
    5501 Fortunes Ridge Dr., 27713
    800-993-5333

Durham Cremation
1125 E. Geer St., 27704
919-683-1497

Quality Cremation Services
448 S. Driver St., 27703
919-383-4427

Elizabeth City

Albermarle Crematorium
P.O. Drawer 405, 27909
919-335-4329

Fayetteville

Highland Funeral Service
610 Ramsey St., 28301
910-484-8108

Rogers & Breece F. Home
500 Ramsey St., 28301
910-483-2191

Goldsboro

Goldsboro Cremation Service
1401 W. Grantham St., 27530
800-672-4748

Greensboro

Guilford Crematory
5926 W. Friendly Ave., 27419
336-299-9171

Westminster Gardens
3601 Whitehurst Rd., 27408
336-288-7329

Greenville

Pitt-Greenville Crematory
2100 E. 5th St., 27858
919-752-2101

Rouse Mortuary Service/Crematory
2111 Dickinson Ave., Ste. N, 27834
919-355-6116

Hendersonville

Jackson Funeral Service/Crematory
P.O. Box 945, 28793
704-693-4261

Shepherd Memorial Park
P.O. Box 765, 28739
704-693-3435

Hickory

Bass-Smith Funeral Home
334 2nd St. NW, 28601
704-332-3015

Jacksonville

Jones Funeral Home
303 Chaney Ave., 28540
910-455-1281

Knightdale

Harold Poole Funeral Service/Crem.
P.O. Box 489, 27545
919-266-3646

Laurinburg

Argyll Crematorium
P.O. Box 187, 28352
910-276-2200

Lumberton

Floyd Mortuary
P.O. Box 1608, 28359
910-738-8144

Moorehead City

Brooks Funeral Home
201 Professional Cir., 28557
919-726-5580

Munden Funeral Home/Crematory
P.O. Box 69, 28557
919-726-8066

New Bern

E. Carolina Crematory
2201 Neuse Blvd., 28560
919-637-3181

Raleigh

Carolina Cremation Service
716 W. North St., 27605
919-828-4311

Raleigh Cremation Services
600 St. Mary's St., 27605
919-832-3760

Southern Pines

Boles Funeral Home/Longleaf Crem.
1345 Old U.S. 1., 28387
910-692-6262

Pines Cremation Service
160 E. New Hampshire, 28387
910-692-6161

Stedman

Cape Fear Crematory
Rt. 1 Box 115A Bunce Rd., 28391
800-541-5284

Tryon

McFarland's Crematory
Hwy. 108 N., 28782
704-859-9341

Wilmington

Andrews Mortuary
4108 S. College Rd., 28401
910-762-7788

Winston-Salem

Cremation Services
7600 N. Point Ct., 27106
336-765-2793

Hayworth-Miller Funeral Home
3315 Silas Creek Pkwy., 27103
336-765-8181

Additional crematories may have been established in this state after the date of publication.

## ❖ State Governance

The North Carolina Board of Mortuary Science has nine members. Three are consumer representatives.

Cemeteries are regulated by the North Carolina Cemetery Commission. It has seven members, two of which are public members.

## ❖ Prepaid Cemetery and Funeral Funds

Only 60% of *cemetery* services and goods must be placed in **trust**. A performance bond can avoid the trusting requirement. **"Constructive delivery"** can also bypass the trusting requirement. "Delivery" usually is accomplished by issuing a certificate of ownership and warehousing the vault and/or marker, although the state is not checking to see if the goods are actually there. Once "delivered," it is almost impossible to get a refund even if the items have never been used. Actually, a purchaser has only 30 days in which to cancel a contract. The laws are mute as to exactly how much one would get back then. If the purchaser defaults on payments, however, the seller may cancel the contract and **refund** the 60% in trust—less anything "delivered" and interest.

**Interest** on the cemetery trust account may be withdrawn by the seller.

An annual **report** of the perpetual care fund must be made to the cemetery commission.

Only 90% of prepaid *funeral* funds must be placed in **trust**. The purchaser should expect to get, within 30 days, a confirmation that the preneed contract has been filed with the state, and a notice to that effect must appear on the preneed contract. Of course, if such a disclosure is missing, what consumer would know enough to realize it? Sellers must send annually to the board a **report** of their preneed accounts.

A consumer may request the cancellation of a preneed contract and get a **refund**—less the permitted 10% that can be retained. Irrevocable preneed funeral contracts may be transferred, with only the 90% in trust available for **transfer**.

Unless the contract was made at a guaranteed price, excess funds at the time of death are to be returned to the estate. With a 10% commission permitted, and funeral inflation exceeding most bank interest, this is a highly unlikely event.

A Preneed **Recovery Fund** is fed by $2 of the $18 fee collected for each preneed contract. This will be used to reimburse consumers in the event of a preneed supplier in default.

## ❖ Consumer Concerns

- The death rate in North Carolina can support approximately 266 full-time mortuaries; there are, however, 686 such establishments. Funeral prices tend to be higher in areas where there are "too many" funeral homes.
- Finance charges are permitted for installment purchases of prepaid cemetery services and merchandise. This is outrageous and should

be repealed immediately! When you finance a car or house, you get to use either. But a finance charge on a lay-away plan before they lay you away?

- Laws should require cemeteries to repurchase an unwanted lot at the original selling price plus 50% of the difference between that and current market price.
- There is no annual reporting requirement to the purchaser of prepaid funeral goods and services, paperwork that might be useful to the family of a deceased to indicate prepayment and which would help to "enforce" trusting requirements.
- There is no provision for an adequate description of funeral goods selected preneed nor a requirement for the substitution—approved by survivors—of equal quality and construction if the selected item is no longer available at the time of death.
- Irrevocable preneed arrangements may not be altered. A provision should be added, "provided that the deceased left sufficient financing to carry out the stated wishes."
- "Constructive delivery" should not be permitted.
- Until the laws are changed to require 100% trusting of all money and interest for prepaid funeral and cemetery goods and services, it is probably a *terrible* idea to prepay for these arrangements in North Carolina. Your own trust account in a bank will be safer.
- There is no provision either forbidding a mark-up on cash advance items or requiring the disclosure of how much the mark-up would be. Consumers may wish to ask for a copy of the invoice for such items.
- North Carolina appears to still permit funeral-casket-price bundling, with all costs presented as one and attached to the casket. This would be in violation of the FTC Funeral Rule, which permits only the nondeclinable "basic" fee to be so included, along with a disclosure that must use specific wording.
- There is no requirement that low-cost caskets be included in any display.
- The 24-hour wait before cremation is totally unnecessary when survivors are in agreement and may be causing additional charges to families for "storage."
- The coroner or medical examiner's permit for cremation in the case of an *anticipated* death from natural causes is totally unnecessary and creates an additional burden and charge for families.

- Identification and tagging of the body at the place of death before removal should be required.
- The FTC Funeral Rule should be adopted by reference to make it more enforceable in this state (pending).
- Ethical standards should be adopted and unethical conduct clearly defined in order for valid consumer complaints to prevail. (See Appendix.)

## ❖ Miscellaneous Information

- Educational requirements for becoming a funeral director/embalmer: mortuary college (1 yr.), pass a state exam, and one year of apprenticeship.
- Crematories are licensed, regulated, and inspected by the Crematory Authority which serves under the Board of Mortuary Science. One does not need to be a funeral director to run a crematory.
- A crematory operator's license may be revoked if guilty of "using profane, indecent or obscene language in the presence of a dead human body, and within the immediate hearing of the family or relatives of a deceased, whose body has not yet been cremated or otherwise disposed of." After that watch out?
- Medical examiners are physicians who are appointed, not elected.
- Preference is given to the expressed wishes of the deceased. You may want to also name a designated deathcare agent for your final arrangements. In situations where you are estranged or distant from next-of-kin, this could be important.

## ❖ Nonprofit Funeral Consumer Information Societies

These consumer groups are run mostly by volunteers. Consequently, contact information may change. If you have difficulty reaching a society or are interested in starting a society in your area, call the FAMSA office: 800-765-0107. Or check the internet directory—

**www.funerals.org/famsa**

Asheville

Blue Ridge Memorial Society
P.O. Box 2601, 28802-2601
704-669-2587

Chapel Hill

Memorial Soc. of the Triangle
P.O. Box 1223, 27514-1223
919-942-6695

Charlotte

Although there is no society here at present, there are several who are interested in starting such a society. Call the FAMSA office if you are willing to help.

Greensboro

Piedmont Mem. & Funeral Soc.
5137 Charleston Rd.
Pleasant Garden, NC 27313
910-674-5501

This is a struggling society and in need of volunteers. It may no longer be in operation when you read this.

Wilmington

Mem. Soc. of Lower Cape Fear
P.O. Box 4262, 28406-4262

~❖~

*This chapter was sent for review to the North Carolina Board of Mortuary Science, the Cemetery Commission, and the Department of Health. No response was received from the Cemetery Commission.*

# In North Dakota

*Please refer to Chapter 8 as you use this section.*

Persons in North Dakota may care for their own dead. The legal authority to do so is found in the Health Code:

> *Title 23-06-02. Who is entitled to custody of body. The person charged with the duty of burying the body of a deceased person is entitled to the custody of such body for the purpose of burying it.*

> *Title 23-06-03. Duty of burial. The duty of burying the body of a deceased person devolves upon the following persons: 1. . . . upon the surviving husband or wife. 2. If the deceased was not married but left kindred, upon the person or persons in the same degree, of adult age, nearest of kin to the deceased living within the state . . . .*

## ❖ Death Certificate

The doctor in attendance, the local health officer, or county coroner will supply and sign the death certificate, stating the cause of death. The remaining information must be supplied, typewritten or in black ink. Do not use a felt-tip pen; the information must carry through to a third copy. The death certificate must be filed with the local registrar within 15 days. When a family is handling all arrangements, the death certificate should be completed and filed at the time of requesting the registrar's signature on the burial-transit permit.

## ❖ Fetal Death

A fetal death report is required when death occurs after 20 weeks of gestation. If there is no family physician involved, the county coroner must sign the fetal death certificate.

## ❖ Transporting and Disposition Permit

The local registrar or sub-registrar in the district where death occurred must sign the burial-transit permit, which is the third page attached to the death certificate.

Board of Funeral Service regulations—not statutes—state that a body may not be "shipped or transported" except under the supervision of a licensed funeral director. However, the Board has authority over licensees only, not over private citizens.

## ❖ Burial

Check with the county or town registrar for local zoning laws regarding home burial. Burial must be in a "properly registered cemetery or in some other place requested by the relatives and friends of the deceased if the same is authorized by the state department of health." The top of the casket must be 3½ feet below the natural surface of the earth. Another sensible guideline is 150 feet from a water supply.

When burial is arranged, the family member acting as the funeral director must detach and sign the burial-transit permit and file it with the registrar of that district within 10 days.

## ❖ Cremation

No additional permit is needed for cremation. Most crematories insist that a pacemaker be removed, and authorization by next-of-kin or an agent of the deceased is required. A disposition plan for the cremated remains must be indicated, but there are no restrictions on what that may be. The crematory will sign the burial-transit permit, which must be filed with the registrar in that district within 10 days.

## ❖ Other Requirements

Disposition must be made within eight days. A body that will not reach its destination within 24 hours must be embalmed. Embalming is required if disposition is not accomplished within 48 hours.

If death is due to anthrax, small pox, cholera, plague, TB, meningococcus, or meningitis, the body must be embalmed.

When death is due to viral hepatitis, TB, AIDS, plague, Creutzfeldt-Jakob, rabies, or meningitis, the body must be tagged: "Blood and body fluids precautions should be observed." The Centers for Disease Control, however, recommend such precautions for *all* deaths.

## ❖ Medical Schools for Body Donation

University of North Dakota
Dept. of Anatomy & Cell Biol.
Medical Science South
Grand Forks, ND 58202
701-777-2101 8-4:30 M-F
    772-7444 or 775-5047 or 772-0484
Moderate need

Cost to family: transportation and embalming (under school direction) over $275
Prior enrollment: not required
Over-enrollment: not occurred
Disposition: cremation; return of cremains by request
Body rejection: autopsy, decomposition, AIDS

## ❖ Crematories

Bismarck

  Bismarck Funeral Home
  3723 Lockport St., 58501
  701-223-4055

  Dakota Cremation Services
  122 E. Rossner Ave., 58502
  701-223-4424

Fargo

  Riverside Cemetery Assn.
  501 21st Ave., 58102
  701-235-2671

Additional crematories may have been established in this state after the date of publication.

## ❖ State Governance

The North Dakota State Board of Funeral Service has three members plus the state health officer. There are no consumer representatives.

The State Department of Health regulates cemeteries.

The Securities Commissioner regulates preneed funeral sales.

## ❖ Prepaid Cemetery and Funeral Funds

A cemetery lot unused for 60 years may be reclaimed by the cemetery if the owner cannot be located or expresses no interest in retaining ownership.

20% of the cost of a lot, mausoleum, or niche space must be put into the perpetual care fund. Not all cemeteries are perpetual care cemeteries and, if not, must so note on signs and paperwork.

50% of *cemetery merchandise* must be placed in **trust**. There is no trusting requirement for cemetery *services* such as the opening-and-closing charge. **"Constructive delivery"** can bypass the trust requirement. That means you will be given title to the merchandise, and it will be placed in a warehouse marked as yours. Few states are checking to see if it is actually there. If you were to change your mind and want a refund, forget it—your money has already been spent. Even if it hasn't, all you'll get back is 50%.

100% of prepaid *funeral* expenses must be placed in **trust**. However, trusting requirements can be avoided with **"Constructive delivery"** of funeral merchandise, too.

A person may request in writing a **refund** or **transfer** of any preneed account. If the casket is in "storage," the amount refunded will be reduced accordingly.

The preneed seller must make an annual **report** of all preneed sales to the Securities Commissioner. Within 90 days, the commissioner will verify the deposits.

A preneed seller must carry a **bond** in an amount deemed "adequate" by the commissioner. Because the cost of bonding in the full amount of preneed accounts being carried is quite expensive, there is motivation to avoid reporting all preneed sales.

## ❖ Consumer Concerns

- The death rate in North Dakota can support approximately 24 full-time mortuaries; there are 111 such establishments. However, given the low density of population over a vast geographic area, mortuary careers are not likely to be full-time work. Unfortunately, because of the low volume of business per mortuary, funeral prices will tend to be higher than elsewhere.
- Laws should require cemeteries to repurchase an unwanted lot at the original selling price plus 50% of the difference between that and current market price.
- Trusting requirements for cemetery merchandise and services should be increased to 100%, with full right of refund.
- Constructive delivery should not be permitted for any cemetery or funeral merchandise.
- There is no provision for an adequate description of funeral goods selected on a guaranteed-price preneed contract nor for a substitution of equal quality and construction if the selected item

is no longer available at the time of death. Any substitution should be with the approval of survivors.

- There is no annual reporting requirement to the purchaser of prepaid funeral goods and services, paperwork that might be useful to the family of a deceased to indicate prepayment and which would help to "enforce" trusting requirements. Consumers have lost money in other states requiring 100% trusting.

- There is no guarantee fund to protect consumers against default of preneed cemetery and funeral purchases.

- Until better trusting is required and other loopholes are closed, it is probably a *terrible* idea to prepay for a funeral in North Dakota.

- Identification and tagging of the body at the place of death before removal should be required, given the regular mix-ups that have been happening at chain-owned establishments with central prep facilities.

- The embalming laws should be repealed. Requiring embalming when death occurs from a communicable disease is not only an offense to some religious groups, it puts the funeral professionals and possibly the environment at risk. The time requirements for disposition without embalming are unnecessarily restrictive and pose an unreasonable burden on those who find this procedure repugnant.

- There is no requirement that low-cost caskets be included in any display.

- There is no provision either forbidding a mark-up on cash advance items or requiring disclosure of how much the mark-up would be.

- The standards for ethical, professional conduct should be strengthened. That would make it easier for a consumer to prevail when filing a valid complaint.

- Complaint procedures are unclear and inadequate. License revocation is the only penalty; there is no provision for a fine.

- There is no law that allows you to state your funeral preferences or for naming a designated agent to make your final arrangements. In situations where you are estranged or distant from next-of-kin, this could be important.

## ❖ Miscellaneous Information

- Educational requirements for becoming a funeral director or embalmer: two years of college, mortuary school, one year of apprenticeship, and an exam.

- Crematories are licensed by the Board of Funeral Service. One does not need to be a funeral director to run a crematory. A crematory used for human remains may not be used to cremate animals or pets.
- A funeral home may not be located on tax-exempt property.
- The 1984 FTC Funeral Rule has been adopted by reference.
- It is a misdemeanor to hold a body for debt.
- The county social services department will provide up to $1,500 for burial expenses for those with insufficient means.

### ❖ Nonprofit Funeral Consumer Information Societies

These consumer groups are run mostly by volunteers. Consequently, contact information may change. If you have difficulty reaching a society or are interested in starting a society in your area, call the FAMSA office: 800-765-0107. Or check the internet directory—

**www.funerals.org/famsa**

Funeral Consumer Information Society of the Dakotas
HCR 66, Box 10
Lemmon, SD 57638

~❖~

*This chapter was reviewed by the Securities Commissioner. It was also sent for review to the North Dakota Department of Health and the North Dakota State Board of Funeral Service. No response was received from the Department of Health.*

I received a letter from the Attorney General's office, at the behest of the Board of Funeral Service. It referred to statutes under Occupations and Professions which state that anyone practicing funeral directing must be licensed and that I was incorrect in stating that families could care for their own dead. I responded by saying that families doing so are not in any business, that once or twice in a lifetime did not constitute a "practice," and that under the health code it would appear that families do have a right to care for their own dead. Mr. Bahr, Assistant Attorney General, responded:

> My concern is not with the accuracy or inaccuracy of your chapter. My concern is with the statement in your chapter indicating the Board of Funeral Service approves the content of the chapter. Please eliminate from your chapter the statement that the North Dakota State Board of Funeral Service reviewed your chapter.

Done.

# In Ohio

*Please refer to Chapter 8 as you use this section.*

Persons and religious groups in Ohio may care for their own dead. The legal authority to do so is found in:

*RC 3705.26—Registration of death with local registrar; certificate of death. Each death which occurs in Ohio shall be registered with the local registrar of vital statistics of the district in which the death occurred by the funeral director or other person in charge of interment or cremation of the remains.*

*RC 4717.10—Exceptions to provisions.... Sections 4717.01-4717.19 of the Revised Code do not prevent or interfere with the ceremonies, customs, religious rights, or religion of any people, denomination, or sect; . . . prevent or interfere with . . . preparing human bodies for burial; prevent or interfere with the use of any place, chapel or private home for the preparation of bodies for burial . . . except in case of a contagious disease, where rules of the local board of health as to preparation for burial shall govern.*

There are no other statutes that might require you to use a funeral director.

## ❖ Death Certificate

The family doctor or a coroner will supply and sign the death certificate within 48 hours, stating the cause of death. The remaining information must be supplied, typewritten or in black ink. The death certificate must be filed with the local registrar within 48 hours and before final disposition.

## ❖ Fetal Death

A certificate of stillbirth is required for each fetal death.

### ❖ Transporting and Disposition Permit

The local registrar or sub-registrar will issue the burial-transit permit. The charge for this is $2.50. This permit must be filed with the registrar in the district of disposition. (Some funeral directors may serve as sub-registrars.)

When a body is brought into the state, a Certificate of Service must be filed with the local registrar after disposition.

### ❖ Burial

Check with the county or town registrar for local zoning laws regarding home burial. There are no state burial statutes or regulations with regard to depth. A sensible guideline is 150 feet from a water supply and at least two feet of earth on top.

When burial is arranged, the family member acting as the funeral director must sign the burial-transit permit and file it with the registrar where the disposition takes place.

### ❖ Cremation

No additional permit is needed for cremation. There will be a 24-hour wait prior to cremation if a pending bill is enacted. Authorization by next-of-kin is usually required, and a pacemaker must be removed. The crematory may offer to file the burial-transit permit.

### ❖ Other Requirements

Ohio has no other requirements controlling the time schedule for the disposition of unembalmed bodies. Weather and reasonable planning should be considered.

The body of a person who has died from a communicable disease must be buried or cremated within 24 hours.

## ❖ Medical Schools for Body Donation

Ohio University
College of Osteopathic Medicine
Athens, OH 45701
614-593-2171  8-5 M-F
614-594-2416 other times
Urgent need

Cost to family: none in Ohio
Prior enrollment: preferred
Over-enrollment: not occurred
Disposition: cremation; return of cremains by request
Body rejection: standard,* fetal death, embalming (except by direction of school), MS, A-L sclerosis, Creutzfeldt-Jakob, Parkinson's, Guillain-Barre, Alzheimer's, and several other diseases

University of Cincinnati
College of Medicine
231 Bethesda Ave., ML 521
Cincinnati, OH 45267
513-872-5678 8:30-5 M-F
or Hamilton Co. Coroner's office:
513-872-5612

Cost to family: transportation
Prior enrollment: not required
Over-enrollment: shared
Disposition: burial or return by request
Body rejection: autopsy (check first), burn victim, decomposition, meningitis, AIDS, under 21, previous embalming (accepts almost all prior enrollees)

Case Western Reserve
School of Medicine
2119 Abington Rd.
Cleveland, OH 44106
216-368-3430 or 221-9330

Cost to family: transportation beyond 75 miles
Prior enrollment: required
Over-enrollment: shared
Disposition: cremation; return of cremains by request
Body rejection: standard,* under 18, previous embalming, obesity, emaciation, major surgery, missing body parts

Ohio State University
College of Medicine
Dept. of Cell Biol., Neurobiol. & Anat.
333 W. 10th Ave.
Columbus, OH 43210
614-292-4831
or ask for University Hospital Morgue
Donations adequate

Cost to family: transportation
Prior enrollment: preferred
Over-enrollment: not occurred
Disposition: cremation; return of cremains by request
Body rejection: standard,* under 18, previous embalming

Wright State University
North Dayton, OH 45431

Repeated requests for information have not been returned from this school.

Northeastern Ohio Universities
College of Medicine (NEOUCOM)
Dept. of Anatomy
4209 S.R. 44, P.O. Box 95
Rootstown, OH 44272-0095
216-325-2511 ext. 253 or 255
Moderate need

Cost to family: none
Prior enrollment: required
Over-enrollment: not shared
Disposition: cremation; return of cremains by request
Body rejection: over 10 hrs. after death, embalming, standard,* excessive edema, missing limbs, major surgery, obesity, emaciation, over-enrollment

Medical College of Ohio
3000 Arlington Ave.
C.S. 10008
Toledo, OH 43699
419-381-4109 or 4172
Moderate need

Cost to family: transportation, $60 enrollment fee
Prior enrollment: required
Over-enrollment: shared
Disposition: cremation; return of cremains by request
Body rejection: standard*

* autopsy, decomposition, mutilation, severe burn victim, meningitis, hepatitis, AIDS, and other contagious or communicable diseases

## ❖ Crematories

Akron

Adams Funeral Home
791 E. Market St., 44305
330-535-9186

Akron Crematory
2399 Gilchrist Rd., 44305
330-784-5475

Summit Cremation Service
85 N. Miller Rd., 44313
330-867-4141

Ashtabula

Ashtabula County Cremation Svc.
4524 Elm Ave., 44004
440-992-2191

Bedford Heights

Hillcrest Memorial Park Cemetery
26700 Aurora, 44146
440-232-0035

Brookfield

Brook Park Cremation Center
6919 Warren-Sharon Rd., 44403
330-448-2412

Canton

CRW Professional Service & Crem.
4225 16th St. NW, 44708
216-477-0499

Chesterland

Tri-County Cremation Service
P.O. Box 61, 44026
440-729-1908

Cincinnati

Arlington Memorial Gardens
2145 Compton Rd., 45231
513-729-1383

Baxter Cremation Service
909 E. Ross Ave., 45217
513-641-1010

Cincinnati Cremation Co.
525 W. ML King Dr., 45220
513-861-1021

Spring Grove Memorial Mausoleum
4521 Spring Grove, 45232
513-541-0600

Cleveland

Baldwin Funeral Chapel & Crem.
1490 Crawford Rd., 44106
216-229-6363

Chambers Funeral Homes
4420 Rocky River Dr., 44135
216-251-6566

Cremation Services, Inc.
1612 Leonard St., 44113
216-861-2334

Great Lakes Crematory
4701 Hinckley Ind. Pkwy., 44109
216-398-8400

Greenfield Crematory
5475 Lake Ct., 44114
216-391-6628

Highland Park Cemetery/Crematory
21400 Chagrin, 44122
216-921-4010

Jakubs & Son Funeral Home
936 E. 185th St., 44119
216-531-7770

Lakewood Crematory
1575 W. 117th St., 44107
216-221-3380
Memorial Abbey Mausoleum
4700 Broadview, 44109
216-351-1476

NE Ohio Crematory
15707 St. Clair Ave., 44110
216-451-1070

Universal Circle Crematory
2165 E. 89th St., 44106
216-791-0770

Columbus

Columbus Crematory
229 E. State St., 43215
614-224-6105

Cook and Son
1631 Parsons, 43207
614-444-7861

Green Lawn Cemetery Assn.
1000 Greenlawn Ave., 43223
614-444-1123

Spears Funeral Home
2693 W. Broad St., 43204
614-274-5092

Cridersville

Cridersville Crematory
311 W. Main St., 45806
419-645-4501

Cuyahoga Falls

North Lawn Memorial Gardens
P.O. Box 1059, 44223
216-929-2884

Dayton

Routsong Funeral Home
6 Oakwood Ave., 45409
513-293-4137

Woodland Cemetery Assn.
118 Woodland Ave., 45409
513-228-3221

Delaware

Mid Ohio Cremation Service
92 N. Sandusky, 43015
614-362-1611

Galloway

Sunset Cemetery
P.O. Box 134, 43119
614-878-4692

Hamilton

Rose Hill Burial Park
2421 Princeton Rd., 45011
513-895-3278

Hillsboro

Turner & Son Funeral Home
602 N. High St., 45133
513-393-2124

Holgate

S & S Crematory
209 N. Wilheim St., 43527
419-264-3401

Kettering

David's Cemetery Assn.
4600 Mad River Rd., 45429
513-434-2255

Lima

Siferd Funeral Homes
506 N. Cable Rd., 45805
419-224-2101

Lorain

AFFSCO Crematory
1155 Reed Ave., 44052
440-244-5288

Mansfield

Mansfield Memorial Park
2507 Park Ave. W., 44906
419-529-4433

No. Central Ohio Cremation Service
98 S. Diamond St., 44902
419-522-5211

Maple Heights

Blessing Funeral Home
16222 Broadway Ave., 44137
216-475-2626

Martin's Ferry

Crummitt & Son
2nd St., 43935
614-633-9381

Mentor

NE Ohio Crematory
7474 Mentor Ave., 44060
216-942-1702

Ohio Crematory Center
9340 Pinecone Dr., 44060
216-352-8100

Miamisburg

Bell Crematory Service
1019 S. Main St., 45342
513-866-2444

Mt. Vernon

Grohe Funeral Home & Crematory
108 N. Main, 43050
614-392-4956

North Olmsted

Sunset Memorial Park
6265 Columbia Rd., 44070
216-777-0450

Oregon

Hoeflinger Funeral Home
3500 Navarre Ave., 43616
419-691-6768

Parma

Brookside Cremation Service
7501 Ridge Rd., 44129
216-741-7700

Peninsula

Northlawn Memorial Gardens
4441 State Rd. 44264
216-929-2884

Portsmouth

F. C. Daehler Mortuary
915-923 Ninth St., 45662
614-353-4146

Sandusky

Sandusky Cremation Service
2001 Columbus Ave., 44870
419-625-4221

Springfield

Northfield Cremation Service
830 N. Limestone, 45503
513-323-6439

Rose Hill Cemetery & Crematory
4781 S. Charleston, 45502
513-322-5172

Struthers

Western Reserve Cremation Service
26 Sexton St., 44471
216-744-4161

Sylvania

Toledo Memorial Park
6382 Monroe., 43560
419-882-7151

Toledo

Bennett-Emmert Funeral Home
3434 Secor Rd., 43606
419-535-7726

Toledo Cremation Service
1021 Warwick Ave., 43607
419-537-1133

Woodlawn Cemetery
1502 W. Central Ave., 43606
419-472-2186

Van Wert

Van Wert Crematory
722 S. Washington, 45891
419-238-1112

Westlake

West Shore Cremation Service
2914 Dover Center Rd., 44145
216-871-0711

Worthington

Rutherford-Corbin Crematory
517 High St., 43085
614-885-4006

Youngstown

Lake Park Cemetery Assn.
1459 E. Midlothian Blvd., 44502
216-782-4221

Additional crematories may have been established in this state after the date of publication.

## ❖ State Governance

The Board of Embalmers and Funeral Directors has seven members. Two are consumer representatives, at least one of whom must be 60 years of age or older.

The Ohio Cemetery Dispute Resolution Committee hears complaints against cemeteries. Most Ohio cemeteries are operated by municipalities or church groups.

### ❖ Prepaid Cemetery and Funeral Funds

If you purchase a burial vault ahead of time, 60% must be placed into **trust**. "**Constructive delivery**" can bypass trusting requirements. If you wish to cancel this purchase after the first week, your **refund** will be 60% of whatever is in trust, plus 80% of the interest. There are no trusting requirements for *cemetery* services.

100% of prepaid *funeral* goods and services must be placed into **trust** with **interest** to accrue. "**Constructive delivery**" can bypass the trusting requirement. If you are given a certificate saying that "your" casket is being stored at the funeral home, forget about changing your mind, because the money for that has been spent and won't go into trust.

If you do want to **cancel** your preneed arrangement, how much you get will depend on a second factor, too: Was it a guaranteed-price arrangement? If so, you'll get back only 90% of the principal left in trust and 80% of the interest.

An example might make this easier to understand. You paid $5,000 for a guaranteed-price funeral; $2,500 was for a casket; and the funeral home gave you a certificate saying that your casket was in storage for you there. But your daughter moves to Oregon, and you decide you'd like to be near her. What will you get back after three years? Only $2,500 went into the trust (the other $2,500 paid for the casket). At maybe 5% interest, you've added $394 to your account. But, at 80%, you'll get only $315 of that. Add 90% of the $2,500 you paid that actually ever made it into trust—$2,250—and you'll get a check for $2,565. Oh, yes, where should they ship your casket? At your expense, of course.

If you made this arrangement irrevocable, you'd better hope you won't want to follow your daughter to Oregon—there's no provision for **transferring** an irrevocable preneed plan.

## ❖ Consumer Concerns

- The death rate in Ohio can support approximately 427 full-time mortuaries; there are, however, 1,271. Funeral prices tend to be higher in areas where there are "too many" funeral homes.
- Laws should require cemeteries to repurchase an unwanted lot at the original selling price plus 50% of the difference between that and current market price, if the value has increased. If the value of the lot has decreased below the original selling price, the cemetery should repurchase the lot at 75% of the current worth.
- All purchase money for burial vaults should be placed in trust, with adequate provision for cancellation and refund; "constructive delivery" should be forbidden.
- There is no annual reporting requirement to the purchaser of prepaid funeral goods and services, paperwork that might be helpful to the family of a deceased to indicate prepayment and which would help to "enforce" trusting requirements.
- There is no state protection in the case of default of prepaid funeral monies.
- There is no provision for an adequate description of funeral goods selected preneed nor for a substitution of equal quality if the selected item is no longer available at the time of death. Survivors should be permitted to approve any substitution.
- Until "constructive delivery" is eliminated and adequate provisions for refund or transfer of all prepaid funeral money plus interest are enacted, it is probably a *terrible* idea to prepay for a funeral in Ohio.
- Identification and tagging of the body at the place of death before removal should be required (legislation pending).
- There is no provision either forbidding a mark-up on cash advance items or requiring the disclosure of how much the mark-up would be.
- There is no requirement that low-cost caskets be included in any display.
- The standards for professional conduct should be strengthened. That would make it easier for a consumer to prevail when filing a valid complaint.
- Complaint procedures are unclear and inadequate.
- The FTC Funeral Rule should be adopted by reference to make it more enforceable in this state.
- If you die with limited funds and no prepaid funeral arrangements, look who gets your money and in what order:

—the lawyers handling your estate

—$2,000 to the funeral director

—support for surviving spouse and minor children

—taxes

—the doctor and hospital

—another $1,000 for the funeral director if more is owed . . .

## ❖ Miscellaneous Information

- Educational requirements for an embalmer: two years of college (pending legislation would increase this to four), one year of mortuary college, and one year of apprenticeship. For a funeral director: bachelor's degree and two years of apprenticeship.
- Pending legislation would give crematory regulation to the state Board of Embalmers and Funeral Directors. It would add a person knowledgeable about crematory operation to that board. One does not need to be a funeral director to operate a crematory.
- According to the same pending legislation, a person may authorize his/her own cremation. The form must indicate the final disposition of the cremated remains, but there is no restriction on what that may be. The wishes of a spouse may over-ride such authorization.
- Coroners are elected. They must be licensed physicians.
- No person may picket a funeral home, church, or cemetery within one hour before and during a funeral, nor may one picket a funeral procession.
- A commercial pet cemetery must be at least three acres, with a beginning endowment fund of $12,000. Fifty dollars from each lot sale must be added to the fund.
- If no other resources exist, adults who are already receiving state aid can receive $750 toward their funeral expenses. For children under the age of 11, the amount is $500. A family may contribute up to the same amount to help defray either cost.

## ❖ Nonprofit Funeral Consumer Information Societies

These consumer groups are run mostly by volunteers. Consequently, contact information may change. If you have difficulty reaching a society or are interested in starting a society in your area, call the FAMSA office: 800-765-0107. Or check the internet directory—

**www.funerals.org/famsa**

Akron

Mem. Society of Akron-Canton Area
3300 Moorewood Rd., 44333
330-836-4418 or 849-1030

Cincinnati

Mem. Society of Greater Cincinnati
536 Linden St., 45219
513-281-1564

Cleveland

Cleveland Memorial Society
21600 Shaker Blvd.
Shaker Heights, OH 44122
216-751-5515

Columbus

Memorial Society of Columbus Area
(also covers Youngstown)
P.O. Box 14835, 43214-4835
614-436-8911

Toledo

Memorial Society of NW Ohio
2210 Collingwood Blvd., 43620-1147
419-475-1429

~❖~

*This chapter was sent for review to the Ohio Department of Health and the Ohio Cemetery Dispute Resolution Committee. No response was received. A staff member from the Board of Embalmers and Funeral Directors, however, was kind enough to supply several corrections.*

# In Oklahoma

*Please refer to Chapter 8 as you use this section.*

Persons in Oklahoma may care for their own dead. The legal authority to do so is found in:

> *Title 59 § 396.12b Conduct of Funeral Services . . . A. Each funeral conducted within this state shall be under the personal supervision of a duly-licensed funeral director. . . .*
>
> *C. Nothing in this section regarding the conduct of funerals or personal supervision of a licensed director . . . shall apply to persons related to the deceased by blood or marriage.*

While the statutes are pretty clear about your rights, it may come as a surprise to clergy that those in the funeral business apparently aspire to a role of spiritual leadership, as the rules promulgated by the Funeral Board read:

> *235:10-1-2 . . . "Funeral Service" means a ritual or ceremony conducted with a body or bodies present with said ritual or ceremony conducted prior to final disposition. A funeral service shall be conducted by a licensed funeral director . . .*

At the risk of meddling with religion even further, the Funeral Board has decided that those who care for their own dead should skip any funeral or prayers over the dead altogether, for the rules go on:

> *235:10-1-3 When Board rules are not applicable . . . Board rules shall not apply where an individual related to the deceased by blood or marriage provides a burial receptacle and buries the related deceased* **without** *embalming or* **conducting a funeral** *[emphasis added].*

My advice? Go ahead anyway. The courts would surely affirm your right to freely engage in the religious or spiritual activity of your choice—at a time of death or any other time.

### ❖ Death Certificate

The family doctor or a local medical examiner will sign the death certificate within 48 hours, stating the cause of death. The remaining information must be supplied, typewritten or in black ink. The death certificate must be filed with the local registrar within three days and before final disposition.

## ❖ Fetal Death

A fetal death report is required for each fetal death.

## ❖ Transporting and Disposition Permit

The medical examiner will issue a burial-transit permit if the body is to be moved out of state. There is no fee for the permit at this time.

## ❖ Burial

Check with the county registrar for local zoning laws regarding home burial. There are no state burial statutes or regulations with regard to depth. A sensible guideline is 150 feet from a water supply and three feet of earth on top.

## ❖ Cremation

A permit for cremation must be obtained from the medical examiner. The fee for this is $100, the highest in the country. Most crematories insist that a pacemaker be removed, and authorization by next-of-kin usually is required. The crematory will return the disposition authorization to the issuing registrar.

## ❖ Other Requirements

Oklahoma has no other requirements controlling the time schedule for the disposition of unembalmed bodies. Weather and reasonable planning should be considered. If the person died of a contagious or communicable disease, the doctor in attendance should be consulted.

## ❖ Medical Schools for Body Donation

Oklahoma University
Health Sciences Center
P.O. Box 26901
Oklahoma City, OK 73190
405-271-2424 or 6666
Moderate need

Cost to family: transportation beyond state
Prior enrollment: required
Over-enrollment: not shared
Disposition: cremation/burial or scattering; return of cremains by request
Body rejection: autopsy, meningitis, hepatitis, AIDS or other, under 18, cavity embalming

Oklahoma State University
College of Osteopathic Medicine
1111 W. 17th
Tulsa, OK 74107
918-582-1972
Moderate need

Cost to family: transportation outside state
Prior enrollment: not required
Over-enrollment: shared
Disposition: cremation/scattering return of cremains by request
Body rejection: autopsy, decomposition, AIDS

## ❖ Crematories

Bartlesville

Regional Cremation Service
1600 SE Washington, 74006
918-333-4300

Broken Arrow

Sloans Mortuary/Crematory
728 W. Elgin., 74012
918-258-0900

Lawton

Southwest Cremation Service
632 -C- Ave., 73501
405-353-2940

Oklahoma City

Area Cremation Service
1145 W. Britton Rd., 73114
405-843-5521

Oklahoma Cremation Service
6934 S. Western Ave.
P.O. Box 19267, 73144
405-634-4711

Oklahoma Mortuary Services
2524 NW 2nd, 73148
405-239-7737

Resthaven F H/Cemetery
700 SW 104th, 73118
405-691-1661

Tonkawa

Area Cremation Service
400 E. Grand Ave., 74653
405-628-2525

Tulsa

American Cremation Services
2211 E. 6th, 74104
918-583-4035

Cremation Society of OK
2103 E. 3rd St., 74104
918-587-7000

Memorial Park
5111 S. Memorial Dr., 74145
918-627-0220

Ninde Cremation Society
3841 S. Peoria, 74105
918-742-5556

Tulsa Cremation Service
3959 E. 31st, 74135
918-743-6396

There may be additional crematories established after publication of this book.

## ❖ State Governance

The Oklahoma State Board of Embalmers and Funeral Directors has seven members. Two are consumer representatives.

Prepaid funeral arrangements are governed by the Department of Insurance. Prepaid cemetery transactions are monitored by the Banking Commissioner.

## ❖ Prepaid Cemetery and Funeral Funds

Although statutes indicate that cemeteries are to be run by not-for-profit corporations, the funeral conglomerates are moving into the Oklahoma cemetery business. As of this writing, SCI owns at least six Oklahoma cemeteries. For a chilling description of the tactics used by the Loewen Group in trying to purchase a Ponca City cemetery from an International Order of Odd Fellows (IOOF) chapter over local objection, be sure to read Chapter 14. What magic permits a company beholden to shareholders to pull this off? A nonprofit "shell" is set up for the purpose of ownership. The nonprofit contracts with the for-profit company to manage the cemetery. *Voilá!*

When purchased preneed, 65% of the retail price of an outer burial container and 110% of the wholesale cost of other *cemetery* merchandise (*i.e.,* markers) must be placed in **trust**, although "**constructive delivery**"—a certificate saying it's in the warehouse—can avoid this requirement. A **refund** would be nearly impossible if you were to change your mind or move. There is no trusting requirement for cemetery services. 10% of lot prices must go to perpetual care. An annual **report** must be made to the banking commissioner. Cemeteries run by religious and benevolent organizations are exempt from these requirements.

Anyone with a high school diploma or equivalent may be hired by a funeral establishment as a telemarketer for selling preneed *funeral* plans. The telemarketer must have a permit from the Department of Insurance and pass a test of Oklahoma rules and laws. No such requirements exist for cemetery sales people.

10% may be pocketed up-front by the seller of preneed *funeral* plans. The balance of the funds must be placed in an insured **trust** fund. Sellers may withdraw up to 1.37% a year for administration. An annual **report** to the commissioner is required.

A consumer may **cancel** a funeral contract and claim a **refund** of the "net value"—money paid plus **interest,** less the 10% "commission" and administrative fees. For a $5,000 prepaid funeral, you would get back—after five years—only about $300 more than you paid. If 100% had been placed in trust, the value of the plan would be nearly $1,000 more in five years (assuming a 5% interest rate), even permitting the 1.37% administrative fee.

Those selling preneed funeral arrangements must supply a **bond** or letter of credit in the amount of $300,000 or 15% of the funds collected, whichever is less. Fifteen percent is hardly adequate protection against default.

## ❖ Restrictive Casket Sales

This heading shows up in only seven state chapters: Alabama, Georgia, Idaho, Louisiana, Oklahoma, South Carolina, and Virginia.

For years, caskets have been the major profit-maker for an undertaker, and mark-up on caskets was often 500-700% or more. As word leaked out about actual casket costs, some entrepreneurs saw an opportunity to cut the price and still make a "fair" profit, knowing that consumers were growing resentful. In the mid '90s, the retail casket business was born. Although I certainly support a free-market concept, I—for one—didn't think the public would shop anywhere but at a funeral home for a casket. Boy, was I wrong! The retail casket market is exploding, and consumers are now saving thousands of dollars on over-night delivery of attractive, well-made, quality caskets that are available from sources all around the country, when casket prices in their area are too high.

The Federal Trade Commission encourages this, permitting consumers to purchase from a funeral home *only* those goods and services wanted. As of 1994, it forbids a funeral home from charging a handling fee if a consumer purchases an item or service elsewhere.[1] The FTC does

---

[1] Funeral homes with nearby casket stores have been dropping their casket prices and upping their service charges to offset the loss. Others offer a discounted package if you purchase the casket from the funeral home. The National Casket Retailers Association has filed a complaint with the FTC charging that falsely inflated service charges that are conditionally discounted later are hiding the illegal handling fee.

not address who may sell a casket, but it has very specific language that does oblige a funeral home to accept a casket provided by the consumer.

When Stone Casket Company—an Oklahoma City casket distributor—began losing funeral home customers to the manipulative tactics of other distributors, the folks there decided to start selling caskets directly to the public. Didn't that make the "good ol' boys" hoppin' mad! What to do? The state funeral board filed a restraining order, and the store was forced to close—temporarily.

Seems that the statutory definition of a "funeral director" in Title 59 § 396.2 -2.(d) indicates that funeral directors sell funeral service merchandise. Well, of course. The statute goes on to define "funeral service merchandise or funeral services" as "those products and services normally provided by funeral establishments." If one were to ask what *normal* was 100 years ago (when local artisans made the caskets and a group of women came in to lay out the dead), it would be very different from what is in practice today. Do Oklahoma legislators have some special gift of foresight indicating that Oklahoma citizens will no longer tolerate change? The funeral industry certainly didn't want change, however. Citing this statute, the Funeral Board decided that **only** licensed funeral directors could sell funeral merchandise.[2]

Outer burial boxes sold by cemeteries are exempted from "funeral service merchandise." And the law is not being applied to wholesalers and distributors of caskets, even though they are not specifically exempt. So, someone in Oklahoma must be aware that it doesn't take any special training, knowledge, or skill to sell a box (although hiding or disparaging the inexpensive ones seems to be a prevalent "skill"). A casket is, after all, just a fancy box—a jewel box, to be more exact, according to my unabridged dictionary.

If one were going to enforce this restrictive *funeral merchandise* law, it wouldn't be fair to apply it selectively, would it? Wouldn't that also mean the corner stationery store may no longer sell guest books or

---

[2] One is tempted to offer the Funeral Board a lesson in logic. A simple example serves the purpose: All Catholics are Christians, but not all Christians are Catholics. All funeral directors sell caskets, but must all caskets be sold by funeral directors?

thank-you cards? What about burial clothing? And funeral flowers? Or the flag-case to hold a veteran's flag?

Protected—they thought—by something as basic as the Oklahoma constitution, Stone Casket took the case to court. The Oklahoma constitution states: "Perpetuities and monopolies are contrary to the genius of a free government, and shall never be allowed . . ." and it protects the right of "all persons . . . the enjoyment of the gains of their own industry." The judge agreed. The Funeral Board—behaving more like an industry patsy than a protector of consumers—appealed. Stone Casket Company is still waiting for its right to enjoy the gains of its industry.

Clearly, any restriction on who may sell caskets or other funeral supplies is a restraint of trade that subverts the FTC's provision specifically permitting consumers to purchase from the funeral provider *only* the goods and services desired. Until legislators get down to business and change the laws or the Funeral Board changes its interpretation, you may want to order your casket from another state via the internet or get directions for building your own:

**www.funerals.org/famsa/caskets.htm**

Or call Catskill Casket Co. in East Meredith, New York: 888-531-5151. Joe White, a minister, and his wife Gail, a teacher, ship affordable caskets for overnight delivery anywhere in the country. They'll be glad to send you a brochure of their casket selection or refer you to another retailer if they don't carry what you want.

## ❖ Consumer Concerns

- The death rate in Oklahoma can support approximately 133 full-time mortuaries; there are, however, 350. Funeral prices tend to be higher in areas where there are "too many" funeral homes.
- The laws should be amended to more readily permit church groups and others—when embalming is not desired—to care for the dead.
- Retail casket sales should be permitted. (High school graduates, by the way, may sell caskets preneed via telephone, as long as they are hired by a funeral director to do so.)
- Laws should require cemeteries to repurchase an unwanted lot at the original selling price plus 50% of the difference between that and current market price.

- All prepaid funeral and cemetery money (100%) should be placed in trust. If an elderly parent needed to move to another state—perhaps to be cared for by an adult child—a more reasonable amount would be available.
- Preneed funeral consumers should get annual reports indicating the institution of deposit and value (purchase price plus interest) of all prepaid funeral monies. Such documents could be important to survivors who otherwise might not know about prepaid accounts. Annual reporting is likely to enforce the trusting requirement.
- There is insufficient statutory provision to protect consumers against default of prepaid funeral agreements if funds were never put in trust. A guarantee fund should be established.
- There is no requirement that when merchandise is selected on a guaranteed-price, preneed agreement that a clear description is given and that merchandise of equal quality and construction must be substituted if the original item selected is not available. Survivors should approve any substitution.
- Until better preneed laws are passed that increase trusting and include adequate provisions for substitution, transfer and cancellation, it is probably a *terrible* idea to prepay for a funeral.
- Identification and tagging of the body at the place of death before removal should be required.
- There is no requirement that low-cost caskets be included in any display.
- There is no restriction on taking a mark-up on cash advance items nor any requirement to disclose how much it is if a mark-up is taken. Consumers may wish to request an invoice for such charges.
- There is no law that allows you to state your funeral preferences or for naming a designated agent to make your final arrangements. In situations where you are estranged or distant from next-of-kin, this could be important.
- The ethical standards for funeral directors need to be well-defined and expanded. See Appendix.
- The procedures for handling funeral complaints seem totally inadequate. Initially, only one funeral board member, along with the executive secretary, examine the complaint to determine if the complaint should be referred to the full board. According to Rule 235:10-9-5, "After a complaint has been filed, all interested persons are prohibited from discussing the complaint with any member of the Board or the hearing officer, if one has been designated." If one of the consumer representatives was not the initial investigating

board member, a complainant presumably may not contact the consumer rep in an effort to bring the complaint before the full board. "Resolutions" of complaints do not require the consent of the complainant. In Vermont, one complainant felt the penalty (a written apology while denying any wrong-doing) was little more than a tap on the wrist, when a much more severe punishment was probably merited. The funeral director had lied and used scare tactics to manipulate the family's choices.

• The FTC Funeral Rule should be adopted by reference to make it more enforceable in this state.

### ❖ Miscellaneous Information

• The educational requirements for becoming a funeral director/embalmer in Oklahoma are: an associate's degree (60 credits or about 2 years) in mortuary science, a passing grade of 75% or better on state written and oral exams, and one year of apprenticeship.

• Crematories are licensed by the Department of Health. A funeral director's license is not required to operate a crematory.

• Medical examiners are appointed, not elected.

### ❖ Nonprofit Funeral Consumer Information Societies

Although there are no FAMSA-affiliated funeral-planning societies in Oklahoma as of this writing, you may check the internet directory—**www.funerals.org/famsa**—or call the national office to see if any have since been started: 1-800-765-0107. Or let the FAMSA office know if you are willing to help start such a society. The FAMSA office may have a limited list of ethically-priced mortuaries in Oklahoma. You may also check with the Memorial Society of North Texas: 800-371-2222.

~❖~

*This chapter was sent for review to the Oklahoma Department of Banking, the Department of Insurance, the Department of Public Health, and the State Funeral Board. No response was received.*

# In Oregon

*Please refer to Chapter 8 as you use this section.*

Persons in Oregon may care for their own dead. The legal authority to do so is found in:

*Title 97.120 (2) A majority of persons within the first applicable listed class among the following listed classes that is available at the time of death or, if there is no majority, the eldest willing and able member of that class, in the absence of actual notice of a contrary direction by the decedent . . . or actual notice of opposition by completion of a written instrument by a majority of the members or the eldest willing and able member of a prior class, may direct any lawful manner of disposition . . . : (a) The spouse of the decedent. (b) A son or daughter of the decedent 18 years of age or older. (c) Either parent of the decedent. (d) A brother or sister of the decedent 18 years of age or older. (e) A guardian of the decedent at the time of his death. (f) A person in the next degree of kindred to the decedent. (g) The personal representative of the estate of the decedent. (h) The person nominated as the personal representative of the decedent in the decedent's last will. (i) A public health officer.*

Written wishes of the decedent or a prearranged funeral can override the above.

## ❖ Death Certificate

A report of the death must be filed with (or mailed to) the registrar within 24 hours by the person having custody of the body. The form will be supplied by the registrar (or a funeral director on weekends).

The family doctor or a local medical examiner will supply and sign the death certificate within 48 hours, stating the cause of death. The remaining information must be supplied, typewritten or in black ink. Do not use a felt-tip pen; the information must carry through to the fourth copy. The death certificate must be filed with the county registrar within five days and (usually) prior to final disposition. There is a $7.00 charge for filing the death certificate.

### ❖ Fetal Death

A fetal death report is required when death occurs after 20 weeks of gestation, or when a weight of 350 grams, and must be filed as above. If there is no family physician involved, the local medical examiner must sign the fetal death certificate.

### ❖ Transporting and Disposition Permit

A body may be moved with the consent of a physician or medical examiner. The family member acting as the funeral director must fill in the parts under "disposition" on the first (white) page. The attached yellow-page carbon serves as a burial-transit permit. The fourth (green) copy is retained by the cemetery or crematory.

An identification tag—a round metal disc—is required. The tag must be attached to the body receptacle and remain with the body throughout final disposition. The identification number must be recorded on the upper left-hand corner of the death certificate. During working weekday hours, the identification tag can be obtained from the county registrar. The person obtaining the tag must sign line *20a* on the certificate of death. If death has occurred when it would be unwise to wait for the next working day, one of the tags assigned to a funeral home will be needed. In that case the funeral service licensee must sign line *20a* and will be billed the $7.00 charge for filing the death certificate.

### ❖ Burial

Check with the county clerk for local zoning laws regarding home burial. There are no state burial statutes or regulations with regard to depth. A sensible guideline is 150 feet from a water supply and at least two feet of earth on top.

Before burial, the person in charge must sign the burial-transit permit and return it within ten days to the registrar of the county in which death occurred.

### ❖ Cremation

No additional permit for cremation is needed. If a person has not authorized cremation prior to death, authorization by next-of-kin is usually required, and a pacemaker must be removed. The crematory will sign the burial-transit permit, which must then be returned to the registrar of the county in which death occurred.

## ❖ Other Requirements

Administrative rules for funeral service practitioners require that a body that will not reach its destination within 24 hours be embalmed, refrigerated, or placed in a sealed casket. Families caring for their own dead would not be bound by such a regulation,[1] but reasonable planning and weather should be considered.

Administrative rules also require: "No public or private funeral shall be held over the remains of any deceased unrefrigerated body . . . later than 24 hours after the death of such deceased body, unless such deceased body shall have first been embalmed by a licensed embalmer. If a public or private funeral service and/or public viewing is desired after the 24-hour period, the unembalmed body shall not be removed from refrigeration for longer than a total of six hours. No public or private funeral service or public viewing shall be held over the remains of an unwashed deceased human body." The regulation that requires bathing is another excuse to mandate charges consumers may not decline. While bathing may be desirable, it should not be required and certainly exceeds the authority of the board. Again, this is a regulation that applies to the funeral business, *not* to private families caring for their own dead.

If the person died of a contagious or communicable disease, the body must be embalmed. If religious custom prohibits embalming, a sealed casket must be used for shipment by common carrier.

## ❖ Medical Schools for Body Donation

Oregon Health Science University
School of Medicine
3181 SW Sam Jackson Park Rd.
Portland, OR 97201
503-494-7811 or 8302
Urgent need
Also serves Western State Chiropractic.

Cost to family: arterial embalming and transportation
Prior enrollment: not required
Over-enrollment: shared
Disposition: cremation; return of cremains by request
Body rejection: standard,* obesity

* autopsy, decomposition, mutilation, severe burn victim, meningitis, hepatitis, AIDS, and other contagious or communicable diseases

---

[1] The office of the state mortuary board contests this statement. However, the powers and duties of the board granted by statutory authority is limited to licensees and those in the business of funeral practice and does not extend to private citizens.

## ❖ Crematories

Ashland

Litwiller-Simonsen Crematory
1811 Ashland St., 97520
541-482-2816

Astoria

Hughes-Ransom Crematory
576 12th St., 97103-4182
503-325-2535

North Coast Crematory
1165 Franklin Ave., 97103
503-325-1611

Baker City

Eastern Oregon Pioneer Crem.
P.O. Box 726, 97814
541-523-3677

Bend

Cascade Crematory
P.O. Box 663, 97709
541-382-5552

Central Oregon Cremation Assn.
105 NW Irving, 97709
541-382-2471

Deschutes Memorial Gardens
63875 Nwy. 97N., 97708
541-382-5592

Brookings

Litty Funeral Directors
517 Railroad St., 97415
503-469-2752

Scantlin Crematory
2 Ross Rd., 97415
541-469-9797

Coos Bay

Ocean View Memory Gardens
1525 NW Ocean Blvd., 97420
541-267-7182

Corvallis

DeMoss-Durdan Garden Chapel
815 NW Buchanan, 97330
541-754-6255

Cottage Grove

Smith-Lund-Mills Crematory
123 S. 7th St., 97424
541-942-0185

Dallas

Sunset Crematory
287 SW Washington St., 97338
503-623-3286

Eugene

Chapel of Memories
3745 W. 11th Ave., 97402
541-687-1431

Lane Crematorium
1100 Charnelton St., 97401
503-484-1435

Musgrove Crematory
1152 Olive St., 97401
541-686-2818

Rest-Haven Crematorium
3986 S. Willamette St., 97405
541-345-8521

Florence

Siuslaw Valley Crematory
1675 First St., 97439
503-997-3416

Grants Pass

Chapel of the Valley Crematory
2065 Upper River Rd., 97526
541-479-7581

Hillcrest Crematory
141 NW -C- St., 97526
541-476-6868

Hull & Hull Funeral Directors
612 NW -A- St., 97526
541-476-4453

Gresham

Columbia Crematorium
520 W. Powell Blvd., 97030
503-665-2128

Hermiston

Hermiston Crematory
685 Hermiston Ave., 97838
541-567-6474

Klamath Falls

Eternal Hills Mem. Gardens
4711 Hwy. 39, 97603
541-884-3668

Klamath Cremation Service
2680 Memorial Dr., 97601
503-884-3456

Pyramid Cremations
444 Hillside Ave., 97601
541-882-2426

Lebanon

Central Linn Crematory
86 W. Grant St., 97355
541-258-2123

Lincoln City

Pacific View Mem. Gardens
P.O. Box 854, 97367
541-994-4562

Medford

Funeral Alternatives
550 Business Park Dr., 97504
541-779-2842

Hillcrest Memorial Park
2201 N. Phoenix Rd., 97504
541-773-6162

Siskiyou Memorial Park
2100 Siskiyou Blvd., 97504
541-283-1980

Myrtle Creek

Mt. View Crematory
428 N. Old Pacific Hwy., 97457
541-863-3148

Newport

Central Coast Crematorium
915 NE Yaquina Hts. Dr., 97365
541-265-2751

Portland

Caldwell's Cremation Service
20 NE 14th Ave., 97232
503-232-4111

Central Crematorium
2025 SE 10th Ave., 97214
503-232-1961

Little Chapel of the Chimes
430 N. Killingsworth St., 97217
503-283-1976

Oregon Crematory
1424 NE 80th Ave., 97213
503-252-5882

Portland Cremation Center
3605 SE 22nd Ave., 97202
503-736-1000

Portland Memorial
6705 SE 14th St., 97282
503-236-4141

River View Cemetery Assn.
8421 SW Macadam Ave., 97219
503-246-4251

Riverview Abbey Mausoleum
0319 SW Taylors Ferry Rd., 97219
503-244-7577

Ross Hollywood Chapel
4733 NE Thompson, 97213
503-281-1800

Wilhelm Crematory
6637 SE Milwaukie Ave., 97202
503-235-3103

Prineville

Prineville Heritage Crematory
199 E. 10th, 97754
541-447-5459

Reedsport

Lower Umpqua Crematory
2300 Frontage Rd., 97467
503-271-5550

Roseburg

Wilson's Chapel of Roses
965 W. Harvard Blvd., 97470
541-673-4455

Salem

City View Crematory
690 Hoyt St. S, 97302
503-363-8652

Springfield

Buell Chapel Crematorium
320 N. 6th St., 97477
541-747-4131

The Dalles

Win-Quatt Crematory
1100 Kelly Ave., 97058
541-296-3234

Tigard

Willamette Crematory
11831 SW Pacific Hwy., 97223
503-636-1206

Tillamook

Tillamook County Crematory
1414 3rd St., 97141
503-842-7557

Woodburn

Valley Crematorium
1050 N. Boones Ferry Rd., 97071
503-981-9501

Additional crematories may have been established in this state after the date of publication.

## ❖ State Governance

The Oregon State Mortuary and Cemetery Board has eleven members. Three are morticians, three are cemeterians, one is a crematory operator, and four are public members, one of whom must be a senior citizen.

Crematories are licensed, regulated, and inspected by the Mortuary and Cemetery Board. One does not need to be a funeral director to run a crematory.

## ❖ Prepaid Cemetery and Funeral Funds

Door-to-door or telephone solicitations are not permitted for preneed sales.

Of prepaid money for *cemetery merchandise*—markers and vaults—66⅔% must be placed in **trust.** A cemetery must post a $10,000 bond or letter of credit to protect this trust fund, a totally insufficient and piddley amount (although there is a consumer protection fund). "**Constructive delivery**" can avoid any trusting requirement and would make a **refund** impossible if you were to change your mind. Of course, all you'd get back anyway is the 66⅔% plus interest.

90% of a guaranteed-price *funeral* contract and 100% of a non-guaranteed funeral contract must be placed in **trust.** Presumably, any prepaid *cemetery services* must be trusted in like proportion. "Constructive delivery" of the casket can avoid the trusting requirement, which might be a real problem if you were to die in another state, for example. The service money could be transferred, but the other funeral director might be told to come pick up your casket.

An amount not to exceed 25% of the interest may be withdrawn each year for the expense of maintaining the account or for taxes. The amount in trust, plus interest, is fully **refundable** if the contract is not irrevocable. There is no provision for transfer of an irrevocable trust.

A Funeral and Cemetery **Consumer Protection Fund** is financed by a $5 assessment for each prepaid contract. Unfortunately, it is not available to anyone who prepaid prior to establishment of the fund in the 1980s. There have been no claims on this fund since its inception.

### ❖ Consumer Concerns

- The death rate in Oregon can support approximately 115 full-time mortuaries; there are 171 such establishments. Given the low density of population over a large geographic area, mortuary careers are not likely to be full-time work. Unfortunately, because of the low volume of business at some mortuaries, funeral prices will tend to be higher than elsewhere.
- Laws should require cemeteries to repurchase an unwanted lot at the original selling price plus 50% of the difference between that and current market price.
- There is no annual reporting requirement to the purchaser of prepaid funeral goods and services, paperwork that might be helpful to the family of a deceased to indicate prepayment and would help to "enforce" trusting requirements.

- There is no provision for an adequate description of funeral goods selected preneed nor for a substitution of equal quality if the selected item is no longer available at the time of death.
- In spite of the Consumer Protection Fund and until the Oregon laws are changed to eliminate constructive delivery, it is probably a *very unwise* idea to prepay for a funeral or any cemetery merchandise and services in this state, given the raw deal a consumer would get in trying to transfer or back out of such a purchase. Your own trust account in a bank will be safer.
- Identification and tagging of the body at the place of death before removal should be required, given the regular mix-ups that have been happening at chain-owned establishments with central prep facilities.
- The regulation requiring embalming or refrigeration after 24 hours should be eliminated, to avoid unnecessary charges for the first 48 hours or so. The regulation requiring embalming when death occurs from a contagious or communicable disease should be repealed. This is not only an offense to some religious groups, it puts the funeral professionals and possibly the environment at risk. Immediate disposition would be a more responsible option for *infectious* diseases.
- There is no provision either forbidding a mark-up on cash advance items or requiring the disclosure of how much the mark-up would be.
- There is no requirement that low-cost caskets be included in any display.
- Ethical standards should be expanded and clearly defined in order for valid consumer complaints to prevail.
- Complaint procedures seem unclear and inadequate, although the governing office says it is eager to work with consumers. The number there is 503-731-4040.
- The FTC Funeral Rule should be adopted by reference to carry more weight in this state, although the state says it is already being rigorously enforced.

## ❖ Miscellaneous Information

- Educational requirements for becoming a funeral practitioner: associate's degree, a state exam, and one year of apprenticeship. For embalmers: mortuary school, both the national and state exams, and one year of apprenticeship.

- Regulations require that "free" offers to veterans and others disclose all conditions and not be misleading (such as conditioning a "free" item on the purchase of another or marking up prices over the usual price before promoting a "discount").
- A body may not be detained before payment of the funeral bill.
- A person may indicate directions for disposition prior to death. There is case law precedence that such wishes will prevail.
- Medical examiners are physicians who are appointed to the position.

## ❖ Nonprofit Funeral Consumer Information Societies

These consumer groups are run mostly by volunteers. Consequently, contact information may change. If you have difficulty reaching a society or are interested in starting a society in your area, call the FAMSA office: 800-765-0107. Or check the internet directory—

**www.funerals.org/famsa**

Oregon Memorial Association
P.O. Box 649
Madras, OR 97741
541-475-5520 or   800-475-5520

~❖~

*This chapter was reviewed by the State Mortuary and Cemetery Board. It was also sent to the Health Division of Human Resources, but no response was received.*

# In Pennsylvania

*Please refer to Chapter 8 as you use this section.*

Persons in Pennsylvania may care for their own dead. One relevant law states:

> *Chapter 35 Title 450.501: The person in charge of interment or of removal of the dead body or fetal remains from the registration district shall file the death certificate with any registrar who shall be authorized to issue certified copies of such death.*

## ❖ Death Certificate

The family doctor, county coroner, or a local medical examiner will sign the death certificate stating the cause of death. The remaining information must be supplied, typewritten or in black ink. The death certificate must be filed with the local registrar within 96 hours of death and before final disposition.

## ❖ Fetal Death

A fetal death certificate is required for each fetal death that occurs after 16 weeks gestation. If there is no family physician involved, the local coroner must sign the fetal death certificate.

## ❖ Transporting and Disposition Permit

The local registrar will issue the authorization for disposition. The death certificate must be obtained first.

## ❖ Burial

Check with local municipalities for local zoning laws regarding home burial. The top of the coffin must be two feet below the natural surface of the earth. Although not mentioned, it is a good idea to pick a site that is at least 150 feet from a water supply. Pennsylvania law prohibits burial of the dead on any land draining into a stream which furnishes any part of the water supply of a municpality unless at least one mile from the city.

When burial is arranged, the family member in charge must sign the authorization for disposition and file the second copy with the Division of Vital Statistics within 10 days. The first copy is to be retained by the crematory, cemetery, property owner (if home burial), or the Humanity Gifts Registry.

## ❖ Cremation

The county coroner must receive notice prior to cremation and provided an opportunity to view the body if there are any questions. In the case of anticipated deaths, coroner authorization may be granted by telephone. There is a 24-hour wait before cremation. Most crematories insist that a pacemaker be removed, and authorization by next-of-kin usually is required. The crematory will file the disposition authorization with the local registrar.

## ❖ Other Requirements

Under the standards of practice and professional responsibilities of funeral directors, the statutes require embalming or refrigeration (35°–40°) after 24 hours. So you're stuck with paying for one or the other when you use a funeral home. No such requirements are mentioned in the Public Health statutes, and no one's likely to be running around with a stop-watch when families are caring for their own dead. Weather and reasonable planning should be considered.

Embalming is required when death is due to amebiasis, anthrax, cholera, diphtheria, plague, poliomyelitis, scarlet fever, shigellosis, smallpos, typhoid fever, paratyphoid fever, salmonellosis "or other known or suspected communicable diseases," the worst possible circumstance under which to embalm.

## ❖ Medical Schools for Body Donation

One agency coordinates all body donations within the state.

Human Gifts Registry
130 S. 9th St.
Philadelphia, PA 19107
215-922-4440
Urgent need

Cost to family: transportation over $50, refrigeration over weekend
Prior enrollment: Preferred
Over-enrollment: shared
Disposition: cremation; return of cremains by request
Body rejection: autopsy, surgery, infectious diseases, embalming, emaciation, obesity, trauma

## ❖ Crematories

Allentown

Cedar Hill Memorial Park
1700 Airport Rd., 18103
610-266-1600

Greenwood Cemetery
2010 Chew St., 18104
610-434-8304

Athens

Tioga Point Crematory
802 N. Main St., 18810
717-888-8286 or
800-472-9938

Bala-Cynwyd

West Laurel Cemetery
215 Belmont, 19004
215-483-1122

Bridgeport

King of Prussia Crematory
805 DeKalb St., 19405
610-272-1773

Clarion

NW Penn. Crematory
330 Wood St., 16214
814-226-7738

Davidsville

Countryside Crematory
Rt. 403, 15928
814-479-4120

Erie

Cremation Services
620 W. 10th St., 16502
814-454-4551

Erie Cemetery Crematory
2116 Chestnut St., 16502
814-459-2463

Harrisburg

E. Harrisburg Cemetery
2260 Herr, 17109
717-233-6789

Johnstown

Forest Lawn Memorial Park
1530 Frankstown Rd., 15902
814-535-8258

Lancaster

Greenwood Cemetery
719 Highland Ave., 17603
717-392-1224

Lansdale

Lansdale Crematory
Derstine/Cannon Ave., 19446
215-855-3314 FH

Lewistown

Hoenstine Crematory
75 Logan St., 17044
717-248-8311

Media

Cremation Specialist
Monroe & Baker, 19063
610-532-2308

New Castle

De Carbo Crematory
3000 Wilmington Rd., 16105
412-658-4711

Philadelphia

Chelten Hills Cemetery
1701 E. Washington, 19138
215-548-2400

Philadelphia Crematories
5301 Tacony St., 19137
215-533-2223

Sunset Memorial Park
P.O. Box 11508, 19116
215-673-0572

Pittsburgh

Allegheny Cemetery
4734 Butler St., 15201
412-682-1624

Homewood Cemetery
Dallas/Aylesboro, 15217
412-421-1822

Penn. Cremation Society
2630 W. Liberty Ave., 15216
412-531-4000

Pittsburgh Cremation Service
147 Cemetery Ln., 15237
412-931-1317

Tennessee Cremation Service
2630 W. Liberty Ave., 15216
412-531-4000

Plymouth Meeting

Geo. Washington Mem. Park
Stenton & Butler, 19462
215-828-1417

Reading

Am. Burial & Cremation
247 Penn St., 19601
610-374-4505 or
(in PA) 800-328-1307

Charles Evans Cemetery
1119 Center, 19601
610-372-1563

Henninger Crematory
229 N. 5th St., 19601
610-373-4500

Robinson Township

Tri-state Cremation Service
Bx 15551, Moon Run, 15244
412-787-1800

Saxonburg

Fox Crematory
410 W. Main St., 16056
412-352-1133

Schaeferstown

Con O Lite Vault & Crematory
P.O. Box 158, 17088
717-949-3280

Sharon Hill

Mount Lawn/Lincoln Memorial
84th & Hook Rd., 19079
610-729-8222

Somerton

Sunset Memorial Park
County Line Rd., 19116
215-673-0572

Southampton

Delaware Valley Crematory
Street & 2nd, 18966
215-357-1101

State College

Oakwood Crematory
2401 S. Atherton St., 16801
814-237-0259

Stroudsburg

HG Smith Crematory
Dereher Ave., 18360
717-420-9599

Sunbury

Pomfret Manor Cemetery
900 Packer St., 17801
717-286-1741

Uniontown

Silbaugh Vault Co.
542 Morgantown Rd., 15401
412-437-3002

Upper Darby

Montrose Cemetery
8504 W. Chester Pk., 19082
610-789-2988

Warwick

American Cremation Service
1859 Stout Dr., 18974
215-443-7171

Washington

Washington Cemetery
498 Park Ave., 15301
412-225-1040

Waynesboro

Cumberland Valley Crem.
50 S. Broad St., 17268
717-762-2811

West Chester

Ferris Cremation Service
899 Fernhill Rd., 19380
610-692-3868

Wilkes-Barre

Maple Hill Crematory
68 E. St. Mary Rd., 18702
717-823-2614

York

Heffner Crematory
1551 Kenneth Rd., 17404
717-767-1551

There may be additional crematories established in this state after the date of publication.

## ❖ State Governance

The Pennsylvania State Board of Funeral Directors has nine members. Two are public representatives.

Cemeteries are supposedly regulated by the Real Estate Commission. Other than environmental compliance, crematories are not regulated in Pennsylvania.

## ❖ Prepaid Cemetery and Funeral Funds

Other than a requirement to put 15% of lot sales into the perpetual care fund, there are apparently no consumer protection laws for *cemetery* transactions. One reference book I have suggests that 70% of the retail price for cemetery merchandise and services must be placed in **trust**, but "**constructive delivery**" can bypass the trusting requirement.

100% of prepaid *funeral* funds are to be placed in **trust**—in a bank, savings and loan, or trust company—along with accumulated **interest**. The seller must make a **report** of all such agreements to the Funeral Board within 90 days.

## ❖ Consumer Concerns

- The death rate in Pennsylvania can support approximately 511 full-time mortuaries; there are, however, 1,845. Funeral prices tend to be higher in areas where there are "too many" funeral homes.
- Laws should require cemeteries to repurchase an unwanted lot at the original selling price plus 50% of the difference between that and current market price.
- Cemetery transactions should be regulated, with protection for prepaid merchandise and services. Consumers should be entitled to a full refund plus interest.
- Although Pennsylvania requires 100% of prepaid funeral money to be put in trust, preneed funeral consumers should get an annual report indicating the institution of deposit and value (purchase price plus interest) of all these funds. Such documents could be important to survivors who might not know about prepaid accounts otherwise. Embezzlement of funds that never made it into trust accounts has already happened in Vermont, Colorado, Massachusetts, and—yes—Pennsylvania, as well as other states. This reporting would be an additional discouragement.
- There is insufficient statutory provision to protect consumers against default of prepaid funeral agreements if funds were never put in trust. A guarantee fund should be established.
- There is no statutory provision to allow for the transfer of an irrevocable funeral account should a person move or want to change which funeral home to use. There is no provision for refund of revocable trusts.
- When a prepaid funeral policy specifies particular merchandise, there is no protection for consumers if that item is no longer available. Consumers should be guaranteed a substitution of equal quality and design that meets the approval of survivors.
- Until the preneed laws have been improved, it is probably a *terrible* idea to prepay for a funeral or any cemetery merchandise and services in Pennsylvania.
- There is no requirement that low-cost caskets be included in a casket display.
- There is no restriction on taking a mark-up on cash advance items nor a requirement to disclose the extent of any mark-up taken.
- Identification and tagging of the body at the place of death before removal should be required.

- The embalming or refrigeration requirement should be changed to 72 hours or eliminated—to permit greater family choice. At 24 hours, it allows a funeral home to make an additional and unnecessary charge, even for the most minimal of arrangements. There has been no public health problem in the states without such a requirement.
- The statute requiring embalming when death involves communicable diseases should be repealed. Not only will the funeral staff and possibly the public health be at risk, such a requirement does not acknowledge religious or personal objections to embalming. The state should also distinguish between "communicable" and "contagious." Requiring immediate disposition is appropriate for contagious or infectious diseases.
- There is no law that allows you to state your funeral preferences or for naming a designated agent to make your final arrangements. In situations where you are estranged or distant from next-of-kin, this could be important.
- The ethical standards for funeral directors need to be defined and expanded. See Appendix.
- Although there is a requirement that funeral agreement forms comply with the FTC Rule, Pennsylvania has not adopted any of the other provisions of the Funeral Rule, limiting the state's authority to enforce consumer protection under the Rule. Indeed, a 1997 visit to 67 Philadelphia-area funeral homes by the FTC found that 19 (almost 30%) did not offer price information in a timely way and therefore were not in compliance with the federal regulations.

## ❖ Miscellaneous Information

- Educational requirements for becoming a funeral director in Pennsylvania: two years of college plus one year of mortuary college, a state exam and the national exam, and a minimum of one year of internship after college.
- Funeral complaints may be filed with the Professional and Occupational Affairs Complaint Office, 800-822-2113 (PA) or 717-787-8503. Or with the Bureau of Consumer Protection in the Attorney General's Office, 717-787-9707.
- Inquiries regarding the interment, transportation, and disinterment of dead bodies and fetal remains may be directed to the Division of Vital Records at 724-656-3121.
- Coroners are elected (or appointed) and need not be physicians. Many are funeral directors.

- It is "unlawful to erect or establish any slaughter house, manure or bone dust factory, soap factory, distillery or tannery within two hundred yards" of a cemetery.

## ❖ Nonprofit Funeral Consumer Information Societies

These consumer groups are run mostly by volunteers. Consequently, contact information may change. If you have difficulty reaching a society or are interested in starting a society in your area, call the FAMSA office: 800-765-0107. Or check the internet directory—

**www.funerals.org/famsa**

Erie

Memorial Society of Erie
Box 3495, 16508-3495
814-456-4433

Harrisburg

Mem. Soc. Greater Harrisburg
1280 Clover Ln., 17113
717-564-8507

Philadelphia

Mem. Soc. of Greater Philadelphia
2125 Chestnut St., 19103
215-567-1065

Pittsburgh

Pittsburgh Memorial Society
605 Morewood Ave., 15213
412-621-4740

State College

Memorial Society of Central PA
780 Waupelani Dr. Ext., 15801
814-237-7605

~❖~

*This chapter was reviewed and corrected by the Pennsylvania Department of Health, and minor corrections were made for the Funeral Board, but staff for both agencies did not want to give the impression that the Department or Board "approved" the chapter. This chapter was also sent to the Real Estate Board.*

Apparently, the Real Estate Board—which controls cemeteries—has no interest in what Pennsylvania consumers will be reading on these topics. No response was received.

# In Rhode Island

*Please refer to Chapter 8 as you use this section.*

Persons in Rhode Island may care for their own dead. The legal authority to do so is found in:

*Title 23-3-18 Permits. The funeral director, his duly authorized agent or person acting as such, who first assumes custody of the dead body or fetus shall prepare a burial-transit permit prior to final disposition.*

*Title 23-4-10 Disposition of deceased bodies. The office of state medical examiners shall, after any postmortem examination or autopsy, promptly release the deceased body to the relatives or representatives of the deceased.*

There are no other statutes that might require you to use a funeral director.

## ❖ Death Certificate

The family doctor will furnish and sign the death certificate "immediately" (or a medical examiner within 48 hours), stating the cause of death. The remaining information must be supplied, typewritten or in black ink. The death certificate must be filed with the local registrar within seven days.

## ❖ Fetal Death

A fetal death report is required when death occurs after 20 weeks of gestation. If there is no family physician involved when a death occurs, the local medical examiner must sign the fetal death certificate.

## ❖ Transporting and Disposition Permit

The funeral director or person acting as such prepares the burial-transit permit.

## ❖ Burial

Check with the county or town registrar for local zoning laws regarding home burial. There are no state burial statutes or regulations with regard to depth. A sensible guideline is 150 feet from a water supply and three feet of earth on top.

## ❖ Cremation

A cremation permit from the medical examiner is required. There may be a charge of no more than $20 for this. There is a 24-hour waiting period prior to cremation unless the deceased died of a contagious or infectious disease. Authorization by next-of-kin is usually required, and a pacemaker must be removed.

## ❖ Other Requirements

A body held by a funeral home must be embalmed or refrigerated within 48 hours of death. Rhode Island has no other requirements controlling the time schedule for the disposition of unembalmed bodies. Weather and reasonable planning should be considered.

If the person died of a contagious or communicable disease, the doctor in attendance should be consulted.

## ❖ Medical Schools for Body Donation

Brown University
Division of Biology & Medicine
Providence, RI 02912
401-863-3355
   863-1000, after hours
Moderate need

Cost to family: no set policy
Prior enrollment: required
Over-enrollment: not shared
Disposition: cremation; cremains returned by request
Body rejection: handled on a case-by-case basis

## ❖ Crematories

Central Falls

  Moshassuck Cemetery
  978 Lonsdale Ave., 02063
  401-723-1087

East Greenwich

  Bayside Cremation Service
  02818
  401-884-5050

East Providence

  East Bay Crematory
  901 Broadway, 02914
  401-438-1135

Greenville

  Blue Hills Crematory
  2 Church St., 02828
  401-949-0180

No. Scituate

   Cremation Service
   P.O. Box 216, 02857
   401-934-2276

Scituate

   Winfield & Sons Funeral Home
   Rte. 116, 02857
   401-647-5421

No. Smithfield

   Cremation Service of NE
   P.O. Box 216, 02857
   401-647-5421

Tiverton

   AA Cremation Service
   19 Rock St., 02878
   401-624-7627

Providence

   Swan Point Cemetery & Crematory
   585 Blackstone Blvd., 02906
   401-272-1314

Additional crematories may have been established in this state after the date of publication.

## ❖ State Governance

The Rhode Island Board of Funeral Directors and Embalmers has five members. Two are consumer representatives, and three are embalmers.

The majority of cemeteries in Rhode Island are operated by towns or churches, with towns having the ultimate authority to regulate burial grounds.

Crematories are licensed, regulated, and inspected by the Board of Health. One does not need to be a funeral director to run a crematory.

## ❖ Prepaid Cemetery and Funeral Funds

Sale of cemetery lots may not be for profit. 20% of the lot price must be put into the perpetual care fund.

100% of prepaid *funeral* money must be placed in **escrow**, with the **interest** and income to accrue.

If a purchaser defaults on installment payments, the seller may retain, as **liquidated damages,** 5% of the amount in escrow or $200—whichever is greater. If you have already paid $5,000 toward a $7,000 funeral contract, it would be better to cancel. Why? If a purchaser wishes to **cancel** a prepaid funeral contract, the seller may retain the greater of $200 or only 2.5% of the amount in escrow, not 5%. Of course, if you have arranged a modest exit and were planning on spending only $750 for an immediate cremation, the $200 cancellation or liquidation fee seems exorbitant.

A funeral contract may be **transferred**, apparently without penalty. If selected merchandise is not available at the time of death, the funeral service provider must **substitute** items equal or superior in quality of material and workmanship. If excess funds remain after calculating goods and services at today's prices, the remainder must be returned to the estate, unlikely given the high rate of funeral inflation.

### ❖ Consumer Concerns

- The death rate in Rhode Island can support approximately 38 full-time mortuaries; there are 127. Funeral prices tend to be much higher in an area where there are "too many" funeral homes.
- Laws should require cemeteries to repurchase an unwanted lot at the original selling price plus 50% of the difference between that and current market price, if the value has increased. If the value of the lot has decreased below the original selling price, the cemetery should repurchase the lot at 75% of the current worth.
- There is no annual reporting requirement to the purchaser of prepaid funeral goods and services, paperwork that might be helpful to the family of a deceased to indicate prepayment and would help to "enforce" trusting requirements.
- The statutes do provide for substitution of merchandise, but a clear description of such merchandise should be mandated with substitution to be made on approval of survivors.
- The penalty for cancelling or defaulting on a prepaid funeral plan should be eliminated.
- There is no state protection for consumers in the event that a provider defaults on a prepaid funeral. In other states that required 100% trusting, consumers were without funeral funds when funeral homes there went out of business.
- Until there is better protection for preneed funeral consumers, it is probably *unwise* to prepay for a funeral in Rhode Island.
- The 24-hour wait before cremation is totally unnecessary when survivors are in agreement and may be causing additional charges to families for "storage."
- The coroner or medical examiner's permit for cremation in the case of an *anticipated* death from natural causes is unnecessary and creates an additional burden and charge for families.

- Identification and tagging of the body at the place of death before removal should be required, given the regular mix-ups that have occurred at chain-owned establishments with central prep facilities.
- There is no requirement that low-cost caskets be included in any display.
- There is no provision either forbidding a mark-up on cash advance items or requiring disclosure of how much the mark-up would be.
- The standards for ethical, professional conduct should be strengthened. That would make it easier for a consumer to prevail when filing a valid complaint.
- Complaint procedures are unclear and inadequate. Fines are limited to $500, although up to six months in jail may result from violations. Reducing jail time and increasing the fine makes far more sense for the kind of mischief found in this industry.
- There is no law that allows you to state your funeral preferences or for naming a designated agent to make your final arrangements. In situations where you are estranged or distant from next-of-kin, this could be important.

## ❖ Miscellaneous Information

- Educational requirements for becoming a funeral director or embalmer: associate's degree, mortuary college, the national exam, a practical exam, and two years of internship (rather than the more typical one year). That's one way to get cheap help.
- No funeral home may operate on the grounds of or contiguous to a cemetery. Cemetery operators may not be in the business of funeral directing.
- Violation of the FTC Funeral Rule is referenced under unprofessional conduct.
- Medical examiners are physicians who are appointed to the job.
- The town in which death occurred shall see that a body is "decently buried," if the family is without funds. Costs may be recovered from the town of residence.

## ❖ Nonprofit Funeral Consumer Information Societies

These consumer groups are run mostly by volunteers. Consequently, contact information may change. If you have difficulty reaching a society or are interested in starting a society in your area, call the FAMSA office: 800-765-0107. Or check the internet directory—

**www.funerals.org/famsa**

Memorial Society of Rhode Island
119 Kenyon Ave.
East Greenwich, RI 02818

~❖~

*This chapter was sent for review to the Department of Health and the Board of Funeral Directors and Embalmers, but no response was received.*

# In South Carolina

*Please refer to Chapter 8 as you use this section.*

Persons in South Carolina may care for their own dead. The legal authority to do so is found in:

> *Title 40-19-190 (B): No public officer or employee, the official of any public institution, physician, surgeon, or any other person having a professional relationship with any decedent shall send or cause to be sent to any funeral establishment or to any person licensed for the practice of funeral service the remains of any deceased person without having first made due inquiry as to the desires of the next of kin and of the persons who may be chargeable with the funeral and expenses of the decedent. If any kin is found, his authority and directions shall govern except in those instances where the deceased made his prior arrangements in writing.*

There are no other statutes that might require you to use a funeral director.

## ❖ Death Certificate

The family doctor will supply and sign the death certificate within 48 hours, stating the cause of death. The remaining information must be supplied, typewritten or in black ink. The death certificate must be filed with the local registrar within five days.

## ❖ Fetal Death

A fetal death report is required when death occurs after 20 weeks of gestation or when the weight is 350 grams or more; the report must be filed as above. If there is no family physician involved, the local medical examiner must sign the fetal death certificate.

## ❖ Transporting and Disposition Permit

A body may be moved with the consent of a physician or medical examiner. The local registrar, deputy, or sub-registrar will issue the authorization for disposition. When death has occurred in a hospital, the subregistrar from whom to obtain the permit will be located there. If death occurred outside of an institution, the coroner of the county serves as sub-registrar. This authorization must be obtained within 72 hours of death and prior to final disposition of the body.

## ❖ Burial

Check with the municipal or county officials for local zoning laws regarding home burial. The top of the casket must be at least ten inches below the surface of the earth. A sensible guideline is 150 feet from a water supply, too.

## ❖ Cremation

There is a 24-hour wait prior to cremation unless the death was from infectious disease, in which case the waiting period can be waived by the doctor or medical examiner. A cremation permit must be obtained from the medical examiner in Charleston or Greenville County. A certified copy of the death certificate must accompany the burial-removal-transit permit when requesting this. There is no fee for the permit to cremate. Authorization by next-of-kin is usually required, and a pacemaker must be removed.

## ❖ Other Requirements

South Carolina has no other requirements controlling the time schedule for the disposition of unembalmed bodies. Weather and reasonable planning should be considered.

If the person died of a contagious or communicable disease, the doctor in attendance should be consulted.

## ❖ Medical Schools for Body Donation

Medical University of SC
Dept. of Anatomy
171 Ashley Ave.
Charleston, SC 29425
803-792-3521
Moderate to high need

Cost to family: none; transportation provided within state
Prior enrollment: required
Over-enrollment: not yet
Disposition: cremation; return of cremains by request and expense of family
Body rejection: standard,* other at discretion of university

University of South Carolina
School of Medicine
Dept. of Developmental Biol. & Anat.
Columbia, SC 29208
803-733-3369
803-777-7000
Donations exceed need at this time

Cost to family: none; transportation
  provided within state
Prior enrollment: required
Over-enrollment: not yet
Disposition: cremation; no return of
  cremains
Body rejection: standard,* previous em-
  balming

* autopsy, decomposition, mutilation, severe burn victim, meningitis, hepatitis, AIDS, and
other communicable or contagious diseases

## ❖ Crematories (All crematories are owned by funeral homes.)

Charleston

  John Libertos Crematory
  11 Cunnington Ave., 29405
  803-722-2555

Columbia

  Dunbar Cremation Service
  1527 Gervais St., 29202
  803-771-7990

  Shives Funeral Home/Crematory
  5202 Colonial Dr., 29203
  803-754-6290
  800-464-6008

Easley

  Robinson Cremation
  1st St., 29640
  803-859-4001

Greenville

  Mackey Cremation Service
  311 Century Dr., 29602
  864-271-8604

Greer

  Piedmont Funeral Service/Crematory
  101 Summit Dr., 29651
  803-439-3185

Hilton Head

  Island Funeral Home & Crematory
  4 Cardinal Rd., 29902
  803-681-4400

Lancaster

  Cauthen Funeral Home
  4100 W. Meeting St., 29720
  803-283-4141
  800-541-4211

Lexington

  Caughman-Harmon Funeral Home
  503 N. Lake Dr., 29072
  803-359-6118

Murrells Inlet

  Goldfinch Crematory
  11528 Hwy 17 Bypass, 29576
  803-651-3295

Myrtle Beach

  Bullard Funeral Home & Crematory
  701 65th St. & Somerset, 29578
  803-449-3341

  McMillon-Small Crematory
  P.O. Box 7506, 29577
  803-449-3396

North Charleston

J. Henry Stuhr Crematory
2180 Greenridge Rd., 29418
803-723-2524

Pickens

Dillard Funeral Home
123 N. Catherine St., 29671
803-878-6371

Spartanburg

J. F. Floyd Mortuary
235 N. Church St., 29304
803-582-5451

Summerville

James A. Dyal Funeral Home
303 S. Main St., 29483
803-873-4040

Tri-County Cremation Center
11000 Dorchester Rd., 29485
803-821-4888
800-432-0801

Additional crematories may have been established in this state after the date of publication.

## ❖ State Governance

The South Carolina Board of Funeral Service has eleven members. Two are consumer representatives. Six of the remaining members may be recommended to the governor by the South Carolina Funeral Directors Association. Three may be recommended by the South Carolina Morticians Association. One has to wonder what political pull it took to give one private trade organization twice as much clout as another in choosing government appointees. Only a funeral establishment may run a crematory in South Carolina

Preneed funeral transactions are regulated by the state Board of Financial Institutions and the statutes for which it is responsible appear to be far more consumer-friendly than those that were probably enacted at the behest of the funeral industry.

There is no longer a state cemetery board to enforce the cemetery laws. Complaints could be directed to the Attorney General's office.

## ❖ Prepaid Cemetery and Funeral Funds

Only the wholesale cost for prepaid *cemetery merchandise* such as vaults and markers must be placed into **trust**. There is no trusting requirement for prepaid services such as opening-and-closing or installation charges. The seller may withdraw from the **interest** sufficient funds to cover the cost of operating the trust; one has to wonder what that means, as there is little cost to letting money sit in the bank. **"Constructive delivery"** can bypass the trusting requirements.

Only after a cemetery contract is fully paid may a purchaser cancel the contract. And what can you expect to get back in a **refund**? Only the wholesale cost—if the item hasn't been "delivered"—and the interest, "less reasonable commission fees and administrative costs." Seems to me the initial profit was already too much of a "commission."

The cemetery must make an annual **report** to the Cemetery Board of all prepaid trust funds.

In-person or telephone solicitations for *preneed funeral sales* are not permitted. The consumer must invite the contact. There is no such restriction for cemetery sales, which surely will be noted by companies with funeral/cemetery combo operations.

Since 1989, 100% of all prepaid funeral money must be placed into **trust**. If a funeral director has sold a vault, 100% of that, too, must be placed into trust. The seller may withdraw 10% of the interest to cover administrative costs.

If a purchaser fails to make installment payments in a timely way, the seller may retain 10% of what was paid and cancel the arrangement for a refund of the remaining amount.

If the contract is a guaranteed-price agreement and selected merchandise is not available at the time of death, "the provider shall make available to the purchaser or his representative merchandise of equal or greater value. The purchaser or his representative is entitled to approve any **substitutions**." While the approval of survivors is commendable in this statute, there is a problem with the wording "equal or greater value." A casket that cost $750 ten years ago would probably cost $1,750 today. For a $750 "value" today, undertakers are likely to exhibit what many call their "welfare caskets." I am told by one of the examiners from the Finance Board that preneed contracts will include a detailed description of the merchandise selected and that there is an obligation to offer substitutes of equal quality and construction. But a consumer may need to be wary; "Windsor 482B" is not a sufficient casket description.

A purchaser may **cancel** a revocable contract at any time. The seller has a right to retain 10% of the earnings in the final year before termination. If the contract is irrevocable, the purchaser has a 30-day period in which it may be cancelled. After that, it may be **transferred**, but the seller may retain 10% of the contract amount and 10% of the earnings in the final year.

Preneed sellers must be licensed by the state and post a bond of $10,000 to $50,000. Only 224 of the 395 funeral homes are so licensed; many of the others are probably very small part-time funeral homes that do minimal preneed sales and that would find the cost of licensing and bonding not cost-effective.

A copy of each preneed contract must be mailed to the state on a form approved by the state. This year (1998) the Finance Department has found two unlicensed funeral homes selling preneed, with the money not in trust. "Consumers must educate themselves," said Barrett Swygert, the examiner.

### ❖ Restrictive Casket Sales

This heading shows up in only seven state chapters: Alabama, Georgia, Idaho, Louisiana, Oklahoma, South Carolina, and Virginia. (An Oklahoma state court determined in 1997 that restrictions on casket sales were illegal, but the ruling is now under appeal by the funeral board.)

For years, caskets were the major profit-maker for an undertaker, and mark-up on caskets was often 500-700% or more. As word leaked out about actual casket costs, some entrepreneurs saw an opportunity to cut the price and still make a "fair" profit, knowing that consumers were growing resentful. In the mid '90s, the retail casket business was born. Although I certainly support a free-market concept, I—for one—didn't think the public would shop anywhere but at a funeral home for a casket. Boy, was I wrong! The retail casket market is exploding, and consumers are now saving thousands of dollars on overnight delivery of attractive, well-made, quality caskets that are available from sources all around the country.

The Federal Trade Commission encourages this, permitting consumers to purchase from a funeral home *only* those goods and services wanted. As of 1994, it forbids a funeral home from charging a handling fee if a consumer purchases an item or service elsewhere.[1] The FTC does not address who may sell a casket, but it has very specific language that does oblige a funeral home to accept a casket provided by the consumer.

That must have made some of the good ol' boys hoppin' mad! With business-like calculation, new statutes were quietly passed, and one can almost imagine the unctuous placations used to justify them.

One of South Carolina's cremation statutes enacted in 1994—*§32-8-335: "Alternative container"*—requires, among other things, that a body be delivered to a crematory in a simple container and that a casket may not be required for cremation. But tacked onto one sentence, hidden in the middle of this otherwise very reasonable statute, are a dozen extra words that create a rather grandiose requirement: . . . *only a licensed funeral director or a funeral establishment may sell preneed and at-need merchandise.* And the statutory definition of "merchandise"? *"Funeral merchandise" means that personal property used in connection with the transportation, conduct of funerals, and final disposition of a dead human body, including, but not limited to, the receptacle into which the body is directly placed but does not mean mausoleum crypts, interment receptacles preset in a cemetery, and columbarium niches.*

Apparently, these statutes are being used to tell those who would like to open retail casket stores that they may not. ***But not limited to*** potentially gives a funeral home the corner on some other markets of ***personal property.*** Would that mean that the corner stationery store may no longer sell guest books or thank-you cards? What about burial clothing? And funeral flowers? Or the flag-case to hold a veteran's flag? If one is going to enforce this restrictive "merchandise" law, it wouldn't be fair to apply it selectively, would it?

Generally, burdensome laws will be sustained by the courts only if there are reasons of public health, vital statistics, or legal/criminal concerns. Just how does the state of South Carolina justify controlling who may

---

[1] Funeral homes with nearby casket stores have been dropping their casket prices and upping their service charges to off-set the loss. Others offer a discounted package if you purchase the casket from the funeral home. The National Casket Retailers Association has filed a complaint with the FTC charging that falsely inflated service charges which are conditionally discounted later are hiding the illegal handling fee.

sell a box—which is all a casket is. What if we call it a "hope chest" instead? Who may sell it then? No law against burying a body in a hope chest.

Until legislators come to the rescue for consumers and change the laws, you may want to order your casket from another state via the internet or get directions for building your own:

**www.funerals.org/famsa/caskets.htm**

Or call Catskill Casket Co. in East Meredith, New York: 888-531-5151. Joe White, a minister, and his wife Gail, a teacher, ship affordable caskets for overnight delivery anywhere in the country. They'll be glad to send you a brochure of their caskets or tell you about other retailers if they don't carry a casket you want.

## ❖ Consumer Concerns

- The death rate in South Carolina can support approximately 135 full-time mortuaries; there are, however, 395. Funeral prices tend to be higher in areas where there are "too many" funeral homes.
- 100% of all cemetery merchandise purchases should be placed in trust; a purchaser should have a full right of refund at any time, along with the interest. "Constructive delivery" should not be permitted.
- Laws should require cemeteries to repurchase an unwanted lot at the original selling price plus 50% of the difference between that and current market price.
- Annual reporting to the purchaser of prepaid funeral goods and services should be required. This paperwork might be useful to the family to indicate prepayment and would help to "enforce" trusting requirements.
- There is no state protection in the case of default of prepaid funeral monies.
- Until the South Carolina laws are changed to require 100% trusting of all money and interest for prepaid cemetery goods *and services* and adequate substitution of funeral merchandise that meets the approval of survivors, it is probably a *terrible* idea to prepay for these arrangements. Your own trust account in a bank will be safer.
- Only a funeral establishment may run a crematory in South Carolina, which is clearly a restraint of trade by the undertakers—to limit competition and low-cost choices. Cremation cost for a consumer is generally higher in the few states where independent crematories

are not allowed. In England and in many U.S. states, a crematory has been traditionally situated on or near cemetery grounds and run by a cemeterian. The knowledge and skills for running a crematory do not require apprenticeship as a funeral director, a college degree, nor training in embalming. Mortuary curricula do not generally cover the running of a crematory, nor is the operation of a crematory covered by the national funeral directors' exam, which further indicates the absurdity of this restriction. Therefore, South Carolina statutes should be amended to allow others to offer this service to the public. A requirement for training by the manufacturer would be consistent with the task involved and is, indeed, already included in the South Carolina statutes! One does not need to be a funeral director to be so trained.

- The coroner or medical examiner's permit for cremation in the case of an *anticipated* death from natural causes is totally unnecessary and creates an additional burden for families.

- Identification and tagging of the body at the place of death before removal should be required.

- There is no provision either forbidding a mark-up on cash advance items or requiring the disclosure of how much the mark-up would be. Consumers may wish to ask for a copy of the invoice for these items.

- There is no requirement that low-cost caskets be included in any display.

- Complaint procedures are unclear and inadequate. Funeral complaints that result in a "private reprimand" are confidential, even if a party is found guilty of violating a statute or regulation. That's one way to keep the mischief quiet.

- Provisions of Chapter 19 (re embalmers and funeral directors) do not apply to the burial of paupers, according to 40-19-240. One is hard-put to figure out what this meant unless perhaps one doesn't have to worry about "unprofessional conduct" with the poor.

- The standards for ethical, professional conduct should be strengthened. That would make it easier for a consumer to prevail when filing a valid complaint. (See Ethical Standards in the Appendix.)

- The FTC Funeral Rule should be adopted by reference to make it more enforceable in this state. Furthermore, the statutes that describe funeral pricing bundled with the casket price should be eliminated, as the FTC Rule requires itemization of funeral services.

## ❖ Miscellaneous Information

- Educational requirements for becoming a mortician: high school diploma, one year of mortuary school, two years of apprenticeship, and a passing exam grade. Two years of apprenticeship—instead of the more usual one year—provide a cheap source of labor for the industry.
- Preference is given to the written wishes of the deceased. A person may authorize his or her own cremation. You may wish to designate a deathcare agent for your final arrangements. In situations where you are estranged or distant from next-of-kin, this could be important.
- A crematory operator may not remove dental gold or any other item of value, including body parts.
- Coroners are elected and need not be MDs. Medical examiners are appointed and are licensed physicians.

## ❖ Nonprofit Funeral Consumer Information Societies

These consumer groups are run mostly by volunteers. Consequently, contact information may change. If you have difficulty reaching a society or are interested in starting a society in your area, call the FAMSA office: 800-765-0107. Or check the internet directory—
**www.funerals.org/famsa**

Columbia (has information for most of the state)

Memorial Society of the Midlands
1716 Ashford Ln., 29210
803-772-7054

~❖~

*This chapter was reviewed by the Department of Health—Vital Statistics, the Board of Funeral Service, and the State Board of Financial Institutions.*

# In South Dakota

*Please refer to Chapter 8 as you use this section.*

Persons in South Dakota may care for their own dead. The legal authority to do so is found in:

> *Title 34-25-25: . . . The funeral director or person acting as such who first assumes custody of a dead body shall file the death certificate.*

> *Title 34-26-14: The person charged by law with the duty of burying the body of a deceased person is entitled to the custody of such body . . . .*

> *Title 34-26-16: The duty of burying the body of a deceased person . . . devolves upon the persons hereinafter specified: (1) . . . the husband or wife; (2) . . . person or persons in the same degree nearest of kin to the decedent, being of adult age . . . .*

There are no other statutes that might require you to use a funeral director.

## ❖ Death Certificate

The doctor in attendance will supply and sign the death certificate within 24 hours, stating the cause of death. The remaining information must be supplied, typewritten or in permanent ink. Use a ballpoint pen; there are two copies. The death certificate(s) must be filed with the local registrar within three days (and prior to removal from the state if that is planned). If the doctor does not have a death certificate, one may be obtained from the local registrar.

## ❖ Fetal Death

A fetal death report is required when death occurs at a weight of 500 grams or more. If there is no family physician involved, the local coroner must sign the fetal death certificate.

## ❖ Transporting and Disposition Permit

The local registrar will issue the burial-transit permit. It must be filed with the registrar of the district in which disposition occurs.

## ❖ Burial

Check with the county or town registrar for local zoning laws regarding home burial. There are no state burial statutes or regulations with regard to depth. The common practice in South Dakota is six feet deep. The burial site should be 150 feet or more from a water supply. If burial is on private land, a map designating the burial ground must be recorded with the land records.

When burial is arranged, the family member acting as the funeral director must sign the burial permit and file the original with the registrar (department of health) within ten days. The third copy is retained by the cemetery. In the case of home burial, the county registrar may request this copy for recording.

## ❖ Cremation

There is a 24-hour wait prior to cremation; this will be waived when death is due to infectious disease. No additional permit for cremation is required. A pacemaker must be removed, and authorization by next-of-kin or agent is required if the deceased did not authorize cremation prior to death. The crematory will sign the permit for disposition, which then must be filed with the local registrar within ten days.

The authorizing agent must specify the planned disposition for the cremated remains. If disposition is not in a designated cemetery or public waterway, they may be scattered, buried, or stored on private property with the written consent of the owner.

## ❖ Other Requirements

South Dakota has no requirements controlling the time schedule for family disposition of unembalmed bodies as long as it is within a "reasonable" time. Weather and prudent planning should be considered.

The Board of Funeral Service has a regulation requiring embalming or refrigeration after 24 hours if disposition has not occurred. This would apply to any body in the possession of a mortician, but the Board of Funeral Service has no jurisdiction over private individuals, according to the Attorney General's office.

If the person died of a contagious or communicable disease, the doctor in attendance should be consulted.

## ❖ Medical Schools for Body Donation

University of South Dakota
Department of Anatomy
School of Medicine
Vermillion, SD 57069
605-677-5321 or
605-677-5141
If no answer, call 624-3932
Moderate need

Cost to family: arterial embalming*; transportation at 30¢ per mile each way if the university collects the body
Prior enrollment: not required
Over-enrollment: has not occurred
Disposition: cremation/burial in a local cemetery; return by request, at expense of the family
Body rejection: autopsy, trauma, organ donation, infectious diseases

*The gentleman who runs the body donation program is a retired funeral director and wants to "keep peace" with the morticians. Therefore, he feels they should at least get the first round of embalming business. "Besides, we usually have to travel long distances to get the bodies—" (and embalming would be required after 24 hours if in the possession of a mortician). He is aware that some funeral homes charge outrageous fees—in addition to the embalming fee—and says people should shop around. Survivors who are making arrangements with a mortuary should make clear, in writing, that you are requesting *arterial embalming only.* If any of the other funereal-type embalming procedures are used, the body will be unusable for medical study and will be rejected. I was told they would not accept a body from a family, although I could not find in the university's printed literature any requirement that the body had to be embalmed first or any restriction against who may deliver a body. Perhaps this is negotiable on a case-by-case basis.

## ❖ Crematories

Rapid City

Behrens Mortuary & Crematory
632 St. Francis, 57709
605-343-0145

Sioux Falls

Hills of Rest Memorial Park
300 Chapel Hill Rd., 57103
605-338-6551

Miller Funeral Home
507 So. Main St., 57102
605-336-2640

Sturgis

Black Hill Crematory
1440 Junction Ave., 57785
605-347-3986

Additional crematories may have been established in this state after the date of publication.

## ❖ State Governance

The South Dakota Board of Funeral Services has seven members, two of whom are consumer representatives. The Secretary of Health also serves on the board, making a total of eight.

Crematories are licensed and inspected by the Department of Health. One does not need to be a funeral director to run a crematory.

Most cemeteries in South Dakota are operated by municipalities. There is no cemetery board.

## ❖ Prepaid Cemetery and Funeral Funds

Cemeteries must not be run for-profit. If a cemetery is not a perpetual care cemetery, all printed material must state that fact. Otherwise, 20% of the lot or interment space price must be placed in perpetual care.

Only 70% of prepaid *cemetery* goods and services must be placed in **trust**. That would make it difficult to get a full refund on a vault, for example, if you changed your mind about body burial and were choosing cremation instead. In fact, there is no statutory provision for cancellation and refunds.

If the contract was for a guaranteed price, 85% of the cost for *funeral* goods and services purchased preneed must be placed in **trust**. If it was not at a guaranteed price, 100% must be placed in trust.

A purchaser, on 30 days notice, may **cancel** a preneed funeral contract. The amount of **refund** will be determined by what was placed in trust— either 85% or 100%—plus all **interest**.

Funeral directors and cemeteries must make an annual **report** to the state Board of Funeral Service for all preneed sales.

## ❖ Consumer Concerns

- The death rate in South Dakota can support approximately 27 full-time mortuaries; there are 135. However, given the low density of population over a vast geographic area, mortuary careers are not likely to be full-time work. Because of the low volume of business per mortuary, funeral prices will tend to be higher than elsewhere.

- Laws should require cemeteries to repurchase an unwanted lot at the original selling price plus 50% of the difference between that and current market price.
- Trusting laws for cemetery and funeral purchases should be increased to 100% for all contracts.
- There is no provision for transfer of irrevocable funeral contracts.
- There is no provision for an adequate description of funeral goods selected preneed nor for a substitution of equal quality and construction if the selected item is no longer available at the time of death. Substitution should be on approval of survivors.
- There is no annual reporting requirement to the purchaser of prepaid funeral goods and services, paperwork that might be useful to the family to indicate prepayment and would help to "enforce" trusting requirements.
- There is no state protection for consumers in case of default on prepaid funeral funds that were never put into trust.
- Until the preneed cemetery and funeral laws are improved, it is probably a *terrible* idea to prepay for a funeral in South Dakota.
- The regulations require that at least ten caskets be on display, but there is no requirement that low-cost caskets be included in that display.
- There is no provision either forbidding a mark-up on cash advance items or requiring the disclosure of how much the mark-up would be. Consumers may wish to request a copy of the invoice for these purchases.
- Identification and tagging of the body at the place of death before removal should be required.
- The standards for ethical, professional conduct should be strengthened. That would make it easier for a consumer to prevail when filing a complaint. (See Appendix.)
- Complaint procedures are unclear and inadequate. There is no provision for levying a fine when regulations or statutes are violated, only revocation of a license—something rarely done.
- The statutes provide that the Board of Funeral Services may comply or exempt themselves from the 1984 FTC Funeral Rule. A strange provision, indeed. The Funeral Rule should be adopted by reference.

## ❖ Miscellaneous Information

- Educational requirements for funeral service practitioner: two years (60 semester credits) of mortuary college, one year of traineeship, plus state and national exams.
- There is a statutory duty to comply with the disposition wishes of the decedent. You may want to designate a deathcare agent for your final arrangements. In situations where you are estranged or distant from next-of-kin, this could be important.
- Coroners are elected and are not usually physicians. The Department of Health may appoint death investigators—physicians and nurse practitioners who are trained in forensic pathology.

## ❖ Nonprofit Funeral Consumer Information Societies

These consumer groups are run mostly by volunteers. Consequently, contact information may change. If you have difficulty reaching a society or are interested in starting a society in your area, call the FAMSA office: 800-765-0107. Or check the internet directory—

**www.funerals.org/famsa**

Funeral Consumer Information Society of the Dakotas
HCR 66 Box 10
Lemmon, SD 57638
605-374-5336

~❖~

*This chapter was sent for review
to the South Dakota Board of Funeral Services,
but no response was received.*

# In Tennessee

*Please refer to Chapter 8 as you use this section.*

Persons in Tennessee may care for their own dead. The legal authority to do so is found in:

> *Title 68-3-502: (3b) The funeral director or person acting as such who first assumes custody of the dead body shall file the death certificate.*

> *Title 62-5-102 (b): Nothing herein shall be constituted to prevent or interfere with the ceremonies, customs, religious rites, or religion of any people, denomination, or sect, or to prevent or interfere with any church or synagogue from having their own committee or committees prepare human bodies for burial or to the families, friends or neighbors of deceased persons who prepare and bury their dead without charge.*

There are no other statutes that might require you to use a funeral director.

## ❖ Death Certificate

The family doctor or a local medical examiner will sign the death certificate within 48 hours, stating the cause of death. The remaining information must be supplied, typewritten or in unfading black ink. The death certificate must be filed with the local registrar of vital records within five days and usually before final disposition.

## ❖ Fetal Death

A fetal death report is required when death occurs after 22 weeks of gestation or when the weight is 500 grams or more. If there is no family physician involved, the local medical examiner must sign the fetal death report. The report must be filed with the Department of Health within ten days.

## ❖ Transporting and Disposition Permit

A body may be moved with the consent of a physician or medical examiner. The registrar where the death certificate is to be filed can issue a burial-transit permit for cremation or removal from the state if the death certificate is not yet complete. However, persons handling death arrangements without the use of a funeral director should try to obtain the death certificate before disposition.

## ❖ Burial

Family burial grounds are permitted. Check with the local registrar for zoning laws regarding home burial. There are no state burial statutes regarding depth. A sensible guideline is 150 feet from a water supply and at least two feet of earth on top.

## ❖ Cremation

While no additional permit for cremation is mandated by state law, a crematory will require you to obtain a permit from the registrar in the local county Health Department. Most crematories insist that a pacemaker be removed, and authorization from next-of-kin usually is required.

## ❖ Other Requirements

Tennessee has no other requirements controlling the time schedule for the disposition of unembalmed bodies. Weather and reasonable planning should be considered.

If the person died of a contagious or communicable disease, the doctor in attendance should be consulted.

## ❖ Medical Schools for Body Donation

East Tennessee State Univ.
Dept. of Anatomy & Cell Biol.
Quillen College of Medicine
Box 70582
Johnson City, TN 38614
615-929-6241 M-F, 8-5 or
615-929-4480
Moderate need

Cost to family: transportation beyond 30 mi. or if other than contract mortician
Prior enrollment: required
Over-enrollment: occasionally shared
Disposition: cremation/burial or scattering; return of cremains by request
Body rejection: standard*, under 18, embalming, over 200 lbs.

University of Tennessee
Knoxville, TN

Requests for information from this school have not been returned.

University of Tennessee
Department of Anatomy
875 Monroe Ave.
Memphis, TN 38163
901-448-5965 days, or
901-528-5500

Cost to family: transportation if not
  pre-enrolled
Prior enrollment: preferred
Over-enrollment: not happened
Disposition: cremation; return of cre-
  mains by request
Body rejection: standard*, obesity or
  emaciation

Meharry Medical College
1005 Todd Blvd.
Nashville, TN 37208
615-327-6308

Cost to family: transportation over
  $1/mi./200 mi. radius
Prior enrollment: not required
Over-enrollment: shared
Disposition: cremation; return of cre-
  mains by request
Body rejection: standard*, obesity

Vanderbilt Anatomical
  Donation Program
201 Light Hall
Nashville, TN 37232-0685
615-322-7948 (24 hrs.)
Low need at present but check

Cost to family: transportation beyond
  50 mi.
Prior enrollment: required
Over-enrollment: not yet
Disposition: cremation/burial; return
  of cremains by request
Body rejection: standard*

* autopsy, decomposition, mutilation, severe burn victim, infectious diseases, AIDS

❖ **Crematories** (All crematories are run by funeral directors.)

Bristol

  Heritage Crematory
  2223 Volunteer Pkwy., 37620
  615-764-7123

Hendersonville

  Cole & Garrett
  182 W. Main, 37075
  615-824-8605

Johnson City/Gray

  Snyder Memorial Gardens
  5913 Kinsport Hwy., 37615
  423-477-7911

Knoxville

  Highland Memorial Cemetery
  5315 Kingston Pike, 37919
  615-584-5890

  Holly Hills Mem. Pk./ FH
  Chapman Hwy./Simpson Rd.
  615-573-7177

Maryville

  East Tenn. Cremation Co.
  Rte. 8, Box 431, 37801
  615-970-2087

Memphis

Forest Hill Crematory
P.O. Box 34577, 38184
901-382-1000

Memphis Memorial Park
5668 Poplar Ave., 38117
901-767-8930

Additional crematories may have been established in this state after the date of publication.

## ❖ State Governance

The Tennessee State Board of Funeral Directors and Embalmers has seven members. There is one consumer representative. Members must constitute a geographic representation, at least one must be 60 years of age or older, and at least one must be of a racial minority.

Crematories must be affiliated with a licensed funeral home.

Preneed funeral arrangements, including those for cemeteries, are regulated by the commissioner of Commerce and Insurance.

## ❖ Prepaid Cemetery and Funeral Funds

20% of lot purchase price and 10% of the cost for mausoleum, crypt, and niche space must be put into an endowment care fund. Cemeteries may charge a maintenance fee ("memorial care") for markers, which will be at the same rate for all regardless of where the marker was purchased. Cemeteries must be maintained "so as to reflect respect for the memory of the dead in keeping with the reasonable sensibilities of survivors."

Unless "delivered," 120% of the wholesale cost of *cemetery* goods and services must be placed in trust when sold preneed. A certificate of delivery (with storage in a warehouse, for example) can bypass the trusting requirement. This is called "**constructive delivery**," and a refund is not likely should you change your mind. Cemetery merchandise would include markers but not vaults, which must be sold by a funeral director.

In the case of default by a purchaser, a cemetery may retain all payments as **liquidated damages**.

Burial *insurance* may not name a specific funeral home as the provider.

Discounted preneed arrangements are not permitted.

100% of prepaid *funeral* money must be placed in **trust** in a federally insured institution. The would include money for the purchase of vault.

Even if the prepaid arrangement is irrevocable, funds may be **transferred** to any licensed funeral home. Revocable arrangements may be **cancelled** with full return of payments and **interest**.

## ❖ Consumer Concerns

- The death rate in Tennessee can support approximately 207 full-time mortuaries; there are, however, 436. Funeral prices tend to be higher in areas where there are "too many" funeral homes.

- Laws should require cemeteries to repurchase an unwanted lot at the original selling price plus 50% of the difference between that and current market price, if the value has increased. If the value of the lot has decreased below the original selling price, the cemetery should repurchase the lot at 75% of the current worth.

- All prepaid funds for cemetery services and merchandise should be placed into trust with a full right of refund with interest. "Constructive delivery" should not be permitted. Until the laws are changed, it is probably a *terrible* idea to prepay for these cemetery items.

- When a prepaid funeral policy specifies particular merchandise, there is no protection for consumers if that item is no longer available. Consumers should be guaranteed a substitution of equal quality and design, with an accurate description on the original agreement. Survivors should approve any substitution.

- Preneed funeral consumers should get an annual report indicating the institution of deposit and value (purchase price plus interest) of all prepaid funeral monies. Such documents could be important to survivors who might not know about prepaid accounts otherwise and are a deterrent against default. Although the original preneed contract must name the institution where monies will be deposited, the seller is free to move the funds without notice.

- There is no statutory provision to protect consumers against default of prepaid funeral agreements if funds were never put in trust.

- Without an adequate provision for substitution of funeral merchandise and better reporting and protection for trust funds, it is probably an *unwise* idea to prepay for funeral services in this state.

- Re-use of a casket or any portion of a casket (as in rental caskets) is not permitted. This regulation should be repealed.

- There is no law that allows you to state your funeral preferences or for naming a designated agent to make your final arrangements. In situations where you are estranged or distant from next-of-kin, this could be important.
- There is no requirement that low-cost caskets be included in a casket display.
- The regulation regarding cash advance items is somewhat vague. While it appears that a *mark-up* on cash advance items is not permitted, retaining a regular discount *is* permitted, provided that the funeral home reveals that it gets a discount. The amount of the discount may not necessarily be disclosed, however. Funeral flowers come to mind as costs that may be easily inflated to families while providing a "discount" to undertakers.
- Crematories must be affiliated with a licensed funeral home. This is unnecessarily restrictive and burdensome and increases the cost of cremation for consumers. Crematories do not need embalming facilities, for example, and the running of a crematory is not part of the curriculum at most mortuary schools.
- Ethical standards should be expanded and clearly defined in order for valid consumer complaints to prevail. (See Appendix.)
- Complaint procedures are not adequately documented in law or regulation. The Department of Consumer Affairs works primarily to mediate complaints. Formal action is brought only if Tennessee law has been violated.

### ❖ Miscellaneous Information

- The educational requirements for becoming a funeral director in Tennessee are a high school diploma and two years of apprenticeship, or one year of mortuary school and one year of apprenticeship. All must pass a state-approved exam with a score of 75% or better. For embalmers, one year of mortuary college and one year of apprenticeship are required.
- Each body must be tagged with identification.
- Funeral establishments must abide by the FTC Funeral Rule.

## ❖ Nonprofit Funeral Consumer Information Societies

These consumer groups are run mostly by volunteers. Consequently, contact information may change. If you have difficulty reaching a society or are interested in starting a society in your area, call the FAMSA office: 800-765-0107. Or check the internet directory—

**www.funerals.org/famsa**

Chattanooga

Memorial Society of Chattanooga
3224 Navajo Dr., 37411
423-624-2985

Knoxville

East Tenn. Memorial Society
P.O. Box 10507, 37939

Nashville

Middle Tenn. Memorial Society
1808 Woodmont Blvd., 37215
615-329-0823
888-254-3872

~❖~

*This chapter was sent for review to the Tennessee Department of Public Health, the Commissioner of Commerce and Insurance, and the State Funeral Board, but no response was received.*

# In Texas

*Please refer to Chapter 8 as you use this section.*

Persons in Texas may care for their own dead. The legal authority to do so is found in the Health and Safety Code:

> *Chapter 711.002 Unless a decedent has left directions in writing for the disposition of the decedent's remains . . . , the following persons, in the priority listed, have the right to control the disposition . . . . (1) the person designated in a written instrument; (2) the decedent's surviving spouse; (3) any one of the decedent's surviving adult children; (4) either one of the decedent's surviving parents . . .*

There are no other statutes which might require you to use a funeral director.

### ❖ Death Certificate; Report of Death

The funeral director or person acting as such must file a *report of death* form with the local registrar where death occurred and within 24 hours. This form is prescribed by the Department of Health, one copy of which serves as the authority to transport a body within the state. The attending physician, certain other physicians, or a person conducting an inquest will sign the *death certificate* stating the cause of death. The remaining information must be supplied, typewritten or in black ink. The death certificate must be filed with the local registrar within ten days.

### ❖ Fetal Death

A certificate of stillbirth (fetal death) is required if death occurs after 20 weeks of gestation or more. A fetal death certificate must be filed within five days.

### ❖ Transporting and Disposition Permit

The local registrar or deputy registrar will issue a burial-transit permit. The death certificate must be filed first.

## ❖ Burial

Check with the city manager or administrator for zoning laws regarding home burial. H & S code 711.008 sets forth limitations regarding proximity to a municipal boundary based on population of the area. The top of the casket must be not less than two feet below the surface of the earth. A sensible guideline is 150 feet from a water supply.

## ❖ Cremation

Once the burial-transit permit is acquired, no additional permit for cremation is needed. There is a 48-hour wait before cremation unless the person died of a contagious disease. The local medical examiner, or—if none—a justice of the peace, may waive the waiting period. Most crematories insist that a pacemaker be removed, and authorization by next-of-kin usually is required. Persons may authorize their own cremations.

Texas statute (Health and Safety code, chapter 711.002) states that next-of-kin or your agent has a duty to "inter" your remains—which apparently includes cremated remains. Funeral and cemetery sales people are likely to use this to coerce you into purchasing a lot or niche space. However, there are no "cremains police" checking to see what you decide to do and no statutory penalty for doing whatever you might want otherwise. In fact, one may leave authority to your agent to follow "special directions." It's a good thing there are no specific laws against scattering, as some medical schools in Texas routinely take unclaimed cremated remains for an ocean voyage, and the consumer information pamphlet distributed by the Texas Funeral Service Commission suggests that a number of options are available including private scattering.

## ❖ Other Requirements

One portion of the Health and Safety Code says a body must be embalmed or refrigerated (to 34°–40°) after 24 hours unless it is in a sealed container. Another part of the code—relating to body donation—says an "unclaimed" body must be embalmed within 24 hours. Why not refrigeration? It may be an impossible task in a scattered society to determine whether a body will be "claimed" within 24 hours and whether embalming would be approved. Refrigeration is a far more effective method of body preservation.

If the person died of a contagious or communicable disease, the doctor in attendance should be consulted.

## ❖ Institutions for Body Donation

Texas A & M University
Dept. of Human Anatomy
Medical College
College Station, TX 77843
409-845-4914 or 822-1571
Low need

Cost to family: transport beyond 100 miles
Prior enrollment: preferred but not required
Over-enrollment: shared
Disposition: cremation; return of cremains by request
Body rejection: autopsy, burn victim, decomposition, hepatitis, AIDS

University of Texas
Southwestern Medical School
5323 Harry Hines Blvd.
Dallas, TX 75235-9143
214-648-2221

Cost to family: transportation beyond 250 mi.
Prior enrollment: preferred but not always required
Over-enrollment: shared with permission
Disposition: cremation; return of cremains by request
Body rejection: HIV, jaundice, burn victim, hepatitis, decomposition

University of North Texas
Health Science Center, FTW
Dept. of Anatomy, 2-202
3500 Camp Bowie Blvd.
Ft. Worth, TX 76107
817-735-2047
Moderate need

Cost to family: transportation beyond 50 mi.
Prior enrollment: preferred
Over-enrollment: shared
Disposition: cremation/burial in university crypt; return of cremains by request
Body rejection: standard,* under 18, syphilis, infectious cases, suicide, missing body parts (sometimes), major trauma

University of Texas
Medical Branch at Galveston
Galveston, TX 77550
409-761-1293 or 1011

Cost to family: transportation beyond 300 mi.
Prior enrollment: not required
Over-enrollment: shared
Disposition: cremation/burial at sea; return of cremains by request
Body rejection: AIDS, hepatitis, meningitis, decomposition, autopsy (usually)

Baylor College of Medicine
Dept. of Cell Biology
Texas Medical Center
Houston, TX 77030
713-799-4930
Low need

Cost to family: transportation beyond 100 mi./over $130 (usually)
Prior enrollment: usually required
Over-enrollment: shared
Disposition: cremation/ scattered at Brookside Memorial Park; return of cremains by request
Body rejection: standard,* under 21, suicide, trauma, other communicable diseases

University of Texas
Medical School
Health Science Center
Dept. of Anatomy
P.O. Box 20708
Houston, TX 77225
713-449-6511

Cost to family: transportation beyond 250 mi.
Prior enrollment: not required
Over-enrollment: shared
Disposition: cremation; return of cremains by request
Body rejection: standard,* under 14, morbid obesity

Texas Tech University
School of Medicine
Lubbock, TX 79430
806-743-2700 or
806-743-3111
Moderate need

Cost to family: transportation beyond 300 mi.
Prior enrollment: required
Over-enrollment: shared
Disposition: cremation; return of cremains by request
Body rejection: standard*

Texas Chiropractic College
5912 Spencer Hwy.
Pasadena, TX 77505
713-487-1170    8-5 M-F
Low need

Cost to family: some transportation
Prior enrollment: not required
Over-enrollment: shared
Disposition: cremation
Body rejection: standard*, missing body parts

University of Texas
Health Science Center
7703 Floyd Curis Dr.
San Antonio, TX 78284-7762
512-691-6533
Low need

Cost to family: transportation beyond 100 mi.
Prior enrollment: required, beginning in Jan.; closed when need is met
Over-enrollment: shared
Disposition: cremation/burial of cremains in university plot; return of cremains by request
Body rejection: autopsy, burn victim, hepatitis, Creutzfeldt-Jakob, etc., herpes, drowning, homicide, suicide, trauma, obesity, emaciation

* autopsy, decomposition, mutilation, severe burn victim, meningitis, hepatitis, AIDS

## ❖ Crematories

Allen

Ridgeview Crematory
2525 Central Expwy. N at
   Ridgeview Rd., 75013
972-424-7834

Amarillo

Memorial Park Cem/FH
6966 I-40 E., 79104
806-374-3709

Memory Gardens
I-27 & McCormick, 79119
806-622-0106

Arlington

Moore FH/Cemetery
1219 N. Davis Dr., 76012
817-275-2711

Austin

Capitol Memorial Park
14619 I-35 N, 78664
512-251-4118

Onion Creek Memorial Park
11610 Chapel Ln., 78748
512-282-3893

Beaumont

Haven of Rest Crematory
Hwy 90/Green Pond, 77704
409-892-3456

Big Spring

Trinity Memorial Park
S. Hwy. 87, 79720
915-267-8243

Boerne

Daniel Schallau
P.O. Box 1821, 78006
512-249-8495

Brownsville

South Texas Crematory
4464 Old Port Isabel, 78521
512-831-4217

Bryan

Callaway-Jones Crematory
3001 S. College, 77801
409-822-3717

Burnet

Clements-Wilcox
P.O. Box 206, 78611
512-756-2222

Colleyville

Blue Bonnet Hills Mcm. Park
5725 Colleyville Blvd., 76034
817-281-8751

Corpus Christi

Clifford Jackson Crematory
4202 Kostoryz Rd., 78415
512-852-8233

Seaside Crematory
4357 Ocean Dr., 78412
512-992-9411

Dallas

Dallas Crematory Service
8004 Scyene Rd., 75227
800-257-1395

Crown Hill Mem. Park
9700 Webb Chapel, 75220
214-357-3985

Laurel Land Mem. Park
6000 S. Thornton Freeway, 75232
214-371-1336

Restland Memorial Park
Greenville/Restland, 75231
214-235-7111

El Paso

Evergreen East Cemetery
East Montana, 79902
915-532-5511

Ft. Worth

Cremation Service
1908 M.L. King Freeway, 76104
817-335-3535

Greenwood Mem. Park
3100 White Settlement
817-336-0584

Laurel Land Mem. Park
71100 Crowley, 76115
817-293-1350

Mt. Olivet Cemetery
2301 N. Sylvania St., 76111
817-336-0584

Gonzales

Onion Creek Mem. Park
820 St. Peter, 78629
512-672-2838

Hitchcock

Galveston Memorial Park
Mem. Dr./ FM 519, 77563
409-986-7409

Houston

Brookside Memorial Park
13401 Eastex Freeway, 77039
713-449-6511

Crespo Funeral Home
4136 Broadway Blvd., 77087
713-644-3831

Earthman Resthaven Cem.
13102 N. Freeway, 77060
713-443-0063

Forest Park Lawndale Cemetery
6900 Lawndale St., 77023
713-928-5141

Golden Era Service
1790 S. Tower
Pennzoil Place, 77002
713-227-4418

Memorial Oaks Cemetery
13001 Katy Hwy., 77079
713-497-2210

Niday Funeral Homes
4136 Broadway Blvd., 77087
713-644-3831

Resthaven Mem. Gardens
13102 N. Freeway, 77060
713-443-0063

South Park Crematory
12400 Telephone, 77017
713-485-2711

Kerrville

Kerrville Funeral Home
1221 Junction Hwy., 78028
210-895-5111

Kilgore

East Texas Crematory
Hwy. 31 W., 75662
903-984-2525

Lamarque

Mainland Crematory
2501 Main St., 77568
409-938-7475

Lewisville

Martin-Oaks Crematory
1230 Kingston, 75067
214-434-1121

Lubbock

Resthaven
5740 W. 19th St., 79416
806-791-6200

Mexia

Clark Manor Mem. Chapel
315 S. Hwy. 14, 76667
817-562-2878

Pearland

Southpark FH/Cemetery
1310 N. Main St., 77581
713-485-2711

Pharr

Palm Valley Crematory
P.O. Box 644, 78577
512-787-5222

Plugerville

Capitol Memorial Park
14619 I-35 N., 78664
512-251-4118

San Antonio

Crematory Associates
P.O. Box 200606
210-661-3991

Memorial Funeral Home
1614 El Paso St., 78207
210-226-4071

Mission Burial Park
1700 SE Military Dr., 78218
512-924-4242

Sunset Memorial Park
1701 Austin, 78218
512-828-2811

Temple

Bellwood Crematory
Hwy. 36 W., 76501
817-778-8441

Van

Fairway Crematory
Hwy. 16 W., 75790-0518
903-963-8831

Vidor

Restlawn FH/Crematory
1750 Hwy. 12, 77662
409-769-8005

Additional crematories may have been established in this state after the date of publication.

## ❖ State Governance

The Texas Funeral Service Commission has nine members. Five are public members.

The Department of Banking regulates perpetual-care cemeteries and preneed trust transactions. The Insurance Department regulates funeral insurance.

### ❖ Prepaid Cemetery and Funeral Funds

A portion of each lot sale must be dedicated to perpetual care in most cemeteries (municipal, religious, and fraternal are excluded).

The cemetery laws have a very peculiar exclusion buried in Chapter 715—"Certain Historic Cemeteries." A nonprofit corporation may petition the district court to take over and restore a cemetery that's more than 75 years old if there is no existing organization actively maintaining the cemetery. Unlike other cemeteries, however, these may not establish crematories.

The preneed purchase of *cemetery* services and vaults are treated like other preneed *funeral* purchases, with 90% **trusting** required. Advance purchase of markers and monuments, however, is not protected. That is, there are no trusting requirements and no provision for a **refund** if you were to change your mind.

Although the Texas Department of Banking is supposed to be regulating the preneed *funeral* business, it's clear the funeral industry is calling the shots via the legislature. I was shocked at what I found buried in the Texas statutes and am alarmed that a large number of seniors and their survivors will be faced with huge disappointments, especially over the next ten years or so.

In 1993, the statutes were amended to permit a one-time raid of prepaid funeral accounts. Undertakers were allowed to claim and withdraw anything over and above 110% of what a consumer had paid. "Excess earnings" they called it. "Legalized embezzlement" would be more like it. In the four months prior to the end of the year, there was a huge sucking sound at the banks: the funeral industry claimed and received more than $58.6 million! If a trust account had been earning 5% a year, it should have generated enough to offset the 10% commission the undertaker had already claimed and to add 10% more, in just four years or so. Therefore, thoughtful folks who had paid for their funerals, say, ten years earlier *lost six years of interest* in this grand give-away to the funeral industry. Some obviously lost a lot more. The depth of this dastardly deed is yet to come, I fear. As these elders begin to die, where is the interest that should have been accumulating to cover funeral inflation? Maybe anyone getting stuck with an added tab for a funeral that was supposed to be fully paid-for prior to 1994 should mail the bill to a local legislator for a reverse "contribution"!

Why do I think your survivors might get an extra bill? If you paid $750 for a casket ten years ago and there was no accurate description of what kind of casket you chose,[1] your family is likely to be shown "the welfare casket" today (or a year from today) because—after all—there simply isn't a whole lot in your prepaid funeral account, certainly not enough to cover inflation. The same casket today is probably $1,750.

The outrageous deeds of the 1993 legislature didn't stop with the Raid-o Grande. Funeral homes may now add **finance charges** to installment preneed sales. When you finance a car, house, or other retail purchase, you get to use the item. But a finance charge on a lay-away plan before they lay you away? The undertaker gets a commission, the undertaker gets the interest even if you cancel, *and* the undertaker now wants you to pay a little extra for the bother of cashing more than one check!

As of this writing, 90% of your preneed *funeral* money is supposed to be placed in **trust**. The seller gets to keep a 10% **commission** right away. If you are making installment payments, however, the mortician doesn't get just 10% of each payment; undertakers can keep 50% of what is paid until the commission is in their pockets.

(To its credit, Texas does not permit **"constructive delivery,"** a mechanism by which trusting requirements are avoided in other states.)

Preneed sellers must make an annual **report** of their trust accounts to the Banking Commissioner, but individual accounts may be co-mingled in a single trust. Therefore, don't expect to get a lot of information from the commissioner on your share of this trust fund. Only the funeral director knows. The funeral director also may withdraw money for all sorts of "expenses"—taxes, inspection fees, and administration—as long as they are "reasonable," whatever that means.

---

[1] The Administrative rules as of 1997 do require that each preneed contract now include a description of funeral merchandise selected preneed and a notation that an item of equal quality will be supplied if the selected merchandise is no longer available at the time of death. The description requirement isn't too bad as far as it goes—material used for casket construction including gauge of metal or type of wood, sealing feature (if mentioned on price list), and lining material. But a quick look at a couple of casket price lists shows that there can be a $500-$1,000 difference between one 18-gauge, crepe-lined steel sealer and another.

A purchaser may **cancel** a revocable agreement, but kiss the **interest** and 10% commission good-bye. (Statutes give all interest to the undertaker, regardless, which is probably why the industry felt entitled to raid the preneed accounts in '93.)

If you made your agreement irrevocable—prior to moving into a retirement or nursing home perhaps, better hope your daughter doesn't move to another area and suggest that you move to a nursing home in that area, too. And don't take any trips out of the immediate area that might risk your death in a far-away place. These contracts are *not* required to be **transferable**. Only by the good will of the first funeral home would another get paid. Even then, all that a new funeral home is likely to get is 90% of what you paid. The original seller is entitled to keep the interest and the 10% commission. By the way, if your family didn't know about a prepaid irrevocable account and used another provider at the time of your death, there is no statutory provision for a refund. In practice, the Banking Department says, there shouldn't be a problem.

Oh, yes, if you are paying on installment and still owe a balance, don't forget to let the funeral home know if you *have* moved. If the funeral home can't find you for three years, it can take the interest and declare your prepaid funeral funds "abandoned" (if the Banking Commissioner agrees). Although the principal goes to the state, the state will owe you nothing—nada—unlike the practice in Canadian provinces that protects a consumer's interest under such circumstances.

A guaranty fund of sorts was established (as of 1988) to protect consumers from mortuary default on prepaid funeral accounts sold by licensed establishments—not cemetery purchases. In most states, that's to help out if a rascal took off with your money and it was never put into trust, but it wouldn't cover situations in which your funeral funds might have been turned over to the state. In Texas, however, it doesn't cover you if you have the misfortune of purchasing a preneed agreement from someone who is not licensed by the state to sell preneed. Preneed sellers need a license to steal?

What about funeral insurance, you might ask? If you were to question the current cash value of your policy—especially before the premiums are fully paid—you'll find that the mortician has taken a hefty commission, leaving a much smaller sum for your benefit than you might imagine.

Watch out for the greedy double-dippers, too. Once an undertaker has collected an initial 10% on a trust account, your 90% can be used to purchase funeral insurance. *Voilà!* A second commission for the mortician. Yes, you will get a right-of-refusal letter, but if you ignore the deadline on this "negative notice" and don't say "no" in time, your account will automatically be moved—a little or a lot lighter than before.

Of death and taxes: For years, the IRS has held that you must declare on your Income Tax Return the interest income from any prepaid funeral trust because it will be used for your benefit. In 1997, a new provision went into effect that allows the funeral home to declare the interest. Because in Texas you are unlikely to get your interest if you were to cancel a preneed contract or die somewhere else, you may wish to return the 1099 tax form the funeral home sends you and politely tell the funeral home that you wish to take advantage of the new provision and let the mortuary report the interest. Although the funeral home may not be forced to do so under current rules, it would be a terrible public relations boo-boo if it refused.

## ❖ Consumer Concerns

- The death rate in Texas can support approximately 563 full-time mortuaries; there are, however, over 1,200. Funeral prices tend to be higher in areas where there are "too many" funeral homes.
- Finance charges are permitted for installment purchases of prepaid funeral and cemetery arrangements. This should be repealed immediately!
- 100% of prepaid cemetery goods and services should be placed in trust, with an adequate provision for cancellation and refund.
- The trusting requirement for preneed funeral purchases also should be increased to 100%, *with all interest retained in the account until need*. Funeral agreements should be fully transferable *with interest,* and—in the case of revocable contracts—fully refundable, with all interest returned to the buyer.
- There is no annual reporting requirement to the purchaser of prepaid funeral goods and services. This paperwork would not only be helpful to the family of a deceased to indicate prepayment, it would let you know how much you actually still have to pay for your funeral.
- The substitution of equal quality requirement when an item chosen preneed is no longer available should be made with the approval of the survivors.

- In spite of the Guaranty Fund and until the Texas laws are changed, it is probably a *terrible* idea to prepay for a funeral or any cemetery merchandise and services in this state, given the raw deal a consumer would get in trying to transfer or back out of such a purchase. Your own trust account in a bank will be safer, will be portable, and will accumulate interest regularly. You may be able to make it irrevocable if assets need to be sheltered for Medicaid eligibility.

- The 48-hour wait before cremation is totally unnecessary when survivors are in agreement and is causing additional charges to families for "storage" or embalming. That the waiting period may be waived in case of disease would indicate that an earlier cremation is probably in the interest of the public health.

- Identification and tagging of the body at the place of death before removal should be required.

- The standards for ethical, professional conduct should be strengthened. That would make it easier for a consumer to prevail when filing a valid complaint. (See Ethical Standards in the Appendix.)

- The Funeral Commission has prepared an information brochure for consumers that funeral directors must give to persons inquiring about funeral arrangements. It also spells out the procedure for filing complaints. It is vague and weak in spelling out the pitfalls of prepaying for a funeral in Texas, and that portion should be rewritten.

- Crematories may be constructed only on the grounds of cemeteries. This kind of business restriction should be either changed in the legislature or challenged in court. Generally, states have a right to make limiting laws only for the public good. There is no justification for effectively limiting crematory operation to cemeterians, and the practice in other states bears proof.

## ❖ Miscellaneous Information

- Educational requirements for funeral directors: high school plus mortuary college, national exam, state exam, and one year of apprenticeship.

- There is a statutory duty to comply with the written wishes of the decedent. Ideally, one should use the state's Body Disposition Authorization form. One may also use the "Appointment of Agent to Control Disposition of Remains," and using both is a good idea. Although such wishes may be challenged in court, weight is given to the wishes of the decedent.

- A casket display must include a reasonable selection of at least five adult caskets, with the least expensive one visibly displayed in the same general manner as all other caskets.
- If there is a fee for obtaining cash advance items, it must be disclosed in advance.
- The language of the FTC Funeral Rule has been adopted in the Funeral Service Commission rules, making it more enforceable in Texas.
- Medical examiners are appointed physicians. Justices of the peace are elected.

## ❖ Nonprofit Funeral Consumer Information Societies

These consumer groups are run mostly by volunteers. Consequently, contact information may change. If you have difficulty reaching a society or are interested in starting a society in your area, call the FAMSA office: 800-765-0107. Or check the internet directory—

**www.funerals.org/famsa**

Austin

> Austin Mem. & Burial Info. Soc.
> P.O. Box 4382, 78765-4382
> 512-480-0555

Corpus Christi

> Memorial Society of S. Texas
> 3125 Horne Rd., 78415
> 800-371-2221

Dallas, Denton, Fort Worth, Lubbock, Tyler, Wichita Falls

> Memorial Society of North Texas
> 4015 Normandy, Dallas, 75205
> 214-528-6006 or 800-371-2221

Houston

> Houston Area Memorial Society
> 5200 Fannin St., 77004-5899
> 713-526-4267

San Antonio

> San Antonio Memorial Society
> 7150 Interstate 10W, 78213
> 210-341-2213

Waco

> Central TX Chapter of N TX Soc.
> 4209 N. 27th St., 76708-1509
> 800-371-2221

~❖~

*This chapter was sent for fact-checking and review to the Texas
Department of Banking, the Texas Funeral Service Commission, and
the Texas Department of Health.*

A staffer for the Department of Banking was good enough to make
a few corrections (as did the Department of Health). She added,
however, "There are many opinions in this section, and—as a state
agency—we must remain neutral." There was no response from the Texas
Funeral Service Commission.

# In Utah

*Please refer to Chapter 8 as you use this section.*

Persons in Utah may care for their own dead. The legal authority to do so is found in:

*Title 26-2-13 (4): The funeral director or person acting as the funeral director who first assumes custody of the dead body shall file the certificate of death.*

*Title 26-2-17 (3): A burial-transit permit shall be issued by the registrar of the district where the certificate of death or fetal death is filed, for bodies to be transported out of the state for final disposition and when disposition is made by a person other than a licensed funeral director.*

## ❖ Death Certificate

The attending physician will supply and sign the death certificate within 72 hours, stating the cause of death. The remaining information must be supplied, typewritten or in black ink. The death certificate must be filed with the local registrar within five days of death and prior to final disposition.

## ❖ Fetal Death

A fetal death report is required for each fetal death. If there is no family physician involved, the local medical examiner must sign the fetal death certificate.

## ❖ Transporting and Disposition Permit

The local registrar will issue the burial-transit permit. This will be required before a body can be released from a hospital. After usual business hours, a law enforcement officer or someone "on call" will supply the permit. Unless moved by a funeral director, a body must be encased in a container or plastic pouch.

## ❖ Burial

Check with the county or town registrar for local zoning laws regarding home burial. There are no state burial statutes or regulations with regard to depth. A sensible guideline is 150 feet from a water supply and three feet of earth on top.

After burial, the family member acting as the funeral director must sign the burial-transit permit and file it with the registrar where disposition takes place, by the 10th of the following month.

## ❖ Cremation

No additional permit is required for cremation. Authorization by next-of-kin is usually required, and a pacemaker must be removed. The crematory may offer to file the burial-transit permit.

## ❖ Other Requirements

There are no statutes that require embalming when a family is handling a death. Weather and reasonable planning should be considered. If the person died of a contagious or communicable disease, the doctor in attendance should be consulted.

## ❖ Medical Schools for Body Donation

University of Utah
Department of Anatomy
50 N. Medial Dr.
Salt Lake City, UT 84132
801-581-6728  8-5 M-F
    581-2121 other times.

Cost to family: transportation outside 50-mile radius
Prior enrollment: not required
Over-enrollment: shared
Disposition: cremation; no return of cremains
Body rejection: standard,* obesity, jaundice, young child/infant

* autopsy, decomposition, mutilation, severe burn victim, meningitis, hepatitis, AIDS, and other contagious or communicable diseases

## ❖ Crematories

Nephi

Capital Memorial Gardens
435-692-3588

Ogden

Aultorest Memorial Park
836 36th St., 84403
801-394-5556

Lindquist & Son
3408 Washington Blvd., 84401
801-394-6667

Salt Lake City

Deseret Mortuary
36 East 700 South, 84111
801-566-1249

Independent Prof. Services
4555 S. Redwood Rd., 84123
801-263-8200

Lake Hills Crematory
10055 S. State St., 84070
801-566-1249

Neil O'Donnell & Son
372 East 100 South, 84111
801-363-6641

Larkin Sunset Lawn Mortuary
2350 East 1300 South, 84106
801-582-1582

Salt Lake Mem. Mausoleum & Mort.
1001 11th Ave., 84103
801-363-7065

Additional crematories may have been established in this state after the date of publication.

## ❖ State Governance

The Utah Board of Funeral Service has five members. One is a consumer representative.

The Preneed Funeral Arrangement Licensing Board consists of three funeral establishment representatives, one preneed sales agent, one owner of an endowment care cemetery, and two public members.

There is no cemetery board or regulation of cemetery purchases.

Crematories are not regulated. One does not need to be a funeral director to run a crematory.

## ❖ Prepaid Cemetery and Funeral Funds

Cemetery lots that have not been used or cared for in 60 years are considered abandoned and may be reclaimed by the cemetery.

There is no statutory protection for preneed *cemetery* transactions. Therefore, the money you spend for vaults, markers, and cemetery services may be spent by the cemetery right away. Let's hope you won't want to change your mind and seek a refund. Let's also hope the cemetery doesn't go out of business.

Any preneed *funeral* contract must be a "guaranteed product contract." In one part of the statutes, it states that a preneed contract may not be revoked by either party once paid in full. Later statutes imply that a purchaser may revoke the contract and get a **refund**, but how much one might get is not at all clear from the statutes. The consumer may be at the mercy of the contract fine-print.

100% of preneed funeral funds must be placed into **trust. Interest** may be withdrawn for "reasonable" expenses for administering the trust by the institution holding funds and by the seller of the prepaid funeral plan for expenses associated with the sale of the plan, accounting, and reporting.

A seller of preneed funeral arrangements must make an annual **report** to the state.

### ❖ Consumer Concerns

- The death rate in Utah can support approximately 44 full-time mortuaries; there are 97 such establishments. Given the low density of population over a vast geographic area, mortuary careers are not likely to be full-time work in most areas. Unfortunately, because of the low volume of business per mortuary, funeral prices will tend to be higher than elsewhere.
- Laws should require cemeteries to repurchase an unwanted lot at the original selling price plus 50% of the difference between that and current market price.
- All preneed contracts appear to be irrevocable, unless the provider fails to supply the goods and services selected. There is also no provision for transferring a contract. This is an absurd limitation of consumer rights, especially given the changing ownership in the funeral industry.
- There is no provision for an adequate description of funeral goods selected on a guaranteed-price preneed contract nor for a substitution of equal quality if the selected item is no longer available at the time of death. Survivors should be permitted to approve any substitution.
- There is no state protection in the case of default of prepaid funeral monies.
- There is no annual reporting requirement to the purchaser of prepaid funeral goods and services, paperwork that might be helpful

to the family of a deceased to indicate prepayment and which would help to "enforce" trusting requirements.

- Until there is more flexibility and better protection, it is probably a *terrible* idea to prepay for a funeral in Utah.
- There is no requirement that low-cost caskets be included in any display.
- Identification and tagging of the body at the place of death before removal should be required, given the regular mix-ups that have been happening at chain-owned establishments with central prep facilities.
- The standards for ethical, professional conduct are almost nonexistent. These should be spelled out to make it easier for a consumer to prevail when filing a valid complaint.
- Complaint procedures are unclear and inadequate.

## ❖ Miscellaneous Information

- Educational requirements for becoming a funeral director: associate's degree in mortuary science (2 years), an exam, and one year (and 50 embalmings) of apprenticeship.
- A personal representative may be named to carry out the wishes of a decedent.
- Cash advance items must be billed in the actual amount of charges paid by the funeral home including discounts and rebates.
- There is a statutory obligation to abide by the FTC Funeral Rule.
- A body may be held for funeral expenses.
- No surface coal mining is permitted within 100 feet of a cemetery.

## ❖ Nonprofit Funeral Consumer Information Societies

Although there are no memorial societies in Utah as of this writing, you may check the internet directory—**www.funerals.org/famsa**—or call the national office to see if any have since been started: 1-800-765-0107. Or let the FAMSA office know if you are willing to help start one. FAMSA may have a limited list of ethically-priced mortuaries in Utah to which referrals can be made while monitoring consumer satisfaction.

~❖~

*This chapter was sent for review to the Utah Department of Health, the Preneed Funeral Arrangement Licensing Board, and the Board of Funeral Service. There was no response from the Department of Health, and the latter two declined review or comment.*

# In Vermont

*Please refer to Chapter 8 as you use this section.*

Persons in Vermont may care for their own dead. The legal authority to do so is found in:

> *Title 18, Section 5207. Certificate furnished family; burial permit. The physician or person filling out the certificate of death, within thirty-six hours after death, shall deliver the same to the family of the deceased, if any, or the undertaker or person who has charge of the body. Such certificate shall be filed with the person issuing the certificate of permission for burial, entombment or removal obtained by the person who has charge of the body before such dead body shall be buried, entombed or removed from the town. . . .*

There are no other statutes that might require you to use a funeral director.

## ❖ Death Certificate

The doctor last in attendance or a medical examiner will supply and sign the death certificate, stating the cause of death. The remaining information must be supplied, typewritten or in black ink. The death certificate must be filed with the town clerk where death occurred.

## ❖ Fetal Death

A fetal death report is required when death occurs after 20 weeks of gestation or when the weight is 400 grams or more.

## ❖ Transporting and Disposition Permit

The town clerk (or any law enforcement officer after hours) will issue a burial-transit permit. Funeral directors often serve as deputies and sign their own burial-transit permits. The burial-transit permit must be filed with the town clerk in the town of disposition.

## ❖ Burial

Check with the town clerk on zoning laws regarding home burial. If burial is planned for private land set aside for the use of the immediate family, the town clerk will need a map of the location to record in the land records. (A hand-drawn map will usually suffice.) The bottom (not the top) of the casket must be five feet below the natural surface of the earth (three-and-a-half feet for infants). Burial must be at least 100 feet from a drilled well and 150 feet from shallow wells or streams. The burial site must be at least 25 feet from a power line.

When burial is arranged, the family member acting as the funeral director must sign the burial-transit permit and file it with the clerk of the town in which burial will occur.

For a pamphlet on home burial, call 800-882-2437 or write to:

Vermont Department of Health
108 Cherry St.
Burlington, VT 05401

## ❖ Cremation

A cremation permit ($10) from the medical examiner is required. Authorization by next-of-kin is usually required, and a pacemaker must be removed. The crematory will file the burial-transit permit.

## ❖ Other Requirements

Vermont has no other requirements controlling the time schedule for the disposition of unembalmed bodies. Weather and reasonable planning should be considered.

If the person died of a contagious or communicable disease, the doctor in attendance should be consulted. Disposition may be under the instructions of the local health officer.

## ❖ Institutions for Body Donation

University of Vermont
Department of Anatomy & Neurobiol.
Burlington, VT 05405
802-656-2230 8-5 M-F
   656-3473 other times
Moderate need

Cost to family: transportation (must be
   listed on funeral home price list)
Prior enrollment: preferred
Over-enrollment: shared
Disposition: cremation; return of cre-
   mains by request
Body rejection: standard*

\* autopsy, decomposition, mutilation, severe burn victim, meningitis, hepatitis, AIDS, and
other contagious or communicable diseases

## ❖ Crematories

Bennington

   Vermont Cremation Service
   213 W. Main St., 05201
   802-442-4329

Brattleboro

   Eternal Flame Crematory
   239 Old Ferry Rd., 05301
   802-254-3508

Burlington area

   Adirondack-Burlington Cremation
   75 Allen Rd., S. Burlington, 05403
   802-862-9006

Middlebury

   Sanderson's Funeral Service
   117 S. Main St., 05753
   802-388-2311

St. Johnsbury

   Mt. Pleasant Cemetery
   39 Mt. Pleasant Ave., 05819
   802-748-3063 or 800-547-7462

White River Junction

   Knight's Funeral Home
   43 Taft Ave., 05001
   802-295-2100

Additional crematories may have been established in this state after
the date of publication.

## ❖ State Governance

The Vermont Board of Funeral Service has five members. Two are
consumer representatives.

Almost all Vermont cemeteries are run by local towns or churches.

Other than meeting environmental requirements, crematories are not
regulated in Vermont.

## ❖ Prepaid Cemetery and Funeral Funds

Cemeteries may not be operated for private gain. It seems unfortunate
that there is statutory provision for moving a cemetery, "when it is

impracticable [for a town] to preserve a burial ground in proper condition."

Although each cemetery must have the lots mapped out and numbered, many old town cemeteries are poorly recorded.[1] When the whereabouts of a lot owner has been unknown for 20 years, the cemetery agency may, through the probate court, regain title. If a claim from one entitled to the lot arises within 17 years after that, the lot will be made available, or, if sold, the proceeds of the sale will go to the claimant.

100% of prepaid *funeral* money must be placed in **trust** with **interest** to accrue. **Administrative fees**—the lesser of one-half the earnings or 2% of the account—may be withdrawn each year.

A purchaser may **transfer** an irrevocable contract to a new provider, but the seller may retain 5% of the assets.

Although a funeral provider "may" substitute merchandise of equal quality if the selected item is no longer available, it is not a requirement. Survivors must be "notified" when a **substitution** is made, but survivor approval is not mandated.

A funeral seller must instruct the escrow agent to send a **report** annually to the purchaser showing all transactions and the balance of the account.[2]

---

[1] In a Bridgewater cemetery, one man's grave was accidently unearthed when excavation began for his wife's. The town Cemetery Commission denied any wrong-doing, but that seemed like a white-wash to the daughter, who'd been given three different stories as to whether there was damage to her dad's casket or not.

[2] Annual reports must be issued by the institution or escrow agent holding the money. The first year such reports were required, one Vermont funeral director simply cranked out reports on his own computer. Troubled by the $100 administrative fee that had been subtracted, one elderly gentleman contacted an Council on Aging advocate. Irregularities were quickly apparent: Instead of posting the last quarter of 1996 interest as of December 31, 1996, it was posted January 1, 1997 in order to qualify for a $100 service fee rather than a mere $50. There were also such outrageously generous interest "deposits" for some years (23.2%) that one had to wonder if the funeral director was playing the ponies with this money, or was the whole thing a bogus report.

There is a **Funeral Services Trust Account** to protect preneed consumers against default of the funeral provider.

### ❖ Consumer Concerns

- The death rate in Vermont can support approximately 20 full-time mortuaries; there are 68 such establishments. Funeral prices tend to be higher in areas where there are "too many" funeral homes.
- Laws should require cemeteries to repurchase an unwanted lot at the original selling price plus 50% of the difference between that and current market price, if the value has increased. If the value of the lot has decreased below the original selling price, the cemetery should repurchase the lot at 75% of the current worth.
- Description of merchandise purchased preneed should be detailed, with a requirement to substitute an item of equal quality and construction, with approval of survivors.
- Administrative fees should be eliminated or drastically reduced for preneed accounts. Such withdrawals significantly reduce the amount available against inflation. Transfer fees should be eliminated.
- Although Vermont now has annual reporting and a protection fund, it may be unwise to prepay for a funeral until penalties and fees are abolished and substitution issues are improved.
- The medical examiner's permit for cremation in the case of an *anticipated* death from natural causes is totally unnecessary and creates an additional burden and charge for families.
- Identification and tagging of the body at the place of death before removal should be required, given the regular mix-ups that have been happening at chain-owned establishments with central prep facilities.
- There is no provision either forbidding a mark-up on cash advance items or requiring the disclosure of how much the mark-up would be. Consumers may wish to ask for receipts for these charges.
- There is no law that allows you to state your funeral preferences or for naming a designated agent to make your final arrangements. In situations where you are estranged or distant from next-of-kin, this could be important.
- The standards for ethical, professional conduct should be strengthened. That would make it easier for a consumer to prevail when filing a valid complaint.

## ❖ Miscellaneous Information

- Educational requirements for becoming a funeral director: national exam and assisting at 30 funerals. For embalmer: two years of college (at least one of which is mortuary study), one year of apprenticeship, and a national exam.
- There is no licensing or regulation of crematories in Vermont other than environmental requirements.
- Regulations require that the least expensive casket be shown on display or by photograph. (This is not always the done, according to some reports.)
- Medical examiners are appointed physicians.
- The FTC Funeral Rule has been adopted by reference. In addition, the General Price List (GPL) must include the costs for private family viewing and body donation. The address and phone number for registering a complaint must be on the GPL, along with a statement that state help with funeral expenses may be available to those who qualify.
- If a person without funds has no headstone after three years, the town must erect one.
- Cemeteries must be fenced. "If a person or estate is damaged by cattle, horses, sheep or swine breaking into a public burial ground and injuring a grave, headstone, monument, shrubbery or flowers, for want of a legal fence around such burial ground, such person or estate may recover of the town double the amount of damages."

## ❖ Nonprofit Funeral Consumer Information Societies

These consumer groups are run mostly by volunteers. Consequently, contact information may change. If you have difficulty reaching a society or are interested in starting a society in your area, call the FAMSA office: 800-765-0107. Or check the internet directory—

**www.funerals.org/famsa**

Memorial Society of Vermont
1630 Clark Road
East Montpelier, VT 05651-4529
800-805-0007 or 802-476-4300

~❖~

*This chapter was sent for review to the Board of Funeral Service and the Department of Health—Vital Statistics. No response was received.*

# In Virginia

*Please refer to Chapter 8 as you use this section.*

Persons in Virginia may care for their own dead. The legal authority to do so is found in:

*Title 32.1-263-B. The funeral director or person who first assumes custody of a dead body shall file the certificate of death with the registrar.*

There are no other statutes that might require you to use a funeral director.

## ❖ Death Certificate

The family doctor or a medical examiner will sign the death certificate within 24 hours, stating the cause of death. The remaining information must be supplied, typewritten or in black ink. The death certificate (two copies) must be filed with the local registrar within three days and before final disposition or removal from the state.

Virginia is researching electronic death registration. When that is adopted the procedure will change somewhat. Check with the local registrar or health department.

## ❖ Fetal Death

A fetal death report is required for each fetal death. If there is no family physician involved, the local medical examiner must sign the fetal death certificate.

## ❖ Transporting and Disposition Permit

A body may be moved with medical permission. A burial-transit permit is required only for out-of-state disposition. The death certificate must be obtained first. In all cases the local registrar must sign line 30 of the death certificate before disposition.

## ❖ Burial

The state requires no additional permit for disposition by burial. There are no state burial statutes regarding depth. A sensible guideline is 150 feet from a water supply and at least two feet of earth on top. Check with the local registrar for zoning laws regarding home burial.

Family graveyards, abandoned after 25 years, may be moved with the permission of the circuit court if there is no objection. That's too bad and unsettling, to say the least. In many if not most other states, a burial site becomes a permanent easement on the land.

## ❖ Cremation

A permit for cremation or burial at sea must be obtained from the medical examiner. The usual fee for this is $50. There is a 24-hour wait before cremation or burial at sea unless visual identification is made by next-of-kin. Most crematories insist that a pacemaker be removed, and authorization by next-of-kin is usually required.

## ❖ Other Requirements

Virginia has no other requirements controlling the time schedule for the disposition of unembalmed bodies. Weather and reasonable planning should be considered.

If the person died of a contagious or communicable disease, the doctor in attendance should be consulted.

## ❖ Medical Schools for Body Donation

There is one agency to handle body donations in this state.

State Anatomy Program
Department of Health
Richmond, VA 23219
804-786-2479 or 786-2474 or
   786-3774

Cost to family: transportation over
   $25
Prior enrollment: not required
Over-enrollment: shared statewide
Disposition: cremation
Body rejection: autopsy, decomposi-
   tion, mutilation, severe burn vic-
   tim, meningitis, hepatitis, AIDS,
   other contagious diseases

## ❖ Crematories

Alexandria

Metropolitan Crematorium
5517 Vine St., 22310
703-971-0806

Everly-Wheatley Funeral Service
1500 W. Braddock Rd., 22302
703-998-9200

Mount Comfort Cemetery
6600 S. Kings Hwy., 22306
703-765-3800

Arlington

Northern VA Crematory
3901 Fairfax Dr., 22203
703-522-1441

Bedford

Blue Ridge Cremation Svc.
320 N. Bridge St., 24523
703-586-3443

Berryville

Enders Crematory
P.O. Box 106, 22611
703-955-1062

Cedar Bluffs

Richlands Tazewell Crem.
210 Cedar Valley Dr., 24609
703-964-4011

Charlottesville

Teague Cremation Service
2260 Ivy Rd., 22901
804-977-0005

Dale City

Potomac Crematory
4143 Dale Blvd., 22193
703-680-1234

Fairfax

Everly Funeral Home
10565 Main St., 22030
703-385-1110

Fairfax Memorial Park
9900 Braddock Rd., 22032
703-323-5202

Glen Allen

Bennett Funeral Home
11020 W. Broad St., 23060
804-270-1402

Hampton

Hampton Memorial Gardens
155 Butler Farm Rd., 23666
804-766-1063

Parklawn Memorial Park
2539 N. Armistead Ave. 23666
804-838-2068

Harrisonburg

Harrisonburg Cremation Service
141 Patterson, 22801
703-434-1359

Kyger & Trobaugh Crematory
903 S. Main St., 22801
703-434-1359

Lindsay Cremation Chapel
473 S. Main St., 22801
703-434-7318

Newport News

Newport Crematory
12746 Nettles Dr., 23606
804-596-2222

Norfolk

Colonial Crematory
1501 Colonial Ave., 23517
804-623-9928

Richmond

Cremation Society of VA
8621 Sanford Dr., 23228
804-262-8267

Forest Lawn
4000 Alma Ave., 23222
804-321-7655

Greenwood Cemetery
14101 Patterson Ave., 23233
804-784-5214

Roanoke

John M. Oakey
318 Church Ave. SW, 24007
540-982-2100

Salem

Sherwood Memorial Park
1045 Lynchburgh Tpk. 24153
703-389-2171

Virginia Beach

Lynn Haven Crematory
3600 Virginia Blvd., 23452
804-463-0150

Waynesboro

Augusta Cremation Service
618 N. Main St., 22980
703-949-8383

Winchester

Jones Funeral Home
228 S. Pleasant Valley, 22601
703-662-2523

Omps Crematory Service
1600 Amherst St., 22601
703-662-6633

Woodbridge

Mountcastle Funeral Home
13318 Occoquan Rd., 22191
703-494-2000

There may be other crematories established since publication of this book.

## ❖ State Governance

The Virginia State Board of Funeral Directors and Embalmers has nine members. There are two consumer representatives.

A state Cemetery Board was established in 1997, in spite of heavy lobbying against it by corporate-owned cemeteries. It remains to be seen whether the chains will be successful in thwarting new regulations—regulations that might limit solicitations or increase trusting requirements, for example.

Crematories are licensed by the Board of Funeral Directors and Embalmers. One does not need to be a funeral director to run a crematory. Virginia also licenses body transport services.

## ❖ Prepaid Cemetery and Funeral Funds

All cemeteries, including pet cemeteries, must have perpetual care funds.

There currently is very little oversight of cemetery business in Virginia. Only 40% of the amount received for preneed *cemetery* "property or services" must be placed in **trust**. "**Constructive delivery**" can bypass the trusting requirement. There is *no* provision for cancellation and refund of preneed cemetery arrangements at this time.

Virginia regulations prohibit a funeral licensee from in-person communication to **solicit** preneed funeral arrangements, including by phone. A consumer must initiate any contact. No such restrictions apply to cemetery sales. As funeral conglomerates buy up both cemeteries and funeral homes, their avid preneed marketers can wear a "cemetery hat" and ignore such a restriction. Consumers receiving un-requested sales calls should tighten a hold on their wallets. Once you're sitting there in person to buy a cemetery lot, the "hats" can change.

A preneed *funeral* contract must have several pages of consumer information disclosures attached. The disclosures are done in an easy-to-read question-and-answer format. The address where complaints may be filed is also included.

**Finance charges** are prohibited on funeral preneed purchases.

100% of the money paid for *funeral* goods and services that will be supplied at a non-guaranteed price must be placed in **trust**. If prices have been guaranteed, only 90% needs to be placed in trust.

A consumer may cancel a funeral contract within 30 days for a full refund including interest. After 30 days, the seller may keep 10% of what was paid but must return all **interest**. The contract may be **transferred** to any provider, presumably minus the 10%.

Funeral directors selling preneed plans must carry a performance **bond** sufficient to cover the risk of loss and have evidence of such on the premises. A chronological list of all preneed contracts must be kept, but there is no annual **reporting** requirement to the state and consumer. Although the Funeral Board inspects funeral homes every three years and reviews preneed record-keeping, there is no way for the state to know that *all* preneed arrangements have been recorded. With the high cost of bonding, there is an inherent motivation to acknowledge or record fewer preneed accounts than have actually been sold. Prepaid funeral money has vanished in other states, including those with 100% trusting requirements.

If selected merchandise is not available at the time of death, **substitution** of items similar in style and at least equal in quality of material and workmanship is required. The survivor may do the selecting; this is one of the few states with such a provision and should be emulated by all others.

### ❖ Restrictive Casket Sales

This heading shows up in only seven state chapters: Alabama, Georgia, Idaho, Louisiana, Oklahoma, South Carolina, and Virginia. (An Oklahoma state court determined in 1997 that restrictions on casket sales were illegal, now under appeal by the funeral board.)

For years, caskets were the major profit-maker for an undertaker, and mark-up on caskets was often 500-700% or more. As word leaked out about actual casket costs, some entrepreneurs saw an opportunity to cut the price and still make a "fair" profit, knowing that consumers were growing resentful. In the mid '90s, the retail casket business was born. Although I certainly support a free-market concept, I—for one—didn't think the public would shop anywhere but at a funeral home for a casket. Boy, was I wrong! The retail casket market is exploding, and consumers are now saving thousands of dollars on over-night delivery of attractive, well-made, quality caskets that are available from sources all around the country, when casket prices in their areas are too high.[1]

The Federal Trade Commission encourages this, permitting consumers to purchase from a funeral home *only* those goods and services wanted. Since 1994, it has forbidden a funeral home from charging a handling fee if a consumer purchases an item or service elsewhere. The FTC

---

[1] Funeral homes with nearby casket stores have been dropping their casket prices and upping their service charges to off-set the loss. Others offer a discounted package if you purchase the casket from the funeral home. The National Casket Retailers Association has filed a complaint with the FTC charging that falsely inflated service charges which are conditionally discounted later are hiding the illegal handling fee.

does not address who may sell a casket, but it has very specific language that does oblige a funeral home to accept a casket provided by the consumer.

So what's the problem in Virginia? The following appears in *Title 320-01-2:1 Definitions*: "*Practice of funeral services*" *means engaging in the care and disposition of the human dead, the preparation of the human dead for the funeral service, burial, or cremation, the making of arrangements for the funeral service or for the financing of the funeral service **and** [emphasis added] the selling or making of financial arrangements for the sale of funeral supplies to the public.*" My reading of this definition—with the use of the word **and**, not *or*—leads me to believe that one must do all of these to be practicing funeral services. Apparently, however, one small portion of this definition—*sale of funeral supplies to the public*—is being used to claim that one must be licensed as a funeral director to sell such supplies.

If one is going to enforce this restrictive *funeral supplies* law, it wouldn't be fair to apply it selectively, would it? Wouldn't that also mean the corner stationery store may no longer sell guest books or thank-you cards? What about burial clothing? And funeral flowers? Or the flag-case to hold a veteran's flag?

Generally, burdensome laws will be sustained by the courts only if there are reasons of public health, vital statistics, or legal/criminal concerns. Just how does the state of Virginia justify controlling who may sell a box—which is all a casket is? What if we call it a "hope chest" instead? Who may sell it then? No law against burying someone in a hope chest.

Clearly, any restriction on who may sell caskets or other funeral supplies in Virginia is a restraint of trade that subverts the FTC's provision specifically permitting consumers to purchase *only* the goods and services desired from the funeral provider. Until legislators get down to business and change the laws or the Funeral Board changes its interpretation, there is nothing to stop you from ordering your casket from another state via the internet or getting directions for building your own:

**www.funerals.org/famsa/caskets.htm**

Not on the internet? Call Catskill Casket Co. in East Meredith, New York: 888-531-5151. Joe White, a minister, and his wife Gail, a teacher, ship affordable caskets for overnight delivery anywhere in the country.

They'll be glad to send you a brochure of their casket selection or refer you to another retailer if they don't carry what you want.

## ❖ Consumer Concerns

- The death rate in Virginia can support approximately 211 full-time mortuaries; there are, however, 474. Funeral prices tend to be higher in areas where there are "too many" funeral homes.
- Laws should require cemeteries to repurchase an unwanted lot at the original selling price plus 50% of the difference between that and current market price.
- There is no annual reporting requirement to the purchaser of prepaid funeral or cemetery goods and services, paperwork that might be useful to the family of a deceased to indicate prepayment. Such reporting would help to "enforce" the required trusting, as well.
- The 10% penalty for transferring a funeral plan should be abolished.
- Until the Virginia laws are changed to require 100% trusting of all money and interest for prepaid *cemetery goods and services* and better oversight for cemetery transactions in general, it is probably a *terrible* idea to prepay for any cemetery arrangements over and above the purchase of a lot. A trust account in a bank will be safer.

There is some effort for legislative change under way at the time of this writing—to increase trusting to 90–100%, among other things. However, certain wording in the proposed legislation leaves a loophole for "constructive delivery"—definitely a no-no for consumers because it reduces trusting requirements. If merchandise has been "delivered" to a warehouse, it is almost impossible to get a refund should you change your mind later. If there are industry people trying to derail and weaken this legislation, one has to assume they are up to no good! Ethical businesses will have no problem going to bat for consumers.

- There is no provision either forbidding a mark-up on cash advance items or requiring the disclosure of how much the mark-up would be. Consumers may want to ask for a copy of the invoice for cash advance items.
- There is no requirement that low-cost caskets be included in any display.
- Virginia regulations incorporate the FTC language only in regard to pricing disclosures. There is no mention of banning deceptive practices such as the misrepresentation of state or cemetery laws

or "tying" (conditioning the purchase of one item on the purchase of another). The FTC Funeral Rule should be adopted by reference. When new amendments to the Rule are enacted, they could then serve the people of Virginia without further legislation. Without such reference, those portions of the Rule will be difficult to enforce in this state.

- Identification and tagging of the body at the place of death before removal should be required.
- The medical examiner's permit for cremation in the case of an *anticipated* death from natural causes is totally unnecessary and creates an additional burden and charge for families.
- The standards for ethical, professional conduct should be strengthened. That would make it easier for a consumer to prevail when filing a complaint.

## ❖ Miscellaneous Information

- The educational requirements for becoming a funeral director in Virginia are mortuary school and one year of apprenticeship. All must pass a state exam and the national exam.
- Medical examiners are physicians who are appointed.
- Any person may designate in writing who will be responsible for making disposition arrangements after death.
- Complaints may be filed with the following:

  Board of Funeral Directors and Embalmers
  c/o Enforcement Division
  6606 W. Broad St. 4th floor
  Richmond, VA 23230-1717
  804-662-9957 or 800-533-1560 (toll-free)

- There is some General Relief money to assist those in need at a time of death. It is administered through local social service departments. Average amount provided: $554.

## ❖ Nonprofit Funeral Consumer Information Societies

These consumer groups are run mostly by volunteers. Consequently, contact information may change. If you have difficulty reaching a society or are interested in starting a society in your area, call the FAMSA office: 800-765-0107. Or check the internet directory—

**www.funerals.org/famsa**

Arlington

> Memorial Society of No. Virginia
> 4444 Arlington Blvd., 22204
> 703-271-9240

Charlottesville

> Mem. Planning Soc. of Piedmont
> 717 Rugby Rd., 22903
> 804-293-8179

Richmond area

> Funeral Consumer Info. Soc. of VA
> P.O. Box 3712, Glen Allen, 23058
> 804-745-3682

Virginia Beach

> Memorial Society of the Tidewater
> P.O. Box 4621, 23454-4621
> 757-428-6900

~❖~

*This chapter was reviewed by the Executive Director for the Board of Funeral Directors and Embalmers. It was also sent for review to the Virginia Department of Health.*

A testy Mr. Harris called me after receiving this chapter and made it clear in no uncertain terms that the Health Department people were unwilling to "review" the Virginia chapter and that I definitely could not print that they had. When I asked what was troubling, he commented on the section I'd written about restrictive casket sales. I was certainly surprised that the Health Department had any interest in who may or may not sell a casket, let alone work up a big snit over what I'd written. I suggested that since the part of the chapter that would be of public health concern came at the beginning of the chapter, I could move any comment on review for accuracy to just after that section. Mr. Harris adamantly refused any such idea. "You just don't get it," he fumed. "We don't want to have anything to do with it."

State Health Commissioner Randolph Gordon, M.D. was a little more sanguine in his letter that followed shortly:

*. . . I expect that this edition of your book will prove to be a helpful resource for those involved with or interested in the care of the deceased. However, as Doug Harris, of my office, explained to you by telephone yesterday, this Department declines your offer to review the excerpt relating to Virginia and emphatically refuses to appear as if it sanctions those provisions that discuss purported shortcomings in Virginia law. . . . I applaud your efforts to provide a useful resource that includes provocative analysis. But, ultimately, you alone bear the responsibility of ensuring the accuracy of what you write and remain accountable for what you propose. . . . I wish you success in this endeavor.*

Thank you, Dr. Gordon.

# In Washington

*Please refer to Chapter 8 as you use this section.*

Persons in Washington may care for their own dead. The legal authority to do so is found in:

> *68.50.160: If the decedent has not made a prearrangement as set forth in subsection (2) of this section or the costs of executing the decedent's wishes . . . exceeds a reasonable amount or directions have not been given by the decedent, the right to control the disposition of the remains of a deceased person vests in . . . (a) the surviving spouse, (b) the surviving adult children of the decedent, (c) the surviving parents of the decedent, (d) the surviving siblings of the decedent, (e) a person acting as a representative of the decedent under the signed authorization of the decedent.*

There are no other statutes that might require you to use a funeral director.

## ❖ Death Certificate

The family doctor or a local medical examiner will sign the death certificate within 48 hours, stating the cause of death. (You may get a blank certificate from the local registrar.) The remaining information must be supplied, typewritten or in black ink. The death certificate must be filed with the local registrar within 72 hours and before final disposition. There will be a $1 charge for filing the death certificate in a county other than the county where death occurred.

## ❖ Fetal Death

A fetal death report is required when death occurs after 20 weeks of gestation. If there is no family physician involved, the local medical examiner must sign the fetal death certificate. The fetal death certificate must be filed within five days. All other procedures apply if disposition is handled by the family.

### ❖ Transporting and Disposition Permit

The local registrar will issue the burial-transit permit. This authorization must be obtained within 72 hours of death and prior to final disposition of the body. After usual business hours, check with the medical examiner's office.

### ❖ Burial

Unless one owns an island, home burial is not permitted, a strange limitation given the vast regions of unpopulated, rural areas where such might be desirable. There are, however, inexpensive county cemeteries where a family might be allowed to handle the burial. The sexton will file the burial-transit permit.

### ❖ Cremation

The burial-transit permit serves as a permit for cremation. Authorization by next-of-kin (or the decedent prior to death) is required, and a pacemaker must be removed. The crematory will file the burial-transit permit.

The crematory must make a note of the casket in which the body is cremated.

### ❖ Other Requirements

Embalming or refrigeration is required if disposition has not been accomplished within 24 hours.

If the person died of a contagious or communicable disease, the doctor in attendance should be consulted. Death from cholera or plague requires embalming or cremation.

### ❖ Medical Schools for Body Donation

University of Washington
Department of Biological Structure
SM-20
Seattle, WA 98195
206-543-1860
   548-3300 after hours
High need

Cost to family: transportation outside King county
Prior enrollment: preferred
Over-enrollment: shared
Disposition: cremation; return of cremains by request
Body rejection: standard,* previous embalming, obesity, cancer

* autopsy, decomposition, mutilation, severe burn victim, meningitis, hepatitis, AIDS, and other contagious or communicable diseases

## ❖ Crematories

Aberdeen

Fern Hill Cemetery
End of Roosevelt, 98520
360-533-2930

Whiteside Funeral Chapels/Crem.
109 E. 2nd St., 98520
360-532-9582

Anacortes

Evans Funeral Chapel
1105 32nd St., 98221
360-293-3311

Auburn

Yahn & Son Crematory
P.O. Box 7, 98071

Bellevue

Green's Funeral Home
1215 145th St. SE, 98009
425-747-1567

Bellingham

Veroske-Jerns-Leveck
James & Sunset, 98225
360-734-0070

Bremerton

Forest Lawn Cemetery
5409 Kitsap, 98310
360-373-3132

Miller Woodlawn Memorial Park
5505 Kitsap Way, 98310
360-377-7648

Colville

Danekas Funeral Chapel
155 W. First Ave., 99114

East Wenatchee

Cascade Memorial Center
378 Eastmont, 98802
509-886-9000

Telford's Chapel of the Valley
P.O. Box 7236, 98802

Ellensburg

Steward & Williams
301 E. 3rd, 98926
509-926-3141

Everett

Cypress Lawn Memorial Park
1615 SE Everett Mall Way, 98204
425-353-7141

Purdy & Walters with Cassidy
P.O. Box 1320, 98206
206-252-2191

Ferndale

Greenacres Memorial Park
5700 Northwest Rd., 98248
206 384-3401

Gig Harbor

Haven of Rest Crematory
P.O. Box 156, 98335

Issaquah

Flintoft's Services
540 E. Sunset Way., 98027

Kelso

Green Hills Memorial Garden
1939 Mt. Brynion Rd., 98626
206-636-0540

Kennewick

Desert Lawn Memorial Park
1401 S. Union, 98336
509-783-9532

Kent

Horizon Services
1317 S. Central Ave. #L, 98032

Moses Lake

Central Cremation Service
416 S. Ash St., 98837

Kayser's Chapel of Memories
831 S. Pioneer Way, 98837

Mt. Vernon

Hawthorne Lawn Memorial Park
P.O. Box 398, 98273
360-424-1154

Mt. Vernon Cemetery
1200 E. Fir St., 98273
360-336-6845

Oak Harbor

Burley Funeral Chapel
6374 60th NW, 98277
360-675-3192

Olympia

Forest Memorial Gardens
2501 Pacific Ave., 98506
360-943-6363

Olympic Cremation Assn.
202 E. 9th, 98501
206-357-4404

Port Angeles

Drennan-Ford Funeral Home
663 Monroe Rd., 98362
360-457-1210

Mt. Angeles Cemetery
105 W. Fourth, 98362
360-452-6255

Port Orchard

Pendleton-Gilchrist Funeral Home
P.O. Box 107, 98366

Port Townsend

Kosec Funeral Home & Crematory
1615 Parkside Dr., 98368
360-385-2642

Puyallup

Powers Funeral Home & Crematory
120 W. Pioneer Ave., 98371
253-845-0536

Renton

Greenwood Memorial Park
350 Monroe Ave. NE, 98056

Mt. Olivet Cemetery
100 Blaine Ave. NE, 98057
206-255-0323

Richland

Einan's Funeral Home & Crematory
915 Bypass Hwy., 99352
509-943-1114

Seattle

Acacia Memorial Park
15000 Bothwell Way NE, 98155
206-362-5525

Arthur Wright Funeral Home
520 W. Raye St., 98133
206-282-5500

Bleitz Funeral Home & Crematory
316 Florentia St., 98109
206-282-5220

Bonney Watson
1732 Broadway, 98122
206-322-0013

Butterworth Manning Ashmore
300 E. Pine St., 98122
206-622-0949

Evergreen-Washelli Memorial Park
11111 Aurora Ave. N, 98133
206-362-5200

Forest Lawn Cemtery
6701 30th Ave. SW, 98126
206-932-0050

Wiggen & Son Mortuary
Bayside Crematory
2003 NW 57th, 98107

Yarrington's White Center
10708 16th Ave. SW, 98146
206-242-2771

Shelton

McComb & Batstone Funeral Home
703 Railroad Ave., 98584
206-426-4803

Spanaway

Fir Lane Memorial Park
Heritage Crematory
924 E. 176th St., 98387

Spokane

Ball & Dodd Crematory
5th & Division, 99202
509-624-4234

Cremation Society of Washington
E. 1821 Sprague Ave., 99202
509-535-6005

Hennessey-Smith Funeral Home
2203 N. Division St., 99207
509-328-2600

Hennessey Valley Funeral Home
1315 N. Pines, 99206

Heritage Crematory
North 508 Government Way, 99210

Riplinger Funeral Home
4305 N. Division St., 99207
509-483-8558

Thornhill Valley Funeral Home
1400 S. Pines, 99206
509-924-2211

Tacoma

Mountain View Memorial Park
4100 Steilacoom Blvd. SW, 98499
253-584-0252

Oakwood Funeral Home/Crematory
5210 S. Alder St., 98409
253-473-2900

Tacoma Cemeteries
9212 Chamers Creek Rd.W, 98467

Tacoma Mausoleum Assn.
S. 53rd & Cedar Sts., 98409
253-474-9574

Vancouver

Park Hill Cemetery/Crematory
5915 E. Mill Plain Blvd., 98661
360-696-8156

Walla Walla

Colonial-Dewitt Crematory
19 E. Birch St., 99362
509-529-4447

Mountain View Funeral Chapel
1551 Dalles-Military Rd., 99362

Professional Funeral Dir./Crem.
2112 S. Second St., 99362
509-522-1625

Wenatchee

Evergreen Memorial Park
P.O. Box 2307, 98807

Jones & Jones
21 S. Chelan Ave., 98801
509-662-2119

Yakima

Terrace Heights Memorial Park
3001 Terrace Heights Rd., 98901
509-453-1961

Additional crematories may have been established in this state after the date of publication.

## ❖ State Governance

The Washington Board of Funeral Directors and Embalmers has five members. One is a public member, and four are funeral directors.

The Washington Cemetery Board has six members: three are cemeterians, two are people with legal, accounting, or other professional experiences that relates to the duties of the board, and one is a public member.

The same administrator serves both boards.

Crematories affiliated with funeral homes are regulated by the funeral board. All others are regulated by the cemetery board.

## ❖ Prepaid Cemetery and Funeral Funds

Only 50% of prepaid *cemetery goods and services* (or wholesale and actual cost, if more) must be placed in **trust. "Constructive delivery"** is permitted and can bypass the trusting requirement. "Delivery" usually is accomplished by issuing a certificate of ownership and warehousing the vault and/or marker, although the state is not checking regularly to see if the goods are actually there. Once "delivered," it is almost impossible to get a refund even if the items have never been used.

A consumer may cancel a cemetery agreement, but only 50%—minus what was spent on "delivered" items—will be **refunded**.

If no claim has been made on a prepaid account for 50 years, the money must be placed in the endowment fund. The cemetery remains obligated, however, for the selected services.

Cemeteries and funeral homes must make an **annual report** of prepaid accounts to the cemetery board.

90% of a prepaid *funeral* contract must be placed into **trust**. The preneed contract must name the institution where money will be deposited along with contact information. "Reasonable fees," not to exceed 1% of the trust, may be withdrawn for administration, provided that the value of the trust is not diminished.

Substitution of funeral merchandise must be equal or better, according to the state-approved preneed contract, but that may be difficult to enforce because such a provision is not in the statutes or rules.

A consumer may **cancel** a preneed agreement within the first 30 days for a full **refund** of all moneys paid. After that, only 90% plus remaining **interest** will be refunded.

## ❖ Consumer Concerns

- The death rate in Washington can support approximately 165 full-time mortuaries; there are 201. Funeral prices tend to be higher in areas where there are "too many" funeral homes.
- Laws should require cemeteries to repurchase an unwanted lot at the original selling price plus 50% of the difference between that and current market price.
- Cemetery trusting should be increased to 100%, with full right to a refund of money paid plus interest. "Constructive delivery" should not be permitted.
- There is no regulation for an adequate description of funeral goods selected preneed nor for a substitution of equal quality approved by survivors if the selected item is no longer available at the time of death.
- There is no annual reporting requirement to the purchaser of prepaid funeral goods and services, paperwork that might be helpful to the family of a deceased to indicate prepayment and would help to "enforce" trusting requirements.
- There is no state protection for consumers in case of default on prepaid funeral funds that were never put into trust.
- Until there is an increase in the trusting requirements and better provisions for substitution, it is probably a *terrible* idea to prepay for a funeral in Washington.
- There is no requirement that low-cost caskets be included in any display.
- The laws requiring embalming or refrigeration after 24 hours and for certain infectious diseases should be repealed. This is not only an offense to some religious groups, it puts the funeral professionals and possibly the environment at risk. The climate in much of Washington makes it realistic to handle a death over several days without embalming. This would be especially important to those caring for their own dead.

- A body must be identified and tagged, but this should be required before removal.
- The standards for ethical, professional conduct should be strengthened. That would make it easier for a consumer to prevail when filing a valid complaint.
- Complaint procedures are unclear and inadequate.
- The FTC Funeral Rule should be adopted by reference to make it more enforceable in this state.
- All cremations must occur in a licensed facility. This will limit the wishes of some Buddhists who would prefer outdoor cremations.

## ❖ Miscellaneous Information

- Educational requirements for becoming a funeral director: two years of college and one year of apprenticeship. For an embalmer: two years of college including mortuary college and two years of apprenticeship.
- Preference is given to the written (and witnessed) wishes of the deceased. Prepaid or prearranged funerals may not be substantially altered by survivors.
- Cash advance items must be billed in the same amount as paid by the funeral home.
- Medical examiners are physicians who are appointed; coroners are elected and do not need to be physicians but may not be an active funeral provider. The county prosecutor assumes the coroner's duties in many counties. The situation varies from one area to another.
- It is illegal to hold a body for debt.

## ❖ Nonprofit Funeral Consumer Information Societies

These consumer groups are run mostly by volunteers. Consequently, contact information may change. If you have difficulty reaching a society or are interested in starting a society in your area, call the FAMSA office: 800-765-0107. Or check the internet directory—

**www.funerals.org/famsa**

Seattle

People's Memorial Assn.
2366 Eastlake Ave. E., Areis Bldg. #409, 98102
206-325-0489

Spokane

Yakima

Spokane Memorial Assn.
P.O. Box 13613, 99213-3613
509-924-8400

Funeral Assn. of Central WA
1916 N. 4th St., 98901
509-248-4533

~❖~

*This chapter was reviewed by the Administrator for Washington Board of Funeral Directors and Embalmers and the Cemetery Board.*

# In West Virginia

*Please refer to Chapter 8 as you use this section.*

Families and members of a religious group in West Virginia may care for their own dead. The following statutes are relevant:

> *Title 30-6-8: Duty of public officers . . . No public officer, employee, physician or surgeon, or any other person having a professional relationship with the deceased shall send, or cause to be sent, to any funeral director . . . the body of any deceased person without having first made due inquiry as to the desires of the next of kin, or any persons who may be chargeable with the funeral expenses of such deceased person; and if any such kin or person can be found, his authority and direction shall be received as to the disposal of said corpse.*

> *Title 30-6-9: (re embalmers and funeral directors) . . . No provision of this article shall apply to or interfere with . . . the customs or rites of any religious sect in the burial of its dead.*

There are no other statutes that might require you to use a funeral director.

## ❖ Death Certificate

The family doctor, local health officer, or medical examiner will supply and sign the death certificate within 24 hours, stating the cause of death. The remaining information must be supplied, typewritten or in black ink with a ball-point pen. There are four copies. The first two pages must be sent to the state Department of Vital Statistics within three days and before final disposition. After verification for accuracy, that office will file the second page with the County. A hospital may retain the fourth copy.

## ❖ Fetal Death

A fetal death report is required when death occurs after 20 weeks of gestation and must be filed as above.

### ❖ Transporting and Disposition Permit

The third page (blue) of the death certificate serves as the burial-transit permit once the signature of the pronouncing medical staff person has been received.

### ❖ Burial

Check with the county or town registrar for local zoning laws regarding home burial. There are no state burial statutes or regulations with regard to depth. A sensible guideline is 150 feet from a water supply and at least three feet of earth on top.

When burial is arranged, the family member acting as the funeral director should sign the permit for disposition and retain it as a record. When there is no person in charge of the burial ground, the words "No person in charge" should be written across the face of the permit.

### ❖ Cremation

A permit for cremation must be obtained from the county medical examiner. There is a modest fee for this. Authorization by next-of-kin is usually required, and a pacemaker must be removed. The crematory operator will retain the burial-transit permit.

One must get permission from the person running a cemetery in order to deposit or bury cremated remains there.

### ❖ Other Requirements

West Virginia has no other requirements controlling the time schedule for the disposition of unembalmed bodies. Weather and reasonable planning should be considered.

If the person died of a contagious or communicable disease, the physician in attendance should be consulted.

## ❖ Medical Schools for Body Donation

Marshall University
School of Medicine
Human Gift Registry
Huntington, WV 25704
304-429-6788 or 525-8121
Donations exceed need at the present
time

Cost to family: transportation outside
state (state sets rate for reimburse-
ment within)
Prior enrollment: required
Over-enrollment: shared
Disposition: cremation; return of cre-
mains by request
Body rejection: standard,* previous em-
balming, sepsis, TB, Creutzfeldt-
Jakob, fetal death


WV School of Osteopathic Medicine
400 N. Lee St.
Lewisburg, WV 24901
304-645-6270

Cost to family: transportation beyond
150 miles
Prior enrollment: not required
Over-enrollment: shared
Disposition: cremation; return of cre-
mains by request
Body rejection: standard*


Human Gift Registry
WV University
4052 Robt. C. Byrd Health Sci. Ctr. N.
P.O. Box 9131
Morgantown, WV 26506
304-293-6322

Cost to family: transportation outside
150 miles (state has transportation
contract)
Prior enrollment: preferred
Over-enrollment: not shared
Disposition: cremation; return of cremains by request
Body rejection: standard,* under 18,
herpes, TB, therapeutic radio nu-
clide treatment


* autopsy, decomposition, mutilation, severe burn victim, meningitis, hepatitis, AIDS, other
infectious diseases

## ❖ Crematories

Beckley

Blue Ridge Memorial Gardens
Beckley-Mt. Hope Rd., 25802
304-256-8625

Keyser-Bryant Funeral Home/Crem.
1000 Johnstown, 25801
304-252-8642

Charleston

Barlow Bonsall Funeral Home/Crem.
1118 Virginia St. E., 25301
304-342-8135

Martinsburg

Rosedale Funeral Home/Crematory
Rt. 7 Box 210A, 25401
304-263-4922

Mineral Wells

Mid-Ohio Valley Cremation Services
Mineral Wells, 26150
304-489-1320
800-315-2050

Morgantown

Omega Crematory
153 Spruce St., 26505
304-292-8664

Princeton

Seaver Funeral Service/Crematory
1507 N. Walker St., 24740
304-425-2282

Additional crematories may have been established in this state after the date of publication.

## ❖ State Governance

The West Virginia Board of Embalmers and Funeral Directors has seven members, one of whom is a lay member.

The Attorney General's office regulates preneed funeral transactions. Cemetery preneed is regulated by the State Tax Department.

Crematories are not licensed or regulated at the time of this writing. One does not need to be a funeral director to operate a crematory.

## ❖ Prepaid Cemetery and Funeral Funds

Only 40% of prepaid *cemetery goods and services* must be placed in **trust**. "**Constructive delivery**" can bypass the trusting requirement altogether for vaults and markers. There's no indication that the state has a procedure for verifying that these are waiting for you in the warehouse, so the cemetery probably feels free to pocket all your money right away. (In one state, there were only 200 of the 500 pre-sold vaults in stock when someone finally went to check.) If you've paid for a vault and the opening-and-closing charges for a full body burial, it's probably unlikely that you'd get much if any money back if you later decided on cremation instead—with only modest interment needs—or had moved on to other places and relationships in your life and wanted to cancel the whole deal and sell the lot.

Oh, yes, **interest** may be withdrawn for "any appropriate trustee and auditor fees, commissions and costs."

Cemetery vendors may sell **unconstructed mausoleum space** for up to seven years before construction must start—or until 80% of the space has been sold, whichever comes first. If each sale represents a simple 50% mark-up over cost, then 100% of the construction money will have been raised after selling half or 50% of the crypts. An investor, however, can wait a little longer, selling the next 30% of the crypts, collecting

60% of the total profit to be made without ever having had to build or maintain a thing. State laws seem strangely silent on any trusting requirements for the money from preconstruction mausoleum sales or how to protect consumers in case of default.

How long construction might take doesn't seem to have been considered, either. Funeral directors tell me that most preneed plans are used within six years. Wonder where they'll put the bodies in the meantime? You might want to ask before purchasing anything that hasn't been built. Or ask how to get your money and interest back if you change your mind.

A preneed seller of *funeral plans* may not make in-person **solicitations**, including by telephone. Contact must be invited by the purchaser. No such restrictions exist for *cemetery sales,* so you can be sure that those companies owning combo operations will send their "cemetery" sales reps to your door. Of course, while they are there . . . .

A preneed seller may retain 10% of the prepaid *funeral funds* as a commission. I'm told I'm not supposed to call this a *commission,* though—it's "to offset administrative and operating costs," wrote the auditor for the Preneed Funeral Division. She says that the majority of funeral directors put 100% into **trust**, but I don't find it particularly reassuring that the state doesn't *require* that 100% be placed into trust or that 100% will stay there. The commission (or whatever you want to call it) can be taken first if you are paying on an installment plan. In other words, on a $5,000 funeral, the funeral director can pocket the first $500. After that, the rest of the funds must be placed in trust.

A preneed seller must make biennial **reports** to the Attorney General's office. Although there is no statutory provision making it a requirement, I'm told that the Attorney General's office will notify a consumer when a preneed plan has been filed in that office.

A purchaser may **cancel** a preneed contract and receive a refund of the 90% in trust plus interest. There is a provision for **transferring** a contract, which would be useful for those with an irrevocable agreement, but you can count on only 90% plus interest being transferred.

A provider is obligated to provide those goods and services contracted for in a preneed arrangement *even if they are not desired by the next-of-kin.* This is a two-edged sword. On the one hand, it's one way for the deceased to make sure that his or her wishes are carried out. Well, sort of. One family did not have the funds to ship a body to Iowa, purchase a vault, and open the grave—services that were not paid for in the initial contract but necessary to complete the original plan. Obviously, an alternative had to be considered. "Otherwise," said the niece, "I'm not sure what you're going to do with an embalmed little old lady at your funeral home. There simply isn't any money left to get her out of there." Next-of-kin should not be bound by a contract for which there are not sufficient funds to carry out the wishes. Another woman wanted to change her father's plans—he'd outlived all his friends and few relatives were nearby, so who would show up for a viewing? When the funeral home refused to modify arrangements, she got up to leave. "Where are you going?" the funeral director asked. "I'm going to find another funeral home," she replied. "But we've got your father's body," said the undertaker. With more aplomb than most could muster at a time of death she shot back, "And what are you going to do with it?" A second funeral home—far more accommodating—picked up the body a short time later.

When a preneed contract is offered at a guaranteed price, the funeral home must make up the difference in any cost at the time of honoring the contract. Although the statutes provide that excess funds must be returned to the estate, that is unlikely with the current rate of funeral inflation.

There is no provision for an adequate description of merchandise selected preneed nor any provision for a **substitute** of equal quality and construction that would be pleasing to the family, not just something of equal "value." This clearly leaves the undertaker free to pull mischief, particularly if the undertaker will be stuck footing the bill. A $750 casket chosen 10 years ago is likely to cost $1,750 today, and a casket "valued" at $750 today may be the one the undertaker refers to as "the welfare casket," one he'll suggest as the one that comes with the contract . . . unless, of course, the family would like to pay for "something a little nicer."

A buyer will be assessed a fee of $20 for each preneed contract purchased, of which $8 goes to the Preneed Guarantee Fund. This protection against default is quite limited, unfortunately. If multiple claims are made and the total exceeds the amount in the Fund, claimants will get only a *pro rata* share. West Virginia would be wise to adopt the Vermont plan that is structured to cover all loss to funeral consumers.

## ❖ Consumer Concerns

- The death rate in West Virginia can support approximately 82 full-time mortuaries; there are, however, 315. Funeral prices tend to be higher in areas where there are "too many" funeral homes.
- There is no state board governing cemeteries. This is a serious omission with the rapid growth of corporate-owned cemeteries. One legislative remedy would be to change the name of the current funeral board to one of "Funeral and Cemetery Services." Then change the make-up of the board to three morticians, three cemeterians who have *no* affiliation with mortuaries, three consumer advocates, and a monument dealer.
- Laws should require cemeteries to repurchase an unwanted lot at the original selling price plus 50% of the difference between that and current market price.
- The provisions for financing the Preneed Guarantee Fund should be modified to adequately cover all consumer loss.
- 100% of prepaid funeral funds should be placed in trust, with interest to accrue and be fully refundable for revocable contracts.
- An adequate description of preneed merchandise selected should be included in the contract if the price is guaranteed, with a provision for substitution of equal quality and construction, satisfactory to the family, if the selected item is not available at the time of death.
- There is no annual reporting requirement to the purchaser of prepaid funeral goods and services, paperwork that might be useful to the family of a deceased to indicate prepayment. It would help to enforce any trusting requirements, as well.
- Until the West Virginia laws are changed to require 100% trusting of all money and interest for prepaid funeral and cemetery goods and services, it is probably a *terrible* idea to prepay for these arrangements. Your own or a shared trust account in the bank will be safer and may be made irrevocable if you need to shelter assets.
- The coroner or medical examiner's permit for cremation in the case of an *anticipated* death from natural causes is totally unnecessary and creates an additional burden and charge for families.
- Identification and tagging of the body at the place of death before removal should be required.

- There is no provision either forbidding a mark-up on cash advance items or requiring the disclosure of how much the mark-up would be. Consumers may wish to ask for a copy of the invoice for such charges.
- There is no requirement that low-cost caskets be included in any display.
- Although a mortician is obliged to honor the wishes of the deceased in a prefunded funeral arrangement, there is no provision for advance directives that would confer the decision-making authority to another in situations where funeral plans were not already paid for. A designated agent for deathcare and funeral arrangements might also be important in situations where you are estranged or distant from next-of-kin.
- The standards for ethical, professional conduct should be strengthened. That would make it easier for a consumer to prevail when filing a valid complaint. (See Ethical Standards in the Appendix.)
- The FTC Funeral Rule should be adopted by reference to make it more enforceable in this state.

## ❖ Miscellaneous Information

- Educational requirements for funeral director: two years of college (60 semester hours) plus mortuary college, national exam, exam of state laws, and one year of apprenticeship.
- Medical examiners are appointed and must be licensed physicians.
- Although complaint procedures are unclear, the Attorney General's office does have a Consumer Hotline: 800-368-8808.

## ❖ Nonprofit Funeral Consumer Information Societies

The Maryland society serves the northern part of the state. Although there is no nonprofit consumer society in West Virginia, the FAMSA office has located an affordable cooperating mortician in the southwest part of West Virginia to whom inquiries can be referred. If you are interested in starting a society in your area, call the FAMSA office: 800-765-0107. Or check the internet directory—

**www.funerals.org/famsa**

For northern WV:

Memorial Society of Maryland
9601 Cedar Ln.
Bethesda, MD 20814
800-564-0017

For the rest of the state:

Call the FAMSA office.

~❖~

*This chapter was reviewed by the Attorney General's office—Consumer Protection Division and the Board of Embalmers and Funeral Directors. A few details were checked by telephone with the Department of Health—Vital Statistics.*

# In Wisconsin

*Please refer to Chapter 8 as you use this section.*

Families in Wisconsin may care for their own dead. The legal authority to do so is found in:

> *Title 69.18(1)(a) Any one of the following may move a body for the purpose of final disposition: . . . 2. A member of the decedent's immediate family who personally prepares for and conducts the final disposition of the decedent.*

There are no other statutes that might require you to use a funeral director.

A pamphlet, "Burial by Immediate Family Members," is available from the Wisconsin Center for Health Statistics, P.O. Box 309, Madison, WI 53701.

## ❖ Death Certificate

The attending doctor will sign the death certificate, in black ink, within six days stating the cause of death. In some counties, the coroner must certify the cause when death occurred at home. The remaining information must be supplied, typewritten or in black ink. The death certificate must be filed with the local registrar within two days of medical certification.

## ❖ Fetal Death

A fetal death report is required when death occurs after 20 weeks of gestation or when the weight is 350 grams or more. The fetal death report must be filed with the registrar within five days. No forms or documents are required by law for fetal disposition unless transported out of the state, in which case the Report for Final Disposition must accompany the remains.

### ❖ Transporting and Disposition Permit

The Report for Final Disposition may be obtained from the local registrar or from a funeral director. A body may be moved from a hospital or nursing home by the immediate family only if the family is conducting the burial. In that case, you will also need the Notice of Removal of a Human Corpse from an Institution. If the institution does not have this form, a funeral director or the local registrar may be asked to supply one.

The Report for Final Disposition must be mailed to the local Registrar within 24 hours (or—in Kenosha, Manitowoc, Milwaukee, Neenah, Oshkosh, Racine, Sheboygan, or West Allis—to the City Health Officer). One copy must also be sent to the coroner or medical examiner, located through the office of the county sheriff.

### ❖ Burial

Check with the county or town registrar for local zoning laws regarding home burial. There are no state burial statutes or regulations with regard to depth. A sensible guideline is 150 feet from a water supply and three feet of earth on top.

When burial is arranged, the family member acting as the funeral director must sign the Report for Final Disposition and retain one copy as a record for two years.

### ❖ Cremation

A cremation permit from the coroner or medical examiner is required. Although the state fee for a coroner investigating a death is $25, a charge of $50 to families for this is not uncommon at this writing. In Milwaukee, the charge is $115. There is a 48-hour waiting period prior to cremation. Authorization by next-of-kin is usually required, and a pacemaker must be removed.

One must get permission from the person running a cemetery in order to deposit or bury cremated remains. However, there are no state laws restricting where you may scatter cremains.

## ❖ Other Requirements

Wisconsin has no other requirements controlling the time schedule for the disposition of unembalmed bodies. Weather and reasonable planning should be considered.

The Health Department may regulate disposition when death was caused by a contagious or infectious disease. The doctor in attendance should be consulted.

## ❖ Medical Schools for Body Donation

University of Wisconsin
Medical School
Dept. of Anatomy
1300 University Ave.
Madison, WI 53706
608-262-2888 days
608-262-2800 or 0143
Moderate need

Cost to family: none, university picks up body within state
Prior enrollment: encouraged
Over-enrollment: will share but has not happened
Disposition: cremation; return of cremains by request
Body rejection: standard,* under 18, obesity, recent major surgery

Medical College of Wisconsin
Dept. of Cell Biol. & Anatomy
Anatomical Gift Registry
8701 Watertown Plank Rd.
P.O. Box 26509
Milwaukee, WI 53226
414-257-8261
Moderate need

Cost to family: transportation; administrative fee
Prior enrollment: preferred but not required
Over-enrollment: shared
Disposition: cremation/scattering in school park; no return of cremains
Body rejection: standard,* under 18, previous embalming, obesity, systemic cancer

* autopsy, decomposition, mutilation, severe burn victim, AIDS, meningitis, hepatitis, other infectious diseases

## ❖ Crematories

Appleton

Wichmann Funeral Home
537 N. Superior St., 54911
414-739-1231

Brookfield

Lakeshore Burial Vault Co.
12780 W. Lisbon Rd., 53005
414-781-6262

Wisconsin Memorial Park
13235 W. Capitol Dr., 53005
414-781-7474

Eau Claire

Eau Claire Mem. Crem. Services
2222 London Rd., 54701
715-832-6244

Fond du Lac

Parkview Cremations
524 N. Park Ave., 54935
414-922-5110

Green Bay

Memorial Crematory
701 N. Baird, 54302
414-432-5579

Proko-Wall Funeral Home
1630 E. Mason St., 54302
414-468-4111

Hayward

Hayward Cremation Service
304 W. 3rd St., 54843
715-634-2609

Janesville

Milton Lawns Mem. Park
2200 Milton Ave., 53545
608-754-4222

Kenosha

Southport Crematory
1119 60th St., 53140
414-654-3533

Kimberly

Heart of the Valley Crematory
101 N. Elm St., 54136
800-622-6208 (WI)

La Crosse

Cremation Associates
1425 Jackson, 54601
608-782-0030

Oak Grove Crematory
1081 Cedar Rd., 54601
608-782-5244

Madison

Cress Funeral Service
3610 Speedway Rd., 53705
608-238-3434

FLS Crematory
6021 University, 53705
608-238-8406

Forest Hill Crematory
1 Speedway Rd., 53705
608-233-5455

Manitowoc

Jens Funeral Home/Crematory
1122 S. 8th St., 54220
414-682-1568

Reinbold & Pfeffer Funeral Home
818 State St., 54220
414-682-0118

Mequon

Schmidt & Bartlet Funeral Service
10280 N. Pt. Washington Rd. 53092
414-241-8085

Milwaukee

Forest Home Cemetery
2405 W. Forest Home Ave., 53215
414-645-2632

Valhalla Memorial Park
5402 N. 91st St., 53225
414-462-3300

Minocqua

Bolger Funeral Home
212 Chicago St., 54548
715-356-3200

Monroe

Cremation Service Unlimited
921 15th Ave., 53566
608-328-8376

Oak Creek

Forest Hill Memorial Park
3301 E. Forest Hill Ave., 53154
414-762-4446

Oshkosh

Lakeview Memorial Park
2786 Algoma, 54901
414-235-5655

Plover/Stevens Point

Jens & Jensky Funeral Home
2800 Plover Rd., 54467
715-344-2023

Ripon

Central WI Crematory
515 Mayparty Dr., 54971
414-748-2623

Sheboygan

Ballhorn Crematory
1201 N. 8th, 53081
414-457-4455

Sun Prairie

Cress Cremation Services
1310 Emerald Terr., 53590
608-837-9054

Superior

Superior Crematory Service
1528 Ogden Ave., 54880
715-394-4721

Wausau

Brainard Funeral Home
522 Adams, 54401
715-845-5525

Wauwatosa

Schmidt & Bartelt
10121 W. North Ave., 53226
414-774-5010

West Allis

John Borgward FH/Crematory
1603 S. 81st St., 53214
414-476-2010

Additional crematories may have been established in this state after the date of publication.

## ❖ State Governance

The Wisconsin Funeral Directors Examining Board has six members. Two are consumer representatives. This board regulates funeral homes and funeral preneed.

Cemeteries and cemetery preneed transactions are regulated by the Department of Regulation and Licensing.

Crematory construction is regulated by the Department of Commerce, but they are not otherwise regulated.

## ❖ Prepaid Cemetery and Funeral Funds

If a cemetery lot appears "abandoned" after 50 years and the cemetery cannot locate the owner or heirs, the lot may be resold.

Funeral home owners may not also own cemeteries in Wisconsin, but the corporate boys simply ignored the law, and purchased both. In 1997, the state ordered Loewen and SCI to divest one or the other. SCI is appealing. Loewen put its funeral homes up for sale, presumably because there is considerably more income from cemetery operations, according to the stockholders' annual report and witnessed by shocked consumers getting gouged at the graveyard. One funeral director offered to buy back his funeral homes. Loewen said "no." The mortician even offered $1 million more than Loewen paid for them. The answer was still "no." The funeral homes in question are now owned by the newly-formed Charon Group based in Illinois.

At least 40% (or wholesale cost, whichever is greater) of preneed *cemetery* purchases must be placed in **trust**. When paying by installment, 40% of each payment must be placed in trust. "**Constructive delivery**" can bypass the trusting requirement with a warehouse receipt. Is the state inspecting warehouses to see if your marker is really there? Money for undeveloped burial space also must be placed in trust in the same proportion. However, a "letter of credit" from a financial institution or **bond** can eliminate any trusting requirements for the undeveloped cemetery space.

Outer burial containers (vaults) are not included in the cemetery merchandise category (as they are in most other states), and 100% of the vault price must be placed in trust, as applies to *funeral* preneed merchandise.

Cemetery preneed sellers must **report** on preneed accounts annually to the Department of Regulation and Licensing.

Religious and certain nonprofit cemeteries are exempt from most of the preneed sales and reporting requirements.

Preneed **solicitation** door-to-door is not permitted. The consumer must request the contact. A prospective purchaser may not be contacted in a health-care facility or similar institution.

100% of prepaid *funeral* money must be placed in separate **trust** accounts with the **interest** accruing. The depositor must be supplied with evidence showing that the funds have been deposited.

Funeral insurance is also permitted as a funding vehicle. If there is a sales commission to be paid, that fact must be disclosed, but not the amount.

Only $2,000 of the funeral funds paid may be considered "irrevocable." An irrevocable agreement may be **transferred** at any time. This limit is fairly low if a vault is included in the "funeral" merchandise.

A purchaser may **cancel** a non-irrevocable prenced funeral agreement at any time and request a refund of the amount paid plus interest. This does not apply to *cemetery* purchases.

## ❖ Consumer Concerns

- The death rate in Wisconsin can support approximately 180 full-time mortuaries; there are 590 such establishments. Funeral prices tend to be higher in areas where there are "too many" funeral homes.
- Laws should require cemeteries to repurchase an unwanted lot at the original selling price plus 50% of the difference between that and current market price.
- Trusting requirements for cemetery merchandise and services should be increased to 100%, with full right of refund for revocable arrangements. Constructive delivery should not be permitted.
- There is no provision for an adequate description of funeral goods selected preneed or for a substitution of equal quality if the selected item is no longer available at the time of death. Survivors should approve any substitution.
- Although the purchaser of a prenced funeral agreement must be supplied with evidence showing that the funds have been deposited, there is no requirement for an annual report to the buyer that would indicate that the funds are still there. Such paperwork would help to enforce the trusting requirement and could be useful to survivors.
- Because of inadequate substitution provisions, limited reporting, and no state protection in case a provider defaults, it is probably *unwise* to prepay for a funeral in Wisconsin. It is probably a *terrible* idea to prepay for any cemetery merchandise and services.
- The 48-hour wait before cremation is totally unnecessary when survivors are in agreement and is causing additional charges to families for "storage."
- The coroner or medical examiner's permit for cremation in the case of an *anticipated* death from natural causes is totally unnecessary and creates an additional burden and charge for families.

- Identification and tagging of the body at the place of death before removal should be required.
- Except for cemetery charges, there is no provision either forbidding a mark-up on cash advance items or requiring the disclosure of how much the mark-up would be.
- There is no requirement that low-cost caskets be included in any display.
- In some parts of the state, medical examiners are appointed to investigate deaths. In other areas, elected coroners are in charge. Some coroners may even be funeral directors. There is only a $50 fine if a funeral director/coroner serves as the funeral director for a body whose death the coroner investigated.
- The standards for ethical, professional conduct should be strengthened. That would make it easier for a consumer to prevail when filing a complaint.
- Complaint procedures are unclear and inadequate.
- There is no law that allows you to state your funeral preferences or for naming a designated agent to make your final arrangements. In situations where you are estranged or distant from next-of-kin, this could be important.

### ❖ Miscellaneous Information

- Educational requirements for a funeral director: two years of college, at least one of which is in mortuary science, one year of apprenticeship, and an exam.
- No funeral director or operator of a funeral home may operate a cemetery or have a financial interest in a cemetery. The giant funeral chains are contesting this restriction.
- The FTC Funeral Rule has been incorporated in the funeral regulations.

### ❖ Nonprofit Funeral Consumer Information Societies

These consumer groups are run mostly by volunteers. Consequently, contact information may change. If you have difficulty reaching a society or are interested in starting a society in your area, call the FAMSA office: 800-765-0107. Or check the internet directory—

**www.funerals.org/famsa**

Egg Harbor

Memorial Societies of Wisc.
6900 Lost Lake Rd. 54209-9231
920-868-3136
800-374-1109 (WI only)
Serves all of the state outside of the Milwaukee area.

Milwaukee

Funeral Consumer Info. Soc. of
  Milwaukee area
13001 W. North Ave.
Brookfield, WI 53005
414-782-3535

~❖~

*This chapter was reviewed by the Department of Regulation and Licensing. No response was received from the Department of Health Statistics.*

# In Wyoming

*Please refer to Chapter 8 as you use this section.*

Persons in Wyoming may care for their own dead. The legal authority to do so is found in:

> *Title 35-1-418(b): The funeral director or person acting as such who first assumes custody of a dead body shall file the death certificate.*

There are no other statutes that might require you to use a funeral director.

### ❖ Death Certificate

The local registrar will supply the death certificate. It must be signed by the attending physician or coroner within 24 hours, stating the cause of death. The remaining information must be supplied, typewritten or in permanent ink. Do not use a felt-tip pen; there are four copies. The third (pink) copy is for the records of the person acting as the funeral director. The remaining portions of the death certificate must be filed with the local registrar within three days or before removal from the state.

### ❖ Fetal Death

A fetal death report is required if death occurs after 20 weeks of gestation. If there is no family physician involved, the local coroner must sign the fetal death certificate. All other procedures apply if disposition is handled by the family.

### ❖ Transporting and Disposition Permit

A body may be moved with the consent of a physician, medical examiner, or county coroner. The fourth page (green) of the death certificate serves as the burial-transit permit and must be signed by the registrar in the district where death occurred before accompanying the body to its final disposition.

## ❖ Burial

Check with the local registrar for local zoning laws regarding home burial. There are no state burial statutes or regulations with regard to depth. A sensible guideline is 150 feet from a water supply and three feet of earth on top. The burial-transit permit must be filed with the registrar in the district of disposition within ten days.

Land that has been surveyed and platted may be recorded in the county clerk's office as a cemetery. Such land is tax-exempt.

## ❖ Cremation

The burial-transit permit is sufficient for cremation. There is a 24-hour waiting period before cremation unless a coroner's permit has been obtained. Authorization by next-of-kin is usually required, and a pacemaker must be removed.

Any person in charge of disposition may witness the cremation.

## ❖ Other Requirements

When a body is in the possession of a funeral director, it must be embalmed or refrigerated within 36 hours.

If death has occurred from a communicable, contagious, or infectious disease, the body must be prepared by an embalmer. Bodies shipped by common carrier must be embalmed.

## ❖ Medical Schools for Body Donation

There are no medical schools in Wyoming.

## ❖ Crematories

Casper

Wyoming Cremation Services
710 E. 2nd St., 82601
307-234-0234

Cheyenne

Cheyenne Memorial Services
2015 Warren Ave., 82001
307-632-2462

Sunset Park Crematory
2323 Care Ave., 82001
307-634-1568

Additional crematories may have been established in this state after the date of publication.

## ❖ State Governance

The Wyoming State Board of Embalming has five members including one from the State Board of Health. There are no consumer representatives.

Prepaid funerals are regulated by the Insurance Department.

There is no state board governing cemeteries (pending change).

## ❖ Prepaid Cemetery and Funeral Funds

Privately-owned *cemeteries* must establish a perpetual care fund. 20% of each interment space sale must go toward perpetual care. A **bond** in the amount of 5% of all amounts received must be maintained as protection against default. An annual **report** must be made to the commissioner of Insurance.

100% of prepaid *funeral* funds must be placed in **deposit,** "in such types of investments which men of prudence, discretion and intelligence would acquire or retain for their own account." This is the only statutory provision regarding preneed purchases. There are, however, regulations that spell out other conditions for preneed transactions.

Each preneed agreement must be a guaranteed-price contract, with no further money due.

Regulations permit the funeral seller to withdraw and keep all **interest.** Furthermore, the seller may retain a **penalty** of 20% if the buyer needs or wishes to **transfer** the contract to another funeral home. For those who travel outside their immediate area, this could be a serious potential problem. There is a strangely-worded provision that "If no request for performance of the contract shall have been received by the contract seller from the next of kin or legal representative of the decedent within seventy-two hours after the death of the decedent, then the contract seller shall cause such services to be performed and such goods supplied in the manner provided in the contract. ..." If the buyer dies in, say, high-priced Palm Beach, Florida, is the seller obligated to pay whatever it takes for the Florida funeral director to provide the services? That seems unfair to the Wyoming funeral director on the one hand, but perhaps it's just desserts if the Wyoming funeral director has been pocketing all the interest and would have kept 20% otherwise.

Sellers must make an annual **report** to the Commissioner. The Insurance Department is regularly auditing preneed record-keeping, according to a local funeral director.

Sellers must maintain a bond in the amount of 5% of preneed trust agreements, hardly sufficient to protect consumers against default.

## ❖ Consumer Concerns

- The death rate in Wyoming can support approximately 15 full-time mortuaries; there are 35 such establishments. Given the low density of population over a vast geographic area, mortuary careers are not likely to be full-time work. Unfortunately, because of the low volume of business per mortuary, funeral prices will tend to be higher than elsewhere.
- No grave-side services are permitted at the Oregon Trail State Veterans' Cemetery. Services must be conducted in a designated chapel or patio area. This seems an odd and disconcerting restriction.
- Laws should require cemeteries to repurchase an unwanted lot at the original selling price plus 50% of the difference between that and current market price.
- Laws should provide that a consumer may cancel a preneed contract and get a refund or transfer arrangements without penalty or loss of interest.
- Laws should require substitution of equal quality and construction—approved by the family—if selected funeral merchandise is not available at the time of death.
- Consumers should get an annual report of preneed accounts, paperwork that might be useful to next-of-kin and that would help to enforce the trusting requirement.
- A guarantee fund should be established to protect consumers against the default of funeral providers.
- Until there is adequate protection, it is probably a *terrible* idea to prepay for a funeral in Wyoming.
- The law requiring preparation by an embalmer when death occurs from a communicable or contagious disease should be amended. The implication is that the body will be embalmed under the worst possible circumstances for doing so. This is not only an offense to some religious groups, it puts the funeral professionals and possibly

the environment at risk. The law should distinguish between "communicable" and "contagious." Those who have cared for those ailing from AIDS prior to death should be able to do so after death.

- There is no provision either forbidding a mark-up on cash advance items or requiring the disclosure of how much the mark-up would be. Consumers may wish to ask for an invoice for these purchases.
- There is no requirement that low-cost caskets be included in any display.
- Identification and tagging of the body at the place of death before removal should be required.
- Complaint procedures are unclear and inadequate.
- The standards for ethical, professional conduct should be strengthened. That would make it easier for a consumer to prevail when filing a valid complaint.
- It would appear that the only choices the Embalming Board has in response to a complaint are a letter of warning, setting conditions on a license, or revocation. The ability to levy fines should be added as a deterrent.

## ❖ Miscellaneous Information

- The educational requirements for becoming an embalmer in Wyoming are one year of college, a year of mortuary school, and one year of apprenticeship. The board will conduct a test of the applicants, which may include a practicum. There are no educational requirements for becoming a funeral director but the applicant must pass a test of state rules and regulations and health information.
- Crematories are licensed, regulated, and inspected by the State Board of Embalming. One does not need to be a mortician to run a crematory.
- The FTC Funeral Rule has been adopted by reference.
- Rental caskets are permitted.
- There is case law requiring survivors to comply with the written wishes of the decedent. You may wish to name a designated agent for your final arrangements. In situations where you are estranged or distant from next-of-kin, this could be important.
- Coroners are elected. There is no requirement that the coroner be medically trained, and funeral directors may run for the job.
- It is unprofessional conduct to use "profane, indecent or obscene language in the presence of a dead human body, or within the immediate hearing of the family or relatives of a deceased, whose

body has not yet been interred or otherwise disposed of." After that, watch out?

### ❖ Nonprofit Funeral Consumer Information Societies

Although there are no memorial societies in Wyoming as of this writing, you may check the internet directory—

**www.funerals.org/famsa**

—or call the national office to see if any have since been started: 1-800-765-0107. Or let the FAMSA office know if you are willing to help start one. The FAMSA office may have a limited list of ethically-priced mortuaries in Wyoming to which referrals can be made.

~❖~

*This chapter was reviewed by the Department of Insurance and the Department of Public Health.*

# Part III

# Appendix

# Ethical Standards & Unprofessional Conduct
## Filing a Complaint

In Indiana, a funeral director must "act with compassion." Unfortunately, it's not so easy to legislate what constitutes "compassion." It's easier—based on consumer complaints—to identify what is *unprofessional conduct*, as many states have done. The majority of the following appear scattered in the laws or regulations of one state or another, but no state has any list so comprehensive:

## Unprofessional Conduct

—uses fraud, deceit, misrepresentation, overreaching, intimidation, or other forms of vexatious conduct to influence funeral choices

—takes undue advantage of a person's ignorance or emotional vulnerability

—makes false or misleading statements of the legal requirement as to the necessity of any particular burial merchandise or services

—creates false or unjustified expectations

—makes statements that are misleading or deceiving because of only a partial disclosure of relevant facts

—exploits a person's fears in order to sell more expensive items

—claims or implies that embalming protects the public health

—claims or implies that embalming preserves the body for more than a brief period

—claims or implies that certain caskets and vaults will protect or preserve the body

—claims or implies that there is only one acceptable way to arrange a funeral or that one way is more acceptable than another

—fails consider the wishes of the family and/or the family's financial limitations

—fails to offer the same courtesy and consideration for those receiving public assistance with funeral costs as is offered to others; uses the term "welfare" funeral

—disparages low-cost options or choices

—treats any person differently to his/her detriment because of race, creed, color, national origin, religion, gender-orientation, or cause of death

—fails to determine the cultural and religious preferences of the family

—shows lack of respect for cultural or religious customs

—fails to honor requests and make adjustments that are not unreasonable, even if they may seem unusual or different

—makes assumptions and decisions for the family without first determining exact wishes

—makes disparaging comments on the condition of any dead human body entrusted to his or her care

—fails to treat with dignity and respect the body of the deceased, any member of the family or relatives of the deceased, any employee, or any other person encountered while within the scope of practice, employment, or business

—fails to ascertain next-of-kin with legal responsibility for funeral arrangements before providing services

—fails to determine if all next-of-kin of the same legal order are in agreement before services are provided

—alters funeral arrangements without the explicit permission of the person who has contracted for those arrangements

—misrepresents the availability or delay in obtaining merchandise

—fails to make available three low-cost caskets in the same general manner as the other caskets are displayed

—represents a for-profit business as a "society"

—refuses to surrender the body (or cremated remains) upon the express order of the person lawfully entitled to the custody, whether or not the funeral bill has been paid

—uses funeral merchandise previously sold without prior written permission of the person selecting or paying for the use of the merchandise

—fails to return all personal items that were with the body at the time of removal

—fails to maintain confidentiality

—solicits future sales during or immediately after at-need arrangements

—uses uninvited, in-person or telephone solicitations

—sells supposedly at a substantial discount when in fact the actual price has been increased to cover the supposed discount

—represents that the price is a special price to the purchaser only, if another purchaser would be given the same price

—obtains a purchaser's signature on a sales contract written in English if the purchaser cannot read or speak English, unless there is a disinterested person present who can explain fully to the purchaser what he or she is buying

—fails to disclose the charge for services in obtaining cash-advance items if not billed at actual cost

—fails to follow all provisions of the FTC Funeral Rule

By having an explicit list of unacceptable behaviors, funeral providers are likely to be more mindful of their actions. When the standards aren't specific enough, consumer complaints are often dismissed.

To meet the needs of consumers, each state should require that a toll-free phone number and address for filing a funeral complaint appear on the General Price List (GPL). Each state should have a pamphlet to mail out on "How to File a Complaint." It should be a required hand-out for preneed sales people. The list of unprofessional behaviors should be included, with a request to identify which (if any) are involved with the complaint, along with a narrative report.

It is important for a state to have the ability to order a refund of money paid, to cancel a debt, or to levy a fine when a mortician is guilty of unprofessional conduct. The fine should be sufficiently large to be a deterrent, not just a nuisance. In some cases, requiring additional education might be appropriate.[1] In far too many states, the only recourse is to suspend a license to practice—something that is rarely done. If the only remedy is too extreme, many who are guilty will go unpunished. The Illinois office handling complaints asks consumers what remedy they are seeking—a nice touch, I thought. A complaint form might list the following:

```
As a remedy I am seeking:
___ loss of license                 ___ probation
___ refund/cancellation of debt $_____
___ fine of $2,000 per violation for ___ violations
___ a public, written apology
___ other _____
```

Almost all states provide for a hearing at which the funeral director can explain things and defend his/her actions. But then the Funeral Board makes the ultimate decision on any penalty, if merited, usually without input from the people involved. I would like to see the settlement process open to the public, with active participation of all parties. Some consumers may need to be educated about what are reasonable expectations. While it won't be perfect all the time, the

---

[1] An e-mail from a priest to FAMSA expressed astonishment that there is no training of religious customs in mortuary schools. Nor are there any such questions on the national exam. To their credit, I have seen funeral directors exchange information on on-line bulletin boards—*e.g.*, "What should I expect from a Hindu service?" Various religious rituals and beliefs about death would be a good topic for continuing education classes. Likewise, funeral directors need to be sensitive to those who have rejected formal religious affiliation. One young father was incensed that a funeral director had placed a bible on display after he thought he had made it clear that his wife's ceremony would be without any religious overtones. The same funeral director failed to call the Eye Bank as had been requested. The husband was terribly dismayed that his wife's last wishes were never honored. A course in eye-enucleation should be required for all funeral directors—a "penalty" this thoughtful Wisconsin husband would have welcomed.

consumer should walk away feeling that the state is listening and is really concerned about consumer rights and ethical standards in the funeral business. The conscientious practitioners in the funeral industry should welcome an open process, too.

~❖~

## Filing a Complaint

If you have a funeral or cemetery complaint, you will need to file it with the appropriate agency. Generally, a *state* office is where to begin. It is a good idea to send a copy of the complaint to the regional office of the Federal Trade Commission, too (see next section). And send a copy to the FAMSA office. That allows us to track the kinds of problems consumers are having.

It is important to be as explicit as possible when filing a complaint and to couch it in terms that reference the state or federal laws. "It was a bad funeral" isn't specific enough. The FAMSA office can help you with the correct references: 800-765-0107.

# FTC Funeral Rule: A Consumer's Guide

Since 1994, the following federal regulations apply to funeral transactions. Not every state has adopted the Rule, which means that state personnel will have difficulty enforcing the Rule in some states, although federal staff may. Generally, however, the FTC acts only when there's a *pattern* of mischief, not on single violations or on behalf of individuals. It is nevertheless important to send copies of any complaints to the FTC.

- **You must be given prices over the telephone when you inquire.**

- **You must be given a General Price List (GPL)** when you visit in person and at the *beginning* of any discussion for funeral arrangements. There are 16 items that are required to be on the GPL:

  Basic services of funeral director & staff (a nondeclinable fee)
  Embalming
  Other preparation of the body
  Transfer of remains to funeral home
  Use of facilities and staff for viewing
  Use of facilities and staff for funeral ceremony
  Use of facilities and staff for memorial service
  Use of equipment and staff for graveside service
  Hearse
  Limousine
  Casket price range
  Outer burial container price range
  Direct cremation
  Immediate burial
  Forwarding remains
  Receiving remains

- **The GPL must contain a disclosure that embalming is not usually required by law.**

- **There must be a disclosure on your statement if the funeral home takes a fee when paying for "cash advance" items on your behalf.** This is a tepid remark few would notice or understand: "We charge you for our services in obtaining. . . ." You'll have to ask, however, to find out how much is charged.

- **You have a right to choose an alternative container for cremation.** A casket is not required.

- **You do not have to purchase any goods or services you don't want.** You may purchase a casket anywhere, for example. The funeral home may not charge you an extra fee if you do.

- **A funeral provider may not claim that embalming or caskets preserve the body or lie about state laws.**

- **You must be given a Statement of Funeral Goods and Services Selected *before* any services are provided**—so you will know what the total cost will be ahead of time and can change your mind if you want.

## Federal Trade Commission Offices

FTC
11000 Wilshire Blvd., Suite 13209
Los Angeles, CA 90024
310-575-7575

FTC
901 Market St., Suite 570
San Francisco, CA 94103
415-744-7920

FTC
1405 Curtis St., Suite 2900
Denver, CO 80202-2393
303-844-2271

FTC
6th & Pennsylvania Ave. NW
Washington, DC 20580
202-326-2222
TDD 202-326-2502

FTC
1718 Peachtree St. NW, Suite #1000
Atlanta, GA 30367
404-347-4836

FTC
55 E. Monroe St., Suite 1437
Chicago, IL 60603
312-353-4423

FTC
101 Merrimac St., Suite 810
Boston, MA 02114-4719
617-424-5960

FTC
150 William St., Suite 1300
New York, NY 10038
212-264-1207

FTC
668 Euclid Ave., Suite 520-A
Cleveland, OH 44114
216-522-4207

FTC
100 N. Central Expressway, Suite 500
Dallas, TX 75201
214-767-5501

FTC
2806 Federal Bldg.
915 Second Ave.
Seattle, WA 98174
206-220-6363

# Death Certificate Instructions

If you assume responsibility for death arrangements without the use of a funeral director, it will be up to you to be certain that a death certificate is properly completed and filed in the appropriate municipal or state office.

All death certificates are based on the U.S. Standard Certificate of Death, although there may be slight variations in some states. The 1978 revision of the certificate is current as of this writing.

The death certificate usually will be provided, and partially filled out, by medical authorities. In most cases, the person doing this will be the attending physician, the family doctor, or the coroner or medical examiner. In a few states, the physician expects the funeral director to supply the death certificate. If that is the case, you will have to obtain a blank death certificate from the department of health. In some states, under specific circumstances when a death is expected, the death certificate may be filled out ahead of time and signed by a registered nurse when the patient dies. If you have any question about this, check with your family doctor.

Medical authorities will fill out only the portion of the certificate having to do with medical information, including the cause of death. The remainder is filled out by the "funeral director or person acting as such." If you fill it out, you are the "person acting as such."

The personal (non-medical) information must be provided by a specific family member or friend, who is referred to on the form as the "informant." Even if the form is filled out by a funeral director, the "informant" should be certain that the information is accurate and complete. When there is no funeral director, the "person acting as such" is often also the "informant."

The form is not complex. However, it must be completed in a careful, conscientious manner. Any error or omission, **even in the portion that is filled out by a doctor,** can delay your plans for disposition of the body or subject family members to questioning at a later date.

The following general and line-by-line instructions are condensed from the guidelines provided to funeral directors and doctors by the U. S. Department of Health and Human Services. Please do not be deterred by the length of the instructions; the form is much shorter. But since every death is different, it seems important to list the rules covering as many contingencies as possible.

## General Instructions

The persons responsible for providing the information are: a) the attending physician or medical examiner or coroner, and b) the "informant." In designating an "informant," the following order of preference should be used, if possible: the spouse, one of the parents, one of the children of the decedent, another relative or close person who has knowledge of the facts.

*Type all entries whenever possible.* If a typewriter cannot be used, print legibly in black ink.

*Complete each item,* following the specific instructions for that item.

*Do not make alterations or erasures or use "white out."*

*Obtain all signatures as (in person) originals.* Rubber stamps or other facsimile signatures are not acceptable.

*File the original certificate with the registrar or office of vital statistics.* Reproductions or duplicates are not acceptable. Certified copies may be obtained from the registrar, for a fee, for use in probate, Social Security notifications, and any other purpose for which proof of death is necessary.

*Avoid abbreviations* except those recommended in the specific item instructions.

*Verify the spelling of names,* especially those that have different spellings for the same sound (Smith or Smyth, Gail or Gayle, Wolf or Wolfe, etc.).

If problems arise that are not covered by these instructions, check with the state office of vital statistics or with a local registrar.

## Line-by-Line Instructions

The items below will be included on any death certificate, although the sequence may vary in some cases. The only significant exception is that a different form is used for fetal death reports. Included are instructions for the sections which must be completed by the physician or coroner. A complaint by registrars is that doctors—whose priority is keeping people alive and healthy—sometimes make hasty errors on death certificates. Since an error, even a simple one such as a signature on the wrong line, can delay body disposition, it may be worthwhile to check the medical portions of the form. The numbers on the form may vary slightly, depending on the state and whether it originated with an attending physician or coroner.

*1. Decedent—Name: First, Middle, Last.* Do not abbreviate.

*2. Sex. Enter "male" or "female."* Do not leave blank.

*3. Date of Death (Month, Day, Year).* Enter the full or abbreviated name of the month (Jan., Feb., March, *etc.*). Do not use a number for a month. If the person died at midnight, the date of death is considered to be at the end of one day, rather than the beginning of the next.

*4. Race—White, Black, American Indian, etc.* (specify). For groups other than those listed in the question, the national origin of the decedent should be listed (Chinese, Japanese, Korean, *etc.*). The information provided on this line is used for studies of health characteristics of minority groups, planning and evaluation of health programs, and in making population estimates.

*5. Age.* There are three lines, only **one** of which should be filled out. *5a* is used if the decedent was over a year old. The person's age in years, as of the last birthday, should be entered. *5b* is used for infants who died between one day and one year of age. Enter the age in completed months, or if less than one month, completed days. *5c* is used when an infant dies within the first day after birth. Enter the age in hours, or if less than one hour, in minutes.

*6. Date of Birth (Month, Day, Year).* Use the full or abbreviated name of the month, rather than a number.

**7. *Place of Death.*** In *7a* and *7b,* indicate the county and city or town where death occurred. In *7c,* indicate the hospital or other institution where the person died. If death occurred at home or at another location, indicate the street address. *7d* should be filled out if the person was pronounced dead at a hospital or other institution. It indicates whether the person was dead on arrival, or whether the person was being treated as an inpatient, outpatient, emergency room patient, *etc.* If death occurred in a moving conveyance other than *en route* to a hospital, enter as the place of death the address where the body was first removed from the conveyance. If death occurred in international waters or airspace, or in a foreign country, contact the state office of vital statistics for instructions.

**8. *State of Birth.*** (If not in the U.S., name the *country*.) If you know the person was born in the U.S. but don't know which state, enter "U.S.—unknown." If no information at all is available regarding the place of birth, enter "Unknown." *Do not leave this space blank.*

**9. *Citizen of What Country.*** If the decedent was born or naturalized as a U.S. citizen, simply enter U.S.A. If the person was a citizen of another country, filling out this item will allow notification of officials of that country.

**10. *Married, Never Married, Widowed, Divorced*** (specify). Enter the marital status at the time of death. A person is legally married even if separated. If marital status cannot be determined, enter "Unknown." *Do not leave this space blank.*

**11. *Surviving Spouse (if wife, include maiden name).*** If the person was married, this information is necessary for insurance and other survivor benefits.

**12. *Was Decedent Ever in U.S. Armed Forces?*** (Specify Yes or No.) If veteran status cannot be determined, enter "Unknown." *Do not leave blank.*

**13. *Social Security Number.*** This is useful for identification and facilitates any Social Security claims.

**14. *Occupation and Industry of Decedent.*** This information should be filled in if the person was 14 or more years of age—even if he or she was retired, disabled, or institutionalized at time of death. Line *14a* lists the person's "usual occupation." This does not necessarily mean the person's last occupation before death. Enter the kind of work the person did during most of his or her working life, such as claim adjuster, farmhand, coal miner, housewife, civil engineer, *etc.* "Retired" is not an acceptable entry. "Student" is an appropriate entry if the person was a student at the time of death and was never regularly employed. Line *14b* lists the kind of business or industry to which the usual occupation was related, such as insurance, farming, hardware store, government, *etc.* Do not enter the name of the firm or organization.

*15. Residence of Decedent.* This is where the person actually resided, and may be different from the "home state," "voting residence," "legal residence," or "mailing address." Never enter a temporary residence such as one used during a visit, business trip, or vacation. However, the place of residence during a tour of military duty or attendance at college is not considered temporary, and should be entered as the residence on the death certificate. Also, persons who at the time of death were living in institutions where individuals usually stay for long periods of time, such as nursing homes, mental institutions, penitentiaries, or hospitals for the chronically ill, are residents of the location of the institution. If the decedent is a child, residence is the same as that of the parents (or custodial parent) or legal guardian, unless the child was living in an institution where individuals usually stay for long periods of time, as indicated above.

The residence information is divided into lines *15a* through *15e.* The individual lines are for the state; the county; the city or town; the street and number (if no number and street name, enter RFD number or post office box number); and whether the person resided within the municipal boundaries of the city or town.

*16-17. Parentage.* Enter the full names—first, middle, and last—of the decedent's father and mother. The mother's maiden name is requested. The justification for this is that the information is useful in tracing of family trees.

*18. Identity of informant.* Enter the name and full mailing address of the person who furnished the personal facts about the decedent and his or her family. If you are the principal source of information, enter your own name and mailing address. The "informant" may be contacted if there are inquiries to correct or to complete any items on the death certificate.

**19. *Type and place of Disposition.*** Line *19a* asks whether the type of disposition was burial, cremation, entombment, removal, or other specified disposition. If a body is to be used by a hospital or medical school for scientific or educational purposes, enter "Removal—Donation," and specify the name and location of the institution in the later lines. Line *19b* asks the name of cemetery, crematory, or institution, and *19c* asks the location (city, town, and state).

**20. *Funeral Service Licensee Information.*** Line *20a* is signed by the "funeral service licensee or person acting as such." If no funeral director is involved and you are completing the death certificate, your signature should appear here. Line *20b* asks the "name of facility." If no funeral director is involved, you may avoid confusion by entering your relationship to the deceased or, if you are working with a church group, the name of the church group. Similarly, on line *20c*—which asks the "address of facility"—you may wish to enter your home address or the address of the church group.

**21. *Certification: Physician.*** This should be filled out by the attending physician or family doctor. If certification is required by the medical examiner or coroner, this space should be left blank. As the "person acting as funeral director," your only role is to be sure the lines are filled in correctly to avoid later inconvenience for you or family members. Line *21a* asks for the signature of the doctor who certifies the death. Line *21b* asks the date (month, day, and year) the certificate was signed. The full or abbreviated name of the month, rather than a number, must be used. Line *21c* asks the exact time of death (hours and minutes), according to local time. If daylight savings time is the prevailing time where death occurs, it should be used. "12 noon" or "12 midnight" should be entered as such; otherwise "A.M." or "P.M." should be noted. Line *21d* asks the "name of attending physician if other than certifier." If the certifier is the attending physician, that space should be left blank.

**22. *Certification: Medical Examiner or Coroner.*** This should be filled out *instead of 21* if a medical examiner or coroner is involved. Lines *22a* through *22c* are identical to their counterparts in *21.* Lines *22d* and

*22e* ask the month, day, year, hour, and minute the person was pronounced dead.

**23. *Name and Address of Certifier.*** The name and address of the person whose signature appears in items *21a* or *22a* should be typed or printed in this space.

**24. *Registrar—Signature and Date Received.*** The local official (registrar) will sign and date the form here at the time it is filed.

**25. *Cause of Death.*** This section must be filled out by the physician, coroner, or medical examiner whose signature appeared on lines *21a* or *22a*. It is extremely important that the section be filled out properly, so the "person acting as funeral director" should review it to be sure there are no hasty errors. The section is divided into two parts.

***Part I.*** Only one cause of death is to be entered on each line of Part I. The general mode of dying (e.g., heart failure, respiratory failure, senility, or old age) should not be stated at all since it is no more than a symptom of the fact that death occurred. Most everyone gets old, and heart and respiratory failure occur in 100% of the deaths.

Line *a* asks the immediate cause of death. This is the disease, injury, or complication that directly preceded death. It can be the sole entry in the cause of death statement if only one condition was present at death. *There must always be an entry on line a.* In the case of violent death, enter the result of the external cause (*e.g.*, fracture of vault of skull, crushed chest, *etc.*). In the case of a specific cancer or injury, the site should be noted as well (*e.g.*, pancreas, left lung, *etc.*).

Line *b* asks what disease, injury, or complication, if immediate cause of any, gave rise to the direct or immediate cause of death reported above. This condition must be considered to have been the antecedent to the immediate cause. If it is believed to have prepared the way for the immediate cause, it can be considered as antecedent even if a long interval of time has elapsed since its onset. In case of injury, the form of external violence or accident is antecedent to an injury entered on line *a* and should be entered on line *b* although the two events are almost simultaneous (*e.g.*, automobile accident, struck by falling tree, *etc.*).

Line *c* asks what condition, if any, gave rise to the antecedent condition on line *b*. If the decedent had more than three causally related conditions leading to death, the person should add lines *d, e, etc.* The final line should state the condition which the physician feels is the underlying cause of death, *i.e.,* the condition that started the sequence of events between normal health and the immediate cause of death. Health departments complain that this section is often in default by the medical persons completing the certificate. If the attending physician is other than the usual family doctor, your help may be invaluable in giving the medical history needed here.

Space is provided at the end of lines *a, b,* and *c* for recording the interval between onset and death for the immediate cause, antecedent condition, if any, and underlying cause. These intervals usually are established by the physician on the basis of information available. The time of onset may be obscure or entirely unknown, in which case the physician can state that the interval is "unknown." *This space should not be left blank.*

*Part II.* Record on this line any other important disease or condition that was present at the time of death that may have contributed to death but was not related to the immediate cause of death. For example, a patient who died of metastasis from carcinoma of the breast may also have had a hypertensive heart disease that contributed to the death. In this case, the hypertensive heart disease would be entered in Part II as a contributory cause of death.

*26. Autopsy.* Enter "Yes" if a partial or complete autopsy was performed. Otherwise, enter "No." *Do not leave this space blank.*

*27. Was Case Referred to Medical Examiner or Coroner?* Complete this item when the cause of death is certified by an attending physician. Enter "Yes" if the medical examiner or coroner was contacted in reference to the case; otherwise enter "No."

*28. Accident or Injury.* Fill out this section if death resulted from an accident or injury. In most instances, such deaths are certified by a medical examiner or coroner, who will complete this section. Otherwise, it should be completed by the attending physician. In line *28a,* specify whether death was caused by accident, suicide, homicide, undetermined, or is pending investigation. In lines *28b* and *28c,* enter the year, month, day, and exact time of the injury. (As always, use the full or abbreviated name of the month, not a number.) Line *28d* asks for a description of how the injury occurred. Use a concise statement, such as, "fell off ladder while painting house." Line *28e* asks whether the injury occurred at work. Enter "Yes," "No," or "Unknown." In line *28f* enter the type of place where the injury occurred (home, farm, street, factory, office building, etc.) In line *28g*, enter the complete address of the location of the injury.

*Origin or Descent.* An additional question regarding origin or descent is asked on the death certificates of many, but not all, states. The question takes two forms. The first is: "Was the decedent of Spanish origin?" Specify "Yes" or "No." If "Yes," specify Mexican, Cuban, Puerto Rican, *etc.* The second form of the question is: "Origin or descent" (*e.g.,* Italian, Mexican, Puerto Rican, English, Cuban, *etc.*). Specify. For the purposes of this question, origin or descent refers to the nationality group of decedents or their ancestors before their arrival in the United States (except for American Indians and Alaskan natives). There is no set rule as to how many generations are to be taken into account in determining ethnic origin. A person's origin may be reported based on the origin of a parent, grandparent, or some far-removed ancestor. The response is to reflect what the person considered himself or herself to be, and is not based on percentages of ancestry. Multiple origins (*e.g.,* English-German) may be entered if the person identified with both or all. If the person did not particularly identify with a foreign birthplace or nationality group, it is entirely appropriate to enter "American."

It is *not* appropriate to enter the name of a religious group (Jewish, Moslem, Protestant, *etc.*). The question refers only to country of origin or nationality group.

It should also be noted that this question is entirely separate from the racial question *4.* In some cases (*e.g.,* Japanese, Chinese, *etc.*), the answers may be the same, but responses to both questions are requested.

# A Good Neighbor's List
## for a Time of Death

These things helped me the most:

• One friend came in right away and cleaned my house. She knew me well enough to know where little things went and never asked a thing as she silently and efficiently put things in order or made coffee. Thank you, Donna.

• A canned ham and frozen food were among the many gifts my neighbors brought. Sometimes it was weeks or months later that I needed the break, and it was with loving gratitude that I relished those thoughtful items long after the time of death. One neighbor who doesn't smoke brought me cigarettes (bless you, Nancy), and others even thought to bring ordinary staples—rice, raisins, tea, a casserole.

• Flowers made me feel better. The ones I appreciated most were not the big fancy arrangements, but those which had been picked out flower by flower, like the favorites in John's garden.

• I will always be grateful for the money I was given. Our families were scattered all over the U. S., and my telephone bill was exorbitant for months.

• Don't ask for mementos right away. I needed to cling for a bit. After losing my husband, I resented people asking for his things. If something is special, there is always a tactful way to let a person know how you feel.

• Even if you don't know what to say, the calls and the cards do count. I had never been one to send cards or call because, after all, what can anyone possibly say at a time like that? But the personal notes from those who shared their thoughts were the ones I kept. And it did help to know that others cared even a little.

• My neighbors took my kids long and often. I needed that, and my children did, too.

• My friends let me talk. And they listened—in my case, for months!

• One of the most special gestures came from my white-haired friend, Faire Edwards, a widow of many years and living modestly on her Social Security income. I met her on the street one day not long after John's death. She threw an arm around me with a quick hug, then started pawing through her pocketbook. Out came a five-dollar bill. "Spend it on yourself," she said. "Spoil yourself with some indulgence. Don't you dare spend it on peanut butter." It was not so much the money—though with Faire's income that was a lot—but she understood and encouraged me to take the time I needed to heal my grieving. I've passed along that $5 bill many times since.

# Resources & References: There's more

The following organizations and literature will be useful to those of you eager to add to your death and funeral education. Some, but not all, have been quoted or otherwise acknowledged in the text.

## Consumer-Oriented Organizations & Publications

**Funeral and Memorial Societies of America,** publishes the *FAMSA Newsletter,* quarterly, $10 in the U.S., $15 in Canada. P.O. Box 10, Hinesburg, VT 05461. It an ideal way to stay abreast of what is happening to funeral consumers nationwide. FAMSA has a wide range of funeral-planning literature and pamphlets, including:

*Veterans' Funeral & Burial Benefits—Including Spouses and Dependent Children.* Copyright ©1997. FAMSA pamphlet. The most comprehensive and concise guide available in one publication.

*Recycling Medical Devices.* Copyright ©1998. FAMSA pamphlet. Instructions for recycling pacemakers, hearing-aids, etc.

**Choice in Dying,** 475 Riverside Dr., Room 1852, New York, NY 10115. Phone: 212-870-2003.

If you are unable to obtain a state-specific copy of the Living Will or Durable Power of Attorney for Healthcare, here's your source. These are critical documents for end-of-life treatment issues that may improve the quality of declining years by allowing you to express your choices in legally-binding documents.

**The Hemlock Society,** P.O. Box 101810, Denver, CO 80250. Phone: 800-247-7521.

The new Aggressive Pain Control Project should be of interest to all, regardless of your opinion on suicide or "choosing your own time."

*The American Way of Death Revisited,* by Jessica Mitford. Copyright ©1998. New York: Alfred A. Knopf.

Wickedly witty! The American way of death, indeed. Although updated, only a few things have changed from the first edition 35 years ago. Shocking revelations and British humor are still intact.

*Death Notification: A Practical Guide,* by R. Moroni Leash, MSW. Copyright ©1994. Hinesburg, VT: Upper Access, Inc.

If it's your job to notify a family that a death is expected or has occurred, how do you do it right? Written for those in the helping professions—medical and ER staff, hospital social workers, law enforcement personnel, to name a few. The powerful vignettes offer practical guidelines and suggestions.

*Dealing Creatively with Death: A Manual of Death Education and Simple Burial,* by Ernest Morgan. 14th edition in progress. Copyright ©1998 or 1999. Zinn Publications.

Morgan's classic book covers a wide range of subjects: death education, living with dying, bereavement, the right to die, simple burial and cremation, death ceremonies, and how the dead can help the living. Personal stories are included.

*Death to Dust: What Happens to Dead Bodies,* by Kenneth V. Iserson, M.D. Copyright ©1994. Galen Press, Ltd., Tucson, AZ

It's hard to imagine how someone could be curious enough to fill 709 pages with details on a subject that most others avoid. Thoroughly researched and well indexed, this tome will surely answer any question you might have: "How will they know when I'm really dead?" to "Will the worms crawl in?"

*A Plain Pine Box: A Return to Simple Jewish Funerals and Eternal Traditions,* by Rabbi Arnold M. Goodman. Copyright ©1981. KTAV Publishing House, Inc., 900 Jefferson St., Box 6249, Hoboken, NJ 07030-7205.

The story of how one Jewish congregation decided to offer free funerals to its members. That decision divided the Jewish community—especially when the local Jewish funeral home refused to cooperate. The plan, however, served as an inspiration to many others.

## Industry Publications and Organizations

Many of these weekly or monthly publications make for interesting reading. All organizations claim to be concerned with consumer issues:

*American Funeral Director,* a glossy monthly trade magazine, $28. Kates-Boylston Publications, Inc., 100 Wood Ave. S., Iselin, NJ 08830; 908-767-9300.

*Death Care Business Advisor,* a twice-a-month trade newsletter, $185. LRP Communications, 747 Dresher Rd., P.O. Box 980, Horsham, PA 19044-0980; 215-784-0860.

*Funeral Monitor,* a weekly trade newsletter, $199 yr. Abbot and Hast Publications, Inc., 761 Lighthouse Ave., Suite A, Monterey, CA 93940-1003; 408-657-9403 or 800-453-1199.

*Funeral Service Insider,* weekly trade newsletter, $295. United Communications Group, 11300 Rockville Pike, Ste. 1100, Rockville, MD 20852-3030; 301-816-8950.

*Mortuary Management,* a glossy monthly trade magazine, 11 issues a year, $33. Abbot and Hast Publications, Inc., 761 Lighthouse Ave., Suite A, Monterey, CA 93940-1003; 408-657-9403 or 800-453-1199.

~❖~

**Cremation Association of North America (CANA),** 401 N. Michigan, Chicago, IL 60611. 312-644-6610

**International Order of the Golden Rule,** P.O. Box 3586, Springfield, IL 62708. 217-793-3322. Funeral home membership by invitation only.

**International Cemetery & Funeral Association,** 1895 Preston White Dr., Suite 220, Reston, VA 20191-5434. 703-391-8400 or 800-645-7700. Publishes *Cemetery & Funeral Management,* a glossy monthly trade magazine, $45.

**Jewish Funeral Directors of America,** Seaport Landing, 150 Lynnway, Suite 506, Lynn, MA 01902. 617-477-9300.

**National Funeral Directors and Morticians Association**, 3951 Snapfinger Parkway, Suite 570, Decatur, GA 30035. 404-286-6680. Primarily black funeral directors.

**National Funeral Directors Association**, 13625 Bishop's Dr., Brookfield, WI 53003; 414-789-1880 or 800-228-6332. Publishes *The Director*, a glossy monthly trade magazine, $26.

**National Selected Morticians**, 5 Revere Dr., Suite 340, Northbrook, IL 60062-8009; 847-559-9569. Membership by invitation only.

# Glossary & Useful Terms

**air tray:** Two-pieced shipping container for a body or for a casketed body. Also, an uncovered container used for placing a body into a cremation chamber, generally made from cardboard or cardboard and plywood.

**alternative container:** an inexpensive body container; funeral directors often use the term "minimum" container. This can be a box made of cardboard or plywood; some are covered with cloth.

**arrangements:** a word used to cover all preparations for a funeral and for the disposition of a dead body.

**ashes:** a misused term for what is left after cremation; the residue is bone fragments which resemble broken sea shells when not pulverized. See *cremains.*

**attending physician:** the doctor who is present at the time of death; sometimes this can be the family doctor responsible for a person's care even if not actually present at the moment of death.

**autopsy:** examination or dissection of a body to determine the cause of death, sometimes requiring lengthy chemical analysis or laboratory procedures.

**bequeathal/bequest:** an after-death gift. Often refers to assets one might dispose of in a will, but also used for body donation.

**body donation:** the bequest of a human body to a medical school for the purpose of anatomical study necessary in training doctors, including osteopaths, chiropractors, and dentists. In addition to the teaching of basic anatomy courses, scientific research may be a part of the medical school program; in many cases this amounts to a loan since the body or cremains may be returned to the family by request when study is complete.

**burial-transit permit:** the form that usually accompanies a body to its final disposition; sometimes it is attached to a death certificate and sometimes it is a separate document. This permit may indicate that the death either has been investigated by a medical examiner or does not need to be; it is also a way for a state to record where final disposition takes place.

**cadaver:** a dead body. The term is used most often in reference to a body donated for medical study.

**casket/coffin:** the box used for containing a body after death. The least expensive ones are cardboard or simple, unfinished wood; the most expensive may be copper or bronze with ornate handles, elaborate cloth lining, and an adjustable inner-spring mattress. Regardless of how well sealed a coffin may be, decomposition is to be expected, even when a body is embalmed.

**casket retailer:** a non-funeral home vendor of caskets. In 1994, the FTC forbid funeral homes from levying a casket handling charge if consumers purchased a casket elsewhere. Purchasing a casket from a retailer may—or may not—save the consumer money.

**CDC:** Centers for Disease Control. Tracks mortality rates, causes of death, among other things.

**coffin vault:** a large one-piece tank, usually concrete but sometimes metal or fiberglass, which is lowered by machine into a grave-site excavation; after the coffin is placed inside, a lid is added. The purpose in using such an item is to keep the ground from settling after decomposition. Extra soil is carted away, and grounds maintenance is simplified. Originally intended to deter grave-robbers, there is no significant effect on body preservation. Coffin vaults usually cost twice the price of a grave liner and serve the same function. No state law requires a coffin vault or liner, but cemetery policy may, even when a metal casket is used.

**columbarium:** a building, usually adorned with stained glass windows and other aesthetic embellishments, containing as many as several hundred small chambers for cremated remains. The door behind which an urn is placed may be marked with a bronze plaque bearing the name of the deceased.

**constructive delivery:** When you are given a title, deed, or warehouse receipt for a casket, vault, or marker, the item is then considered "delivered" to you, even though you have not yet used it. This bit of mischief is used to avoid putting the money in trust. Once "delivered," it's almost impossible to get a refund. Few states are checking warehouses to see if the items are actually there. In one state when the authorities went to check, many were missing.

**common carrier:** public transportation such as railroad or airplane. Shipping of a body by common carrier usually requires a hermetically sealed container or, in some states, embalming.

**coroner:** usually an elected official who must investigate the circumstances surrounding the cause of death when other than natural cause is suspected. The coroners in some states are not required to have medical training and may refer the case to a state pathologist or medical examiner for study. In some states, the coroner may be a funeral director, posing the potential for conflict of interest.

**corpse:** a dead body.

**cremains or cremated remains:** the bone fragments remaining after the cremation process, a more accurate term than *ashes.* Most crematories now pulverize these fragments into small granular particles.

**cremation:** reduction of body mass by the use of heat or fire; only mineral content remains.

**cremation society:** a for-profit business, "borrowing" the respect enjoyed by the nonprofit groups. Memorial societies endorse choice, not just cremation.

**crematory/crematorium/crematoria:** A facility for reducing the body to mineral residue using intense heat.

**crypt:** part of a vaulted chamber into which a casket is placed. Originally, a crypt was below ground, but in current cemetery practices, an above-ground space in a mausoleum is referred to as a crypt.

**decomposition:** the natural process of disintegration of any once-living matter.

**disposition/final disposition:** the last resting place of a dead human body. Because few states have statutes governing the final plans for cremated remains, the cremation process itself is usually considered final disposition. Body donation is usually considered final disposition even if the remains or cremated remains are to be returned to a family. Body burial is the most common form of disposition in the U. S. at this time, but the cremation rate is increasing rapidly.

**embalm:** to inject a body with chemicals to temporarily retard decay and to restore the body to a life-like condition for the purpose of public viewing. Routine embalming is not required by law in any state and serves no public health purpose. However, laws in a few states still require embalming when death is from a communicable or contagious disease. Hawaii and several Canadian provinces forbid embalming under those circumstances. Embalming (or a sealed casket) is likely to be required for transportation by common carrier. The type of embalming used to delay funeral arrangements for several days does not preserve a body much beyond that time. Read the chapter on body donation for a description of medical embalming, which is quite different.

**designated agent:** the person to whom you delegate the right to make after-death decisions and funeral arrangements on your behalf. The designated agent's authority will supersede that of next-of-kin in some states but not all.

**durable power of attorney:** a document that gives to another person the right to make decisions for you when you are no longer able. The rights may be restricted to healthcare, for example, or finance, perhaps, but not healthcare.

**embalmer:** a person who has received training in body preservation. In some states, an embalmer's license is additional to or separate from the license required to operate as a funeral director. A medical school might need an embalmer on its staff, but it would not need a funeral director.

**FAMSA:** Funeral and Memorial Societies of America, a nonprofit educational organization that monitors the funeral industry for consumers.

**fetal death:** a miscarriage or spontaneous termination of pregnancy before birth. In some states an abortion must be reported as a fetal death. Fetal death reports are used primarily for statistical purposes.

**FTC:** Federal Trade commission. See the description of the FTC "Funeral Rule" earlier in the Appendix.

**funeral:** the ceremony held at a time of death. Usually a funeral is planned within a religious context and with the body present. It also is considered an occasion for family and friends to share in the grieving process and to acknowledge regard for the deceased.

**funeral board :** a state-authorized board that licenses funeral directors and embalmers. The state funeral board will often be instrumental in writing legislation for that state regarding the practice of funeral directing. The board is generally in charge of regulating those practices.

**funeral director:** a person whose services may be hired to make some or all of the arrangements at a time of death. In some states, a funeral director is not necessarily an embalmer. Also used: mortician, undertaker.

**GPL:** The General Price List—a menu of funeral options from which you may choose. Required by the Federal Trade Commission to be given at the beginning of any funeral arrangements.

**grave liner:** see *coffin vault.* A grave liner is usually assembled at the grave-site from several pieces. It costs about half the amount of a coffin vault and serves the same function.

**hermetically sealed:** airtight. The primary purpose of a hermetically-sealed casket is to prevent the escape of noxious odors which may develop during decomposition. An embalmed body will continue to decay even inside an air-tight container.

**hospice:** originally a shelter for travellers, later for the sick and poor. In current U.S. practice, a hospice organization functions as a support group and can assist the family in caring for a terminally ill person at home and in preparation for death.

**interment:** burial.

**inurnment:** placement of cremated remains in an urn; burial or placement of an urn in a niche.

**irrevocable:** you may not cancel an irrevocable funeral plan. This option is used to legally shelter funds for funeral expenses. In some states, you may transfer an irrevocable plan to another funeral provider.

**Living Will:** a document in which you may designate the treatments you wish to avoid when death is impending. May not be honored by the medical staff without an aggressive family member to intervene. Without your written request, it would be difficult for relatives to convince the hospital to turn off a respirator or stop force-feeding even though the outlook is admittedly hopeless.

**mausoleum:** named after a Turkish king who built one for his sister/wife. One of the original seven wonders of the world. This structure may contain only those crypts of a family or it may be a building large enough to contain several hundred crypts.

**medical examiner:** a physician trained for investigation into the cause of death.

**memorial society:** a nonprofit funeral information group, usually run by volunteers. Such a group often does price surveys of area funeral homes and cemeteries. Some operate as cooperative buyers' clubs and have negotiated discounts for members at cooperating mortuaries. All can assist a person in making pre-death funeral plans or arrangements. Memorial societies also make an effort to educate the public in a wide variety of matters regarding death and funeral arrangements and may be monitoring state laws. Not to be confused with for-profit "cremation societies."

**memorial service:** a funeral service without a body present.

**morgue:** a place for the temporary storage of a dead body, usually refrigerated.

**mortician:** a funeral director/embalmer.

**mortuary:** a funeral home.

**mortuary arts:** the ability to restore a dead body to a life-like pose. Mortuary science deals especially with temporary body preservation.

**next-of-kin:** the relative(s) in nearest blood or marriage relationship. The exact order may vary somewhat from state to state, but a common sequence is spouse, adult children, parents, adult siblings.

**niche:** a small wall-chamber for cremains, usually side-by-side with many others. See *columbarium.*

**nondeclinable:** a fee that you must pay, regardless of what goods and services you are selecting.

**obituary:** the written notice of a death published by a newspaper.

**organ donation:** the removal after death of a body part that can be transplanted to a living person in need.

**over-enrollment:** more body donations than are needed at a given time. Because a person who has signed a body bequest may have had strong feelings favoring a particular school, some schools are reluctant to share surplus donations to others. However, the need for body donations varies greatly and is far from adequate in many colleges.

**pacemaker:** an electronic device that is surgically implanted beneath the skin to regulate heartbeat. The batteries that power a pacemaker can explode during cremation. See the Resources list in the Appendix for those wishing to recycle pacemakers.

**perpetual care:** maintenance of a cemetery forever. Town or city cemeteries may be taken care of by tax money. Large for-profit cemeteries usually charge an additional sum for this; the money is invested, with the investment income applied to maintenance costs.

**pre-need:** funeral arrangements made and often paid for before death.

**prior enrollment:** the bequest or "will" signed before death when you wish to donate your body to medical science. Some medical schools require this. Other medical schools will accept a donation by next-of-kin after death.

**protective:** a word frequently used in labelling caskets that have a sealing gasket. Hardly protective, however, as the body will putrefy in the anaerobic environment instead of drying out as would otherwise occur.

**pyre:** a pile of wood on which a body is placed for burning, a common funeral rite in India.

**registrar:** the official who keeps the important records for that municipality. Often includes birth, death, and marriage certificates, as well as deeds. In some areas, this may be a town clerk or county clerk. For the purposes of recording vital statistics, it also may be a local health officer.

**remains:** a dead body or its collected parts (after a disaster).

**refrigeration:** an acceptable alternative to embalming in most states and far more effective in retarding decomposition when the body must be held for more than a few days.

**retort:** a cremation chamber

**sealer/sealed casket:** a gasketed casket. Also called "protective."

**shroud:** the clothing or cloth used to wrap a dead body.

**Totten trust:** a pay-on-death savings account.

**undertaker:** funeral director; the term *undertaker* is no longer in vogue among those in the business, although many statutes still include this word.

**unattended death:** a death without a physician present, the cause of which may require investigation. In some states, this is interpreted more liberally: *i.e.,* the death of a person who has been regularly under a physician's care and whose death was anticipated need not be investigated.

**urn:** a container for cremains, usually covered. An elaborate urn may be somewhat like a vase, and many are made of metal. If the family has not chosen such a purchase, the "urn" used to deliver cremains is a simple box.

**trust or trusting:** investing funeral funds in a dedicated account, usually in a federally-insured institution.

**vault:** see coffin vault. This word is also used to describe the chamber a cemetery uses to hold a body until spring burial.

**viewing:** a ritual that allows friends and relatives to see the dead person. Close family members who may not have been present at the time of death often feel the need to see a body in accepting the reality of death. May be done privately or as part of a public viewing or visitation.

**visitation:** a time when friends can pay their respects to the bereaved, usually before the formal funeral ceremonies. If the casket is present, it will be closed, unlike that for a "viewing."

**vital statistics:** the record of births, deaths, and marriages that every state is required to keep.

# Index